BERLITZ

S0-DQW-154

portuguese-english
english-portuguese
dictionary

dicionário
português-inglês
inglês-português

By the staff of Editions Berlitz

Library of Congress Catalog Card Number: 78-78080

4th printing 1986
Printed in Switzerland

Contents

Índice

Preface

In selecting the 12.500 word-concepts in each language for this dictionary, the editors have had the traveller's needs foremost in mind. This book will prove invaluable to all the millions of travellers, tourists and business people who appreciate the reassurance a small and practical dictionary can provide. It offers them—as it does beginners and students—all the basic vocabulary they are going to encounter and to have to use, giving the key words and expressions to allow them to cope in everyday situations.

Like our successful phrase books and travel guides, these dictionaries—created with the help of a computer data bank—are designed to slip into pocket or purse, and thus have a role as handy companions at all times.

Besides just about everything you normally find in dictionaries, there are these Berlitz bonuses:

- imitated pronunciation next to each foreign-word entry, making it easy to read and enunciate words whose spelling may look forbidding

- a unique, practical glossary to simplify reading a foreign restaurant menu and to take the mystery out of complicated dishes and indecipherable names on bills of fare

- useful information on how to tell the time and how to count, on conjugating irregular verbs, commonly seen abbreviations and converting to the metric system, in addition to basic phrases.

While no dictionary of this size can pretend to completeness, we expect the user of this book will feel well armed to affront foreign travel with confidence. We should, however, be very pleased to receive comments, criticism and suggestions that you think may be of help in preparing future editions.

Prefácio

Ao seleccionarem as 12.500 referências em cada língua para este dicionário, os editores pensaram sobretudo nas necessidades dos viajantes. Este livro será de um valor inestimável para os milhões de turistas e homens de negócios que apreciarão a confiança que lhes pode dar um pequeno e prático dicionário. O dicionário oferece-lhes, assim como aos principiantes e estudantes, todo o vocabulário de base que vão encontrar e que deverão utilizar, e as palavras-chave e expressões que lhes permitirão enfrentar situações correntes.

Como os nossos apreciados livros de frases e guias de viagem, estes dicionários – criados com a ajuda de um banco de dados de computador – são feitos de maneira a caberem facilmente no bolso ou no saco de mão e a serem prontamente acessíveis em qualquer momento.

Para além de quase tudo o que normalmente se encontra num dicionário, estão incluídas as seguintes vantagens da edição Berlitz:

- a pronúncia simulada que aparece junto a cada vocábulo na língua estrangeira, o que torna fácil a leitura e a enunciação de palavras com uma ortografia complicada

- um único e prático glossário destinado a simplificar a leitura da ementa de um restaurante estrangeiro e a tornar compreensíveis os nomes misteriosos e complicados das iguarias e os termos indecifráveis que nela aparecem

- informação útil sobre a maneira de dizer as horas e de contar, sobre a conjugação de verbos irregulares e abreviaturas mais comuns, para além das frases de base.

Embora nenhum dicionário deste tamanho possa ter a pretensão de ser completo, esperamos que o leitor se sinta preparado para enfrentar com confiança as suas viagens ao estrangeiro. Teríamos o maior prazer, no entanto, em receber comentários, críticas e sugestões que o leitor julgue úteis à preparação de edições futuras.

portuguese-english
português-inglês

Abbreviations

adj	adjective	*n*	noun
adv	adverb	*nAm*	noun (American)
Am	American		
art	article	*num*	numeral
Br	Brazilian	*p*	past tense
conj	conjunction	*pl*	plural
f	feminine	*plAm*	plural (American)
fBr	feminine (Brazilian)		
fpl	feminine plural	*pp*	past participle
fplBr	feminine plural (Brazilian)	*pr*	present tense
		pref	prefix
m	masculine	*prep*	preposition
mBr	masculine (Brazilian)	*pron*	pronoun
mpl	masculine plural	*v*	verb
mplBr	masculine plural (Brazilian)	*vAm*	verb (American)
		vBr	verb (Brazilian)

Introduction

This dictionary has been designed to take account of your practical needs. Unnecessary linguistic information has been avoided. The entries are listed in alphabetical order, regardless of whether the entry is printed in a single word or in two or more separate words. As the only exception to this rule, a few idiomatic expressions are listed alphabetically as main entries, according to the most significant word of the expression. When an entry is followed by sub-entries, such as expressions and locutions, these are also listed in alphabetical order.

Each main-entry word is followed by a phonetic transcription (see guide to pronunciation). Following the transcription is the part of speech of the entry word whenever applicable. If an entry word is used as more than one part of speech, the translations are grouped together after the respective part of speech.

Irregular plurals are given in brackets after the part of speech.

Whenever an entry word is repeated in irregular forms or sub-entries, a tilde (~) is used to represent the full word. In plurals of long words, only the part that changes is written out fully, whereas the unchanged part is represented by a hyphen (-).

Entry word:	Plural
abre-latas *m* (pl ~)	abre-latas
actual *adj* (pl -ais)	actuais

An asterisk (*) in front of a verb indicates that it is irregular. For more details, refer to the list of irregular verbs.

The dictionary is based on the Portuguese written and spoken in Portugal. All words and uses of words that are exclusively Brazilian have been marked as such.

Guide to Pronunciation

Each main entry in this part of the dictionary is followed by a phonetic transcription which shows you how to pronounce the words. This transcription should be read as if it were English. It is based on Standard British pronunciation, though we have tried to take account of General American pronunciation also. Below, only those letters and symbols are explained which we consider likely to be ambiguous or not immediately understood.

The syllables are separated by hyphens, and stressed syllables are printed in *italics*.

Of course, the sounds of any two languages are never exactly the same, but if you follow carefully our indications, you should be able to pronounce the foreign words in such a way that you'll be understood. To make your task easier, our transcriptions occasionally simplify slightly the sound system of the language while still reflecting the essential sound differences.

Consonants

bh	an indistinct **b**-sound, slightly like a **v**
dh	an indistinct **d**-sound, slightly like **th** in **th**is
g	always hard, as in **go**
ġ	an indistinct **g**-sound, like a soft, voiced version of **ch** in Scottish lo**ch**
lʸ	like **lli** in mi**lli**on
ng	as in si**ng**, not as in fi**ng**er (no g-sound!)
ñ	as in Spanish se**ñ**or, or like **ni** in o**ni**on
r	like Scottish **r** (rolled with the tip of the tongue)
rr	a strongly rolled **r**
s	always hard, as in **so**
zh	a soft, voiced **sh**, like **s** in plea**s**ure

Vowels and Diphthongs

ah	a short version of the **a** in c**a**r, i.e. a sound between **a** in c**a**t and **u** in c**u**t
eh	like **e** in g**e**t
er	more or less as in oth**er**, without any **r**-sound

i	like **i** in b**i**t
igh	as in h**igh**
o	always as in h**o**t (Standard British pronunciation)
oa	as in r**oa**d (but a *pure* vowel, i.e. the lips and tongue don't move while you're pronouncing it)
oo	as in r**oo**t
ou	as in l**ou**d

1) Portuguese vowels are fairly short.

2) Raised letters (e.g. **er**ee, ʸ**oo**) should be pronounced only fleetingly.

3) Portuguese contains nasal vowels, which we transcribe with a vowel symbol plus **ng** (e.g. **ahng**). This **ng** should *not* be pronounced, and serves solely to indicate nasal quality of the preceding vowel. A nasal vowel is pronounced simultaneously through the mouth and the nose. It can calso be part of a diphthong (e.g. **erng**ʷ).

Brazilian Pronunciation

Brazilian Portuguese differs from the Portuguese spoken in Portugal in several important respects. The Brazilian pronunciation is slower and the words are less linked together than in Portugal. Unstressed vowels sound clearer when spoken by Brazilians, while in Portugal they are rapidly slurred over; **s** and **z** at the end of a syllable tend to be pronounced like **s** in **s**it and **z** in ra**z**or (rather than like **sh** in **sh**ut or **s** in plea**s**ure). Vowel groups or diphthongs are often simplified.

A

a (er) *pron* her; *prep* to, at; on

abadia (er-bher-*dhee*-er) *f* abbey

abaixar (er-bhigh-*shahr*) *v* lower

abaixo (er-*bhigh*-shoo) *adv* over; down

abaixo-assinado (er-*bhigh*-shoo-er-see-*nah*-dhoo) *m* the undersigned

abajur (er-bher-*zhoor*) *m* lampshade

abalroamento (er-bhahl-rrwer-*mayngn*-too) *m* collision

abanar (er-bher-*nahr*) *v* *shake

abandonar (er-bherngn-doo-*nahr*) *v* *leave, abandon, desert, *leave behind

abastado (er-bhersh-*tah*-dhoo) *adj* well-to-do, well-off

abastecimento (er-bhersh-ter-see-*mayngn*-too) *m* supply

abatido (er-bher-*tee*-dhoo) *adj* down, discouraged

abcesso (erbh-*seh*-soo) *m* abscess

abelha (er-*bhay*-lᵞer) *f* bee

abençoar (er-bhayngn-*swahr*) *v* bless

aberração (er-bhee-rrer-*serng*ʷ) *f* (pl -ções) aberration

aberto (er-*bhehr*-too) *adj* open

abertura (er-bherr-*too*-rer) *f* overture; opening

abibe (er-*bhee*-bher) *m* pewit

abismo (er-*bheezh*-moo) *m* abyss

abóbada (er-*bho*-bher-dher) *f* vault; arch

*abolir (er-bhoo-*leer*) *v* abolish

aborrecer (er-bhoo-rrer-*sayr*) *v* annoy

aborrecido (er-bhoo-rrer-*see*-dhoo) *adj* boring; unpleasant; bored; annoyed

aborrecimento (er-bhoo-rrer-see-*mayngn*-too) *m* annoyance

aborto (er-*bhoar*-too) *m* abortion; miscarriage

abotoaduras (er-bhoo-twer-*dhoo*-rersh) *fplBr* cuff-links *pl*

abotoar (er-bhoo-*twahr*) *v* button

abraçar (er-bhrer-*sahr*) *v* hug, embrace

abraço (er-*bhrah*-soo) *m* embrace, hug; grip

abrandar (er-bhrerngn-*dahr*) *v* slow down

abre-garrafas (ah-bhrer-ger-*rrah*-fersh) *m* (pl ~) bottle opener

abre-latas (ah-bhrer-*lah*-tersh) *m* (pl ~) tin-opener, can opener

abreviatura (er-bhrer-vᵞer-*too*-rer) *f* abbreviation

abrigar (er-bhree-*gahr*) *v* shelter

abrigo (er-*bhree*-goo) *m* cover, shelter

Abril (er-*bhreel*) April

abrir (er-*bhreer*) *v* open; unlock; turn on

absolutamente (erbh-soo-loo-ter-*mayngn*-ter) *adv* absolutely

absoluto (erbh-soo-*loo*-too) *adj* sheer; total

absolvição (erbh-soal-vee-*serng*ʷ) *f* (pl -ções) acquittal

abstémio (erbhsh-*teh*-mʸoo) *m* teetotaller

***abster-se de** (erbhsh-*tayr*-ser) abstain from

abstracto (erbhsh-*trah*-too) *adj* abstract

absurdo (er-bher-*soor*-dhoo) *adj* absurd; foolish

abundância (er-bhoongn-*derng*-sʸer) *f* plenty, abundance

abundante (er-bhoongn-*derngn*-ter) *adj* plentiful, abundant

abuso (er-bhoo-zoo) *m* abuse; misuse

abutre (er-*bhoo*-trer) *m* vulture

acabado (er-ker-*bhah*-dhoo) *adj* over, finished; ~ **de** just

acabar (er-ker-*bhahr*) *v* finish; stop, end

academia (er-ker-dher-*mee*-er) *f* academy; ~ **das belas-artes** art school

acalmar (er-kahl-*mahr*) *v* calm down; **acalmar-se** calm down

acampamento (er-kerngm-per-*mayngn*-too) *m* camp

acampar (er-kerngm-*pahr*) *v* camp

acaso (er-*kah*-zoo) *m* chance; **ao** ~ at random; **por** ~ by chance

acção (ah-*serng*ʷ) *f* (pl acções) action, deed; share; **acções** stocks and shares

aceder (er-ser-*dhayr*) *v* grant; consent

aceitar (er-say-*tahr*) *v* accept

acelerador (er-ser-ler-rer-*dhoar*) *m* accelerator

acelerar (er-ser-ler-*rahr*) *v* accelerate

acenar (er-ser-*nahr*) *v* wave

acender (er-sayngn-*dayr*) *v* *light; turn on

acento (er-*sayngn*-too) *m* accent

acentuar (er-sayngn-*twahr*) *v* stress, emphasize

acepipe (er-ser-*pee*-per) *m* delicacy; **acepipes** hors-d'œuvre

ácer (*ah*-sehr) *m* maple

acerca de (er-*sayr*-ker) about

acertar (er-serr-*tahr*) *v* *hit; adjust

acessível (er-ser-*see*-vehl) *adj* (pl -eis) accessible; attainable

acesso (er-*seh*-soo) *m* access; entrance, approach

acessório (er-ser-*so*-rʸoo) *adj* additional; **acessórios** accessories *pl*

achaque (er-*shah*-ker) *m* ailment

achar (er-*shahr*) *v* consider; *find; a-chados e perdidos** lost and found

acidentado (er-see-dhayngn-*tah*-dhoo) *adj* hilly; bumpy

acidental (er-see-dhayngn-*tahl*) *adj* (pl -ais) accidental

acidente (er-see-dhayngn-ter) *m* accident

ácido (*ah*-see-dhoo) *m* acid

acima (er-*see*-mer) *adv* up

aclamar (er-kler-*mahr*) *v* cheer

aclarar (er-kler-*rahr*) *v* clarify

acne (*ahk*-ner) *f* acne

aço (*ah*-soo) *m* steel; ~ **inoxidável** stainless steel

acolher (er-koo-lʸayr) *v* welcome; lodge

acolhimento (er-koo-lʸee-*mayngn*-too) *m* welcome; reception

acomodação (er-koo-moo-dher-*serng*ʷ) *f* (pl -ções) accommodation

acomodar (er-koo-moo-*dhahr*) *v* accommodate

acompanhar (er-kawngm-per-*ñahr*) *v* accompany; conduct, escort

aconchegado (er-kawng-sher-*gah*-dhoo) *adj* cosy

aconselhar (er-kawng-sɪ-lʸahr) *v* advise; recommend

acontecer (er-kawngn-ter-sayr) *v* happen, occur

acontecimento (er-kawngn-ter-see-mayngn-too) m event; happening

acordado (er-koor-dhah-dhoo) adj awake

acordar (er-koor-dahr) v *awake; *wake; wake up

acordo (er-koar-doo) m agreement; settlement; **de acordo!** all right!; okay!

acostumar (er-koosh-too-mahr) v accustom

acreditar (er-krer-dhee-tahr) v believe

acrescentar (er-krısh-sayngn-tahr) v add; increase

acta (ah-ter) f minutes

actividade (ah-tee-vee-dhah-dher) f activity

activo (ah-tee-voo) adj active

acto (ah-too) m act

actor (ah-toar) m actor

actriz (ah-treesh) f actress

actuação (ah-twer-serng ᵂ) f (pl -cões) appearance, performance

actual (ah-twahl) adj (pl -ais) topical; present

actualmente (ah-twahl-mayngn-ter) adv now; at present

actuar (ah-twahr) v operate

açúcar (er-soo-kahr) m sugar; **torrão de ~** lump of sugar

acusação (er-koo-zer-serng ᵂ) f (pl -cões) charge

acusado (er-koo-zah-dhoo) m accused

acusar (er-koo-zahr) v accuse, charge; blame

adaptar (er-dahp-tahr) v adapt; **~ a** suit

adega (er-dhay-ger) f wine-cellar

adepto (er-dhehp-too) m supporter

adequado (er-dher-kwah-dhoo) adj appropriate

***aderir a** (er-dher-reer) join

adesivo (er-dher-zee-voo) m adhesive tape

adestrar (er-dhısh-trahr) v train; drill

adeus (er-dhayᵒᵒsh) m farewell; **adeus!** good-bye!

adiamento (er-dhᵞer-mayngn-too) m delay; postponement

adiantadamente (er-dhᵞerngn-tah-dher-mayngn-ter) adv in advance

adiantado (er-dhᵞerngn-tah-dhoo) adj advanced

adiantamento (er-dhᵞerngn-ter-mayngn-too) m advance

adiantar (er-dhᵞerngn-tahr) v advance

adiante (er-dhᵞerngn-ter) adv before; onward, forward; **~ de** ahead of

adiar (er-dhᵞahr) v postpone; adjourn, delay, *put off

adição (er-dhee-serng ᵂ) f (pl -cões) addition

adicional (er-dhee-sᵞoo-nahl) adj (pl -ais) additional

adicionar (er-dhee-sᵞoo-nahr) v add

adivinha (er-dher-vee-ñer) f riddle

adivinhar (er-dher-vee-ñahr) v guess

adjectivo (er-jeh-tee-voo) m adjective

administração (erdh-mer-neesh-trer-serng ᵂ) f (pl -cões) administration; direction

administrar (erdh-mer-neesh-trahr) v manage; administer

administrativo (er-dh-mer-neesh-trer-tee-voo) adj administrative

admiração (erdh-mee-rer-serng ᵂ) f (pl -cões) admiration; wonder

admirador (erdh-mee-er-dhoar) m fan

admirar (erdh-mee-rahr) v admire

admissão (erdh-mee-serng ᵂ) f (pl -sões) admission

admitir (erdh-mer-teer) v admit; acknowledge

adoçar (er-dhoo-sahr) v sweeten

adolescente (er-dhoo-lısh-sayngn-ter) m teenager

adoptar (er-dho-tahr) v adopt

adorar (er-dhoo-*rahr*) v worship

adorável (er-dhoo-*rah*-vehl) adj (pl -eis) adorable

adormecer (er-dhoor-mer-*sayr*) v *put to sleep; *fall asleep

adormecido (er-dhoor-mer-*see*-dhoo) adj asleep

adquirir (erdh-ker-*reer*) v acquire; *buy

adulto (er-*dhool*-too) adj adult, grown-up; m adult, grown-up

advérbio (erdh-*vehr*-bhⱽoo) m adverb

adversário (erdh-verr-*sah*-rⱽoo) m opponent

adverso (erdh-*vehr*-soo) adj averse

*advertir (erdh-verr-*teer*) v caution, warn

advogado (erdh-voo-*gah*-dhoo) m solicitor, barrister, attorney, lawyer

advogar (erdh-voo-*gahr*) v plead

aéreo (er-*eh*-rⱽoo) adj airy; **correio ~** airmail

aeroporto (er-eh-roo-*poar*-too) m airport

afastado (er-fersh-*tah*-dhoo) adj out of the way

afável (er-*fah*-vehl) adj (pl -eis) friendly

afecção (er-fehk-*serng*ʷ) f (pl -cões) affection

afectado (er-feh-*tah*-dhoo) adj affected

afectar (er-feh-*tahr*) v affect

afectuoso (er-feh-*twoa*-zoo) adj affectionate

afeição (er-fay-*serng*ʷ) f (pl -cões) affection

afiado (er-fⱽ*ah*-dhoo) adj sharp

afiar (er-fⱽ*ahr*) v sharpen

afinal (er-fee-*nahl*) adv finally; at last

afirmar (er-feer-*mahr*) v claim

afirmativo (er-feer-mer-*tee*-voo) adj affirmative

aflição (er-flee-*serng*ʷ) f (pl -cões) grief

afligir-se (er-flee-*zheer*-ser) v worry

afluente (er-flwayngn-ter) m tributary

afogador (er-foo-ger-*dhoar*) mBr choke

afogar (er-foo-*gahr*) v drown; **afogar-se** *be drowned

afortunado (er-foor-too-*nah*-dhoo) adj fortunate; lucky

África (*ah*-free-ker) f Africa; **África do Sul** South Africa

africano (er-free-*ker*-noo) adj African; m African

afrouxar (er-froa-*shahr*) v slow down

afugentar (er-foo-zhayngn-*tahr*) v chase

afundar-se (er-foongn-*dahr*-ser) v *sink

agarrar (er-ger-*rrahr*) v seize, grip, grasp, *catch; *take; **agarrar-se** *hold on

agência (er-*zhayng*-sⱽer) f agency; **~ de colocação** employment exchange; **~ de informações** information bureau; **~ de turismo** tourist office; **~ de viagens** travel agency

agenda (er-*zhayng*-der) f diary; notebook; agenda

agente (er-*zhayng*-ter) m agent; **~ de viagens** travel agent; **~ imobiliário** house agent

ágil (*ah*-zheel) adj (pl ágeis) supple

agir (er-*zheer*) v act

agitação (er-zhee-ter-*serng*ʷ) f (pl -cões) unrest

agora (er-*go*-rer) adv now; **até ~ so** far; **de ~ em diante** henceforth

Agosto (er-*goash*-too) August

agradar (er-grer-*dhahr*) v please

agradável (er-grer-*dhah*-vehl) adj (pl -eis) agreeable, nice, pleasant, enjoyable, pleasing

agradecer (er-grer-dher-*sayr*) v thank

agradecido (erg-rer-dher-*see*-dhoo) *adj* thankful

agrafo (er-*grah*-foo) *m* staple

agrário (er-*grah*-rᵞoo) *adj* agrarian

*agredir (er-grer-*dheer*) *v* attack, assault

agressivo (er-grer-*see*-voo) *adj* aggressive

agrião (er-grᵞerng^w) *m* (pl -iões) watercress

agrícola (er-*gree*-koo-ler) *adj* agrarian

agricultor (er-gree-kool-*toar*) *m* farmer

agricultura (er-gree-kool-*too*-rer) *f* agriculture

agrupar (er-groo-*pahr*) *v* arrange; group

água (*ah*-gwer) *f* water; ~ **corrente** running water; ~ **doce** fresh water; ~ **do mar** sea-water; ~ **gasificada** soda-water; ~ **gelada** iced water; ~ **mineral** mineral water; ~ **oxigenada** peroxide; ~ **potável** drinking-water

aguaceiro (er-gwer-*say*-roo) *m* downpour, shower

água-forte (ah-gwer-*for*-ter) *f* etching

aguarela (er-gwer-*reh*-ler) *f* water-colour

agudo (er-*goo*-dhoo) *adj* acute; pointed

aguentar (er-gwayngn-*tahr*) *v* *hold up, *put up with

águia (*ahg*-ᵞer) *f* eagle

agulha (er-*goo*-lᵞer) *f* needle; spire

ai (er-ee) *adv* there

ainda (er-*eengn*-der) *adv* yet, still; ~ **agora** just now, a moment ago; ~ **assim** nevertheless; ~ **bem** fortunately; ~ **que** though

aipo (*igh*-poo) *m* celery

ajoelhar (er-zhwɪ-*lᵞahr*) *v* *kneel

ajuda (er-*zhoo*-dher) *f* assistance, aid

ajudante (er-zhoo-*dherngn*-ter) *m* helper

ajudar (er-zhoo-*dhahr*) *v* help, aid

ajustar (er-zhoosh-*tahr*) *v* adjust

ajuste (er-*zhoosh*-ter) *m* settlement

alabote (er-ler-*bo*-ter) *m* halibut

alargar (er-lerr-*gahr*) *v* widen

alarido (er-ler-*ree*-dhoo) *m* racket

alarmar (er-lerr-*mahr*) *v* alarm

alarme (er-*lahr*-mer) *m* alarm; ~ **de incêndio** fire-alarm

alavanca (er-ler-*verngñ*-ker) *f* lever; ~ **das mudanças** gear lever

albergue (ahl-*behr*-ger) *m* hostel; ~ **de juventude** youth hostel

álbum (*ahl*-bhoong) *m* album

alcachofra (ahl-ker-*shoa*-frer) *f* artichoke

alcançar (ahl-kerng-*sahr*) *v* reach; achieve

alcance (ahl-*kerng*-ser) *m* reach, range

alçapão (ahl-ser-*perng^w*) *m* (pl -pões) hatch

alcatrão (ahl-ker-*trerng^w*) *m* tar

alce (*ahl*-ser) *m* moose

álcool (*ahl*-kwol) *m* (pl -ois) alcohol; ~ **desnaturado** methylated spirits; **lamparina de** ~ spirit stove

alcoólico (ahl-*kwo*-lee-koo) *adj* alcoholic; *m* alcoholic

alcunha (ahl-*koo*-ñer) *f* nickname

aldeia (ahl-*day*-er) *f* village

aldeola (ahl-*dᵞo*-ler) *f* hamlet

alegrar (er-ler-*grahr*) *v* cheer up

alegre (er-*leh*-grer) *adj* joyful, merry, gay, cheerful

alegria (er-ler-*gree*-er) *f* joy, gaiety; gladness

aleijado (er-lay-*zhah*-dhoo) *adj* crippled

além (er-*lerng*ᵞ) *adv* beyond; ~ **de** past, beyond; besides; ~ **disso** besides; furthermore, moreover; **mais** ~ further

Alemanha (er-ler-*merng*-ñer) *f* Germany

alemão (er-ler-*merng*ʷ) *adj* (f -mã; pl -ães) German; *m* German

alergia (er-lerr-*zhee*-er) *f* allergy

alfabeto (ahl-fer-*bheh*-too) *m* alphabet

alface (ahl-*fah*-ser) *f* lettuce

alfaiate (ahl-fee-*ʸah*-ter) *m* tailor

alfândega (ahl-*ferng*-der-ger) *f* Customs *pl*

alfinete (ahl-fee-*nay*-ter) *m* pin; ~ **de segurança** safety-pin; **prender com alfinetes** pin

alforreca (ahl-foo-*rreh*-ker) *f* jelly-fish

algarismo (ahl-ger-*reezh*-moo) *m* figure; number; digit

álgebra (*ahl*-zher-bhrer) *f* algebra

algemas (ahl-*zhay*-mersh) *fpl* handcuffs *pl*

algibeira (ahl-zhee-*bhay*-rer) *f* pocket

algo (*ahl*-goo) *adv* somewhat, a little; *pron* something, anything

algodão (ahl-goo-*dherng*ʷ) *m* (pl -dões) cotton; cotton-wool; **de** ~ cotton

alguém (ahl-*gerng*ʸ) *pron* someone, somebody

algum (ahl-*goong*) *pron* some; any

alguns (ahl-*goongsh*) *adj* some

alho (*ah*-lʸoo) *m* garlic

ali (er-*lee*) *adv* over there; **para** ~ there

aliado (er-*lʸah*-dhoo) *m* associate; **Aliados** Allies *pl*

aliança (er-*lʸerng*-ser) *f* alliance; wedding-ring

alicate (er-lee-*kah*-ter) *m* pliers *pl*

alicerce (er-lee-*sehr*-ser) *m* base, foundation

alimentação (er-lee-mayngn-ter-*serng*ʷ) *f* (pl -ções) fare, food

alimentar (er-lee-mayngn-*tahr*) *v* *feed; adj* alimentary; **intoxicação** ~ food poisoning

alimentício (er-lee-mayngn-*tee*-sʸoo) *adj* nourishing

alimento (er-lee-*mayngn*-too) *m* food

alínea (er-*lee*-nʸer) *f* paragraph

aliviar (er-lee-*vʸahr*) *v* relieve

alívio (er-*lee*-vʸoo) *m* relief

alma (*ahl*-mer) *f* soul

almanaque (*ahl*-mer-*nah*-ker) *m* almanac

almirante (ahl-mee-*rerng*-ter) *m* admiral

almoçar (ahl-moo-*sahr*) *v* lunch

almoço (ahl-*moa*-soo) *m* dinner, lunch, luncheon; **pequeno** ~ breakfast

almofada (ahl-moo-*fah*-dher) *f* pillow; cushion; ~ **eléctrica** heating pad

almofadão (ahl-moo-fer-*dherng*ʷ) *m* (pl -dões) pillow

almofadinha (ahl-moo-fer-*dhee*-ñer) *f* pad

alocução (er-loo-koo-*serng*ʷ) *f* (pl -ções) speech

alojamento (er-loo-zher-*mayngn*-too) *m* accommodation, lodgings *pl*

alojar (er-loo-*zhahr*) *v* accommodate

alongar (er-lawng-*gahr*) *v* lengthen

alperche (ahl-*pehr*-sher) *m* apricot

alpinismo (ahl-pee-*neezh*-moo) *m* mountaineering

altar (ahl-*tahr*) *m* altar

alteração (ahl-ter-rer-*serng*ʷ) *f* (pl -ções) alteration

alterar (ahl-ter-*rahr*) *v* alter

altercar (ahl-terr-*kahr*) *v* dispute

alternado (ahl-terr-*nah*-dhoo) *adj* alternate

alternativa (ahl-terr-ner-*tee*-ver) *f* alternative

altifalante (ahl-tee-fer-*lerngn*-ter) *m* loud-speaker

altitude (ahl-tee-*too*-dher) *f* altitude

altivo (ahl-*tee*-voo) *adj* haughty

alto (*ahl*-too) *adj* tall, high; loud; *m*

lump; **alto!** stop!

altura (ahl-*too*-rer) *f* height

alugar (er-loo-*gahr*) *v* lease, rent, hire, *let; **para** ~ for hire

aluguer (er-loo-*gehr*) *m* letting; ~ **de carros** car hire

alumiar (er-loo-m*Y*ahr) *v* illuminate

aluno (er-*loo*-noo) *m* pupil, scholar

alvará (ahl-ver-*rah*) *m* patent

alvo (*ahl*-voo) *m* target; mark

âmago (*er*-mer-goo) *m* heart

amaldiçoar (er-mahl-dee-*swahr*) *v* curse

amamentar (er-mer-mayngn-*tahr*) *v* nurse

amanhã (ah-mer-*ñerng*) *adv* tomorrow

amanhecer (ah-mer-ñer-*sayr*) *m* day-break

amante (er-*merngn*-ter) *m* lover; *f* mistress

amar (er-*mahr*) *v* love

amarelo (er-mah-*reh*-loo) *adj* yellow

amargo (er-*mahr*-goo) *adj* bitter

amarrotar (er-mer-rroo-*tahr*) *v* crease

ama-seca (er-mer-*say*-ker) *f* nurse

amável (er-*mah*-vehl) *adj* (pl -eis) amiable, kind

âmbar (*erngm*-bahr) *m* amber

ambicionar (erngm-bee-s*Y*oo-*nahr*) *v* wish, *strive for

ambicioso (erngm-bee-s*Y*oa-zoo) *adj* ambitious

ambiente (erngm-b*Y*ayngn-ter) *m* atmosphere

ambíguo (erngm-*bee*-gwoo) *adj* ambiguous

ambos (*erngm*-boosh) *pron* either, both

ambulância (erngm-boo-*lerng*-s*Y*er) *f* ambulance

ameaça (er-m*Y*ah-ser) *f* threat

ameaçador (er-m*Y*er-ser-*dhoar*) *adj* threatening

ameaçar (er-m*Y*er-*sahr*) *v* threaten

ameixa (er-*may*-sher) *f* plum; ~ **passada** prune

amêndoa (er-*mayngn*-dwer) *f* almond

amendoim (er-mayngn-*dweeng*) *m* peanut

América (er-*meh*-ree-ker) *f* America; ~ **Latina** Latin America

americano (er-mer-ree-*ker*-noo) *adj* American; *m* American

ametista (er-mer-*teesh*-ter) *f* amethyst

amianto (er-m*Y*erngn-too) *m* asbestos

amiga (er-*mee*-ger) *f* friend

amígdalas (er-*meeg*-der-lersh) *fpl* tonsils *pl*

amigdalite (er-*meeg*-dher-lee-ter) *f* tonsilitis

amigo (er-*mee*-goo) *m* friend

amimar (er-mee-*mahr*) *v* *spoil; fondle

amistoso (er-meesh-*toa*-zoo) *adj* friendly

amizade (ah-mee-*zah*-dher) *f* friendship

amnistia (er-mnersh-*tee*-er) *f* amnesty

amoníaco (er-moo-*nee*-er-koo) *m* ammonia

amontoar (er-mawngn-*twahr*) *v* pile

amor (er-*moar*) *m* love; darling; **meu** ~ sweetheart

amora (er-*mo*-rer) *f* mulberry; ~ **silvestre** blackberry

amortecedor (er-moor-ter-ser-*dhoar*) *m* shock absorber

amostra (er-mosh-trer) *f* sample; specimen

ampliação (erngm-pl*Y*er-*serng*ʷ) *f* (pl -ções) extension; enlargement

ampliar (erngm-pl*Y*ahr) *v* enlarge; extend

amplo (*erngm*-ploo) *adj* extensive; broad

amuleto (er-moo-*lay*-too) *m* charm

analfabeto (er-nahl-fer-*bheh*-too) *m* illiterate

analisar (er-ner-lee-*zahr*) *v* analyse;

*break down

análise (er-*nah*-lee-zer) *f* analysis

analista (er-ner-*leesh*-ter) *m* analyst

análogo (er-*nah*-loo-goo) *adj* similar

anamnese (er-nerm-*neh*-zer) *f* history of a disease

ananás (er-ner-*nahsh*) *m* pineapple

anão (er-*nerng*ʷ) *m* (f anã; pl anões) dwarf

anarquia (er-nerr-*kee*-er) *f* anarchy

anatomia (er-ner-too-*mee*-er) *f* anatomy

anca (*erng*ñ-ker) *f* hip

anchova (erng-*shoa*-ver) *f* anchovy

ancinho (erng-*see*-ñoo) *m* rake

âncora (*erng*-koo-rer) *f* anchor

andaime (erng-*digh*-mer) *m* scaffolding

andar (erng-*dahr*) *v* *go, walk, step; *m* pace, gait; floor, storey; apartment *nAm;* ~ **com** associate with; ~ **térreo** *Br* ground floor

andorinha (erng-doo-*ree*-ñer) *f* swallow

anedota (er-ner-*dho*-ter) *f* joke

anel (er-*nehl*) *m* (pl anéis) ring; ~ **de noivado** engagement ring

anemia (er-ner-*mee*-er) *f* anaemia

anestesia (er-nɪsh-ter-*zee*-er) *f* anaesthesia

anestésico (er-nɪsh-*teh*-zee-koo) *m* anaesthetic

anexar (er-nehk-*sahr*) *v* annex

anexo (er-*nehk*-soo) *m* enclosure, annex

ângulo (*erng*-goo-loo) *m* angle

animado (er-nee-*mah*-dhoo) *adj* crowded; lively

animal (er-nee-*mahl*) *m* (pl -ais) animal; beast; ~ **de estimação** pet; ~ **de rapina** beast of prey

animar (er-nee-*mahr*) *v* cheer up

aniversário (er-nee-verr-*sah*-rʸoo) *m* anniversary

anjo (*erng*-zhoo) *m* angel

ano (er-noo) *m* year; ~ **bissexto** leap-year; **Ano Novo** New Year

anoitecer (er-noi-ter-*sayr*) *m* dusk

anónimo (er-*no*-nee-moo) *adj* anonymous

anormal (er-noor-*mahl*) *adj* (pl -ais) abnormal

anotar (er-noo-*tahr*) *v* note; *write down

ansiedade (erng-sʸay-*dhah*-dher) *f* anxiety

ansioso (erng-sʸoa-zoo) *adj* anxious

antecedente (erng-ter-ser-*dhayng*-ter) *adj* former

antecipadamente (erng-ter-see-pah-dher-*mayng*-ter) *adv* in advance

do anteguerra (doo erng-ter-*geh*-rer) pre-war

antena (erng-*tay*-ner) *f* aerial

anteontem (erng-ter-*awng*-terngʸ) *adv* the day before yesterday

antepassado (erng-ter-per-*sah*-dhoo) *m* ancestor

anterior (erng-ter-rʸoar) *adj* previous; prior

anteriormente (erng-ter-rʸoar-*mayng*-ter) *adv* formerly

antes (*erng*-tɪsh) *adv* before; rather, sooner; ~ **de** before; ~ **que** before

antibiótico (erng-tee-*bhʸo*-tee-koo) *m* antibiotic

anticongelante (erng-tee-kawng-zher-*lerng*-ter) *m* antifreeze

antigamente (erng-tee-ger-*mayng*-ter) *adv* formerly

antigo (erng-*tee*-goo) *adj* former; antique; ancient

antiguidade (erng-tee-gwee-*dhah*-dher) *f* antiquity; antique

antipatia (erng-tee-per-*tee*-er) *f* dislike, antipathy

antipático (erng-tee-*pah*-tee-koo) *adj* unfriendly, nasty

antiquado (erɴgn-tee-*kwah*-dhoo) *adj* quaint. old-fashioned, ancient

antiquário (erɴgn-tee-*kwah*-rⱽoo) *m* antique dealer

antisséptico (erɴgn-tee-*sehp*-tee-koo) *m* antiseptic

antologia (erɴgn-too-loo-*zhee*-er) *f* anthology

anual (er-*nwahl*) *adj* (pl -ais) annual; yearly

anualmente (er-nwahl-*mayɴg*-ter) *adv* per annum

anuário (er-nwah-rⱽoo) *m* annual

anular (er-noo-*lahr*) *v* cancel

anunciar (er-noong-sⱽahr) *v* announce

anúncio (er-*noong*-sⱽoo) *m* announcement; advertisement; commercial

anzol (erɴg-*zol*) *m* (pl anzóis) fishing hook

apagado (er-per-*gah*-dhoo) *adj* dull

apagar (er-per-*gahr*) *v* extinguish; *put out

apaixonado (er-pigh-shoo-*nah*-dhoo) *adj* in love; passionate

apalpar (er-pahl-*pahr*) *v* *feel

apanhar (er-per-*ñahr*) *v* *catch; pick up

aparafusar (er-*pah*-rer-foo-*zahr*) *v* screw

apara-lápis (er-pah-rer-*lah*-peesh) *m* (pl ~) pencil-sharpener

aparar (er-per-*rahr*) *v* trim

aparecer (er-per-rer-*sayr*) *v* appear

aparelho (er-per-*ray*-lⱽoo) *m* apparatus; appliance

aparência (er-per-*rayng*-sⱽer) *f* appearance; look, semblance

aparentado (er-per-rayɴgn-*tah*-dhoo) *adj* related

aparente (er-per-*rayɴgn*-ter) *adj* apparent

aparentemente (er-per-rayɴgn-ter-*mayɴgn*-ter) *adv* apparently

aparição (er-per-ree-*serɴg*ʷ) *f* (pl -cões) apparition

apartamento (er-perr-ter-*mayɴg*-too) *m* flat; suite; apartment *nAm*

***apear-se** (er-pⱽahr-ser) *v* *get off

apelido (er-per-*lee*-dhoo) *m* surname; family name; *mBr* nickname; ~ **de solteira** maiden name

apelo (er-*pay*-loo) *m* appeal

apêndice (er-*payɴgn*-dee-ser) *m* appendix

apendicite (er-payɴg-dee-*see*-ter) *f* appendicitis

aperceber (er-perr-ser-*bhayr*) *v* perceive

aperitivo (er-per-ree-*tee*-voo) *m* aperitif; **aperitivos** appetizer

apertado (er-perr-*tah*-dhoo) *adj* narrow, tight

apertar (er-perr-*tahr*) *v* tighten; **apertar-se** tighten

aperto (er-*payr*-too) *m* clutch, grasp; ~ **de mão** handshake

apesar de (er-per-*zahr* der) despite, in spite of

apetecer (er-per-ter-*sayr*) *v* *feel like

apetite (er-per-*tee*-ter) *m* appetite

apetitoso (er-per-tee-*toa*-zoo) *adj* appetizing

apinhado (er-pee-*ñah*-dhoo) *adj* crowded

apito (er-*pee*-too) *m* whistle

aplanar (er-pler-*nahr*) *v* level

aplaudir (er-plou-*dheer*) *v* clap; cheer

aplausos (er-*plou*-zoosh) *mpl* applause

aplicação (er-plee-ker-*serɴg*ʷ) *f* (pl -cões) application; diligence

aplicado (er-plee-*kah*-dhoo) *adj* diligent

aplicar (er-plee-*kahr*) *v* apply; **aplicar-se a** apply to

apogeu (er-poo-*zhay*ᵒᵒ) *m* peak; height, zenith

apoiar-se (er-poa-ⱽahr-ser) *v* *lean

apólice (er-*po*-lee-ser) f policy

apontador (er-pawngn-ter-*doar*) mBr pencil-sharpener

apontamento (er-pawngn-ter-*mayngn*-too) m note

apontar (er-pawngn-*tahr*) v point, point out; ~ **para** aim at

aposta (er-*posh*-ter) f bet

apostar (er-*posh-tahr*) v *bet

apreciação (er-prer-sYer-*serngw*) f (pl -ções) appreciation

apreciar (er-prer-*sYahr*) v appreciate

apreender (er-prYayngn-*dayr*) v impound

aprender (er-prayngn-*dayr*) v *learn

apresentação (er-prer-zayngn-ter-*serngw*) f (pl -ções) introduction

apresentar (er-prer-zayngn-*tahr*) v present, introduce; **apresentar-se** report; appear

apressadamente (er-prer-sah-dher-*mayngn*-ter) adv in a hurry

apressado (er-prer-*sah*-dhoo) adj hasty

apressar-se (er-prer-*sahr*-ser) v rush, hurry, hasten

apropriado (er-proo-prYah-dhoo) adj suitable, convenient, proper, fit, appropriate

aprovação (er-proo-ver-*serngw*) f (pl -ções) approval

aprovar (er-proo-*vahr*) v approve; consent

aproveitar-se (er-proo-vay-*tahr*-ser) v profit; *take advantage of

aproximadamente (er-pro-see-mah-dher-*mayngn*-ter) adv approximately; about

aproximado (er-pro-see-*mah*-dhoo) adj approximate

aproximar-se (er-pro-see-*mahr*-ser) v approach

aptidão (erp-tee-*dherngw*) f (pl -dões) faculty

aquecedor (er-keh-ser-*dhoar*) m heater; ~ **de imersão** immersion heater

aquecer (er-keh-*sayr*) v warm, heat

aquecimento (er-keh-see-*mayngn*-too) m heating; ~ **central** central heating

aquele (er-*kay*-ler) adj that; pron that, that one; **aqueles** those

aqui (er-*kee*) adv here; ~ **está** here you are

aquilo (er-*kee*-loo) pron that

aquisição (er-ker-zee-*serngw*) f (pl -ções) acquisition

ar (ahr) m sky, air; **ao** ~ **livre** outdoors; ~ **condicionado** air-conditioning; **corrente de** ~ draught

árabe (*ah*-rer-bher) adj Arab; m Arab

Arábia Saudita (er-*rah*-bhYer sou-*dee*-ter) Saudi Arabia

arado (er-*rah*-dhoo) m plough

arame (er-*rer*-mer) m wire

aranha (er-*rer*-ñer) f spider; **teia de** ~ cobweb, spider's web

arbitrário (err-bhee-*trah*-rYoo) adj arbitrary

árbitro (*ahr*-bhee-troo) m umpire

arborizado (err-bhoo-ree-*zer*-dhoo) adj wooded

arbusto (err-*bhoosh*-too) m shrub; bush

arca (*ahr*-ker) f chest

arcada (err-*kah*-dher) f arcade

arcebispo (err-ser-*bheesh*-poo) m archbishop

archote (err-*sho*-ter) m torch

arco (*ahr*-koo) m arch, bow

arco-íris (ahr-koo-*ee*-reesh) m (pl ~) rainbow

arder (err-*dayr*) v *burn

ardil (err-*deel*) m (pl -is) ruse

ardósia (err-do-zYer) f slate

área (*ahr*-Yer) f area

areia (er-*ray*-er) f sand

arejamento (er-rer-zher-*mayng*-too) *m* ventilation

arejar (er-rer-*zhahr*) *v* air, ventilate

arenoso (er-rer-*noa*-zoo) *adj* sandy

arenque (er-*rayngng*-ker) *m* herring

Argélia (err-zheh-lYer) *f* Algeria

argelino (err-zher-*lee*-noo) *adj* Algerian; *m* Algerian

Argentina (err-zhayngn-*tee*-ner) *f* Argentina

argentino (err-zhayngn-*tee*-noo) *adj* Argentinian; *m* Argentinian

argila (err-*zhee*-ler) *f* clay

argumentar (err-goo-mayngn-*tahr*) *v* argue

argumento (err-goo-*mayng*-too) *m* argument

árido (*ah*-ree-dhoo) *adj* arid

arinca (ah-*reeng*-ker) *f* haddock

aritmética (er-reet-*meh*-tee-ker) *f* arithmetic

arma (*ahr*-mer) *f* arm, weapon

armação (err-mer-*serng*ᵂ) *f* (pl -ções) frame

armadilha (err-mer-*dhee*-lYah) *f* trap

armado (err-*mer*-dhoo) *adj* armed

armador (err-mer-*dhoar*) *m* shipowner

armadura (err-mer-*dhoo*-rer) *f* armour

armar (err-*mahr*) *v* arm

armarinho (ahr-mah-*ree*-ñoo) *mBr* haberdashery

armário (err-*mah*-rYoo) *m* closet, cupboard

armazém (err-mer-*zerng*Y) *m* warehouse; depository, store-house, depot; department store

armazenagem (err-mer-zer-*nah*-zherng*Y*) *f* storage

armazenar (err-mer-zer-*nahr*) *v* store

armazenista (err-mer-zer-*neesh*-ter) *m* wholesale dealer

aroma (er-*roa*-mer) *m* aroma

arqueado (err-kʸ*ah*-dhoo) *adj* arched

arquejar (err-kɪ-*zhahr*) *v* pant

arqueologia (err-kʸoo-loo-*zhee*-er) *f* archaeology

arqueólogo (err-kʸo-loo-goo) *m* archaeologist

arquitecto (err-kee-*teh*-too) *m* architect

arquitectura (err-kee-teh-*too*-rer) *f* architecture

arquivo (err-*kee*-voo) *m* archives *pl*; file

arrancar (er-rrerng-*kahr*) *v* extract

arranha-céus (er-rrer-ñer-*seh*-oosh) *m* (pl ~) skyscraper

arranhão (er-rrer-*nerng*ᵂ) *m* (pl -hões) graze, scratch

arranhar (er-rrer-*ñahr*) *v* scratch

arranjar (er-rrerng-*zhahr*) *v* arrange; **arranjar-se com** *make do with

arrastar (er-rrersh-*tahr*) *v* drag, haul

arrecadação (er-rrer-ker-dher-*serng*ᵂ) *f* (pl -ções) shed

arredondado (er-rrer-dhawngn-*dah*-dhoo) *adj* rounded

arredores (er-rrer-*dhoa*-rɪsh) *mpl* surroundings *pl*, environment; outskirts *pl*

arreliar (er-rrer-lYahr) *v* tease; annoy

arremessar (er-rrer-mer-*sahr*) *v* toss

arrendamento (er-rrayngn-dah-*mayng*-too) *m* lease

arrendar (er-rrayngn-*dahr*) *v* rent; lease

arrependimento (er-rrer-payngn-dee-*mayng*-too) *m* repentance

arrepio (er-rrer-*pee*ᵒᵒ) *m* shiver

arriscado (er-rreesh-*kah*-dhoo) *adj* risky

arriscar (er-rreesh-*kahr*) *v* risk

arrogante (er-rroo-*gerng*n-ter) *adj* snooty

arrojado (er-rroo-*zhah*-dhoo) *adj* bold

arroz (er-*rroash*) *m* rice

arruinar (er-rrwee-*nahr*) *v* ruin

arrumador (er-rroo-mer-*dhoar*) *m* usher

arrumadora (er-rroo-mer-*dho*-rer) *f* usherette

arrumar (er-rroo-*mahr*) *v* tidy up

arte (*ahr*-ter) *f* art; **artes e ofícios** arts and crafts

artéria (ahr-*teh*-r ^{Y} er) *f* artery; $\sim$ **principal** thoroughfare

artesanato (ahr-ter-zer-*nah*-too) *m* handicraft

articulação (ahr-tee-koo-ler-*serng* ^{W}) *f* (pl -ções) joint

artificial (err-ter-fι-*s* ^{Y} *ahl*) *adj* (pl -ais) artificial

artifício (err-ter-*fee*-s ^{Y} oo) *m* artifice

artigo (err-*tee*-goo) *m* article, item; **artigos de toalete** toiletry

artista (err-*teesh*-ter) *m* artist; *f* artist

artístico (err-*teesh*-tee-koo) *adj* artistic

árvore (*ahr*-voo-rer) *f* tree; $\sim$ **de cames** camshaft

asa (ah-zer) *f* wing

ascendência (ersh-sayngn-*dayng*-s ^{Y} er) *f* origin

ascender (ersh-sayngn-*dayr*) *v* ascend

ascensão (ersh-sayng-*serng* ^{W}) *f* (pl -sões) ascent

ascensor (ersh-sayng-*soar*) *m* lift

asfalto (ersh-*fahl*-too) *m* asphalt

Ásia (er-z ^{Y} er) *f* Asia

asiático (er-z ^{Y} ah-tee-koo) *adj* Asian; *m* Asian

asilo (er-*zee*-loo) *m* asylum

asma (*ahzh*-mer) *f* asthma

asneira (erzh-*nay*-rah) *f* rubbish; blunder; mistake

aspas (*ahsh*-persh) *fpl* quotation marks

aspecto (ersh-*peh*-too) *m* aspect; look

áspero (*ahsh*-per-roo) *adj* rough, harsh

aspirador (ersh-pee-rer-*dhoar*) *m* vacuum cleaner

aspirar (ersh-pee-*rahr*) *v* aim at, aspire; hoover; $\sim$ **a** aim at

aspirina (ersh-pee-*ree*-ner) *f* aspirin

assaltar (er-sahl-*tahr*) *v* burgle

assalto (er-*sahl*-too) *m* assault, attack

assar (er-*sahr*) *v* roast

assassinar (er-ser-see-*nahr*) *v* murder

assassínio (er-ser-*see*-n ^{Y} oo) *m* assassination

assassino (er-ser-*see*-noo) *m* murderer

assaz (er-*sahsh*) *adv* enough, sufficiently; rather

asseado (er-s ^{Y} *ah*-dhoo) *adj* neat; tidy

assegurar (er-ser-goo-*rahr*) *v* assure

assembleia (er-sayngm-*blay*-er) *f* assembly, meeting

assemelhar-se (er-ser-mι-l ^{Y} *ahr*-ser) *v* resemble

assento (er-*sayngn*-too) *m* seat; chair

assim (er-*seeng*) *adv* so; thus; $\sim$ **como** as well as; $\sim$ **por diante** and so on; $\sim$ **que** as soon as

assinalar (er-see-ner-*lahr*) *v* indicate

assinante (er-see-*nerngn*-ter) *m* subscriber

assinar (er-see-*nahr*) *v* sign

assinatura (er-see-ner-*too*-rer) *f* signature; subscription; $\sim$ **de temporada** season-ticket

assistência (er-seesh-*tayng*-s ^{Y} er) *f* attendance; assistance, relief

assistente (er-seesh-*tayngn*-ter) *m* assistant

assistir (er-seesh-*teer*) *v* assist; $\sim$ **a** assist at; attend

assobiar (er-soo-bh ^{Y} *ahr*) *v* whistle

associação (er-soo-s ^{Y} er-*serng* ^{W}) *f* (pl -ções) association; club, society

associar (er-soo-s ^{Y} *ahr*) *v* associate; **associar-se a** join

assoprar (er-soo-*prahr*) *v* *blow

assunto (er-*soongn*-too) *m* matter; theme, concern, affair, subject, business

assustado (er-soosh-*tah*-dhoo) *adj* frightened; afraid

assustador (er-soosh-ter-*dhoar*) *adj* scary; creepy

assustar (er-soosh-*tahr*) *v* frighten; scare; **assustar-se** *be frightened

astronomia (ersh-troo-noo-*mee*-er) *f* astronomy

astuto (ersh-*too*-too) *adj* clever; sly

atacador (ah-tah-ker-*dhoar*) *m* shoe-lace, lace

atacar (er-ter-*kahr*) *v* attack, assault; *strike

atalho (er-*tah*-lYoo) *m* trail

ataque (er-*tah*-ker) *m* attack, fit; stroke

atar (er-*tahr*) *v* tie; bundle, *bind, attach, fasten; ~ **num molho** bundle

atarefado (er-ter-rer-*fah*-dhoo) *adj* busy

até (er-*teh*) *prep* till; until, to; ~ **a-gora** so far; ~ **que** till

atenção (er-tayng-*serng*ʷ) *f* (pl -ções) attention; notice, consideration; **prestar** ~ mind; **prestar** ~ **a** attend to; *pay attention to, mind

atencioso (er-tayng-sYoa-zoo) *adj* considerate; thoughtful

atender (er-tayngn-*dayr*) *v* attend on

atento (er-*tayngn*-too) *adj* attentive

aterrador (er-ter-rrer-*dhoar*) *adj* terrifying

aterrar (er-ter-*rrahr*) *v* land

aterrorizar (er-ter-rroo-ree-*zahr*) *v* terrify

atestado (er-tɪsh-*tah*-dhoo) *adj* chock-full; *m* certificate; ~ **de saúde** health certificate

atestar (er-tɪsh-*tahr*) *v* fill up

ateu (er-*tay*ᵒᵒ) *m* (f ateia) atheist

atingir (er-teeng-*zheer*) *v* attain; *hit

atirar (er-tee-*rahr*) *v* *throw, *cast

atitude (er-tee-*too*-dher) *f* attitude;

position

Atlântico (ert-*lerngn*-tee-koo) *m* Atlantic

atleta (ert-*leh*-ter) *m* athlete

atletismo (ert-ler-*teezh*-moo) *m* athletics *pl*

atmosfera (ert-moosh-*feh*-rer) *f* atmosphere

atómico (er-*to*-mee-koo) *adj* atomic

átomo (*ah*-tuu-muu) *m* atom

atordoado (er-toor-*dhwah*-dhoo) *adj* dizzy, giddy

atormentar (er-toor-mayngn-*tahr*) *v* torment

atracar (er-trer-*kahr*) *v* moor

atracção (er-trah-*serng*ʷ) *f* (pl -ções) attraction

atractivo (er-trah-*tee*-voo) *m* attraction

atraente (er-trer-*ayngn*-ter) *adj* attractive

***atrair** (er-trer-*eer*) *v* attract

atrás (er-*trahsh*) *adv* behind; back; ~ **de** behind

atrasado (er-trer-*zah*-dhoo) *adj* late; overdue

atrasar (er-trer-*zahr*) *v* delay

atraso (er-*trah*-zoo) *m* delay

através (er-trer-*vehsh*) *adv* across, through; ~ **de** through

atravessar (er-trer-ver-*sahr*) *v* cross, pass through; *go through

atrevido (er-trer-*vee*-dhoo) *adj* bold

***atribuir** (er-tree-*bhweer*) *v* allot ~ **a** assign to

átrio (*ah*-trYoo) *m* lobby

atroz (er-*trosh*) *adj* horrible

atum (er-*toong*) *m* tuna

audácia (ou-*dhah*-sYer) *f* nerve

audiência (erᵒᵒ-dhYayng-sYer) *f* audience

auditório (erᵒᵒ-dhee-*to*-rYoo) *m* auditorium

audível (ou-*dhee*-vehl) *adj* (pl -eis)

audible

aula (ou-ler) f lesson

aumentar (ou-mayngn-tahr) v increase; raise

aumento (ou-mayngn-too) m increase; rise; raise nAm; ~ **de salário** raise nAm

aurora (ou-ro-rah) f dawn

auscultador (oush-kool-ter-dhoar) m receiver; stethoscope

ausência (ou-zayng-sYer) f absence

ausente (ou-zayngn-ter) adj absent; away

Austrália (oush-trah-lYer) f Australia

australiano (oush-trer-lYer-noo) adj Australian; m Australian

Áustria (oush-trYer) f Austria

austríaco (oush-tree-er-koo) m Austrian, adj Austrian

autêntico (ou-tayngn-tee-koo) adj authentic; original

autocarro (ou-too-kah-rroo) m coach, bus

auto-estrada (ou-tōōeesh-trah-dher) f motorway; highway nAm

automático (ou-too-mah-tee-koo) adj automatic; **distribuidor ~ de selos** stamp machine

automatização (ou-too-mer-tee-zer-serngw) f (pl -cões) automation

automobilismo (ou-too-moo-bhee-leezh-moo) m motoring

automobilista (ou-too-moo-bhee-leesh-ter) m motorist

automóvel (ou-too-mo-vehl) m (pl -eis) automobile; motor-car; **andar de ~** *ride

autonomia (ou-too-noo-mee-er) f self-government

autónomo (ou-to-noo-moo) adj independent, autonomous

autópsia (ou-top-sYer) f autopsy

autor (ou-toar) m author

autoridade (ou-too-ree-dhah-dher) f

authority

autoritário (ou-too-ree-tah-rYoo) adj authoritarian

autorização (ou-too-ree-zer-serngw) f (pl -cões) permission, authorization, permit; ~ **de residência** residence permit; ~ **de trabalho** work permit; labor permit Am

autorizar (ou-too-ree-zahr) v license; ~ **a** allow to; ***estar autorizado** *be allowed

auto-serviço (ou-too-serr-vee-soo) m self-service

auxiliar (ou-see-lYahr) v assist, aid

avalanche (er-ver-lerng-sher) f avalanche

avaliação (er-ver-lYer-serngw) f (pl -cões) appreciation

avaliar (er-ver-lYahr) v value; appreciate, evaluate

avançar (er-verng-sahr) v *get on, advance; *go ahead, *go on

avanço (er-verng-soo) m lead; advance

avante (er-verngn-ter) adv forward

avarento (er-ver-rayngn-too) adj avaricious

avaria (er-ver-ree-er) f breakdown

avariado (er-ver-rYah-dhoo) adj out of order, broken

avariar-se (er-ver-rYahr-ser) v *break down

ave (ah-ver) f bird; ~ **marinha** seabird; **aves de criação** poultry, fowl

aveia (er-vay-er) f oats pl

avelã (er-ver-lerng) f hazelnut

avenida (er-ver-nee-dher) f avenue

avental (er-vayngn-tahl) m (pl -ais) apron

aventura (er-vayngn-too-rer) f adventure; affair

aventurar (er-vayngn-too-rahr) v venture

aversão (er-verr-serngw) f (pl -sões)

dislike, aversion

do avesso (doo er-*veh*-soo) inside out

avestruz (er-vish-*troosh*) f ostrich

avião (er-v*Yerng*ᵂ) m (pl aviões) aeroplane; aircraft, plane; airplane nAm; ~ **a jacto** jet

avisar (er-vee-*sahr*) v caution, warn; notify

aviso (er-*vee*-zoo) m warning; notice

avistar (er-veesh-*tahr*) v *see

avó (er-*vo*) f grandmother; **avozinha** grandmother

avô (er-*voa*) m grandfather; granddad; **avós** grandparents pl; **avozinho** grandfather

à-vontade (ah-vawngn-*tah*-dher) m at ease, ease

azáfama (er-*zah*-fer-mer) f bustle

azar (er-*zahr*) m bad luck; chance

azedo (er-*zay*-dhoo) adj sour

azeite (er-*zay*-ter) m olive oil

azeitona (er-zay-*toa*-ner) f olive

azia (er-*zee*-er) f heartburn

azinhaga (er-zee-*ñah*-ger) f lane

azoto (er-*zoa*-too) m nitrogen

azul (er-*zool*) adj (pl azuis) blue

azulejo (er-zoo-*lay*-zhoo) m tile

B

bacalhau (ber-ker-*lᶌou*) m cod

bacia (ber-*see*-er) f basin

baço (*bah*-soo) adj mat, dull, dim

bacon (*bay*-kern) m bacon

bactéria (berk-*teh*-rᶌer) f bacterium

baga (*bah*-ger) f berry

bagageira (ber-ger-*zhay*-rer) f luggage rack

bagagem (ber-*ger*-zherngᶌ) f baggage, luggage; ~ **de mão** hand luggage; hand baggage Am

baía (ber-*ee*-er) f bay

bailado (bigh-*lah*-dhoo) m ballet

baile (*bigh*-ler) m ball

bainha (ber-*ee*-ñer) f hem

bairro (*bigh*-rroo) m district, quarter; ~ **pobre** slum

baixa-mar (bigh-sher-*mahr*) f low tide

baixar (bigh-*shahr*) v lower

baixo (*bigh*-shoo) adj short; low; m bass; **em** ~ below; downstairs; **para** ~ down; downwards, downstairs

bala (*bah*-ler) f bullet

balança (ber-*lerng*-ser) f scales; weighing-machine

balançar (ber-lerng-*sahr*) v *swing; **balançar-se** *swing

balancé (ber-lerng-*seh*) m seesaw

balanço (ber-*lerng*-soo) m balance; mBr swing

balão (ber-*lerng*ᵂ) m (pl balões) balloon

balas (*bah*-lersh) fplBr sweets

balaustrada (ber-loush-*trah*-dher) f rail

balbuciar (bahl-boo-s*ᶌahr*) v falter

balcão (bahl-*kerng*ᵂ) m (pl -cões) counter; circle

balde (*bahl*-der) m bucket, pail

balé (bah-*leh*) mBr ballet

baleia (ber-*lay*-er) f whale

baliza (ber-*lee*-zer) f goal

balofo (ber-*loa*-foo) adj flaccid

baloiçar (ber-loi-*sahr*) v rock

baloiço (ber-*loi*-soo) m swing

bambu (berngm-boo) m bamboo

banana (ber-*ner*-ner) f banana

banco (*berng*-koo) m bench; bank

banda (*berng*n-der) f band

bandeira (berngn-*day*-rer) f flag

bandido (berng-*dee*-dhoo) m bandit

banhar-se (ber-*ñahr*-ser) v bathe

banheira (ber-*ñay*-rer) f bathtub

banheiro (ber-*ñay*-roo) mBr bathroom

banho (*ber*-ñoo) m bath; ~ **turco**

Turkish bath; **tomar ~ bathe; to-mar um ~ de sol** sunbathe; **touca de ~** bathing-cap; **traje de ~** *Br* bathing-suit

banquete (berng-kay-ter) *m* banquet

baptismo (bah-*teezh*-moo) *m* christening, baptism

baptizar (bah-tee-*zahr*) *v* christen, baptize

bar (bahr) *m* saloon, bar; public house

baralhar (ber-rer-*lᵞahr*) *v* shuffle

barato (ber-*rah*-too) *adj* cheap, inexpensive

barba (*bahr*-ber) *f* beard; *fazer a ~ shave

barbaridade (berr-ber-ree-*dhah*-dher) *f* barbarity

***barbear-se** (berr-*bᵞahr*-ser) *v* shave

barbeiro (berr-*bay*-roo) *m* barber

barco (*bahr*-koo) *m* boat; **~ a motor** launch, motor-boat; **~ a remos** rowing-boat; **~ a vapor** steamer; **~ à vela** sailing-boat

barítono (ber-*ree*-too-noo) *m* baritone

barómetro (ber-*ro*-mer-troo) *m* barometer

barquinho (berr-*kee*-ño) *m* dinghy

barra (*bah*-rrer) *f* bar; rail

barraca (ber-*rrah*-ker) *f* shed

barragem (ber-*rrah*-zhernɡᵞ) *f* dam

barreira (ber-*rray*-rer) *f* barrier; **~ de protecção** crash barrier

barrete (ber-*rray*-ter) *m* cap

barrica (ber-*rree*-ker) *f* keg

barriga (ber-*rree*-ger) *f* stomach; **~ da perna** calf

barril (ber-*rreel*) *m* (pl -is) cask; barrel

barro (*bah*-roo) *m* terracotta

barroco (ber-*rroa*-koo) *adj* baroque

barulho (ber-*roo*-lᵞoo) *m* noise

base (*bah*-zer) *f* basis, base

***basear** (ber-z*ᵞahr*) *v* base

basebol (*bayz*-bhol) *m* baseball

basílica (ber-*zee*-lee-ker) *f* basilica

bastante (bersh-*ternɡn*-ter) *adj* sufficient, enough; *adv* quite, rather, pretty, fairly

bastar (bersh-*tahr*) *v* *do, suffice

bastardo (bersh-*tahr*-dhoo) *m* bastard

bata (*bah*-ter) *f* smock

batalha (ber-*tah*-lᵞer) *f* battle

batata (ber-*tah*-ter) *f* potato; **batatas fritas** chips

batedeira (ber-ter-*dhay*-rer) *f* mixer

bater (ber-*tayr*) *v* *beat; whip, bump, knock, tap, smack, *strike, slap, *hit; **~ as palmas** clap

bateria (ber-ter-*ree*-er) *f* battery

baton (bah-*tawng*) *m* lipstick

baú (ber-*oo*) *m* trunk

baunilha (bou-*nee*-lᵞer) *f* vanilla

bêbado (*bay*-bher-dhoo) *adj* drunk

bebé (beh-*bheh*) *m* baby; **alcofa de ~** carry-cot; **carrinho de ~** pram; baby carriage *Am*

beber (ber-*bhayr*) *v* *drink

beberete (ber-bher-*ray*-ter) *m* cocktail

bebida (ber-*bhee*-dher) *f* beverage, drink; **~ não alcoólica** soft drink; **bebidas alcoólicas** spirits, liquor

beco (*bay*-koo) *m* alley; **~ sem saída** cul-de-sac

bege (behzh) *adj* beige

beijar (bay-*zhahr*) *v* kiss

beijo (*bay*-zhoo) *m* kiss

beira (*bay*-rer) *f* bank; **à ~ de** on the edge of

beira-mar (bay-rer-*mahr*) *f* seashore; shore

beira-rio (bay-rer-*rree*ᵒᵒ) *f* riverside

belas-artes (beh-lerz-*ahr*-tısh) *fpl* fine arts

belbutina (behl-boo-*tee*-ner) *f* velveteen

beleza (ber-*lay*-zer) *f* beauty

belga (*behl*-ger) *adj* Belgian; *m* Belgian

Bélgica (behl-zhee-ker) f Belgium

beliche (ber-lee-sher) m bunk, berth

beliscar (ber-leesh-kahr) v pinch

belo (beh-loo) adj fine, beautiful; handsome

bem (berngY) adv well; **bem!** well!; **está bem!** all right!

bem-estar (berngY-ish-tahr) m comfort; welfare

benção (bayng-serngW) f (pl ~s) blessing

*bendizer (berngY-dee-zayr) v bless

beneficiar (ber-ner-fee-sYahr) v benefit

beneficiário (ber-ner-fee-sYah-rYoo) m payee

benefício (ber-neh-fee-koo) m benefit, profit

bengala (bayngng-gah-ler) f cane; walking-stick

bengaleiro (bayngng-ger-lay-roo) m hat rack

bens (bayngeesh) mpl possessions; goods pl, belongings pl

benvindo (berngY-veengn-doo) adj welcome

berço (bayr-soo) m cradle

beringela (ber-reeng-zheh-ler) f eggplant

berlinde (berr-leengn-der) m marble

berma (behr-mer) f roadside

berrar (ber-rrahr) v yell

berro (beh-rroo) m yell

betão (ber-terngW) m concrete

beterraba (ber-ter-rrah-bher) f beet; beetroot

bétula (beh-too-ler) f birch

bexiga (ber-shee-ger) f bladder; **bexigas doidas** chicken-pox

bíblia (bee-bhlYer) f bible

biblioteca (bee-bhlYoo-teh-ker) f library

bicha (bee-sher) f queue; ***fazer ~**
queue

bicho (bee-shoo) m worm; animal

bicicleta (bee-see-kleh-ter) f cycle, bicycle; **~ a motor** moped; motorbike nAm

bico (bee-koo) m point; nozzle; beak

bicudo (bee-koo-dhoo) adj pointed

biela (bYeh-ler) f piston-rod

bife (bee-fer) m steak

bifurcação (bee-foor-ker-serngW) f (pl -cões) road fork, fork

bifurcar (bee-foor-kahr) v fork

bigode (bee-go-dher) m moustache

bilha (bee-lYer) f pitcher

bilhar (bee-lYahr) m billiards pl

bilhete (bee-lYay-ter) m ticket; **~ de gare** platform ticket; **~ gratuito** free ticket; **~ postal** postcard

bilheteira (bee-lYer-tay-rer) f box-office; **~ automática** ticket machine; **~ de reservação** box-office

bilheteria (bee-lYer-ter-ree-er) fBr box-office

bilião (bee-lYerngW) m (pl -iões) billion

bilíngue (bee-leeng-gwer) adj bilingual

bílis (bee-leesh) f bile; gall; **vesícula biliar** gall bladder

binóculo (bee-no-koo-loo) m binoculars pl; field glasses

biologia (bYoo-loo-zhee-er) f biology

biombo (bYawngm-boo) m screen

biscoito (beesh-koi-too) m biscuit; cookie nAm

bispo (beesh-poo) m bishop

bloco (blo-koo) m block; **~ de notas** writing-pad; pad; **~ de papel** writing-pad; **~ habitacional** house block Am

*bloquear (bloo-kYahr) v block

blusa (bloo-zer) f blouse

boate (bwaht) f nightclub

bobagem (boa-bhah-zherngY) fBr rubbish

bobina (boo-*bhee*-ner) f spool; ~ **de ignição** ignition coil

boca (*boa*-ker) f mouth

bocadinho (poa-koo-*shee*-ñoo) m bit

bocado (boo-*kah*-dhoo) m bite; fragment; morsel, part, lump

bocejar (boo-sı-*zhahr*) v yawn

bode (*bo*-dher) m goat; ~ **expiatório** scapegoat

bofetada (boo-fer-*tah*-dher) f slap

boi (boi) m ox

bóia (*bo*-ᵞer) f buoy

boina (*boi*-ner) f beret

bola (*bo*-ler) f ball; ~ **de futebol** football

bolacha (boo-*lah*-sher) f waffle; ~ **de baunilha** wafer

bolbo (*boal*-bhoo) m bulb

boletim (boo-ler-*teeng*) m bulletin; ~ **meteorológico** weather forecast

bolha (*boa*-lᵞer) f bubble; blister

Bolívia (boo-*lee*-vᵞer) f Bolivia

boliviano (boo-lee-vᵞah-noo) adj Bolivian; m Bolivian

bolo (*boa*-loo) m cake

bolor (boo-*loar*) m mildew

bolorento (boo-loo-*rayngn*-too) adj mouldy

bolota (boo-*lo*-ter) f acorn

bolsa (*boal*-ser) f pouch, bag; stock market, exchange, stock exchange; ~ **de estudos** scholarship; ~ **de valores** stock exchange

bolso (*boal*-soo) m pocket

bom (bawng) adj (f boa; pl bons) good; kind; well; nice; **é boa!** indeed!

bomba (*bawngm*-ber) f bomb; pump; ~ **de água** water pump; ~ **de gasolina** petrol pump; fuel pump Am: ***dar à** ~ pump

*bombardear (bawngm-berr-dᵞahr) v bomb

bombazina (bawngm-ber-*zee*-ner) f corduroy

*bombear (bawngm-bᵞahr) vBr pump

bombeiros (bawngm-*bay*-roosh) mpl fire-brigade

bombom (bawng-*bawng*) m chocolate

bombordo (bawngm-*boar*-dhoo) m port

bonde (*boan*-der) mBr tram, streetcar nAm

bondoso (bawngn-*doa*-zoo) adj good-natured; kind

boné (boo-*neh*) m cap

boneca (boo-*neh*-ker) f doll

bonito (boo-*nee*-too) adj pretty; nice, fair, good-looking

boquilha (boo-*kee*-lᵞer) f cigarette-holder

borboleta (boor-boo-*lay*-ter) f butterfly

borbulha (boor-*boo*-lᵞer) f pimple

borda (*bor*-dher) f verge, edge, brim, border, rim

bordado (boor-*dah*-dhoo) m embroidery

bordar (boor-*dahr*) v embroider

bordel (boor-*dehl*) m (pl -déis) brothel

a bordo (er *bor*-doo) aboard

borracha (boo-*rrah*-sher) f rubber; eraser

borrão (boo-*rrerng*ʷ) m (pl -rões) blot

borrego (boo-*rray*-goo) m lamb

bosque (*boash*-ker) m wood

bota (*bo*-ter) f boot; **botas de esqui** ski boots

botânica (boo-*ter*-nee-ker) f botany

botão (boo-*terng*ʷ) m (pl botões) button; push-button; bud; ~ **de colarinho** collar stud; **botões de punho** cuff-links pl; **casa de** ~ buttonhole

boutique (boo-*tee*-ker) f boutique

bowling (*boa*-leeng) *m* bowling

braço (*brah*-soo) *m* arm; **de ~ dado** arm-in-arm

brado (*brah*-dhoo) *m* cry

braguilha (brer-*gee*-lYah) *f* fly

bramir (brer-*meer*) *v* roar

branco (*brerng*-koo) *adj* white; **em ~** blank

brando (*brerngn*-dhoo) *adj* tender, soft; smooth

Brasil (brer-*zeel*) *m* Brazil

brasileiro (brer-zee-*lay*-roo) *adj* Brazilian; *m* Brazilian

brecha (*breh*-sher) *f* breach; gap

breve (*breh*-ver) *adj* brief; **dentro em ~** shortly; **em ~** soon

brevemente (breh-ver-*mayngn*-ter) *adv* shortly, soon

bridge (breej) *m* bridge

briga (*bree*-ger) *f* quarrel, dispute

brilhante (bree-*lYerngn*-ter) *adj* brilliant; *m* diamond

brilhar (bree-*lYahr*) *v* *shine; glow

brilho (*bree*-lYoo) *m* glare; glow

brincar (breeng-*kahr*) *v* play

brinco (*breeng*-koo) *m* earring

brinde (*breengn*-der) *m* toast

brinquedo (breeng-*kay*-dhoo) *m* toy

brioche (bree-osh) *m* bun

brisa (*bree*-zer) *f* breeze

britânico (bree-*ter*-nee-koo) *adj* British; *m* Briton

broca (*bro*-ker) *f* drill

brocar (broo-*kahr*) *v* bore; drill

broche (*bro*-sher) *m* brooch

brochura (broo-*shoo*-rer) *f* brochure

bronquite (brawng-*kee*-ter) *f* bronchitis

bronze (*brawng*-zer) *m* bronze; **de ~** bronze

bronzeado (brawng-z*Yah*-dhoo) *adj* tanned

bruços (*broo*-soosh) *mpl* breaststroke; **de ~** face downwards

bruma (*broo*-mer) *f* haze

brutal (broo-*tahl*) *adj* (pl -ais) brutal

bruto (*broo*-too) *adj* gross; *m* brute

bruxa (*broo*-sher) *f* witch

bufete (boo-*fay*-ter) *m* buffet

bule (*boo*-ler) *m* teapot

Bulgária (bool-*gah*-rYer) *f* Bulgaria

búlgaro (*bool*-ger-roo) *adj* Bulgarian; *m* Bulgarian

buraco (boo-*rah*-koo) *m* hole

burguês (boor-*gaysh*) *adj* middle-class, bourgeois

burla (*boor*-ler) *f* swindle

burlão (boor-*lerng*W) *m* (pl -lões) swindler

burlar (boor-*lahr*) *v* swindle

burocracia (boo-roo-krer-*see*-er) *f* bureaucracy

burro (*boo*-rroo) *m* ass, donkey

busca (*boosh*-ker) *f* search

buscar (boosh-*kahr*) *v* look for; ***ir ~** fetch; collect

bússola (*boo*-soo-ler) *f* compass

busto (*boosh*-too) *m* bust

buzina (boo-zee-ner) *f* horn; hooter

buzinar (boo-zee-*nahr*) *v* hoot

búzio (*boo*-zYoo) *m* winkle

C

cá (kah) *adv* here

cabana (ker-*bher*-ner) *f* cabin; hut

cabeça (ker-*bhay*-ser) *f* head; **~ do motor** cylinder head

cabeçalho (ker-bher-*sah*-lYoo) *m* headline

cabeçudo (ker-bhay-*soo*-dhoo) *adj* head-strong

cabedal (ker-bher-*dhahl*) *m* (pl -ais) leather

cabeleireiro (ker-bay-lay-*ray*-roo) *m* hairdresser

cabelo (ker-*bhay*-loo) *m* hair; ~ pos-tiço hair piece

cabeludo (ker-bher-*loo*-dhoo) *adj* hairy

*caber (ker-*bhayr*) *v* *be contained in: fit in

cabide (ker-*bhee*-dher) *m* hanger; coat-hanger

cabina (ker-*bhee*-ner) *f* booth, cabin; ~ telefónica telephone booth

cabo (*kah*-bhoo) *m* handle; cape; cable

cabra (*kah*-bhrer) *f* goat

caça (*kah*-ser) *f* chase, hunt; game

caçador (ker-ser-*dhoar*) *m* hunter

caçar (ker-*sahr*) *v* hunt; ~ furtiva-mente poach

caçarola (ker-ser-ro-ler) *f* saucepan

cacete (ker-*say*-ter) *m* club, cudgel

cachimbo (kah-*sheengm*-boo) *m* pipe

cada (*kah*-dher) *adj* each, every; ~ um everyone

cadáver (ker-*dhah*-vehr) *m* corpse

cadeado (ker-dh^yah-dhoo) *m* padlock

cadeia (ker-*dhay*-er) *f* chain; gaol

cadeira (ker-*dhay*-rer) *f* chair; ~ de braços armchair; ~ de lona deck chair; ~ de rodas wheelchair

cadela (kah-*dheh*-ler) *f* bitch

café (ker-*feh*) *m* coffee; café

cafeína (ker-feh-*ee*-ner) *f* caffeine

cafetaria (ker-fer-*ter*-r^yer) *f* cafeteria

cafeteira (ker-fer-*tay*-rer) *f* coffee-pot; ~ de filtro percolator

câibra (*kerng^ym*-brer) *f* cramp

*cair (ker-*eer*) *v* *fall; deixar ~ drop

cais (kighsh) *m* wharf, quay, dock

caixa (*kigh*-sher) *f* box; pay-desk; cashier; *m* carton; cashier; ~ de cartão carton; ~ de ferramenta tool-box; ~ de fósforos match-box; ~ de papelão *Br* carton; ~ de primeiros socorros first-aid kit; ~ de tintas paint-box; ~ de velo-cidades gear-box; ~ económica savings bank

cal (kahl) *f* lime

calado (kah-*lah*-dhoo) *adj* silent; *es-tar ~ *be silent

calafrio (kah-ler-*free^{oo}*) *m* chill

calamidade (kah-ler-mee-*dhah*-dher) *f* calamity

calar (ker-*lahr*) *v* silence; calar-se *keep quiet

calçada (kahl-*sah*-dher) *f* causeway

calçado (kahl-*sah*-dhoo) *m* footwear

calcanhar (kahl-ker-*ñahr*) *m* heel

calcar (kahl-*kahr*) *v* stamp

calças (*kahl*-sersh) *fpl* slacks *pl*, trousers *pl*; pants *plAm*; ~ de es-qui ski pants; ~ de ganga jeans *pl*

calcinhas (kahl-*see*-ñersh) *fpl* knickers *pl*, panties *pl*

cálcio (*kahl*-s^yoo) *m* calcium

calções (kahl-*sawng*-ish) *mpl* shorts *pl*; briefs *pl*; ~ de banho swim-ming-trunks *pl*; ~ de ginástica gym-trunks

calculador (kahl-koo-ler-*dhoar*) *m* ad-ding-machine

calcular (kahl-koo-*lahr*) *v* calculate, reckon

cálculo (*kahl*-koo-loo) *m* calculation; ~ biliar gallstone

calendário (ker-layngn-*dah*-r^yoo) *m* calendar

calfe (*kahl*-fer) *m* calf skin

calista (ker-*leesh*-ter) *m* chiropodist

calmante (kahl-*merngn*-ter) *m* tran-quillizer

calmo (*kahl*-moo) *adj* calm, quiet; se-date

calo (*kah*-loo) *m* callus; corn

calor (ker-*loar*) *m* warmth, heat

caloria (ker-loo-*ree*-er) *f* calorie

calúnia (ker-loo-n^yer) *f* slander

calvinismo (kahl-vee-*neezh*-moo) *m* Calvinism

cama (*ker*-mer) *f* bed; ~ de acampa-

mento camp-bed; cot *nAm;* ~ **e mesa** room and board; **duas camas** twin beds

camada (ker-*mah*-dher) *f* layer

camafeu (ker-mer-*fay*⁰⁰) *m* cameo

câmara municipal (ker-mer-rer mooner-see-*pahl*) town hall

camarada (ker-mer-*rah*-dher) *m* comrade

câmara-de-ar (ker-mer-rer-*dhahr*) *f* inner tube

camarão (ker-mer-*rerngʷ*) *m* (pl -rões) shrimp; ~ **grande** prawn

cambiante (kerngm-*bʸerngn*-ter) *m* nuance

câmbio (*kerngm*-bʸoo) *m* exchange rate; **casa de** ~ money exchange, exchange office

cambota (kerngm-*bo*-ter) *f* crankshaft

camelo (ker-*may*-loo) *m* camel

camião (ker-*mʸerngʷ*) *m* (pl -iões) lorry; truck *nAm*

caminhar (ker-mee-*ñahr*) *v* step, walk

caminho (ker-*mee*-ñoo) *m* way; **a** ~ **de** bound for; **a meio** ~ halfway; **beira do** ~ wayside

caminho-de-ferro (ker-mee-ñoo-der-*feh*-roo) *m* railway; railroad *nAm*

camisa (ker-*mee*-zer) *f* shirt; vest; ~ **de dormir** nightdress

camiseta (ker-mee-*zay*-ter) *f Br* undershirt

camisola (ker-mee-*zo*-ler) *f* sweater, jumper; *f Br* nightdress; ~ **interior** undershirt

campainha (kerngm-per-*ee*-ñer) *f* bell; ~ **da porta** doorbell

campanário (kerngm-per-*nah*-rʸoo) *m* steeple

campanha (kerngm-*per*-ñer) *f* campaign

campeão (kerngm-*pʸerngʷ*) *m* (pl -eões) champion

campismo (kerngm-*peezh*-moo) *m* camping; **parque de** ~ camping site

campista (kerngm-*peesh*-ter) *m* camper

campo (*kerngm*-poo) *m* field; country, countryside; ~ **de aviação** airfield

camponês (kerngm-poo-*naysh*) *m* peasant

camurça (ker-*moor*-ser) *f* suede

cana (*ker*-ner) *f* cane; reed

Canadá (ker-*nah*-dher) *m* Canada

canadiano (ker-ner-dʸer-noo) *adj* Canadian; *m* Canadian

canal (ker-*nahl*) *m* (pl -ais) channel; canal; **Canal da Mancha** English Channel

canalizador (ker-ner-lee-zer-*dhoar*) *m* plumber

canário (ker-*nah*-rʸoo) *m* canary

canção (kerng-*serngʷ*) *f* (pl -ções) song; ~ **popular** folk song

cancela (kerng-*seh*-ler) *f* barrier; gate

cancelamento (kerng-ser-ler-*mayngn*-too) *m* cancellation

cancelar (kerng-ser-*lahr*) *v* cancel

cancro (*kerng*-kroo) *m* cancer

candeeiro (kerngm-*dʸay*-roo) *m* lamp; ~ **de mesa** reading-lamp

candelabro (kerngm-der-*lah*-bhroo) *m* candelabrum

candidato (kerngm-dee-*dhah*-too) *m* candidate

candidatura (kerngm-dee-dhah-*too*-rer) *f* application

caneca (ker-*neh*-ker) *f* mug

canela (ker-*neh*-ler) *f* cinnamon; shin-bone

caneta (ker-*nay*-ter) *f* pen; ~ **de tinta permanente** fountain-pen; ~ **esferográfica** ballpoint-pen

canga (*kerng*-ger) *f* yoke

canguru (*kerng*-goo-roo) *m* kangaroo

cânhamo (*ker*-ñer-moo) *m* hemp; canvas

canhão (ker-*ñerng*ʷ) *m* (pl -hões) gun

canhoto (ker-*ñoa*-too) *adj* left-handed

canil (ker-*neel*) *m* (pl -is) kennel

canivete (ker-nee-*veh*-ter) *m* pocket-knife, penknife

cano (*ker*-noo) *m* pipe; tube

canoa (ker-*noa*-er) *f* canoe

cansaço (kerng-*sah*-soo) *m* tiredness

cansado (kerng-*sah*-dhoo) *adj* weary, tired

cansar (kerng-*sahr*) *v* tire

cantar (kerng-*tahr*) *v* *sing

canteiro (kerng-*tay*-roo) *m* flowerbed

cantina (kerng-*tee*-ner) *f* canteen

canto (*kerng*-too) *m* singing; corner

cantor (kerng-*toar*) *m* singer

cantora (kerng-*toa*-rer) *f* singer

cão (kerng ʷ) *m* (pl cães) dog; ∼ **de cego** guide-dog; **casota do** ∼ kennel

caos (*koush*) *m* chaos

caótico (ker-*o*-tee-koo) *adj* chaotic

capa (*kah*-per) *f* cape; cover; jacket, sleeve; ∼ **de chuva** *Br* raincoat, mackintosh

capacete (ker-per-*say*-ter) *m* helmet

capacidade (ker-per-see-*dhah*-dher) *f* capacity; ability; faculty

capataz (ker-per-*tahsh*) *m* foreman

capaz (ker-*pahsh*) *adj* able, capable; *ser ∼ de *be able to

capela (ker-*peh*-ler) *f* chapel

capelão (ker-per-*lerng*ʷ) *m* (pl -ães) chaplain

capelista (ker-per-*leesh*-ter) *m* haberdashery

capital (ker-pee-*tahl*) *adj* (pl -ais) capital; *f* capital; *m* capital

capitalismo (ker-pee-ter-*leez*-moo) *m* capitalism

capitão (ker-pee-*terng*ʷ) *m* (pl -ães) captain

capitulação (ker-pee-too-ler-*serng*ʷ) *f* (pl -ções) capitulation

capricho (ker-*pree*-shoo) *m* fancy, whim, fad

cápsula (*kahp*-soo-ler) *f* capsule

captura (kerp-too-rer) *f* capture

capturar (kerp-too-*rahr*) *v* capture

capuz (ker-*poosh*) *m* hood

caqui (ker-*kee*) *m* khaki

cara (*kah*-rer) *f* face

caracol (ker-rer-*kol*) *m* (pl -cóis) snail; curl

carácter (ker-*rah*-tehr) *m* character

característica (ker-rer-ter-*reesh*-tee-ker) *f* characteristic; quality; feature

característico (ker-rer-ter-*reesh*-tee-koo) *adj* characteristic; typical

caracterizar (ker-rer-ter-ree-*zahr*) *v* mark, characterize

caramelo (ker-rer-*meh*-loo) *m* caramel; toffee

caranguejo (ker-rerng-*gay*-zhoo) *m* crab

caravana (kah-rah-*ver*-ner) *f* caravan; trailer *nAm*

carburador (kerr-boo-rer-*dhoar*) *m* carburettor

carcaça (kerr-*kah*-ser) *f* wreck

carcereiro (kerr-ser-ray-roo) *m* jailer

cardápio (kahr-*dhahp*-Yoo) *mBr* menu

cardeal (kerr-dhᵞahl) *m* (pl -ais) cardinal; *adj* cardinal

cardo (*kahr*-doo) *m* thistle

careca (ker-reh-ker) *adj* bald

carecer de (ker-rer-*sayr*) lack

carência (ker-*rayngs*ᵞer) *f* shortage, lack, want

careta (ker-ray-ter) *f* grin

carga (*kahr*-ger) *f* cargo, freight; charge

cargo (*kahr*-goo) *m* office, duty, function

caridade (ker-ree-*dhah*-dher) *f* charity

caril (ker-*reel*) *m* curry

carimbo (ker-*reengm*-boo) *m* stamp

Carnaval (kerr-ner-*vahl*) *m* (pl -ais) carnival

carne (*kahr*-ner) *f* flesh; meat; ~ **de carneiro** mutton; ~ **de porco** pork; ~ **de vaca** beef

carneiro (kerr-*nay*-roo) *m* sheep, ram

caro (*kah*-roo) *adj* dear, expensive; precious

caroço (ker-*roa*-soo) *m* pip; stone

carpa (*kahr*-per) *f* carp

carpinteiro (kerr-peengn-*tay*-roo) *m* carpenter

carrasco (ker-*rrahsh*-koo) *m* executioner

carregador (ker-rrer-ger-*dhoar*) *m* porter

carregamento (ker-rrer-ger-*mayngn*-too) *m* cargo, charge, load

carregar (ker-rrer-*gahr*) *v* charge, load; press; ~ **em** press

carreira (ker-*rray*-rer) *f* career

carreiro (ker-*rray*-roo) *m* path

carrilhão (ker-rree-*lYerng*w) *m* (pl -hões) chimes *pl*

carro (*kah*-rroo) *m* car; **carrinho de mão** wheelbarrow; ~ **de desporto** sports-car

carroça (ker-*rro*-ser) *f* cart

carroçaria (ker-rroo-ser-*rree*-er) *f* body-work

carro-esporte (kah-rroo-ısh-*por*-ter) *mBr* sportscar

carrossel (ker-rroo-*sehl*) *m* (pl -séis) merry-go-round

carruagem (ker-*rrwah*-zherngY) *f* coach, carriage

carruagem-cama (ker-rrwah-zherngY-ker-mer) *f* sleeping-car, Pullman

carruagem-restaurante (ker-rrwah-zherngY-rrısh-tou-rerngn-ter) *f* dining-car

carta (*kahr*-ter) *f* letter; ~ **de condução** driving licence; ~ **de crédito** letter of credit; ~ **de jogar** play-

ing-card; ~ **de recomendação** letter of recommendation; ~ **registada** registered letter; ~ **verde** green card

cartão (kerr-*terng*w) *m* (pl -tões) cardboard; card; ~ **de crédito** credit card; charge plate *Am;* ~ **de visita** visiting-card; **de** ~ cardboard

cartaz (kerr-*tahsh*) *m* placard; poster

carteira (kerr-*tay*-rer) *f* wallet, pocket-book; bag; desk; ~ **de escola** desk; ~ **de motorista** *Br* driving licence

carteiro (kerr-*tay*-roo) *m* postman

cárter (*kahr*-terr) *m* crankcase

cartilagem (kerr-tee-*lah*-zherngY) *f* cartilage

cartucho (kerr-*too*-shoo) *m* cartridge

carvalho (kerr-*vah*-lYoo) *m* oak

carvão (kerr-*verng*w) *m* coal; ~ **de lenha** charcoal

casa (*kah*-zer) *f* house; ~ **de banho** bathroom; ~ **de campo** cottage, country house; ~ **de repouso** rest-home; ~ **flutuante** houseboat; **dentro de** ~ indoors; **dona de** ~ housewife; mistress; **em** ~ at home; **em** ~ **de** with; **lida da** ~ housekeeping, housework; **para** ~ home

casacão (ker-zer-*kerng*w) *m* (pl -cões) coat; cloak

casaco (ker-*zer*-koo) *m* coat; jacket; ~ **de malha** cardigan; ~ **de peles** fur coat; ~ **desportivo** sports-jacket, blazer

casa-forte (kah-zer-*for*-ter) *f* vault

casal (ker-*zahl*) *m* (pl -ais) farmhouse; married couple

casamento (ker-zer-*mayngn*-too) *m* marriage; wedding

casar-se (ker-*zahr*-ser) *v* marry

casca (*kahsh*-ker) *f* bark; peel, skin;

shell; ~ **de noz** nutshell

cascalho (kersh-*kah*-lYoo) *m* gravel

casco (*kahsh*-koo) *m* hoof

caseiro (ker-*zay*-roo) *adj* home-made

casino (ker-*zee*-noo) *m* casino

caso (*kah*-zoo) *m* case; instance, event; ~ **que** in case; **em** ~ **algum** by no means; **em** ~ **de** in case of; *****fazer ~ de** *pay attention to

caspa (*kahsh*-per) *f* dandruff

casquilho (kersh-*kee*-lYoo) *m* socket

cassino (kah-*see*-noo) *mBr* casino

castanha (kersh-*ter*-ñer) *f* chestnut

castanho (kersh-*ter*-ñoo) *adj* brown; ~ **claro** fawn; ~ **encarniçado** auburn

castelo (kersh-*teh*-loo) *m* castle

castigar (kersh-tee-*gahr*) *v* punish

castigo (kersh-*tee*-goo) *m* penalty, punishment

casto (*kahsh*-too) *adj* chaste

castor (kersh-*toar*) *m* beaver

casual (ker-*zwahl*) *adj* (pl -ais) casual

catacumba (ker-ter-*koom*-ber) *f* catacomb

catálogo (ker-*tah*-loo-goo) *m* catalogue

catarro (ker-*tah*-rroo) *m* catarrh

catástrofe (ker-*tahsh*-troo-fer) *f* calamity, disaster, catastrophe

catedral (ker-ter-*dhrahl*) *f* (pl -ais) cathedral

categoria (ker-ter-goo-*ree*-er) *f* category; sort

categórico (ker-ter-*go*-ree-koo) *adj* explicit; downright

católico (ker-to-lee-koo) *adj* catholic; Roman Catholic

catorze (ker-*toar*-zer) *num* fourteen

caução (kou-*serng*W) *f* (pl -ções) guarantee, bail

cauda (kou-dher) *f* tail

causa (*kou*-zer) *f* reason, cause; case; ~ **judicial** lawsuit; **por** ~ **de** be-

cause of, for; on account of

causar (kou-*zahr*) *v* cause

cautela (kou-*teh*-ler) *f* caution

cavaco (ker-*vah*-koo) *m* chat

cavala (ker-*vah*-ler) *f* mackerel

cavaleiro (ker-ver-*lay*-roo) *m* horseman, rider; knight

cavalheiro (ker-ver-*lYay*-roo) *m* gentleman

cavalho-de-batalha (ker-vah-loo-der-ber-*tah*-lYer) *m* hobby-horse

cavalo (ker-*vah*-loo) *m* horse; ~ **de corridas** race-horse

cavalo-vapor (ker-vah-loo-ver-*poar*) *m* horsepower

*****cavaquear** (ker-ver-*kYahr*) *v* chat

cavar (ker-*vahr*) *v* *dig

cave (*kah*-ver) *f* basement; cellar

caverna (kah-*vehr*-ner) *f* cavern; cave

caviar (ker-*vYahr*) *m* caviar

cavidade (kah-vee-*dhah*-dher) *f* cavity

cavilha (kah-*vee*-lYer) *f* bolt

caxemira (ker-sher-*mee*-rer) *f* cashmere

cebola (ser-*bhoa*-ler) *f* onion; bulb

cebolinho (ser-bhoo-*lee*-ñoo) *m* chives *pl*

ceder (ser-*dhayr*) *v* indulge, *give in

cedo (*say*-dhoo) *adv* early

cegar (ser-*gahr*) *v* blind

cego (*seh*-goo) *adj* blind

cegonha (ser-*goa*-ñer) *f* stork

ceia (*say*-er) *f* supper

ceifa (*say*-fer) *f* harvest

ceifar (*say*-fahr) *v* harvest

celebração (ser-ler-bhrer-*serng*W) *f* (pl -ções) celebration

celebrar (ser-ler-*bhrahr*) *v* celebrate

celebridade (ser-ler-bhree-*dhah*-dher) *f* celebrity

celeiro (ser-*lay*-roo) *m* barn

celibatário (ser-lee-bher-*tah*-rYoo) *m* bachelor

celibato (ser-lee-*bhah*-too) *m* celibacy

celofane (ser-loo-*fer*-ner) *m* cellophane

célula (*seh*-loo-ler) *f* cell

cem (serng▼) *num* hundred

cemitério (ser-mee-*teh*-rᵛoo) *m* cemetery, churchyard, graveyard

cena (*say*-ner) *f* scene

cenário (ser-*nah*-rᵛoo) *m* setting

cenoura (ser-*noa*-rer) *f* carrot

censura (sayng-*soo*-rer) *f* censorship; reproach; blame

censurar (sayng-soo-*rahr*) *v* reproach; blame; censor

centavo (sayng-*tah*-voo) *m* 1/100 of an escudo or a cruzeiro

centena (sayng-*tay*-ner) *f* some hundred

centímetro (sayng-*tee*-mer-troo) *m* centimetre

central (sayng-*trahl*) *adj* (pl -ais) central; **~ eléctrica** power-station; **~ telefónica** telephone exchange

centralizar (sayng-trer-lee-*zahr*) *v* centralize

centro (*sayng*-troo) *m* centre; **~ comercial** shopping centre; **~ da cidade** town centre; **~ de saúde** health centre; **~ recreativo** recreation centre

cera (*say*-rer) *f* wax

cerâmica (ser-*rer*-mee-ker) *f* pottery, ceramics

cerca (*sayr*-ker) *f* fence; **~ de** about

cercar (serr-*kahr*) *v* surround; encircle

cerco (*sayr*-koo) *m* siege

cereal (ser-rᵛahl) *m* (pl -ais) grain; **cereais** cereals *pl*

cérebro (*seh*-rer-bhroo) *m* brain

cereja (ser-*ray*-zher) *f* cherry

cerimónia (ser-ree-*mo*-nᵛer) *f* ceremony; **sem ~** informal

certamente (sehr-ter-*mayng*-ter) *adv* surely, naturally

certeza (serr-*tay*-zer) *f* certainty; **com ~** of course

certidão (serr-tee-*dherng*ᵂ) *f* (pl -dões) certificate

certificado (serr-ter-fee-*kah*-dhoo) *m* certificate

certificar (serr-ter-fee-*kahr*) *v* certify; **certificar-se de** ascertain

certo (*sehr*-too) *adj* sure, certain; correct; **certos** some

cerveja (serr-*vay*-zher) *f* ale, beer; **fábrica de ~** brewery; **fabricar ~** brew

cervejaria (serr-vı-zher-*ree*-er) *f* pub

cessar (ser-*sahr*) *v* quit, stop, discontinue, cease

cesta (*saysh*-ter) *f* hamper

cesto (*saysh*-too) *m* basket; **~ dos papéis** wastepaper-basket

cetim (ser-*teeng*) *m* satin

céu (seh⁰⁰) *m* heaven, sky

cevada (ser-*vah*-dher) *f* barley

chá (shah) *m* tea; **salão de ~** tea-shop

chalé (shah-*leh*) *m* chalet

chaleira (sher-*lay*-rer) *f* kettle

chama (*sher*-mer) *f* flame

chamada (sher-*mah*-dher) *f* call; **~ interurbana** trunk-call; **~ local** local call; **~ telefónica** telephone call

chamar (sher-*mahr*) *v* cry, call; name; recall; **chamar-se** *be called

chaminé (sher-mee-*neh*) *f* chimney

champanhe (sherngm-*per*-ñer) *m* champagne

champô (sherngm-*poa*) *m* shampoo

chantagem (sherng-*tah*-zherngᵛ) *f* blackmail; ***fazer ~** blackmail

chão (sherngᵂ) *m* (pl ~s) floor

chapa (*shah*-per) *f* sheet; plate; **~ da matrícula** registration plate

chapéu (sher-*peh*⁰⁰) *m* hat; **chapeleira de senhoras** milliner

charco (*shahr*-koo) *m* puddle

charlatão (shahr-ler-*terng*ᵂ) *m* (pl -ães) quack

charneca (shahr-*neh*-ker) *f* heath; moor

charuto (sher-*roo*-too) *m* cigar

chassi (sher-*see*) *m* chassis

chave (*sher*-ver) *f* key; ~ **de parafusos** screw-driver; ~ **de porcas** spanner; ~ **de trinco** latchkey

chave-inglesa (shah-ver-eeng-*glay*-zer) *f* wrench

chávena *f* cup; ~ **de chá** teacup

checo (*sheh*-koo) *adj* Czech; *m* Czech

Checoslováquia (sheh-ko-zhloo-*vah*-kᵞer) *f* Czechoslovakia

chefe (*sheh*-fer) *m* chief; boss, leader, manager; chieftain; ~ **de estação** station-master; ~ **de estado** head of state; ~ **de mesa** head-waiter

chegada (sher-*gah*-dher) *f* arrival, coming

chegado (sher-*gah*-dhoo) *adj* near

chegar (sher-*gahr*) *v* arrive

cheio (*shay*-oo) *adj* full

cheirar (shay-*rahr*) *v* *smell; ~ **mal** *stink, *smell

cheiro (*shay*-roo) *m* smell; **mal cheiroso** smelly

cheque (*sheh*-ker) *m* cheque; check *nAm;* **livro de cheques** chequebook; check-book *nAm*

chicote (shee-*ko*-ter) *m* whip

chifre (*shee*-frer) *m* horn

Chile (*shee*-ler) *m* Chile

chileno (shee-*lay*-noo) *adj* Chilean; *m* Chilean

China (*shee*-ner) *f* China

chinês (shee-*naysh*) *adj* Chinese; *m* Chinese

chocante (shoo-*kerng*-ter) *adj* revolting, shocking

chocar (shoo-*kahr*) *v* shock; bump, collide; ~ **com** knock against

chocolate (shoo-koo-*lah*-ter) *m* chocolate

choque (*sho*-ker) *m* shock; crash, collision

chorar (shoo-*rahr*) *v* *weep, cry

chover (shoo-*vayr*) *v* rain

chumbo (*shoo*ngm-boo) *m* lead

chupar (shoo-*pahr*) *v* suck

churrasqueira (shoo-rrah-*shkay*-rer) *f* grill-room

chuva (*shoo*-ver) *f* rain; ~ **miudinha** drizzle

chuvada (shoo-*vah*-dher) *f* cloud-burst

chuvoso (shoo-*voa*-zoo) *adj* rainy

cicatriz (see-ker-*treesh*) *f* scar

ciclista (see-*kleesh*-ter) *m* cyclist

ciclo (*see*-kloo) *m* cycle

cidadania (see-dher-dher-*nee*-er) *f* citizenship

cidadão (see-dher-*dherng*ᵂ) *m* (pl ~s) citizen

cidade (see-*dhah*-dher) *f* town, city

ciência (sᵞayng-sᵞer) *f* science; **ciências naturais** physics

ciente (sᵞayng-ter) *adj* aware

científico (sᵞayng-*tee*-fee-koo) *adj* scientific

cientista (sᵞayng-*teesh*-ter) *m* scientist

cigano (see-*ger*-noo) *m* gipsy

cigarreira (see-ger-*rray*-rer) *f* cigarette-case

cigarro (see-*gah*-rroo) *m* cigarette

cilindro (see-*leengn*-droo) *m* cylinder

cima (*see*-mer) *m* summit; **em ~** above; up; overhead, upstairs; **em ~ de** on top of; **para ~** up, upwards; upstairs; **por ~** over; **por ~ de** over

cimento (see-*mayngn*-too) *m* cement

cimo (*see*-moo) *m* top

cinco (*seeng*-koo) *num* five

cinema (see-*nay*-mer) *m* pictures, cinema

cinquenta (seeng-kwayngn-ter) *num* fifty

cinta (seengn-ter) *f* girdle

cintilante (seengn-tee-lerngn-ter) *adj* sparkling

cinto (seengn-too) *m* belt; ~ **de ligas** suspender belt; ~ **de segurança** safety-belt, seat-belt

cintura (seengn-too-rer) *f* waist

cinza (seeng-zer) *f* ash

cinzeiro (seeng-zay-roo) *m* ashtray

cinzel (seeng-zehl) *m* (pl -zéis) chisel

cinzento (see-zayngn-too) *adj* grey

circo (seer-koo) *m* circus

circuito turístico (seer-koo̅ᵉᵉ-too too-reezh-tee-koo) tour

circulação (seer-koo-ler-serngᵂ) *f* (pl -cões) circulation

círculo (seer-koo-loo) *m* ring, circle; club; ~ **eleitoral** constituency

circundar (seer-koongn-dahr) *v* circle

circunstância (seer-koongsh-terngsʸer) *f* circumstance; condition

cirurgião (see-roor-zhʸerngᵂ) *m* (pl -iões) surgeon

cisne (seezh-ner) *m* swan

cistite (seesh-tee-ter) *f* cystitis

citação (see-ter-serngᵂ) *f* (pl -cões) quotation

citadino (see-ter-dhee-noo) *m* townspeople *pl*

citar (see-tahr) *v* quote

ciúme (sʸoo-mer) *m* jealousy

ciumento (sʸoo-mayngn-too) *adj* envious, jealous

cívico (see-vee-koo) *adj* civic

civil (see-veel) *adj* (pl -is) civil, civilian; *m* civilian

civilização (see-ver-lee-zer-serngᵂ) *f* (pl -cões) civilization

civilizado (see-ver-lee-zah-dhoo) *adj* civilized

clareira (kler-ray-rer) *f* clearing

claro (klah-roo) *adj* bright, light, clear; plain

classe (klah-ser) *f* class, form; ~ **média** middle class; ~ **turística** tourist class

clássico (klah-see-koo) *adj* classical

classificar (kler-ser-fee-kahr) *v* classify; sort, grade, assort

cláusula (klou-soo-ler) *f* clause

clavícula (kler-vee-koo-ler) *f* collarbone

clemência (kler-mayng-sʸer) *f* mercy

clérigo (kleh-ree-goo) *m* clergyman

cliente (klʸayngn-ter) *m* customer, client

clima (klee-mer) *m* climate

clínica (klee-nee-ker) *f* clinic

cloro (klo-roo) *m* chlorine

clube (kloo-bher) *m* club; **automóvel** ~ automobile club; ~ **náutico** yacht-club; ~ **nocturno** cabaret

coador (kwer-dhoar) *m* strainer

coagular (kwer-goo-lahr) *v* coagulate

cobarde (koo-bhahr-der) *adj* cowardly; *m* coward

cobertor (koo-bherr-toar) *m* blanket

cobiçar (koo-bhee-sahr) *v* desire

cobrador (koo-bhrer-dhoar) *m* conductor

cobre (ko-bher) *m* copper

*****cobrir** (koo-bhreer) *v* cover

coçado (koo-sah-dhoo) *adj* threadbare

cocaína (koo-ker-ee-ner) *f* cocaine

*****fazer cócegas** (fer-zayr ko-ser-gersh) tickle

coche (koa-sher) *m* coach, carriage

coco (koa-koo) *m* coconut

côdea (koa-dhʸer) *f* crust

código (ko-dhee-goo) *m* code; ~ **postal** zip code *Am*

codorniz (koo-dhoor-neesh) *f* quail

coelho (kway-lʸoo) *m* rabbit

coerência (kwer-rayng-sʸer) *f* coherence

cofre-forte (ko-frer-*for*-ter) *m* safe

cogumelo (koo-goo-*meh*-loo) *m* mushroom; toadstool

coincidência (kweeng-see-*dhayng*-s^yer) *f* concurrence, coincidence

coincidir (kweeng-see-*dheer*) *v* coincide

coisa (*koi*-zer) *f* thing; **alguma ~** something; **entre outras coisas** among other things; **qualquer ~** anything

cola (*ko*-ler) *f* glue, gum

colaborador (koo-ler-bhoo-rer-*dhoar*) *adj* co-operative; *m* collaborator

colar (koo-*lahr*) *v* paste; *stick; *m* beads, necklace

colarinho (koo-ler-*ree*-ñoo) *m* collar

colcha (*koal*-sher) *f* quilt; counterpane

colchão (koal-*sherng*^w) *m* (pl -hões) mattress

colecção (koo-leh-*serng*^w) *f* (pl -ções) collection; **~ de obras de arte** art collection

coleccionador (koo-leh-s^yoo-ner-*dhoar*) *m* collector

coleccionar (koo-leh-s^yoo-*nahr*) *v* gather, collect

colectivo (koo-leh-*tee*-voo) *adj* collective

colector (koo-leh-*toar*) *m* collector

colega (koo-*leh*-ger) *m* colleague; **~ de classe** *Br* class-mate; **~ de turma** class-mate

colégio (koo-*leh*-z^yoo) *m* college; **~ interno** boarding-school

coleira (koo-*lay*-rer) *f* collar

cólera (*ko*-ler-rer) *f* anger

colete (koo-*lay*-ter) *m* waistcoat; vest *nAm*; **~ salva-vidas** life jacket

colheita (koo-l^y*ay*-ter) *f* crop, harvest

colher¹ (koo-l^y*ayr*) *f* spoon; **~ de chá** teaspoon; **~ de sopa** soup-spoon, tablespoon

colher² (koo-l^y*ayr*) *v* pick; gather

colherada (koo-l^yer-*rah*-dher) *f* spoonful

colidir (koo-lee-*dheer*) *v* collide, crash

colina (koo-*lee*-ner) *f* hill

colisão (koo-lee-*zerng*^w) *f* (pl -sões) collision

collants (koo-*lerngnsh*) *mpl* tights *pl*

colmeia (koal-*may*-er) *f* beehive

colocar (koo-loo-*kahr*) *v* *put; *lay, place

Colômbia (koo-*lawngm*-b^yer) *f* Colombia

colombiano (koo-lawngm-b^yer-noo) *adj* Colombian; *m* Colombian

colónia (koo-*lo*-n^yer) *f* colony; **~ de férias** holiday camp

colorido (koo-loo-*ree*-dhoo) *adj* colourful

***colorir** (koo-loo-*reer*) *v* colour, paint

coluna (koo-*loo*-ner) *f* pillar, column; **~ de direcção** steering-column

com (kawng) *prep* with

coma (*koa*-mer) *m* coma

comandante (koo-merngn-*derngn*-ter) *m* commander, captain

comandar (koo-merngn-*dahr*) *v* command

comando (koo-merngn-doo) *m* order

combate (kawngm-*bah*-ter) *m* battle, struggle, combat

combater (kawngm-ber-*tayr*) *v* combat; *fight, battle

combinação (kawngm-bee-ner-*serng*^w) *f* (pl -ções) combination

combinar (kawngm-bee-*nahr*) *v* combine

comboio (kawngm-*boi*-oo) *m* train; **~ correio** stopping train; **~ de mercadorias** goods train; **~ de passageiros** passenger train; **~ directo** through train; **~ nocturno** night train; **~ rápido** express train; **~ suburbano** local train

combustível (kawɴgm-boosh-*tee*-vehl) *m* (pl -eis) fuel

começar (koo-mer-*sahr*) *v* *begin, commence, start

começo (koo-*mer*-soo) *m* start

comédia (koo-*meh*-dhᵞer) *f* comedy; ~ **musical** musical comedy

comediante (koo-mer-*dh*ᵞerɴg-ter) *m* comedian

comemoração (koo-mer-moo-rer-*serɴg*ʷ) *f* (pl -ções) commemoration

comentar (koo-mayɴgn-*tahr*) *v* comment

comentário (koo-mayɴgn-*tah*-rᵞoo) *m* comment

comer (koo-*mayr*) *v* *eat

comercial (koo-merr-*s*ᵞ*ahl*) *adj* (pl -ais) commercial

comerciante (koo-merr-*s*ᵞerɴg-ter) *m* merchant, tradesman, trader

comércio (koo-*mehr*-sᵞoo) *m* commerce; business, trade; ~ **a retalho** retail trade

comestível (koo-mersh-*tee*-vehl) *adj* (pl -eis) edible

cometer (koo-mer-*tayr*) *v* commit

comichão (koo-mee-*sherɴg*ʷ) *f* (pl -hões) itch; ***ter** ~ itch

cómico (*ko*-mee-koo) *adj* comic; *m* comedian

comida (koo-*mee*-dher) *f* food; fare; ~ **congelada** frozen food

comigo (koo-*mee*-goo) with me

comissão (koo-mee-*serɴg*ʷ) *f* (pl -sões) commission; committee

comissário (koo-mee-*sahr*-ᵞoo) *m* commissioner; ~ **de bordo** steward

comité (koo-mee-*teh*) *m* committee

como (*koa*-moo) *conj* as, like; *adv* how; ~ **se** as if

comoção cerebral (koo-moo-*serɴg*ʷ ser-rer-*bhrahl*) concussion

cómoda (*ko*-moo-dher) *f* chest of drawers; bureau *nAm*

comodidade (koo-moo-dhee-*dhah*-dher) *f* comfort

cómodo (*ko*-moo-dhoo) *adj* convenient, easy

comover (koo-moo-*vayr*) *v* move

compacto (kawɴgm-*pahk*-too) *adj* compact

compaixão (kawɴgm-pigh-*sherɴg*ʷ) *f* sympathy

companheiro (kawɴgm-per-*ñay*-roo) *m* companion; associate

companhia (kawɴgm-per-*ñee*-er) *f* company; society; ~ **de aviação** airline; ~ **de navegação** shipping line

comparação (kawɴgm-per-rer-*serɴg*ʷ) *f* (pl -ções) comparison

comparar (kawɴgm-per-*rahr*) *v* compare

compartimento (kawɴgm-perr-tee-mayɴg-too) *m* compartment; ~ **para fumadores** smoker; smoking-compartment

compatriota (kawɴgm-per-*tr*ᵞo-ter) *m* countryman

compêndio (kawɴgm-*payɴg*n-dᵞoo) *m* textbook

compensação (kawɴgm-payɴg-ser-*serɴg*ʷ) *f* (pl -ções) indemnity, compensation

compensar (kawɴgm-payɴg-*sahr*) *v* compensate; *pay; *make good

competência (kawɴgm-per-*tayɴg*-sᵞer) *f* capacity, competence

competente (kawɴgm-per-*tayɴg*n-ter) *adj* qualified, expert, competent

competição (kawɴgm-per-tee-*serɴg*ʷ) *f* (pl -ções) competition

***competir** (kawɴgm-per-*teer*) *v* compete

compilar (kawɴgm-pee-*lahr*) *v* compile

completamente (kawɴgm-pler-ter-

mayngn-ter) *adv* completely; quite, wholly

completar (kawngm-pler-*tahr*) *v* complete

completo (kawngm-*pleh*-too) *adj* complete; utter, total, whole

complexo (kawngm-*pleh*-ksoo) *adj* complex; *m* complex

complicado (kawngm-plee-*kah*-dhoo) *adj* complicated

*****compor** (kawngm-*poar*) *v* *make up, compose

comporta (kawngm-*por*-ter) *f* sluice, lock

comportamento (kawngm-poor-ter-*mayngn*-too) *m* behaviour

comportar-se (kawngm-poor-*tahr*-ser) *v* act

composição (kawngm-poo-zee-*serng*ʷ) *f* (pl -ções) composition; essay

compositor (kawngm-poo-zee-*toar*) *m* composer

compra (*kawngm*-prer) *f* purchase; *****fazer compras** shop

comprador (kawngm-prer-*dhoar*) *m* buyer, purchaser

comprar (kawngm-*prahr*) *v* *buy, purchase

compreender (kawngm-pr ʸayng-*dayr*) *v* *understand; *take, conceive, *see; comprise; ~ **mal** *misunderstand

compreensão (kawngm-prʸayng-*serng*ʷ) *f* (pl -sões) insight; understanding

compreensivo (kawngm-prʸayng-*see*-voo) *adj* sympathetic, understanding

comprido (kawngm-*pree*-dhoo) *adj* long

comprimento (kawngm-pree-*mayngn*-too) *m* length; ~ **de onda** wavelength

comprimido (kawngm-pree-*mee*-dhoo)

m pill; ~ **para dormir** sleeping-pill

comprometer-se (kawngm-proo-mer-*tayr*-ser) *v* engage

compromisso (kawngm-proo-*mee*-soo) *m* compromise; engagement

comum (koo-*moong*) *adj* common; plain

comuna (koo-*moo*-ner) *f* commune

comunicação (koo-moo-nee-ker-*serng*ʷ) *f* (pl -ções) information, communication

comunicado (koo-moo-nee-*kah*-dhoo) *m* communiqué

comunicar (koo-moo-nee-*kahr*) *v* inform, communicate

comunidade (koo-moo-nee-*dhah*-dher) *f* community; congregation

comunismo (koo-moo-*neezh*-moo) *m* communism

comunista (koo-moo-*neesh*-ter) *m* communist

conceber (kawng-ser-*bhayr*) *v* conceive

conceder (kawng-ser-*dayr*) *v* extend, grant

conceito (kawng-*say*-too) *m* idea

concentração (kawng-sayngn-trer-*serng*ʷ) *f* (pl -ções) concentration

concentrar (kawng-sayngn-*trahr*) *v* concentrate

concepção (kawng-sehp-*serng*ʷ) *f* (pl -ções) conception

concerto (kawng-*sayr*-too) *m* concert

concessão (kawng-ser-*serng*ʷ) *f* (pl -sões) concession

concha (*kawng*-sher) *f* sea-shell, shell

conciso (kawng-*see*-zoo) *adj* concise

conclusão (kawng-kloo-*zerng*ʷ) *f* (pl -sões) conclusion; end, issue

concordar (kawng-koor-*dahr*) *v* agree; ~ **com** approve of

concorrência (kawng-koo-*rrayng*-sʸer) *f* rivalry, competition

concorrente (kawng-koo-*rrayngn*-ter)

m competitor

concreto (kawng-*kreh*-too) *adj* concrete; *mBr* concrete

concurso (kawng-*koor*-soo) *m* contest; quiz

condado (kawng-*dah*-dhoo) *m* county

conde (*kawngn*-der) *m* earl, count

condenação (kawngn-der-ner-*serng*ʷ) *f* (pl -ções) conviction

condenado (kawngn-der-*nah*-dhoo) *m* convict

condenar (kawngn-der-*nahr*) *v* sentence; condemn; disapprove

condessa (kawngn-*day*-ser) *f* countess

condição (kawngn-dee-*serng*ʷ) *f* (pl -ções) condition; term; **à ~** on approval

condicional (kawngn-dee-s'oo-*nahl*) *adj* (pl -ais) conditional

condimentado (kawngn-dee-mayngn-*tah*-dhoo) *adj* spiced

*****condizer** (kawngn-dee-*zayr*) *v* fit; **~ com** match

*****condoer-se de** (kawngn-*dwayr*-ser) pity

conduta (kawngn-*doo*-tah) *f* conduct

condutor (kawngn-doo-*toar*) *m* driver

*****conduzir** (kawngn-doo-*zeer*) *v* carry, conduct; *****drive

confederação (kawng-fer-dher-rer-*serng*ʷ) *f* (pl -ções) union

confeitaria (kawng-fay-ter-*ree*-er) *f* sweetshop

confeiteiro (kawng-fay-*tay*-roo) *m* confectioner

conferência (kawng-fer-*rayng*-s'er) *f* conference; lecture; **~ de imprensa** press conference

*****conferir** (kawng-fer-*reer*) *v* check; award

confessar-se (kawng-fer-*sahr*-ser) *v* confess

confiança (kawng-f'*erng*-ser) *f* confidence; trust, faith; **de ~** reliable;

digno de ~ trustworthy; **indigno de ~** unreliable; untrustworthy

confiante (kawng-f'*erngn*-ter) *adj* confident

confiar (kawng-f'*ahr*) *v* commit; entrust; **~ em** trust

confidencial (kawng-fee-dhayng-s'*erl*) *adj* (pl -ais) confidential

confirmação (kawng-feer-mer-*serng*ʷ) *f* (pl -ções) confirmation

confirmar (kawng-feer-*mahr*) *v* confirm

confiscar (kawng-feesh-*kahr*) *v* confiscate

confissão (kawng-fee-*serng*ʷ) *f* (pl -sões) confession

conflito (kawng-*flee*-too) *m* conflict

conforme (kawng-*for*-mer) *adv* according to; in accordance with; *adj* conform

confortar (kawng-foor-*tahr*) *v* comfort

confortável (kawng-foor-*tah*-vehl) *adj* (pl -eis) comfortable

conforto (kawng-*foar*-too) *m* comfort

confundir (kawng-foongn-*deer*) *v* confuse; *****mistake

confusão (kawng-foo-*zerng*ʷ) *f* (pl -sões) confusion; muddle

confuso (kawng-*foo*-zoo) *adj* confused; obscure

congelador (kawng-zher-ler-*dhoar*) *m* deep-freeze

congelar (kawng-zher-*lahr*) *v* *****freeze

congratular (kawng-grer-too-*lahr*) *v* congratulate

congregação (kawng-grer-ger-*serng*ʷ) *f* (pl -ções) congregation

congresso (kawng-*greh*-soo) *m* congress

conhaque (ko-*ñah*-ker) *m* cognac

conhecedor (koo-ñer-ser-*dhoar*) *m* connoisseur

conhecer (koo-ñer-*sayr*) *v* *****know

conhecido (koo-ñer-*see*-dhoo) *adj*

well-known; *m* acquaintance

conhecimento (koo-ñer-see-*mayngn*-too) *m* knowledge; acquaintance

conjectura (kawng-zheh-*too*-rah) *f* guess

conjuntamente (kawng-zhoongn-ter-*mayngn*-ter) *adv* jointly

conjunto (kawng-*zhoon*-too) *adj* joint; *m* a whole

conjura (kawng-*zhoo*-rer) *f* plot

connosco (kawng-*noash*-koo) with us

conquista (kawng-*keesh*-ter) *f* conquest

conquistador (kawng-keesh-ter-*dhoar*) *m* conqueror

conquistar (kawng-keesh-*tahr*) *v* conquer

consciência (kawngsh-s*Y*ayng-s*Y*er) *f* consciousness; conscience

consciente (kawngsh-s*Y*ayngn-ter) *adj* conscious

*conseguir (kawng-ser-*geer*) *v* obtain; manage, succeed in

conselheiro (kawng-ser-l*Y*ay-roo) *m* counsellor; councillor

conselho (kawng-*say*-l*Y*oo) *m* advice; council, counsel; board

consentimento (kawng-sayngn-tee-*mayngn*-too) *m* consent

*consentir (kawng-sayngn-*teer*) *v* agree, consent; allow

consequência (kawng-ser-*kwayng*-s*Y*er) *f* consequence; issue, result; **em ~ de** as a result of

consequentemente (kawng-ser-kwayngn-ter-*mayngn*-ter) *adv* consequently

consertar (kawng-serr-*tahr*) *v* repair, mend

conserto (kawng-*sayr*-too) *m* repair

conservação (kawng-serr-ver-*serng*ʷ) *f* (pl -ções) preservation

conservador (kawng-serr-ver-*dhoar*) *adj* conservative

conservar (kawng-serr-*vahr*) *v* preserve; maintain

conservas (kawng-*sehr*-versh) *fpl* tinned food; **~ em vinagre** pickles *pl*; ***pôr em conserva** preserve

conservatório (kawng-serr-ver-*to*-rʸoo) *m* music academy

consideração (kawng-see-dher-rer-*serng*ʷ) *f* (pl -ções) consideration

considerar (kawng-see-dher-*rahr*) *v* regard, consider, count, reckon

considerável (kawng-see-dher-rah-vehl) *adj* (pl -eis) considerable

consigo (kawng-*see*-goo) with you

consistir em (kawng-seesh-*teer*) consist of

consolação (kawng-soo-ler-*serng*ʷ) *f* (pl -ções) comfort

consolar (kawng-soo-*lahr*) *v* comfort

conspiração (kawngsh-pee-rer-*serng*ʷ) *f* (pl -ções) plot

conspirar (kawngsh-pee-*rahr*) *v* conspire

constante (kawngsh-*terngn*-ter) *adj* constant; even, steadfast

constatar (kawngsh-ter-*tahr*) *v* ascertain; note, diagnose

constipação (kawngsh-tee-per-*serng*ʷ) *f* (pl -ções) cold

constipar-se (kawngsh-tee-*pahr*-ser) *v* *catch a cold

constituição (kawngsh-tee-twee-*serng*ʷ) *f* (pl -ções) constitution

construção (kawngsh-troo-*serng*ʷ) *f* (pl -ções) construction

*construir (kawngsh-*trweer*) *v* *build, construct

cônsul (*kawng*-sool) *m* (pl ~es) consul

consulado (kawng-soo-*lah*-dhoo) *m* consulate

consulta (kawng-*sool*-ter) *f* consultation; appointment

consultar (kawng-sool-*tahr*) *v* consult

consultório (kawng-sool-*to*-rᵞoo) *m* surgery

consumidor (kawng-soo-mee-*dhoar*) *m* consumer

***consumir** (kawng-soo-*meer*) *v* use up

conta (*kawng*-ter) *f* account; bill; bead; check *nAm;* ~ **bancária** bank account

contactar com (kawng-ter-*tahr*) contact

contacto (kawng-*tah*-too) *m* contact; touch

contador (kawng-ter-*dhoar*) *m* meter

contagioso (kawng-ter-zhᵞoa-zoo) *adj* contagious

contanto que (kawng-*terngn*-too ker) provided that

contar (kawng-*tahr*) *v* count; relate, *tell;* ~ **com** rely on

contemporâneo (kawng-tayngm-poo-*rer*-nᵞoo) *adj* contemporary; *m* contemporary

contente (kawng-*tayngn*-ter) *adj* happy, glad, joyful

***conter** (kawng-*tayr*) *v* contain; comprise; restrain

contestar (kawng-tish-*tahr*) *v* dispute

conteúdo (kawng-tᵞoo-dhoo) *m* contents *pl*

contextura (kawng-tish-*too*-rer) *f* texture

contigo (kawng-*tee*-goo) with you

contíguo (kawng-*tee*-gwoo) *adj* neighbouring

continental (kawng-tee-nayngn-*tahl*) *adj* (pl -ais) continental

continente (kawng-tee-*nayngn*-ter) *m* continent

continuação (kawng-tee-nwer-*serng*ᵂ) *f* (pl -ções) sequel

continuamente (kawng-tee-nwer-*mayngn*-ter) *adv* continually, all the time

continuar (kawng-tee-*nwahr*) *v* carry

on, continue; *keep on; *go on, *go ahead

contínuo (kawng-*tee*-nwoo) *adj* continuous; continual

conto (*kawng*-too) *m* tale

contornar (kawng-toor-*nahr*) *v* bypass

contorno (kawng-*toar*-noo) *m* contour, outline

contra (*kawng*-trer) *prep* versus, against

***contrabandear** (kawng-trer-bherngn-d̯ᵞahr) *v* smuggle

contraceptivo (kawng-trer-seh-*tee*-voo) *m* contraceptive

contraditório (kawng-trer-dhee-*to*-rᵞoo) *adj* contradictory

***contradizer** (kawng-trer-dhee-*zayr*) *v* contradict

***contrair** (kawng-trer-*eer*) *v* contract

contralto (kawng-*trahl*-too) *m* alto

contrário (kawng-*trah*-rᵞoo) *adj* opposite, contrary; *m* reverse, contrary; **ao** ~ the other way round; **pelo** ~ on the contrary

contraste (kawng-*trahsh*-ter) *m* contrast

contratar (kawng-trer-*tahr*) *v* engage

contrato (kawng-*trah*-too) *m* agreement, contract; ~ **de arrendamento** lease

contribuição (kawng-tree-bhwee-*serng*ᵂ) *f* (pl -ções) contribution

controlar (kawng-troo-*lahr*) *v* control

controle (kawng-*troa*-ler) *m* control

controverso (kawng-troo-*vehr*-soo) *adj* controversial

contudo (kawng-*too*-dhoo) *conj* however, yet

contusão (kawng-too-*zerng*ᵂ) *f* (pl -sões) bruise

convencer (kawng-vayng-*sayr*) *v* convince; persuade

conveniente (kawng-ver-nᵞayngn-ter)

adj convenient

convento (kawng-*vayngn*-too) *m* cloister, convent; nunnery

conversa (kawng-*vehr*-ser) *f* talk, discussion, conversation; chat

conversação (kawng-verr-ser-*serng*ʷ) *f* (pl -ções) conversation

conversar (kawng-verr-*sahr*) *v* chat

converter (kawng-verr-*tayr*) *v* convert

convés (kawng-*vehsh*) *m* deck; **camarote de** ~ deck cabin; ~ **principal** main deck

convicção (kawng-veek-*serng*ʷ) *f* (pl -ções) conviction, persuasion

convidado (kawng-vee-*dhah*-dhoo) *m* guest

convidar (kawng-vee-*dhahr*) *v* invite; ask

*convir (kawng-*veer*) *v* suit

convite (kawng-*vee*-ter) *m* invitation

convocação (kawng-voo-ker-*serng*ʷ) *f* (pl -ções) summons

convulsão (kawng-vool-*serng*ʷ) *f* (pl -sões) convulsion

cooperação (kwoa-per-rer-*serng*ʷ) *f* (pl -ções) co-operation

cooperador (kwoa-perrer-*dhoar*) *adj* co-operative

cooperativa (kwoa-per-rer-*tee*-ver) *f* co-operative

cooperativo (kwoa-per-rer-*tee*-voo) *adj* co-operative

coordenação (kwoar-der-ner-*serng*ʷ) *f* (pl -ções) co-ordination

coordenar (kwoar-der-*nahr*) *v* co-ordinate

cópia (*ko*-pʸer) *f* copy

copiar (koo-*pʸahr*) *v* copy

copo (*ko*-poo) *m* glass; tumbler; **copinho para os ovos** egg-cup

coquetel (ko-ker-*tehl*) *m* *Br* cocktail

cor (koar) *f* colour; **de** ~ coloured; by heart; **de** ~ **fixa** fast-dyed

coração (koo-rer-*serng*ʷ) *m* (pl -ções) heart; core; **ataque de** ~ heart attack

coragem (koo-*rah*-zherng ʸ) *f* courage; guts

corajoso (koo-rer-*zhoa*-zoo) *adj* brave, courageous

coral (koo-*rahl*) *m* (pl -ais) coral

corante (ko-*rerngn*-ter) *m* colourant

corar (ko-*rahr*) *v* blush

corda (*kor*-der) *f* rope; cord; ***dar** ~ ***wind**

cordão (koor-*derng*ʷ) *m* (pl -dões) string, cord

cordeiro (koor-*dhay*-roo) *m* lamb

cordel (koor-*dehl*) *m* (pl -déis) string

cor-de-laranja (koar-der-ler-*rerng*-zher) *adj* orange

cor-de-rosa (koar-der-*rro*-zer) *adj* pink

cordial (koor-*dʸahl*) *adj* (pl -ais) cordial, amiable

cordilheira (koor-dee-*lʸay*-rer) *f* mountain range

coro (*koa*-roo) *m* choir

coroa (koo-*roa*-er) *f* crown

coroar (koo-*rwahr*) *v* crown

coronel (koo-roo-*nehl*) *m* (pl -néis) colonel

corpete (koor-*pay*-ter) *m* corset

corpo (*koar*-poo) *m* body

corpulento (koor-poo-*layngn*-too) *adj* corpulent; stout

correcção (koo-rreh-*serng*ʷ) *f* (pl -ções) correction

correcto (koo-*reh*-too) *adj* correct; right

corredor (koo-rrer-*dhoar*) *m* corridor

correia (koo-*rray*-er) *f* strap; ~ **de relógio** watch-strap; ~ **de ventoinha** fan belt

correio (koo-*rray*-oo) *m* post, mail; **caixa do** ~ letter-box; pillar-box; mailbox *nAm*; ~ **aéreo** airmail; **correios** postal service; post-office; **deitar no** ~ post; ***pôr no** ~ mail

corrente (koo-*rrayngn*-ter) *adj* current; regular; *f* stream, current; chain; ~ **alterna** alternating current; ~ **contínua** direct current; ***pôr ao** ~ inform

correr (koo-*rrayr*) *v* *run; stream, flow

correspondência (koo-rrish-pawngn-*dayng*-sYer) *f* correspondence; connection

correspondente (koo-rrish-pawngn-*dayng*-ter) *m* correspondent

corresponder (koo-rrish-pawngn-*dayr*) *v* correspond

corretor (koo-rrer-*toar*) *m* broker; ~ **de apostas** bookmaker

corrida (koo-*rree*-dher) *f* race; ~ **de cavalos** horserace; **pista de corridas** race-course, race-track

corrigir (koo-rree-*zheer*) *v* correct

corrimão (koo-rree-*merng*ᵂ) *m* (pl ~s) banisters *pl*

corromper (koo-rrawngm-*payr*) *v* corrupt

corrupção (koo-rroo-*serng*ᵂ) *f* (pl -ções) corruption

corrupto (koo-*rroop*-too) *adj* corrupt

corta-papel (kor-ter-per-*pehl*) *m* paper-knife

cortar (koor-*tahr*) *v* *cut; *cut off, chip

corte¹ (*kor*-ter) *m* cut; ~ **de cabelo** haircut

corte² (*koar*-ter) *f* court

cortejo (koor-*tay*-zhoo) *m* procession

cortês (koor-*taysh*) *adj* courteous

cortina (koor-*tee*-ner) *f* curtain

corvo (*koar*-voo) *m* raven

coser (koo-*zayr*) *v* *sew

cosméticos (koozh-*meh*-tee-koosh) *mpl* cosmetics *pl*

costa (*kosh*-ter) *f* coast; **costas** back

costela (koosh-*teh*-ler) *f* rib

costeleta (koosh-ter-*lay*-ter) *f* cutlet, chop

costumado (er-koosh-too-*mah*-dhoo) *adj* accustomed, customary

costume (koosh-*too*-mer) *m* custom; **como de** ~ as usual; **costumes** morals; ***ter por** ~ *be in the habit of

costura (koosh-*too*-rer) *f* needlework; seam; **sem** ~ seamless

cotovelo (koo-too-*vay*-loo) *m* elbow

cotovia (koo-too-*vee*-ah) *f* lark

couro (*koa*-roo) *m* leather

couve (*koa*-ver) *f* cabbage; **couve-de-bruxelas** sprouts *pl*; **couve-flor** cauliflower

cova (*ko*-ver) *f* pit, hole

coxa (*ko*-sher) *f* thigh

***coxear** (koo-*shYahr*) *v* limp

coxo (*koa*-shoo) *adj* lame

cozer (koo-*zayr*) *v* cook, boil, bake

cozinha (koo-*zee*-ñer) *f* kitchen; **livro de** ~ cookery-book

cozinhar (koo-zee-*ñahr*) *v* cook; ~ **no forno** bake

cozinheiro (koo-zee-*ñay*-roo) *m* cook

cozinheiro-chefe (koo-zee-ñay-roo-*sheh*-fer) *m* chef

crânio (*krer*-nYoo) *m* skull

cratera (krer-*teh*-rer) *f* crater

cravo (*krer*-voo) *m* harpsichord; carnation

creche (*kreh*-sher) *f* nursery

creditar (krer-dhee-*tahr*) *v* credit

crédito (*kreh*-dhee-too) *m* credit

credor (kreh-*dhoar*) *m* creditor

crédulo (*kreh*-dhoo-loo) *adj* credulous

creme (*kreh*-mer) *m* cream; *adj* cream; ~ **de base** foundation cream; ~ **de beleza** face-cream; ~ **de noite** night-cream; ~ **hidratante** moisturizing cream; ~ **para a barba** shaving-cream; ~ **para a pele** skin cream; ~ **para as mãos** hand cream; ~ **para o cabelo** hair

cream
cremoso (krer-*moa*-zoo) *adj* creamy
crença (*krayng*-ser) *f* belief
crepúsculo (krer-*poosh*-koo-loo) *m* twilight
***crer** (krayr) *v* believe
crescer (krish-*sayr*) *v* *grow; increase
crescimento (krish-see-*mayngn*-too) *m* growth
criada (*krⱽah*-dher) *f* maid; ~ **de quarto** chambermaid
criado (*krⱽah*-dhoo) *m* servant; valet, boy, waiter; ~ **de café** waiter; ~ **de quarto** valet
criança (*krⱽerng*-ser) *f* child, kid; ~ **de peito** infant; ~ **pequena** tot; ~ **pequenina** toddler
criar (krⱽahr) *v* create; *bring up, rear; raise, *breed
criatura (krⱽer-*too*-rer) *f* creature
crime (*kree*-mer) *m* crime
criminal (kree-mee-*nahl*) *adj* (pl -ais) criminal
criminalidade (kree-mee-ner-lee-*dhah*-dher) *f* criminality
criminoso (kree-mee-*noa*-zoo) *adj* criminal; *m* criminal
críquete (*kree*-kert) *m* cricket
crise (*kree*-zer) *f* crisis
cristal (kreesh-*tahl*) *m* (pl -ais) crystal; **de** ~ crystal
cristão (kreesh-*terngʷ*) *adj* (pl ~s) Christian; *m* Christian
Cristo (*kreesh*-too) Christ
crítica (*kree*-tee-ker) *f* criticism; review
criticar (kree-tee-*kahr*) *v* criticize
crítico (*kree*-tee-koo) *adj* critical; *m* critic
crocodilo (kroo-koo-*dhee*-loo) *m* crocodile
crómio (*kro*-mⱽoo) *m* chromium
crónico (*kro*-nee-koo) *adj* chronic
cronológico (kroo-noo-*lo*-zhee-koo) *adj* chronological
cru (kroo) *adj* raw
crucificação (kroo-ser-fee-ker-*serngʷ*) *f* (pl -ções) crucifixion
crucificar (kroo-ser-fee-*kahr*) *v* crucify
crucifixo (kroo-ser-*feek*-soo) *m* crucifix
cruel (krwehl) *adj* (pl cruéis) harsh, cruel
cruz (kroosh) *f* cross
cruzada (kroo-*zah*-dher) *f* crusade
cruzamento (kroo-zer-*mayngn*-too) *m* crossroads; junction
cruzar (kroo-*zahr*) *v* cross
cruzeiro (kroo-*zay*-roo) *m* cruise; *mBr* Brazilian monetary unit
Cuba (*koo*-bher) *f* Cuba
cubano (koo-*bhah*-noo) *adj* Cuban; *m* Cuban
cubo (*koo*-bhoo) *m* cube
cuco (*koo*-koo) *m* cuckoo
cuecas (*kweh*-kersh) *fpl* pants *pl*, drawers, briefs *pl*; shorts *plAm*
cuidado (kwee-*dhah*-dhoo) *m* care; ***ter** ~ beware, look out; **tomar** ~ watch out
cuidadoso (kwee-dher-*dhoa*-zoo) *adj* careful
cuidar (kwee-*dahr*) *v* tend; ~ **de** *take care of; look after
culpa (*kool*-per) *f* fault, blame; guilt
culpado (kool-*pah*-dhoo) *adj* guilty
culpar (kool-*pahr*) *v* blame
cultivar (kool-tee-*vahr*) *v* raise, cultivate; *grow
culto (*kool*-too) *adj* cultured; *m* worship
cultura (kool-*too*-rer) *f* culture
cume (*koo*-mer) *m* peak
cumeada (koo-mⱽah-dher) *f* ridge
cúmplice (*koongm*-plee-ser) *m* accomplice
cumprimentar (koongm-pree-mayngn-*tahr*) *v* greet; compliment

cumprimento (koongm-pree-*mayngn*-too) *m* compliment

cumprir (koongm-*preer*) *v* perform

cunha (*koo*-ñer) *f* wedge

cunhada (koo-*ñah*-dher) *f* sister-in-law

cunhado (koo-*ñah*-dhoo) *m* brother-in-law

cupão (koo-*perng*ʷ) *m* (pl cupões) coupon

cupidez (koo-pee-*dhaysh*) *f* greed

cúpula (*koo*-poo-ler) *f* dome

cura (*koo*-rer) *f* cure; recovery

curandeiro (koo-rerngn-*day*-roo) *m* quack

curar (koo-*rahr*) *v* cure; heal; **curar-se** recover

curiosidade (koo-rʸoo-zee-*dhah*-dher) *f* curiosity; curio

curioso (koo-rʸoa-zoo) *adj* curious; inquisitive

curso (*koor*-soo) *m* course; ~ **intensivo** intensive course

curto (*koor*-too) *adj* short

curto-circuito (koor-too-seer-*kōo*ee-too) *m* short circuit

curva (*koor*-ver) *f* turn, bend; turning, curve

curvado (koor-*vah*-dhoo) *adj* curved

curvar (koor-*vahr*) *v* *bend; **curvar-se** *bend down

curvatura (koor-ver-*too*-rer) *f* bend

curvo (*koor*-voo) *adj* curved; bent

***cuspir** (koosh-*peer*) *v* *spit

cuspo (*koosh*-poo) *m* spit

custar (koosh-*tahr*) *v* *cost

custo (*koosh*-too) *m* cost

custódia (koosh-*to*-dhʸer) *f* custody

D

dactilógrafa (dahk-tee-*lo*-grer-fer) *f* typist

dactilografado (dahk-tee-loo-grer-*fah*-dhoo) *adj* typewritten

dactilografar (dahk-tee-loo-grer-*fahr*) *v* type

dado (*dah*-dhoo) *m* data *pl*

daltónico (dahl-*to*-nee-koo) *adj* colour-blind

dança (*derng*-ser) *f* dance; ~ **folclórica** folk-dance

dançar (derng-*sahr*) *v* dance

danificar (der-ner-fee-*kahr*) *v* damage

dano (*der*-noo) *m* damage; mischief; harm

***dar** (dahr) *v* *give; donate

data (*dah*-ter) *f* date

de (der) *prep* from; of; out of; with; off

debaixo (der-*bhigh*-shoo) *adv* below, underneath, beneath; ~ **de** below, under; beneath

debate (der-*bhah*-ter) *m* debate, discussion

debater (der-bher-*tayr*) *v* discuss

débito (*deh*-bhee-too) *m* debit

debruçar-se (der-bhroo-*sahr*-ser) *v* *lean out; *bend down

decência (der-*sayng*-sʸer) *f* decency

decente (der-*sayngn*-ter) *adj* decent

decepcionar (der-seh-sʸoo-*nahr*) *v* *be disappointing

decerto (der-*sehr*-too) *adv* certainly

decidido (der-see-*dhee*-dhoo) *adj* resolute

decidir (der-see-*dheer*) *v* decide

décimo (*deh*-see-moo) *num* tenth; ~ **nono** nineteenth; ~ **oitavo** eighteenth; ~ **primeiro** eleventh; ~ **quarto** fourteenth; ~ **quinto** fifteenth; ~ **segundo** twelfth; ~ **sétimo** seventeenth; ~ **sexto** sixteenth; ~ **terceiro** thirteenth

decisão (der-see-*zerng*ʷ) *f* (pl -sões) decision

declaração (der-kler-rer-*serng*ʷ) f (pl -ções) declaration; statement

declarar (der-kler-*rahr*) v declare; state; ~ **culpado** convict

declive (der-*klee*-ver) m incline

decoração (der-koo-rer-*serng*ʷ) f (pl -ções) decoration

decorar (der-koo-*rahr*) v memorize; decorate

decorativo (der-koo-rer-*tee*-voo) adj decorative

dedal (der-*dhahl*) m (pl -ais) thimble

dedicado a (der-dhee-*kah*-dhoo er) attached to, devoted to

dedicar (der-dhee-*kahr*) v devote, dedicate

dedo (*day*-dhoo) m finger; ~ **do pé** toe; ~ **mínimo** little finger

***deduzir** (der-dhoo-*zeer*) v subtract, deduct; infer, deduce

defeito (der-*fay*-too) m fault

defeituoso (der-fay-*twoa*-zoo) adj defective, faulty

defender (der-fayng-*dayr*) v defend

defensor (der-fayng-*soar*) m advocate, champion

defesa (der-*fay*-zer) f defence; plea

défice (*deh*-fee-ser) m deficit

deficiência (der-fee-s ʸayng-s ʸer) f deficiency

definição (der-fer-nee-*serng*ʷ) f (pl -ções) definition

definido (der-fer-*nee*-dhoo) adj definite

definir (der-fer-*neer*) v define; determine

deformado (der-foor-*mah*-dhoo) adj ·deformed

defraudar (der-frou-*dhahr*) v cheat

defronte de (der-*frawng*-ter der) facing

degelar (der-zher-*lahr*) v thaw

degelo (der-*zhay*-loo) m thaw

degrau (der-*grou*) m step

deitar (day-*tahr*) v *throw; pour; **deitar-se** *lie down, *go to bed; ***estar deitado** *lie

deixar (day-*shahr*) v *leave, *let

delapidado (der-ler-pee-*dher*-dhoo) adj dilapidated

delegação (der-ler-ger-*serng*ʷ) f (pl -ções) delegation

delegado (der-ler-*gah*-dhoo) m delegate

deleite (der-*lay*-ter) m delight

deles (deh-*lish*) their; of them

delgado (dehl-*gah*-dhoo) adj slim

deliberação (der-lee-bher-rer-*serng*ʷ) f (pl -ções) deliberation

deliberado (der-lee-bher-*rah*-dhoo) adj deliberate

deliberar (der-lee-bher-*rahr*) v deliberate

delicado (der-lee-*kah*-dhoo) adj tender, delicate; gentle; sheer; polite

delícia (der-lee-s ʸer) f delight

deliciar (der-lee-s ʸ*ahr*) v delight

delicioso (der-lee-s ʸoa-zoo) adj delicious, delightful; wonderful, lovely

delinquente (der-leeng-*kwayng*-ter) m criminal

demais (der-*mighsh*) adv besides, moreover; ~ **a mais** moreover; **os** ~ the rest, the others

demasiado (der-mer-z ʸ*ah*-dhoo) adv too, too much

demência (der-mayng-s ʸer) f madness

demente (der-*mayng*-ter) adj mad

demissão (der-mee-*serng*ʷ) f (pl -sões) resignation

demitir-se (der-mee-*teer*-ser) v resign

democracia (der-moo-krer-*see*-er) f democracy

democrático (der-moo-*krah*-tee-koo) adj democratic

demolição (der-moo-lee-*serng*ʷ) f (pl -ções) demolition

***demolir** (der-moo-*leer*) v demolish

demonstração (der-mawngsh-trer-serng^w) f (pl -ções) demonstration

demonstrar (der-mawngsh-trahr) v prove, demonstrate; *show

demora (der-mo-rer) f delay

demorar-se (der-moo-rahr-ser) v *be late; *be long; linger

denegar (der-ner-gahr) v deny

denso (dayng-soo) adj dense

dentadura (dayngn-ter-dhoo-rer) f denture; false teeth

dente (dayngn-ter) m tooth

dente-de-leão (dayngn-ter-der-lYerng^w) m dandelion

dentista (dayngn-teesh-ter) m dentist

dentro (dayngn-troo) adv inside; in; ~ de inside; into, in, within; para ~ inwards; por ~ inside, within

deparar com (der-per-rahr) run into

departamento (der-perr-ter-mayngn-too) m department

depenar (der-per-nahr) v *bleed, extort money from; pluck

dependente (der-payngn-dayngn-ter) adj dependant

depender de (der-payngn-dayr) depend on

depois (der-poish) adv afterwards; then; ~ de after; ~ que after

depositar (der-poo-zee-tahr) v deposit; bank

depósito (der-po-zee-too) m deposit; ~ da gasolina petrol tank; ~ de bagagens left luggage office; ~ de gás gasworks; ~ de objectos perdidos lost property office

depressa (der-preh-ser) adv fast, quickly

depressão (der-prer-serng^w) f (pl -sões) depression

deprimente (der-pree-mayngn-ter) adj depressing

deprimido (der-pree-mee-dhoo) adj blue, low, depressed

deprimir (der-pree-meer) v depress

deputado (der-poo-tah-dhoo) m deputy; Member of Parliament

derramar (der-rrer-mahr) v *shed; *spill

derrapar (der-rrer-pahr) v skid

derreter (der-rrer-tayr) v melt

derrota (der-rro-ter) f defeat

derrotar (der-rroo-tahr) v defeat

derrubar (der-rroo-bhahr) v knock down

desabitado (der-zer-bhee-tah-dhoo) adj uninhabited

desabotoar (der-zer-bhoo-twahr) v unbutton

desacostumado (der-zer-koosh-too-mah-dhoo) adj unaccustomed

desafiar (der-zer-fYahr) v dare; challenge

desafio (der-zer-fee^oo) m challenge; match

desagradar (der-zer-grer-dhahr) v displease

desagradável (der-zer-grer-dhah-vehl) adj (pl -eis) disagreeable; unpleasant, nasty; unkind

desajeitado (der-zer-zhay-tah-dhoo) adj clumsy

desalinhado (der-zer-lee-ñah-dhoo) adj untidy

desaparafusar (der-zer-per-rer-foo-zahr) v unscrew

desaparecer (der-zer-per-rer-sayr) v disappear; vanish

desaparecido (der-zer-per-rer-see-dhoo) adj lost; m missing person

desapertar (der-zer-perr-tahr) v loosen

desapontar (der-zer-pawngn-tahr) v disappoint

desaprender (der-zer-prayngn-dayr) v unlearn

desaprovar (der-zer-proo-vahr) v disapprove

desarrazoado (der-zer-rrer-zwah-dhoo)

adj unreasonable

desarrolhar (der-zer-rroo-*lʸahr*) *v* uncork

desassossego (der-zer-soo-*say*-goo) *m* unrest

desastrado (der-zersh-*trah*-dhoo) *adj* awkward

desastre (der-*zahsh*-trer) *m* disaster; accident; ~ **de aviação** plane crash

desastroso (der-zahsh-*troa*-zoo) *adj* disastrous

desatar (der-zer-*tahr*) *v* untie

desavergonhado (der-zer-verr-goo-*ñah*-dhoo) *adj* impudent

desbotar (dɪzh-bhoo-*tahr*) *v* fade

descafeinado (dɪsh-ker-fay-*nah*-dhoo) *adj* decaffeinated

descansar (dɪsh-kerng-*sahr*) *v* rest

descanso (dɪsh-*kerng*-soo) *m* rest

descarado (dɪsh-ker-*rah*-dhoo) *adj* bold; shameless

descarregar (dɪsh-ker-rrer-*gahr*) *v* discharge, unload

descascar (dɪsh-kersh-*kahr*) *v* peel

descendente (dɪsh-sayngn-*dayngn*-ter) *m* descendant

descer (dɪsh-*sayr*) *v* descend; *get off

descida (dɪsh-*see*-dher) *f* descent

descoberta (dɪsh-koo-*bhehr*-ter) *f* discovery

descoberto (dɪsh-koo-*bhayr*-too) *adj* bare

***descobrir** (dɪsh-koo-*bhreer*) *v* discover; detect

descolagem (dɪsh-koo-*lah*-zherngʸ) *f* take-off

descolar (dɪsh-koo-*lahr*) *v* *take off

descolorir (dɪsh-koo-loo-*reer*) *v* discolour; bleach

desconcertar (dɪsh-kawng-serr-*tahr*) *v* overwhelm

desconfiado (dɪsh-kawng-*fʸah*-dhoo) *adj* suspicious

desconfiança (dɪsh-kawng-*fʸerng*-ser) *f* suspicion

desconfiar (dɪsh-kawng-*fʸahr*) *v* mistrust; suspect

desconfortável (dɪsh-kawng-foor-*tah*-vehl) *adj* (pl -eis) uncomfortable

descongelar (dɪsh-kawng-zher-*lahr*) *v* thaw

desconhecido (dɪsh-koo-ñer-*see*-dhoo) *adj* unknown; unfamiliar

descontar (dɪsh-kawngn-*tahr*) *v* cash

descontente (dɪsh-kawngn-*tayngn*-ter) *adj* discontented

desconto (dɪsh-*kawngn*-too) *m* discount; rebate, reduction

descontracção (dɪsh-kawngn-trah-*serngʷ*) *f* (pl -ções) relaxation

descontraído (dɪsh-kawngn-*trer*-ee-dhoo) *adj* easy-going

***descontrair-se** (dɪsh-kawngn-trer-*eer*) *v* relax

descrever (dɪsh-krer-*vayr*) *v* describe

descrição (dɪsh-kree-*serngʷ*) *f* (pl -ções) description

descuidado (dɪsh-kwee-*dhah*-dhoo) *adj* careless; slovenly

descuidar (dɪsh-kwee-*dhahr*) *v* neglect

desculpa (dɪsh-*kool*-per) *f* excuse; apology; **pedir** ~ apologize

desculpar (dɪsh-kool-*pahr*) *v* excuse; **desculpar-se** apologize; **desculpe!** sorry!

desde (*dayzh*-dher) *prep* since; as from; ~ **então** since; ~ **que** since

desdém (dɪzh-*dherngʸ*) *m* contempt

desdobrar (dɪzh-dhoo-*bhrahr*) *v* unfold

desejar (der-zɪ-*zhahr*) *v* desire, wish; want; long for

desejável (der-zɪ-*zhah*-vehl) *adj* (pl -eis) desirable

desejo (der-*zay*-zhoo) *m* desire; wish, longing

desejoso (der-zay-*zhoa*-zoo) *adj* eager

desembarcar (der-zayngm-berr-*kahr*) *v*

land, disembark

desembrulhar (der-zayngm-broo-*lⱽahr*) *v* unwrap

desempacotar (der-zayngm-per-koo-*tahr*) *v* unpack

desempenhar (der-zayngm-per-*ñahr*) *v* perform; execute

desempregado (der-zayngm-prer-*gah*-dhoo) *adj* unemployed

desemprego (der-zayngm-*pray*-goo) *m* unemployment

desencaminhar (der-zayngng-ker-mee-*ñahr*) *v* *mislay

desenhar (der-zɪ-*ñahr*) *v* *draw; sketch, design

desenho (der-*zay*-ñoo) *m* sketch, drawing; pattern; **banda desenhada** comics *pl;* **caderno de ~** sketch-book; **~ animado** cartoon

desenvolver (der-zayng-voal-*vayr*) *v* develop; expand

desenvolvimento (der-zayng-voal-vee-*mayngn*-too) *m* development

desertar (der-zerr-*tahr*) *v* desert

deserto (der-*zehr*-too) *adj* desert; *m* desert

desesperado (der-zɪsh-per-*rah*-dhoo) *adj* hopeless, desperate

desesperar (der-zɪsh-per-*rahr*) *v* despair

desespero (der-zɪsh-*pay*-roo) *m* despair

desfalecido (dɪsh-fer-ler-*see*-dhoo) *adj* faint

desfavorável (dɪsh-fer-voo-*rah*-vehl) *adj* (pl -eis) unfavourable

***desfazer** (dɪsh-fer-*zayr*) *v* *undo; ***desfazer-se de** discard

desfiar (dɪsh-*fⱽahr*) *v* fray

desfiladeiro (dɪsh-fee-ler-*dhay*-roo) *m* mountain pass

desfile (derz-*fee*-ler) *m* parade

desfrutar (dɪsh-froo-*tahr*) *v* enjoy

desgostar (dɪsh-goosh-*tahr*) *v* dis-

please

desgosto (dɪsh-*goash*-too) *m* grief, sorrow; ***ter desgosto** grieve

desgostoso (dɪsh-goosh-*toa*-zoo) *adj* sad

desgraça (dɪsh-*grah*-ser) *f* disaster

desgraçado (dɪsh-grah-*sah*-dhoo) *adj* unfortunate

designação (der-zee-gner-*serng*ʷ) *f* (pl -ções) denomination

designar (der-zeeg-*nahr*) *v* designate; appoint

desigual (der-zee-*gwahl*) *adj* (pl -ais) uneven, unequal

desiludir (der-zee-loo-*dheer*) *v* *let down; disappoint

desilusão (der-zee-loo-*zerng*ʷ) *f* (pl -sões) disappointment

desinfectante (der-zeeng-feh-*terngn*-ter) *m* disinfectant

desinfectar (der-zeeng-feh-*tahr*) *v* disinfect

desinteressado (der-zeeng-ter-rer-*sah*-dhoo) *adj* unselfish

desistir (der-zeesh-*teer*) *v* *give up

desligar (dɪzh-lee-*gahr*) *v* disconnect; switch off

deslizar (dɪzh-lee-*zahr*) *v* *slide, slip

deslize (dɪzh-*lee*-zer) *m* slide

deslocado (dɪsh-loo-*ker*-dhoo) *adj* dislocated

deslocar (dɪzh-loo-*kahr*) *v* move

deslumbrante (dɪzh-loongm-*brerngn*-ter) *adj* glaring

desmaiar (dɪsh-mer-*ⱽahr*) *v* faint

desmantelado (dɪzh-merngn-ter-*lah*-dhoo) *adj* ramshackle

desmobilado (dɪzh-moo-bhee-*lah*-dhoo) *adj* unfurnished

desmoronar-se (dɪzh-moo-roo-*nahr*-ser) *v* collapse

desnecessário (dɪzh-ner-ser-*sah*-rⱽoo) *adj* unnecessary

desocupado (der-zoa-koo-*pah*-dhoo)

adj unoccupied

desodorante (dı-zo-dhoa-*rerng*-ter) *mBr* deodorant

desodorizante (der-zoo-dhoo-ree-*zerng*-ter) *m* deodorant

desolado (der-zoo-*lah*-dhoo) *adj* sorry; desolate

desonesto (der-zoo-*nehsh*-too) *adj* dishonest; crooked

desonra (derz-*awng*-rrer) *f* disgrace; shame

desordem (derz-*or*-derng^Y) *f* disorder, mess; riot

desossar (der-zoo-*sahr*) *v* bone

despachar (dısh-per-*shahr*) *v* despatch; **despachar-se** hurry

despedida (dısh-per-*dhee*-dher) *f* parting; departure

***despedir** (dısh-per-*dheer*) *v* dismiss; fire

despenhar-se (dısh-per-*ñahr*-ser) *v* crash

despensa (dish-*payng*-ser) *f* larder

desperdiçar (dısh-perr-dee-*sahr*) *v* waste

desperdício (dısh-perr-*dee*-s^Yoo) *m* waste

despertador (dısh-perr-ter-*dhoar*) *m* alarm-clock

despertar (dish-perr-*tahr*) *v* wake up; *awake

despesa (dish-*pay*-zer) *f* expense; expenditure; **despesas de viagem** travelling expenses

despido (dısh-*pee*-dhoo) *adj* bare; naked

***despir-se** (dısh-*peer*-ser) *v* undress

desportista (dısh-poor-*teesh*-tah) *m* sportsman

desporto (dısh-*poar*-too) *m* sport; **desportos de inverno** winter sports

desposar (dish-poo-*zahr*) *v* marry

desprender (dısh-prayngn-*dayr*) *v* loosen; unfasten

despreocupado (dısh-pr^Yoo-koo-*pah*-dhoo) *adj* carefree

desprezar (dısh-prer-*zahr*) *v* despise; scorn

desprezo (dısh-*pray*-zoo) *m* contempt; scorn

despropositado (dısh-proo-poo-zee-*tah*-dhoo) *adj* misplaced

desprotegido (dısh-proo-tı-*zhee*-dhoo) *adj* unprotected

destapar (dısh-ter-*pahr*) *v* uncover

destinar (dısh-tee-*nahr*) *v* destine

destinatário (dısh-tee-ner-*tah*-r^Yoo) *m* addressee

destino (dısh-*tee*-noo) *m* fate, destiny, lot; destination

destro (*dehsh*-troo) *adj* skilful

destruição (dısh-trwee-*serng*^w) *f* (pl -ções) destruction

***destruir** (dısh-*trweer*) *v* destroy; wreck

desusado (der-zoo-*zah*-dhoo) *adj* unusual

desvalorização (dızh-ver-loo-ree-zer-*serng*^w) *f* (pl -ções) devaluation

desvalorizar (dızh-ver-loo-ree-*zahr*) *v* devalue

desvanecer (dızh-ver-ner-*sayr*) *v* fade

desvantagem (dızh-verngn-*tah*-zherng^Y) *f* disadvantage

desviar (dızh-v^Yahr) *v* avert; hijack; **desviar-se** deviate

desvio (dızh-*vee*^oo) *m* detour; diversion

detalhado (der-ter-l^Yah-dhoo) *adj* detailed

detalhe (der-*tah*-l^Yer) *m* detail

detective (der-tehk-*tee*-ver) *m* detective

detenção (der-tayng-⊗oo) *f* (pl -ções) custody

detergente (der-terr-*zhayngn*-ter) *m* detergent; ~ **em pó** washing-powder

deteriorável (der-ter-rᵞoo-*rah*-vehl) *adj* (pl -eis) perishable

determinar (der-terr-mee-*nahr*) *v* determine; define; **determinado** definite

detestar (der-tısh-*tahr*) *v* hate, dislike

detido (der-*tee*-dhoo) *m* prisoner

deus (dayᵒᵒsh) *m* god

deusa (dayᵒᵒ-zer) *f* goddess

dever (der-*vayr*) *v* *have to (*must); owe; *m* duty

devido (der-*vee*-dhoo) *adj* due; proper; ∼ **a** owing to

devolver (der-voal-*vayr*) *v* *bring back; *send back

dez (dehsh) *num* ten

dezanove (der-zer-*no*-ver) *num* nineteen

dezasseis (der-zer-*saysh*) *num* sixteen

dezassete (der-zer-*seh*-ter) *num* seventeen

Dezembro (der-*zayngm*-broo) December

dezena (der-*zay*-ner) *f* ten, about ten

dezoito (der-*zoi*-too) *num* eighteen

dia (*dee*-er) *m* day; **bom dia!** hello!; **de** ∼ by day; ∼ **de semana** weekday; ∼ **dos anos** birthday; ∼ **útil** working day; **por** ∼ per day; **qualquer** ∼ some day

diabetes (dᵞer-*bheh*-tersh) *f* diabetes

diabético (dᵞer-*bheh*-tee-koo) *m* diabetic

diabo (dᵞah-bhoo) *m* devil

diabrura (dᵞer-*bhroo*-rer) *f* mischief

diagnosticar (dee-erg-noosh-tee-*kahr*) *v* diagnose

diagnóstico (dee-erg-*nosh*-tee-koo) *m* diagnosis

diagonal (dee-er-goo-*nahl*) *adj* (pl -ais) diagonal; *f* diagonal

diagrama (dee-er-*grah*-mer) *m* diagram

dialecto (dee-er-*leh*-too) *m* dialect

diamante (dᵞer-*merngn*-ter) *m* diamond

diante de (dᵞerngn-ter der) in front of; before

diário (dᵞah-rᵞoo) *adj* daily; *m* diary; daily

diarreia (dᵞer-*rray*-er) *f* diarrhoea

dicionário (dee-sᵞoo-*nah*-rᵞoo) *m* dictionary

dieta (dᵞeh-ter) *f* diet

diferença (dee-fer-*rayng*-ser) *f* difference; contrast, distinction

diferente (dee-fer-*rayngn*-ter) *adj* different; unlike

*diferir (dee-fer-*reer*) *v* vary, differ

difícil (dee-*fee*-sıl) *adj* (pl -ceis) difficult; hard

dificuldade (dee-fee-kool-*dhah*-dher) *f* difficulty; pains

difteria (deef-ter-*ree*-er) *f* diphtheria

*digerir (dee-zher-*reer*) *v* digest

digestão (dee-zhersh-*terng*ʷ) *f* digestion

digestivo (dee-zhersh-*tee*-voo) *adj* digestible

digno de (*dee*-gnoo der) worthy of

*diluir (dee-*lweer*) *v* dissolve; dilute

dimensão (dee-mayng-*serng*ʷ) *f* (pl -sões) extent, size

diminuição (dee-mee-nwee-*serng*ʷ) *f* (pl -cões) decrease; subtraction

*diminuir (dee-mee-*nweer*) *v* reduce; decrease, lessen

Dinamarca (dee-ner-*mahr*-ker) *f* Denmark

dinamarquês (dee-ner-mahr-*kaysh*) *adj* Danish; *m* Dane

dínamo (*dee*-ner-moo) *m* dynamo

dinheiro (dee-*ñay*-roo) *m* money; cash

diploma (dee-*ploa*-mer) *m* certificate, diploma

diplomar-se (dee-ploo-*mahr*-ser) *v* graduate

diplomata (dee-ploa-*mah*-ter) *m* diplomat

dique (*dee*-ker) *m* dike; dam

direcção (dee-reh-*serng*ʷ) *f* (pl -cões) leadership, management, lead, direction; way; **em** ~ **a** towards

directamente (dee-reh-ter-*mayng*-ter) *adv* straight; straight away

directiva (dee-reh-*tee*-ver) *f* directive

directo (dee-*reh*-too) *adj* direct

director (dee-reh-*toar*) *m* executive; manager, director; principal; ~ **de escola** head teacher, headmaster

direita (dee-*ray*-ter) *f* right side; **à** ~ on the right

direito (dee-*ray*-too) *adj* straight, right; upright, right-hand; level; *m* justice, law, right; ~ **administrativo** administrative law; ~ **civil** civil law; ~ **comercial** commercial law; ~ **de importação** duty; ~ **de voto** franchise; ~ **penal** criminal law; **direitos** *pl*; **direitos alfandegários** Customs duty; **direitos de importação** import duty; **isento de direitos** duty-free; **sempre a** ~ straight ahead

dirigente (dee-ree-*zhayng*-ter) *m* leader

dirigir (dee-ree-*zheer*) *v* direct; conduct, head, *lead; **dirigir-se a** address

disciplina (dee-shee-*plee*-ner) *f* discipline

disco (*deesh*-koo) *m* disc; record; ~ **de longa duração** long-playing record

discordar (deesh-koor-*dhahr*) *v* disagree

discreto (deesh-*kreh*-too) *adj* inconspicuous

discurso (deesh-*koor*-soo) *m* speech

discussão (deesh-koo-*serng*ʷ) *f* (pl -sões) discussion; argument

discutir (deesh-koo-*teer*) *v* quarrel; discuss; argue, deliberate

disenteria (dee-zayngn-ter-*ree*-er) *f* dysentery

disfarçar-se (deesh-ferr-*sahr*-ser) *v* disguise

disfarce (deesh-*fahr*-ser) *m* disguise

disforme (deesh-*for*-mer) *adj* deformed

disparar (deesh-per-*rahr*) *v* fire, *shoot

disparatado (deesh-per-rer-*tah*-dhoo) *adj* silly

disparate (deesh-per-*rah*-ter) *m* nonsense; **disparates** rubbish; *dizer **disparates** talk rubbish

dispensar (deesh-payng-*sahr*) *v* exempt; spare; ~ **de** discharge of

dispersar (deesh-perr-*sahr*) *v* scatter

disponível (deesh-poo-*nee*-vehl) *adj* (pl -eis) available

*dispor de** (deesh-*poar*) *have at one's disposal

disposição (deesh-poo-zee-*serng*ʷ) *f* (pl -cões) disposal; mood

dispositivo (deesh-poo-zee-*tee*-voo) *m* apparatus

disposto (deesh-*poash*-too) *adj* willing; inclined; **bem** ~ good-tempered

disputa (deesh-*poo*-ter) *f* dispute; argument

disputar (bree-*gahr*) *v* quarrel

dissolver (dee-soal-*vayr*) *v* dissolve

dissuadir (dee-swer-*dheer*) *v* dissuade from

distância (deesh-*terng*-sʸer) *f* way, space, distance

distante (deesh-*terngn*-ter) *adj* distant; remote, far-away; **o mais** ~ furthest

distensão (deesh-tayng-*serng*ʷ) *f* (pl -sões) sprain

distinção (deesh-teeng-*serng*ʷ) *f* (pl

-ções) distinction; difference

distinguir (deesh-teeng-*geer*) v distinguish

distinto (deesh-*teengn*-too) adj distinct; separate; dignified, distinguished

distracção (deesh-trah-*serng*ʷ) f (pl -ções) amusement

distribuidor (deesh-tree-bhwee-*dhoar*) m distributor

*****distribuir** (deesh-tree-*bhweer*) v *deal, distribute; issue

distrito (deesh-*tree*-too) m district

distúrbio (deesh-*toor*-bʸoo) m disturbance

ditado (dee-*tah*-dhoo) m dictation

ditador (dee-ter-*dhoar*) m dictator

ditafone (dee-ter-*foa*-ner) m dictaphone

ditar (dee-*tahr*) v dictate

divã (dee-*verng*) m couch

diversão (dee-verr-*serng*ʷ) f (pl -sões) diversion; entertainment

diversos (dee-*vehr*-soosh) adj various

divertido (dee-verr-tee-dhoo) adj amusing; entertaining

divertimento (dee-verr-tee-*mayngn*-too) m entertainment, amusement; fun, pleasure

*****divertir** (dee-verr-*teer*) v amuse; entertain

dívida (*dee*-vee-dher) f debt

dividir (dee-vee-*dheer*) v divide; ~ ao meio halve

divino (der-*vee*-noo) adj divine

divisa (der-*vee*-zer) f motto

divisão (der-vee-*zerng*ʷ) f (pl -sões) division; section; room

divorciar-se (dee-voor-sʸahr-ser) v divorce

divórcio (dee-*vor*-sʸoo) m divorce

*****dizer** (dee-*zayr*) v *say; *tell; *querer dizer *mean

doação (dwer-*serng*ʷ) f (pl -ções) do-

nation

doador (dwer-*dhoar*) m donor

dobra (*do*-bhrer) f fold, crease

dobradiça (doo-bhrer-*dhee*-ser) f hinge

dobrar (doo-*bhrahr*) v fold; *bend

o dobro (oo *doa*-bhroo) the double

doca (*do*-ker) f dock

doce (*doa*-ser) adj sweet; m sweet; ~ de fruta jam; ~ de laranja marmalade

documento (doo-koo-*mayngn*-too) m document

doença (*dwayng*-ser) f illness; sickness, disease; ~ **venérea** venereal disease

doente (*dwayngn*-ter) adj ill, sick; m patient

doentio (dwayngn-tee*ᵒᵒ*) adj unhealthy, unsound

*****doer** (*dwayr*) v ache

doido (*doi*-dhoo) adj crazy

dois (doish) num (f duas) two

dólar (*do*-lahr) m dollar

doloroso (doo-loo-*roa*-zoo) adj painful; sore

dom (*dawng*) m gift

domesticado (doo-*mehsh*-tee-*kah*-dhoo) adj tame

domesticar (doo-mɪsh-tee-*kahr*) v tame

doméstico (doo-*mehsh*-tee-koo) adj domestic

domicílio (doo-mee-*see*-lʸoo) m domicile

dominação (doo-mee-ner-*serng*ʷ) f (pl -ções) domination

dominante (doo-mee-*nerngn*-ter) adj leading

dominar (doo-mee-*nahr*) v master

domingo (doo-*meeng*-goo) m Sunday

domínio (doo-*mee*-nʸoo) m field; rule, dominion

donativo (doo-ner-*tee*-voo) m donation

dono (*doa*-noo) *m* master; owner

dor (doar) *f* ache, pain; sore; grief, sorrow; ~ **de barriga** stomach-ache; ~ **de cabeça** headache; ~ **de dentes** toothache; ~ **de estô-mago** stomach-ache; ~ **de gar-ganta** sore throat; ~ **de ouvidos** earache; **dores** labour; **dores nas costas** backache; **sem** ~ painless

*dormir (door-*meer*) *v* *sleep; ~ **de-mais** *oversleep

dormitório (door-mee-*to*-rYoo) *m* dormitory

dose (*do*-zer) *f* dose

dotado (doo-*tah*-dhoo) *adj* talented, gifted

dourado (doa-*rah*-dhoo) *adj* gilt

doutor (doa-*toar*) *m* doctor

doze (*doa*-zer) *num* twelve

dragão (drer-*gerng*ᵂ) *m* (pl -gões) dragon

drama (*drer*-mer) *m* drama

dramático (drer-*mah*-tee-koo) *adj* dramatic

dramaturgo (drer-mer-*toor*-goo) *m* dramatist; playwright

drenar (drer-*nahr*) *v* drain

drogaria (droo-ger-*ree*-er) *f* pharmacy, chemist's; drugstore *nAm*

duche (*doo*-sher) *m* shower

duna (*doo*-ner) *f* dune

duplo (*doo*-ploo) *adj* double

duque (*doo*-ker) *m* duke

duquesa (doo-*kay*-zer) *f* duchess

duração (doo-rer-*serng*ᵂ) *f* (pl -ções) duration

duradouro (doo-rer-*dhoa*-roo) *adj* lasting; permanent

durante (doo-*rerng*n-ter) *prep* for, during

durar (doo-*rahr*) *v* last; continue

duro (*doo*-roo) *adj* hard; tough

dúvida (*doo*-vee-dher) *f* doubt; ***pôr em** ~ query; **sem** ~ undoubtedly

duvidar (doo-vee-*dhahr*) *v* doubt

duvidoso (doo-vee-*dhoa*-zoo) *adj* doubtful

dúzia (*doo*-zYer) *f* dozen

E

e (ee) *conj* and

ébano (*eh*-bher-noo) *m* ebony

eclipse (er-*kleep*-ser) *m* eclipse

eco (*eh*-koo) *m* echo

economia (ee-koo-noo-*meeer*) *f* economy; **economias** savings *pl*

económico (ee-koo-*no*-mee-koo) *adj* economic; thrifty, economical; cheap

economista (ee-koo-noo-*meesh*-ter) *m* economist

economizar (ee-koo-noo-mee-*zahr*) *v* economize

écran (ehk-*rerng*) *m* screen

eczema (ehk-*zay*-mer) *m* eczema

edição (er-dhee-*serng*ᵂ) *f* (pl -ções) edition; issue; ~ **da manhã** morning edition

edificar (ee-dher-fee-*kahr*) *v* erect; construct

edifício (ee-dher-*fee*-sYoo) *m* construction, building

editor (er-dhee-*toar*) *m* publisher

edredão (ee-dhrer-*dherng*ᵂ) *m* (pl -dões) eiderdown

educação (ee-dhoo-ker-*serng*ᵂ) *f* (pl -ções) education

educado (ee-dhoo-*kah*-dhoo) *adj* polite, civil; **bem** ~ well brought-up; **mal** ~ badly brought-up

educar (ee-dhoo-*kahr*) *v* educate; raise, *bring up

efectivamente (ee-feh-tee-ver-*mayng*n-ter) *adv* indeed; as a matter of fact

efectuar (ee-feh-*twahr*) *v* effect

efeito (ee-*fay*-too) *m* effect; **com ~** in fact, in effect

efervescência (ee-ferr-vish-*sayng*-s^yer) *f* fizz

eficaz (er-fee-*kahsh*) *adj* effective

eficiente (er-fee-s^y*ayng*-ter) *adj* efficient

efusivo (ee-foo-*zee*-voo) *adj* hearty

egípcio (er-*zheep*-s^yoo) *adj* Egyptian; *m* Egyptian

Egipto (er-*zheep*-too) *m* Egypt

egocêntrico (ee-goo-*sayng*-tree-koo) *adj* self-centred

egoísmo (ee-*gweezh*-moo) *m* selfishness

egoísta (ee-*gweesh*-ter) *adj* egoistic; selfish

égua (*eh*-gwer) *f* mare

eixo (*ay*-shoo) *m* axle

ela (*eh*-ler) *pron* she; **~ mesma** herself

elaborar (ee-ler-bhoo-*rahr*) *v* elaborate

elas (*eh*-lersh) *pron* they; **~ mesmas** themselves

elasticidade (ee-lersh-ter-see-*dhah*-dher) *f* elasticity

elástico (ee-*lahsh*-tee-koo) *adj* elastic; *m* rubber band, elastic band

ele (*ay*-ler) *pron* he; **~ mesmo** himself

electricidade (ee-lehk-trer-see-*dhah*-dher) *f* electricity

electricista (ee-lehk-trer-*seesh*-ter) *m* electrician

eléctrico (ee-*leh*-tree-koo) *adj* electric; *m* tram; streetcar *nAm*

electrónico (ee-leh-*troa*-nee-koo) *adj* electronic

elefante (ee-ler-*ferngn*-ter) *m* elephant

elegância (ee-ler-*gerng*-s^yer) *f* elegance

elegante (ee-ler-*gerngn*-ter) *adj* smart, elegant

eleger (ee-ler-*zhayr*) *v* elect

eleição (ee-lay-*serng*^w) *f* (pl -ções) election

elementar (ee-ler-mayngn-*tahr*) *adj* primary, elementary

elemento (ee-ler-*mayngn*-too) *m* element

eles (*ay*-lish) *pron* they; **~ mesmos** themselves

elevação (ee-ler-ver-*serng*^w) *f* (pl -ções) rise

elevador (ee-ler-ver-*dhoar*) *m* elevator *nAm*

elfo (*ehl*-foo) *m* elf

eliminar (ee-ler-mee-*nahr*) *v* eliminate

elo (*eh*-loo) *m* link

elogio (ee-loo-*zhee*^{oo}) *m* praise

elucidar (ee-loo-see-*dhahr*) *v* elucidate

em (erng^y) *prep* at; in, inside

emagrecer (ee-mer-grer-*sayr*) *v* slim

emancipação (ee-merng-see-per-*serng*^w) *f* emancipation

embaixada (ayngm-bigh-*shah*-dher) *f* embassy

embaixador (ayngm-bigh-shah-*dhoar*) *m* ambassador

embalagem (ayngm-ber-*lah*-zherng^y) *f* packing

embalar (ayngm-ber-*lahr*) *v* pack up, pack

embaraçado (ayngm-ber-rer-*sah*-dhoo) *adj* embarrassed

embaraçar (ayngm-ber-rer-*sahr*) *v* embarrass

embaraçoso (ayngm-ber-rer-*soa*-zoo) *adj* awkward, embarrassing

embarcação (ayngm-berr-ker-*serng*^w) *f* (pl -ções) embarkation; vessel

embarcar (ayngm-ber-*kahr*) *v* embark

embargo (ayngm-*bahr*-goo) *m* embargo

embeber (ayngm-ber-*bhayr*) *v* soak

emblema (ayngm-*blay*-mer) *m* emblem

embora (ayɴgm-*bo*-rer) *conj* although, though; *adv* off

emboscada (ayɴgm-boosh-*kah*-dher) *f* ambush

embotado (ayɴgm-boo-*tah*-dhoo) *adj* dull

embraiagem (ayɴgm-brer-ʸah-zherngʸ) *f* clutch

embriagado (ayɴgm-bree-er-*gah*-dhoo) *adj* intoxicated

embrulhar (ayɴgm-broo-*lʸahr*) *v* wrap up, pack up; confuse

embrulho (ayɴgm-*broo*-lʸoo) *m* parcel

ementa (ee-*mayng*-ter) *f* menu; ~ **fixa** set menu

emergência (ee-merr-*zhayng*-sʸer) *f* emergency

emigração (er-mee-grer-*serng*ʷ) *f* (pl -ções) emigration

emigrante (er-mee-*gremng*-ter) *m* emigrant

emigrar (er-mee-*grahr*) *v* emigrate

eminente (er-mee-*nayngn*-ter) *adj* outstanding

emissão (er-mee-*serng*ʷ) *f* (pl -sões) issue; broadcast

emissário (er-mee-*sah*-rʸoo) *m* envoy

emissor (er-mee-*soar*) *m* transmitter

emitir (er-mee-*teer*) *v* utter; *broadcast

emoção (ee-moo-*serng*ʷ) *f* (pl -ções) emotion

emocionante (ee-moo-sʸoo-*nengn*-ter) *adj* exciting

empatar (ayɴgm-*pah*-terr) *v* hinder, disturb; tie

empena (ayɴgm-*pay*-ner) *f* gable

empenhar (ayɴgm-per-*ñahr*) *v* pawn

empilhar (ayɴgm-pee-*lʸahr*) *v* pile

empola (ayɴgm-*poa*-ler) *f* blister

empreender (ayɴgm-prʸayɴgn-*dayr*) *v* *undertake

empregada (ayɴgm-prer-*gah*-dher) *f* maid; employee; ~ **de bar** bar-

maid; ~ **de mesa** waitress; ~ **doméstica** housemaid

empregado (ayɴgm-prer-*gah*-dhoo) *m* employee; ~ **de balcão** shop assistant; ~ **de bar** bartender; ~ **de escritório** clerk; ~ **de mesa** waiter; ~ **doméstico** domestic

empregar (ayɴgm-prer-*gahr*) *v* employ, engage; *spend

emprego (ayɴgm-*pray*-goo) *m* employment; job

empreiteiro (ayɴgm-pray-*tay*-roo) *m* contractor

empresa (ayɴgm-*pray*-zer) *f* undertaking, enterprise; business, concern

emprestar (ayɴgm-prɪsh-*tahr*) *v* *lend

empréstimo (ayɴgm-*prehsh*-tee-moo) *m* loan

empurrão (ayɴgm-poo-*rrerng*ʷ) *m* (pl -rões) push

empurrar (ayɴgm-poo-*rrahr*) *v* push

encadernação (ayɴgng-ker-dherr-ner-*serng*ʷ) *f* (pl -ções) binding

encantado (ayɴgng-kerngn-*tah*-dhoo) *adj* delighted

encantador (ayɴgng-kerngn-ter-*dhoar*) *adj* enchanting; sweet, lovely, charming, delightful

encantamento (ayɴgng-kerngn-ter-*mayngn*-too) *m* spell

encantar (ayɴgng-kerngn-*tahr*) *v* bewitch; delight

encanto (ayɴgng-*kerngn*-too) *m* charm; glamour

encaracolado (ayɴgng-ker-rer-koo-*lah*-dhoo) *adj* curly

encaracolar (ayɴgng-ker-rer-koo-*lahr*) *v* curl

encarceramento (ayɴgng-kerr-ser-rer-*mayngn*-too) *m* imprisonment

encarnado (ayɴgng-ker-*nah*-dhoo) *adj* red

encarregar (ayɴgng-ker-rrer-*gahr*) *v* charge; **encarregado de** in charge of; **encarregar-se de** *take charge of

encenador (ayng-ser-ner-*dhoar*) m director

encenar (ayng-ser-*nahr*) v direct

encerrado (ayng-ser-*rrer*-dhoo) adj closed; shut

encerrar (ayng-ser-*rrahr*) v lock up

enchente (ayng-*shayngn*-ter) f flood

encher (ayng-*shayr*) v fill; fill out Am; ~ **de ar** inflate

enciclopédia (ayng-see-kloo-*peh*-dhᵞer) f encyclopaedia

encoberto (ayngng-koo-*bhehr*-too) adj cloudy

encolher (ayngng-koo-*lᵞayr*) v *shrink; **não encolhe** shrinkproof

encomenda (ayngng-koo-*mayngn*-der) f parcel; order; **feito por** ~ made to order

encomendar (ayngng-koo-mayngn-*dahr*) v order

encontrão (ayngng-kawngn-*trerngʷ*) m (pl -rões) bump

encontrar (ayngng-kawngn-*trahr*) v *find; *come across; encounter, *meet

encontro (ayngng-*kawngn*-troo) m encounter; date

encorajar (ayngng-koo-rer-*zhahr*) v encourage

encosta (ayngng-*kosh*-ter) f hillside

encruzilhada (ayngng-kroo-zee-*lᵞah*-dher) f crossing

encurtar (ayngng-koor-*tahr*) v shorten

endereçar (ayngn-der-rer-*sahr*) v address

endereço (ayngn-der-*ray*-soo) m address

endireitar (ayngn-dee-ray-*tahr*) v straighten

endossar (ayngn-doo-*sahr*) v endorse

energia (ee-nerr-*zheeer*) f energy; power; ~ **nuclear** nuclear energy

enérgico (ee-*nehr*-zhee-koo) adj energetic

enevoado (ee-ner-*vwah*-dhoo) adj misty, hazy; foggy

enfadonho (ayng-fer-*dhoa*-ño) adj dull

ênfase (*ayng*-fer-zer) f stress

enfeitiçar (ayng-fay-tee-*sahr*) v bewitch

enfermaria (ayng-ferr-mer-*ree*-er) f infirmary

enfermeira (ayng-ferr-*may*-rer) f nurse

enfermeiro (ayng-ferr-*may*-roo) m male nurse

enfiar (ayng-*fᵞahr*) v thread; pierce

enforcar (ayng-foor-*kahr*) v hang

enfrentar (ayng-frayngn-*tahr*) v face

enfurecer (ayng-foo-rer-*sayr*) v rage

enganar (ayngng-ger-*nahr*) v deceive; cheat, fool; **enganar-se** *be mistaken

engano (ayngng-*ger*-noo) m deceit; mistake

engarrafamento (ayngng-ger-rer-fer-*mayngn*-too) m bottling; obstruction; ~ **de trânsito** traffic jam

engenheiro (ayng-zhɪ-*ñay*-roo) m engineer

engenhoca (ayng-zhɪ-*ño*-ker) f gadget

***engolir** (ayngng-goo-*leer*) v swallow

engomar (ayngng-goo-*mahr*) v starch; **engomado permanente** permanent press

engordar (ayng-goor-*dahr*) v fatten; *grow fat

engraçado (ayngng-grer-*sah*-dhoo) adj humorous, funny

engrossar (ayngng-groo-*sahr*) v thicken

enguia (ayngng-*gee*-er) f eel

enigma (ee-*neeg*-mer) m enigma, mystery; puzzle

enjoado (ayng-*zhwah*-dhoo) adj sick; seasick

enjoo (ayng-*zhoa*-oo) *m* sickness, air-sickness, seasickness

enorme (ee-*nor*-mer) *adj* enormous; huge, immense

enquanto (ayng-*kwerng*-too) *conj* whilst, while

enredo (ayng-*rray*-dhoo) *m* plot

enrolar (ayng-roo-*lahr*) *v* *wind

enrugar (ayng-roo-*gahr*) *v* crease

ensaiar (ayng-ser-*Yahr*) *v* rehearse

ensaio (ayng-*sigh*-oo) *m* rehearsal; essay

enseada (ayng-s*Yah*-dher) *f* inlet, creek

ensinamentos (ayng-see-ner-*mayngn*-toosh) *mpl* teachings *pl*

ensinar (ayng-see-*nahr*) *v* *teach

ensopar (ayng-soo-*pahr*) *v* soak

entalhar (ayng-ter-*lYahr*) *v* carve

no entanto (noo ayng-*terngn*-too) though

então (ayng-*terng*ʷ) *adv* then; **de ~** contemporary

enteada (ayng-t*Yah*-dher) *f* step-daughter

enteado (ayng-t*Yah*-dhoo) *m* stepson, stepchild

entender (ayng-tayngn-*dayr*) *v* *understand

enterrar (ayng-ter-*rrahr*) *v* bury

enterro (ayng-*tay*-rroo) *m* burial

entornar (ayng-toor-*nahr*) *v* *spill

entorpecido (ayng-toor-per-*see*-dhoo) *adj* numb

entrada (ayng-*trah*-dher) *f* entry, way in, entrance; admittance; foyer; **~ proibida** no admittance

entranhas (ayng-*trer*-ñersh) *fpl* insides

entrar (ayng-*trahr*) *v* enter, *go in

entravar (ayng-trer-*vahr*) *v* impede

entre (*ayng*-trer) *prep* between; amid, among

entrega (ayng-*treh*-ger) *f* delivery

entregar (ayng-trer-*gahr*) *v* deliver; hand, *give; commit

entretanto (ayng-trer-*terngn*-too) *adv* meanwhile, in the meantime

entreter (ayng-trer-*tayr*) *v* entertain

entrevista (ayng-trer-*veesh*-ter) *f* interview; appointment

entusiasmo (ayng-too-z*Yahzh*-moo) *m* enthusiasm

entusiasta (ayng-too-z*Yahsh*-ter) *adj* keen

entusiástico (ayng-too-z*Yahsh*-tee-koo) *adj* enthusiastic

envelhecido (ayng-veh-l*Yer*-*see*-dhoo) *adj* old, aged

envenenar (ayng-ver-ner-*nahr*) *v* poison

envergonhado (ayng-verr-goo-*ñah*-dhoo) *adj* embarrassed; ashamed

envernizar (ayng-verr-nee-*zahr*) *v* varnish

enviar (ayng-v*Yahr*) *v* *send, dispatch

envolver (ayng-voal-*vayr*) *v* wrap

envolvido (ayng-voal-*vee*-dhoo) *adj* concerned; involved

enxaguadela (ayng-sher-gwer-*dhay*-ler) *f* rinse

enxaguar (ayng-sher-*gwahr*) *v* rinse

enxaqueca (ayng-sher-*keh*-ker) *f* migraine

enxugar (ayng-shoo-*gahr*) *v* dry

épico (*eh*-pee-koo) *adj* epic

epidemia (er-pee-dher-*mee*-er) *f* epidemic

epilepsia (er-pee-lehp-*see*-er) *f* epilepsy

epílogo (er-*pee*-loo-goo) *m* epilogue

episódio (er-pee-z*oo*-dh*Yoo*) *m* episode

época (*eh*-poo-ker) *f* period; **fora da ~** off season

epopeia (ee-poo-*pay*-er) *f* epic

Equador (ee-kwer-*dhoar*) *m* Ecuador

equador (ee-kwer-*dhoar*) *m* equator

equatoriano (i-kwer-too-r*Yah*-noo) *m*

Ecuadorian

equilíbrio (ee-ker-*lee*-bhr^Yoo) *m* balance

equipa (ı-*kee*-per) *f* team; soccer team

equipamento (ı-kee-per-*mayngn*-too) *m* equipment; outfit, kit, gear; ~ **de pesca** fishing gear

equipar (ı-kee-*pahr*) *v* equip

equitação (ı-kee-ter-*serng*^W) *f* riding; **escola de** ~ riding-school

equitativo (ı-kwee-ter-*tee*-voo) *adj* right

equivalente (ı-kee-ver-*layngn*-ter) *adj* equivalent

equívoco (ı-*kee*-voo-koo) *m* mistake; *adj* ambiguous

erecto (ee-*reh*-too) *adj* erect

erguer (eer-*gayr*) *v* lift; **erguer-se** *rise; *get up

erigir (ee-rer-*zheer*) *v* erect

errado (ee-*rrah*-dhoo) *adj* wrong; false, mistaken; *estar ~ *be wrong

errar (ee-*rrahr*) *v* err; wander

erro (ay-rroo) *m* mistake, error

erudito (ee-roo-*dhee*-too) *adj* learned; *m* scholar

erupção (ee-roop-*serng*^W) *f* (pl -ções) rash

erva (*ehr*-ver) *f* herb; grass; ~ **daninha** weed; **folha de** ~ blade of grass

ervilha (ır-*vee*-l^Yer) *f* pea

esbelto (ızh-*bhehl*-too) *adj* slender

esboçar (ızh-bhoo-*sahr*) *v* sketch

esboço (ızh-*bhoa*-soo) *m* sketch

escada (ısh-*kah*-dher) *f* ladder; stairs *pl*; staircase; ~ **de incêndio** fire-escape; ~ **do portaló** gangway; ~ **rolante** escalator

escala (ısh-*kah*-ler) *f* scale

escalar (ısh-ker-*lahr*) *v* ascend

escama (ısh-*ker*-mer) *f* scale

escândalo (ısh-*kerngn*-der-loo) *m*

scandal

Escandinávia (ısh-kerngn-dee-*ner*-v^Yer) *f* Scandinavia

escandinavo (ısh-kerngn-dee-*nah*-voo) *adj* Scandinavian; *m* Scandinavian

escangalhado (ısh-kerng-ger-*l^Yah*-dhoo) *adj* broken

escangalhar (ısh-kerng-ger-*l^Yahr*) *v* *break

escapar (ısh-ker-*pahr*) *v* slip, escape

escape (ısh-*kah*-per) *m* exhaust; **tubo de** ~ exhaust

escaravelho (ısh-ker-rer-*vay*-l^Yoo) *m* beetle; bug

escarlate (ısh-kerr-*lah*-ter) *adj* scarlet

escárnio (ısh-*kahr*-n^Yoo) *m* scorn

escarpado (ısh-kahr-*pah*-dhoo) *adj* steep

escassez (ısh-ker-*saysh*) *f* scarcity; shortage

escasso (ısh-*kah*-soo) *adj* scarce

escavação (ısh-ker-ver-*serng*^W) *f* (pl -ções) excavation

escavar (ısh-ker-*vahr*) *v* *dig

esclarecer (ısh-kler-rer-*serr*) *v* clarify

esclarecimento (ısh-kler-rer-see-*mayngn*-too) *m* explanation

escocês (ısh-koo-*saysh*) *adj* Scottish, Scotch; *m* Scot

Escócia (ısh-ko-s^Yer) *f* Scotland

escola (ısh-*ko*-ler) *f* school; ~ **secundária** secondary school

escolar (ısh-koo-*lahr*) *f* schoolgirl; *m* schoolboy; *adj* of or pertaining to school

escolha (ısh-*koa*-l^Yer) *f* choice, selection; pick

escolher (ısh-koo-*l^Yayr*) *v* *choose; pick; select; elect

escolta (ısh-*koal*-ter) *f* escort

escoltar (ısh-koal-*tahr*) *v* escort

esconder (ısh-kawngn-*dayr*) *v* *hide; conceal

escorregadela (ısh-koo-rrer-ger-*dheh*-

ler) *f* slip

escorregadio (ish-koo-rrer-ger-*dhee*⁰⁰) *adj* slippery

escorregadouro (ish-koo-rrer-ger-*dhoa*-roo) *m* slide

escorregar (ish-koo-rrer-*gahr*) *v* glide, slip

escova (ish-*koa*-ver) *f* brush; ~ **de cabelo** hairbrush; ~ **de dentes** toothbrush; ~ **de fato** clothesbrush; ~ **de unhas** nailbrush

escovar (ish-koo-*vahr*) *v* brush

escravo (ish-*krer*-voo) *m* slave

escrevaninha (ish-kree-ver-*nee*-ñer) *f* bureau

escrever (ish-krer-*vayr*) *v* *write; ~ à máquina type; por escrito written, in writing

escrita (ish-*kree*-ter) *f* handwriting

escritor (ish-kree-*toar*) *m* writer

escritório (ish-kree-*to*-rʸoo) *m* office; study; **artigos de** ~ stationery

escrivão (ish-kree-*verng*ʷ) *m* (pl -ães) clerk

escultor (ish-kool-*toar*) *m* sculptor

escultura (ish-kool-*too*-rer) *f* sculpture

escuridão (ish-koo-ree-*dherng*ʷ) *f* darkness; gloom

escuro (ish-*koo*-roo) *adj* dark; obscure

escutar (ish-koo-*tahr*) *v* listen

escuteira (ish-koo-*tay*-rer) *f* girl guide

escuteiro (ish-koo-*tay*-roo) *m* boy scout, scout

esfera (ish-*feh*-rer) *f* sphere

esfomeado (ish-foo-mʸah-dhoo) *adj* hungry; famished

esforçar-se (ish-foor-*sahr*-ser) *v* try

esforço (ish-*foar*-soo) *m* strain, effort

esfregar (ish-frer-*gahr*) *v* rub, scrub

esgalhos (izh-gah-lʸoosh) *mpl* antlers *pl*

esgotado (ish-goo-*tah*-dhoo) *adj* sold out

esgoto (ish-*goa*-too) *m* drain, sewer

esgrimir (izh-gree-*meer*) *v* fence

esguicho (izh-*gee*-shoo) *m* squirt

esmagar (izh-mer-*gahr*) *v* mash

esmaltado (izh-mahl-*tah*-dhoo) *adj* enamelled

esmaltar (izh-mahl-*tahr*) *v* enamel

esmalte (izh-*mahl*-ter) *m* enamel

esmeralda (izh-mer-*rahl*-der) *f* emerald

espaçar (ish-per-*sahr*) *v* space

espaço (ish-*pah*-soo) *m* room, space

espaçoso (ish-pah-*soa*-zoo) *adj* spacious; large, roomy

espada (ish-*pah*-dher) *f* sword

espalhafato (ish-per-lʸer-*fah*-too) *m* fuss

espalhar (ish-per-*lʸahr*) *v* *spread; *shed

Espanha (ish-*per*-ñer) *f* Spain

espanhol (ish-per-*ñol*) *adj* (pl -hóis) Spanish; *m* Spaniard

espantar (ish-perng-*tahr*) *v* amaze, astonish

espanto (ish-*perng*-too) *m* astonishment, amazement

espantoso (ish-perng-*toa*-zoo) *adj* astonishing; dreadful

esparadrapo (ish-per-rer-*dhrah*-poo) *mBr* adhesive tape, adhesive bandage, plaster

espargo (ish-*pahr*-goo) *m* asparagus

especial (ish-per-sʸ*ahl*) *adj* (pl -ais) special; particular, peculiar

especialidade (ish-per-sʸer-lee-*dhah*-dher) *f* speciality

especialista (ish-per-sʸer-*leesh*-ter) *m* specialist; expert

especializado (ish-per-sʸer-lee-*zah*-dhoo) *adj* skilled

especializar-se (ish-per-sʸer-lee-*zahr*-ser) *v* specialize

especialmente (ish-per-sʸahl-*mayng*-ter) *adv* especially

especiaria (ish-per-s^yer-*ree*-er) *f* spice

espécie (ish-*peh*-s^yer) *f* species; breed; **toda a ~ de** all sorts of

específico (ish-per-*see*-fee-koo) *adj* specific

espectáculo (ish-peh-*tah*-koo-loo) *m* sight; show, spectacle; **~ de varie-dades** variety show; floor show

espectador (ish-peh-ter-*dhoar*) *m* spectator

especular (ish-per-koo-*lahr*) *v* specu-late

espelho (ish-*pay*-l^yoo) *m* looking-glass, mirror

espera (ish-*peh*-rer) *f* waiting

esperado (ish-per-*rer*-doo) *adj* due

esperança (ish-per-*rerng*-ser) *f* hope

esperançado (ish-per-rerng-*sah*-dhoo) *adj* hopeful

esperar (ish-per-*rahr*) *v* expect; await, wait; hope

esperto (ish-*pehr*-too) *adj* bright; smart, clever

espesso (ish-*pay*-soo) *adj* thick

espeto (ish-*peh*-too) *m* spit

espião (ish-p^y*erng*^w) *m* (pl -iões) spy

espinafres (ish-pee-*nah*-frersh) *mpl* spinach

espingarda (ish-peeng-*gahr*-dher) *f* rifle; gun

espinha (ish-*pee*-ñer) *f* bone; **~ de peixe** fishbone; **~ dorsal** back-bone, spine

espinho (ish-*pee*-ñoo) *m* thorn

espírito (ish-*pee*-ree-too) *m* spirit; soul; ghost

espiritual (ish-per-ree-*twahl*) *adj* (pl -ais) spiritual

espirituoso (ish-per-ree-*twoa*-zoo) *adj* humorous; witty

espirrar (ish-pee-*rrahr*) *v* sneeze

esplanada (ish-pler-*nah*-dher) *f* espla-nade

esplêndido (ish-*playngn*-dee-dhoo) *adj*

splendid; glorious, enchanting, magnificent

esplendor (ish-playngn-*doar*) *m* splen-dour; glare

esponja (ish-*pawng*-zher) *f* sponge

esporte (ish-*por*-ter) *mBr* sport

esposa (ish-*poa*-zer) *f* wife

esposo (ish-*poa*-zoo) *m* husband

espreitar (ish-pray-*tahr*) *v* peep; watch for

espuma (ish-*poo*-mer) *f* froth; foam, lather; **~ de borracha** foam-rub-ber

espumante (ish-poo-*merngn*-ter) *adj* sparkling

espumar (ish-poo-*mahr*) *v* foam

esquadrilha (ish-kwer-*dhree*-l^yer) *f* squadron

esquecer (ish-keh-*sayr*) *v* *forget

esquecido (ish-keh-*see*-dhoo) *adj* for-getful

esqueleto (ish-ker-*lay*-too) *m* skeleton

esquema (ish-*kay*-mer) *m* scheme, diagram

esquerdo (ish-*kayr*-doo) *adj* left; left-hand

esqui (ish-*kee*) *m* ski; skiing; **~ aquático** water ski; **varas de ~** ski sticks

esquiador (ish-k^yer-*dhoar*) *m* skier

esquiar (ish-k^y-*ahr*) *v* ski

esquilo (ish-*kee*-loo) *m* squirrel

esquina (ish-*kee*-ner) *f* corner

esquisito (ish-ker-*zee*-too) *adj* queer

esquivo (ish-*kee*-voo) *adj* shy

esse (*ay*-ser) *adj* that; **esses** those

essência (ee-*sayng*-s^yer) *f* essence

essencial (ee-sayng-s^y*ahl*) *adj* (pl -ais) essential

essencialmente (ee-sayng-s^yahl-*mayngn*-ter) *adv* essentially

estabelecer (ish-ter-bher-ler-*sayr*) *v* es-tablish; found

estábulo (ish-*tah*-bhoo-loo) *m* stable

estação (ısh-ter-*serng*ᵂ) *f* (pl -ções)
station; season; depot *nAm;* **alta ~**
high season; **baixa ~** low season;
~ balnear seaside resort; **~ central** central station; **~ de serviço**
service station, filling station; **plena ~** peak season

estacionamento (ısh-ter-s ᵞoo-ner-*mayngn*-too) *m* parking; **~ proibido**
no parking

estacionar (ısh-ter-s ᵞoo-*nahr*) *v* park

estacionário (ısh-ter-s ᵞoo-nah-r ᵞoo)
adj stationary

estadia (ısh-tah-dh ᵞer) *f* stay

estádio (ısh-*tah*-dh ᵞoo) *m* stadium

estadista (ısh-ter-*dheesh*-ter.) *m*
statesman

estado (ısh-*tah*-dhoo) *m* state; condition; **do ~** national; **~ de emergência** emergency; **Estados Unidos**
United States; the States

estalagem (ısh-ter-*lah*-zherng ᵞ) *f* inn,
roadhouse

estalajadeiro (ısh-ter-ler-zher-*dhay*-roo) *m* inn-keeper

estalar (ısh-ter-*lahr*) *v* crack

estaleiro (ısh-ter-*lay*-roo) *m* shipyard

estalido (ısh-ter-*lee*-dhoo) *m* crack

estampa (ısh-*terngm*-per) *f* engraving

estandarte (ısh-terngn-*dahr*-ter) *m*
banner

estanho (ısh-*ter*-ñoo) *m* pewter, tin

***estar** (ısh-*tahr*) *v* ***be**

estatística (ısh-ter-*teesh*-tee-ker) *f*
statistics *pl*

estátua (ısh-*tah*-twer) *f* statue

estatura (ısh-tah-*too*-rer) *f* figure

estável (ısh-*tah*-vehl) *adj* (pl -eis)
stable; permanent

este¹ (*aysh*-ter) *adj* this; *pron* this;
estes these

este² (*ehsh*-ter) *m* east

estenografia (ısh-ter-noo-grer-*fee*-er) *f*
shorthand

estenógrafo (ısh-ter-*no*-grer-foo) *m*
stenographer

esterco (ısh-*tayr*-koo) *m* dung

estéril (ısh-*teh*-reel) *adj* (pl -eis) sterile

esterilizar (ısh-ter-rer-lee-*zahr*) *v* sterilize

estibordo (ısh-tee-*bhor*-doo) *m* starboard

esticão (ısh-tee-*kerng*ᵂ) *m* (pl -cões)
tug

esticar (ısh-tee-*kahr*) *v* stretch

estilo (ısh-*tee*-loo) *m* style

estima (ısh-*tee*-mer) *f* respect, esteem

estimar (ısh-tee-*mahr*) *v* esteem; estimate

estimativa (ısh-tee-mer-*tee*-ver) *f* estimate; ***fazer a ~** estimate

estimulante (ısh-tee-moo-*lerngn*-ter) *m*
stimulant

estimular (ısh-tee-moo-*lahr*) *v* stimulate

estímulo (ısh-*tee*-moo-loo) *m* impulse

estipulação (ısh-tee-poo-ler-*serng*ᵂ) *f*
(pl -ções) stipulation

estipular (ısh-tee-poo-*lahr*) *v* stipulate

estivador (ısh-tee-ver-*dhoar*) *m* docker

estofar (ısh-too-*fahr*) *v* upholster

estojo (ısh-*toa*-zhoo) *m* case; **~ de**
toalete toilet case

estola (ısh-*to*-ler) *f* stole

estômago (ısh-*toa*-mer-goo) *m* stomach

estore (ısh-*to*-rer) *m* blind

estorninho (ısh-toor-*nee*-ñoo) *m* starling

estorvar (ısh-toor-*vahr*) *v* embarras,
hinder; disturb

estrábico (ısh-*trah*-bhee-koo) *adj*
cross-eyed

estrada (ısh-*trah*-dher) *f* road, drive;
~ com portagem turnpike *nAm;*
~ de circunvalação by-pass; **~ de**
ferro *Br* railway, railroad *nAm;* **~**

em obras road works, road up; **~ principal** main road; highway, thoroughfare

estragar (ish-trer-*gahr*) v *spoil; mess up

estrangeiro (ish-trerng-*zhay*-roo) m alien, stranger, foreigner; adj alien, foreign; **no ~** abroad; **para o ~** abroad

estrangular (ish-trerng-goo-*lahr*) v choke, strangle

estranho (ish-*trer*-ñoo) adj funny; foreign, strange; queer, odd, quaint, peculiar; m alien

estreitar (ish-tray-*tahr*) v tighten

estreito (ish-*tray*-too) adj narrow; tight

estrela (ish-*tray*-ler) f star

estremecimento (ish-trer-mer-see-*mayngn*-too) m shudder

estribo (ish-*tree*-bhoo) m stirrup

estrofe (ish-*tro*-fer) f stanza

estrume (ish-*troo*-mer) m manure

estrumeira (ish-troo-*may*-rer) f dunghill

estrutura (ish-troo-*too*-rer) f structure; fabric

estuário (ish-*twah*-rYoo) m estuary

estudante (ish-too-*dherngn*-ter) m student; f student

estudar (ish-too-*dhahr*) v study

estudo (ish-*too*-dhoo) m study

estufa (ish-*too*-fer) f greenhouse

estupefaciente (ish-too-per-fer-sYayngn-ter) m drug

estupendo (ish-too-*payngn*-doo) adj wonderful

estúpido (ish-*too*-pee-dhoo) adj dumb, stupid

estuque (ish-*too*-ker) m plaster

esvaziar (izh-ver-zYahr) v empty

etapa (ee-*tah*-per) f stage

éter (*eh*-tehr) m ether

eternidade (ee-terr-nee-dhah-der) f eternity

eterno (ee-*tehr*-noo) adj eternal

etíope (ı-*tee*⁰⁰-per) adj Ethiopian; m Ethiopian

Etiópia (ı-tYoa-pYer) f Ethiopia

etiqueta (er-tee-*kay*-ter) f tag, label

etiquetar (er-tee-ker-*tahr*) v label

eu (ay⁰⁰) pron I; **~ mesmo** myself

Europa (ay⁰⁰-ro-per) f Europe

europeu (ay⁰⁰-roo-pay⁰⁰) adj European; m European

evacuar (ee-ver-*kwahr*) v evacuate

evadir (ee-ver-*dheer*) v escape

evangelho (ee-verng-*zheh*-lYoo) m gospel

evaporar (ee-ver-poo-*rahr*) v evaporate

evasão (ee-ver-*zerng*ʷ) f (pl -sões) escape

eventual (ee-vayngn-*twahl*) adj (pl -ais) possible

evidente (er-vee-*dhayngn*-ter) adj evident

evitar (er-vee-*tahr*) v avoid; prevent

evolução (ee-voo-loo-*serng*ʷ) f (pl -ções) evolution

exactamente (ee-zah-ter-*mayngn*-ter) adv exactly

exactidão (ee-zah-tee-*dherng*ʷ) f correctness; precision

exacto (ee-*zah*-too) adj precise, exact; accurate

exagerado (ee-zer-zher-*rah*-dhoo) adj extravagant; excessive

exagerar (ee-zer-zher-*rahr*) v exaggerate

exalar (ee-zer-*lahr*) v exhale

exame (ee-*zer*-mer) m examination; **~ médico** check-up

examinar (ee-zer-mee-*nahr*) v examine

exausto (ee-*zoush*-too) adj over-tired

excedente (ish-ser-*dhayngn*-ter) m remnant, surplus

exceder (ish-ser-*dhayr*) v exceed

excelente (ish-ser-*layngn*-ter) *adj* excellent; fine, first-rate

excêntrico (ish-*sayngn*-tree-koo) *adj* eccentric

excepção (ish-seh-*serng*ʷ) *f* (pl -ções) exception

excepcional (ish-seh-sʸoo-*nahl*) *adj* (pl -ais) exceptional

excepto (ish-*seh*-too) *prep* except

excessivo (ish-ser-*see*-voo) *adj* excessive

excesso (ish-*seh*-soo) *m* excess; ~ **de peso** overweight; ~ **de velocidade** speeding

excitação (ish-see-ter-*serng*ʷ) *f* (pl -ções) excitement

excitar (ish-see-*tahr*) *v* excite

exclamação (ish-kler-mer-*serng*ʷ) *f* (pl -ções) exclamation

exclamar (ish-kler-*mahr*) *v* exclaim

*****excluir** (ish-*klweer*) *v* exclude

exclusivamente (ish-kloo-see-ver-*mayngn*-ter) *adv* exclusively; solely

exclusivo (ish-kloo-*zee*-voo) *adj* exclusive

excursão (ish-koor-*serng*ʷ) *f* (pl -sões) excursion; day trip

execução (ee-zer-koo-*serng*ʷ) *f* (pl -ções) execution

executar (ee-zer-koo-*tahr*) *v* execute, perform, carry out

executivo (ee-zer-koo-*tee*-voo) *adj* executive

exemplar (ee-zayngm-*plahr*) *m* specimen; copy

exemplo (ee-*zayngm*-ploo) *m* example; instance; **por** ~ for instance, for example

exercer (ee-zerr-*sayr*) *v* exercise

exercício (ee-zerr-*see*-sʸoo) *m* exercise

exercitar (ee-zerr-see-*tahr*) *v* exercise; **exercitar-se** practise

exército (ee-*zehr*-see-too) *m* army

exibição (ee-zer-bhee-*serng*ʷ) *f* (pl -ções) exhibition

exibir (ee-zer-*bheer*) *v* exhibit; display, *show

exigência (ee-zɪ-*zhayng*-sʸer) *f* demand

exigente (ee-zɪ-*zhayngn*-ter) *adj* particular, demanding

exigir (ee-zɪ-*zheer*) *v* demand; require

exilado (ɪ-zee-*lah*-dhoo) *m* exile

exílio (ɪ-*zee*-lʸoo) *m* exile

existência (ɪ-zeesh-*tayng*-sʸer) *f* existence

existir (ɪ-zeesh-*teer*) *v* exist

êxito (ay-zee-too) *m* success

exótico (ee-zo-tee-koo) *adj* exotic

expandir (ish-perngn-*deer*) *v* expand

expectativa (ish-peh-ter-*tee*-ver) *f* expectation

expedição (ish-per-dhee-*serng*ʷ) *f* (pl -ções) expedition

*****expedir** (ish-per-*dheer*) *v* dispatch; ship, *send off

experiência (ish-per-rʸayng-sʸer) *f* experiment; trial, experience

experiente (ish-per-rʸayngn-ter) *adj* experienced

experimentar (ish-per-ree-mayngn-*tahr*) *v* try, experiment; test; experience

expiração (ish-pee-rer-*serng*ʷ) *f* (pl -ções) expiry

expirar (ish-pee-*rahr*) *v* expire

explicação (ish-plee-ker-*serng*ʷ) *f* (pl -ções) explanation

explicar (ish-plee-*kahr*) *v* explain

explícito (ish-*plee*-see-too) *adj* express, explicit

*****explodir** (ish-ploo-*dheer*) *v* explode

explorar (ish-ploo-*rahr*) *v* explore; exploit

explosão (ish-ploo-*zerng*ʷ) *f* (pl -sões) blast, explosion; outbreak

explosivo (ish-ploo-*zee*-voo) *adj* explosive; *m* explosive

*expor (ısh-*poar*) *v* exhibit, ***show**, display

exportação (ısh-poor-ter-*serng*ᵂ) *f* (pl -cões) export, exportation

exportar (ısh-poor-*tahr*) *v* export

exposição (ısh-poo-zee-*serng*ᵂ) *f* (pl -cões) display; show, exhibition, exposition; exposure; ~ **de arte** art exhibition

expressão (ısh-prer-*serng*ᵂ) *f* (pl -sões) expression; ~ **idiomática** idiom

expressar (ısh-prer-*sahr*) *v* express

expresso (ısh-*preh*-soo) *adj* express; **distribuição expressa** special delivery

exprimir (ısh-pree-*meer*) *v* express

expulsar (ısh-pool-*sahr*) *v* chase, expel

êxtase (*aysh*-ter-zer) *m* ecstasy

extensão (ısh-tayng-*serng*ᵂ) *f* (pl -sões) extension

extensivo (ısh-tayng-see-voo) *adj* comprehensive

extenso (ısh-*tayng*-soo) *adj* extensive

extenuar (ısh-ter-*nwahr*) *v* exhaust

exterior (ısh-ter-*r*ʸ*oar*) *m* exterior, outside; *adj* exterior, external

externo (ısh-*tehr*-noo) *adj* outward

extinguir (ısh-teeng-*geer*) *v* extinguish

extintor (ısh-teengn-*toar*) *m* fire-extinguisher

*extorquir (ısh-toor-*keer*) *v* extort

extorsão (ısh-toor-*serng*ᵂ) *f* (pl -sões) extortion

extraditar (ısh-trah-dhee-*tahr*) *v* extradite

*extrair (ısh-trer-*eer*) *v* extract

extraordinário (ısh-trer-oor-dhee-*nah*-rʸoo) *adj* extraordinary; exceptional

extravagante (ısh-trer-ver-*gerngn*-ter) *adj* extravagant

extraviar (ısh-trah-*v*ʸ*ahr*) *v* *mislay

extremidade (ısh-trer-mee-*dhah*-dher) *f* end

extremo (ısh-*tray*-moo) *adj* extreme; very; *m* extreme

exuberante (ee-zoo-bher-*rerngn*-ter) *adj* exuberant

F

fã (ferng) *m Br* fan

fábrica (*fah*-bhree-ker) *f* factory; works *pl*, plant, mill

fabricante (fah-bhree-*kerngn*-ter) *m* manufacturer

fabricar (fah-bhree-*kahr*) *v* manufacture

fábula (*fah*-bhoo-ler) *f* fable

faca (*fah*-ker) *f* knife

face (*fah*-ser) *f* cheek

fachada (fer-*shah*-dher) *f* façade

fácil (*fah*-seel) *adj* (pl fáceis) easy

facilidade (fer-ser-lee-*dhah*-dher) *f* facility, ease

facto (*fahk*-too) *m* fact; **de ~** as a matter of fact

factor (fah-*toar*) *m* factor

factura (fah-*too*-rer) *f* invoice

facturar (fah-too-*rahr*) *v* bill

faculdade (fer-kool-*dah*-dher) *f* faculty

facultativo (fer-kool-ter-*tee*-voo) *adj* optional

fada (*fah*-dher) *f* fairy

faia (*figh*-er) *f* beech

faiança (fer-ʸ*erng*-ser) *f* faience; crockery

faina (*figh*-ner) *f* work

faisão (figh-*zerng*ᵂ) *m* (pl -sões) pheasant

faísca (fer-*eesh*-ker) *f* spark

faixa (*figh*-sher) *f* strip; ~ **de rodagem** carriageway

fala (*fah*-ler) *f* speech

falador (fer-ler-*dhoar*) *adj* talkative

falar (fer-*lahr*) *v* *speak; talk

falcão (fahl-*kerng*ʷ) *m* (pl -cões) hawk

falecer (fer-ler-*sayr*) *v* depart, die

falésia (fer-*leh*-sʸer) *f* cliff

falha (*fah*-lʸer) *f* fault; shortcoming

falhar (fer-*lʸahr*) *v* fail

falido (fer-*lee*-dhoo) *adj* bankrupt

falsificação (fahl-ser-fee-ker-*serng*ʷ) *f* (pl -cões) fake

falsificar (fahl-ser-fee-*kahr*) *v* counterfeit, forge

falso (*fahl*-soo) *adj* false; untrue; hypocritical

falta (*fahl*-ter) *f* want, lack; error; offence; **sem ~** without fail

faltar (fahl-*tahr*) *v* fail

fama (*fer*-mer) *f* fame

família (fer-*mee*-lʸer) *f* family

familiar (fer-mee-*lʸahr*) *adj* familiar

famoso (fer-*moa*-zoo) *adj* famous

fanático (fer-*nah*-tee-koo) *adj* fanatical

fanfarra (ferng-*fer*-rrer) *f* brass band

fantasia (ferngn-ter-*zee*-er) *f* fantasy

fantasma (ferngn-*tahzh*-mer) *m* spook, phantom, ghost

fantástico (ferngn-*tahsh*-tee-koo) *adj* fantastic, terrific

fardo (*fahr*-doo) *m* burden, load

farinha (fer-*ree*-ñer) *f* flour

farmacêutico (ferr-mer-*say*ᵒᵒ-tee-koo) *m* chemist

farmácia (ferr-*mah*-sʸer) *f* pharmacy, chemist's; drugstore *nAm*

farmacologia (fahr-mer-koo-loo-*zhee*-er) *f* pharmacology

farol (fer-*rol*) *m* (pl faróis) lighthouse; headlight, headlamp; **~ de nevoeiro** foglamp; **~ traseiro** taillight

farpa (*fahr*-per) *f* splinter

farsa (*fahr*-ser) *f* farce

farto de (*fahr*-too der) tired of, fed up with

fartura (ferr-*too*-rer) *f* plenty

fascinante (fersh-see-*nerng*n-ter) *adj* glamorous

fascinar (fersh-see-*nahr*) *v* fascinate

fascismo (fersh-*seesh*-moo) *m* fascism

fascista (fersh-*seesh*-ter) *adj* fascist; *m* fascist

fase (*fah*-zer) *f* phase; stage

fastidioso (fersh-tee-*dh*ʸoa-zoo) *adj* tedious

fatal (fer-*tahl*) *adj* (pl -ais) fatal, mortal

fatia (fer-*tee*-er) *f* slice

fatigado (fer-tee-*gah*-dhoo) *adj* tired

fatigante (fer-tee-*gerng*n-ter) *adj* tiring

fato (*fah*-too) *m* suit; **~ calça e casaco** pant-suit; **~ de banho** swimsuit, bathing-suit

fato-macaco (fah-too-mer-*kah*-koo) *m* overalls *pl*

favor (fer-*voar*) *m* favour; **a ~ de** on behalf of; **por ~** please; **se faz ~** please

favorável (fer-voo-*rah*-vehl) *adj* (pl -eis) favourable

favorecer (fer-voo-rer-*sayr*) *v* favour

favorito (fer-voo-*ree*-too) *adj* pet; *m* favourite

*fazer (fer-*zayr*) *v* *do; *make; ***fazer-se** *get; *go, *grow

fé (feh) *f* faith

febre (*feh*-bhrer) *f* fever, temperature; **~ dos fenos** hay fever

febril (feh-*breel*) *adj* (pl -is) feverish

fechado (fɪ-*shah*-dhoo) *adj* closed, shut

fechadura (fɪ-sher-⊗oo-rer) *f* lock; **buraco da ~** keyhole

fechar (fɪ-*shahr*) *v* *shut, close; lock up, *shut in; fasten; turn off; **~ a chave** lock

fecho (*fay*-shoo) *m* fastener; ~ **éclair** zip; zipper

federação (fer-dher-rer-*serng*ʷ) *f* (pl -ções) federation

federal (fer-dher-*rahl*) *adj* (pl -ais) federal

feijão (fay-*zherng*ʷ) *m* (pl -jões) bean

feio (*fay*-oo) *adj* ugly

feira (*fay*-rer) *f* fair

feito (*fay*-too) *m* feat

felicidade (fer-ler-see-*dhah*-dher) *f* happiness

felicitação (fer-ler-see-ter-*serng*ʷ) *f* (pl -ções) congratulation

felicitar (fer-ler-see-*tahr*) *v* compliment, congratulate

feliz (fer-*leesh*) *adj* happy

feltro (*fayl*-troo) *m* felt

feminino (fer-mer-*nee*-noo) *adj* feminine; female

fenda (*fayngn*-der) *f* crack; cleft, chasm; slot

fender (fayngn-*dayr*) *v* *split

feno (*fay*-noo) *m* hay

feriado (fer-r*Y*ah-dhoo) *m* holiday

férias (*feh*-r*Y*ersh) *fpl* vacation, holiday; **em** ~ on holiday; **estância de** ~ holiday resort

ferida (fer-*ree*-dher) *f* wound; injury

ferido (fer-*ree*-dhoo) *adj* injured

***ferir** (fer-*reer*) *v* wound; *hurt, injure

fermentar (ferr-mayngn-*tahr*) *v* ferment

feroz (fer-*rosh*) *adj* fierce; wild

ferradura (fer-rrer-*dhoo*-rer) *f* horseshoe

ferragens (fer-rrah-zher^{ee}sh) *fpl* hardware

ferramenta (fer-rrer-*mayngn*-ter) *f* utensil, implement, tool

ferreiro (fer-*rray*-roo) *m* blacksmith, smith

ferro (*feh*-roo) *m* iron; **de** ~ iron; ~ **de engomar** iron; ~ **de frisar** curling-tongs *pl;* ~ **de soldar** soldering-iron; ~ **fundido** cast iron; **não passar a** ~ drip-dry

ferrolho (fer-rroa-l*Y*oo) *m* bolt

ferrugem (fer-rroo-zherng*Y*) *f* rust

ferrugento (fer-rroo-*zhayngn*-too) *adj* rusty

fértil (*fehr*-teel) *adj* (pl -teis) fertile

ferver (ferr-*vayr*) *v* boil

festa (*fehsh*-ter) *f* feast; party

festival (fish-tee-*vahl*) *m* (pl -ais) festival

festivo (fish-*tee*-voo) *adj* festive

feudal (fay^{oo}-*dhahl*) *adj* (pl -ais) feudal

Fevereiro (fer-ver-*ray*-roo) February

fiador (f*Y*er-*dhoar*) *m* guarantor

fiança (f*Y*erng-ser) *f* security

fiar (f*Y*ahr) *v* *spin

fiasco (f*Y*ahsh-koo) *m* failure

fibra (*fee*-bhrer) *f* fibre

ficar (fee-*kahr*) *v* stay, remain; ~ **bem** suit; *become

ficção (feek-*serng*ʷ) *f* (pl -ções) fiction

ficha (*fee*-sher) *f* token, chip; plug

fiel (f*Y*ehl) *adj* (pl fiéis) faithful; loyal

fígado (*fee*-ger-dhoo) *m* liver

figo (*fee*-goo) *m* fig

figura (fee-*goo*-rer) *f* figure

fila (*fee*-ler) *f* file; row, rank, line

filha (*fee*-l*Y*er) *f* daughter

filho (*fee*-l*Y*o) *m* son

filiação (fee-l*Y*er-*serng*ʷ) *f* membership

filiado (fee-l*Y*ah-dhoo) *adj* affiliated

Filipinas (fee-lee-*pee*-nersh) *fpl* Philippines *pl*

filipino (fee-lee-*pee*-noo) *adj* Philippine; *m* Filipino

filmar (feel-*mahr*) *v* film

filme (*feel*-mer) *m* film; movie; ~ **a cores** colour film

filosofia (fee-loo-zoo-*fee*-er) *f* philosophy

filósofo (fee-*lo*-zoo-foo) *m* philosopher

filtrar (feel-*trahr*) *v* strain

filtro (*feel*-troo) *m* filter; ~ **de ar** air-filter; ~ **de óleo** oil filter

fim (feeng) *m* ending, finish, end; issue, aim; **a** ~ **de** so that; **sem** ~ unlimited

fim-de-semana (feeng-der-ser-*mer*-ner) *m* weekend

final (fee-*nahl*) *adj* (pl -ais) final; eventual

finalmente (fee-nahl-*mayngn*-ter) *adv* at last

finanças (fee-*nerng*-sersh) *fpl* finances *pl*

financeiro (fee-nerng-*say*-roo) *adj* financial

financiar (fee-nerng-s*y*ahr) *v* finance

fingir (feeng-*zheer*) *v* pretend

finlandês (feeng-lerngn-*daysh*) *adj* Finnish; *m* Finn

Finlândia (feeng-*lerngn*-d*y*er) *f* Finland

fino (*fee*-noo) *adj* fine; sheer, thin

fio (fee°°) *m* thread; yarn; wire; ~ **de extensão** extension cord; ~ **eléctrico** flex

fiorde (*feeor*-der) *m* fjord

firma (*feer*-mer) *f* firm; company

firme (*feer*-mer) *adj* firm; steady

fiscalização (feesh-ker-lee-zer-*serng*w) *f* supervision

fiscalizar (feesh-ker-lee-*zahr*) *v* control

física (*fee*-zee-ker) *f* physics

físico (*fee*-zee-koo) *adj* physical; *m* physicist

fisiologia (fee-z*y*oo-loo-*zhee*-er) *f* physiology

fita (*fee*-ter) *f* ribbon; tape; ~ **adesiva** adhesive tape; ~ **métrica** tape-measure

fitar (fee-*tahr*) *v* gaze, stare

fivela (fee-*veh*-ler) *f* buckle

fixar (feek-*sahr*) *v* attach; **fixar-se** settle down

fixo (*feek*-soo) *adj* permanent, fixed

flamingo (fler-*meeng*-goo) *m* flamingo

flanela (fler-*neh*-ler) *f* flannel

flauta (*flou*-ter) *f* flute

flexível (flehk-*see*-vehl) *adj* (pl -eis) flexible; supple, elastic

flor (floar) *f* flower

floresta (floo-*rehsh*-ter) *f* forest

florista (floo-*reesh*-ter) *m* florist

fluente (fl*way*ngn-ter) *adj* fluent

fluido (*flwee*-dhoo) *adj* fluid

flutuador (floo-twer-*dhoar*) *m* float

flutuar (floo-*twahr*) *v* float

foca (*fo*-ker) *f* seal

focinho (foo-*see*-ñoo) *m* snout; mouth

foco (*fo*-koo) *m* focus

fogão (foo-*gerng*w) *m* (pl fogões) stove; cooker; ~ **a gás** gas stove; gas cooker

fogo (*foa*-goo) *m* fire; **à prova de** ~ fireproof

foguete (foo-*ger*-ter) *m* rocket

folclore (foalk-*lo*-rer) *m* folklore

folha (*foa*-l*y*er) *f* leaf; sheet; ~ **de ouro** gold leaf

folhetim (foo-l*y*er-*teeng*) *m* serial

fome (*fo*-mer) *f* hunger

fonético (foo-*neh*-tee-koo) *adj* phonetic

fonte (*fawngn*-ter) *f* fountain; source; temple

fora (*fo*-rer) *adv* out; *prep* apart from; **de** ~ outside; ~ **de** out of; outside; **para** ~ outwards

forasteiro (foo-rersh-*tay*-roo) *m* stranger, foreigner

forca (*foar*-ker) *f* gallows *pl*

força (*foar*-ser) *f* force, strength, energy; ~ **armada** military force; ~ **de vontade** will-power; ~ **motriz** driving force

forçar (foor-*sahr*) *v* force, strain

forçosamente (foor-soa-zer-*mayngn*-ter) *adv* by force

forjar (foor-*zhahr*) *v* forge; form; fabricate

forma[1] (*for*-mer) *f* form; shape

forma[2] (*foar*-mer) *f* mould

formal (foor-*mahl*) *adj* (pl -ais) formal

formalidade (foor-mer-lee-*dhah*-dher) *f* formality

formar (foor-*mahr*) *v* shape, form; educate, train

formato (foor-*mah*-too) *m* size

formidável (foor-mee-*dhah*-vehl) *adj* (pl -eis) swell; tremendous, huge

formiga (foor-*mee*-ger) *f* ant

fórmula (*for*-moo-ler) *f* formula

formular (foor-moo-*lahr*) *v* formulate

formulário (foor-moo-*lah*-rᵛoo) *m* form; ~ **de inscrição** registration form

fornecer (foor-ner-*sayr*) *v* supply, furnish, provide

fornecimento (foor-ner-see-*mayngn*-too) *m* supply

forno (*foar*-noo) *m* oven; furnace; **cozer no** ~ bake; **de ir ao** ~ fireproof

forrar (foo-*rrahr*) *v* upholster

forro (*foo*-rroo) *m* lining

fortaleza (foor-ter-*lay*-zer) *f* fortress

forte (*for*-ter) *adj* powerful, strong; loud; *m* fort

fortemente (foar-ter-*mayngn*-ter) *adv* strongly, firmly

fortuna (foor-*too*-ner) *f* fortune

fósforo (*fosh*-foo-roo) *m* match

fosso (*foa*-soo) *m* moat; ditch

fotocópia (fo-toa-*ko*-pᵛer) *f* photostat

fotografar (foo-too-grer-*fahr*) *v* photograph

fotografia (foo-too-grer-*fee*-er) *f* photography; photo, photograph; ~ **de passe** passport photograph

fotógrafo (foo-*to*-grer-foo) *m* photographer

fotómetro (foo-*to*-mer-troo) *m* exposure meter

foz (fosh) *f* mouth

fracassar (frer-ker-*sahr*) *v* fail

fracasso (frer-*kah*-soo) *m* failure

fracção (frah-*serng*ᵂ) *f* (pl -ções) fraction

fraco (*frah*-koo) *adj* feeble, weak, faint; poor

fractura (frah-*too*-rer) *f* fracture; break

fracturar (frah-too-*rahr*) *v* fracture

frágil (*frah*-zheel) *adj* (pl -geis) fragile

fragmento (frerg-*mayngn*-too) *m* fragment; piece

fralda (*frahl*-der) *f* nappy; diaper *n*Am

framboesa (frerng-*bway*-zer) *f* raspberry

França (*frerng*-ser) *f* France

francês (frerng-*saysh*) *adj* French; *m* Frenchman

franco (*frerng*-koo) *adj* open

franco-atirador (frerng-koo-er-tee-rer-*dhoar*) *m* sniper

frango (*frerng*-goo) *m* chicken

franja (*frerng*-zher) *f* fringe

franquia (frerng-*kee*-er) *f* postage

franquiar (frerng-kᵛ*ahr*) *v* stamp

fraqueza (frer-*kay*-zer) *f* weakness

frasco (*frahsh*-koo) *m* flask

frase (*frah*-zer) *f* sentence; phrase

fraternidade (frer-terr-nee-*dhah*-dher) *f* fraternity

fraude (*frou*-dher) *f* fraud

*****frear** (fr*ᵛahr*) *v*Br slow down

freguês (freh-*gaysh*) *m* customer

freira (*fray*-rer) *f* nun

frente (*frayngn*-ter) *f* front; **em** ~ forward; ahead; **em** ~ **de** opposite; **para a** ~ onwards; **sempre em** ~ straight ahead, straight on

frequência (frer-*kwayng*-sʸer) *f* frequency

frequentar (frer-kwayng-*tahr*) *v* mix with

frequente (frer-*kwayng*-ter) *adj* frequent

frequentemente (frer-kwayng-ter-*mayng*-ter) *adv* often, frequently

fresco (*fraysh*-koo) *adj* fresh; chilly, cool

fricção (freek-*serng*ʷ) *f* (pl -ções) friction

frieira (*fr*ʸay-rer) *f* chilblain

frigideira (free-zher-*dhay*-rer) *f* frying-pan

frigorífico (free-goo-*ree*-fee-koo) *m* fridge, refrigerator

frio (*free*ᵒᵒ) *adj* cold; *m* cold

frisar (free-*zahr*) *v* emphasize

fritar (free-*tahr*) *v* fry

fronha (*froa*-nger) *f* pillow-case

fronteira (frawng-*tay*-rer) *f* frontier; border; boundary

frota (*fro*-ter) *f* fleet

frouxo (*froa*-shoo) *adj* limp

fruta (*froo*-ter) *f* fruit

fruto (*froo*-too) *m* fruit

fuga (*foo*-ger) *f* leak; escape

***fugir** (foo-*zheer*) *v* escape

fugitivo (foo-zhee-*tee*-voo) *m* runaway

fumador (foo-mer-*dhoar*) *m* smoker

fumar (foo-*mahr*) *v* smoke

fumo (*foo*-moo) *m* smoke

função (foong-*serng*ʷ) *f* (pl -ções) function

funcionamento (foong-sʸoo-ner-*mayng*-too) *m* operation; working

funcionar (foong-sʸoo-*nahr*) *v* operate, work

funcionário (foong-sʸoo-*nah*-rʸoo) *m* civil servant; clerk; ~ aduaneiro Customs officer

fundação (foongn-der-*serng*ʷ) *f* (pl -ções) foundation

fundamentado (foongn-der-mayngn-*tah*-dhoo) *adj* well-founded

fundamental (foongn-der-mayngn-*tahl*) *adj* (pl -ais) fundamental, basic

fundamento (foongn-der-*mayng*n-too) *m* basis

fundar (foongn-*dahr*) *v* found

fundição (foongn-dee-*serng*ʷ) *f* (pl -ções) ironworks

fundo (*foong*n-doo) *m* bottom, ground; background; fund; *adj* deep

funeral (foo-ner-*rahl*) *m* (pl -ais) funeral

funil (foo-*neel*) *m* (pl -is) funnel

furacão (foo-rer-*kerng*ʷ) *m* (pl -ções) hurricane

furado (foo-*rah*-dhoo) *adj* punctured

furar (foo-*rahr*) *v* pierce, drill

furgão (foor-*gerng*ʷ) *m* (pl -gões) luggage van

furgoneta (foor-goo-*nay*-ter) *f* van; delivery van, pick-up van

fúria (*foo*-rʸer) *f* passion

furibundo (foo-ree-*bhoong*n-doo) *adj* furious

furioso (foo-rʸ*oa*-zoo) *adj* furious

furo (*foo*-roo) *m* puncture; blow-out

furor (foo-*roar*) *m* anger; rage

furúnculo (foo-*roong*-koo-loo) *m* boil

fusco (*foosh*-koo) *adj* hazy

fusível (foo-zee-*vehl*) *m* (pl -eis) fuse

futebol (foo-ter-*bhol*) *m* soccer; **jogo de** ~ football match

fútil (*foo*-teel) *adj* (pl fúteis) petty; insignificant; idle

futuro (foo-*too*-roo) *adj* future; *m* future

G

gabardina (ger-bherr-*dee*-ner) *f* mackintosh

gabar-se (ger-*bhahr*-ser) v boast

gabinete (ger-bhee-*nay*-ter) m cabinet; ~ **de provas** fitting room

gado (*gah*-dhoo) m cattle pl

gafanhoto (ger-fer-*ñoa*-too) m grasshopper

gaiato (ger-*ʸah*-too) m boy

gaivota (gigh-*vo*-ter) f gull, seagull

galeria (ger-ler-*ree*-er) f gallery; ~ **de arte** art gallery

galgo (*gahl*-goo) m greyhound

galinha (ger-*lee*-ñer) f hen; **pele de** ~ goose-flesh

galo (*gah*-loo) m cock

galope (ger-*lo*-per) m gallop

gamba (*gerngm*-ber) f prawn

ganancioso (ger-nerng-*sʸoa*-zoo) adj greedy

gancho (*gerng*-shoo) m hook; peg; ~ **de cabelo** hairpin; bobby pin Am

gangorra (gerng-*goa*-rrer) f Br seesaw

ganhar (loo-*krahr*) v gain; *win; earn, *make

ganhos (ger-*ñoosh*) mpl earnings pl

ganso (*gerng*-soo) m goose

garagem (ger-*rah*-zherngʸ) f garage; *pôr na ~ garage

garagista (ger-rer-*zheesh*-ter) m garage man

garantia (ger-rerngn-*tee*-er) f guarantee

garantir (ger-rerngn-*teer*) v assure, guarantee

garça (*gahr*-ser) f heron

garçom (gahr-*sawng*) m Br waiter

garçonete (gahr-soo-*nay*-ter) f Br waitress

garfo (*gahr*-foo) m fork

gargalhada (gerr-ger-*lʸah*-der) f burst of laughter

garganta (gerr-*gerng*-ter) f throat; gorge

gargarejar (gerr-ger-rı-*zhahr*) v gargle

garoto (ger-*roa*-too) m kid

garra (*gah*-rrer) f claw

garrafa (ger-*rrah*-fer) f bottle; carafe; ~ **termos** vacuum flask

garrafão (ger-rrer-*ferngʷ*) m (pl -fões) carboy

garrido (ger-*rree*-dhoo) adj gay

gás (gahsh) m gas; **gases de escape** exhaust gases

gasolina (ger-zoo-*lee*-ner) f petrol; gas nAm, gasoline nAm; **posto de** ~ petrol station; gas station Am

gastador (gersh-ter-*dhoar*) adj wasteful

gastar (gersh-*tahr*) v *spend; wear out

gasto (*gahsh*-too) adj worn; worn-out

gástrico (*gahsh*-tree-koo) adj gastric

gastrónomo (gahsh-tro-noo-moo) m gourmet

gatilho (ger-*tee*-lʸoo) m trigger

gato (*gah*-too) m cat

gaveta (ger-*vay*-ter) f drawer

gavião (ger-vʸ*erngʷ*) m (pl -iões) hawk

gaze (*gah*-zer) f gauze

geada (zhʸ*ah*-dher) f frost

geladeira (zher-ler-*dhay*-rer) f Br fridge

gelado (zher-*lah*-dhoo) adj freezing; m ice-cream

gelar (zher-*lahr*) v *freeze

geleia (zher-*lay*-er) f jelly; **geléia** Br jam

gelo (*zhay*-loo) m ice

gema (*zhay*-mer) f yolk

gémeos (*zheh*-mʸoosh) mpl twins pl

gemer (zher-*mayr*) v moan, groan

general (zher-ner-*rahl*) m (pl -ais) general

género (*zheh*-ner-roo) m gender; sort, kind; **géneros** victuals pl

generosidade (zher-ner-roo-zee-*dhah*-dher) f generosity

generoso (zher-ner-*roa*-zoo) adj generous; liberal

gengibre (_zhayng-zhee_-bhrer) _m_ ginger

gengiva (_zhayng-zhee_-ver) _f_ gum

génio (_zheh_-nʸoo) _m_ genius

genital (_zher-nee-tahl_) _adj_ (pl -ais) genital

genro (_zhayng_-rroo) _m_ son-in-law

gente (_zhayngn_-ter) _f_ people _pl_; a ~ we; **toda a** ~ everybody, everyone

gentil (_zhayngn-teel_) _adj_ (pl -is) kind

genuíno (_zher-nwee_-noo) _adj_ genuine

geografia (zhʸoo-grer-_fee_-er) _f_ geography

geologia (zhʸoo-loo-_zhee_-er) _f_ geology

geometria (zhʸoo-mer-_tree_-er) _f_ geometry

geração (zher-rer-_serngʷ_) _f_ (pl -ções) generation

gerador (zher-rer-_dhoar_) _m_ generator

geral (zher-_rahl_) _adj_ (pl -ais) universal, general; public; **em** ~ in general

geralmente (zher-rahl-_mayngn_-ter) _adv_ as a rule

germe (_zhehr_-mer) _m_ germ

gesso (_zhay_-soo) _m_ plaster

gestão (zhish-_terngʷ_) _f_ (pl -tões) administration; management

gesticular (zhersh-tee-koo-_lahr_) _v_ gesticulate

gesto (_zhehsh_-too) _m_ sign

gigante (zhee-_gerngn_-ter) _m_ giant

gigantesco (zhee-gerngn-_taysh_-koo) _adj_ gigantic; enormous

gilete (zhee-_leh_-ter) _f_ safety-razor

ginásio (zhee-_nah_-zʸoo) _m_ gymnasium

ginasta (zhee-_nahsh_-ter) _m_ gymnast

ginástica (zhee-_nahsh_-tee-ker) _f_ gymnastics _pl_

ginecologista (zhee-ner-koo-loo-_zheesh_-ter) _f_ gynaecologist

gira-discos (zhee-rer-_deesh_-koosh) _m_ (pl ~) record-player

girar (zhee-_rahr_) _v_ turn around

giz (zheesh) _m_ chalk

glaciar (gler-_sʸahr_) _m_ glacier

glândula (_glerngn_-doo-ler) _f_ gland

global (gloo-_bhahl_) _adj_ (pl -ais) broad; overall

globo (_gloa_-bhoo) _m_ globe

glória (_glo_-rʸer) _f_ glory

gola (_go_-ler) _f_ collar

goleiro (goo-_lay_-roo) _mBr_ goalkeeper

golfe (_goal_-fer) _m_ golf; **campo de** ~ golf-course, golf-links; **clube de** ~ golf-club

golfo (_goal_-foo) _m_ gulf

golo (_goa_-loo) _m_ goal

golpe (_gol_-per) _m_ cut; blow

goma (_goa_-mer) _f_ gum; starch; ~ **de mascar** _Br_ chewing-gum

gôndola (_gawngn_-doo-ler) _f_ gondola

gordo (_goar_-doo) _adj_ fat; stout

gordura (goor-_doo_-rer) _f_ fat, grease

gordurento (goor-doo-_rayngn_-too) _adj_ greasy

gorduroso (goor-doo-_roa_-zoo) _adj_ fatty

gorjeta (goor-_zhay_-ter) _f_ tip, gratuity

gostar de (goosh-_tahr_) like, *be fond of; fancy, care for

gosto (_goash_-too) _m_ taste; zest; **com muito** ~ gladly

gota (_goa_-ter) _f_ drop; gout

governador (goo-verr-ner-_dhoar_) _m_ governor

governanta (goo-verr-_nerngn_-ter) _f_ housekeeper, governess

governante (goo-verr-_nerngn_-ter) _m_ ruler

governar (goo-verr-_nahr_) _v_ govern, rule

governo (goo-_vayr_-noo) _m_ government, rule; ~ **de casa** housekeeping, household

gozar (goo-_zahr_) _v_ enjoy; ~ **com** kid

gozo (_goa_-zoo) _m_ enjoyment

Grã-Bretanha (grerng-bhrer-*ter*-ñer) *f* Great Britain

graça (*grah*-ser) *f* grace; joke

gracioso (grer-s^y*oa*-zoo) *adj* graceful

grade (*grah*-dher) *f* crate

gradeamento (grer-dh^yer-*mayngn*-too) *m* railing

gradual (grer-*dhwahl*) *adj* (pl -ais) gradual

gradualmente (grer-dhwahl-*mayngn*-ter) *adv* gradually

gráfico (*grah*-fee-koo) *adj* graphic; *m* diagram, graph, chart

gralha (*grah*-l^yer) *f* crow

grama (*grer*-mer) *m* gram

gramática (grer-*mah*-tee-ker) *f* grammar

gramatical (grer-mer-tee-*kahl*) *adj* (pl -ais) grammatical

gramofone (grer-moo-*fo*-ner) *m* gramophone

grampo (*grerngm*-poo) *m* clamp; *mBr* staple

grande (*grerngn*-der) *adj* big; great, large, major

grandioso (grerngn-d^y*oa*-zoo) *adj* magnificent; superb, grand

granito (grer-*nee*-too) *m* granite

granizo (grer-*nee*-zoo) *m* hail

grão (grerng^w) *m* (pl ~s) corn, grain

gratidão (grer-tee-*dherng*^w) *f* (pl -dões) gratitude

grato (*grah*-too) *adj* grateful

gratuito (grer-*too*^{ee}-too) *adj* free of charge; gratis

grau (grou) *m* grade, degree; ~ **de latitude** latitude

gravação (grer-ver-*serng*^w) *f* (pl -ções) engraving; recording

gravador (grer-ver-*dhoar*) *m* tape-recorder; engraver; recorder

gravar (grer-*vahr*) *v* engrave; record

gravata (grer-*vah*-ter) *f* tie, necktie

grave (*grah*-ver) *adj* grave; bad, severe; serious

grávida (*grah*-vee-dher) *adj* pregnant

gravidade (grer-vee-*dhah*-dher) *f* gravity

gravura (grer-*voo*-rer) *f* picture, print

graxa (*grah*-sher) *f* shoe polish

Grécia (*greh*-s^yer) *f* Greece

grego (*gray*-goo) *adj* Greek; *m* Greek

grelha (*greh*-l^yer) *f* grate

grelhador (grɪ-l^yer-*dhoar*) *m* grill

grelhar (grɪ-*l^yahr*) *v* grill; roast

greta (*gray*-ter) *f* chink

greve (*greh*-ver) *f* strike; ***fazer ~ *strike**

grilo (*gree*-loo) *m* cricket

gripe (*gree*-per) *f* influenza, flu

gritar (gree-*tahr*) *v* cry; shriek, scream, shout

grito (*gree*-too) *m* cry; shout, scream

groom (groongm) *m* bellboy

grosa (*gro*-zer) *f* gross

groselha (groo-*zeh*-l^yer) *f* currant; ~ **negra** black-currant; ~ **verde** gooseberry

grosseiro (groo-*say*-roo) *adj* gross; coarse, impolite

grosso (*groa*-soo) *adj* big, thick

grossura (groa-*soo*-rer) *f* thickness

grotesco (groo-*taysh*-koo) *adj* ludicrous

grua (*groo*-er) *f* crane

grumo (*groo*-moo) *m* lump

grumoso (groo-*moa*-zoo) *adj* lumpy

grupo (*groo*-poo) *m* group; bunch, party, set

gruta (*groo*-ter) *f* cave, grotto

guarda (*gwahr*-dher) *m* policeman; custodian, attendant, caretaker, guard, warden

guarda-chuva (gwahr-dher-*shoo*-ver) *m* umbrella

guarda-costas (gwahr-dher-*kosh*-tersh) *m* (pl ~) bodyguard

guarda-florestal (gwahr-dher-floo-rɪsh-

tahl) m (pl -ais) forester

guarda-lama (gwahr-dher-*ler*-mer) m mud-guard

guardanapo (gwahr-dher-*nah*-poo) m serviette, napkin; ~ **de papel** paper napkin

guardar (gwerr-*dhahr*) v guard; *keep, *hold; *put away

guarda-redes (gwahr-dher-*ray*-dhish) m goalkeeper

guarda-roupa (gwahr-dher-*roa*-per) m cloakroom, wardrobe

guelra (*gehl*-rrer) f gill

guerra (*geh*-rer) f war

guia (*gee*-er) m guide; guidebook; ~ **linguístico** phrase-book

guiar (g^Yahr) v guide; *drive

guincho (*geeng*-shoo) m shriek

guita (*gee*-ter) f twine

guloseimas (goo-loo-*zay*-mersh) fpl candy nAm

guloso (goo-*loa*-zoo) adj greedy

H

há (ah) ago; ~ **pouco tempo** recently

hábil (*ah*-bheel) adj (pl hábeis) skilled, skilful

habilidade (er-bher-lee-*dhah*-dher) f art, skill, ability

habilidoso (er-bher-lee-*dhoa*-zoo) adj skilful

habilitação (er-bher-lee-ter-*serng*^w) f (pl -ções) qualification

habitação (er-bhee-ter-*serng*^w) f (pl -ções) house

habitante (er-bhee-*terng*n-ter) m inhabitant

habitar (er-bhee-*tahr*) v inhabit

habitável (er-bhee-*tah*-vehl) adj (pl -eis) habitable, inhabitable

hábito (*ah*-bhee-too) m habit; custom

habituado (er-bhee-*twah*-dhoo) adj accustomed

habitual (er-bhee-*twahl*) adj (pl -ais) habitual; common, customary

habitualmente (er-bhee-twahl-*mayngn*-ter) adv usually

harmonia (err-moo-*nee*-er) f harmony

harpa (*ahr*-per) f harp

haste (*ahsh*-ter) f stem

*haver** (er-*vayr*) v *have; exist; *be

hebreu (ee-*bhray*^{oo}) m Hebrew

hélice (*eh*-lee-ser) f propeller

hemorragia (eh-mo-rrer-*zhee*-er) f haemorrhage; ~ **nasal** nosebleed

hemorróidas (eh-mo-*rroi*-dhersh) fpl piles, haemorrhoids pl

hera (*eh*-rer) f ivy

herança (ee-*rerng*-ser) f inheritance

herdar (eer-*dahr*) v inherit

hereditário (ee-rer-dhee-*tah*-r^Yoo) adj hereditary

hermético (eer-*meh*-tee-koo) adj airtight

hérnia (*ehr*-n^Yer) f hernia; ~ **discal** slipped disc

herói (ee-*roi*) m hero

hesitar (er-zee-*tahr*) v hesitate

heterossexual (eh-ter-roo-sehk-*swahl*) adj (pl -ais) heterosexual

hidrogénio (ee-dhro-*zheh*-n^Yoo) m hydrogen

hierarquia (^Yeh-rerr-*kee*-er) f hierarchy

hífen (*ee*-fayn) m hyphen

higiene (ee-zh^Yeh-ner) f hygiene

higiénico (ee-zh^Yeh-nee-koo) adj hygienic

hino (*ee*-noo) m hymn; ~ **nacional** national anthem

hipocrisia (ee-poo-kree-*zee*-er) f hypocrisy

hipócrita (ee-*po*-kree-ter) adj hypocritical; m hypocrite

hipódromo (ee-*po*-dhroo-moo) *m* race-course

hipoteca (ee-poo-*teh*-ker) *f* mortgage

histérico (eesh-*teh*-ree-koo) *adj* hysterical

história (eesh-*to*-r Yer) *f* history; story; ~ **da arte** art history; ~ **de amor** love-story; ~ **de fadas** fairytale

historiador (eesh-too-r Yer-*dhoar*) *m* historian

histórico (eesh-*to*-ree-koo) *adj* historic; historical

hoje (*oa*-zher) *adv* today; ~ **em dia** nowadays

Holanda (oo-*lerng*-der) *f* Holland

holandês (oo-lerng-*daysh*) *adj* Dutch; *m* Dutchman

holofote (oa-loa-*fo*-ter) *m* searchlight

homem (*o*-merng Y) *m* man; ~ **de negócios** businessman

homenagem (oo-mer-*nah*-zherng Y) *f* homage; tribute; **prestar** ~ honour

homicídio (oo-mee-*see*-dh Yoo) *m* murder

homossexual (o-mo-sayk-*swahl*) *adj* (pl -ais) homosexual

honestidade (oo-nehsh-tee-*dhah*-dher) *f* honesty

honesto (oo-*nehsh*-too) *adj* honest

honorário (oo-noo-rah-r Yoo) *m* fee

honra (*awng*-rrer) *f* honour, glory

honrado (awng-*rrah*-dhoo) *adj* honourable

honrar (awng-*rrahr*) *v* honour

honroso (awng-*rroa*-zoo) *adj* honourable

hóquei (*oa*-kay) *m* hockey

hora (*o*-rer) *f* hour; time of day; ~ **a hora** hourly; ~ **de chegada** time of arrival; ~ **de partida** time of departure; ~ **de ponta** rush-hour, peak hour; **horas de abertura** business hours; **horas de**

consulta consultation hours; **horas de serviço** office hours, business hours; **horas de visita** visiting hours; **quarto de** ~ quarter of an hour; **vinte e quatro horas** twenty-four hours

horário (oo-rah-r Yoo) *m* timetable; schedule; ~ **de Verão** summer time

horizontal (oo-ree-zawng-*tahl*) *adj* (pl -ais) horizontal

horizonte (oo-ree-*zawng*-ter) *m* horizon

horripilante (oo-rree-pee-*lerng*-ter) *adj* creepy, horrible

horrível (oo-*rree*-vehl) *adj* (pl -eis) awful, horrible

horror (oo-*rroar*) *m* horror

horroroso (oo-rroo-roa-zoo) *adj* horrible, hideous

horta (*or*-ter) *f* kitchen garden

hortaliça (oorr-ter-*lee*-ser) *f* greens *pl*; **vendedor de** ~ greengrocer

hortelã (oorr-ter-*lerng*) *f* mint

hortelã-pimenta (oorr-ter-lerng-pee-*mayng*-ter) *f* peppermint

horticultura (oorr-tee-kool-*too*-rer) *f* horticulture

hospedar (oosh-per-*dhahr*) *v* lodge; **hospedar-se** stay

hóspede (*osh*-per-dher) *m* guest; lodger

hospedeira (oosh-per-*dhay*-rer) *f* hostess; stewardess

hospedeiro (oosh-per-*dhay*-roo) *m* host; innkeeper

hospital (oosh-pee-*tahl*) *m* (pl -ais) hospital

hospitaleiro (oosh-pee-ter-*lay*-roo) *adj* hospitable

hospitalidade (oosh-pee-ter-lee-*dhah*-dher) *f* hospitality

hostil (oosh-*teel*) *adj* (pl -is) hostile

hotel (o-*tehl*) *m* (pl hotéis) hotel

humanidade (oo-mer-nee-*dhah*-dher) *f* humanity, mankind

humano (oo-*mer*-noo) *adj* human

humedecer (oo-mer-dher-*sayr*) *v* moisten, damp

humidade (oo-mee-*dhah*-dher) *f* moisture, humidity, damp

húmido (*oo*-mee-dhoo) *adj* wet, humid, moist, damp

humilde (oo-*meel*-der) *adj* humble

humor (oo-*moar*) *m* humour; mood; spirit; **bem humorado** good-humoured

húngaro (*oong*-ger-roo) *adj* Hungarian; *m* Hungarian

Hungria (oong-*gree*-er) *f* Hungary

I

iate (*Yah*-ter) *m* yacht

içar (ee-*sahr*) *v* hoist

ícone (ee-koo-ner) *m* icon

icterícia (eek-ter-*ree*-sYer) *f* jaundice

idade (ee-*dhah*-dher) *f* age; **de** ~ elderly; **Idade Média** Middle Ages

ideal (ee-*dh*Yahl) *adj* (pl -ais) ideal; *m* ideal

ideia (ee-*dhay*-er) *f* idea; ~ **luminosa** brain-wave

idêntico (ee-*dhayngn*-tee-koo) *adj* identical

identidade (ee-dhayngn-tee-*dhah*-dher) *f* identity; **bilhete de** ~ identity card

identificação (ee-dhayngn-tee-fee-ker-*serng*w) *f* (pl -ções) identification

identificar (ee-dhayngn-ter-fee-*kahr*) *v* identify

idiomático (ee-dhYoo-*mah*-tee-koo) *adj* idiomatic

idiota (ee-*dh*Yo-ter) *m* idiot; fool; *adj* idiotic

ídolo (ee-dhoo-loo) *m* idol

ignição (eeg-nee-*serng*w) *f* ignition

ignorante (eeg-noo-*rerngn*-ter) *adj* ignorant

ignorar (eeg-noo-*rahr*) *v* ignore

igreja (ee-*gray*-zher) *f* church

igual (ee-*gwahl*) *adj* (pl -ais) alike, equal; even, level

igualar (ee-gwer-*lahr*) *v* equalize; equal

igualdade (ee-gwahl-*dah*-dher) *f* equality

igualmente (ee-gwahl-*mayngn*-ter) *adv* equally; likewise, also, alike

ilegal (ee-ler-*gahl*) *adj* (pl -ais) illegal; unlawful

ilegível (ee-ler-*zhee*-vehl) *adj* (pl -eis) illegible

ileso (ee-*lay*-zoo) *adj* unhurt

ilha (ee-lYer) *f* island

ilícito (ee-*lee*-ser-too) *adj* unauthorized

ilimitado (ee-ler-mee-*tah*-dhoo) *adj* unlimited

iluminação (ee-loo-mee-ner-*serng*w) *f* (pl -ções) lighting, illumination

iluminar (ee-loo-mee-*nahr*) *v* illuminate

ilusão (ee-loo-*zerng*w) *f* (pl -sões) illusion

ilustração (ee-loosh-trer-*serng*w) *f* (pl -ções) picture, illustration

ilustrar (ee-loosh-*trahr*) *v* illustrate

ilustre (ee-*loosh*-trer) *adj* noted; illustrious

imaculado (ee-mer-koo-*lah*-dhoo) *adj* stainless; immaculate

imagem (ee-*mah*-zherngY) *f* image; picture; ~ **reflectida** reflection

imaginação (ee-mer-zhee-ner-*serng*w) *f* (pl -ções) fancy, imagination

imaginar (ee-mer-zhee-*nahr*) *v* imagine; fancy, conceive

imaginário (ee-mer-zhee-*nah*-rYoo) *adj*

imaginary

imediatamente (ee-mer-dhᵞah-ter-*mayng*-ter) *adv* immediately; straight away, at once, instantly

imediato (ee-mer-*dhᵞah*-too) *adj* immediate, prompt

imenso (ee-*mayng*-soo) *adj* immense; vast

imerecido (ee-mer-rer-*see*-dhoo) *adj* unearned

imigração (ee-mee-grer-*serng*ʷ) *f* (pl -cões) immigration

imigrante (ee-mee-*grerng*-ter) *m* immigrant

imigrar (ee-mee-*grahr*) *v* immigrate

imitação (ee-mee-ter-*serng*ʷ) *f* (pl -cões) imitation

imitar (ee-mee-*tahr*) *v* imitate; copy

imodesto (ee-moo-*dhehsh*-too) *adj* immodest

impaciente (eengm-per-sᵞ*ayng*-ter) *adj* impatient; eager

ímpar (*eengm*-pahr) *adj* odd

imparcial (eengm-perr-sᵞ*ahl*) *adj* (pl -ais) impartial

impecável (eengm-per-*kah*-vehl) *adj* (pl -eis) faultless

impedimento (eengm-per-dhee-*mayng*-too) *m* impediment

*impedir (eengm-per-*dheer*) *v* prevent; impede

imperador (eengm-per-rer-*dhoar*) *m* emperor

imperatriz (eengm-per-rer-*treesh*) *f* empress

imperfeição (eengm-perr-fay-*serng*ʷ) *f* (pl -cões) fault, imperfection

imperfeito (eengm-perr-*fay*-too) *adj* imperfect; faulty

imperial (eengm-per-rᵞ*ahl*) *adj* (pl -ais) imperial

império (eengm-*peh*-rᵞoo) *m* empire

impermeável (eengm-perr-mᵞ*ah*-vehl) *adj* (pl -eis) waterproof; rainproof;

m raincoat

impertinência (eengm-perr-tee-*nayng*-sᵞer) *f* impertinence

impertinente (eengm-perr-tee-*nayng*-ter) *adj* impertinent

impessoal (eengm-per-*swahl*) *adj* (pl -ais) impersonal

ímpeto (*eengm*-per-too) *m* impetuosity

impetuoso (eengm-per-*twoa*-zoo) *adj* violent

implicado (eengm-plee-*kah*-dhoo) *adj* involved

implicar (eengm-plee-*kahr*) *v* imply; involve; ~ **com** tease

imponente (eengm-poo-*nayng*-ter) *adj* imposing

impopular (eengm-poo-poo-*lahr*) *adj* unpopular

importação (eengm-poor-ter-*serng*ʷ) *f* (pl -cões) import

importador (eengm-poor-ter-*dhoar*) *m* importer

importância (eengm-poor-*terng*-sᵞer) *f* importance; ***ter** ~ matter

importante (eengm-poor-*terng*n-ter) *adj* important; considerable, capital, big

importar (eengm-poor-*tahr*) *v* import; ~ **em** amount to; **importar-se com** mind

impossível (eengm-poo-*see*-vehl) *adj* (pl -eis) impossible

imposto (eengm-*poash*-too) *m* tax; ~ **sobre a cifra de negócios** turnover tax; ~ **sobre os rendimentos** income-tax; **isento de** ~ tax-free; **lançar impostos** tax

impotência (eengm-poo-*tayng*-sᵞer) *f* impotence

impotente (eengm-poo-*tayng*n-ter) *adj* impotent; powerless

impraticável (eengm-prer-tee-*kah*-vehl) *adj* (pl -eis) impassable

imprensa (eengm-*prayng*-ser) *f* press

impressão (eengm-prer-*serng*ʷ) *f* (pl -sões) impression; ~ **digital** fingerprint

impressionante (eengm-prer-sʸoo-*nerngn*-ter) *adj* striking, impressive

impressionar (eengm-prer-sʸoo-*nahr*) *v* impress; *strike

impresso (eengm-*preh*-soo) *m* printed matter

imprevisto (eengm-prer-*veesh*-too) *adj* unexpected

imprimir (eengm-pree-*meer*) *v* print

impróprio (eengm-*pro*-prʸoo) *adj* improper; wrong

improvável (eengm-proo-*vah*-vehl) *adj* (pl -eis) unlikely, improbable

improvisar (eengm-proo-vee-*zhahr*) *v* improvise

imprudente (eengm-proo-*dhayngn*-ter) *adj* unwise

impulsionar (eengm-pool-sʸoo-*nahr*) *v* propel

impulsivo (eengm-pool-*see*-voo) *adj* impulsive

impulso (eengm-*pool*-soo) *m* urge, impulse

imundo (ee-*moongn*-doo) *adj* filthy

imunidade (ee-moo-nee-*dhah*-dher) *f* immunity

imunizar (ee-moo-nee-*zahr*) *v* immunize

inabitável (ee-ner-bhee-*tah*-vehl) *adj* (pl -eis) uninhabitable

inaceitável (ee-ner-say-*tah*-vehl) *adj* (pl -eis) unacceptable

inacessível (ee-ner-ser-*see*-vehl) *adj* (pl -eis) inaccessible

inadequado (ee-ner-dher-*kwah*-dhoo) *adj* inadequate; unfit, unsuitable

inadvertência (een-erdh-verr-*tayng*-sʸer) *f* oversight

inalar (ee-ner-*lahr*) *v* inhale

incapacitado (eeng-ker-per-see-*tah*-dhoo) *adj* disabled

incapaz (eeng-ker-*pahsh*) *adj* unable, incapable

incêndio (eeng-*sayngn*-dʸoo) *m* fire

incenso (eeng-*sayng*-soo) *m* incense

incerto (eeng-*sehr*-too) *adj* doubtful, uncertain

inchaço (eeng-*shah*-soo) *m* swelling

inchar (eeng-*shahr*) *v* *swell; inflate

incidental (eeng-see-dhayngn-*tahl*) *adj* (pl -ais) incidental

incidente (eeng-see-*dhayngn*-ter) *m* incident

incineração (eeng-see-ner-rer-*serng*ʷ) *f* (pl -ções) cremation

incinerar (eeng-see-ner-*rahr*) *v* cremate

incitar (eeng-see-*tahr*) *v* urge, incite

inclinação (eeng-klee-ner-*serng*ʷ) *f* (pl -ções) gradient; tendency, inclination; ~ **de cabeça** nod

inclinado (eeng-klee-*nah*-dhoo) *adj* slanting; sloping

inclinar (eeng-klee-*nahr*) *v* bow; **inclinar-se** slant

incluir (eeng-*klweer*) *v* include; enclose; count; **tudo incluído** in all

inclusive (eeng-kloo-*zee*-vay) *adv* including

inclusivo (eeng-kloo-*see*-voo) *adj* inclusive

incluso (eeng-*kloo*-zoo) *adj* included

incomestível (eeng-koa-mersh-*tee*-vehl) *adj* (pl -eis) inedible

incomodar (eeng-koo-moo-*dhahr*) *v* disturb; bother; trouble; **incomodar-se** bother

incómodo (eeng-*ko*-moo-dhoo) *m* nuisance, inconvenience, trouble, bother

incompetente (eeng-kawngm-per-*tayngn*-ter) *adj* unqualified, incompetent

incompleto (eeng-kawngm-*pleh*-too)

adj incomplete

incompreensível (eeng-kawngm-prᵞayngn-*see*-vehl) *adj* (pl -eis) puzzling

inconcebível (eeng-kawng-ser-*bhee*-vehl) *adj* (pl -eis) inconceivable

incondicional (eeng-kawngn-dee-sᵞoo-nahl) *adj* (pl -ais) unconditional

inconsciente (eeng-kawngsh-sᵞayngn-ter) *adj* unconscious; unaware

inconveniência (eeng-kawng-ver-nᵞayng-sᵞer) *f* inconvenience

inconveniente (eeng-kawng-ver-nᵞayngn-ter) *adj* inconvenient

incorrecto (eeng-koo-*rreh*-too) *adj* incorrect; inaccurate

incrível (eeng-*kree*-vehl) *adj* (pl -eis) incredible

inculto (eeng-*kool*-too) *adj* waste, uncultivated; uneducated

incurável (eeng-koo-*rah*-vehl) *adj* (pl -eis) incurable

incursão (eeng-koor-*serng*ᵂ) *f* (pl -sões) raid

indagar (eeng-der-*gahr*) *v* inquire, enquire; query

indecente (eeng-der-*sayngn*-ter) *adj* indecent

indefinido (eeng-der-fer-*nee*-dhoo) *adj* indefinite

indemnização (eeng-der-mnee-zer-*serng*ᵂ) *f* (pl -ções) indemnity; compensation

independência (eeng-der-payngn-*dayng*-sᵞer) *f* independence

independente (eeng-der-payngn-*dayngn*-ter) *adj* independent; self-employed

indesejável (eeng-der-zɪ-*zhah*-vehl) *adj* (pl -eis) undesirable

Índia (*eeng*n-dᵞer) *f* India

indiano (eeng-n-*d*ᵞer-noo) *adj* Indian; *m* Indian

indicação (eeng-n-dee-ker-*serng*ᵂ) *f* (pl -ções) indication

indicado (eeng-n-dee-*kah*-dhoo) *adj* proper

indicador (eeng-n-dee-ker-*dhoar*) *m* index finger; indicator; ~ **de direcção** trafficator

indicar (eeng-n-dee-*kahr*) *v* point out, indicate

indicativo (eeng-n-dee-ker-*tee*-voo) *m* area code

índice (*eeng*n-dee-ser) *m* index; table of contents

indiferente (eeng-n-dee-fer-*rayngn*-ter) *adj* indifferent

indígena (eeng-n-*dee*-zher-ner) *m* native

indigestão (eeng-n-dee-zhersh-*terng*ᵂ) *f* (pl -tões) indigestion

indignação (eeng-n-deeg-ner-*serng*ᵂ) *f* (pl -ções) indignation

índio (*eeng*n-dᵞoo) *adj* Indian; *m* Indian

indirecto (eeng-n-dee-*reh*-too) *adj* indirect

indispensável (eeng-n-deesh-payng-*sah*-vehl) *adj* (pl -eis) essential

indisposto (eeng-n-deesh-*poash*-too) *adj* unwell

individual (eeng-n-der-vee-*dhwahl*) *adj* (pl -ais) individual

indivíduo (eeng-n-der-*vee*-dhwoo) *m* individual

Indonésia (eeng-n-doo-*neh*-sᵞer) *f* Indonesia

indonésio (eeng-n-doo-*neh*-zᵞoo) *adj* Indonesian; *m* Indonesian

indulto (eeng-n-*dool*-too) *m* pardon

indústria (eeng-n-*doosh*-trᵞer) *f* industry

industrial (eeng-n-doosh-*tr*ᵞahl) *adj* (pl -ais) industrial

ineficiente (ee-ner-fee-sᵞayngn-ter) *adj* inefficient

inesperado (ee-nɪsh-per-*rah*-dhoo) *adj*

unexpected

inestimável (ee-nısh-tee-*mah*-vehl) *adj* (pl -eis) priceless

inevitável (ee-ner-vee-*tah*-vehl) *adj* (pl -eis) inevitable; unavoidable

inexacto (ee-nee-*zah*-too) *adj* incorrect

inexperiente (ee-nısh-per-r ᵞaᵧngn-ter) *adj* inexperienced

inexplicável (ee-nısh-plee-*kah*-vehl) *adj* (pl -eis) unaccountable

infame (eeng-*fer*-mer) *adj* foul

infantaria (eeng-ferngn-ter-*ree*-er) *f* infantry

infecção (eeng-feh-*serng*ᵂ) *f* (pl -cões) infection

infeccioso (eeng-feh-sᵞoa-zoo) *adj* infectious

infectar (eeng-feh-*tahr*) *v* infect; *become septic

infelicidade (eeng-fer-ler-see-*dhah*-dher) *f* misery, misfortune

infeliz (eeng-fer-*leesh*) *adj* unhappy

infelizmente (eeng-fer-leezh-*maynᵍn*-ter) *adv* unfortunately

inferior (eeng-fer-*rᵞoar*) *adj* bottom, inferior

inferno (eeng-*fehr*-noo) *m* hell

infiel (eeng-fᵞehl) *adj* (pl -iéis) unfaithful

infinitivo (eeng-fer-nee-*tee*-voo) *m* infinitive

infinito (eeng-fer-*nee*-too) *adj* endless, infinite

inflação (eeng-flah-*serng*ᵂ) *f* (pl -cões) inflation

inflamação (eeng-fler-mer-*serng*ᵂ) *f* (pl -cões) inflammation

inflamável (eeng-fler-*mah*-vehl) *adj* (pl -eis) inflammable

influência (eeng-*flwayng*-sᵛer) *f* influence

influenciar (eeng-flwaynng-sᵛahr) *v* influence

influente (eeng-*flwaynng*-ter) *adj* influential

informação (eeng-foor-mer-*serng*ᵂ) *f* (pl -cões) information; enquiry; **agência de informações** inquiry office

informar (eeng-foor-*mahr*) *v* inform; **informar-se** inquire

infortunado (eeng-foor-too-*nah*-dhoo) *adj* unlucky

infortúnio (eeng-foor-*too*-nᵛoo) *m* misfortune

infra-vermelho (eeng-frah-verr-*meh*-lᵛoo) *adj* infra-red

infringir (eeng-freeng-*zheer*) *v* trespass

ingénuo (eeng-*zheh*-nwoo) *adj* naïve, simple

Inglaterra (eeng-gler-*teh*-rrer) *f* England; Britain

inglês (eeng-*glaysh*) *adj* English; *m* Briton, Englishman

ingrato (eeng-*grah*-too) *adj* ungrateful

ingrediente (eeng-grer-dhᵛaynᵍn-ter) *m* ingredient

íngreme (*eeng*-grer-mer) *adj* steep

inicial (ee-nee-sᵛahl) *adj* (pl -ais) initial; *f* initial

iniciar (ee-nee-sᵛahr) *v* *begin

iniciativa (ee-nee-sᵛer-*tee*-ver) *f* initiative

início (ee-*nee*-sᵛoo) *m* beginning

inimigo (ee-ner-*mee*-goo) *m* enemy

ininterrupto (ee-neengn-ter-*rroop*-too) *adj* continuous

injecção (eeng-zheh-*serng*ᵂ) *f* (pl -cões) shot, injection

injectar (eeng-zheh-*tahr*) *v* inject

injuriar (eeng-zhoo-rᵛahr) *v* call names

injustiça (eeng-zhoosh-*tee*-ser) *f* injustice

injusto (eeng-*zhoosh*-too) *adj* unjust; unfair

inocência (ee-noo-*saynᵍ*-sᵛer) *f* innocence

inocente (ee-noo-*sayngn*-ter) *adj* innocent

inoculação (ee-noo-koo-ler-*serng*ᵂ) *f* (pl -ções) inoculation

inocular (ee-noo-koo-*lahr*) *v* inoculate

inofensivo (ee-noo-fayng-*see*-voo) *adj* harmless

inoportuno (ee-noo-poor-*too*-noo) *adj* misplaced

inquebrável (eeng-ker-*bhrah*-vehl) *adj* (pl -eis) unbreakable

inquérito (eeng-*keh*-ree-too) *m* enquiry; inquiry

inquieto (eeng-*kʸeh*-too) *adj* anxious; restless

inquilino (eeng-ker-*lee*-noo) *m* tenant

inquirir (eeng-ker-*reer*) *v* inquire

insatisfatório (eeng-ser-teesh-fer-*to*-rʸoo) *adj* unsatisfactory

insatisfeito (eeng-ser-teesh-*fay*-too) *adj* dissatisfied

inscrever (eengsh-krer-*vayr*) *v* enter; list, book; **inscrever-se** check in; register

inscrição (eengsh-kree-*serng*ᵂ) *f* (pl -ções) inscription

insecticida (eeng-seh-tee-*see*-dher) *m* insecticide

insecto (eeng-*seh*-too) *m* insect; bug *nAm*

inseguro (eeng-ser-*goo*-roo) *adj* unsafe

insensato (eeng-*sayng*-sah-too) *adj* mad

insensível (eeng-sayng-*see*-vehl) *adj* (pl -eis) insensitive; heartless

*****inserir** (eeng-ser-*reer*) *v* insert

insignificante (eeng-seeg-ner-fee-*kerngn*-ter) *adj* unimportant, petty, insignificant

insípido (eeng-*see*-pee-dhoo) *adj* tasteless; dull

insistir (eeng-seesh-*teer*) *v* insist

insolação (eeng-soo-ler-*serng*ᵂ) *f* (pl -ções) sunstroke

insolência (eeng-soo-*layng*-sʸer) *f* insolence

insolente (eeng-soo-*layngn*-ter) *adj* impertinent, insolent

insólito (eeng-*so*-lee-too) *adj* uncommon; strange

insónia (eeng-*so*-nʸer) *f* insomnia

inspecção (eengsh-peh-*serng*ᵂ) *f* (pl -ções) inspection

inspeccionar (eengsh-peh-sʸoo-*nahr*) *v* inspect

inspector (eengsh-peh-*toar*) *m* inspector

inspirar (eengsh-pee-*rahr*) *v* inspire

instalação (eengsh-ter-ler-*serng*ᵂ) *f* (pl -ções) installation

instalar (eengsh-ter-*lahr*) *v* install

instantaneamente (eengsh-terngn-ter-nʸer-*mayngn*-ter) *adv* instantly

instantâneo (eengsh-tern-*ter*-nʸoo) *m* snapshot

instante (eengsh-*terngn*-ter) *m* instant; second, moment

instável (eengsh-*tah*-vehl) *adj* (pl -eis) unsteady; unstable

instinto (eengsh-*teengn*-too) *m* instinct

instituição (eengsh-tee-twee-*serng*ᵂ) *f* (pl -ções) institution, institute

*****instituir** (eengsh-tee-*tweer*) *v* institute; found

instituto (eengsh-tee-*too*-too) *m* institute; ~ **de beleza** beauty parlour

instrução (eengsh-troo-*serng*ᵂ) *f* (pl -ções) tuition, instruction; direction

*****instruir** (eengsh-*trweer*) *v* instruct

instrumento (eengsh-troo-*mayngn*-too) *m* instrument; tool; ~ **musical** musical instrument

instrutivo (eengsh-troo-*tee*-voo) *adj* instructive

instrutor (eengsh-troo-*toar*) *m* instructor

insuficiente (eeng-soo-fee-s^y*ayngn*-ter) *adj* insufficient

insultante (eeng-sool-*terngn*-ter) *adj* offensive

insultar (eeng-sool-*tahr*) *v* insult

insulto (eeng-*sool*-too) *m* insult

insuperável (eeng-soo-per-*rah*-vehl) *adj* (pl -eis) unsurpassed

insuportável (eeng-soo-poor-*tah*-vehl) *adj* (pl -eis) unbearable

insurreição (eeng-soo-rray-*serng*^w) *f* (pl -ções) rising

intacto (eengn-*tah*-too) *adj* intact, whole

inteiramente (eengn-tay-rer-*mayngn*-ter) *adv* entirely; altogether, completely

inteiro (eengn-*tay*-roo) *adj* entire; unbroken, whole

intelecto (eengn-ter-*leh*-too) *m* intellect

intelectual (eengn-ter-leh-*twahl*) *adj* (pl -ais) intellectual

inteligência (eengn-ter-lee-*zhayng*-s^yer) *f* intelligence; brain

inteligente (eengn-ter-lee-*zhayng*-ter) *adj* intelligent; clever; bright; smart

intenção (eengn-tayng-*serng*^w) *f* (pl -ções) intention, purpose

intencional (eengn-tayng-s^yoo-*nahl*) *adj* (pl -ais) intentional

intenso (eengn-*tayng*-soo) *adj* intense

intento (eengn-*tayngn*-too) *m* purpose

interdição (eengn-terr-dee-*serng*^w) *f* (pl -ções) prohibition

interessado (eengn-ter-rer-*sah*-dhoo) *adj* interested

interessante (eengn-ter-rer-*serngn*-ter) *adj* interesting

interessar (eengn-ter-rer-*sahr*) *v* interest

interesse (eengn-ter-*ray*-ser) *m* interest

interferência (eengn-terr-fer-*rayng*-s^yer) *f* interference

***interferir** (eengn-terr-fer-*reer*) *v* interfere

interim (eengn-ter-*reeng*) *m* interim

interior (eengn-ter-*r*^y*oar*) *adj* inner; inside; *m* interior, inside

interlúdio (eengn-terr-*loo*-dh^yoo) *m* interlude

intermediário (eengn-terr-mer-dh^y*ah*-r^yoo) *m* mediator, intermediary; ***servir de ~** mediate

internacional (eengn-terr-nerng-s^yoo-*nahl*) *adj* (pl -ais) international

interno (eengn-*tehr*-noo) *adj* internal; indoor; domestic, resident

interpretar (eengn-terr-prer-*tahr*) *v* interpret

intérprete (eengn-*tehr*-prer-ter) *m* interpreter

interrogar (eengn-ter-rroo-*gahr*) *v* interrogate

interrogativo (eengn-ter-rroo-ger-*tee*-voo) *adj* interrogative

interrogatório (eengn-ter-rroo-ger-*to*-r^yoo) *m* examination; interrogation

interromper (eengn-ter-rrawngm-*payr*) *v* interrupt; *cut off

interrupção (eengn-ter-rroop-*serng*^w) *f* (pl -ções) interruption

interruptor (eengn-ter-rroop-*toar*) *m* switch

intersecção (eengn-terr-sehk-*serng*^w) *f* (pl -ções) intersection

intervalo (eengn-terr-*vah*-loo) *m* space; pause, interval, intermission; break; half-time

***intervir** (eengn-terr-*veer*) *v* intervene

intestino (eengn-tish-*tee*-noo) *m* intestine; gut; **intestinos** bowels *pl*

intimidade (eengn-tee-mee-*dhah*-dher) *f* privacy

íntimo (*eengn*-tee-moo) *adj* intimate; cosy

intolerável (eengn-too-ler-*rah*-vehl) *adj* (pl -eis) intolerable

intriga (eengn-*tree*-ger) *f* intrigue

introdução (eengn-troo-dhoo-*serng*ʷ) *f* (pl -ções) introduction

***introduzir** (eengn-troo-dhoo-*zeer*) *v* introduce

intrometer-se em (eengn-troo-mer-*tayr*-ser) interfere with

intruso (eengn-*troo*-zoo) *m* trespasser

inundação (ee-noongn-der-*serng*ʷ) *f* (pl -ções) flood

inútil (een-*oo*-teel) *adj* (pl -teis) useless

inutilmente (ee-noo-teel-*mayngn*-ter) *adv* in vain

invadir (eeng-ver-*dheer*) *v* invade

inválido (eeng-*vah*-lee-dhoo) *adj* disabled, invalid; *m* invalid

invasão (eeng-ver-*zerng*ʷ) *f* (pl -sões) invasion

inveja (eeng-*veh*-zher) *f* envy

invejar (eeng-vɪ-*zhahr*) *v* envy; grudge

invejoso (eeng-vɪ-*zhoa*-zoo) *adj* envious

invenção (eeng-vayng-*serng*ʷ) *f* (pl -ções) invention

inventar (eeng-vayngn-*tahr*) *v* invent

inventário (eeng-vayngn-tah-rʸoo) *m* inventory

inventivo (eeng-vayngn-*tee*-voo) *adj* inventive

inventor (eeng-vayngn-*toar*) *m* inventor

Inverno (eeng-*vehr*-noo) *m* winter

inverso (eeng-*vehr*-soo) *adj* reverse

inverter (eeng-verr-*tayr*) *v* invert; turn over

investigação (eeng-vɪsh-tee-ger-*serng*ʷ) *f* (pl -ções) enquiry; research, investigation

investigar (eeng-vɪsh-tee-*gahr*) *v* enquire, investigate

investimento (eeng-vɪsh-tee-*mayngn*-too) *m* investment

***investir** (eeng-vɪsh-*teer*) *v* invest

invisível (eeng-ver-zee-vehl) *adj* (pl -eis) invisible

involuntário (eeng-voo-loongn-*tah*-rʸoo) *adj* unintentional

invulgar (eeng-vool-*gahr*) *adj* odd

iodo (ʸoa-dhoo) *m* iodine

***ir** (eer) *v* *go; ~ **buscar** fetch; *get; pick up; *ir-se depart; *ir-se embora *go away

ira (ee-rer) *f* anger

iraniano (ee-rer-nʸer-noo) *adj* Iranian; *m* Iranian

Irão (ee-*rerng*ʷ) *m* Iran

Iraque (ee-*rah*-ker) *m* Iraq

iraquiano (ee-rer-*k*ʸer-noo) *adj* Iraqi; *m* Iraqi

irascível (ee-rersh-*see*-vehl) *adj* (pl -eis) irascible; quick-tempered, hot-tempered

Irlanda (eer-*lern*-der) *f* Ireland

irlandês (eer-lern-*daysh*) *adj* Irish; *m* Irishman

irmã (eer-*merng*) *f* sister

irmão (eer-*merng*ʷ) *m* (pl ~s) brother

ironia (ee-roo-*nee*-er) *f* irony

irónico (ee-ro-nee-koo) *adj* ironical

irreal (ee-rrʸahl) *adj* (pl -ais) unreal

irreflectido (ee-rrer-fleh-*tee*-dhoo) *adj* rash

irregular (ee-rrer-goo-*lahr*) *adj* irregular; uneven

irrelevante (ee-rrer-ler-*verngn*-ter) *adj* insignificant

irreparável (ee-rrer-per-*rah*-vehl) *adj* (pl -eis) irreparable

irrevogável (ee-rrer-voo-*gah*-vehl) *adj* (pl -eis) irrevocable

irritado (ee-rree-*tah*-dhoo) *adj* cross

irritante (ee-rree-*terngn*-ter) *adj* an-

noying
irritar (ee-rree-*tahr*) *v* irritate; annoy
irritável (ee-rree-*tah*-vehl) *adj* (pl -eis) irritable
isca (*eesh*-ker) *f* bait
isenção (ee-zayng-*serng*ᵂ) *f* (pl -ções) exemption
isentar (ee-zayng-*tahr*) *v* exempt
isento (ee-*zayng*-too) *adj* exempt
islandês (eezh-lerng-*daysh*) *adj* Icelandic; *m* Icelander
Islândia (eezh-*lerng*-dᵛah) *f* Iceland
isolado (ee-zoo-*lah*-dhoo) *adj* isolated
isolador (ee-zoo-ler-*dhoar*) *m* insulator
isolamento (ee-zoo-ler-*mayng*-too) *m* isolation; insulation
isolar (ee-zoo-*lahr*) *v* isolate; insulate
isqueiro (eesh-*kay*-roo) *m* cigarette-lighter, lighter
Israel (eezh-rrer-*ehl*) *m* Israel
israeliano (eezh-rrer-ay-*l*ᵛ*er*-noo) *adj* Israeli; *m* Israeli
isso (*ee*-soo) *pron* that
istmo (*eesht*-moo) *m* isthmus
Itália (ee-*tah*-lᵛer) *f* Italy
italiano (ee-ter-*l*ᵛ*er*-noo) *adj* Italian; *m* Italian
itálico (ee-*tah*-lee-koo) *m* italics *pl*
itinerante (een-tee-ner-*rerng*-ter) *adj* itinerant
itinerário (ee-tee-ner-*rah*-rᵛoo) *m* itinerary

J

já (zhah) *adv* at once, immediately; already; ~ **não** any more; ~ **que** because
jacto (*zhahk*-too) *m* jet
jade (*zhah*-dher) *m* jade
jamais (zher-*mighsh*) *adv* ever
Janeiro (zher-*nay*-roo) January

janela (zher-*neh*-ler) *f* window; ~ **de madeira** shutter
jangada (zherng-*gah*-dher) *f* raft
jantar (zherng-*tahr*) *m* dinner; *v* dine
jante (*zherng*-ter) *f* rim
Japão (zher-*perng*ᵂ) *m* Japan
japonês (zher-poo-*naysh*) *adj* Japanese; *m* Japanese
jardim (zherr-*deeng*) *m* garden; ~ **infantil** kindergarten; ~ **público** public garden; ~ **zoológico** zoological gardens
jardineiro (zherr-dee-*nay*-roo) *m* gardener
jarra (*zhah*-rrer) *f* jar
jarro (*zhah*-roo) *m* jug
jaula (*zhou*-ler) *f* cage
jeitoso (zhay-*toa*-zoo) *adj* handy
jersey (*zherr*-seh) *m* jersey
joalharia (zhwer-lᵛer-*ree*-er) *f* jewellery
joalheiro (zhwer-lᵛ*ay*-roo) *m* jeweller
joelho (zhway-lᵛoo) *m* knee
jogada (zhoo-*gah*-dher) *f* move
jogador (zhoo-ger-*dhoar*) *m* player
jogar (zhoo-*gahr*) *v* play
jogo (*zhoa*-goo) *m* game, play; set; **campo de jogos** recreation ground; ~ **das damas** draughts
jóia (*zho*-ᵛer) *f* jewel; gem; **jóias** jewellery
jóquei (*zho*-kay) *m* jockey
Jordânia (zhoor-der-nᵛer) *f* Jordan
jordaniano (zhoor-der-nᵛ*er*-noo) *adj* Jordanian; *m* Jordanian
jornal (zhoor-*nahl*) *m* (pl -ais) paper, newspaper; journal; ~ **da manhã** morning paper
jornalismo (zhoor-ner-*leezh*-moo) *m* journalism
jornalista (zhoor-ner-*leesh*-ter) *m* journalist
jorro (*zhoa*-rroo) *m* spout
jovem (*zho*-verng ᵛ) *adj* young

jovial (zhoo-v^yahl) adj (pl -ais) jolly; cheerful

jubileu (zhoo-bhee-lay^{oo}) m jubilee

judaico (zhoo-dhigh-koo) adj Jewish

judeu (zhoo-dhay^{oo}) m Jew

judicioso (zhoo-dhee-syoa-zoo) adj judicious

Jugoslávia (zhoo-go-zhlah-v^yer) f Yugoslavia

jugoslavo (zhoo-go-zhlah-voo) adj Yugoslav; m Yugoslav

juiz (zhweesh) m judge

juízo (zhwee-zoo) m sense; judgment

julgamento (zhool-ger-mayngn-too) m judgment; trial

julgar (zhool-gahr) v judge

Julho (zhoo-l^yoo) July

junção (zhoong-serng^w) f (pl -ções) junction

junco (zhoong-koo) m rush

Junho (zhoo-ñoo) June

júnior (zhoo-n^yoar) adj junior

junquilho (zhoong-kee-l^yoo) m daffodil

juntar (zhoongn-tahr) v join; attach, enclose; add

junto (zhoongn-too) adj joined; joint; ~ a next to; por~ wholesale

juntos (zhoongn-toosh) adv together

juramento (zhoo-rer-mayngn-too) m oath, vow

jurar (zhoo-rahr) v *swear, vow

júri (zhoo-ree) m jury

jurídico (zhoo-ree-dhee-koo) adj legal

jurista (zhoo-reesh-ter) m lawyer

juro (zhoo-roo) m interest

justamente (zhoosh-ter-mayngn-ter) adv just; rightly; exactly

justiça (zhoosh-tee-ser) f justice

justo (zhoosh-too) adj righteous, just, right; proper, fair, appropriate

juvenil (zhoo-ver-neel) adj (pl -nis) juvenile

juventude (zhoo-vayngn-too-dher) f youth

L

lá (lah) adv there

lã (lerng) f wool; de ~ woollen; ~ cardada worsted

lábio (lah-bh^yoo) m lip

labirinto (ler-bher-reengn-too) m labyrinth, maze

laboratório (ler-bhoo-rer-to-r^yoo) m laboratory; ~ de línguas language laboratory

labutar (ler-bhoo-tahr) v labour

laca para o cabelo (lah-ker per-rer oo ker-bhay-loo) hair-spray

laço (lah-soo) m link; bow tie

lado (lah-dhoo) m side; way; ao ~ next-door; ao ~ de beside; de ~ aside; sideways; do outro ~ de across; em qualquer ~ anywhere; em todo o ~ anywhere, everywhere; no outro ~ across; noutro ~ elsewhere

ladrão (ler-dhrerng^w) m (pl -rões) thief; burglar, robber

ladrar (ler-dhrahr) v bark, bay

lago (lah-goo) m lake

lagoa (ler-goa-er) f small lake

lagosta (ler-goash-ter) f lobster

lágrima (lah-gree-mer) f tear

laguna (ler-goo-ner) f lagoon

lama (ler-mer) f mud

lamacento (ler-mer-sayngn-too) adj muddy

lamber (lerngm-bayr) v lick

lambril (lerngm-breel) m (pl -is) panelling

lamechice (ler-mer-shee-ser) f tearjerker

lamentar (ler-mayngn-tahr) v regret

lamentável (ler-mayngn-tah-vehl) adj

(pl -eis) lamentable

lâmina (*ler*-mee-ner) *f* blade; ~ **de barbear** razor-blade

lâmpada (*ler*ngm-per-dher) *f* light bulb; ~ **de flash** flash-bulb; ~ **de tempestade** hurricane lamp

lança (*ler*ng-ser) *f* spear

lançamento (ler*ng*-ser-*may*ngn-too) *m* launching; throw; entry

lançar (ler*ng*-*sahr*) *v* *cast, *throw, toss; launch

lance (*ler*ng-ser) *m* cast

lanche (*ler*ng-sher) *m* tea, snack

lanterna (ler*ng*n-*tehr*-ner) *f* lantern; ~ **de bolso** torch; ~ **de mão** flash-light

lapela (ler-*peh*-ler) *f* lapel

lápide (*lah*-pee-dher) *f* gravestone

lápis (*lah*-peesh) *m* (pl ~) pencil; ~ **para os olhos** eye-pencil

lar (lahr) *m* home

laranja (ler-*rer*ng-zher) *f* orange

lareira (ler-*ray*-rer) *f* fireplace, hearth

largo (*lahr*-goo) *adj* broad, wide

largura (lerr-*goo*-rer) *f* breadth, width

laringite (ler-reeng-*zhee*-ter) *f* laryngitis

lasca (*lahsh*-ker) *f* chip

lascar (lersh-*kahr*) *v* chip

lastimar (lersh-tee-*mahr*) *v* deplore

lata (*lah*-ter) *f* tin, can; canister

latão (ler-*ter*ng^W) *m* brass; **utensílios de** ~ brassware

lavabos (ler-*vah*-bhoosh) *mpl* washroom *nAm*; ~ **das senhoras** powder-room; ~ **dos homens** men's room

lava-louça (lah-ver-*loa*-ser) *m* (pl ~s) sink

lavandaria (ler-ver*ng*-der-*ree*-er) *f* laundry; ~ **automática** launderette

lavar (ler-*vahr*) *v* wash; ~ **a loiça** wash up

lavatório (ler-ver-*to*-r^Yoo) *m* washstand; wash-basin

lavável (ler-*vah*-vehl) *adj* (pl -eis) washable

lavrador (ler-vrer-*dhoar*) *m* farmer

lavrar (ler-*vrahr*) *v* plough

laxante (ler-*sher*ng-ter) *m* laxative

leal (l^Yahl) *adj* (pl leais) loyal; true

leão (l^Yer*ng*^W) *m* (pl leões) lion

lebre (*leh*-bhrer) *f* hare

legação (ler-ger-*ser*ng^W) *f* (pl -ções) legation

legado (ler-*gah*-doo) *m* legacy

legal (ler-*gahl*) *adj* (pl -ais) legal; lawful

legalização (ler-ger-lee-zer-*ser*ng^W) *f* (pl -ções) legalization

legenda (l^-*zhay*ngn-der) *f* subtitle

legítimo (l^-zhee-tee-moo) *adj* legitimate, legal

legível (l^-*zhee*-vehl) *adj* (pl -eis) legible

legume (ler-*goo*-mer) *m* vegetable

lei (lay) *f* law

leigo (*lay*-goo) *m* layman

leilão (lay-*ler*ng^W) *m* (pl -lões) auction

leitão (lay-*ter*ng^W) *m* (pl -tões) piglet

leitaria (lay-ter-*ree*-er) *f* dairy

leite (*lay*-ter) *m* milk; **batido de** ~ milk-shake

leiteiro (lay-*tay*-roo) *m* milkman

leitoso (lay-*toa*-zoo) *adj* milky

leitura (lay-*too*-rer) *f* reading

lema (*lay*-mer) *m* slogan

lembrança (layngm-*brer*ng-ser) *f* remembrance

lembrar (layngm-*brahr*) *v* remind; **lembrar-se** remember

leme (*leh*-mer) *m* rudder, helm

lenço (*layng*-soo) *m* handkerchief; ~ **da cabeça** scarf; ~ **de assoar** handkerchief; ~ **de papel** tissue; ~ **do pescoço** scarf

lençol (layng-*sol*) *m* (pl -çóis) sheet

lente (*layng*n-ter) *f* lens; **lentes de contacto** contact lenses; ~ **zoom** zoom lens

lento (*layng*n-too) *adj* slow; slack

lepra (*leh*-prer) *f* leprosy

leque (*leh*-ker) *m* fan

*ler (layr) *v* *read

lesão (ler-*zerng*ʷ) *f* (pl lesões) injury

lesar (ler-*zahr*) *v* wrong

letra (*lay*-trer) *f* letter; draft

levantar (ler-verng*n-tahr*) *v* raise, lift; *bring up; cash, *draw; **levantar-se** *rise; *get up

levar (ler-*vahr*) *v* *take; *bear; *take away; ~ **a mal** resent

leve (*leh*-ver) *adj* light

levedura (ler-ver-*dhoo*-rer) *f* yeast

lhe (lᵞer) *pron* him; her; **lhes** them

libanês (lee-bher-*naysh*) *adj* Lebanese; *m* Lebanese

Líbano (*lee*-bher-noo) *m* Lebanon

liberal (lee-bher-*rahl*) *adj* (pl -ais) liberal

liberdade (lee-bherr-*dhah*-dher) *f* freedom, liberty

Libéria (lee-*bheh*-rᵞer) *f* Liberia

liberiano (lee-bher-rᵞer-noo) *adj* Liberian; *m* Liberian

libertação (lee-bherr-ter-*serng*ʷ) *f* (pl -cões) liberation; delivery

libra (*lee*-bhrer) *f* pound

lição (lee-*serng*ʷ) *f* (pl lições) lesson

licença (lee-*sayng*-ser) *f* licence, permit, permission; leave

licor (lee-*koar*) *m* liqueur

lida (*lee*-dher) *f* work

liga (*lee*-ger) *f* league, union

ligação (lee-ger-*serng*ʷ) *f* (pl -cões) connection; affair

ligadura (lee-ger-*dhoo*-rer) *f* bandage; band

ligar (lee-*gahr*) *v* *bind; connect, switch on, plug in, turn on; link

ligeiro (lee-*zhay*-roo) *adj* slight; gentle; swift; light

lilás (lee-*lahsh*) *adj* mauve

lima (*lee*-mer) *f* file; lime; ~ **de unhas** nail-file

limão (lee-*merng*ʷ) *m* (pl limões) lemon

limiar (lee-*m*ᵞ*ahr*) *m* threshold

limitar (lee-mee-*tahr*) *v* limit

limite (lee-*mee*-ter) *m* limit; bound, boundary

limonada (lee-moo-*nah*-dher) *f* lemonade

limpa-cachimbos (leeng*m*-per-ker-*sheeng*m-boosh) *m* (pl ~) pipe cleaner

limpa-chaminés (leeng*m*-per-sher-mee-*nehsh*) *m* (pl ~) chimney-sweep

limpar (leeng*m*-*pahr*) *v* clean; wipe; ~ **a seco** dry-clean

limpeza (leeng*m*-*pay*-zer) *f* cleaning

limpo (*leeng*m-poo) *adj* clean

lindo (*leeng*n-doo) *adj* lovely

língua (*leeng*-gwer) *f* tongue; language; ~ **materna** mother tongue, native language

linguado (leeng-*gwah*-dhoo) *m* sole

linguagem (leeng-*gwah*-zherng ᵞ) *f* speech

linha (*lee*-ñer) *f* line; thread; ~ **de passajar** darning wool; ~ **principal** main line

linho (*lee*-ñoo) *m* linen

liquidação (lee-kee-dher-*serng*ʷ) *f* (pl -cões) clearance sale

liquidar (lee-kee-*dhahr*) *v* *pay off; destroy

líquido (*lee*-kee-dhoo) *adj* liquid; net; *m* fluid; ~ **dentífrico** mouthwash

lírio (*lee*-rᵞoo) *m* lily

liso (*lee*-zoo) *adj* smooth; level; even

lista (*leesh*-ter) *f* list; ~ **de espera** waiting-list; ~ **de preços** price-list; ~ **dos telefones** telephone directory; telephone book *Am;* ~ **dos vinhos** wine-list; ~ **telefónica** telephone directory; telephone book *Am*

literário (lee-ter-*rah*-rᵞoo) *adj* literary

literatura (lee-ter-er-*too*-rer) *f* literature

litígio (lee-*tee*-zhᵞoo) *m* dispute, quarrel

litoral (lee-too-*rahl*) *m* sea-coast

litro (*lee*-troo) *m* litre

livrar (loo-*vrahr*) *v* deliver

livraria (lee-vrer-*ree*-er) *f* bookstore

livre (*lee*-vrer) *adj* free

livreiro (lee-*vray*-roo) *m* bookseller

livro (*lee*-vroo) *m* book; ~ **de bolso** paperback; ~ **de reclamações** complaints book

lixa (*lee*-sher) *f* sandpaper

lixo (*lee*-shoo) *m* garbage; trash; refuse; litter, rubbish; **caixote do** ~ rubbish-bin, dustbin; **lata de** ~ *Br* rubbish-bin, dustbin

lobo (*loa*-bhoo) *m* wolf

local (loo-*kahl*) *adj* (pl -ais) local; *m* premises *pl;* spot

localidade (loo-ker-lee-*dhah*-dher) *f* locality

localização (loo-ker-lee-zer-*serng*ᵂ) *f* (pl -ções) location

localizar (loo-ker-lee-*zahr*) *v* locate

loção (loo-*serng*ᵂ) *f* (pl loções) lotion; ~ **fixadora** setting lotion; ~ **para depois da barba** aftershave lotion

locomotiva (loo-koo-moo-*tee*-ver) *f* engine, locomotive

lógica (*lo*-zhee-ker) *f* logic

lógico (*lo*-zhee-koo) *adj* logical

logo (*lo*-goo) *adv* immediately; soon; ~ **que** when

loiça (*loi*-ser) *f* crockery, pottery

loira (*loi*-rer) *f* blonde

loiro (*loi*-roo) *adj* fair

loja (*lo*-zher) *f* store, shop; ~ **de artigos fotográficos** camera shop; ~ **de brinquedos** toyshop; ~ **de ferragens** hardware store; ~ **de vinhos** off-licence

lojista (loo-*zheesh*-ter) *m* shopkeeper

lona (*loa*-ner) *f* canvas

longe (*lawng*-zher) *adv* far; **de** ~ by far

longínquo (lawng-*zheeng*-kwoo) *adj* far-off

longitude (lawng-zhee-*too*-dher) *f* longitude

longitudinalmente (lawng-zhee-too-dhee-nerl-*mayng*-ter) *adv* lengthways

longo (*lawng*-goo) *adj* long; **ao** ~ **de** along

lotaria (loo-ter-*ree*-er) *f* lottery

lote (*lo*-ter) *m* batch

louco (*loa*-koo) *adj* crazy; insane, lunatic

loucura (loa-*koo*-rer) *f* lunacy

louro (*loa*-roo) *adj* blond

louvar (loa-*vahr*) *v* praise

louvor (loa-*voar*) *m* glory

lua (*loo*-er) *f* moon

lua-de-mel (*loo*-er-der-mehl) *f* honeymoon

luar (lwahr) *m* moonlight

lubrificação (loo-bhrer-fee-ker-*serng*ᵂ) *f* (pl -ções) lubrication; **sistema de lubrificação** lubrication system

lubrificar (loo-bhrer-fee-*kahr*) *v* lubricate; grease

lúcio (*loo*-sᵞoo) *m* pike

lucrativo (loo-krer-*tee*-voo) *adj* profitable

lucro (*loo*-kroo) *m* profit; gain, benefit; **lucros** winnings

lugar (loo-*gahr*) *m* place; room; seat; ~ **de nascimento** place of birth; ***ter** ~ *take place

lumbago (loongm-*bah*-goo) *m* lumbago

luminoso (loo-mee-*noa*-zoo) *adj* luminous

lupa (*loo*-per) *f* magnifying glass

lúpulo (*loo*-poo-loo) *m* hop

lustro (*loosh*-troo) *m* gloss

lustroso (loosh-*troa*-zoo) *adj* glossy

luta (*loo*-ter) *f* strife; combat, fight; contest, battle, struggle; ~ **de boxe** boxing match

lutar (loo-*tahr*) *v* *fight; struggle

luto (*loo*-too) *m* mourning

luva (*loo*-ver) *f* glove; **luvas sem dedos** mittens *pl*

luxo (*loo*-shoo) *m* luxury

luxuoso (loo-*shwoa*-zoo) *adj* luxurious

luz (loosh) *f* light; ~ **da retaguarda** rear-light; ~ **de estacionamento** parking light; ~ **do dia** daylight; ~ **do sol** sunlight; **luzes de travão** brake lights; ~ **lateral** sidelight

M

maca (*mah*-ker) *f* stretcher

maçã (mer-*serng*) *f* apple; ~ **do rosto** cheek-bone

macacão (mer-ker-*kerng*ʷ) *mBr* (pl -cões) overalls *pl*

macaco (mer-*kah*-koo) *m* monkey; jack

maçador (mer-ser-*dhoar*) *adj* boring, annoying; troublesome, inconvenient; unpleasant; *m* bore

maçaneta (mer-ser-*nay*-ter) *f* handle, knob

maçar (mer-*sahr*) *v* bore; bother

machado (mer-*shah*-dhoo) *m* axe

macho (*mah*-shoo) *m* mule; male animal

maciço (mer-*see*-soo) *adj* massive; solid

macio (mer-*see*ᵒᵒ) *adj* mellow

maço (*mah*-soo) *m* mallet

madeira (mer-*dhay*-rer) *f* wood; **de** ~ wooden; ~ **de construção** timber

madrasta (mer-*dhrahsh*-ter) *f* stepmother

madre-pérola (mah-dhrer-*peh*-roo-ler) *f* mother-of-pearl

madrugada (mer-dhroo-*gah*-dher) *f* dawn

maduro (mer-*dhoo*-roo) *adj* ripe, mature

mãe (merngʸ) *f* mother

maestro (mer-*ehsh*-troo) *m* conductor

magia (mer-*zhee*-er) *f* magic

mágico (*mah*-zhee-koo) *adj* magic

magistrado (mer-zheesh-*trah*-dhoo) *m* magistrate

magnânimo (merg-*ner*-nee-moo) *adj* generous

magnético (merg-*neh*-tee-koo) *adj* magnetic

magneto (merg-*neh*-too) *m* magneto

magnífico (merg-*nee*-fee-koo) *adj* magnificent; gorgeous, splendid

magoar (mer-*gwahr*) *v* *hurt; bruise

magro (*mah*-groo) *adj* lean, thin

Maio (*mah*-ʸoo) May

maior (mer-*ʸor*) *adj* major, superior; main; of age; ~ **parte** bulk

maioria (mer-ʸoo-*ree*-er) *f* majority

mais (mighsh) *adj* more; most; *adv* plus; ~ **de** over; **não** ~ no longer

maiúscula (mer-*ʸoosh*-koo-ler) *f* capital letter

major (mer-*zhor*) *m* major

mal (mahl) *m* (pl ~es) evil; wrong, harm; ailment; *adv* barely, hardly; ***fazer** ~ **a** harm; ~ **sucedido** unsuccessful

mala (*mah*-ler) *f* bag; case, suitcase; boot; trunk *nAm*; ~ **de mão** handbag

malaio (mer-*ligh*-oo) *adj* Malaysian; *m* Malay

malandro (mer-*lerngn*-droo) *m* rascal

malária (mer-*lah*-r*Y*er) *f* malaria

Malásia (mer-*lah*-z*Y*er) *f* Malaysia

malcriado (mahl-kr*Y*ah-dhoo) *adj* impertinent

maldade (mahl-*dah*-dher) *f* mischief

*****maldizer** (mahl-dee-*zayr*) *v* curse

maleável (merl-*Y*ah-vehl) *adj* (pl -eis) supple; flexible

mal-entendido (mahl-eengn-tayngn-*dee*-dhoo) *m* misunderstanding

malévolo (mer-*leh*-voo-loo) *adj* spiteful

malha (*mah*-l*Y*er) *f* mesh; *****fazer** ~ knit; **malhas** hosiery

malícia (mer-lee-s*Y*er) *f* mischief

malicioso (mer-lee-s*Y*oa-zoo) *adj* malicious

maligno (mer-*leeg*-noo) *adj* malignant; ill

maluco (mer-*loo*-koo) *adj* foolish; mad

mamífero (mer-*mee*-fer-roo) *m* mammal

mamute (mer-*moo*-ter) *m* mammoth

manada (mer-*nah*-dher) *f* herd

mancha (*merng*-sher) *f* stain, spot; speck, blot; **sem** ~ spotless

manchar (merng-*shahr*) *v* stain

mandar (merngn-*dahr*) *v* order, command; *****send**; *****have**; ~ **vir** *****send** for

mandato (merngn-*dah*-too) *m* mandate

maneira (mer-*nay*-rer) *f* way, manner; fashion; **de qualquer** ~ anyway; any way

manejar (mer-n*I*-*zhahr*) *v* handle

manejável (mer-n*I*-zhah-vehl) *adj* (pl -eis) manageable

manequim (mer-ner-*keeng*) *m* model, mannequin

manga (*merng*-ger) *f* sleeve

manha (*mer*-ñer) *f* trick

manhã (mer-*ñerng*) *f* morning; **esta** ~ this morning

manhoso (mer-*ñoa*-zoo) *adj* cunning

mania (mer-*nee*-er) *f* craze

manicura (mer-nee-*koo*-rer) *f* manicure

manifestação (mer-nee-fish-ter-*serng*^w) *f* (pl -ções) demonstration

manifestar (mer-nee-fish-*tahr*) *v* demonstrate; express

manjedoura (merng-zher-*dhoa*-rer) *f* manger

manso (*merng*-soo) *adj* tame

manteiga (merngn-*tay*-ger) *f* butter

*****manter** (merngn-*tayr*) *v* maintain; *****keep**

manual (mer-*nwahl*) *adj* (pl -ais) manual; *m* handbook

manuscrito (mer-noosh-*kree*-too) *m* manuscript

manutenção (mer-noo-tayng-*serng*^w) *f* maintenance, upkeep

mão (*merng*^w) *f* (pl ~s) hand; **em segunda** ~ second-hand; **feito à** ~ hand-made; **palma da** ~ palm

mapa (*mah*-per) *m* map; ~ **de estradas** road map; ~ **marítimo** chart

maquilhagem (mer-kee-*lah*-zherng*Y*) *f* make-up

máquina (*mah*-kee-ner) *f* machine, engine; ~ **de barbear** shaver, electric razor; ~ **de costura** sewing-machine; ~ **de escrever** typewriter; ~ **de filmar** camera; ~ **de lavar** washing-machine; ~ **fotográfica** camera

maquinaria (mer-kee-ner-*ree*-er) *f* machinery

mar (mahr) *m* sea

maravilha (mer-rer-vee-l*Y*er) *f* marvel

maravilhar-se (mer-rer-vee-l*Y*ahr-ser) *v* marvel

maravilhoso (mer-rer-vee-l*Y*oa-zoo) *adj*

marvellous; fine, wonderful

marca (*mahr*-ker) f mark; sign; tick; brand; ~ **de fábrica** trademark

marcar (merr-*kahr*) v mark; tick off; score

marceneiro (merr-ser-*nay*-roo) m joiner

marcha (*mahr*-sher) f march; *****fazer** ~ **à ré** Br reverse; *****fazer** ~ **atrás** reverse; ~ **atrás** reverse

marchar (mar-*shahr*) v march

Março (*mahr*-soo) March

marco (*mahr*-koo) m landmark; ~ **miliário** milestone

maré (mer-*reh*) f tide; ~ **baixa** low tide; ~ **cheia** high tide

marfim (merr-*feeng*) m ivory

margarina (merr-ger-*ree*-ner) f margarine

margem (*mahr*-zherngʸ) f margin; river bank, shore

marido (mer-*ree*-dhoo) m husband

marinha (mer-*ree*-ñer) f navy

marinheiro (mer-ree-*ñay*-roo) m sailor, seaman

mariposa (mer-ree-*poa*-zer) f butterfly stroke

marisco (mer-*reesh*-koo) m shellfish

marítimo (mer-*ree*-tee-moo) adj maritime

mármore (*mahr*-moo-rer) m marble

maroto (mer-*roa*-too) adj naughty, mischievous

Marrocos (mer-*roa*-koosh) m Morocco

marroquino (mer-rroa-*kee*-noo) adj Moroccan; m Moroccan

martelar (merr-ter-*lahr*) v thump

martelo (merr-*teh*-loo) m hammer

mártir (*mahr*-teer) m martyr

mas (mersh) conj but; only, yet

máscara (*mahsh*-ker-rer) f mask; ~ **facial** face-pack

masculino (mersh-koo-*lee*-noo) adj

masculine, male

massa (*mah*-ser) f dough, batter; mass

massagem (mer-*sah*-zherngʸ) f massage; ~ **facial** face massage

massagista (mer-ser-*zheesh*-ter) m masseur

massajar (mer-ser-*zhahr*) v massage

mastigar (mersh-tee-*gahr*) v chew

mastro (*mahsh*-troo) m mast

mata (*mah*-ter) f grove

mata-borrão (mah-ter-bhoo-*rrerng*ʷ) m (pl -rões) blotting paper

matar (mer-*tahr*) v kill

mate (*mah*-ter) adj dim, mat

matemática (mer-ter-*mah*-tee-ker) f mathematics

matemático (mer-ter-*mah*-tee-koo) adj mathematical; m mathematician

matéria (mer-*teh*-rʸer) f matter

material (mer-ter-*rʸahl*) adj (pl -ais) substantial, material; m material

matéria-prima (mer-teh-rʸer-*pree*-mer) f raw material

mato (*mah*-too) m brush

matrimonial (mer-tree-moo-*nʸahl*) adj (pl -ais) matrimonial

matrimónio (mer-tree-*mo*-nʸoo) m matrimony

maturidade (mer-too-ree-*dhah*-dher) f maturity

mau (mou) adj (f má) evil, bad; ill, wicked; ~ **génio** temper

mausoléu (mou-zoo-*leh*ᵒᵒ) m mausoleum

maxila (mahk-*see*-ler) f jaw

máximo (*mah*-see-moo) adj utmost; **no** ~ at most

me (mer) pron me; myself

mecânico (mer-ker-*nee*-koo) adj mechanical; m mechanic

mecanismo (mer-ker-*neezh*-moo) m mechanism; machinery

mecha (*meh*-sher) f fuse

medalha (mer-*dhah*-l*Y*er) *f* medal

média (*meh*-dh*Y*er) *f* average, mean; **em** ~ on the average

mediano (mer-*dh*Y*er*-noo) *adj* medium

medicamento (mer-dhee-ker-*mayngn*-too) *m* drug, medicine

medicina (mer-dhee-*see*-ner) *f* medicine

médico (*meh*-dhee-koo) *m* physician, doctor; *adj* medical; ~ **de clínica geral** general practitioner

medida (mer-*dhee*-dher) *f* measure; gauge, size; **feito à** ~ tailor-made

medidor (mer-dee-*doar*) *mBr* meter

medieval (mer-dh*Y*er-*vahl*) *adj* (pl -ais) mediaeval

médio (*meh*-dh*Y*oo) *adj* average, medium; middle

mediocre (mer-*dhee^oo*-krer) *adj* mediocre, second-rate

***medir** (mer-*dheer*) *v* measure

meditar (mer-dhee-*tahr*) *v* meditate

Mediterrâneo (mer-dhee-ter-*rrer*-n*Y*oo) *m* Mediterranean

medo (*may*-dhoo) *m* fear, fright; **com** ~ afraid; **meter** ~ frighten; ***ter** ~ *be afraid

medonho (mer-*dhoa*-ño) *adj* frightful, terrible

medula (mer-*dhoo*-ler) *f* marrow

medusa (mer-*dhoo*-zer) *fBr* jelly-fish

meia (*may*-er) *f* stocking; **meias de descanso** support hose

meia-calça (may-er-*kahl*-ser) *f* pantyhose

meia-noite (may-er-*noi*-ter) *f* midnight

meio (*may*-oo) *adj* half; *m* midst, middle; means; *adv* half; ~ **ambiente** environment, milieu; **no** ~ **de** amid; **por** ~ **de** by means of

meio-dia (may-oo-*dhee*-er) *m* noon, midday

meio-fio (may-*Y*oo-*fee^oo*) *mBr* curb

mel (mehl) *m* honey

melancia (mer-ler*ng*-*see*-er) *f* watermelon

melancolia (mer-ler*ng*-koo-*lee*-er) *f* melancholy

melancólico (mer-ler*ng*-*ko*-lee-koo) *adj* sad

melão (mer-*ler*ng^w) *m* (pl melões) melon

melhor (m*ı*-l*Y*oar) *adj* better; superior; **o** ~ best, the best

melhoramento (m*ı*-l*Y*oo-rer-*mayngn*-too) *m* improvement

melhorar (m*ı*-l*Y*oo-*rahr*) *v* improve

melindrar-se por (mer-leengn-*drahr*-ser) resent

melodia (mer-loo-*dhee*-er) *f* melody; tune

melodioso (mer-loo-dh*Y*oa-zoo) *adj* tuneful

melodrama (mer-loo-*drer*-mer) *m* melodrama

melro (*mehl*-rroo) *m* blackbird

membrana (may*ng*m-*brer*-ner) *f* diaphragm

membro (*may*ng*m*-broo) *m* limb; associate, member

memorando (mer-moo-*rer*ng*n*-doo) *m* memo

memorável (mer-moo-*rah*-vehl) *adj* (pl -eis) memorable

memória (mer-*mo*-r*Y*er) *f* memory

memorial (mer-moo-r*Y*ahl) *m* (pl -ais) memorial

menção (may*ng*-*ser*ng^w) *f* (pl -ções) mention

mencionar (may*ng*-s*Y*oo-*nahr*) *v* mention

mendigar (may*ng*n-dee-*gahr*) *v* beg

mendigo (may*ng*n-*dee*-goo) *m* beggar

menina (mer-*nee*-ner) *f* miss; small girl; **a** ~ you

menino (mer-*nee*-noo) *m* small boy

menor (mer-*nor*) *adj* minor; inferior;

under age; *m* minor

menos (may-noosh) *adj* less, fewer; *adv* less; *prep* but; **pelo ~** at least

menosprezar (may-noosh-prer-*zahr*) *v* underestimate

mensageiro (mayng-ser-*zhay*-roo) *m* messenger

mensagem (mayng-*sah*-zherngʸ) *f* message

mensal (mayng-*sahl*) *adj* (pl -ais) monthly

menstruação (mayngsh-trwer-*serng*ʷ) *f* (pl -cões) menstruation

mental (mayngn-*tahl*) *adj* (pl -ais) mental

mente (*mayngn*-ter) *f* mind

*mentir (mayngn-*teer*) *v* lie

mentira (mayngn-*tee*-rer) *f* lie

mercado (merr-*kah*-dhoo) *m* market

mercadoria (merr-ker-dhoo-*ree*-er) *f* merchandise; **mercadorias** goods *pl*; wares *pl*

mercearia (merr-sʸer-*ree*-er) *f* grocer's; **artigos de ~** groceries *pl*; **~ fina** delicatessen

merceeiro (merr-sʸay-roo) *m* grocer

mercúrio (merr-*koo*-rʸoo) *m* mercury

merecer (mer-rer-*sayr*) *v* deserve; merit

mergulhar (merr-goo-*lʸahr*) *v* dive

meridional (mer-ree-dhʸoo-*nahl*) *adj* (pl -ais) southerly

mérito (*meh*-ree-too) *m* merit

mês (maysh) *m* month

mesa (*may*-zer) *f* table

mesmo (*mayzh*-moo) *adj* same; *adv* even

mesquinho (mish-*kee*-ño) *adj* stingy; mean

mesquita (mish-*kee*-ter) *f* mosque

mestre (*mehsh*-trer) *m* master; teacher

meta (*meh*-ter) *f* finish

metade (mer-*tah*-dher) *f* half

metal (mer-*tahl*) *m* (pl -ais) metal

metálico (mer-*tah*-lee-koo) *adj* metal

meter (mer-*tayr*) *v* *put

meticuloso (mer-tee-koo-*loa*-zoo) *adj* precise

metódico (mer-*to*-dhee-koo) *adj* methodical

método (*meh*-too-dhoo) *m* method

métrico (*meh*-tree-koo) *adj* metric

metro (*meh*-troo) *m* metre

metropolitano (mer-troo-poo-lee-*ter*-noo) *m* underground; subway *nAm*

meu (may°°) *adj* (f minha) my

mexer (mɪ-*shayr*) *v* stir; touch; **mexer-se** move

mexericar (mɪ-sher-ree-*kahr*) *v* gossip

mexerico (mɪ-sher-*ree*-koo) *m* gossip

mexicano (mɪ-shee-*ker*-noo) *adj* Mexican; *m* Mexican

México (*meh*-shee-koo) *m* Mexico

mexilhão (mɪ-shee-*lʸerng*ʷ) *m* (pl -hões) mussel

micróbio (mee-*kro*-bhʸoo) *m* germ

microfone (mee-kro-*fo*-ner) *m* microphone

migalha (mee-*gah*-lʸer) *f* crumb

mil (meel) *num* thousand

milagre (mee-*lah*-grer) *m* wonder, miracle

milagroso (mee-ler-*groa*-zoo) *adj* miraculous

milha (*mee*-lʸer) *f* mile

milho (*mee*-lʸoo) *m* maize; **maçaroca de ~** corn on the cob

milionário (mee-lʸoo-nah-rʸoo) *m* millionaire

militar (mer-lee-*tahr*) *adj* military

mim (meeng) *pron* me

mina (*mee*-ner) *f* mine; pit

mineiro (mee-*nay*-roo) *m* miner

mineral (mee-ner-*rahl*) *m* (pl -ais) mineral

minério (mee-*neh*-rʸoo) *m* ore

miniatura (mee-nʸer-*too*-rer) *f* miniature

mínimo (*mee*-nee-moo) *adj* least; *m* minimum; **no ~** at the very least

ministério (mer-neesh-*teh*-rʸoo) *m* ministry

ministro (mer-*neesh*-troo) *m* minister

minoria (mee-noo-*ree*-er) *f* minority

minucioso (mee-noo-sʸoa-zoo) *adj* thorough

minúsculo (mee-*noosh*-koo-loo) *adj* minute, tiny

minuto (mee-*noo*-too) *m* minute

míope (*mee*ᵒᵒ-per) *m* short-sighted

miserável (mee-zer-*rah*-vehl) *adj* (pl -eis) miserable

miséria (mee-*zeh*-rʸer) *f* misery

misericórdia (mee-zer-ree-*kor*-dhʸer) *f* mercy

misericordioso (mee-zer-ree-koor-dhʸoa-zoo) *adj* merciful

missa (*mee*-ser) *f* Mass

mistério (meesh-*teh*-rʸoo) *m* mystery

misterioso (meesh-ter-*rʸoa*-zoo) *adj* mysterious

mistura (meesh-*too*-rer) *f* mixture

misturado (meesh-too-*rah*-dhoo) *adj* mixed; miscellaneous

misturar (meesh-too-*rahr*) *v* mix

mito (*mee*-too) *m* myth

mobilar (moo-bhee-*lahr*) *v* furnish

mobília (moo-*bhee*-lʸer) *f* furniture

moca (*mo*-ker) *f* club

moção (moo-*serng*ʷ) *f* (pl moções) motion

mochila (moo-*shee*-ler) *f* rucksack, knapsack

mocho (*moa*-shoo) *m* owl

moço (moa-soo) *m* boy; **~ de hotel** *Br* page-boy

moda (*mo*-dher) *f* fashion; **fora de ~** out of date; **na ~** fashionable

modelar (moo-dher-*lahr*) *v* model

modelo (moo-*dhay*-loo) *m* model

moderado (moo-dher-*rah*-dhoo) *adj* moderate

moderno (moo-*dhehr*-noo) *adj* modern

modéstia (moo-*dhehsh*-tʸer) *f* modesty

modesto (moo-*dhehsh*-too) *adj* modest

modificação (moo-dher-fee-ker-*serng*ʷ) *f* (pl -ções) change

modificar (moo-dher-fee-*kahr*) *v* modify; change

modista (moo-*dheesh*-ter) *f* dressmaker

modo (*mo*-dhoo) *m* way, manner; **de ~ nenhum** by no means; **de ~ que** so that; **de qualquer ~** at any rate, anyhow; **doutro ~** otherwise, else; **~ de emprego** directions for use

moeda (*mweh*-dher) *f* coin; currency; **~ estrangeira** foreign currency

***moer** (mwayr) *v* *grind

mohair (mo-*ehr*) *m* mohair

moinho (*mwee*-ño) *m* mill; **~ de vento** windmill

moita (*moi*-ter) *f* scrub

mola (*mo*-ler) *f* spring

molar (moo-*lahr*) *m* molar

moldar (moal-*dahr*) *v* model

moldura (moal-*doo*-rer) *f* frame

mole (*mo*-ler) *adj* soft

moleiro (moo-*lay*-roo) *m* miller

molhado (moo-lʸah-dhoo) *adj* wet; damp, moist

molhar (moo-lʸahr) *v* soak

molhe (*mo*-lʸer) *m* pier, jetty

molho¹ (*mo*-lʸoo) *m* bundle

molho² (moa-lʸoo) *m* gravy, sauce; **pôr de ~** soak

momentâneo (moo-mayngn-ter-nʸoo) *adj* momentary

momento (moo-*mayngn*-too) *m* moment; while; **~ decisivo** turning-point

monarca (moo-*nahr*-ker) *m* ruler, monarch

monarquia (moo-nerr-*kee*-er) *f* monarchy

monetário (moo-ner-*tah*-rⱽoo) *adj* monetary

monge (*mawng*-zher) *m* monk

monólogo (moo-*no*-loo-goo) *m* monologue

monopólio (moo-noo-*po*-lⱽoo) *m* monopoly

monótono (moo-*no*-too-noo) *adj* monotonous

montanha (mawⱨgn-*ter*-ñer) *f* mountain

montanhoso (mawⱨgn-ter-*ñoa*-zoo) *adj* mountainous

montão (mawⱨgn-*terng*ʷ) *m* (pl -tões) heap

montar (mawⱨgn-*tahr*) *v* assemble; ~ **a cavalo** *ride

monte (*mawⱨgn*-ter) *m* mount; heap; **cume do** ~ hilltop

montículo (mawⱨgn-*tee*-koo-loo) *m* mound

montra (*mawⱨgn*-trer) *f* shop-window

monumento (moo-noo-*mayⱨgn*-too) *m* monument

morada (moo-*rah*-dher) *f* home

morador (moo-rer-*dhoa*-rer) *m* occupant

moral (moo-*rahl*) *adj* (pl -ais) moral; *f* moral; *m* spirits

moralidade (moo-rer-lee-*dhah*-dher) *f* morality

morango (moo-*rerng*-goo) *m* strawberry

morar (moo-*rahr*) *v* live

mordedura (moor-der-*dhoo*-rer) *f* bite

morder (moor-*dayr*) *v* *bite

morena (moo-*ray*-ner) *f* brunette

moreno (moo-*ray*-noo) *adj* dark

morfina (moor-*fee*-ner) *f* morphia, morphine

morno (*moar*-noo) *adj* lukewarm

morrer (moo-*rrayr*) *v* die

mortal (moor-*tahl*) *adj* (pl -ais) mortal; fatal

morte (*mor*-ter) *f* death

morto (*moar*-too) *adj* dead

mosaico (moo-*zigh*-koo) *m* mosaic

mosca (*moash*-ker) *f* fly

mosquiteiro (moosh-kee-*tay*-roo) *m* mosquito-net

mosquito (moosh-*kee*-too) *m* mosquito

mossa (*mo*-ser) *f* dent

mostarda (moosh-*tahr*-der) *f* mustard

mosteiro (moosh-*tay*-roo) *m* monastery

mostrar (moosh-*trahr*) *v* *show; display

motel (mo-*tehl*) *m* (pl motéis) motel

motim (moo-*teeng*) *m* mutiny

motivo (moo-*tee*-voo) *m* motive; occasion, cause

motocicleta (mo-to-see-*klay*-ter) *f* motor-cycle

motor (moo-*toar*) *m* motor; engine; **cobertura do** ~ bonnet; hood *nAm;* ~ **a jacto-propulsão** turbojet; ~ **de arranque** starter motor

motorista (moo-too-*reesh*-ter) *m* chauffeur; ~ **de táxi** cab-driver, taxi-driver

móvel (*mo*-vehl) *adj* (pl -eis) mobile; movable

mover (moo-*vayr*) *v* move

movimentado (moo-vee-mayⱨgn-*tah*-dhoo) *adj* busy

movimento (moo-vee-*mayⱨgn*-too) *m* motion, movement

mudança (moo-*dherng*-ser) *f* variation, change; move

mudar (moo-*dhahr*) *v* vary; change, transform; ~ **de roupa** change clothes; ~ **de velocidade** change gear; **mudar-se** move

mudo (*moo*-dhoo) *adj* mute, dumb;

speechless

muito (*moong^yn*-too) *adv* very, quite; much; *adj* much; **muitos** many

mulato (moo-*lah*-too) *f* mulatto

muleta (moo-*lay*-ter) *f* crutch

mulher (moo-*l^yayr*) *f* woman, wife; ~ **a dias** cleaning woman

mulo (*moo*-loo) *m* mule

multa (*mool*-ter) *f* fine, ticket

multidão (mool-tee-*dherng^w*) *f* (pl -dões) crowd

multiplicação (mool-tee-plee-ker-*serng^w*) *f* (pl -ções) multiplication

multiplicar (mool-tee-plee-*kahr*) *v* multiply

mundial (moongn-*d^yahl*) *adj* (pl -ais) global, world-wide

mundo (*moongn*-doo) *m* world

municipal (moo-ner-see-*pahl*) *adj* (pl -ais) municipal

municipalidade (moo-ner-see-per-lee-*dhah*-dher) *f* municipality

murmurar (moor-moo-*rahr*) *v* whisper

muro (*moo*-roo) *m* wall

músculo (*moosh*-koo-loo) *m* muscle

musculoso (moosh-koo-*loa*-zoo) *adj* muscular

museu (moo-*zay^{oo}*) *m* museum; ~ **das ceras** waxworks *pl*

musgo (*moozh*-goo) *m* moss

música (*moo*-zee-ker) *f* music; ~ **pop** pop music

musical (moo-zee-*kahl*) *adj* (pl -ais) musical; **comédia** ~ musical

músico (*moo*-zee-koo) *m* musician

musselina (moo-ser-*lee*-ner) *f* muslin

mutuamente (moo-twer-*mayngn*-ter) *adv* each other

mútuo (*moo*-twoo) *adj* mutual

N

nacional (ner-s^yoo-*nahl*) *adj* (pl -ais) national

nacionalidade (ner-s^yoo-ner-lee-*dhah*-dher) *f* nationality

nacionalizar (ner-s^yoo-ner-lee-*zahr*) *v* nationalize

nada (*nah*-dher) *pron* nothing

nadador (ner-dher-*dhoar*) *m* swimmer

nadar (ner-*dhahr*) *v* *swim

nádega (*nah*-dher-ger) *f* buttock

não (nerng^w) *adv* no; not; ~ **obstante** nevertheless

narcose (nerr-*ko*-zer) *f* narcosis

narcótico (nerr-*ko*-tee-koo) *m* narcotic

narina (ner-*ree*-ner) *f* nostril

nariz (ner-*reesh*) *m* nose

narrativa (ner-rrer-*tee*-ver) *f* tale

nascente (nersh-*sayngn*-ter) *f* spring

nascer (nersh-*sayr*) *v* *be born

nascido (nersh-*see*-dhoo) *adj* born

nascimento (nersh-see-*mayngn*-too) *m* birth

nata (*nah*-ter) *f* cream

natação (ner-ter-*serng^w*) *f* swimming

Natal (ner-*tahl*) *m* (pl -ais) Xmas, Christmas

nativo (ner-*tee*-voo) *m* native

nato (*nah*-too) *adj* natural

natural (ner-too-*rahl*) *adj* (pl -ais) natural

naturalmente (ner-too-rahl-*mayngn*-ter) *adv* naturally; of course

natureza (ner-too-*ray*-zer) *f* nature; essence

náusea (*nou*-z^yer) *f* nausea

naval (ner-*vahl*) *adj* (pl -ais) naval

navegação (ner-ver-ger-*serng^w*) *f* navigation

navegar (ner-ver-*gahr*) *v* sail, navigate

navegável (ner-ver-*gah*-vehl) *adj* (pl -eis) navigable

navio (ner-*vee*-oo) *m* ship; vessel, boat

navio-cisterna (ner-vee^{oo}-seesh-*tayr*-ner) *m* tanker

neblina (ner-*bhlee*-ner) *f* mist

necessário (ner-ser-*sah*-r^Yoo) *adj* necessary; requisite

necessidade (ner-ser-see-*dhah*-dher) *f* necessity; requirement, want, need

necessitar (ner-ser-see-*tahr*) *v* need

negar (ner-*gahr*) *v* deny

negativo (ner-ger-*tee*-voo) *adj* negative; *m* negative

negligência (ner-glee-*zhayng*-s^Yer) *f* neglect

negligente (ner-glee-*zhayngn*-ter) *adj* neglectful; careless

negociação (ner-goo-s^Yer-*serng*^w) *f* (pl -ções) negotiation

negociante (ner-goo-s^Y*erngn*-ter) *m* dealer; ~ **de tecidos** draper

*****negociar** (ner-goo-s^Y*ahr*) *v* negotiate; trade

negócio (ner-*go*-s^Yoo) *m* business; deal: *****fazer negócios com** *****deal with; **movimento de negócios** turnover; **para negócios** on business; **viagem de negócios** business trip

negro (*nay*-groo) *m* Negro

nem ... nem (nerng^Y) neither ... nor; **nem um nem outro** neither

nenhum (nɪ-*ñoong*) *adj* no; *pron* none

néon (*neh*-awng) *m* neon

nervo (*nayr*-voo) *m* nerve

nervoso (nerr-*voa*-zoo) *adj* nervous

neta (*neh*-ter) *f* granddaughter; grandchild

neto (*neh*-too) *m* grandson

neurose (nay^{oo}-*ro*-zer) *f* neurosis

neutral (nay^{oo}-*trahl*) *adj* (pl -ais) neutral

neutro (*nay*^{oo}-troo) *adj* neuter; neutral

nevado (ner-*vah*-dhoo) *adj* snowy

nevar (ner-*vahr*) *v* snow

neve (*neh*-ver) *f* snow; **tempestade de** ~ blizzard, snowstorm

névoa (*nehv*-wer) *f* haze

nevoeiro (ner-*vway*-roo) *m* mist, fog

nevralgia (ner-vrahl-*zhee*-er) *f* neuralgia

nicotina (nee-koo-*tee*-ner) *f* nicotine

Nigéria (nee-*zheh*-r^Yer) *f* Nigeria

nigeriano (nee-zher-r^Yer-noo) *adj* Nigerian; *m* Nigerian

ninguém (neeng-*gerng*^Y) *pron* no one, nobody

ninhada (nee-*ñah*-dher) *f* litter

ninho (*nee*-ñoo) *m* nest

níquel (*nee*-kehl) *m* nickel

nível (*nee*-vehl) *m* (pl -eis) level; ~ **de vida** standard of living

nivelar (nee-ver-*lahr*) *v* level

nó (no) *m* knot; lump; *****dar um** ~ tie; *****fazer um** ~ knot; ~ **corrediço** loop; ~ **dos dedos** knuckle

nobre (*no*-bhrer) *adj* noble

nobreza (noo-*bhray*-zer) *f* nobility

noção (noo-*serng*^w) *f* (pl noções) notion; idea

nocivo (noo-*see*-voo) *adj* harmful

nocturno (no-*toor*-noo) *adj* nightly

nódoa (*no*-dhwer) *f* spot, stain; ~ **negra** bruise

nogado (noo-*gah*-dhoo) *m* nougat

noite (*noi*-ter) *f* night; evening; **de** ~ by night; **durante a** ~ overnight; **esta** ~ tonight

noiva (*noi*-ver) *f* fiancée; bride

noivado (noi-vah-dhoo) *m* engagement

noivo (*noi*-voo) *adj* engaged; *m* fiancé; bridegroom

nojento (noo-*zhayngn*-too) *adj* revolting

nome (*noa*-mer) *m* name; denomination; **em** ~ **de** on behalf of, in the name of; ~ **de batismo** _Br_ Christian name; ~ **próprio** first name, Christian name

nomeação (noo-m ^{Y} er-_serng_ ^{W}) _f_ (pl -ções) nomination; appointment

*nomear (noo-m ^{Y} _ahr_) _v_ name; mention; nominate, appoint

nominal (noo-mee-_nahl_) _adj_ (pl -ais) nominal

nono (_noa_-noo) _num_ ninth

nordeste (nor-_dehs_-ter) _m_ north-east

nórdico (_nor_-dhee-koo) _adj_ northern

norma (_nor_-mer) _f_ standard; rule

normal (nor-_mahl_) _adj_ (pl -ais) regular, normal; standard

noroeste (no-_rwehs_-ter) _m_ north-west

norte (_nor_-ter) _m_ north; **do** ~ northerly

Noruega (no-_rweh_-ger) _f_ Norway

norueguês (no-rway-_gaysh_) _adj_ Norwegian; _m_ Norwegian

nos (noosh) _pron_ us, to us, ourselves

nós (noosh) _pron_ we; us; ~ **próprios** ourselves

nosso (_no_-soo) _adj_ our

nostalgia (noosh-tahl-_zhee_-er) _f_ homesickness

nota (_no_-ter) _f_ note; mark; ~ **de banco** banknote; ~ **de encomenda** order-form

notar (noo-_tahr_) _v_ notice

notário (noo-tah-r ^{Y} oo) _m_ notary

notável (noo-tah-vehl) _adj_ (pl -eis) remarkable, striking, noticeable; considerable

notícia (noo-tee-s ^{Y} er) _f_ news; notice

noticiar (noo-tee-s ^{Y} ah-r ^{Y} oo) _m_ news

notificar (noo-ter-fee-_kahr_) _v_ notify

notório (noo-to-r ^{Y} oo) _adj_ notorious

Nova Zelândia (_no_-ver zer-_lerngn_-d ^{Y} er) New Zealand

nove (_no_-ver) _num_ nine

Novembro (noo-_vayngm_-broo) No-

vember

noventa (noo-_vayngn_-ter) _num_ ninety

novo (_noa_-voo) _adj_ new; **de** ~ again

noz (nosh) _f_ nut; walnut; ~ **moscada** nutmeg

nu (noo) _adj_ nude; naked, bare; _m_ nude

nuance (_nwerng_-ser) _f_ nuance

nublado (noo-_bhlah_-dhoo) _adj_ cloudy, overcast

nuca (_noo_-ker) _f_ nape of the neck

nuclear (noo-kl ^{Y} ahr) _adj_ nuclear

núcleo (noo-kl ^{Y} oo) _m_ core, nucleus

nulo (_noo_-loo) _adj_ void

numeral (noo-mer-_rahl_) _m_ (pl -ais) numeral

número (_noo_-mer-roo) _m_ number; quantity; act; ~ **de matrícula** registration number

numeroso (noo-mer-_roa_-zoo) _adj_ numerous

nunca (_noong_-ker) _adv_ never

nutritivo (noo-tree-_tee_-voo) _adj_ nutritious

nuvem (_noo_-verng ^{Y}) _f_ cloud

nylon (_nigh_-lon) _m_ nylon

O

o¹ (oo) _art_ (f a) the _art_

o² (oo) _pron_ it, him; ~ **que** what; ~ **quê** what

oásis (_wah_-zeesh) _m_ oasis

obedecer (oo-bher-dher-_sayr_) _v_ obey

obediência (oo-bher-dh ^{Y} ayng-s ^{Y} er) _f_ obedience

obediente (oo-bher-dh ^{Y} ayngn-ter) _adj_ obedient

obesidade (oo-bher-zee-_dhah_-dher) _f_ fatness

obeso (oo-_bheh_-zoo) _adj_ corpulent

objecção (oobh-zheh-_serng_ ^{W}) _f_ (pl

-ções) objection; **fazer ~ a mind**

objectar (oobh-zheh-*tahr*) *v* object

objectivo (oobh-zheh-*tee*-voo) *adj* objective; *m* design, goal, objective; target

objecto (oobh-*zheh*-too) *m* object

oblíquo (oo-*bhlee*-kwoo) *adj* slanting

oblongo (oobh-*lawng*-goo) *adj* oblong

obra (o-bhrer) *f* work; **~ de arte** work of art

obra-prima (obh-rer-*pree*-mer) *f* masterpiece

obrigação (oobh-ree-ger-*serng*ᵂ) *f* (pl -ções) bond

obrigado (oobh-ree-*gah*-dhoo) *adj* obliged; **obrigado!** thank you!

obrigar (oobh-ree-*gahr*) *v* oblige; compel, force

obrigatório (oobh-ree-ger-*to*-rᵞoo) *adj* compulsory, obligatory

obsceno (oobhsh-*say*-noo) *adj* obscene

obscuro (oobhsh-*koo*-roo) *adj* dim; obscure

observação (oobh-serr-ver-*serng*ᵂ) *f* (pl -ções) observation; remark

observar (oobh-serr-*vahr*) *v* observe; view, note, watch; remark

observatório (oobh-serr-ver-*to*-rᵞoo) *m* observatory

obsessão (oobh-ser-*serng*ᵂ) *f* (pl -sões) obsession

obstáculo (oobhsh-*tah*-koo-loo) *m* obstacle

obstinado (oobhsh-tee-*nah*-dhoo) *adj* dogged, obstinate

*obstruir (oobhsh-*trweer*) *v* block

*obter (oobh-*tayr*) *v* obtain; *get

obturação (oobh-too-rer-*serng*ᵂ) *f* (pl -ções) filling

obtuso (oobh-*too*-zoo) *adj* dumb

óbvio (*obh*-vᵞoo) *adj* obvious; apparent

ocasião (oo-ker-zᵞ*erng*ᵂ) *f* (pl -iões) occasion; chance

ocasionalmente (oo-ker-zᵞoo-nahl-mayng-ter) *adv* occasionally

oceano (oo-s*ᵞer*-noo) *m* ocean; **Oceano Pacífico** Pacific Ocean

ocidental (oo-see-dhayng-*tahl*) *adj* (pl -ais) western, westerly

ocidente (oo-see-*dhayng*-ter) *m* west

ocioso (oo-s*ᵞoa*-zoo) *adj* idle

oco (*oa*-koo) *adj* hollow

ocorrência (oo-koo-*rrayng*-sᵞer) *f* occurrence

oculista (o-koo-*leesh*-ter) *m* optician; oculist

óculos (*o*-koo-loosh) *mpl* glasses; spectacles; **~ escuros** sun-glasses *pl;* **~ para mergulhar** diving goggles

ocultar (oo-kool-*tahr*) *v* conceal

ocupação (oo-koo-per-*serng*ᵂ) *f* (pl -ções) business, occupation

ocupado (oo-koo-*pah*-dhoo) *adj* occupied; engaged, busy

ocupar (oo-koo-*pahr*) *v* occupy; *take up; **ocupar-se de** attend to; look after

*odiar (oo-dh*ᵞahr*) *v* hate

ódio (*o*-dhᵞoo) *m* hatred, hate

odor (oo-*dhoar*) *m* odour

oeste (*wehsh*-ter) *m* west

ofender (oo-fayng-*dayr*) *v* offend; wound, injure; *hurt

ofensa (oo-*fayng*-ser) *f* offence

ofensiva (oo-fayng-*see*-ver) *f* offensive

ofensivo (oo-fayng-*see*-voo) *adj* offensive

oferecer (oo-fer-rer-*sayr*) *v* present, offer

oferta (oo-*fehr*-ter) *f* offer; supply; gift

oficial (oo-fee-s*ᵞahl*) *adj* (pl -ais) official; *m* officer; **~ de diligências** bailiff

oficina (oo-fee-*see*-ner) *f* workshop

ofício (oo-*fee*-sʸoo) *m* trade

oficioso (oo-fee-sʸoa-zoo) *adj* unofficial

oitavo (oi-*tah*-voo) *num* eighth

oitenta (oi-*tayngn*-ter) *num* eighty

oito (*oi*-too) *num* eight

olá! (o-*lah*) hello!

olaria (oo-ler-*ree*-er) *f* earthenware

*olear (oo-*lʸahr*) *v* lubricate

óleo (*ol*-ʸoo) *m* oil; ~ **capilar** hair-oil; ~ **combustível** fuel oil; ~ **de bronzear** suntan oil; ~ **de lubrificação** lubrication oil; ~ **de mesa** salad-oil

oleoso (oo-lʸoa-zoo) *adj* oily; greasy

olhadela (oo-lʸer-*dheh*-ler) *f* look

olhar (oo-*lʸahr*) *v* look; *m* look; ~ **para** look at

olho (*oa*-lʸoo) *m* eye

ombro (*awngm*-broo) *m* shoulder

omeleta (oa-mer-*lay*-ter) *f* omelette

omitir (oo-mee-*teer*) *v* omit; *leave out, fail

omnipotente (om-nee-poo-*tayngn*-ter) *adj* omnipotent

onda (*awngn*-der) *f* wave

onde (*awngn*-der) *adv* where; ~ **quer que** wherever; ~ **quer que seja** anywhere

*ondear (awngn-*dʸahr*) *v* wave

ondulação (awngn-doo-ler-*serngʷ*) *f* (pl -ções) wave

ondulado (awngn-doo-*lah*-dhoo) *adj* wavy

ondulante (awngn-doo-*lerngn*-ter) *adj* undulating

ônibus (*o*-nee-bhoosh) *mBr* (pl ~) coach; bus

ónix (*oa*-neeks) *m* onyx

ontem (*awngn*-terngʸ) *adv* yesterday

onze (*awng*-zer) *num* eleven

opala (oo-*pah*-ler) *f* opal

ópera (o-per-rer) *f* opera; opera house

operação (oo-per-rer-*serngʷ*) *f* (pl -ções) operation; surgery

operar (oo-per-*rahr*) *v* operate

operário (oo-per-rah-rʸoo) *m* workman; labourer

opereta (oo-per-*ray*-ter) *f* operetta

opinião (oo-pee-nʸerngʷ) *f* (pl -iões) opinion; view

*opor (oo-*poar*) *v* object; ***opor-se** oppose; ***opor-se a** object to

oportunidade (oo-poor-too-nee-*dhah*-dher) *f* opportunity; chance

oportuno (oo-poor-*too*-noo) *adj* convenient

oposição (oo-poo-zee-*serngʷ*) *f* (pl -ções) opposition

oposto (oo-*poash*-too) *adj* opposite

oprimir (oo-pree-*meer*) *v* oppress; press

optimismo (op-tee-*meezh*-moo) *m* optimism

optimista (op-tee-*meesh*-ter) *adj* optimistic; *m* optimist

óptimo (o-tee-moo) *adj* excellent

oração (oo-rer-*serngʷ*) *f* (pl -ções) prayer

oral (oo-*rahl*) *adj* (pl orais) oral

orçamento (oor-ser-*mayngn*-too) *m* budget

ordem (or-derngʸ) *f* order; method; command; congregation; **em** ~ in order; ~ **postal** money order

ordenado (oor-der-*nah*-dhoo) *m* salary, pay

ordenar (oor-der-*nahr*) *v* sort, arrange; order

ordinário (oor-dee-nah-rʸoo) *adj* vulgar; simple; common

orelha (oo-*ray*-lʸer) *f* ear

órfão (or-ferngʷ) *m* (pl ~s) orphan

orgânico (oor-*ger*-nee-koo) *adj* organic

organização (oor-ger-nee-zer-*serngʷ*) *f* (pl -ções) organization

organizar (oor-ger-*nee*-zahr) *v* arrange, organize

orgão (or-gerng^w) *m* (pl ~s) organ

orgulho (oor-goo-l^Yoo) *m* pride

orgulhoso (oor-goo-l^Yoa-zoo) *adj* proud

oriental (oo-r^Yayngn-tahl) *adj* (pl -ais) easterly; oriental, eastern

orientar-se (oo-r^Yayngn-tahr-ser) *v* orientate

oriente (oo-r^Yayngn-ter) *m* Orient

origem (oo-ree-zherng^Y) *f* origin; rise

original (oo-ree-zhee-nahl) *adj* (pl -ais) original

originalmente (oo-ree-zhee-nahl-mayngn-ter) *adv* originally

orla (or-ler) *f* edge

ornamental (oor-ner-mayngn-tahl) *adj* (pl -ais) ornamental

ornamento (oor-ner-mayngn-too) *m* ornament

orquestra (or-kehsh-trer) *f* orchestra

ortodoxo (oo-toa-dhok-soo) *adj* orthodox

ortografia (or-toa-grer-free-er) *f* spelling

orvalho (oor-vah-l^Yoo) *m* dew

os (oosh) *pron* them

osso (oa-soo) *m* bone

ostra (oash-trer) *f* oyster

ou (oa) *conj* or; **ou ... ou** either ... or

ouriço (oa-ree-soo) *m* hedgehog

ouriço-do-mar (oa-ree-soo-doo-mahr) *m* sea-urchin

ourives (oa-ree-vish) *m* goldsmith; silversmith

ouro (oa-roo) *m* gold; **de ~** golden; **mina de ~** goldmine

ousar (oa-zahr) *v* dare

outeiro (oa-tay-roo) *m* hillock

Outono (oa-toa-noo) *m* autumn; fall *nAm*

outro (oa-troo) *adj* different, other; **um ~** another

Outubro (oa-too-bhroo) October

ouvido (oa-vee-dhoo) *m* hearing

ouvinte (oa-veengn-ter) *m* listener; auditor

***ouvir** (oa-veer) *v* *hear

ova (o-ver) *f* roe

oval (oo-vahl) *adj* (pl ovais) oval

ovelha (oo-vay-l^Yer) *f* sheep

ovo (oa-voo) *m* egg; **gema de ~** egg-yolk

oxigénio (ok-see-zheh-n^Yoo) *m* oxygen

P

pá (pah) *f* spade; shovel

paciência (per-s^Yayng-s^Yer) *f* patience

paciente (per-s^Yayngn-ter) *adj* patient

pacífico (per-see-fee-koo) *adj* pacifist

pacifismo (per-ser-feezh-moo) *m* pacifism

pacifista (per-ser-feesh-ter) *m* pacifist

pacote (per-ko-ter) *m* packet

padaria (per-dher-ree-er) *f* bakery

padeiro (pah-day-roo) *m* baker

padrão (per-dhrerng^w) *m* (pl -rões) pattern; standard

padrasto (per-dhrahsh-too) *m* stepfather

padre (pah-dhrer) *m* priest; father

padrinho (per-dhree-ñoo) *m* godfather

pagamento (per-ger-mayngn-too) *m* payment

pagão (per-gerng^w) *adj* (pl ~s) pagan, heathen; *m* pagan, heathen

pagar (per-gahr) *v* *pay; **pago adiantado** prepaid; **porte pago** post-paid

página (pah-zhee-ner) *f* page

pai (pigh) *m* father; dad; **pais** parents *pl*; **pais adoptivos** foster-parents *pl*

painel (pigh-nehl) *m* (pl -néis) panel; **~ de instrumentos** dashboard

país (per-eesh) *m* country, land; **~ natal** native country

paisagem (pigh-*zah*-zherng^y) *f* landscape; scenery; ~ **marítima** seascape

Os Países Baixos (oosh per-*ee*-zızh *bhigh*-shoosh) the Netherlands

paixão (pigh-*sherng*^w) *f* (pl -xões) passion

paizinho (pigh-*zee*-ñoo) *m* daddy

palacete (per-ler-*say*-ter) *m* mansion

palácio (per-*lah*-s^yoo) *m* palace

paladar (per-ler-*dhahr*) *m* taste

palavra (per-*lah*-vrer) *f* word

palco (*pahl*-koo) *m* stage

palerma (per-*lehr*-mer) *adj* silly

palestra (per-*lehsh*-trer) *f* lecture

paletó (per-ler-*to*) *mBr* jacket

palha (*pah*-l^yer) *f* straw

palhaço (per-l^y*ah*-soo) *m* clown

pálido (*pah*-lee-dhoo) *adj* pale

palito (per-*lee*-too) *m* toothpick

palmada (pahl-*mah*-dher) *f* smack

palmeira (pahl-*may*-rer) *f* palm

palpável (pahl-*pah*-vehl) *adj* (pl -eis) palpable

pálpebra (*pahl*-per-bhrer) *f* eyelid

palpitação (pahl-pee-ter-*serng*^w) *f* (pl -ções) palpitation

pancada (perng-*kah*-dher) *f* knock; bump, blow

pancadinha (perng-kah-*dhee*-ñah) *f* tap

panela (per-*neh*-ler) *f* pan; ~ **de pressão** pressure-cooker

pânico (*per*-nee-koo) *m* panic

pano (*per*-noo) *m* cloth; curtain; ~ **da loiça** tea-cloth; ~ **turco** terry cloth

pântano (*perng*-ter-noo) *m* marsh, swamp, bog

pantanoso (perng-ter-*noa*-zoo) *adj* marshy

pantufa (perng-*too*-fer) *f* slipper

pão (perng^w) *m* (pl pães) bread; loaf; ~ **integral** wholemeal bread

pãozinho (perng^w-*zee*-ñoo) *m* (pl pãezinhos) roll

papa (*pah*-per) *m* pope

papagaio (per-per-*gigh*-oo) *m* parrot

papeira (per-*pay*-rer) *f* mumps

papel (per-*pehl*) *m* (pl -éis) paper; **de** ~ paper; ~ **carbono** *Br* carbon paper; ~ **de carta** notepaper; ~ **de embrulho** wrapping paper; ~ **de máquina** typing paper; ~ **de parede** wallpaper; ~ **higiénico** toilet-paper; ~ **para escrever** writing-paper; notepaper; ~ **químico** carbon paper

papelão (per-per-*lerng*^w) *mBr* cardboard

papelaria (per-per-ler-*ree*-er) *f* stationer's

papoila (per-*poi*-ler) *f* poppy

papoula (per-*poa*-ler) *f* poppy

paquete (per-*kay*-ter) *m* liner; pageboy

paquistanês (per-keesh-ter-*naysh*) *adj* Pakistani; *m* Pakistani

Paquistão (per-kee-*shterng*^w) *m* Pakistan

par (pahr) *adj* even; *m* couple, pair

para (*per*-rer) *prep* for, to, at, in order to; ~ **com** towards; ~ **que** so that; ~ **quê** what for; ~ **trás** backwards

parabéns (per-rer-*bherng*^ysh) *mpl* congratulations *pl*

pára-brisas (pah-rer-*bhree*-zersh) *m* (pl ~) windscreen; windshield *nAm*; **limpa** ~ windscreen wiper

pára-choques (per-rer-*sho*-kersh) *m* (pl ~) bumper; fender

parada (per-*rah*-dher) *f* parade; *fBr* stop

parafuso (per-rer-*foo*-zoo) *m* screw

paragem (per-*rer*-zherng^y) *f* stop; ~ **de táxis** taxi stand *Am*

parágrafo (per-*rah*-grer-foo) *m* paragraph

paralelo (per-rer-*leh*-loo) *adj* parallel; *m* parallel

paralisar (per-rer-lee-*zahr*) *v* paralyse

paralisia infantil (per-rer-lee-*zee*-er eeng-ferngn-*teel*) polio

paralítico (per-rer-*lee*-tee-koo) *adj* lame

parar (per-*rahr*) *v* stop; pull up, halt

pára-sol (pah-rer-*sol*) *m* (pl -sóis) sunshade

parceiro (perr-*say*-roo) *m* partner

parcela (pahr-*seh*-ler) *f* plot

parcial (pahr-sᵞahl) *adj* (pl -ais) partial

parcialmente (pahr-sᵞahl-*mayngn*-ter) *adv* partly

parcómetro (perr-*ko*-mer-troo) *m* parking meter

pardal (perr-*dahl*) *m* (pl -ais) sparrow

parecer (per-rer-*sayr*) *v* appear; look, seem; *m* opinion, view

paredão (per-rer-*dherng*ʷ) *m* (pl -dões) embankment

parede (per-*ray*-dher) *f* wall

parente (per-*rayngn*-ter) *m* relative, relation

pargo (*pahr*-goo) *m* bream

parlamentar (perr-ler-mayngn-*tahr*) *adj* parliamentary

parlamento (perr-ler-*mayngn*-too) *m* parliament

paróquia (per-*ro*-kᵞer) *f* parish

parque (*pahr*-ker) *m* park; ~ **de campismo** camping site; ~ **de estacionamento** car park; parking lot *Am;* ~ **nacional** national park

parte (*pahr*-ter) *f* part; share; **à** ~ apart, separately; **em** ~ partly; **em** ~ **alguma** nowhere; **em qualquer** ~ somewhere; ~ **de cima** top; ~ **superior** top side; **por toda a** ~ everywhere; throughout

parteira (perr-*tay*-rer) *f* midwife

participação (pahr-ter-see-per-*serng*ʷ) *f* (pl -ções) announcement; participation

participante (pahr-ter-see-*perngn*-ter) *m* participant

participar (perr-ter-see-*pahr*) *v* notify; report; participate

particular (perr-*tee*-koo-*lahr*) *adj* private; individual; special; **em** ~ in particular

particularidade (perr-tee-koo-ler-ree-*dhah*-dher) *f* detail; peculiarity

particularmente (perr-tee-koo-lerr-*mayngn*-ter) *adv* specially

partida (per-*tee*-dher) *f* departure; **ponto de** ~ starting-point

partido (perr-*tee*-dhoo) *adj* broken; *m* party; side

partilhar (perr-tee-*lᵞahr*) *v* share

partir (perr-*teer*) *v* *break, crack; *leave, depart, pull out, *set out; check out; **a** ~ **de** from, as from

parto (*pahr*-too) *m* childbirth, delivery

parvo (*pahr*-voo) *adj* foolish

Páscoa (*persh*-kwer) *f* Easter

passa (*pah*-ser) *f* raisin; ~ **de Corinto** currant

passado (per-*sah*-dhoo) *adj* past; *m* past

passageiro (per-ser-*zhay*-roo) *m* passenger

passagem (per-*sah*-zherng ᵞ) *f* passage; aisle; ~ **de nível** level crossing, crossing; ~ **de pedestres** *Br* pedestrian crossing; crosswalk *nAm;* ~ **de peões** pedestrian crossing; crosswalk *nAm;* ~ **estreita** bottleneck

passajar (per-ser-*zhahr*) *v* darn

passaporte (per-ser-*por*-ter) *m* passport; **inspecção de passaportes** passport control

passar (per-*sahr*) *v* pass; *spend; **deixar** ~ overlook; **não** ~ **a ferro**

drip-dry, wash and wear; ~ **a fer-ro** iron; press; ~ **por** pass by; *go through

pássaro (*pah*-ser-roo) m small bird

passatempo (pah-ser-*tayngm*-poo) m hobby

passeante (per-s^yerngn-ter) m walker

***passear** (per-s^yahr) v walk

passeio (per-*say*-oo) m stroll, walk; promenade; trip; pavement, foot-path; sidewalk nAm; **beira do ~** curb; ~ **de carro** drive

passivo (per-*see*-voo) adj passive

passo (*pah*-soo) m pace; move, step; gait

pasta (*pahsh*-ter) f paste; briefcase, attaché case; ~ **da escola** satchel; ~ **de dentes** toothpaste

pastagem (persh-*tah*-zherng^y) f pasture

pastar (persh-*tahr*) v graze

pastelaria (persh-ter-ler-*ree*-er) f pastry shop; pastry

pastilha (persh-*tee*-l^yer) f tablet; ~ **elástica** chewing-gum

pastor (persh-*toar*) m shepherd; parson, minister, rector; clergyman

pata (*pah*-ter) f paw

patente (per-*tayngn*-ter) f patent; rank

patife (per-*tee*-fer) m villain, bastard, rascal

patim (per-teeng) m skate

patinagem (per-tee-*nah*-zherng^y) f roller-skating; skating

patinar (per-tee-*nahr*) v skate

patinhar (per-tee-*ñahr*) v wade

pátio (*pah*-t^yoo) m yard

pato (*pah*-too) m duck

patrão (per-*trerng*^w) m (pl -rões) master; boss, employer

pátria (*pah*-tr^yer) f fatherland, native country

patriota (per-*tr^yo*-ter) m patriot

patroa (per-*troa*-er) f mistress

patrulha (per-troo-l^yer) f patrol

patrulhar (per-troo-l^yahr) v patrol

pau (pou) m stick

pausa (*pou*-zer) f pause

pavão (per-*verng*^w) m (pl pavões) peacock

pavilhão (per-vee-l^y*erng*^w) m (pl -hões) pavilion; ~ **de caça** lodge

pavimentar (per-vee-mayngn-*tahr*) v pave

pavimento (per-vee-*mayngn*-too) m pavement

pavor (per-*voar*) m horror

paz (pahsh) f peace

pé (peh) m foot; **a ~** on foot, walking; **em ~** upright, erect; ***estar de ~** *stand

peão (p^y*erng*^w) m (pl peões) pedestrian; pawn; **interdito a peões** no pedestrians

peça (*peh*-ser) f piece; **de duas peças** two-piece; ~ **de teatro** play; ~ **num acto** one-act play; ~ **sobresselente** spare part

pecado (per-*kah*-dhoo) m sin

pechincha (pɪ-*sheeng*-sher) f bargain

peculiar (per-koo-l^y*ahr*) adj peculiar

pedaço (per-*dhah*-soo) m scrap, bit; ~ **grosso** chunk

pedal (per-*dhahl*) m (pl -ais) pedal

pé-de-cabra (peh-dher-*kahbh*-rer) m crowbar

pedestre (per-*dhehsh*-trer) mBr pedestrian

pedicuro (per-dhee-*koo*-roo) m pedicure

pedido (per-*dhee*-dhoo) m request; application; ~ **de socorro** distress signal

***pedir** (per-*dheer*) v ask; beg; charge; ~ **boleia** hitchhike; ~ **carona** Br hitchhike; ~ **emprestado** borrow

pedra (*peh*-dhrer) f stone; **de ~**

stone; ~ **de isqueiro** flint; ~ **preciosa** gem; stone; ~ **tumular** tombstone

pedra-pomes (peh-dhrer-*poa*-mish) f pumice stone

pedregulho (per-dhrer-*goo*-lᵞoo) m boulder

pedreira (per-*dhray*-rer) f quarry

pedreiro (per-*dhray*-roo) m bricklayer

pega¹ (*peh*-ger) f handle

pega² (*pay*-ger) f magpie

pegajoso (per-ger-*zhoa*-zoo) adj sticky

pegar (per-*gahr*) v *stick

peito (*pay*-too) m chest; breast, bosom

peitoril (pay-too-*reel*) m (pl -is) window-sill

peixaria (pay-sher-*ree*-er) f fish shop

peixe (*pay*-sher) m fish; ~ **miúdo** whitebait

pele (*peh*-ler) f skin; hide; fur; furs; **de** ~ leather

peleiro (per-*lay*-roo) m furrier

pelica (per-*lee*-ker) f kid

pelicano (per-lee-*ker*-noo) m pelican

película (per-*lee*-koo-ler) f film

pêlo (*pay*-loo) m hair

pélvis (*pehl*-veesh) f pelvis

pena (*pay*-ner) f regret; feather; ~ **de morte** death penalty; **que pena!** what a pity!; *ter ~ **de** pity

penalidade (per-ner-lee-*dhah*-dher) f penalty; **grande** ~ penalty kick

pender (payn̄g-*dayr*) v *hang

pendurar (payn̄g-doo-*rahr*) v *hang

peneira (per-*nay*-rer) m sieve

peneirar (per-nay-*rahr*) v sieve; sift

penetrar (per-ner-*trahr*) v penetrate

penhorista (pɪ-ñoo-*reesh*-ter) m pawnbroker

penicilina (per-nee-see-*lee*-ner) f penicillin

península (per-*neeng*-soo-ler) f peninsula

pensador (payn̄g-ser-*dhoar*) m thinker

pensamento (payn̄g-ser-*mayn̄g*-too) m thought; idea

pensão (payn̄g-*sern̄g*ʷ) f (pl -sões) pension; board; boarding-house, guest-house; ~ **alimentícia** alimony; ~ **completa** full board, bed and board, board and lodging

pensar (payn̄g-*sahr*) v *think; guess; dress; ~ **em** *think of

pensativo (payn̄g-ser-*tee*-voo) adj thoughtful

pensionista (payn̄g-sʸoo-*neesh*-ter) m boarder

penso (*payn̄g*-soo) m dressing; ~ **higiénico** sanitary towel; ~ **rápido** plaster

pente (*payn̄g*-ter) m comb; ~ **de bolso** pocket-comb

penteado (payn̄g-tʸah-dhoo) m hairdo

***pentear** (payn̄g-tʸahr) v comb

Pentecostes (payn̄g-ter-*kosh*-tɪsh) m Whitsun

penugem (per-*noo*-zhern̄gᵞ) f down

pepino (per-*pee*-noo) m cucumber

pequeno (per-*kay*-noo) adj little, small; petty, minor

pêra (*pay*-rer) f pear

perca (*pehr*-ker) f perch

perceber (perr-ser-*bhayr*) v *understand; *take, *see; sense, realize; ~ **mal** *misunderstand

percentagem (perr-sayn̄g-*tah*-zhern̄gᵞ) f percentage

percepção (perr-seh-*sern̄g*ʷ) f (pl -ções) perception

perceptível (perr-seh-*tee*-vehl) adj (pl -eis) perceptible; noticeable

percevejo (perr-ser-*vay*-zhoo) m bug

perda (*payr*-dher) f loss

perdão (perr-*dhern̄g*ʷ) m (pl -dões) pardon; grace; **perdão!** sorry!

***perder** (perr-*dhayr*) v *lose; miss

perdido (perr-*dhee*-dhoo) *adj* lost; missing

perdiz (perr-*dheesh*) *f* partridge

perdoar (perr-*dhwahr*) *v* *forgive

perecer (per-rer-*sayr*) *v* perish

peregrinação (per-rer-gree-ner-*serng*ʷ) *f* (pl -cões) pilgrimage

peregrino (per-rer-*gree*-noo) *m* pilgrim

perfeição (perr-fay-*serng*ʷ) *f* (pl -cões) perfection

perfeito (perr-*fay*-too) *adj* perfect; faultless

perfume (perr-*foo*-mer) *m* perfume; scent

perfurar (perr-foo-*rahr*) *v* pierce

pergunta (perr-*goongn*-ter) *f* question; inquiry, query

perguntar (perr-goongn-*tahr*) *v* ask; enquire; ~ **a si próprio** wonder

perícia (per-ree-sʸer) *f* skill

perigo (per-*ree*-goo) *m* peril, danger; risk; distress

perigoso (per-ree-*goa*-zoo) *adj* perilous, dangerous; risky

periódico (per-rʸo-dhee-koo) *adj* periodical; *m* periodical

período (per-*ree*ᵒᵒ-dhoo) *m* period; term

periquito (pɪ-ree-*kee*-too) *m* parakeet

perito (per-*ree*-too) *adj* skilled; *m* expert

perjúrio (perr-*zhoo*-rʸoo) *m* perjury

permanecer (perr-mer-ner-*sayr*) *v* stay

permanente (perr-mer-*nayngn*-ter) *adj* permanent; *f* permanent wave

permitir (perr-mee-*teer*) *v* permit; allow; **permitir-se** afford

perna (*pehr*-ner) *f* leg; **barriga da** ~ calf; **de pernas para o ar** upside-down

pérola (*peh*-roo-ler) *f* pearl

perpendicular (perr-payngn-dee-koo-*lahr*) *adj* perpendicular

persa (*pehr*-ser) *adj* Persian; *m* Persian

*perseguir (pehr-ser-*geer*) *v* chase

perseverar (per-ser-ver-*rahr*) *v* *keep up

Pérsia (*pehr*-sʸer) *f* Persia

persiana (perr-sʸer-ner) *f* blind; shutter

persistir (perr-seesh-*teer*) *v* insist

personalidade (perr-soo-ner-lee-*dhah*-dher) *f* personality

perspectiva (perrsh-peh-*tee*-ver) *f* prospect; perspective

perspicaz (perrsh-pee-*kahsh*) *adj* keen

perspiração (perrsh-pee-rer-*serng*ʷ) *f* perspiration

persuadir (perr-swer-*dheer*) *v* persuade

pertencer (perr-tayng-*sayr*) *v* belong; ~ **a** belong to

perto (*pehr*-too) *adv* near; ~ **de** near; by

perturbação (perr-toor-bher-*serng*ʷ) *f* (pl -cões) disturbance

perturbar (perr-toor-*bhahr*) *v* embarrass; disturb

peru (per-*roo*) *m* turkey

peruca (per-*roo*-ker) *f* wig

pesado (per-*zah*-dhoo) *adj* heavy

pesar (per-*zahr*) *v* weigh

pesca (*pehsh*-ker) *f* fishing industry; **aparelho de** ~ fishing tackle; **cana de** ~ fishing rod; **licença de** ~ fishing licence; **linha de** ~ fishing line

pescada (pɪsh-*kah*-dher) *f* whiting

pescador (pɪsh-ker-*dhoar*) *m* fisherman

pescar (pɪsh-*kahr*) *v* fish; ~ **à linha** angle

pescoço (pɪsh-*koa*-soo) *m* neck

peso (*pay*-zoo) *m* weight

pesquisar (pɪsh-kee-*zahr*) *v* search

pêssego (*pay*-ser-goo) *m* peach

pessimismo (per-see-*meezh*-moo) *m* pessimism

pessimista (per-see-*meesh*-ter) *adj* pessimistic; *m* pessimist

pessoa (per-*soa*-er) *f* person; **pessoas** people *pl;* **por ~** per person; **qualquer ~** anyone, anybody; **uma ~** one

pessoal¹ (per-*swahl*) *m* personnel, staff

pessoal² (per-*swahl*) *adj* (*pl* -ais) personal; private

pestana (pish-*ter*-ner) *f* eyelash

pétala (*peh*-ter-ler) *f* petal

petição (per-tee-*serng*ʷ) *f* (*pl* -ções) petition

petróleo (per-*tro*-lʸoo) *m* petroleum; paraffin, oil; **poço de ~** oil-well

peúga (pʸoo-ger) *f* sock

pianista (pʸer-*neesh*-ter) *m* pianist

piano (pʸer-noo) *m* piano; **~ de cauda** grand piano

picada (pee-*kah*-dher) *f* sting; bite

picadela (pee-ker-*dheh*-ler) *f* sting

picante (pee-*kerng*n-ter) *adj* spicy, savoury

picar (pee-*kahr*) *v* prick; *sting; chop, mince

picareta (pee-ker-*ray*-ter) *f* pick-axe

piedade (pʸay-*dhah*-dher) *f* pity

pijama (pee-*zher*-mer) *m* pyjamas *pl*

pilar (pee-*lahr*) *m* pillar; column

pilha (*pee*-lʸer) *f* stack, pile; **~ eléctrica** battery

piloto (pee-*loa*-too) *m* pilot

pílula (*pee*-loo-ler) *f* pill

pimenta (pee-*mayng*n-ter) *f* pepper

pinça (*peeng*-ser) *f* tweezers *pl*

pincel (peeng-*sehl*) *m* (*pl* -céis) brush; paint-brush; **~ da barba** shaving-brush

pingente (peeng-*zhayng*n-ter) *m* pendant

pinguim (peeng-*gweeng*) *m* penguin

pinheiro (pee-*ñay*-roo) *m* fir-tree

pintar (peeng-*tahr*) *v* paint; dye

pintarroxo (peengn-ter-*rroa*-shoo) *m* robin

pintor (peengn-*toar*) *m* painter

pintura (peengn-*too*-rer) *f* painting; **~ a óleo** oil-painting

pio (*pee*ᵒᵒ) *adj* pious

piolho (pʸoa-lʸoo) *m* louse

pioneiro (pʸoo-*nay*-roo) *m* pioneer

pionés (pʸoo-*nehsh*) *m* drawing-pin; thumbtack *nAm*

pior (pʸor) *adj* worse; *adv* worse, worst; **o ~** worst, the worst

pipa (*pee*-per) *f* barrel

piquenicar (pee-ker-nee-*kahr*) *v* picnic

piquenique (pee-ker-nee-ker) *m* picnic

pirata (pee-*rah*-ter) *m* pirate

pires (*pee*-rish) *m* saucer

pisca-pisca (peesh-ker-*peesh*-ker) *m* indicator

piscina (peesh-*see*-ner) *f* swimming pool

piso (*pee*-zoo) *m* floor

pista (*peesh*-ter) *f* trail; ring; track; **~ de descolagem** runway

pistão (peesh-*terng*ʷ) *m* (*pl* -tões) piston; **segmento do ~** piston ring

pistola (peesh-*to*-ler) *f* pistol

pitoresco (pee-too-*raysh*-koo) *adj* picturesque; scenic

planador (pler-ner-*dhoar*) *m* glider

planalto (pler-*nahl*-too) *m* plateau

***planear** (pler-nʸahr) *v* plan; devise

planeta (pler-*nay*-ter) *m* planet

planetário (pler-ner-*tah*-rʸoo) *m* planetarium

planície (pler-nee-sʸer) *f* plain

plano (*pler*-noo) *adj* flat, even, plane; smooth, level; *m* plan, scheme, project; **primeiro ~** foreground

planta (*plerng*n-ter) *f* plant; map

plantação (plerngn-ter-*serng*ʷ) *f* (*pl* -ções) plantation

plantar (pler*ng*n-*tahr*) v plant

plástico (*plahsh*-tee-koo) m plastic; **de ~** plastic

plataforma (pler-ter-*for*-mer) f platform

plateia (pler-*tay*-er) f stall; orchestra seat *Am*

platina (pler-*tee*-ner) f platinum

plural (ploo-*rahl*) m (pl -ais) plural

pneu (pnay°°) m tire, tyre; **~ furado** flat tyre; **~ sobresselente** spare tyre

pneumático (pnay°°-*mah*-tee-koo) adj pneumatic; inflatable

pneumonia (pnay°°-moo-*nee*-er) f pneumonia

pó (po) m powder; **~ de talco** talc powder; **pós dentífricos** toothpowder

pobre (*po*-bhrer) adj poor

pobreza (poo-*bhray*-zer) f poverty

poço (*po*-soo) m well; **~ de petróleo** oil-well

pó-de-arroz (po-der-er-*rroash*) m face-powder; **borla de ~** powder-puff; **caixa de ~** powder compact

poder (poo-*dhayr*) m power; might, authority; **~ executivo** executive

*poder (poo-*dhayr*) v *may; *might, *be able to; *can

poderoso (poo-dher-*roa*-zoo) adj mighty, powerful

podre (*poa*-dhrer) adj rotten

poeira (*pway*-rer) f dust

poeirento (pway-*rayng*n-too) adj dusty

poema (*pway*-mer) m poem

poesia (pwı-*zee*-er) f poetry

poeta (*pweh*-ter) m poet

pois (*poish*) conj because; **~ bem** granted, so be it

polaco (poo-*lah*-koo) adj Polish; m Pole

polegar (poo-ler-*gahr*) m thumb

polícia (poo-*lee*-s°er) f police pl; m policeman; **delegacia de ~** *Br* police-station; **posto da ~** police-station

pólio (*po*-l°oo) f polio

*polir (poo-*leer*) v polish

política (poo-*lee*-tee-ker) f politics; policy

político (poo-*lee*-tee-koo) adj political; m politician

polivalente (poo-lee-ver-*layng*n-ter) adj all-round

Polónia (poo-*loa*-n°er) f Poland

pólo norte (*po*-loo *nor*-ter) North Pole

pólo sul (*po*-loo sool) South Pole

poltrona (poal-*troa*-ner) f armchair, easy chair

poluição (poo-lwee-*serng*ʷ) f (pl -ções) pollution

polvo (*poal*-voo) m octopus

pólvora (*pol*-voo-rer) f gunpowder

pomar (poo-*mahr*) m orchard

pombo (*pawng*m-boo) m pigeon

ponderado (pawng-der-*rah*-dhoo) adj sober

ponderar (pawng-der-*rahr*) v consider, *think over

pónei (*po*-nay) m pony

ponta (*pawng*n-ter) f tip

pontada (pawng-*tah*-dher) f stitch

pontapé (pawng-ter-*peh*) m kick; ***dar um ~** kick; **~ de saída** kick-off

ponte (*pawng*n-ter) f bridge; **~ levadiça** drawbridge; **~ pênsil** suspension bridge

pontiagudo (pawng-t°er-*goo*-dhoo) adj pointed

ponto (*pawng*n-too) m stitch; point; period; item, issue; **~ de congelação** freezing-point; **~ de encontro** meeting-place; **~ de interesse** sight; **~ de interrogação** question mark; **~ e vírgula** semi-colon; **~**

final full stop

pontual (pawngn-*twahl*) adj (pl -ais) punctual

popelina (po-per-*lee*-ner) f poplin

população (poo-poo-ler-*serng*ᵂ) f (pl -ções) population

popular (poo-poo-*lahr*) adj popular; vulgar

populoso (poo-poo-*loa*-zoo) adj populous

por (poor) prep by; for; past

***pôr** (poar) v *put; *set; *lay

porão (poo-*rerng*ᵂ) m (pl porões) hold; *mBr* basement; cellar

porca (*por*-ker) f nut

porção (poor-*serng*ᵂ) f (pl -ções) portion; helping

porcaria (poor-ker-*ree*-er) f muck

porcelana (poor-ser-*ler*-ner) f porcelain; china

porcento (poor-*sayngn*-too) m percent

porco (*poar*-koo) m pig; adj foul, dirty; **pele de ~** pigskin

porco-espinho (poar-koo-eesh-*pee*-ñoo) m porcupine

porque (*poor*-ker) conj because; as, for

porquê (poor-*kay*) adv why

porquinho-da-índia (poor-kee-ñoo-der-*eengn*-dᵞer) m guinea-pig

porta (*por*-ter) f door; gate; **~ corrediça** sliding door; **~ giratória** revolving door

portador (poor-ter-*dhoar*) m bearer

portagem (poor-ter-*zherng*ᵞ) f toll

porta-moedas (por-ter-*mweh*-dhersh) m (pl **~**) purse

portanto (poor-*terngn*-too) conj so; therefore

portão (poor-*terng*ᵂ) m (pl -tões) gate

portar-se (poor-*tahr*-ser) v behave; **~ mal** misbehave

portátil (poor-*tah*-teel) adj (pl -teis)

portable

porteiro (poor-*tay*-roo) m doorman, porter, door-keeper; concierge, janitor

porte pago (*por*-ter pah-goo) postage paid

porto (*poar*-too) m harbour, port; **~ marítimo** seaport

Portugal (poor-too-*gahl*) m Portugal

português (poor-too-*gaysh*) adj Portuguese; m Portuguese

posição (poo-zee-*serng*ᵂ) f (pl -ções) position

positivo (poo-zee-*tee*-voo) adj positive; m positive

possante (poo-*serngn*-ter) adj strong

posse (*po*-ser) f possession

possesso (poo-*seh*-soo) adj possessed

possibilidade (poo-ser-bher-lee-*dhah*-dher) f possibility

possibilitar (poo-ser-bher-lee-*tahr*) v enable

possível (poo-*see*-vehl) adj (pl -eis) possible; attainable

***possuir** (poo-*sweer*) v possess; own

postal (poosh-*tahl*) m (pl -ais) card; **~ ilustrado** picture postcard, postcard

posta-restante (posh-ter-rish-*terngn*-ter) poste restante

poste (*posh*-ter) m pole, post; **~ de iluminação** lamp-post; **~ indicador** milepost, signpost

posto (*poash*-too) m post; station; **~ de socorros** first-aid post

potável (poo-*tah*-vehl) adj (pl -veis) for drinking

potência (poo-*tayng*-sᵞer) f power; capacity

pouco (*poa*-koo) adj little; **daqui a ~** shortly; **dentro em ~** presently; **poucos** few; **um ~ mais** some more

poupado (poa-*pah*-dhoo) adj economical

poupar (poa-*pahr*) v save

pousada (poa-*zah*-dher) f inn

pousar (poa-*zahr*) v *lay; place, *set, *put

povo (*poa*-voo) m people; nation, folk

praça (*prah*-ser) f square; ~ **de táxis** taxi rank; ~ **de touros** bullring; ~ **do mercado** market-place

praça-forte (prah-ser-*for*-ter) f stronghold

prado (*prah*-dhoo) m meadow

praga (*prah*-ger) f curse; plague

praguejar (prer-ger-*zhahr*) v curse

praia (*prigh*-er) f beach; ~ **para nudistas** nudist beach

prancha (*prerng*-sher) f plank; ~ **de surf** surf-board

prata (*prah*-ter) f silver; **de** ~ silver; **pratas** silverware

prateleira (prer-ter-*lay*-rer) f shelf

prática (*prah*-tee-ker) f practice

praticamente (prah-tee-ker-*mayngn*-ter) adv practically

praticar (prer-tee-*kahr*) v practise; commit

prático (*prah*-tee-koo) adj practical

prato (*prah*-too) m plate, dish; course; ~ **de sopa** soup-plate

prazer (prer-*zayr*) m pleasure; joy, fun

precário (prer-*kah*-rʸoo) adj precarious, critical

precaução (prer-kou-*serng*ʷ) f (pl -ções) precaution

***precaver-se** (prer-ker-*vayr*-ser) v beware

precedente (prer-ser-*dhayngn*-ter) adj last, previous, preceding

preceder (prer-ser-*dhayr*) v precede

preceptor (prer-seh-*toar*) m tutor

precioso (prer-sʸoa-zoo) adj precious

precipício (prer-ser-*pee*-sʸoo) m precipice

precipitação (prer-ser-pee-ter-*serng*ʷ) f (pl -ções) precipitation

precipitado (prer-ser-pee-*tah*-dhoo) adj rash

precipitar-se (prer-ser-pee-*tahr*-ser) v dash

precisão (prer-see-*zherng*ʷ) f (pl -sões) need; precision

precisar (prer-see-*zahr*) v need

preciso (prer-*see*-zoo) adj precise

preço (*pray*-soo) m price; cost, charge; rate; **baixa de preços** slump; **fixar o** ~ **de** price; ~ **da viagem** fare; ~ **de compra** purchase price; ~ **de entrada** entrance-fee; ~ **do bilhete** fare

preconceito (prer-kawng-*say*-too) m prejudice

predecessor (prer-dher-ser-*soar*) m predecessor

prédio (*preh*-dhʸoo) m building; house; ~ **de andares** block of flats, apartment house Am; ~ **de apartamentos** Br apartment house Am

***predizer** (prer-dhee-*zayr*) v predict

preencher (prʸayng-*shayr*) v fill in; fill out Am

preferência (prer-fer-*rayng*-sʸer) f preference; ***dar** ~ **a** prefer

preferido (prer-fer-*ree*-dhoo) adj favourite

***preferir** (prer-fer-*reer*) v prefer

preferível (prer-fer-*ree*-vehl) adj (pl -eis) preferable

prefixo (prer-*feek*-soo) m prefix

prega (*preh*-ger) f crease

pregar¹ (preh-*gahr*) v preach

pregar² (prer-*gahr*) v nail

prego (*preh*-goo) m nail

preguiçoso (prer-gee-*soa*-zoo) adj lazy

preia-mar (*pray*-er-mahr) f high tide

prejudicar (prer-zhoo-dhee-*kahr*) v

harm

prejudicial (prer-zhoo-dhee-s^Yahl) adj (pl -ais) hurtful, harmful

prejuízo (prer-zhwee-zoo) m harm

preliminar (prer-ler-mee-nahr) adj preliminary

prematuro (prer-mer-too-roo) adj premature

prémio (preh-m^Yoo) m prize; award; premium; ~ **de consolação** consolation prize

prender (prayng-dayr) v attach, fasten; imprison, arrest

prenome (prer-noa-mer) mBr first name

preocupação (pr^Yoo-koo-per-serng^W) f (pl -cões) trouble; concern; worry; care

preocupado (pr^Yoo-koo-pah-dhoo) adj worried; concerned

preocupar-se com (pr^Yoo-koo-pahr-ser) care about

preparação (prer-per-rer-serng^W) f (pl -cões) preparation; background

preparado (prer-per-rah-dhoo) adj prepared; ready

preparar (prer-per-rahr) v prepare; cook

preposição (prer-poo-zee-serng^W) f (pl -cões) preposition

presbitério (prizh-bhee-teh-r^Yoo) m parsonage, vicarage

prescrever (prish-krer-vayr) v prescribe

presença (prer-zayng-ser) f presence

presente (prer-zayngn-ter) adj present; m present; gift

presidente (prer-zee-dhayngn-ter) m chairman, president; ~ **da Câmara** mayor

pressa (preh-ser) f haste, hurry; speed; **com** ~ in haste

pressão (prer-serng^W) f (pl -sões) pressure; ~ **atmosférica** atmos-

pheric pressure; ~ **do óleo** oil pressure; ~ **dos pneus** tyre pressure

prestação (prish-ter-serng^W) f (pl -cões) instalment; **pagar a prestações** *pay on account

prestar (prish-tahr) v render; ~ **contas de** account for

prestidigitador (prish-tee-dher-zhee-ter-dhoar) m magician

prestígio (prish-tee-zh^Yoo) m prestige

presumível (prer-zoo-mee-vehl) adj (pl -eis) presumable

presunçoso (prer-zoong-soa-zoo) adj presumptuous

presunto (prer-zoongn-too) m ham

pretender (prer-tayngn-dayr) v pursue

pretensão (prer-tayngn-serng^W) f (pl -sões) claim

pretensioso (prer-tayngn-s^Yoa-zoo) adj conceited

pretenso (prer-tayng-soo) adj so-called

pretexto (prer-taysh-too) m pretext, pretence

preto (pray-too) adj black

***prevenir** (prer-ver-neer) v anticipate; warn

preventivo (prer-vayngn-tee-voo) adj preventive

***prever** (prer-vayr) v anticipate; forecast

prévio (preh-v^Yoo) adj previous

previsão (prer-vee-zerng^W) f (pl -sões) outlook; forecast

prima (pree-mer) f cousin

primário (pree-mah-r^Yoo) adj primary

Primavera (pree-mer-veh-rer) f spring; springtime

primeiro (pree-may-roo) num first; adj primary, foremost; adv at first; before

primeiro-ministro (pree-may-roo-mer-neesh-troo) m Prime Minister, pre-

mier
primo (*pree*-moo) *m* cousin
primordial (pree-moor-*dᵞahl*) *adj* (pl -ais) primary
princesa (preeng-*say*-zer) *f* princess
principal (preeng-se-*pahl*) *adj* (pl -ais) principal; chief, leading, main; cardinal; **sector ~ mains** *pl*.
principalmente (preeng-see-perl-*mayngn*-ter) *adv* especially, mainly; mostly
príncipe (*preeng*-see-per) *m* prince
principiante (preeng-see-pᵞ*erngn*-ter) *m* beginner; learner
principiar (preeng-see-pᵞ*ahr*) *v* commence, *begin
princípio (preeng-*see*-pᵞoo) *m* beginning; principle
prioridade (prᵞoo-ree-*dhah*-dher) *f* priority; right of way
prisão (pree-*zerng*ʷ) *f* (pl -sões) arrest; jail, prison; **~ de ventre** constipation
prisioneiro (pree-zᵞoo-*nay*-roo) *m* prisoner; **~ de guerra** prisoner of war
privado (pree-*vah*-dhoo) *adj* private
privar de (pree-*vahr* der) deprive of
privilégio (prer-vee-*leh*-zhᵞoo) *m* privilege
problema (proo-*bhlay*-mer) *m* problem; question
proceder (proo-ser-*dhayr*) *v* proceed
procedimento (proo-ser-dhee-*mayngn*-too) *m* process
processo (proo-*seh*-soo) *m* process; lawsuit; procedure
procissão (proo-see-*serng*ʷ) *f* (pl -sões) procession
proclamar (proo-kler-*mahr*) *v* proclaim
procura (proo-*koo*-rer) *f* demand
procurar (proo-koo-*rahr*) *v* hunt for, look for, search, *seek; look up
pródigo (*pro*-dhee-goo) *adj* lavish

produção (proo-dhoo-*serng*ʷ) *f* (pl -cões) production; output; **~ em série** mass production
produto (proo-*dhoo*-too) *m* product; produce; **~ de limpeza** cleaning fluid; **produtos alimentícios** foodstuffs *pl*
produtor (proo-dhoo-*toar*) *m* producer
***produzir** (proo-dhoo-*zeer*) *v* produce; generate
professar (proo-fer-*sahr*) *v* confess
professor (proo-fer-*soar*) *m* teacher, schoolmaster, master; professor
professora (proo-fer-*soa*-rer) *f* teacher
profeta (proo-*feh*-ter) *m* prophet
profissão (proo-fee-*serng*ʷ) *f* (pl -sões) profession
profissional (proo-fee-sᵞoo-*nahl*) *adj* (pl -ais) professional
profundidade (proo-foongn-dee-*dhah*-dher) *f* depth
profundo (proo-*foongn*-doo) *adj* deep; profound
programa (proo-*grer*-mer) *m* programme
***progredir** (proo-gray-*dheer*) *v* *get on; *make progress
progressista (proo-grer-*seesh*-ter) *adj* progressive
progressivo (proo-grer-*see*-voo) *adj* progressive
progresso (proo-*greh*-soo) *m* progress
proibido (prwee-*bhee*-dhoo) *adj* prohibited; **~ entrar** no entry; **~ fumar** no smoking
proibir (prwee-*bheer*) *v* *forbid; prohibit
proibitivo (prwee-bhee-*tee*-voo) *adj* prohibitive
projecto (proo-*zheh*-too) *m* project; design
projector (proo-zheh-*toar*) *m* spotlight
prolongamento (proo-lawng-ger-*mayngn*-too) *m* extension

prolongar (proo-lawng-*gahr*) v extend; renew

promessa (proo-*meh*-ser) f promise

prometer (proo-mer-*tayr*) v promise

promoção (proo-moo-*serng*ʷ) f (pl -ções) promotion

promontório (proo-mawng-*to*-rʸoo) m headland

promover (proo-moo-*vayr*) v promote

pronome (proo-*noa*-mer) m pronoun

pronto (*prawng*-too) adj prompt; ready

pronúncia (proo-*noong*-sʸer) f pronunciation

pronunciar (proo-noong-sʸ*ahr*) v pronounce

propaganda (proo-per-*gerng*-der) f propaganda

propenso (proo-*payng*-soo) adj inclined

*propor (proo-*poar*) v propose

proporção (proo-poor-*serng*ʷ) f (pl -ções) proportion

proporcional (proo-poor-sʸoo-*nahl*) adj (pl -ais) proportional

proporcionar (proo-poor-sʸoo-*nahr*) v furnish, provide

propositado (proo-poo-zee-*tah*-dhoo) adj on purpose

propósito (proo-*po*-zee-too) m purpose; **a ~** by the way; **de ~** on purpose

proposta (proo-*posh*-ter) f proposal, proposition

propriedade (proo-prʸay-*dhah*-dher) f property; estate

proprietário (proo-prʸay-*tah*-rʸoo) m owner, proprietor; landlord

próprio (*pro*-prʸoo) adj own

propulsionar (proo-pool-sʸoo-*nahr*) v propel

prospecto (proosh-*peh*-too) m prospectus

prosperidade (proosh-per-ree-*dhah*-dher) f prosperity

próspero (*prosh*-per-roo) adj prosperous

*prosseguir (proo-ser-*geer*) v carry on; continue, pursue, proceed

prostituta (proosh-tee-*too*-ter) f whore, prostitute

protecção (proo-teh-*serng*ʷ) f (pl -ções) protection

proteger (proo-tɪ-*zhayr*) v protect

proteína (proa-tay-*ee*-ner) f protein

protelação (proo-ter-ler-*serng*ʷ) f (pl -ções) respite

protestante (proo-tɪsh-*terng*-ter) adj Protestant

protestar (proo-tɪsh-*tahr*) v protest

protesto (proo-*tehsh*-too) m protest

prova (*pro*-ver) f proof; token, evidence; experiment, test; print

provar (proo-*vahr*) v prove; try on; taste

provável (proo-*vah*-vehl) adj (pl -eis) probable; likely

provavelmente (proo-vah-vehl-*mayng*-ter) adv probably

proveniência (proo-ver-nʸ*ayng*-sʸer) f origin

provérbio (proo-*vehr*-bhʸoo) m proverb

*prover de (proo-*vayr* der) furnish with

província (proo-*veeng*-sʸer) f province

provincial (proo-veeng-sʸ*ahl*) adj (pl -ais) provincial

provisão (proo-vee-*zerng*ʷ) f (pl -sões) supply; **provisões** provisions pl

provisório (proo-vee-*zo*-rʸoo) adj provisional; temporary

provocar (proo-voo-*kahr*) v cause

proximidades (pro-ser-mee-*dhah*-dhersh) fpl vicinity

próximo (*pro*-see-moo) adj nearby, close; next; oncoming

prudente (proo-*dhayngn*-ter) *adj* cautious; wary

prurido (proo-*ree*-dhoo) *m* itch

psicanalista (psee-ker-ner-*leesh*-ter) *m* psychoanalyst; analyst

psicologia (psee-koo-loo-*zhee*-er) *f* psychology

psicológico (psee-koo-*lo*-zhee-koo) *adj* psychological

psicólogo (psee-*ko*-loo-goo) *m* psychologist

psiquiatra (psee-k*ʸah*-trer) *m* psychiatrist

psíquico (*psee*-kee-koo) *adj* psychic

publicação (poo-bhlee-ker-*serngʷ*) *f* (pl -ções) publication

publicar (poo-bhlee-*kahr*) *v* publish

publicidade (poo-bhlee-see-*dhah*-dher) *f* advertising, publicity

público (*poo*-bhlee-koo) *adj* public; *m* public

pulmão (pool-*merngʷ*) *m* (pl -mões) lung

pulo (*poo*-loo) *m* hop

pulóver (poo-*loa*-vehr) *m* pullover

púlpito (*pool*-pee-too) *m* pulpit

pulseira (pool-*say*-rer) *f* bracelet, bangle

pulso (*pool*-soo) *m* wrist; pulse

pulverizador (pool-ver-ree-zer-*dhoar*) *m* atomizer

punhado (poo-*ñah*-dhoo) *m* handful

punho (*poo*-ñoo) *m* fist; cuff

puro (*poo*-roo) *adj* pure; sheer; neat, clean; ~ **sangue** thoroughbred

purulento (poo-roo-*layngn*-too) *adj* purulent

pus (poosh) *m* pus

puxar (poo-*shahr*) *v* *draw; pull; ~ **o lustro a** brush

puzzle (*per*-zler) *m* puzzle

Q

quadrado (kwer-*dhrah*-dhoo) *adj* square; *m* square; check

quadriculado (kwer-dhree-koo-*lah*-dhoo) *adj* chequered

quadrilha (kwer-*dhree*-lʸer) *f* gang

quadro (*kwah*-dhroo) *m* picture; board; cadre; ~ **de distribuição** switchboard; ~ **preto** blackboard

qual (kwahl) *pron* (pl quais) which

qualidade (kwer-lee-*dhah*-dher) *f* quality; **de primeira** ~ first-class; first-rate

qualificado (kwer-ler-fee-*kah*-dhoo) *adj* qualified

qualificar-se (kwer-ler-fee-*kahr*-ser) *v* qualify

qualquer (kwahl-*kehr*) *adj* any; whichever

quando (*kwerngn*-doo) *adv* when; *conj* when; ~ **muito** at most; ~ **quer que** whenever

quantia (kwerngn-*tee*-er) *f* amount

quantidade (kwerngn-tee-*dhah*-dher) *f* number, quantity; lot, amount

quanto (*kwerngn*-too) *adv* how much; ~ **a** as regards; ~ **mais ... mais** the ... the; **quantos** how many

quarenta (kwer-*rayngn*-ter) *num* forty

quarentena (kwer-rayngn-*tay*-ner) *f* quarantine

quarta-feira (kwahr-ter-*fay*-rer) *f* Wednesday

quartel (kwahr-*tehl*) *m* (pl -téis) barracks *pl*

quartel-general (kwahr-tehl-zher-ner-*rahl*) *m* headquarters *pl*

quarto (*kwahr*-too) *num* fourth; *m* quarter; chamber, room; bedroom; ~ **das crianças** nursery; ~ **de banho** bathroom; ~ **de hóspedes** spare room, guest-room; ~ **de**

vestir dressing-room; ~ e pequeno almoço bed and breakfast; ~ individual single room

quase (*kwah*-zer) *adv* almost; nearly

quatro (*kwah*-troo) *num* four

que (ker) *pron* that; which, who; *adv* how; *conj* that; as, than

quebra-cabeças (keh-bhrer-ker-*bhay*-sersh) *m* (pl ~) jigsaw puzzle

quebradiço (ker-bhrer-*dhee*-soo) *adj* fragile

quebra-nozes (keh-bhrer-*no*-zersh) *m* (pl ~) nutcrackers *pl*

quebrar (ker-*bhrahr*) *v* crack; fracture, *break

queda (*keh*-dher) *f* fall; ~ de água waterfall

queijo (*kay*-zhoo) *m* cheese

queimadura (kay-mer-*dhoo*-rer) *f* burn; ~ do sol sunburn

queimar (kay-*mahr*) *v* *burn

queixa (*kay*-sher) *f* complaint

queixar-se (kay-*shahr*-ser) *v* complain

queixo (*kay*-shoo) *m* chin

quem (kerng^Y) *pron* who; a ~ whom; ~ quer que whoever

Quénia (*kayng*-n^Yah) *m* Kenya

quente (*kayng*n-ter) *adj* warm, hot

*querer (ker-*rayr*) *v* want

querido (ker-*ree*-dhoo) *adj* beloved, dear; *m* darling, sweetheart

querosene (kay-roa-*zeh*-ner) *m* kerosene

quer ... quer (kehr) whether ... or

questão (kish-*terng*^W) *f* (pl -tões) question; matter, issue

quiçá (kee-*ser*) *adv* perhaps

quieto (k^Y-eh-too) *adj* quiet

quilate (kee-*lah*-ter) *m* carat

quilha (kee-l^Yer) *f* keel

quilo (kee-loo) *m* kilogram

quilograma (kee-loo-*grer*-mer) *m* kilogram

quilometragem (kee-loo-mer-*trah*-zherng^Y) *m* distance in kilometres

quilómetro (kee-*lo*-mer-troo) *m* kilometre

química (kee-mee-ker) *f* chemistry

químico (kee-mee-koo) *adj* chemical

quinina (kee-*nee*-ner) *f* quinine

quinta (*keeng*n-ter) *f* farm

quinta-feira (keeng^n-ter-*fay*-rer) *f* Thursday

quinto (*keeng*n-too) *num* fifth

quinze (*keeng*-zer) *num* fifteen

quinzena (keeng-*zay*-ner) *f* fortnight

quiosque (k^Yosh-ker) *m* kiosk; ~ de jornais newsstand; ~ de livros bookstand

quota (*kwo*-ter) *f* quota

quotidiano (kwoo-tee-*dh*^Yer-noo) *adj* everyday, daily

R

rã (rrerng) *f* frog

rabanete (rrer-bher-*nay*-ter) *m* radish

rábano (*rrah*-bher-noo) *m* turnip; ~ silvestre horseradish

rabo (*rrah*-bhoo) *m* bottom

raça (*rrah*-ser) *f* race, breed

ração (rrer-*serng*^W) *f* (pl rações) ration

racial (rrer-s^Yahl) *adj* (pl -ais) racial

raciocinar (rrer-s^Yoo-see-*nahr*) *v* reason

radiador (rrer-dh^Yer-*dhoar*) *m* radiator

radical (rrer-dhee-*kahl*) *adj* (pl -ais) radical

rádio (*rrah*-dh^Yoo) *m* wireless, radio

radiografar (rrah-dh^Yoo-grer-*fahr*) *v* X-ray

radiografia (rrah-dh^Yoo-grer-*fee*-er) *f* X-ray

rainha (rrer-*ee*-ñer) *f* queen

raio (*rrigh*-oo) *m* ray, beam; radius;

spoke

raiva (*rrigh*-ver) *f* rabies; rage

raivoso (rrigh-*voa*-zoo) *adj* mad

raiz (rrer-*eesh*) *f* root

rajada (rrer-*zhah*-dher) *f* blow, gust

ralador (rrer-ler-*dhoar*) *m* grater

ralhar (rrer-*lYahr*) *v* scold

raminho (rrer-*mee*-ñoo) *m* twig

ramo (*rrer*-moo) *m* bough, branch; bunch, bouquet

rampa (*rrerngm*-per) *f* ramp

rançoso (rrerng-*soa*-zoo) *adj* rancid

ranger (rrerng-*zhayr*) *v* creak

rapariga (rrer-per-*ree*-ger) *f* girl

rapaz (rrer-*pahsh*) *m* boy; lad

rapidamente (rrer-pee-dher-*mayngn*-ter) *adv* soon; rapidly

rapidez (rrer-pee-*dhaysh*) *f* speed; haste

rápido (*rrah*-pee-dhoo) *adj* rapid; quick, fast, swift

rápidos (*rrah*-pee-dhoosh) *mpl* rapids *pl*

raposa (rrah-*poa*-zer) *f* fox

raptor (rrerp-*toar*) *m* hijacker

raqueta (rrer-*kay*-ter) *f* racquet

raramente (rrer-rer-*mayngn*-ter) *adv* rarely; scarcely, seldom

raro (*rrah*-roo) *adj* rare; infrequent, uncommon

rasgão (rrerzh-*gerngw*) *m* (pl -gões) tear

rasgar (rrerzh-*gahr*) *v* rip; *tear

raso (*rrah*-zoo) *adj* flat

raspar (rrersh-*pahr*) *v* grate, scrape

rastejar (rrersh-tı-*zhahr*) *v* crawl, *creep

rasto (*rrahsh*-too) *m* trace; *seguir o ~ de trace

ratazana (rrer-ter-*zer*-ner) *f* rat

rato (*rrah*-too) *m* mouse

ravina (rrer-*vee*-ner) *f* glen

razão (rrer-*zerngw*) *f* (pl razões) reason; wits *pl*, sense; *ter ~ * be

right

razoável (rrer-*zwah*-vehl) *adj* (pl -eis) reasonable

razoavelmente (rrer-zwah-vehl-*mayngn*-ter) *adv* fairly

reabilitação (rree-er-bher-lee-ter-*serngw*) *f* (pl -cões) rehabilitation

reacção (rreeah-*serngw*) *f* (pl -cões) reaction

real (rrYahl) *adj* (pl reais) true; factual, actual, substantial; royal

realejo (rrYer-*lay*-zhoo) *m* street-organ

realidade (rrYer-lee-*dhah*-dher) *f* reality; na ~ really

realista (rrYer-*leesh*-ter) *adj* matter-of-fact

realização (rrYer-lee-zer-*serngw*) *f* (pl -cões) achievement; direction

realizar (rrYer-lee-*zahr*) *v* realize, accomplish; implement, carry out; achieve

realizável (rrYer-lee-*zah*-vehl) *adj* (pl -eis) feasible, realizable

realmente (rrYahl-*mayngn*-ter) *adv* really; actually

rebanho (rrer-*bher*-ñoo) *m* flock

rebelião (rrer-bher-*lYerngw*) *f* (pl -iões) revolt; rebellion

rebentar (rrer-bhayngn-*tahr*) *v* *burst, crack

rebocador (rrer-bhoo-ker-*dhoar*) *m* tug

rebocar (rrer-bhoo-*kahr*) *v* tow, tug

reboque (rrer-*bho*-ker) *m* trailer

rebuçado (rrer-bhoo-*sah*-dhoo) *m* sweet; candy *nAm*; **rebuçados** sweets

rebuscar (rrer-bhoosh-*kahr*) *v* search

recado (rrer-*kah*-dhoo) *m* message, errand

recarga (rrer-*kahr*-ger) *f* refill

***recear** (rrer-*sYahr*) *v* fear

receber (rrer-ser-*bhayr*) *v* receive; entertain

receio (rrer-*say*-Yoo) *m* fear

receita (rrer-*say*-ter) *f* revenue; recipe; prescription

receitar (rrer-say-*tahr*) *v* prescribe

recente (rrer-*sayngn*-ter) *adj* recent

recentemente (rrer-sayngn-ter-*mayngn*-ter) *adv* lately, recently

receoso (rrer-sᵛ-oa-zoo) *adj* frightened

recepção (rrer-seh-*serng*ʷ) *f* (pl -cões) reception; receipt, reception office

recepcionista (rrer-seh-sᵛoo-*neesh*-ter) *f* receptionist

recessão (rrer-seh-*serng*ʷ) *f* recession

recheado (rrer-*shᵛah*-dhoo) *adj* stuffed

recheio (rrer-*shay*-oo) *m* filling, stuffing

recibo (rrer-*see*-bhoo) *m* receipt

recife (rrer-*see*-fer) *m* reef

recipiente (rrer-see-pᵛ*ayngn*-ter) *m* container

recíproco (rrer-*see*-proo-koo) *adj* mutual

recital (rrer-see-*tahl*) *m* (pl -ais) recital

recolha (rrer-*koa*-lᵛer) *f* collection

recomeçar (rrer-koo-mer-*sahr*) *v* recommence; resume

recomendação (rrer-koo-mayngn-der-*serng*ʷ) *f* (pl -cões) recommendation

recomendar (rrer-koo-mayngn-*dahr*) *v* recommend

recompensa (rrer-kawngm-*payng*-ser) *f* prize, reward

recompensar (rrer-kawngm-payng-*sahr*) *v* reward

reconciliação (rrer-kawng-see-lᵛer-*serng*ʷ) *f* (pl -cões) reconciliation

reconhecer (rrer-koo-ñer-*sayr*) *v* recognize, acknowledge; confess, admit

reconhecido (rrer-koo-ñer-*see*-dhoo)

adj grateful

reconhecimento (rrer-koo-ñer-see-*mayngn*-too) *m* recognition; gratitude

recordação (rrer-koor-dher-*serng*ʷ) *f* (pl -cões) memory, remembrance; souvenir

recordar (rrer-koor-*dhahr*) *v* remind; **recordar-se** recall, remember; recollect

recorde (rrer-*kor*-dher) *m* record

recreação (rer-krᵛer-*serng*ʷ) *f* (pl -cões) recreation

recreio (rrer-*kray*-oo) *m* playground

recruta (rrer-*kroo*-ter) *m* conscript, recruit

rectangular (rreh-terng-goo-*lahr*) *adj* rectangular

rectângulo (rreh-*terng*-goo-loo) *m* oblong, rectangle

rectificação (rreh-tee-fee-ker-*serng*ʷ) *f* (pl -cões) correction

recto (*rreh*-too) *adj* right; straight; *m* rectum

recuar (rrer-*kwahr*) *v* pull back; reverse

recuperação (rrer-koo-per-rer-*serng*ʷ) *f* (pl -cões) recuperation; recovery

recuperar (rrer-koo-per-*rahr*) *v* recover

recusa (rrer-*koo*-zer) *f* refusal

recusar (rrer-koo-*zahr*) *v* refuse; reject, deny

redactor (rrer-dhah-*toar*) *m* editor

rede (*rray*-dher) *f* net; network; hammock; ~ **da bagagem** luggage rack; ~ **de pesca** fishing net; ~ **rodoviária** road system

redigir (rrer-dher-*zheer*) *v* *write

redimir (rrer-dher-*meer*) *v* redeem

redondo (rrer-*dhawngn*-doo) *adj* round

em redor (erngᵛ rrer-*dhor*) surrounding

redução (rrer-dhoo-*serng*ʷ) *f* (pl

-ções) reduction, discount, rebate

*reduzir (rrer-dhoo-*zeer*) *v* reduce; *cut

reembolsar (rr^yayngm-boal-*sahr*) *v* reimburse; refund, *repay

reembolso (rr^yayngm-*boal*-soo) *m* refund, repayment

refeição (rrer-fay-*serng*^w) *f* (pl -ções) meal; ~ ligeira snack

refém (rrer-*ferng*^y) *m* hostage

referência (rrer-fer-*rayng*-s^yer) *f* reference; ponto de ~ landmark

referente a (rrer-fer-*rayngn*-ter) concerning; about

*referir a (rrer-fer-*reer*) refer to

refinaria (rrer-fee-ner-*ree*-er) *f* refinery; ~ de petróleo oil-refinery

*reflectir (rrer-fleh-*teer*) *v* reflect; *think

reflector (rrer-fleh-*toar*) *m* reflector

reflexão (rrer-flehk-*serng*^w) *f* (pl -xões) reflection

Reforma (rrer-*for*-mer) *f* reformation

reformado (rrer-foor-*mah*-dhoo) *adj* retired

*refrear (rrer-*fr*^y*ahr*) *v* curb

refrescar (rrer-frish-*kahr*) *v* refresh

refresco (rrer-*fraysh*-koo) *m* refreshment

refúgio (rrer-*foo*-zh^yoo) *m* shelter, cover

regata (rrer-*gah*-ter) *f* regatta

*regatear (rrer-ger-*t*^y*ahr*) *v* bargain

região (rrer-zh^y*erng*^w) *f* (pl -iões) region; zone, country, district, area; ~ arborizada woodland

regime (rrer-*zhee*-mer) *m* régime; rule, government

regional (rri-zh^yoo-*nahl*) *adj* (pl -ais) regional

registar (rri-zheesh-*tahr*) *v* register; book, record; registar-se check in

registo (rri-*zheesh*-too) *m* record; registration

regra (*rreh*-grer) *f* rule; em ~ as a rule

regressar (rrer-grer-*sahr*) *v* *get back, *go back

regresso (rrer-*greh*-soo) *m* return; viagem de ~ return journey

régua (*rreh*-gwer) *f* ruler

regulamentação (rrer-goo-ler-mayngn-ter-*serng*^w) *f* (pl -ções) regulation

regulamento (rrer-goo-ler-*mayngn*-too) *m* regulation; arrangement

regular (rrer-goo-*lahr*) *v* regulate; *adj* regular

regularizar (rrer-goo-ler-ree-*zahr*) *v* settle

rei (rray) *m* king

reinado (rray-*nah*-dhoo) *m* reign

reinar (rray-*nahr*) *v* reign

reino (*rray*-noo) *m* kingdom

reitor (rray-*toar*) *m* headmaster, principal; rector

reitoria (rray-too-*ree*-er) *f* rectory

reivindicação (rray-veengn-dee-ker-*serng*^w) *f* (pl -ções) claim

reivindicar (rray-veengn-dee-*kahr*) *v* claim

rejeitar (rri-zhay-*tahr*) *v* turn down, reject

relação (rrer-ler-*serng*^w) *f* (pl -ções) report; relation, connection, reference; relações intercourse

relâmpago (rrer-*lerngm*-per-goo) *m* lightning; flash

relance (rrer-*lerng*-ser) *m* glance

*relancear (rrer-lerng-s^y*ahr*) *v* glance

relatar (rrer-ler-*tahr*) *v* report

relativamente (rrer-ler-tee-ver-*mayngn*-ter) *adv* quite; ~ a regarding

relativo (rrer-ler-*tee*-voo) *adj* relative; comparative; ~ a regarding, with reference to

relato (rrer-*lah*-too) *m* account

relatório (rrer-ler-*to*-r^yoo) *m* report

relevante (rrer-ler-*verngn*-ter) *adj* important

relevo (rrer-*lay*-voo) *m* relief; importance

religião (rrer-lee-*zh*Yerng*W*) *f* (pl -iões) religion

religioso (rrer-lee-*zh*Yoa-zoo) *adj* religious

relíquia (rrer-*lee*-kYer) *f* relic

relógio (rrer-*lo*-zhYoo) *m* watch; clock; ~ **de bolso** pocket-watch; ~ **de pulso** wrist-watch

relojoeiro (rrer-loo-*zhway*-roo) *m* watch-maker

reluzente (rrer-loo-*zayngn*-ter) *adj* bright

*reluzir (rrer-loo-*zeer*) *v* *shine

relva (*rrehl*-ver) *f* lawn

relvado (rrehl-*vah*-dhoo) *m* lawn

remanescente (rrer-mer-nɪsh-*sayngn*-ter) *m* remnant; remainder

remar (rrer-*mahr*) *v* row

remédio (rrer-*meh*-dhYoo) *m* remedy

remendar (rrer-mayngn-*dhahr*) *v* mend; patch

remessa (rrer-*meh*-ser) *f* consignment; remittance

remeter (rrer-mer-*tayr*) *v* remit

remo (*rray*-moo) *m* oar; paddle

remoção (rrer-moo-*serng*W) *f* (pl -ções) removal

remoto (rrer-*mo*-too) *adj* remote

remover (rrer-moo-*vayr*) *v* remove

remuneração (rrer-moo-ner-rer-*serng*W) *f* (pl -ções) remuneration

remunerar (rrer-moo-ner-*rahr*) *v* remunerate

rena (*rray*-ner) *f* reindeer

renda (*rrayngn*-der) *f* lace; rent; ***fazer** ~ crochet

render (rrayngn-*dayr*) *v* yield; **render-se** surrender

rendição (rrayngn-dee-*serng*W) *f* (pl -ções) surrender

rendimento (rrayngn-dee-*mayngn*-too) *m* income, revenue; **rendimentos** earnings *pl*

renome (rrer-*noa*-mer) *m* reputation

renovar (rrer-noo-*vahr*) *v* renew

rentável (*rrayngn*-tah-vehl) *adj* (pl -eis) paying

renunciar (rrer-noong-s*Y*ahr) *v* *give up

reparação (rrer-per-rer-*serng*W) *f* (pl -ções) reparation

reparar (rrer-per-*rahr*) *v* repair; mend, fix; ~ **em** notice

repartição (rrer-perr-tee-*serng*W) *f* (pl -ções) agency

repartir (rrer-perr-*teer*) *v* divide

repelente (rrer-per-*layngn*-ter) *adj* repellent, repulsive

de repente (der rrer-*payngn*-ter) suddenly

repentinamente (rrer-payngn-tee-ner-*mayngn*-ter) *adv* suddenly

repentino (rrer-payngn-*tee*-noo) *adj* sudden

repertório (rrer-perr-*to*-rYoo) *m* repertory

repetição (rrer-per-tee-*serng*W) *f* (pl -ções) repetition

repetidamente (rrer-per-tee-dher-*mayngn*-ter) *adv* again and again

*repetir (rrer-per-*teer*) *v* repeat

repleto (rrer-*pleh*-too) *adj* full up; chock-full

repórter (rrer-*por*-tehr) *m* reporter

repousar (rrer-poa-*zahr*) *v* rest

repreender (rrer-prYayngn-*dayr*) *v* scold, reprimand

representação (rrer-prer-zayngn-ter-*serng*W) *f* (pl -ções) representation; performance, show

representante (rrer-prer-zayngn-*terngn*-ter) *m* agent

representar (rrer-prer-zayngn-*tahr*) *v* represent; act

representativo (rrer-prer-zayngn-ter-tee-voo) *adj* representative

reprimir (rrer-pree-*meer*) *v* suppress; curb

reprodução (rrer-proo-dhoo-*serng*ᵂ) *f* (pl -ções) reproduction

*reproduzir (rrer-proo-dhoo-*zeer*) *v* reproduce

reprovar (rrer-proo-*vahr*) *v* reject; fail

réptil (*rrehp*-teel) *m* (pl -teis) reptile

república (rreh-*poo*-bhlee-ker) *f* republic

republicano (rreh-poo-bhlee-*ker*-noo) *adj* republican

repugnância (rrer-poog-*nerng*-sᵛer) *f* dislike

repugnante (rrer-poog-*nerng*-ter) *adj* repellent; disgusting

reputação (rrer-poo-ter-*serng*ᵂ) *f* (pl -ções) reputation, fame

*requerer (rrer-ker-*rayr*) *v* request; demand

requintado (rrer-keengn-*tah*-dhoo) *adj* exquisite, delicious

rés-do-chão (rrehzh-doo-*sherng*ᵂ) *m* ground floor

reserva (rrer-*zehr*-ver) *f* store, reserve; booking, reservation; qualification; **de ~** spare; **~ natural** game reserve

reservar (rrer-zehr-*vahr*) *v* reserve; book

reservatório (rrer-zerr-ver-*to*-rYoo) *m* reservoir

resgate (rrizh-*gah*-ter) *m* ransom

residência (rrer-zee-*dhayng*-sᵛer) *f* residence

residente (rrer-zee-*dhayng*n-ter) *m* resident; *adj* resident

residir (rrer-zee-*dheer*) *v* reside

resina (rrer-*zee*-ner) *f* resin

resistência (rrer-zeesh-*tayng*-sᵛer) *f* resistance; strength; stamina

resistir (rrer-zeesh-*teer*) *v* resist

resmungar (rrizh-moong-*gahr*) *v* grumble

resoluto (rrer-zoo-*loo*-too) *adj* resolute; determined

resolver (rrer-zoal-*vayr*) *v* solve; settle; decide

respectivo (rrish-peh-*tee*-voo) *adj* respective

respeitante a (rrish-pay-*terng*n-ter er) as regards

respeitar (rrish-pay-*tahr*) *v* respect

respeitável (rrish-pay-*tah*-vehl) *adj* (pl -eis) respectable

respeito (rrish-*pay*-too) *m* respect; regard; **a ~ de** about; **com ~ a** regarding; ***dizer ~ a** concern; touch; **no que diz ~ a** as regards

respeitoso (rrish-pay-*toa*-zoo) *adj* respectful

respiração (rrish-pee-rer-*serng*ᵂ) *f* respiration; breath, breathing

respirar (rrish-pee-*rahr*) *v* breathe

responder (rish-pawng-*dayr*) *v* answer, reply; **~ a** answer

responsabilidade (rrish-pawng-ser-bher-lee-*dhah*-dher) *f* responsibility; liability

responsável (rrish-pawng-*sah*-vehl) *adj* (pl -eis) responsible; liable

resposta (rrish-*posh*-ter) *f* answer, reply; **em ~** in reply; **sem ~** unanswered

ressaca (rrer-*sah*-ker) *f* undercurrent; *mBr* hangover

ressonar (rrer-soo-*nahr*) *v* snore

restabelecer-se (rrish-ter-bher-ler-*sayr*-ser) *v* recover

restabelecimento (rısh-ter-bher-ler-see-*mayng*n-too) *m* recovery

restante (rrish-*terng*n-ter) *adj* remaining; *m* remainder

restaurante (rrish-tou-*rerng*n-ter) *m* restaurant

resto (*rrehsh*-too) *m* rest; remainder

restrição (rrish-tree-*serng*ʷ) *f* (pl -ções) limitation, restriction

resultado (rrer-zool-*tah*-dhoo) *m* result; effect, outcome, issue; score

resultar (rrer-zool-*tahr*) *v* result; appear

resumo (rrer-*zoo*-moo) *m* summary, résumé, survey

retaguarda (rreh-ter-*gwahr*-dher) *f* rear

retalhista (rrer-ter-lʸeesh-ter) *m* retailer

*reter (rrer-*tayr*) *v* restrain

retina (rrer-*tee*-ner) *f* retina

retirar (rrer-tee-*rahr*) *v* *withdraw

retrato (rrer-*trah*-too) *m* portrait

retretes (rrer-*tray*-tersh) *fpl* toilet

reumatismo (rrayᵒᵒ-mer-*teezh*-moo) *m* rheumatism

reunião (rrʸoo-n*ʸerng*ʷ) *f* (pl -iões) meeting; assembly, rally

reunir (rrʸoo-*neer*) *v* reunite; unite; join; gather, assemble

revelação (rrer-ver-ler-*serng*ʷ) *f* (pl -ções) revelation

revelar (rrer-ver-*lahr*) *v* reveal; *give away; develop; **revelar-se** prove

revendedor (rrer-vayngn-der-*dhoar*) *m* retailer

*rever (rrer-*vayr*) *v* overhaul, revise

reverso (rrer-*vehr*-soo) *m* reverse

revés (rrer-*vehsh*) *m* reverse; **de ~ askew**

reviravolta (rrer-vee-rer-*vol*-ter) *f* reverse

revisor (rrer-vee-*zoar*) *m* ticket collector

revista (rrer-*veesh*-ter) *f* review, magazine; revue; **~ mensal** monthly magazine

revistar (rrer-veesh-*tahr*) *v* search

revogar (rrer-voo-*gahr*) *v* cancel

revolta (rrer-*vol*-ter) *f* revolt, rebellion

revoltante (rrer-voal-*terngn*-ter) *adj* revolting

revoltar-se (rrer-voal-*tahr*-ser) *v* revolt

revolução (rrer-voo-loo-*serng*ʷ) *f* (pl -ções) revolution

revolucionário (rrer-voo-loo-sʸoo-*nah*-rʸoo) *adj* revolutionary

revólver (rrer-*vol*-vehr) *m* gun, revolver

rezar (rrer-*zahr*) *v* pray

riacho (rrʸah-shoo) *m* brook

ribeiro (rree-*bhay*-roo) *m* stream

rico (*ree*-koo) *adj* rich; wealthy

ridicularizar (rree-dhee-koo-ler-ree-*zahr*) *v* ridicule

ridículo (rree-*dhee*-koo-loo) *adj* ludicrous, ridiculous

rigoroso (rree-goo-*roa*-zoo) *adj* severe, strict; bleak

rim (rreeng) *m* kidney

rima (*ree*-mer) *f* rhyme

rímel (*ree*-mehl) *m* mascara

rinoceronte (rree-noo-ser-*rawngn*-ter) *m* rhinoceros

rio (*ree*ᵒᵒ) *m* river; **~ abaixo** downstream; **~ acima** upstream

riqueza (rree-*kay*-zer) *f* wealth, riches *pl*; pet

*rir (rreer) *v* laugh

risada (rree-*zah*-dher) *f* laughter

risca (*rreesh*-ker) *f* stripe; parting; **às riscas** striped

riscar (rreesh-*kahr*) *v* scratch

risco (*rreesh*-koo) *m* line; scratch; risk, hazard, chance

riso (*rree*-zoo) *m* laugh

ritmo (*rreet*-moo) *m* rhythm; pace

rival (rree-*vahl*) *m* (pl -ais) rival

rivalidade (rree-ver-lee-*dhah*-dher) *f* rivalry

rivalizar (rree-ver-lʸe-*zahr*) *v* rival

robalo (rroo-*bhah*-loo) *m* roach; bass

robusto (rroo-*bhoosh*-too) *adj* solid, robust

rocha (*rro*-sher) *f* rock

rochoso (rroo-*shoa*-zoo) *adj* rocky

roda (*rro*-dher) *f* wheel; ~ **sobresselente** spare wheel

rodar (rroo-*dhahr*) *v* turn

***rodear** (rroo-*dh*Yahr) *v* circle, encircle; surround

rodovalho (rroo-dhoo-*vah*-lYoo) *m* brill

rola (*rroa*-ler) *f* turtle dove

rolar (rroo-*lahr*) *v* roll

roldana (rroal-*der*-ner) *f* pulley

roleta (rroo-*lay*-ter) *f* roulette

rolha (*rroa*-lYer) *f* cork; stopper

roliço (rroo-*lee*-soo) *adj* plump

rolo (*rroa*-loo) *m* roll; curler

romance (rroo-*merng*-ser) *m* romance; novel; ~ **policial** detective story

romancista (rroo-merng-*seesh*-ter) *m* novelist

romântico (rroo-*merngn*-tee-koo) *adj* romantic

rombo (*rrawngm*-boo) *adj* blunt

Roménia (rroo-meh-nYer) *f* Rumania

romeno (rroo-*may*-noo) *adj* Rumanian; *m* Rumanian

romper (rrawngm-*payr*) *v* *break; *tear

rosa (*rro*-zer) *f* rose

rosado (rroo-*zah*-dhoo) *adj* rose

rosário (rroo-*zah*-rYoo) *m* rosary; beads

rosnar (rroozh-*nahr*) *v* growl

rosto (*rroash*-too) *m* face; **feição do** ~ feature

rota (*rro*-ter) *f* route; course

rotação (rroo-ter-*serng*ʷ) *f* (pl -ções) revolution

rotim (rroo-*teeng*) *m* rattan

rotina (rroo-*tee*-ner) *f* routine

rótula (*rro*-too-ler) *f* kneecap

rotunda (rroo-*toongn*-der) *f* roundabout

roubar (rroa-*bhahr*) *v* *steal; rob

roubo (*rroa*-bhoo) *m* theft, robbery

rouco (*rroa*-koo) *adj* hoarse

rouge (roozh) *m* rouge

roupa (*rroa*-per) *f* clothes *pl*; **lavar a** ~ washing; ~ **branca** linen; ~ **de cama** bedding; ~ **interior** underwear, lingerie; ~ **para lavar** laundry; washing

roupão (rroa-*perng*ʷ) *m* (pl -pões) dressing-gown; ~ **de banho** bathrobe

roupeiro (rroa-*pay*-roo) *m* wardrobe; closet *nAm*

rouxinol (rroa-shee-*nol*) *m* (pl -nóis) nightingale

rua (*rroo*-er) *f* road, street; ~ **principal** main street

rubi (rroo-*bhee*) *m* ruby

rubrica (rroo-*bhree*-ker) *f* column

rubricar (rroo-bhree-*kahr*) *v* initial

rude (*rroo*-dher) *adj* rude

ruga (*rroo*-ger) *f* wrinkle

rugido (rroo-*zhee*-dhoo) *m* roar

rugir (rroo-*zheer*) *v* roar

rugoso (rroo-*goa*-zoo) *adj* uneven

ruibarbo (rrwee-*bhahr*-bhoo) *m* rhubarb

ruído (rrwee-*ee*-dhoo) *m* noise

ruidoso (rrwee-*dhoa*-zoo) *adj* noisy

ruína (rrwee-ner) *f* destruction, ruin, ruination; ruins

rulote (rroa-*lot*) *f* caravan

rumor (rroo-*moar*) *m* rumour; roar

rural (rroo-*rahl*) *adj* (pl -ais) rural

Rússia (*rroo*-sYer) *f* Russia

russo (*rroo*-soo) *adj* Russian; *m* Russian

rústico (*rroosh*-tee-koo) *adj* rustic

S

sábado (*sah*-bher-dhoo) *m* Saturday

sabão (ser-*bherng*ʷ) *m* (pl sabões) soap; ~ **da barba** shaving-soap; ~

em pó soap powder

sabedoria (ser-bher-dhoo-*ree*-er) f wisdom; knowledge

*****saber** (ser-*bhayr*) v *know; *be able to; **a saber** namely; ~ **a** taste

sabonete (ser-bhoo-*nay*-ter) m toilet soap

sabor (ser-*bhoar*) m flavour

*****saborear** (ser-bhoo-rʸ*ahr*) v appreciate

saboroso (ser-bhoo-*roa*-zoo) adj savoury; tasty, enjoyable

saca (*sah*-ker) f sack

sacar (ser-*kahr*) v *draw

sacarina (ser-ker-*ree*-ner) f saccharin

saca-rolhas (sah-ker-*rroa*-lʸersh) m (pl ~) corkscrew

saco (*sah*-koo) m bag; ~ **das compras** shopping bag; ~ **de gelo** icebag; ~ **de mão** grip nAm; ~ **de papel** paper bag

saco-cama (*sah*-koo-ker-mer) m sleeping-bag

sacrificar (ser-krer-fee-*kahr*) v sacrifice

sacrifício (ser-krer-*fee*-sʸoo) m sacrifice

sacrilégio (ser-kree-*leh*-zhʸoo) m sacrilege

sacristão (ser-kreesh-*terng*ʷ) m (pl -stães) sexton

*****sacudir** (ser-koo-*dheer*) v *shake

safira (ser-*fee*-rer) f sapphire

sagrado (ser-*grah*-dhoo) adj holy, sacred

saia (*sigh*-er) f skirt; ~ **de baixo** slip

saibro (*sigh*-bhroo) m grit

saída (ser-*ee*-dher) f exit, way out; issue; ~ **de emergência** emergency exit

*****sair** (ser-*eer*) v *go out; check out

sal (sahl) m (pl sais) salt; **sais de banho** bath salts

sala (*sah*-ler) f drawing-room; hall; ~ **de aula** classroom; ~ **de concertos** concert hall; ~ **de espera** waiting-room; ~ **de estar** living-room, sitting-room; ~ **de exposições** showroom; ~ **de fumo** smoking-room; ~ **de jantar** dining-room; ~ **de leitura** reading-room

salada (ser-*lah*-dher) f salad

salão (ser-*lerng*ʷ) m (pl salões) salon; lounge; ~ **de baile** ballroom; ~ **de banquetes** banqueting-hall; ~ **de beleza** beauty salon

salário (ser-*lah*-rʸoo) m salary; wages pl, pay

saldo (*sahl*-doo) m balance; **saldos** sales

saleiro (ser-*lay*-roo) m salt-cellar

salgado (sahl-*gah*-dhoo) adj salty

saliva (ser-*lee*-ver) f spit

salpicar (sahl-pee-*kahr*) v splash

salsa (*sahl*-ser) f parsley

salsicha (sahl-*see*-sher) f sausage

saltar (sahl-*tahr*) v jump; *leap; skip

saltitar (sahl-tee-*tahr*) v hop; skip

salto (*sahl*-too) m jump, leap; heel; ~ **de esqui** ski-jump

salvação (sahl-ver-*serng*ʷ) f rescue

salvador (sahl-ver-*dhoar*) m saviour

salvar (sahl-*vahr*) v rescue, save

sanatório (ser-ner-*to*-rʸoo) m sanatorium

sandália (serng-*dah*-lʸer) f sandal

sanduíche (serng-*dwee*-sher) f sandwich

sangrar (serng-*grahr*) v *bleed

sangue (*serng*-ger) m blood

sanitário (ser-nee-*tah*-rʸoo) adj sanitary; m lavatory

santo (*serng*-too) m saint

santo-e-senha (serng-too-twee-*say*-ñer) m password

santuário (serng-*twah*-rʸoo) m shrine

são (serng^w) adj (pl ~s) healthy

sapataria (ser-per-ter-ree-er) f shoe-shop

sapateiro (ser-per-tay-roo) m shoe-maker

sapato (ser-pah-too) m shoe; sapatos de ginástica gym shoes; plimsolls pl, sneakers plAm; sapatos de ténis tennis shoes

sapo (sah-poo) m toad

sarampo (ser-rerngm-poo) m measles

sarapintado (ser-rer-peengn-tah-dhoo) adj spotted

sarar (ser-rahr) v heal

sardinha (serr-dhee-ñer) f sardine

satélite (ser-teh-lee-ter) m satellite

satisfação (ser-teesh-fer-serng^w) f (pl -ções) satisfaction

*satisfazer (ser-teesh-fer-zayr) v satis-fy

satisfeito (ser-teesh-fay-too) adj satis-fied; pleased, content

saudação (sou-dher-serng^w) f (pl -ções) greeting

saudar (sou-dhahr) v salute

saudável (sou-dhah-vehl) adj (pl -eis) wholesome

saúde (ser-oo-dher) f health

saudita (sou-dhee-ter) adj Saudi Arabian

sauna (sou-ner) f sauna

se (ser) pron himself, herself, itself, oneself, yourself; themselves; your-selves; conj if; whether; ~ bem que though

seara (s^yah-rer) f cornfield

sebe (seh-bher) f hedge

seca (seh-ker) f drought

secador (ser-ker-dhoar) m dryer; ~ de cabelo hair-dryer

secar (ser-kahr) v dry; drain

secção (sehk-serng^w) f (pl -ções) sec-tion; division

seco (say-koo) adj dry

secretária (ser-krer-tah-r^yer) f secre-tary; bureau, desk

secretário (ser-krer-tah-r^yoo) m secre-tary; clerk

secreto (ser-kreh-too) adj secret

século (seh-koo-loo) m century

secundário (ser-koongn-dah-r^yoo) adj secondary; subordinate

seda (say-dher) f silk; ~ artificial rayon

sedativo (ser-dher-tee-voo) m sedative

sede¹ (seh-dher) f seat

sede² (say-dher) f thirst

sedento (ser-dhayngn-too) adj thirsty

sedimento (ser-dhee-merngn-too) m deposit

sedoso (ser-dhoa-zoo) adj silken

*seduzir (ser-dhoo-zeer) v seduce

segredo (ser-gray-dhoo) m secret

em seguida (erng^y ser-gee-dher) after-wards, then

seguinte (ser-geengn-ter) adj next; following

*seguir (ser-geer) v follow; a seguir presently; *fazer seguir forward; ~ o rasto de trace

segunda-feira (ser-goongn-der-fay-rer) f Monday

segundo (ser-goongn-doo) num sec-ond; m second; prep according to

segurança (ser-goo-rerng-ser) f secur-ity; safety

segurar (ser-goo-rahr) v *hold; grasp; insure

seguro (ser-goo-roo) adj secure; safe; sound; m insurance; apólice de ~ insurance policy; ~ de viagem travel insurance; ~ de vida life in-surance

seio (say-oo) m bosom

seis (saysh) num six

seixo (say-shoo) m pebble

seja ... seja (say-zher) either ... or

sela (seh-ler) f saddle

selecção (ser-leh-*ser^oo*) *f* (pl -ções) choice, selection

seleccionado (ser-leh-s^Yoo-*ner*-dhoo) *adj* select

seleccionar (ser-leh-s^Yoo-*nahr*) *v* select

selecto (ser-*leh*-too) *adj* select

selo (*say*-loo) *m* seal; stamp; ~ **postal** postage stamp

selva (*sehl*-ver) *f* jungle

selvagem (sehl-*vah*-zherng^Y) *adj* wild, savage

sem (serng^Y) *prep* without

semáforo (ser-*mah*-foo-roo) *m* traffic light

semana (ser-*mer*-ner) *f* week

semanal (ser-mer-*nahl*) *adj* (pl -ais) weekly

***semear** (ser-m^Y*ahr*) *v* *sow

semelhança (ser-mı-l^Yerng-ser) *f* resemblance, similarity

semelhante (ser-mı-l^Yerng-ter) *adj* like, alike; similar

semente (ser-*mayng*-ter) *f* seed

semi- (ser-mee) semi

semi-círculo (ser-mee-*seer*-koo-loo) *m* semicircle

sempre (*sayngm*-prer) *adv* always, ever; ~ **que** whenever

senado (ser-*nah*-dhoo) *m* senate

senador (ser-ner-*dhoar*) *m* senator

senão (ser-*nerng*^w) *conj* otherwise

senhor (sı-*ñoar*) mister; sir; **o** ~ you; **os senhores** you

senhora (sı-*ñoa*-rer) *f* madam; **a** ~ you

senhoria (sı-ñoa-*ree*-er) *f* landlady

senhorio (sı-*ñoo*-*ree*-oo) *m* landlord

senil (ser-*neel*) *adj* (pl -is) senile

sensação (sayng-ser-*serng*^w) *f* (pl -ções) feeling, sensation

sensacional (sayng-ser-s^Yoo-*nahl*) *adj* (pl -ais) sensational

sensato (sayng-*sah*-too) *adj* sensible; down-to-earth

sensível (sayng-*see*-vehl) *adj* (pl -eis) sensitive

senso (*sayng*-soo) *m* reason

sentar-se (sayngn-*tahr*-ser) *v* *sit down; *estar sentado* *sit

sentença (sayngn-*tayng*-ser) *f* sentence, verdict

sentido (sayngn-*tee*-dhoo) *m* sense; **sem** ~ meaningless; senseless; ~ **único** one-way traffic

sentimental (sayng-tee-mayngn-*tahl*) *adj* (pl -ais) sentimental

***sentir** (sayngn-*teer*) *v* *feel; sense

separação (ser-per-rer-*serng*^w) *f* (pl -ções) division

separadamente (ser-per-rah-dher-*mayng*n-ter) *adv* apart; separately

separado (ser-per-*rah*-dhoo) *adj* separate

separar (ser-per-*rahr*) *v* separate; divide, part, detach

septicemia (sehp-tee-*seh*-m^Yer) *f* blood-poisoning

séptico (*sehp*-tee-koo) *adj* septic

sepultura (ser-pool-*too*-rer) *f* grave

sequência (ser-*kwayng*-s^Yer) *f* sequence

ser (sayr) *m* being, creature; ~ **humano** human being

***ser** (sayr) *v* *be; ~ **preciso** *be necessary

sereia (ser-*ray*-er) *f* mermaid

sereno (ser-*ray*-noo) *adj* serene

série (*seh*-r^Yer) *f* series, sequence

seriedade (ser-r^Yay-*dhah*-dher) *f* seriousness; gravity

seringa (ser-*reeng*-ger) *f* syringe

sério (*seh*-r^Yoo) *adj* serious

sermão (serr-*merng*^w) *m* (pl -mões) sermon

serpente (serr-*payng*n-ter) *f* snake

serpentear (serr-payngn-t^Y*ahr*) *v* *wind

serra (seh-rrer) f saw; mountain range

serração (ser-rrer-serng^w) f (pl -cões) saw-mill

serradura (ser-rrer-dhoo-rer) f saw-dust

serviço (serr-vee-soo) m service; **prestar** ~ render services; ~ **de chá** tea-set; ~ **de jantar** dinner-service; ~ **de quarto** room service

***servir** (serr-veer) v serve; wait on; *be of use

sessão (ser-serng^w) f (pl -sões) session

sessenta (ser-saynggn-ter) num sixty

seta (seh-ter) f arrow

sete (seh-ter) num seven

Setembro (ser-tayngm-broo) September

setenta (ser-tayngn-ter) num seventy

setentrional (ser-tayngn-tr^yoo-nahl) adj (pl -ais) northern

sétimo (seh-tee-moo) num seventh

seu (say^{oo}) adj (f sua) his; her; your

severo (ser-veh-roo) adj strict; harsh

sexo (sehk-soo) m sex

sexta-feira (saysh-ter-fay-rer) f Friday

sexto (saysh-too) num sixth

sexual (sehk-swahl) adj (pl -ais) sexual

sexualidade (sehk-swer-lee-dhah-dher) f sex, sexuality

siamês (s^yer-maysh) adj Siamese

sifão (see-ferng^w) m (pl sifões) siphon, syphon

significado (seeg-ner-fee-kah-dhoo) m meaning

significar (seeg-ner-fee-kahr) v *mean

significativo (seeg-ner-fee-ker-tee-voo) adj significant

sílaba (see-ler-bher) f syllable

silêncio (see-layng-s^yoo) m silence; stillness, quiet

silencioso (see-layng-s^yoa-zoo) adj silent; m silencer

sim (seeng) yes

símbolo (seengm-boo-loo) m symbol

simpatia (seengm-per-tee-er) f sympathy

simpático (seengm-pah-tee-koo) adj nice; friendly, pleasant

simples (seengm-plish) adj plain, simple

simplesmente (seengm-plizh-mayngn-ter) adv simply

simular (see-moo-lahr) v simulate

simultaneamente (see-mool-ter-nay-er-mayngn-ter) adv simultaneously

simultâneo (see-mool-ter-n^yoo) adj simultaneous

sinagoga (see-ner-go-ger) f synagogue

sinal (see-nahl) m (pl -ais) signal; token, sign; indication; down payment; *fazer sinais signal; **sinais pessoais** description; ~ **de trânsito** road sign

sincero (seeng-seh-roo) adj honest, sincere

sindicato (seengn-dee-kah-too) m trade-union

sinfonia (seeng-foo-nee-er) f symphony

singular (seeng-goo-lahr) adj singular; m singular

sinistro (see-neesh-troo) adj ominous, sinister; m accident

sino (see-noo) m bell

sinónimo (see-no-nee-moo) m synonym

sintético (seengn-teh-tee-koo) adj synthetic

sintoma (seengn-toa-mer) m symptom

sintonizar (seengn-too-nee-zahr) v tune in

sinuoso (see-nwoa-zoo) adj winding

sirene (see-reh-ner) f siren

Síria (see-r^yer) f Syria

sírio (*see-r Yoo*) *adj* Syrian; *m* Syrian

sistema (*seesh-tay-mer*) *m* system; ~ **de arrefecimento** cooling system; ~ **decimal** decimal system

sistemático (*seesh-ter-mah-tee-koo*) *adj* systematic

sítio (*see-t Yoo*) *m* site; seat; place, spot

situação (*see-twer-serng^w*) *f* (*pl* -ções) situation; position

situado (*see-twer-dhoo*) *adj* situated

slide (*sligh-der*) *m* slide

smoking (*smo-keeng g*) *m* dinner-jacket; tuxedo *nAm*

só (*so*) *adv* only, alone; *adj* single, only

soalheiro (*swer-l Yay-roo*) *adj* sunny

soalho (*swah-l Yoo*) *m* parquet flooring

soar (*swahr*) *v* sound

sob (*soabher*) *prep* under

sobejar (*soobhı-zhahr*) *v* remain, *be left over

soberano (*soo-bher-rer-noo*) *m* sovereign

soberbo (*soo-bhayr-bhoo*) *adj* superb

sobrancelha (*soo-bhrerng-say-l Yer*) *f* eyebrow

sobre (*soa-bhrer*) *prep* on, upon; over, above

sobreexcitado (*soa-bhrer-ısh-see-tah-dhoo*) *adj* overstrung

sobreloja (*soa-bhrer-lo-zher*) *f* mezzanine

sobremesa (*soa-bhrer-may-zer*) *f* dessert

sobrenome (*soa-bhrer-noa-mer*) *m* surname

sobrescrito (*soa-bhrısh-kree-too*) *m* envelope

*sobressair (*soa-bhrer-ser-eer*) *v* excel; attract attention

sobresselente (*soa-bhrer-ser-layng ng-ter*) *adj* spare

sobretaxa (*soa-bhrer-tah-sher*) *f* surcharge

sobretudo (*soa-bhrer-too-dhoo*) *adv* most of all; *m* topcoat, overcoat

sobrevivência (*soa-bhrer-vee-vayng-s Yer*) *f* survival

sobreviver (*soa-bhrer-vee-vayr*) *v* survive

sobrinha (*soo-bhree-ñah*) *f* niece

sobrinho (*soo-bhree-ñah*) *m* nephew

sóbrio (*so-bhr Yoo*) *adj* sober

socar (*soo-kahr*) *v* punch

social (*soo-s Yahl*) *adj* (*pl* -ais) social

socialismo (*soo-s Yer-leezh-moo*) *m* socialism

socialista (*soo-s Yer-leesh-ter*) *adj* socialist; *m* socialist

sociedade (*soo-s Yay-dhah-dher*) *f* society; community; company

sócio (*so-s Yoo*) *m* associate; partner

soco (*soa-koo*) *m* punch

socorrer (*soo-koo-rrayr*) *v* help

socorro (*soo-koa-rroo*) *m* help; **primeiros socorros** first-aid

soda (*so-dher*) *f* soda-water

sofá (*soo-fah*) *m* sofa

sofrer (*soo-frayr*) *v* suffer

sofrimento (*soo-free-mayng ng-too*) *m* suffering; affliction

sogra (*so-grer*) *f* mother-in-law

sogro (*soa-groo*) *m* father-in-law; **sogros** parents-in-law *pl*

sol (*sol*) *m* sun; sunshine; **nascer do** ~ sunrise; **pôr do** ~ sunset

sola (*so-ler*) *f* sole

solar (*soo-lahr*) *m* manor-house

soldado (*soal-dah-dhoo*) *m* soldier

soldadura (*soal-der-dhoo-rer*) *f* joint

soldar (*soal-dahr*) *v* solder; weld

solene (*soo-leh-ner*) *adj* solemn

*soletrar (*soo-ler-trahr*) *v* *spell

solha (*soa-l Yer*) *f* plaice

solícito (*soo-lee-see-too*) *adj* obliging

sólido (*so-lee-dhoo*) *adj* firm, solid; *m*

solid
solitário (soo-lee-*tah*-rⱽoo) *adj* lonely
solo (*so*-loo) *m* ground; earth, soil
soltar (soal-*tahr*) *v* unfasten
solteirão (soal-tay-*rrerng*ʷ) *m* (pl -rões) elderly bachelor
solteiro (soal-*tay*-roo) *adj* single
solteirona (soal-tay-*roa*-ner) *f* spinster
solto (*soal*-too) *adj* loose
solução (soo-loo-*serng*ʷ) *f* (pl -ções) solution
soluço (soo-*loo*-soo) *m* hiccup
solúvel (soo-*loo*-vehl) *adj* (pl -eis) soluble
som (sawng) *m* sound; **à prova de ~** soundproof
soma (*soa*-mer) *f* amount, sum; **~ global** lump sum
somar (soo-*mahr*) *v* add up
sombra (*sawng*m-brer) *f* shadow, shade; **~ para os olhos** eyeshadow
sombrio (*sawng*m-bree°°) *adj* sombre; gloomy, shady
somente (so-*mayng*n-ter) *adv* only; merely
soneca (soo-*neh*-ker) *f* nap
sonhar (soo-*ñahr*) *v* *dream
sonho (*soa*-ñoo) *m* dream
sono (*soa*-noo) *m* sleep
sonolento (soo-noo-*layng*n-too) *adj* sleepy
sopa (*soa*-per) *f* soup
soprar (soo-*prahr*) *v* *blow
sopro (*soa*-proo) *m* breath
soro (*soa*-roo) *m* serum
***sorrir** (soo-*rreer*) *v* smile; ***sorrir-se** grin
sorriso (soo-*rree*-zoo) *m* smile
sorte (*sor*-ter) *f* lot, destiny, fortune; chance; luck
sorteio (soor-*tay*-oo) *m* draw
sortido (soor-*tee*-dhoo) *m* assortment
sortimento (soor-tee-*mayng*n-too) *m*
assortment
sorvete (soor-*vay*-ter) *mBr* ice-cream
sorvo (*soar*-voo) *m* sip
sossegado (soo-ser-*gah*-dhoo) *adj* restful; quiet
sossego (soo-*say*-goo) *m* leisure; quiet, peace
sótão (so-*terng*ʷ) *m* (pl ~s) attic
sotaque (soo-*tah*-ker) *m* accent
soutien (soo-tⱽang) *m* brassiere, bra
soviético (soo-vⱽeh-tee-koo) *adj* Soviet
sozinho (so-*zee*-ñoo) *adj* alone
suaili (swigh-*lee*) *m* Swahili
suar (swahr) *v* sweat; perspire
suave (*swah*-ver) *adj* mild, gentle, smooth
suavizar (swer-vee-*zahr*) *v* soften
subalimentação (soo-bher-lee-mayngn-ter-*serng*ʷ) *f* malnutrition
súbdito (*soobh*-dhee-too) *m* subject
subida (soo-*bhee*-dher) *f* ascent; rise, climb
***subir** (soo-*bheer*) *v* ascend; mount, *rise; **~ para** *get on
sublinhar (soobh-lee-*ñahr*) *v* underline; stress
submarino (soobh-mer-*ree*-noo) *adj* underwater; *m* submarine
***submergir** (soobh-merr-*zheer*) *v* overwhelm; submerge
submeter (soobh-mer-*tayr*) *v* subject
subordinado (soo-bhoor-dhee-*nah*-dhoo) *adj* subordinate
subornar (soo-bhoor-*nahr*) *v* bribe
suborno (soo-*bhoar*-noo) *m* bribery
subsequente (soobh-ser-*kwayng*n-ter) *adj* subsequent
subsídio (soobh-*see*-dhⱽoo) *m* subsidy; grant, allowance
subsistência (soobh-seesh-*tayng*-sⱽer) *f* livelihood
substância (soo-bhısh-*terng*-sⱽer) *f* substance

substancial (soo-bhısh-ter~~ng~~-s^yahl) *adj*
(pl -ais) substantial

substantivo (soo-bhısh-ter~~ng~~-tee-voo)
m noun

*substituir (soo-bhısh-tee-*tweer*) *v* replace, substitute

substituto (soo-bhısh-tee-*too*-too) *m*
substitute; deputy

subterrâneo (soobh-ter-*rrer*-n^yoo) *adj*
underground

subtil (soobh-*teel*) *adj* (pl -is) subtle

*subtrair (soobh-trer-*eer*) *v* deduct,
subtract

suburbano (soo-bhoor-*bher*-noo) *adj*
suburban

subúrbio (soo-*bhoor*-bh^yoo) *m* suburb

subvenção (soobh-vay~~ng~~-ser~~ng~~^w) *f* (pl
-ções) grant

sucata (soo-*kah*-ter) *f* scrap-iron

suceder (soo-ser-*dhayr*) *v* succeed;
happen, occur

sucesso (soo-*seh*-soo) *m* success; hit

sucumbir (soo-koo~~ng~~m-*beer*) *v* collapse, succumb

sucursal (soo-koor-*sahl*) *f* (pl -ais)
branch

sudoeste (soo-*dhwehsh*-ter) *m* south-
west

Suécia (*sweh*-s^yer) *f* Sweden

sueco (*sweh*-koo) *adj* Swedish; *m*
Swede

sueste (*swehsh*-ter) *m* south-east

suéter (*sweh*-tehr) *mBr* sweater

suficiente (soo-fee-s^yay~~ng~~-ter) *adj*
sufficient; enough; adequate

sufocante (soo-foo-*ker~~ng~~*-ter) *adj*
stuffy

sufocar (soo-foo-*kahr*) *v* choke

sufrágio (soo-frah-zh^yoo) *m* suffrage

*sugerir (soo-zher-*reer*) *v* suggest

sugestão (soo-zhısh-ter~~ng~~^w) *f* (pl
-tões) suggestion

Suíça (*swee*-ser) *f* Switzerland

suíças (*swee*-sersh) *fpl* whiskers pl,
sideburns *pl*

suicídio (swee-*see*-dh^yoo) *m* suicide

suíço (*swee*-soo) *adj* Swiss; *m* Swiss

sujar (soo-*zhahr*) *v* dirty

sujeito (soo-*zhay*-too) *adj* subordinate; liable; *m* individual; subject;
~ **a** subject to; liable to; ~ **a taxas** dutiable

sujidade (soo-zhee-*dhah*-dher) *f* dirt

sujo (*soo*-zhoo) *adj* soiled, dirty; unclean

sul (sool) *m* south; **do** ~ southern

sul-americano (sool-er-mer-ree-*ker*-
noo) *adj* Latin-American

sulco (*sool*-koo) *m* groove

sumarento (soo-mer-*ray~~ng~~n*-too) *adj*
juicy

sumo (*soo*-moo) *m* juice; squash

suor (swor) *m* perspiration, sweat

superar (soo-peh-*rahr*) *v* exceed,
*outdo

superficial (soo-pehr-fee-s^yahl) *adj* (pl
-ais) superficial

superfície (soo-perr-*fee*-s^yer) *f* surface

supérfluo (soo-*pehr*-flwoo) *adj* redundant, superfluous

superintendente (soo-perr-ee~~ng~~n-
tay~~ng~~n-*day~~ng~~n*-ter) *m* supervisor

superintender (soo-perr-ee~~ng~~n-tay~~ng~~n-
dayr) *v* supervise

superior (soo-per-r^yoar) *adj* superior;
upper; top

superlativo (soo-perr-ler-tee-voo) *adj*
superlative; *m* superlative

supermercado (soo-pehr-merr-*kah*-
dhoo) *m* supermarket

superstição (soo-perr-shtee-ser~~ng~~^w) *f*
(pl -ções) superstition

supervisão (soo-pehr-vee-zer~~ng~~^w) *f*
supervision

suplementar (soo-pler-may~~ng~~n-*tahr*)
adj extra, additional

suplemento (soo-pler-*may~~ng~~n*-too) *m*
supplement

suplicar (soo-plee-*kahr*) v beg

*supor (soo-*poar*) v assume, suppose; guess; **supondo que** supposing that

suportar (soo-poor-*tahr*) v support; endure, sustain, *bear; suffer

suporte (soo-*por*-ter) m support

supositório (soo-poo-zee-*to*-rˠoo) m suppository

surdo (*soor*-dhoo) adj deaf

surgir (soor-*zheer*) v *arise

surpreender (soor-prˠaɥŋn-*dayr*) v surprise; amaze; *catch

surpresa (soor-*pray*-zer) f surprise

suspeita (soosh-*pay*-ter) f suspicion

suspeitar (soosh-pay-*tahr*) v suspect

suspeito (soosh-*pay*-too) adj suspect; m suspect

suspender (soosh-payŋn-*dayr*) v discontinue; suspend

suspensão (soosh-payŋ-*serŋ*ʷ) f (pl -sões) suspension

suspensórios (soosh-payŋ-*so*-rˠoosh) mpl braces pl; suspenders plAm

sussurrar (soo-soo-*rrahr*) v whisper

sussurro (soo-*soo*-rroo) m whisper

*suster (soosh-*tayr*) v *hold up

susto (*soosh*-too) m scare, fright

sutura (soo-*too*-rer) f stitch

suturar (soo-too-*rahr*) v *sew up

T

tabacaria (ter-bher-ker-*ree*-er) f cigar shop; tobacconist, tobacconist's

tabaco (ter-*bhah*-koo) m tobacco; **bolsa de ~** tobacco pouch; **~ para cachimbo** pipe tobacco; **~ para cigarro** cigarette tobacco

tabela (ter-*bheh*-ler) f table; chart; **~ de conversão** conversion chart

taberna (ter-*bhehr*-ner) f tavern; pub

tabique (ter-*bhee*-ker) m partition

tabu (ter-*bhoo*) m taboo

tábua (*tah*-bhwer) f board

tabuleiro (ter-bhoo-*lay*-roo) m tray; **~ de damas** draught-board; **~ de xadrez** checkerboard nAm

taça (*tah*-ser) f cup

tacanho (ter-*ker*-ñoo) adj narrow-minded

táctica (*tah*-tee-ker) f tactics pl

tacto (*tah*-too) m touch

tagarela (ter-ger-*reh*-ler) m chatterbox

tailandês (tigh-lerŋn-*daysh*) adj Thai; m Thai

Tailândia (tigh-*lern*-dˠer) f Thailand

tainha (ter-*ee*-ñer) f mullet

tal (tahl) adj (pl tais) such; **~ como** such as

tala (*tah*-ler) f splint

talão (ter-*lerŋ*ʷ) m (pl talões) stub, counterfoil; coupon; heel

talento (ter-*layŋ*-too) m talent

talha (*tah*-lˠer) f wood-carving; **obra de ~** carving

talher (ter-*lˠehr*) m cutlery; **preço do ~** cover charge

talho (*tah*-lˠoo) m butcher

talismã (ter-leezh-*merŋ*) m lucky charm

talvez (tahl-*vaysh*) adv maybe, perhaps

tamanco (ter-*merŋ*-koo) m wooden shoe

tamanho (ter-*mer*-ñoo) m size; **~ extra-grande** outsize

tâmara (*ter*-mer-rer) f date

também (terŋgm-*berŋ*ˠ) adv as well, also, too; **~ não** neither

tampa (*terŋgm*-per) f top; lid, cover

tampão (terŋgm-*perŋ*ʷ) m (pl -pões) tampon

tangerina (terŋg-zher-*ree*-ner) f mandarin, tangerine

tangível (terŋg-zhee-vehl) adj (pl -eis) tangible

tanque (*terng*-ker) *m* pond; tank

tanto (*terng*n-too) *adv* as much; as; **tanto ... como** both ... and; **um ~** rather; pretty; somewhat

tão (terng*w*) *adv* such, so; as

tapar (ter-*pahr*) *v* cover

tapeçaria (ter-per-ser-*ree*-er) *f* tapestry

tapete (ter-*pay*-ter) *m* mat; rug; carpet

tarde (*tahr*-dher) *f* afternoon; *adv* late; **esta ~** this afternoon

tardio (tahr-*dhee*ᵒᵒ) *adj* late

tarefa (tah-*reh*-fer) *f* duty, task

tareia (ter-*ray*-er) *f* spanking

tarifa (tah-*ree*-fer) *f* tariff; rate; **~ de estacionamento** parking fee; **~ nocturna** night rate

tartaruga (terr-ter-*roo*-ger) *f* turtle

taxa (*tah*-sher) *f* Customs duty, charge; **~ de desconto** bank-rate; **~ de serviço** service charge; **~ do câmbio** rate of exchange

táxi (*tahk*-see) *m* taxi; cab; **ponto de táxis** *Br* taxi rank, taxi stand *Am*

taxímetro (terk-*see*-mer-troo) *m* taximeter

te (ter) *pron* you; yourself

teatro (*t*ᵞ*ah*-troo) *m* theatre; drama; **~ de fantoches** puppet-show; **~ de variedades** variety theatre

tecelão (ter-ser-*lerng*ʷ) *m* (pl ~s) weaver

tecer (ter-*sayr*) *v* *weave

tecido (ter-*see*-dhoo) *m* textile; material, tissue, fabric

técnica (*tehk*-nee-ker) *f* technique

técnico (*tehk*-nee-koo) *adj* technical; *m* technician

tecnologia (tehk-noo-loo-*zhee*-er) *f* technology

tecto (*teh*-too) *m* ceiling

teimoso (tay-*moa*-zoo) *adj* stubborn, obstinate; pig-headed

tela (*teh*-ler) *f* screen

telefonar (ter-ler-foo-*nahr*) *v* ring up, phone; call; call up *Am*

telefone (ter-ler-*fo*-ner) *m* phone, telephone

telefonema (ter-ler-foo-*nay*-mer) *m* telephone call

telefonia (ter-ler-foo-*nee*-er) *f* radio

telefonista (ter-ler-foo-*neesh*-ter) *f* telephonist; telephone operator

telegrafar (ter-ler-grer-*fahr*) *v* cable, telegraph

telegrama (ter-ler-*grer*-mer) *m* cable, telegram

telémetro (ter-*leh*-mer-troo) *m* rangefinder

teleobjectiva (teh-leh-oabh-zheh-*tee*-ver) *f* telephoto lens

telepatia (ter-ler-per-*tee*-er) *f* telepathy

telesqui (teh-leh-*shkee*) *m* ski-lift

televisão (ter-ler-vee-*zerng*ʷ) *f* (pl -sões) television; **aparelho de ~** television set

telha (*tay*-lᵞer) *f* tile

telhado (tɪ-*l*ᵞ*ah*-dhoo) *m* roof; **~ de colmo** thatched roof

tema (*tay*-mer) *m* theme

temer (ter-*mayr*) *v* dread

temerário (ter-mer-*rah*-rᵞoo) *adj* daring

temor (ter-*moar*) *m* dread

temperar (tayngm-per-*rahr*) *v* flavour

temperatura (tayngm-per-rer-*too*-rer) *f* temperature; **~ ambiente** room temperature

tempestade (tayngm-pɪsh-*tah*-dher) *f* storm, tempest

tempestuoso (tayngm-pɪsh-*twoa*-zoo) *adj* stormy; thundery

templo (*tayngm*-ploo) *m* temple

tempo (*tayngm*-poo) *m* time; weather; **a ~** in time; **de tempos a tempos** now and then; **~ livre** spare time

temporal (tayngm-poo-*rahl*) *m* (pl -ais) gale

temporário (tayngm-poo-*rah*-r^Yoo) *adj* temporary

tenaz (ter-*nahsh*) *f* tongs *pl*; pincers *pl*

tencionar (tayng-s^Yoo-*nahr*) *v* intend

tenda (*tayngn*-der) *f* tent; stall

tendão (tayngn-*derng*ʷ) *m* (pl -dões) tendon, sinew

tendência (tayngn-*dayng*-s^Yer) *f* tendency; ***ter ~** tend

tender (tayngn-*dayr*) *v* *be inclined to; **~ para** tend to

ténis (*teh*-neesh) *m* tennis; **campo de ~** tennis-court; **~ de mesa** table tennis

tenro (*tayng*-rroo) *adj* tender

tensão (tayng-*serng*ʷ) *f* (pl -sões) tension; pressure, strain, stress; **~ arterial** blood pressure

tenso (*tayng*-soo) *adj* tense

tentação (tayngn-ter-*serng*ʷ) *f* (pl -ções) temptation

tentar (tayngn-*tahr*) *v* try, tempt; attempt

tentativa (tayngn-ter-*tee*-ver) *f* try, attempt

tentilhão (tayngn-tee-*l^Yerng*ʷ) *m* (pl -hões) finch

teologia (t^Yoo-loo-*zhee*-er) *f* theology

teoria (t^Yoo-*ree*-er) *f* theory

teórico (t^Yo-ree-koo) *adj* theoretical

tépido (*teh*-pee-dhoo) *adj* tepid

*ter (tayr) *v* *have; **~ ares** look; **~ de** *have to; *be obliged to, *must, *be bound to, need to; **~ em stock** stock; **~ êxito** manage, succeed

terapia (ter-rer-*pee*-er) *f* therapy

terça-feira (tayr-ser-*fay*-rer) *f* Tuesday

terceiro (terr-*say*-roo) *num* third

terebentina (ter-rer-bhayngn-*tee*-ner) *f* turpentine

termas (*tehr*-mersh) *f pl* spa

terminal (terr-mee-*nahl*) *m* (pl -ais) terminal

terminar (terr-mee-*nahr*) *v* finish, end; expire; accomplish

termo[1] (*tayr*-moo)ʳ *m* term

termo[2] (*tehr*-moo) *m* thermos flask

termómetro (terr-*mo*-mer-troo) *m* thermometer

termóstato (terr-*mosh*-ter-too) *m* thermostat

terno (*tehr*-noo) *adj* tender; gentle; *mBr* suit

terra (*teh*-rrer) *f* earth; soil; land; **a ~** ashore; **em ~** ashore; **~ firme** mainland; **tremor de ~** earthquake

terraço (teh-*rrah*-soo) *m* terrace

terreno (ter-*rray*-noo) *m* terrain; grounds

território (ter-rree-*to*-r^Yoo) *m* territory

terrível (ter-*rree*-vehl) *adj* (pl -eis) terrible; awful, frightful, dreadful

terror (ter-*rroar*) *m* terror

terrorismo (ter-rroo-*reezh*-moo) *m* terrorism

terrorista (ter-rroo-*reesh*-ter) *m* terrorist

tese (*teh*-zer) *f* thesis

teso (*tay*-zoo) *adj* stiff; broke

tesoura (ter-*zoa*-rer) *f* scissors *pl*; **~ de unhas** nail-scissors *pl*

tesoureiro (ter-zoa-*ray*-roo) *m* treasurer

tesouro (ter-*zoa*-roo) *m* treasure; **~ público** treasury

testa (*tehsh*-ter) *f* forehead

testamento (tɪsh-ter-*mayngn*-too) *m* will

teste (*tehsh*-ter) *m* test

testemunha (tɪsh-ter-*moo*-ñer) *f* witness; **~ ocular** eye-witness

testemunhar (tɪsh-ter-moo-*ñahr*) *v* testify

teu (tay^{oo}) *adj* (f tua) your; **teus** your

têxteis (*taysh*-taysh) *mpl* drapery

texto (*taysh*-too) *m* text

tez (taysh) *f* complexion

tia (*tee*-er) *f* aunt

tifo (*tee*-foo) *m* typhoid

tigela (tee-*zheh*-ler) *f* basin, bowl

tigre (*tee*-grer) *m* tiger

tijolo (tee-*zhoa*-loo) *m* brick

tília (*tee*-l^yah) *f* lime; limetree

timbre (*teengm*-brer) *m* tone

timidez (tee-mee-*dhehsh*) *f* timidity; shyness

tímido (*tee*-mee-dhoo) *adj* timid; shy

timoneiro (tee-moo-*nay*-roo) *m* steersman, helmsman

tímpano (*teengm*-per-noo) *m* eardrum

tingir (teeng-*zheer*) *v* dye; **não tinge** fast-dyed

tinta (*teengn*-ter) *f* ink; dye, paint; ~ de água water-colour

tinturaria (teengn-too-rer-*ree*-er) *f* drycleaner's

tio (tee^{oo}) *m* uncle

típico (*tee*-pee-koo) *adj* characteristic, typical

tipo (*tee*-poo) *m* type; fellow, guy, chap

tiragem (tee-rer-*zherng*^y) *f* issue

tirano (tee-*rer*-noo) *m* tyrant

tira-nódoas (tee-rer-*no*-dhwersh) *m* (pl ~) stain remover

tirar (tee-*rahr*) *v* *take out, *take away

tiritar (tee-ree-*tahr*) *v* tremble, shiver

tiro (*tee*-roo) *m* shot

título (*tee*-too-loo) *m* title; degree; heading

toalha (*twah*-l^yer) *f* towel; ~ de banho bath towel; ~ de mesa tablecloth

toca (*to*-ker) *f* den

toca-discos (to-ker-*dheesh*-koosh) *mBr* (pl ~) record-player

tocante (too-*kerngn*-ter) *adj* touching

tocar (too-*kahr*) *v* touch; play; *ring; não ~ *keep off

todavia (toa-dher-*vee*-er) *conj* but; however; still

todo (*toa*-dhoo) *adj* entire, all; *m* whole; de ~ at all; ~ o mundo *Br* everyone, everybody

toldo (*toal*-doo) *m* awning; ~ impermeável tarpaulin

tolerável (too-ler-rah-*vehl*) *adj* (pl -eis) tolerable

tolo (*toa*-loo) *adj* foolish; *m* fool

tom (tawng) *m* tone; shade

tomar (too-*mahr*) *v* *catch, *take; ~ conta de *take over

tomate (too-*mah*-ter) *m* tomato

tomilho (too-mee-l^yoo) *m* thyme

tonelada (too-ner-*lah*-dher) *f* ton

tónico (*to*-nee-koo) *m* tonic; ~ capilar hair tonic

tontura (tawngn-*too*-rer) *f* giddiness

tópico (*to*-pee-koo) *m* topic

topo (*toa*-poo) *m* height

toque (*to*-ker) *m* touch

toranja (too-*rerng*-zher) *f* grapefruit

torção (toor-*serng*^w) *f* (pl -ções) twist

torcedor (toor-ser-*dhoar*) *mBr* supporter

torcedura (toor-ser-*dhoo*-rer) *f* wrench

torcer (toor-*sayr*) *v* twist; sprain, wrench; torcer-se sprain; torcido crooked

tordo (*toar*-dhoo) *m* thrush

tormento (toor-*mayngn*-too) *m* torment

tornar-se (toor-*nahr*-ser) *v* *get; *become

torneio (toor-*nay*-oo) *m* tournament

torneira (toor-*nay*-rer) *f* tap; faucet *nAm*

em torno de (erng^y *toar*-noo der) round

tornozelo (toor-noo-*zeh*-loo) *m* ankle

toro (*toa*-roo) *m* log

torrada (too-*rrah*-dher) *f* toast

torre (*toa*-rrer) *f* tower

torto (*toar*-too) *adj* crooked

tortura (toor-*too*-rer) *f* torture

torturar (toor-too-*rahr*) *v* torture

tosse (*to*-ser) *f* cough

*****tossir** (too-*seer*) *v* cough

total (too-*tahl*) *adj* (pl -ais) total; utter; *m* total

totalitário (too-ter-lee-*tah*-r^yoo) *adj* totalitarian

totalizador (too-ter-lee-zer-*dhoar*) *m* totalizator

totalmente (too-terl-*mayngn*-ter) *adv* completely; altogether

toucador (toa-ker-*dhoar*) *m* dressing-table

tourada (toa-*rah*-dher) *f* bullfight

touro (*toa*-roo) *m* bull

tóxico (*tok*-see-koo) *adj* toxic

trabalhador (trer-bher-l^yer-*dhoar*) *adj* industrious; *m* worker

trabalhar (trer-bher-*l^yahr*) *v* work; ~ **demais** overwork

trabalho (trer-*bah*-l^yoo) *m* work, labour; job; difficulty; ~ **manual** handwork; handicraft

traça (*trah*-ser) *f* moth

traço (*trah*-soo) *m* dash; trait; ~ **caracterial** characteristic

tractor (trer-*toar*) *m* tractor

tradição (trer-dhee-*serng*^w) *f* (pl -cões) tradition

tradicional (trer-dhee-s^yoo-*nahl*) *adj* (pl -ais) traditional

tradução (trer-dhoo-*serng*^w) *f* (pl -cões) translation

tradutor (trer-dhoo-*toar*) *m* translator

*****traduzir** (trer-dhoo-*zeer*) *v* translate; interpret

tragédia (trer-*zheh*-dh^yer) *f* tragedy; drama

trágico (*trer*-zhee-koo) *adj* tragic

traição (trigh-*serng*^w) *f* (pl -cões) treason

traidor (trigh-*dhoar*) *m* traitor

*****trair** (trer-*eer*) *v* betray

traje (*trah*-zher) *m* dress; ~ **a rigor** evening dress; ~ **nacional** national dress

tralha (*trah*-l^yer) *f* junk

tranquilidade (trerng-kwee-lee-*dhah*-dher) *f* quiet

tranquilizar (trerng-kwee-lee-*zahr*) *v* reassure

tranquilo (trerng-*kwee*-loo) *adj* tranquil; calm, peaceful, still, quiet

transacção (trerng-zah-*serng*^w) *f* (pl -cões) transaction

transatlântico (trerng-zert-*lerngn*-tee-koo) *adj* transatlantic

*****fazer transbordo** (fer-zayr trerngz-*bhoar*-doo) change

transeunte (trerng-z^y*oongn*-ter) *m* passer-by

*****transferir** (trerngsh-fer-*reer*) *v* transfer; postpone

transformador (trerngsh-foor-mer-*dhoar*) *m* transformer

transformar (trerngsh-foor-*mahr*) *v* transform; ~ **em** turn into

*****transgredir** (trerngzh-grer-*dheer*) *v* offend, violate

transição (trerng-zee-*serng*^w) *f* (pl -cões) transition

trânsito (*trerng*-zee-too) *m* traffic

translúcido (trerngzh-*loo*-see-dhoo) *adj* sheer; translucent

transmissão (trerngzh-mee-*serng*^w) *f* (pl -sões) transmission

transmitir (trerngzh-mee-*teer*) *v* transmit

transparente (trersh-per-*rangn*-ter) *adj* transparent

transpiração (trerngsh-pee-rer-*serng*ʷ) f perspiration

transpirar (trerngsh-pee-*rahr*) v perspire

transportar (trerngsh-poor-*tahr*) v transport; carry

transporte (trerngsh-*por*-ter) m transportation, transport

transtornado (trerngsh-toor-*nah*-dhoo) adj *upset

transtornar (trerngsh-toor-*nahr*) v *upset

transversal (trerngzh-verr-*sahl*) f (pl -ais) side-street

trapalhada (trer-per-*lʸah*-dher) f mess; muddle; *fazer ~ muddle

trapo (*trah*-poo) m rag; cloth

traquete (trer-*kay*-ter) m foresail

traseiro (trer-*zay*-roo) m bottom

tratado (trer-*tah*-dhoo) m essay; treaty

tratamento (trer-ter-*mayngn*-too) m treatment; ~ de beleza beauty treatment

tratar (trer-*tahr*) v treat; handle; ~ com *deal with; ~ de nurse, *take care of; attend to, see to

*tratear (trou-*tʸahr*) v hum

travão (trer-*verng*ʷ) m (pl -vões) brake; tambor do ~ brake drum; ~ de mão hand-brake; ~ de pé foot-brake

travar (trer-*vahr*) v slow down; break

travessa (trer-*veh*-ser) f dish

travessão (trer-ver-*serng*ʷ) m (pl -sões) hair-grip

travessia (trer-verr-*see*-er) f crossing, passage

travesso (trer-*vay*-soo) adj naughty

*trazer (trer-*zayr*) v *bring

trecho (*tray*-shoo) m stretch; extract; excerpt, passage

treinador (tray-ner-*dhoar*) m coach

treinar (tray-*nahr*) v train

treino (*tray*-noo) m training

trela (*treh*-ler) f lead, leash

trem (trerng*ʸ*) m Br train

tremendo (trer-*mayngn*-doo) adj terrible

tremer (trer-*mayr*) v shiver, tremble

trémulo (*treh*-moo-loo) adj shivery

trenó (trer-*no*) m sleigh; sledge

trepar (trer-*pahr*) v climb

três (traysh) num three; ~ quartos three-quarter

trevas (*treh*-versh) fpl dark

trevo (*tray*-voo) m clover, shamrock

treze (*tray*-zer) num thirteen

triangular (tree-erng-goo-*lahr*) adj triangular

triângulo (tree-*erng*-goo-loo) m triangle

tribo (*tree*-bhoo) f tribe

tribuna (tree-*bhoo*-ner) f stand; pulpit

tribunal (tree-bhoo-*nahl*) m (pl -ais) law court; court

tributar (tree-bhoo-*tahr*) v raise

tricotar (tree-koo-*tahr*) v *knit

trigésimo (tree-*zheh*-zee-moo) num thirtieth

trigo (*tree*-goo) m wheat; corn

trimestral (tree-mɪsh-*trahl*) adj (pl -ais) quarterly

trimestre (tree-*mehsh*-trer) m quarter

trinchar (treeng-*shahr*) v carve

trinta (*treengn*-ter) num thirty

tripulação (tree-poo-ler-*serng*ʷ) f (pl -ções) crew

triste (*treesh*-ter) adj sad

tristeza (treesh-*tay*-zer) f sorrow, sadness

triturar (tree-too-*rahr*) v *grind

triunfante (trʸoong-*ferngn*-ter) adj triumphant

triunfar (trʸoong-*fahr*) v triumph

triunfo (trʸoong-foo) m triumph

troar (trwahr) v thunder

troca (*tro*-ker) f exchange

troça (tro-ser) f mockery

trocar (troo-kahr) v change, exchange; switch; swap

troçar (tro-sahr) v mock, ridicule

troco (troa-koo) m change

troleicarro (tro-lay-kah-rroo) m trolley-bus

trombeta (trawngm-bay-ter) f trumpet

trompa (trawngm-per) f horn

tronco (trawng-koo) m trunk

trono (troa-noo) m throne

tropas (tro-persh) fpl troops pl

tropeçar (troo-per-sahr) v stumble

tropical (troo-pee-kahl) adj (pl -ais) tropical

trópicos (tro-pee-koosh) mpl tropics pl

trotineta (tro-tee-neh-ter) f scooter

trovão (troo-verngᵂ) m (pl -vões) thunder

trovoada (troo-vwah-dher) f thunderstorm

truque (troo-ker) m trick

truta (troo-ter) f trout

tu (too) pron you; ~ **mesmo** yourself

tubarão (too-bher-rerngᵂ) m (pl -rões) shark

tuberculose (too-bherr-koo-lo-zer) f tuberculosis

tubo (too-bhoo) m tube; ~ **respirador** snorkel

tudo (too-dhoo) pron everything; ~ **o que** whatever

tulipa (too-lee-per) f tulip

tumor (too-moar) m growth, tumour

túmulo (too-moo-loo) m tomb

túnel (too-nehl) m (pl -eis) tunnel

túnica (too-nee-ker) f tunic

Tunísia (too-nee-zee-er) f Tunisia

tunisino (too-nee-see-noo) adj Tunisian; m Tunisian

turba (toor-bher) f crowd

turbina (toor-bhee-ner) f turbine

turbulento (toor-bhoo-layngn-too) adj rowdy

turco (toor-koo) adj Turkish; m Turk

turismo (too-reezh-moo) m tourism

turista (too-reesh-ter) m tourist

turno (toor-noo) m gang, shift

Turquia (toor-kee-er) f Turkey

tutela (too-teh-ler) f custody

tutor (too-toar) m tutor, guardian

tweed (tweed) m tweed

U

úlcera (ool-ser-rer) f ulcer; sore; ~ **gástrica** gastric ulcer

ulmeiro (ool-may-roo) m elm

ulterior (ool-ter-rʸoar) adj further; subsequent

ultimamente (ool-tee-mer-mayngn-ter) adv lately

último (ool-tee-moo) adj ultimate, last

ultraje (ool-trah-zher) m outrage; offence

ultramarino (ool-trer-mer-ree-noo) adj overseas

ultrapassar (ool-trer-per-sahr) v pass, *overtake; **ultrapassagem proibida** no overtaking

ultravioleta (ool-trer-vʸoo-lay-ter) adj ultraviolet

um (oong) num (f uma) one; art a art; **mais** ~ another; ~ **ou outro** either

umbigo (oongm-bee-goo) m navel

unânime (oo-ner-nee-mer) adj unanimous; like-minded

unguento (oong-gwayngn-too) m ointment, salve

unha (oo-ñer) f nail; **arranjar as unhas** manicure

união (oo-nʸerngᵂ) f (pl uniões)

union; **União Soviética** Soviet Union

unicamente (oonee-ker-*mayngn*-ter) *adv* exclusively

único (*oo*-nee-koo) *adj* sole, unique

unidade (oo-nee-*dhah*-der) *f* unit; unity; ~ **monetária** monetary unit

unido (oo-*nee*-dhoo) *adj* joint

uniforme (oo-nee-*for*-mer) *adj* uniform; *m* uniform

unilateral (oo-nee-ler-ter-*rahl*) *adj* (pl -ais) one-sided

unir (oo-*neer*) *v* unite; join; connect

universal (oonee-verr-*sahl*) *adj* (pl -ais) universal

universidade (oo-nee-verr-see-*dhah*-der) *f* university

universo (oo-nee-*vehr*-soo) *m* universe

uns (oongsh) *pron* (f umas) some

untar (oongn-*tahr*) *v* lubricate

urbano (oor-*bher*-noo) *adj* urban

urgência (oor-*zhayng*-s^{y}er) *f* urgency

urgente (oor-*zhayngn*-ter) *adj* urgent; pressing

urina (oo-*ree*-ner) *f* urine

urso (*oor*-soo) *m* bear

Uruguai (oo-roo-*gwer*^{ee}) *m* Uruguay

uruguaio (oo-roo-*gwigh*-oo) *adj* Uruguayan; *m* Uruguayan

urzal (oor-*zahl*) *m* moor

urze (*oor*-zay) *f* heather

usar (oo-*zahr*) *v* use; employ; *wear

uso (*oo*-zoo) *m* use; usage

usual (oo-*zwahl*) *adj* (pl -ais) usual; customary, ordinary

utensílio (oo-tayng-*seel*-^{y}oo) *m* utensil

utente (oo-*tayng*-ter) *m* user

útero (*oo*-ter-roo) *m* womb

útil (*oo*-teel) *adj* (pl úteis) useful; helpful

utilidade (oo-ter-lee-*dhah*-dher) *f* utility; use

utilizar (oo-ter-lee-*zahr*) *v* utilize; employ

utilizável (oo-ter-lee-*zah*-vehl) *adj* (pl -eis) usable

uvas (*oo*-versh) *fpl* grapes *pl*

V

vaca (*vah*-ker) *f* cow; **pele de** ~ cowhide

vacilante (ver-see-*lerngn*-ter) *adj* unsteady; shaky

vacilar (ver-see-*lahr*) *v* falter

vacinação (ver-see-ner-*serng*^{w}) *f* (pl -ções) vaccination

vacinar (ver-see-*nahr*) *v* vaccinate

vácuo (*vah*-kwoo) *m* vacuum

vadiagem (ver-*dh*^{y}*ah*-zherng^y) *f* vagrancy

vadiar (ver-*dh*^{y}*ahr*) *v* tramp

vadio (ver-*dhee*^{oo}) *m* tramp

vaga (*vah*-ger) *f* vacancy

***vagabundear** (ver-ger-bhoongn-*dh*^{y}*ahr*) *v* roam

vagabundo (ver-ger-*bhoongn*-doo) *m* tramp

vagão (ver-*gerng*^{w}) *m* (pl vagões) waggon

vagar (ver-*gahr*) *v* vacate; *m* leisure

vago (*vah*-goo) *adj* vacant; faint; vague; obscure, dim

***vaguear** (ver-*g*^{y}*ahr*) *v* wander

vaidoso (vigh-*dhoa*-zoo) *adj* vain; proud

vale (*vah*-ler) *m* valley; voucher; ~ **postal** postal order

valente (ver-*layngn*-ter) *adj* brave; plucky

valentia (ver-layngn-*tee*-er) *f* courage

***valer** (ver-*layr*) *v* *be worth; ~ **a pena** *be worth-while

valeta (ver-*lay*-ter) *f* gutter

valete (ver-*leh*-ter) *m* knave

válido (*vah*-lee-dhoo) *adj* valid

valioso (ver-*lⁱoa*-zoo) *adj* valuable

valor (ver-*loar*) *m* value; worth; **de ~** valuable; **sem ~** worthless; **valores** valuables

valsa (*vahl*-ser) *f* waltz

válvula (*vahl*-voo-ler) *f* valve

vantagem (ver*ng*n-*tah*-zherng ʸ) *f* profit, advantage; benefit

vantajoso (ver*ng*n-ter-*zhoa*-zoo) *adj* advantageous

vão (ver*ng*ʷ) *adj* (f vã; pl ~s) vain

vapor (ver-*poar*) *m* vapour, steam

vaporizador (ver-poo-ree-zer-*dhoar*) *m* atomizer

vara (*vah*-rer) *f* rod

varanda (ver-*rer*ng-der) *f* veranda; balcony

varão (ver-*rer*ngʷ) *m* (pl varões) rod

variação (ver-rʸer-*ser*ngʷ) *f* (pl -ções) variation

variado (ver-*rʸah*-dhoo) *adj* varied

variar (ver-*rʸahr*) *v* vary

variável (ver-*rʸah*-vehl) *adj* (pl -eis) variable

varicela (ver-ree-*seh*-ler) *f* chickenpox

variedade (ver-rʸay-*dhah*-dher) *f* variety; **teatro de variedades** music-hall

varíola (ver-*ree*ᵒᵒ-ler) *f* smallpox

vários (*vah*-rʸoosh) *adj* several

variz (vah-*reesh*) *f* varicose vein

varrer (ver-*rrayr*) *v* *sweep

vasilha (ver-*zee*-ger) *f* vessel

vaso (*vah*-zoo) *m* vase; pot; **~ sanguíneo** blood-vessel

vassoura (ver-*soa*-rer) *f* broom

vasto (*vahsh*-too) *adj* vast; extensive; wide, broad

vau (vou) *m* ford

vazar (ver-*zahr*) *v* *shed, leak; empty

vazio (ver-*zee*ᵒᵒ) *adj* empty

veadinho (vʸer-*dhee*-ño) *m* fawn

veado (vʸah-dhoo) *m* deer

vegetariano (vɪ-zher-ter-rʸer-noo) *m* vegetarian

veia (*vay*-ʸer) *f* vein

veículo (vay-ee-koo-loo) *m* vehicle

vela (*veh*-ler) *f* sail; yachting; candle; **~ de ignição** sparking-plug

veleidade (ver-lay-*dhah*-dher) *f* whim

velhice (vɪ-*lⁱee*-ser) *f* old age

velhíssimo (vɪ-*lⁱee*-see-moo) *adj* ancient

velho (*veh*-lⁱoo) *adj* old; aged; ancient; stale; **mais ~** elder; **o mais ~** eldest

velhote (veh-*lⁱo*-ter) *adj* old

velocidade (ver-loo-see-*dhah*-dher) *f* speed, rate; gear; *ir com ~ *speed; **limitação de ~** speed limit; **~ de cruzeiro** cruising speed; **~ máxima** speed limit

velocímetro (ver-loo-*see*-mer-troo) *m* speedometer

velocípede (ver-loo-*see*-per-dher) *m* cycle

veloz (ver-*losh*) *adj* rapid

veludo (ver-*loo*-dhoo) *m* velvet

vencedor (vayng-ser-*dhoar*) *adj* winning; *m* winner

vencer (vayng-*sayr*) *v* *win; *overcome

vencido (vayng-*see*-dhoo) *adj* due

vencimento (vayng-see-*mayng*n-too) *m* expiry; salary

venda (*vayng*n-der) *f* sale; **à ~** for sale; **~ por grosso** wholesale

vendável (vayng-*dah*-vehl) *adj* (pl -eis) saleable

vendedor (vayng-der-*dhoar*) *m* salesman; **~ de aves de criação** poulterer; **~ de jornais** newsagent

vendedora (vayng-der-*dhoa*-rer) *f* salesgirl

vender (vayng-*dayr*) *v* *sell; **~ a retalho** retail

veneno (ver-*nay*-noo) *m* poison

venenoso (ver-ner-*noa*-zoo) *adj* poisonous

veneração (ver-ner-rer-*serng*w) f respect

venerável (ver-ner-*rah*-vehl) adj (pl -eis) venerable

Venezuela (ver-ner-*zway*-ler) f Venezuela

venezuelano (ver-ner-zway-*ler*-noo) adj Venezuelan; m Venezuelan

ventilação (vayngn-tee-ler-*ser*oo) f (pl -ções) ventilation

ventilador (vayngn-tee-ler-*dhoar*) m fan, ventilator

ventilar (vayngn-tee-*lahr*) v ventilate

vento (*vayngn*-too) m wind

ventoso (vayngn-*toa*-zoo) adj gusty, windy

ventre (*vayngn*-trer) m belly; **prisão de** ~ constipation

***ver** (vayr) v *see; notice

Verão (ver-*rerng*w) m (pl -rões) summer; **pleno** ~ (high) summer

verbal (verr-*bhahl*) adj (pl -ais) verbal

verbo (*verr*-bhoo) m verb

verdade (verr-*dhah*-dher) f truth

verdadeiramente (verr-dher-dhay-rer-*mayngn*-ter) adv really

verdadeiro (verr-dher-*dhay*-roo) adj true; very, real; actual

verde (*vayr*-dher) adj green

veredicto (ver-rer-*dhee*-too) m verdict

vergonha (verr-*ewoa*-ñer) f shame; **que vergonha!** shame!; ***ter** ~ *be ashamed

verídico (ver-*ree*-dhee-koo) adj truthful

verificar (ver-rer-fee-*kahr*) v verify; check

verme (*vehr*-mer) m worm

vermelho (verr-*meh*-lyoo) adj crimson, red

verniz (verr-*neesh*) m varnish; lacquer; ~ **de unhas** nail-polish

verosímil (vay-roa-*see*-meel) adj (pl

-meis) credible

versão (verr-*serng*w) f (pl -sões) version

verso (*vehr*-soo) m verse

vertente (vehr-*tayngn*-ter) f slope

verter (verr-*tayr*) v pour; leak

vertical (verr-tee-*kahl*) adj (pl -cais) vertical

vertigem (verr-*tee*-zherngy) f vertigo; dizziness

vespa (*vaysh*-per) f wasp

veste (*vehsh*-ter) f robe

vestiário (vish-*tYah*-rYoo) m checkroom *nAm*

vestíbulo (vish-*tee*-bhoo-loo) m hall; lobby

vestido (vish-*tee*-dhoo) m dress; gown, frock; ***trazer** ~ *wear; ~ **comprido** robe

***vestir** (vish-*teer*) v dress; *put on; ***vestir-se** dress

vestuário (vish-*twah*-rYoo) m clothes pl; ~ **de desporto** sportswear

veterinário (ver-ter-ree-*nah*-rYoo) m veterinary surgeon

véu (veh°°) m veil

vez (vaysh) f time; turn; **alguma** ~ some time; **às vezes** sometimes; **de** ~ **em quando** occasionally; **duas vezes** twice; **em** ~ **de** instead of; **muitas vezes** often; **outra** ~ again; **uma** ~ once; **uma** ~ **mais** once more

via (*vee*-er) prep via; f track; lane; ~ **férrea** railway; railroad *nAm*; ~ **navegável** waterway

viaduto (vYer-*dhoo*-too) m viaduct

viagem (*vYah*-zherngy) f voyage; trip, journey; passage; ~ **de regresso** return journey

viajante (vYer-*zhern*-ter) m traveller

viajar (vYer-*zhahr*) v travel; ~ **de automóvel** motor

vibração (vee-bhrer-*serng*w) f (pl

-ções) vibration

vibrar (vee-*bhrahr*) v vibrate; tremble

vice-presidente (vee-ser-prer-see-*dhayngn*-ter) m vice-president

vicioso (vee-s^{Y}oa-zoo) adj vicious

vida (vee-*dher*) f life; lifetime; **cheio de ~** lively; **com ~** alive

videira (vee-*dhay*-rer) f vine

vidraça (vee-*dhrah*-ser) f window-pane

vidro (vee-*dhroo*) m glass; pane; **de ~** glass; **~ colorido** stained glass

viela (v^{Y}eh-ler) f lane

viga (vee-ger) f beam

vigário (vee-*gah*-r^{Y}oo) m vicar

vigésimo (vee-*zheh*-zee-moo) num twentieth

vigia (vee-*zhee*-er) f porthole

vigiar (vee-zh^{Y}ahr) v patrol; watch

vigilante (vee-zhee-*lerngn*-ter) adj vigilant

vila (vee-ler) f borough; fBr villa

vinagre (vee-*nah*-grer) m vinegar

vindima (veengn-*dee*-mer) f vintage

vingança (veeng-*gerng*-serng) f revenge

vinha (vee-ñer) f vineyard

vinho (vee-ñoo) m wine; **negociante de vinhos** wine-merchant

vinte (veengn-ter) num twenty

viola (v^{Y}o-ler) f guitar

violação (v^{Y}oo-ler-*serng*^{w}) f (pl -ções) violation

violar (v^{Y}oo-*lahr*) v assault, rape

violência (v^{Y}oo-*layng*-s^{Y}er) f violence

violento (v^{Y}oo-*layngn*-too) adj violent; fierce, severe

violeta (v^{Y}oo-*lay*-ter) f violet

violino (v^{Y}oo-*lee*-noo) m violin

*vir (veer) v *come; **~ a ser** *become

viragem (vee-*rah*-zherng^Y) f turn

virar (vee-*rahr*) v turn; **virar-se** turn round

virgem (veer-zherng^Y) f virgin

vírgula (veer-goo-ler) f comma

virilha (ver-*ree*-lYer) f groin

virtude (veer-*too*-dher) f virtue

visão (vee-*zerng*^{w}) f (pl visões) vision

visar (vee-*zahr*) v aim at

visibilidade (vee-zee-bher-lee-*dhah*-dher) f visibility

visita (vee-zee-ter) f visit; call; ***fazer uma ~** a call on

visitante (vee-zee-*terngn*-ter) m visitor

visitar (vee-zee-*tahr*) v visit; call on

visível (vee-zee-vehl) adj (pl -eis) visible

vislumbrar (veezh-loongm-*brahr*) v glimpse

vislumbre (veezh-*loongm*-brer) m glimpse

vison (vee-son) m mink

visor (vee-zoar) m view-finder

vista (veesh-ter) f sight; view; **em ~ de** considering; **ponto de ~** point of view; outlook

visto (veesh-too) m visa; **~ que** since; as

vital (vee-tahl) adj (pl -ais) vital

vitamina (vee-ter-*mee*-ner) f vitamin

vitela (vee-teh-ler) f veal

vitelo (vee-teh-loo) m calf

vítima (vee-tee-mer) f victim; casualty

vitória (vee-to-r^{Y}er) f victory

vitrina (vee-*tree*-ner) f show-case

viúva (v^{Y}oo-ver) f widow

viúvo (v^{Y}oo-voo) m widower

viveiro (vee-vay-roo) m nursery

vivenda (vee-*vayngn*-der) f villa

viver (vee-*vayr*) v live; experience

vivo (vee-voo) adj alive, live; brisk, vivid

vizinhança (vee-zee-*ñerng*-ser) f neighbourhood; vicinity

vizinho (vee-zee-ñoo) adj near; neighbouring; m neighbour

voar (vwahr) v *fly

vocabulário (voo-ker-bhoo-*lah*-r^Yoo) *m* vocabulary

vocal (voo-*kahl*) *adj* (*pl* -ais) vocal

vocalista (voo-ker-*leesh*-ter) *m* vocalist

vocês (vo-*saysh*) *pron* you; ~ **mesmos** yourselves

vogal (voo-*gahl*) *f* (*pl* -ais) vowel

volante (voo-*lerngn*-ter) *m* steering-wheel

volt (voalt) *m* volt

volta (*vol*-ter) *f* way back; turn, curve, bend; round, ride; à ~ about; round; à ~ **de** around; **em** ~ about; **em** ~ **de** about, around; **ida e** ~ round trip *Am*

voltagem (voal-*tah*-zherng^V) *f* voltage

voltar (voal-*tahr*) *v* return; turn round; ~ **atrás** turn back

volume (voo-*loo*-mer) *m* volume; bulk; package

volumoso (voo-loo-*moa*-zoo) *adj* bulky; big

voluntário (voo-loongn-*tah*-r^Yoo) *adj* voluntary; *m* volunteer

volúpia (voo-*loo*-p^Yer) *f* lust

vomitar (voo-mee-*tahr*) *v* vomit

vontade (vawngn-*tah*-dher) *f* will; desire; à ~ casual; **boa** ~ goodwill; **de boa** ~ gladly, willingly; **de má** ~ unwilling; **pouco à** ~ uneasy; ***ter** ~ **de** fancy, *feel like

voo (*voa*-oo) *m* flight; ~ **charter** charter flight; ~ **de regresso** return flight; ~ **nocturno** night flight

vosso (*vo*-soo) *adj* your

votação (voo-ter-*serng*^w) *f* (*pl* -cões) vote

votar (voo-*tahr*) *v* vote

voto (*vo*-too) *m* vote; vow

voz (vosh) *f* voice; **em** ~ **alta** aloud

vulcão (vool-*kerng*^w) *m* (*pl* -cões) volcano

vulgar (vool-*gahr*) *adj* vulgar; ordinary

vulnerável (vool-ner-*rah*-vehl) *adj* (*pl* -eis) vulnerable

X

xadrez (sher-*dhraysh*) *m* chess; **em** ~ chequered

xaile (*shigh*-ler) *m* shawl

xale (*shah*-ler) *m* shawl

xarope (sher-*ro*-per) *m* syrup

xeque! (*sheh*-ker) check!

xícara (*shee*-ker-rer) *fBr* cup

Z

zangado (zerng-*gah*-dhoo) *adj* angry, cross

zaragata (zer-rer-*gah*-ter) *f* row

zebra (*zay*-bhrer) *f* zebra

zelo (*zay*-loo) *m* zeal; diligence

zeloso (zer-*loa*-zoo) *adj* zealous; diligent

zénite (*zeh*-nee-ter) *m* zenith

zero (*zeh*-roo) *m* nought, zero

zinco (*zeeng*-koo) *m* zinc

zodíaco (zoo-*dhee*-er-koo) *m* zodiac

zona (*zoa*-ner) *f* area, zone; ~ **de estacionamento** parking zone; ~ **industrial** industrial area

zoologia (zoo-oa-loo-*zhee*-er) *f* zoology

Menu Reader

Food

à, à moda de in the style of
abacate avocado pear
abacaxi pineapple
abóbora pumpkin (US winter squash)
açafrão saffron
acará, acarajé portion of fritters made of black-eyed bean purée, ground, dried shrimps and hot peppers
acelga swiss chard
acepipes hors d'œuvre
acompanhamento vegetables, side dish
açorda thick soup or side dish where bread is a principal ingredient
  ~ alentejana with poached eggs, garlic, coriander leaves and olive-oil
  ~ de bacalhau with dried cod, sliced and fried in garlic-flavoured olive-oil
  ~ à moda de Sesimbra with fish, garlic and coriander leaves
açúcar sugar
agrião watercress
aipim cassava root
aipo celeriac

alcachofra artichoke
  fundo de ~ bottom
alcaparra caper
alecrim rosemary
aletria 1) vermicelli, thin noodles 2) dessert made with vermicelli
alface lettuce
alheira garlic sausage made of breadcrumbs and different kinds of minced meat
  ~ à transmontana served with fried eggs, fried potatoes and cabbage
alho garlic
  ~ francês/-porro leek
almoço lunch
almôndega ball of fish or meat
alperce apricot
amargo bitter
amêijoas baby clams
  ~ à bulhão pato fried in olive-oil with garlic and coriander
  ~ à espanhola baked in the oven with onions, tomatoes, peppers, garlic and herbs
  ~ ao natural steamed with herbs and served with melted butter and lemon juice
ameixa plum
  ~ seca prune

amêndoa almond

amendoim peanut

amora blackberry

ananás pineapple

anchova anchovy

angu cassava-root flour or maize boiled in water and salt

ao in the style of

arenque herring

arroz rice

  ~ de Cabidela kind of risotto with giblets and chicken blood, flavoured with vinegar

  ~ doce pudding flavoured with cinnamon

  ~ de frango baked with chicken

  ~ de manteiga cooked in water and butter

  ~ de pato no forno duck cooked with bacon and *chouriço* then baked with rice

  ~ tropeiro with *carne de sol*

asparago asparagus

assado roast

atum tuna fish

  bife de ~ cutlet (US steak) marinated in white wine and fried in olive-oil

aveia oats

avelã hazelnut

aves fowl

azeda sorrel

azedo sour

azeite olive-oil

  ~ de dendê palm-oil

azeitona olive

  ~ preta black

  ~ verde (de Elvas) green

babá de moça dessert made of egg yolks poached in coconut milk and syrup

bacalhau cod, usually dried and salted

  ~ à Brás fried with onions and potatoes, then baked with a topping of beaten eggs

  ~ de caldeirada braised with chopped onions, tomatoes, parsley, garlic and coriander (or saffron)

  ~ cozido com todos poached and served with boiled cabbage, onions, potatoes, chickpeas and eggs

  ~ à Gomes de Sá fried with onions, boiled potatoes, garlic and garnished with hard-boiled eggs and black olives

  ~ com leite de coco poached in coconut milk seasoned with coriander

  ~ com natas no forno boiled, then baked with potatoes in a white sauce with cream

  ~ à provinciana a gratin of poached cod, potatoes and *grelos* (or broccoli), topped with minced hard-boiled eggs, flour and port wine

  ~ à transmontana braised with cured pork or *chouriço,* white wine, parsley, garlic and tomatoes

batata potato

  ~ doce yam, sweet potato

  ~ frita chip (US french fry)

  ~ palha matchstick

baunilha vanilla

berbigão type of cockle

beringela aubergine (US egg-plant)

besugo sunfish, type of sea-bream

beterraba beetroot

bifana slice of pork tenderloin usually served in a bun

bife steak, escalope

~ **a cavalo** of beef topped with a fried egg

~ **à cortador** of beef fried in garlic-flavoured butter

~ **de espadarte** swordfish cutlet (US steak) fried with onions and potatoes

~ **à milanesa** breaded escalope of veal

bifinhos de vitela slices of veal fillet served with a Madeira wine sauce

biscoito biscuit (US cookie)

bobó dish made of dried shrimps, onions, cassava root, fish stock, palm-oil, coconut milk and served with bananas and grated coconut

boi beef

bola de Berlim doughnut

bolacha biscuit (US cookie)

~ **de água e sal** cracker

bolinho de bacalhau deep-fried croquette of dried cod and mashed potatoes flavoured with eggs and parsley

bolo cake

~ **caseiro** home-made

~ **podre** flavoured with honey and cinnamon

borracho young pigeon

borrego lamb

(na) brasa charcoal-grilled

brioche yeast bun

broa 1) thick maize-(US corn-). meal cracker 2) type of gingerbread

brócolos broccoli

cabrito kid

~~**montês** roebuck

~ **à ribatejana** marinated and roasted with herbs and paprika

caça game

(à) caçador(a) simmered in white wine with carrots, onions, herbs and sometimes tomatoes

cachorro (quente) hot-dog

cachucho small sea-bream

café da manhã breakfast

caju cashew nut

calamar (sliced) squid

caldeirada fish stewed with potatoes, onions, tomatoes, pimentos, spices, wine and olive-oil

~ **de enguias** eel simmered with potatoes, onions, garlic, bay leaf and parsley

~ **à fragateira** fish, shellfish and mussels simmered in a fish stock with tomatoes and herbs; served on toast

~ **à moda da Póvoa** hake, skate, sea-bass and eel simmered with tomatoes in olive-oil

caldo clear soup, consommé

~ **verde** thick soup made from shredded cabbage, potatoes and *chouriço*

camarões shrimps

~ **à baiana** served in a spicy tomato sauce with boiled rice

~ **grandes** Dublin Bay prawns (US jumbo shrimps)

cambuquira tender shoots of pumpkin (US squash) stewed with meat

canapé small open sandwich

canela cinnamon

canja chicken-and-rice soup

canjica dessert made of peanuts and sweet-corn cooked in milk with cloves and cinnamon and served in fresh coconut milk

capão capon

caqui persimmon

caracóis snails

caracol 1) snail 2) a spiral-shaped bun filled with currants

caranguejo crab

carapau horse mackerel

~ **de escabeche** fried and dipped in a sauce made of vinegar, olive-oil, fried onions and garlic

cardápio menu

caril curry

carne meat

~ **de porco à alentejana** cubes of marinated pork fried with clams

~ **de sol** salted and dried in the sun

carneiro mutton

~ **guisado** stewed with tomatoes, garlic, bay leaf, parsley and often potatoes

carnes frias cold meat (US cold cuts)

caruru 1) green amaranth 2) a dish of minced herbs stewed in oil and spices

castanha chestnut

~ **de caju** cashew nut

(na) cataplana steamed in a copper pan shaped like a big nutshell

cavala mackerel

cebola onion

cebolada fried-onion garnish

cenoura carrot

cereja cherry

cherne black grouper

chicória endive (US chicory)

chispalhada pig's trotters (US feet) stewed with navy beans, cabbage, bacon and blood sausage

chispe pig's trotter (US foot)

chocos com tinta cuttlefish cooked in their own ink

chouriça, chouriço smoked pork

sausage flavoured with paprika

chuchu type of marrow (US summer squash)

churrasco charcoal-grilled meat served in Brazil with *farofa* and a hot-pepper sauce

cocada coconut macaroon

coco coconut

codorniz quail

coelho rabbit

coentro coriander

cogumelo (button) mushroom

colorau paprika (used for colouring)

cominho caraway seed

compota compote, stewed fruit

congro conger eel

conta bill (US check)

coração heart

cordeiro lamb

corvina croaker (fish)

costeleta chop, cutlet

couve cabbage

~**-de-bruxelas** brussels sprouts

~**-flor** cauliflower

~ **galega** galician (with a long stem, big dark green leaves and a slightly bitter taste)

~ **lombarda** savoy

~ **portuguesa** portuguese (like the galician but smaller)

~ **roxa** red

cozido 1) boiled stew 2) boiled 3) cooked

~ **em lume brando** simmered

~ **à portuguesa** beef and pork boiled with *chouriço*, carrots, turnips and cabbage *(couve portuguesa)*

creme cream

~ **de leite** fresh

criação fowl

croissant crescent roll

cru raw

urau mashed sweet-corn cooked in coconut milk with sugar and cinnamon

damasco apricot

dióspiro persimmon

dobrada, dobradinha tripe

doce 1) sweet 2) jam
~ **de laranja** marmalade

dourada guilt-head (fish)

iró eel

iroses fritas fried eel

menta 1) menu 2) set menu

mpada small type of pie

mpadão large type of pie
~ **de batata** shepherd's pie (with minced meat and mashed potato topping)

nchidos assorted pork products made into sausages

endívia chicory (US endive)

nguia eel

nsopado meat or fish casserole served on (or with) slices of bread

entrecosto sparerib

ervilha green pea

escabeche sauce of fried onions, garlic, olive-oil and vinegar

escalfado poached

escalope de vitela escalope of veal, thin, flattened breaded slice of veal

espadarte swordfish

espargo asparagus
ponta de ~ tip

esparregado purée of assorted greens in cream

especiaria spice

espetada kebab

(no) espeto spit-roasted

espinafre spinach

estragão tarragon

estufado braised

esturjão sturgeon

farofa cassava-root meal browned in oil or butter

farófias floating island

fatias slices
~ **da China** cold, baked egg yolks topped with syrup flavoured with lemon and cinnamon
~ **douradas** slices of bread dipped into milk and egg yolk, fried and sprinkled with sugar (US french toast)

favas broad beans
~ **guisadas com chouriço** stewed with *chouriço* and coriander leaves

febras de porco à alentejana pieces of pork fillet grilled with onions, *chouriço* and bacon

feijão bean
~ **branco** navy
~ **catarino** pink
~ **encarnado** red
~ **frade** black-eyed
~ **guisado** stewed with bacon in a tomato sauce
~ **preto** black
~ **tropeiro** black beans fried with chopped *carne de sol* and served with *farofa*
~ **verde** runner (US green)

feijoada dish of dried beans stewed with pig's head and trotters (US feet) bacon, sausages and sometimes vegetables; served in Brazil with *farofa,* rice, sliced oranges and a hot-pepper sauce

fiambre cooked (US boiled) ham

fígado liver
~ **de aves** chicken

figo fig

filete fillet of fish

filhó fritter
  ~ de abóbora of pumpkin purée

fios de ovos dessert of fine golden strands made from beaten egg yolk and melted sugar

folhado sweet puff-pastry delicacy

(no) forno baked

framboesa raspberry

frango chicken
  ~ com farofa served with *farofa* mixed with olives, hard-boiled eggs and giblets
  ~ na púcara chicken cassserole flavoured with port wine, prepared in a special earthenware pot

fresco fresh

fressura de porco guisada casserole of pork offal (US variety meat), sometimes with navy beans

fricassé casserole, usually of lamb or veal in a cream sauce

(na) frigideira sautéed

frio cold

fritada de peixe deep-fried fish

frito 1) fried 2) fritter

fruta fruit
  ~ em calda in syrup
  ~ do conde variety of tropical fruit
  ~ cristalizada candied

fubá maizeflour (US cornflour)

fumado smoked

galantina pressed meat in gelatine

galinha boiling chicken

galinhola woodcock

ganso goose

garoupa large grouper (fish)

gaspacho chilled soup with diced tomatoes, sweet peppers, onions, cucumber and croutons

gelado 1) ice-cream 2) chilled

geleia 1) jelly 2) jam (Brazil)

gengibre ginger

ginja morello cherry

goiaba guava

goiabada guava paste

gombo okra (GB lady's finger)

grão(-de-bico) chickpeas
  ~ com bacalhau stew made of chickpeas, potatoes and dried-cod fillets

gratinado oven-browned

grelhado grilled

grelos turnip greens

groselha red currant

guaraná very sweet tropical fruit

guisado 1) stew 2) stewed

hortaliça fresh vegetables

hortelã mint

incluído included

inhame yam, variety of sweet potato

iscas thinly sliced liver
  ~ à portuguesa marinated in white wine with herbs and garlic then fried

jabuticaba bing cherry

jambu variety of cress

jantar dinner

jardineira mixed vegetables

javali wild boar

lagosta spiny lobster
  ~ americana fried with onions and garlic, flambéed in brandy and served in a sauce flavoured with Madeira wine
  ~ suada with onions, garlic, tomatoes and flavoured with port wine

lagostim Norwegian lobster, langoustine
  ~-do-rio fresh-water crayfish

lampreia lamprey

~ à moda do Minho marinated in "green" wine, port wine, brandy, blood and spices then poached in the marinade and served with rice

lanche snack

laranja orange

lavagante lobster

lebre hare

legumes vegetables
~ **variados** mixed

leitão suck(l)ing pig
~ **à Bairrada** coated with spicy lard and roasted on a spit in a very hot bread-oven
~ **recheado** stuffed with a spicy, brandy-flavoured mince of bacon, *chouriço* and giblets and then roasted

leite-creme blancmange (US pudding) often sprinkled with caramelised sugar

lentilha lentil

lima lime

limão lemon
~ **verde** lime

língua tongue

linguado sole
~ **à meunière** sautéed in butter, served with parsley and lemon-juice
~ **com recheio de camarão** filled with shrimps in a white sauce

linguíça thin pork sausage flavoured with paprika

lista dos vinhos wine list

lombo loin

louro bay leaf

lulas squid
~ **de caldeirada** simmered with white wine, olive-oil, diced potatoes, tomatoes, onions and parsley

~ recheadas braised with a stuffing of eggs, onions and *chouriço*

maçã apple
~ **assada** baked

maçapão, massapão 1) marzipan 2) almond macaroon

macarrão macaroni

macaxeira cassava root

maionese mayonnaise

malagueta hot pepper

mamão papaya

mandioca cassava root

manjar de coco coconut blancmange (US pudding) topped with plum syrup

manjericão basil

manteiga butter

mãozinhas de vitela guisadas calves' trotters (US feet) braised with onions, parsley and vinegar, served with vegetables

maracujá passion fruit

marinado marinated

(à) marinheira with white wine, onions, parsley and sometimes tomatoes

marisco seafood

marmelada quince paste

marmelo quince

massa 1) dough, pastry 2) pasta, all types of noodle

medalhão medallion, small choice cut of meat

medronho arbutus berry

meia desfeita poached pieces of dried cod fried with chickpeas, onions and vinegar, topped with hard-boiled eggs and chopped garlic

mel honey

melancia watermelon

melão melon, usually a honeydew

melon
~ **com vinho do Porto** with port wine
merengue meringue
mero red grouper (fish)
mexilhão mussel
mexerica tangerine
migas meat or fish fried in olive-oil with onions and garlic and thickened with bread
mil-folhas flaky pastry with cream filling (US napoleon)
milho doce sweet-corn
mioleira brains
miolos brains
~ **mexidos com ovos** of lamb fried and served with scrambled eggs
misto mixed
miúdos de galinha chicken giblets
mocotós stewed calves' trotters (US feet), usually served with *farofa* and a hot-pepper sauce
molho sauce
~ **branco** white
~ **de manteiga** with butter and lemon
~ **tártaro** mayonnaise with chopped gherkins, chives, capers, olives
~ **verde** olive-oil and vinegar with chopped spinach, parsley and coriander leaves
com ~ with
sem ~ without
moqueca de peixe fish cooked in an earthenware casserole with coconut milk, palm-oil, coriander leaves, ginger and ground shrimps
morango strawberry
~ **silvestre** wild
morcela black pudding, blood sausage

mortadela mortadella (US Bologna sausage)
mostarda mustard
nabiça turnip greens
nabo turnip
nata(s) fresh cream
~ **batida(s)** whipped
(ao) natural plain, without dressing, sauce, stuffing etc.
nêspera medlar, a small apple-like fruit eaten when over-ripe
noz nut, walnut
~ **moscada** nutmeg
óleo oil
~ **de amendoim** peanut oil
omeleta omelette
~ **simples** plain
osso bone
ostras oysters
~ **recheadas** oystershells stuffed with oysters, onions, garlic, breadcrumbs, egg yolk, lemon juice, spice and then oven-browned
ouriço-do-mar sea-urchin
ovas fish roe
ovos eggs
~ **cozidos** hard-boiled
~ **escalfados** poached
~ **estrelados** fried, sunny side up
~ **mexidos** scrambled
~ **moles** beaten egg yolks cooked in syrup
~ **quentes** soft-boiled
~ **verdes** stuffed with hard-boiled yolks mixed with onions flavoured with vinegar and deep-fried in olive-oil
paçoca 1) roast *carne de sol* ground with cassava root and served with sliced bananas 2) dessert made with roast peanuts crushed with

sweetened cassavaroot meal

paio spicy cured pork fillet presented in a casing

~ **com ervilhas** simmered with peas and chopped onions

palmito palm heart

panado breaded

pão bread

~ **de centeio** rye

~ **de forma** white, for toast

pão-de-ló tea bread (US coffee cake)

pãozinho roll

papos de anjo baked egg yolks topped with syrup

pargo red porgy (fish)

passa (de uva) raisin, sultana

(bem) passado well done

(mal) passado medium

(muito mal) passado rare

pastel usually a type of pie

~ **de bacalhau** deep-fried croquette of dried cod and mashed potatoes flavoured with eggs and parsley

~ **de Belém/de nata** custard pie

~ **folhado** flaky pastry

~ **de massa tenra** soft crust-pastry pie filled with minced meat

~ **de Santa Clara** tartlet with almond-paste filling

~ **de Tentúgal** flaky pastry filled with beaten eggs cooked in syrup

pastelão de palmito e camarão shrimp and palm-heart pie

pato duck

~ **estufado** braised in white wine with onions, parsley and bay leaf

~ **ao tucupi** roasted, braised with carrots and *jambu* in cassava-root juice and served

with fruit

pé de moleque peanut brittle

pé de porco pig's trotters (US feet)

peito breast

peixe fish

~~**espada** cutlass fish, scabbard fish

~~**galo** 1) moonfish 2) John Dory

~ **da horta** runner beans deep-fried in batter

pepino cucumber

pequeno almoço breakfast

pêra pear

perca perch

perceve barnacle

perdiz partridge

~ **à caçador(a)** simmered with carrots, onions, white wine, herbs and often tomatoes

~ **com molho de vilão** poached and served with a cold sauce of olive-oil, vinegar, onions, garlic and chopped parsley

perna leg

pernil ham

pêro variety of eating apple

peru turkey

pescada whiting

~ **cozida com todos** poached and served with boiled potatoes and runner beans

pescadinhas de rabo na boca plate of whitings fried whole

pêssego peach

pevide 1) pip (US seed) 2) salted pumpkin pip (US seed)

picado de carne minced meat

picante hot, spicy, highly seasoned

pimenta peppercorn

piment(ã)o sweet pepper

pinhão pine kernel

pinhoada pine-kernel brittle

piripiri tiny hot peppers (preserved in olive-oil)

polvo octopus

pombo pigeon
 ~ **estufado** braised with bacon, onions and white wine, served with fried bread

porco pork

posta slice of fish or meat

prato 1) plate 2) dish
 ~ **do dia** speciality of the day

preço price

prego small steak often served in a roll

presunto 1) cured ham 2) cooked (US boiled) ham (Brazil)
 ~ **cru** dried ham

pudim pudding
 ~ **de bacalhau** dried-cod loaf, served with tomato sauce
 ~ **flan** caramel custard
 ~ **à portuguesa** custard flavoured with brandy and raisins

puré puree
 ~ **de batata** mashed potatoes

queijada small cottage-cheese tart
 ~ **de Sintra** flavoured with cinnamon

queijinhos do céu marzipan balls rolled in sugar

queijo cheese
 ~ **de Azeitão** soft or hard and made with ewe's milk
 ~ **cabreiro** made with goat's milk
 ~ **cardiga** made with goat's and ewe's milk
 ~ **catupiri** small, white cream cheese
 ~ **flamengo** Dutch type of cheese
 ~ **da ilha** made in the Azores

and not unlike Cheddar
 ~ **de Minas** plain
 ~ **Prata** mild and yellow
 ~ **rabaçal** made with goat's milk
 ~ **requeijão** type of cottage cheese
 ~ **São Jorge** not unlike Cheddar
 ~ **da Serra** made with ewe's milk

quente hot
 ~ **e frio** chocolate-nut (US hot-fudge) sundae

quiabo okra (GB lady's finger)

quindim sweet made with eggs and grated coconut

rabanada slice of bread dipped into egg batter and sprinkled with sugar (US french toast)

rabanete radish

raia skate

rainha-cláudia greengage plum

recheado stuffed

recheio stuffing, forcemeat

refeição meal
 ~ **ligeira** snack

refogado onions fried in olive-oil (base of a stew)

repolho green cabbage

rins kidneys

rissol fritter with minced meat or fish

robalo sea-bass

rodela round slice

rojões à alentejana pork cubes fried with baby clams, diced potatoes and onions

rojões à moda do Minho pork cubes marinated in dry white wine with garlic and paprika, fried and mixed with boiled blood cubes

rolo de carne picada meatloaf

rolos de couve lombarda
savoy-cabbage leaves stuffed with minced or sausage meat

romã pomegranate

rosca ring-shaped white bread

ruivo red gurnard (fish)

sal salt

salada salad
~ **de fruta** fruit
~ **mista** mixed
~ **de pimentos assados** made with grilled sweet peppers
~ **russa** cooked, diced vegetables in mayonnaise

salgado 1) salty 2) salted

salmão salmon
~ **fumado** smoked

salmonete surmullet
~ **grelhado com molho de manteiga** grilled and served with melted butter, chopped parsley and lemon

salsa parsley

salsicha sausage

salva sage

sande, sanduíche sandwich

santola spider-crab
~ **ao natural** boiled in salted water with lemon
~ **recheada** stuffed with its own flesh, generally seasoned with mustard, curry powder, lemon and white wine

sarda mackerel

sardinha sardine

sável shad

seco 1) dry 2) dried

sêmola semolina

sericá alentejano cinnamon soufflé

serviço incluído service included

siri crab

sobremesa dessert

solha plaice

sonho type of doughnut

sopa soup
~ **de agriões** with watercress and potatoes
~ **de coentros** with coriander leaves, bread, poached eggs, olive-oil and garlic
~ **do dia** of the day
~ **de feijão** with kidney beans, cabbage, carrots and rice
~ **de hortaliça** with fresh vegetables
~ **juliana** with shredded vegetables
~ **de rabo de boi** oxtail
~ **de tomate à alentejana** with tomatoes, onions and poached eggs
~ **transmontana** with vegetables, ham, bacon and slices of bread

sorvete ice-cream
~ **com água** water-ice (US sherbet)

sururu type of cockle

suspiro meringue

tainha grey mullet (fish)

tâmara date

tangerina tangerine

tempero seasoning

tenro tender

tigelada dessert of eggs beaten with milk and cinnamon, baked in an earthenware bowl

toranja grapefruit

torrada toast

torrão de ovos marzipan sweet

torta swiss roll
~ **de Viana** filled with lemon curd

tosta mista toasted ham-and-cheese sandwich

toucinho bacon
~ **do céu** kind of marzipan
pudding
tornedó round cut of prime beef
tremoço salted lupine seed
tripas tripe (usually minced)
~ **à moda do Porto** cooked
with assorted pork products,
navy beans and pieces of
chicken; served with rice
trouxa de vitela veal olive (US
veal bird)
trouxas de ovos egg yolks
poached in sweetened water
and topped with syrup
trufa truffle
truta trout
tutano marrow
tutu à mineira puree of black
beans mixed with cassava-root

meal and served with cabbage
and fried bacon
uva grape
~ **moscatel** muscat
vaca beef
vagens runner beans (US green
beans)
variado assorted
vatapá fish and shrimp puree
flavoured with coconut milk
and palm-oil and served with a
peanut-and-cashew sauce
vieira scallop
vinagre vinegar
vitela veal
ximxim de galinha chicken
braised in palm-oil and served
with a sauce of ground shrimp,
sweet peppers, onions, peanuts
and ginger

Drinks

adocicado slightly sweet
água water
~ **de coco** coconut milk
~**-pé** weak wine, made from a
base of watered-down wine
draff
~ **tónica** tonic
água mineral mineral water
~ **com gás/gaseificada** fizzy
(US carbonated)
~ **sem gás** still
aguardente spirit distilled from
vegetable matter or fruit
~ **bagaceira** spirit distilled
from grape husks
~ **de figo** spirit distilled from

figs
~ **de medronho** spirit distilled
from arbutus berries
~ **velha** well-aged brandy
Antiqua Portuguese grape
brandy, aged
aperitivo aperitif
batida long drink (US highball)
of rum, sugar and fruit juice,
usually lemon juice
batido milk-shake flavoured with
a scoop of ice-cream
bebida drink
~ **sem álcool/não alcoólica**
soft drink
~ **espirituosa** spirits

bica black coffee
Borges Portuguese grape brandy, aged
branco white
Bucelas region north of Lisbon which produces the famous dry, straw-coloured *Bucelas* wine
cacau cocoa
cachaça white rum
café coffee
~ **sem cafeína** caffeine-free
~ **duplo** large cup of coffee
~ **frio** iced coffee
~ **com leite** white coffee
~ **puro** genuine coffee
cafezinho strong black coffee
caipirinha white rum served with lemon juice, ice cubes and a slice of lime or lemon
caldo de cana sugar-cane juice
caneca pint-size beer mug
Carcavelos region west of Lisbon producing good fortified wines
carioca small weak coffee
(água de) Castelo fizzy (US carbonated) mineral water
cerveja 1) beer 2) lager
~ **em garrafa** bottled
~ **imperial** draught (US draft)
~ **preta** stout
chá tea
~ **com leite** with milk
~ **com limão** with lemon
~ **de limão** made from an infusion of lemon peel
~ **maté** made from an infusion of the maté-tree leaf and usually served chilled with a slice of lemon
clarete light red wine
Colares region to the north-west of Lisbon, producing good quality red and white wine; the reds have good colour and body and are rich in tanning; the whites have a strong aromatic flavour

conhaque cognac, French brandy
~ **espanhol** Spanish brandy
Constantino Portuguese brandy, aged
copo glass
Cuba livre rum and Coke
Dão some of the best wines of Portugal, normally drunk quite young, come from this region, in the south-east of Oporto; the reds are strong and of good flavour, the whites dry and fruity
doce sweet
meio-~ medium-sweet (usually in reference to sparkling wine)
Douro the upper part of this valley, east of Oporto produces the renowned port wine (see *Porto*) and pleasant table wines
espumante 1) sparkling 2) sparkling wine
Favaios dessert wine similar to muscatel
fino draught (US draft) beer
fresco fresh, chilled
frio cold
galão white coffee served in a big glass
garoto white coffee served in a small cup
garrafa bottle
meia-~ half bottle
gasosa fizzy (US carbonated) soft drink
gelado iced
gelo ice, ice cubes
com ~ with ice
sem ~ without ice

genebra Dutch gin, usually produced under licence

gim gin

ginjinha spirit distilled from morello cherries

girafa draught (US draft) beer served in a fluted glass

guaraná soft drink flavoured with *guaraná,* a very sweet tropical fruit

jarro carafe

jeropiga locally made fortified wine (see also *vinho abafado*)

laranjada orangeade

leite milk

~ **com chocolate** chocolate drink

licor liqueur

limonada type of lemon squash (US lemon drink)

Madeira excellent red and white aperitif and dessert wines are produced on this island; *Sercial* is the driest, and this, with *Verdelho* (medium-dry), can be drunk as an aperitif; *Boal* (or *Bual*) is smoky and less sweet than the rich dark-amber *Malmsey* (or *Malvásia*), which is best served for dessert at room temperature

maduro mature (wine produced from ripe grapes, as opposed to "green wine", see *Minho*)

(suco/sumo de) maracujá passion-fruit (juice)

Mateus rosé famous rosé wine from the district of Trás-os-Montes

mazagrã chilled black coffee served on the rocks with sugar and a slice of lemon

Minho area in the north-west of Portugal where the famous young *vinho verde,* or "green wine", is produced; it is made from unripened grapes; faintly sparkling and acid in taste, very refreshing and with low alcohol content; the whites are more popular than the reds, both should be drunk young and chilled

moscatel 1) muscat grape 2) muscatel, a rich, aromatic dessert wine

pinga 1) wine 2) crude white rum (Brazil)

(vinho do) Porto this famous fortified wine from the upper Douro valley, east of Oporto, is classified by *vintage* and *blend;* the *vintage* ports, only made in exceptional years (indicated on the label), are bottled at least two years after harvesting and then stored to age for 10 to 20 years or more, while the *blended* ports, a subtle mixture of the harvests of different years, are kept in barrels for a minimum of 5 years; there are two types of *blended* ports: the younger *Ruby* variety is full-coloured, full-bodied, and the *Tawny* amber-coloured and delicate; moreover, less sweet, aromatic white ports are also available and are suitable as an aperitif

quente hot

região demarcada controlled and classified wine-producing area, e.g. *Bucelas, Colares, Dão, Douro, Minho,* etc.

seco dry

extra-~ extra-dry

meio-~ medium-dry

Setubal region south of Lisbon noted for its famous dessert wines *(moscatel)* and some good red and rosé table wines

sidra cider

simples neat (US straight)

suco/sumo fruit or vegetable juice

taça long-stemmed glass, cup

tinto red

uísque whisky

vermute vermouth

vinho wine

~ **abafado** locally made fortified wine (see also *jeropiga*)

~ **adamado** sweet wine

~ **da casa** house or carafe wine

~ **espumante natural** sparkling wine produced in a similar fashion to French champagne and available in extra-dry, dry and medium-dry blends

~ **generoso** well-aged and fortified wine, high in alcohol content

~ **licoroso** naturally sweet wine, high in alcohol content e.g. *Moscatel de Setúbal*

~ **da Madeira** Madeira wine (see *Madeira*)

~ **do Porto** port wine (see *Porto*)

~ **da região** local wine

~ **verde** "green wine" (see *Minho*)

xerez sherry

Portuguese Verbs

Three regular conjugations appear below, grouped by families according to their infinitive endings, *-ar, -er* and *-ir*. Verbs which do not follow the conjugations below are considered irregular (see irregular verb list). Note that there are some verbs which follow the regular conjugation of the category they belong to, but present some minor changes in spelling. Examples: *boiar, bóio; tocar, toque; almoçar, almoce; cegar, cegue; dirigir, dirijo; distinguir, distingo*. The personal pronoun is not generally expressed since the verb endings clearly indicate the person.

		1st conj.	2nd conj.	3rd conj.
Infinitive		**am ar**	**tem er**	**part ir**
		(love)	*(fear)*	*(leave for)*
Present	(eu)	am o	tem o	part o
	(tu)	am as	tem es	part es
	(ele)	am a	tem e	part e
	(nós)	am amos	tem emos	part imos
	(vós)	am ais	tem eis	part is
	(eles)	am am	tem em	part em
Imperfect	(eu)	am ava	tem ia	part ia
	(tu)	am avas	tem ias	part ias
	(ele)	am ava	tem ia	part ia
	(nós)	am ávamos	tem íamos	part íamos
	(vós)	am áveis	tem íeis	part íeis
	(eles)	am avam	tem iam	part iam
Past def.	(eu)	am ei	tem i	part i
	(tu)	am aste	tem este	part iste
	(ele)	am ou	tem eu	part iu
	(nós)	am ámos	tem emos	part imos
	(vós)	am astes	tem estes	part istes
	(eles)	am aram	tem eram	part iram
Future	(eu)	am arei	tem erei	part irei
	(tu)	am arás	tem erás	part irás
	(ele)	am ará	tem erá	part irá
	(nós)	am aremos	tem eremos	part iremos
	(vós)	am areis	tem ereis	part ireis
	(eles)	am arão	tem erão	part irão
Conditional	(eu)	am aria	tem eria	part iria
	(tu)	am arias	tem erias	part irias
	(ele)	am aria	tem eria	part iria
	(nós)	am aríamos	tem eríamos	part iríamos
	(vós)	am aríeis	tem eríeis	part iríeis
	(eles)	am ariam	tem eriam	part iriam

Pres. subj.	(eu)	am e	tem a	part a
	(tu)	am es	tem as	part as
	(ele)	am e	tem a	part a
	(nós)	am emos	tem amos	part amos
	(vós)	am eis	tem ais	part ais
	(eles)	am em	tem am	part am
Imp. subj.	(eu)	am asse	tem esse	part isse
	(tu)	am asses	tem esses	part isses
	(ele)	am asse	tem esse	part isse
	(nós)	am ássemos	tem êssemos	part íssemos
	(vós)	am ásseis	tem êsseis	part ísseis
	(eles)	am assem	tem essem	part issem
Present part.		am ando	tem endo	part indo
Past part.		am ado	tem ido	part ido

Auxiliary Verbs

	ser *(be)*		ter *(have)*	
	Present	*Imperfect*	*Present*	*Imperfect*
(eu)	sou	era	tenho	tinha
(tu)	és	eras	tens	tinhas
(ele)	é	era	tem	tinha
(nós)	somos	éramos	temos	tínhamos
(vós)	sois	éreis	tendes	tínheis
(eles)	são	eram	têm	tinham
	Past def.	*Future*	*Past def.*	*Future*
(eu)	fui	serei	tive	terei
(tu)	foste	serás	tiveste	terás
(ele)	foi	será	teve	terá
(nós)	fomos	seremos	tivemos	teremos
(vós)	fostes	sereis	tivestes	tereis
(eles)	foram	serão	tiveram	terão
	Pres. subj.	*Imp. subj.*	*Pres. subj.*	*Imp. subj.*
(eu)	seja	fosse	tenha	tivesse
(tu)	sejas	fosses	tenhas	tivesses
(ele)	seja	fosse	tenha	tivesse
(nós)	sejamos	fôssemos	tenhamos	tivéssemos
(vós)	sejais	fôsseis	tenhais	tivésseis
(eles)	sejam	fossem	tenham	tivessem
	Pres. part.	*Past part.*	*Pres. part.*	*Past part.*
	sendo	sido	tendo	tido

Irregular Verbs

Below is a list of the irregular verbs with the tenses most commonly used in Portuguese. In the listing, a) stands for the present tense, b) for the imperfect, c) for the past definite, d) for the future, e) for the present subjunctive and f) for the past participle. All forms of the present tense are given plus the 1st person of the other tenses unless further irregularities occur in the conjugation of the particular tense.

Unless otherwise indicated, verbs with prefixes (*ab-, ad-, ante-, bem-, circum-, com-, contra-, de-, des-, dis-, em-, entre-, ex-, in-, inter-, intro-, mal-, ob-, per-, pre-, pro-, re-, retro-, sob-, sobre-, sub-, sus-, trans-,* etc.) are conjugated like the stem verb.

Although they are irregular, verbs ending in *-ear, -uzir* and *-uir* do not figure below. All those in *-ear* are conjugated as in *barbear;* those in *-uzir* as in *conduzir* and those in *-uir* as in *constituir,* with the exception of *destruir* and *construir* (see list).

abolir *abrogate, abolish*	a) –, –, –, abolimos, abolis, –; b) abolia; c) aboli; d) abolirei; e) –; f) abolido
acudir *help, assist*	a) acudo, acodes, acode, acudimos, acudis, acodem; b) acudia; c) acudi; d) acudirei; e) acuda; f) acudido
aderir *join, agree*	a) adiro, aderes, adere, aderimos, aderis, aderem; b) aderia; c) aderi; d) aderirei; e) adira; f) aderido
advertir *warn, admonish*	→aderir
agredir *attack*	a) agrido, agrides, agride, agredimos, agredis, agridem; b) agredia; c) agredi; d) agredirei; e) agrida; f) agredido
ansiar *crave for; worry*	a) anseio, anseias, anseia, ansiamos, ansiais, anseiam; b) ansiava; c) ansiei; d) ansiarei; e) anseie, anseies, anseie, ansiemos, ansieis, anseiem; f) ansiado
aprazer[1] *please*	a) apraz; b) aprazia; c) aprouve; d) aprazerá; e) apraza; f) aprazido
barbear *shave*	a) barbeio, barbeias, barbeia, barbeamos, barbeais, barbeiam; b) barbeava; c) barbeei; d) barbearei; e) barbeie, barbeies, barbeie, barbeemos, barbeeis, barbeiem; f) barbeado
bulir *move, touch*	→acudir
caber *fit*	a) caibo, cabes, cabe, cabemos, cabeis, cabem; b) cabia; c) coube, coubeste, coube, coubemos, coubestes, couberam; d) caberei; e) caiba; f) cabido
cair *fall*	a) caio, cais, cai, caímos, caís, caiem; b) caía; c) caí; d) cairei; e) caia; f) caído
cobrir *cover*	a) cubro, cobres, cobre, cobrimos, cobris, cobrem; b) cobria; c) cobri; d) cobrirei; e) cubra; f) coberto/cobrido

---

[1] impersonal

colorir *colour, paint*	→abolir
compelir *compel, force*	→aderir
conduzir *lead, drive*	a) conduzo, conduzes, conduz, conduzimos, conduzis, conduzem; b) conduzia; c) conduzi; d) conduzirei; e) conduza; f) conduzido
constituir *constitute*	a) constituo, constituis, constitui, constituímos, constituís, constituem; b) constituía; c) constituí; d) constituirei; e) constitua; f) constituído
construir *build*	a) construo, constróis, constrói, construímos, construís, constroem; b) construía; c) construí; d) construirei; e) construa; f) construído
consumir *consume*	→acudir
convergir *converge*	→emergir
crer *believe*	a) creio, crês, crê, cremos, credes, crêem; b) cria; c) cri; d) crerei; e) creia; f) crido
cuspir *spit*	→acudir
dar *give*	a) dou, dás, dá, damos, dais, dão; b) dava; c) dei, deste, deu, demos, destes, deram; d) darei; e) dê, dês, dê, demos, deis, dêem; f) dado
demolir *demolish*	→abolir
despir *undress*	→aderir
destruir *destroy*	→construir
digerir *digest*	→aderir
discernir *perceive, see*	→aderir
divertir *amuse*	→aderir
dizer *say*	a) digo, dizes, diz, dizemos, dizeis, dizem; b) dizia; c) disse, dissestes, disse, dissemos, dissestes, disseram; d) direi; e) diga; f) dito
doer *hurt*	→moer (only in 3rd person singular and plural)
dormir *sleep*	→cobrir; f) dormido

emergir
emerge

a) –, emerges, emerge, emergimos, emergis, emergem;
b) emergia; c) emergi; d) emergirei; e) –; f) emergido/
emerso

engolir
swallow

→cobrir; f) engolido

estar
be

a) estou, estás, está, estamos, estais, estão; b) estava;
c) estive, estiveste, esteve, estivemos, estivestes,
estiveram; d) estarei; e) esteja; f) estado

explodir
explode, burst

→abolir

extorquir
extort

→abolir

fazer
do, make

a) faço, fazes, faz, fazemos, fazeis, fazem; b) fazia;
c) fiz, fizeste, fez, fizemos, fizestes, fizeram; d) farei;
e) faça; f) feito

ferir
wound, hurt

→aderir

fugir
run away, escape

a) fujo, foges, foge, fugimos, fugis, fogem; b) fugia;
c) fugi; d) fugirei; e) fuja; f) fugido

gerir
administer, organize

→aderir

haver[1]
have; be

a) há; b) havia; c) houve; d) haverá; e) haja; f) havido

haver de
have to

a) hei-de, hás-de, há-de, havemos de, haveis de, hão-de;
b) havia de; c) –; d) –; e) –; f) –

impelir
drive, force

→aderir

incendiar
set on fire

→ansiar

inserir
insert

→aderir

ir
go

a) vou, vais, vai, vamos, ides, vão; b) ia; c) fui, foste,
foi, fomos, fostes, foram; d) irei; e) vá, vás, vá, vamos,
vades, vão; f) ido

jazer
lie (here lies)

a) jazo, jazes, jaz, jazemos, jazeis, jazem; b) jazia;
c) jazi; d) jazerei; e) jaza; f) jazido

ler
read

a) leio, lês, lê, lemos, ledes, lêem; b) lia; c) li; d) lerei;
e) leia; f) lido

mediar
mediate

→ansiar

medir
measure

a) meço, medes, mede, medimos, medis, medem;
b) media; c) medi; d) medirei; e) meça; f) medido

---

[1] impersonal

mentir	→aderir
lie (tell lies)	
moer	a) moo, móis, mói, moemos, moeis, moem;
grind	b) moía; c) moí; d) moerei; e) moa; f) moído
negociar	→ansiar
negociate	
odiar	→ansiar
hate	
ouvir	a) ouço, ouves, ouve, ouvimos, ouvis, ouvem; b) ouvia;
hear, listen	c) ouvi; d) ouvirei; e) ouça; f) ouvido
pedir	→medir
ask	
perder	a) perco, perdes, perde, perdemos, perdeis, perdem;
lose	b) perdia; c) perdi; d) perderei; e) perca; f) perdido
poder	a) posso, podes, pode, podemos, podeis, podem;
be able to	b) podia; c) pude, pudeste, pôde, pudemos, pudestes,
	puderam; d) poderei; e) possa; f) podido
polir	→abolir
polish	
por	a) ponho, pões, põe, pomos, pondes, põem; b) punha,
put	punhas, punha, púnhamos, púnheis, punham; c) pus,
	puseste, pôs, pusemos, pusestes, puseram; d) porei;
	e) ponha; f) posto
premiar	→ansiar
award	
prevenir	→agredir
prevent; warn	
prover	a) provejo, provês, provê, provemos, provedes,
provide	provêem; b) provia; c) provi; d) proverei; e) proveja;
	f) provido
querer	a) quero, queres, quer, queremos, quereis, querem;
want, wish	b) queria; c) quis, quiseste, quis, quisemos, quisestes,
	quiseram; d) quererei; e) queira; f) querido
reflectir	→aderir
reflect; ponder	
remediar	→ansiar
put right, palliate	
repetir	→aderir
repeat	
requerer	a) requeiro, requeres, requer, requeremos, requereis,
request	requerem; b) requeria; c) requeri; d) requererei;
	e) requeira; f) requerido
rir	a) rio, ris, ri, rimos, rides, riem; b) ria; c) ri; d) rirei;
laugh	e) ria; f) rido

saber	a) sei, sabes, sabe, sabemos, sabeis, sabem; b) sabia;
know	c) soube, soubeste, soube, soubemos, soubestes, souberam; d) saberei; e) saiba; f) sabido
sair	a) saio, sais, sai, saímos, saís, saem; b) saía;
go out	c) saí; d) sairei; e) saia; f) saído
seguir	→aderir
follow	
sentir	→aderir
feel; be sorry	
servir	→aderir
serve	
subir	→acudir
go up, ascend	
sugerir	→aderir
suggest	
tossir	→cobrir; f) tossido
cough	
trair	→cair
betray	
trazer	a) trago, trazes, traz, trazemos, trazeis, trazem;
bring	b) trazia; c) trouxe, trouxeste, trouxe, trouxemos, trouxestes, trouxeram; d) trarei; e) traga; f) trazido
valer	a) valho, vales, vale, valemos, valeis, valem; b) valia;
be worth	c) vali; d) valerei; e) valha; f) valido
ver	a) vejo, vês, vê, vemos, vedes, vêem; b) via; c) vi, viste,
see, watch	viu, vimos, vistes, viram; d) verei; e) veja; f) visto
vestir	→aderir
dress	
vir	a) venho, vens, vem, vimos, vindes, vêm; b) vinha,
come	vinhas, vinha, vínhamos, vínheis, vinham; c) vim, vieste, veio, viemos, viestes, vieram; d) virei; e) venha; f) vindo

Portuguese abbreviations

(a)	*assinado*	signed
a/c	*ao cuidado de*	c/o
a.C., A.C.	*antes de Cristo*	B.C.
A.C.B.	*Automóvel Clube do Brasil*	Brazilian Automobile Association
A.C.P.	*Automóvel Clube de Portugal*	Portuguese Automobile Association
A.D.	*anno Domini*	A.D.
Al.	*alameda*	lane, alley
apart., ap.	*apartamento*	flat, apartment
Av.	*avenida*	avenue; alley
BB	*Banco do Brasil*	Bank of Brazil
B.º	*beco*	cul-de-sac, blind alley
c/	*com; conta*	with; account
c/c	*conta corrente*	current account
c/v	*cave*	basement, cellar
C.ª, Cia, Cⁱᵃ	*companhia*	company
Calç.	*calçada*	paved street
CEE	*Comunidade Económica Europeia*	EEC, Common Market
C.M.	*Câmara Municipal*	Local council
CP	*Caminhos de Ferro Portugueses*	Portuguese Railways
C.P.	*caixa postal*	p.o. box
Cr$	*cruzeiro*	Brazilian monetary unit
C.T.B.	*Companhia Telefônica Brasileira*	Brazilian Telephone Company
C.T.T.	*Correios, Telégrafos e Telefones*	Post Office, Telegraph, Telephone
Cv., ctv.	*centavo*	¹⁄₁₀₀ of an escudo (or a cruzeiro)
c.v.	*cavalo-vapor*	horsepower
D.	*Dona*	Miss, Mrs. (title of courtesy)
d., dto.	*direito*	on the right (part of an address)
d.C., D.C.	*depois de Cristo*	A.D.
D.F.	*Distrito Federal (Brasília)*	Federal District of Brasilia
Dr.	*Doutor*	Doctor

Dra.	*Doutora*	Doctor (fem)
e., esq.	*esquerdo*	left-hand (part of an address)
E.C.T.	*Empresa de Correios e Telégrafos*	Brazilian Post and Telegraph Company
E.F.C.B.	*Estrada de Ferro Central do Brasil*	Brazilian Railways
ENATUR	*Empresa Nacional de Turismo*	Portuguese National Tourist Office
End.	*endereço*	address
E.R.	*Espera resposta*	please reply
Esc.	*escudo*	Portuguese monetary unit
Ex.ª, Excia.	*Excelência*	Excellency
Ex.ma (Sra.)	*Excelentíssima (Senhora)*	title of courtesy (followed by Mrs. or Mr.)
Ex.mo (Sr.)	*Excelentíssimo (Senhor)*	
G.B.	*Estado da Guanabara*	State of Guanabara
G.N.R.	*Guarda Nacional Republicana*	National Republican Guard (police)
h	*hora(s)*	o'clock
Ilma. (Sra.)	*Ilustríssima (Senhora)*	title of courtesy (followed by Mrs. or Mr.)
Ilmo. (Sr.)	*Ilustríssimo (Senhor)*	
L., L.º	*Largo*	square, plaza
Lda., Ltda.	*limitada*	Limited
Lx.ª	*Lisboa*	Lisbon
méd.	*médico*	physician
Men.ª	*Menina*	Miss
n/	*nosso, nossa*	our
Obg., Obr.º	*obrigado*	thank you
P., Pr.	*praça*	square
pág., p.	*página*	page
R.	*rua*	street
r/c	*rés-do-chão*	ground floor
reg.º	*registado; regulamento*	registered; regulation
Rem., Rem.te	*remetente*	sender
Revmo.	*Reverendíssimo*	Reverend Father
R.P.	*Rádio-Patrulha*	Police-Patrol

R.S.F.F.	*responda se faz favor*	please reply, R.S.V.P.
RTI	*Rádio e Televisão Independente*	Independent Portuguese Broadcasting Company
RTP	*Rádio e Televisão Portuguesa*	Portuguese Broadcasting Company
s/	*sem; seu, sua*	without; your
S., Sto.	*São, Santo*	saint
S.A.	*Sociedade Anónima*	Incorporated
s.f.f.	*se faz favor*	please
S.P.	*Estado de São Paulo*	State of São Paulo
Sr., Sra.	*Senhor, Senhora*	Mr., Mrs.
Sta.	*Santa*	saint (fem)
Tr., Trav.	*travessa*	by-lane, passageway
v/	*vosso, vossa*	your
v.	*você*	you
v.°	*verso*	back, reverse
V.S.F.F.	*volte se faz favor*	please turn over

Numerals

Cardinal numbers		Ordinal numbers	
0	zero	1.	primeiro
1	um	2.	segundo
2	dois	3.	terceiro
3	três	4.	quarto
4	quatro	5.	quinto
5	cinco	6.	sexto
6	seis	7.	sétimo
7	sete	8.	oitavo
8	oito	9.	nono
9	nove	10.	décimo
10	dez	11.	décimo primeiro
11	onze	12.	décimo segundo
12	doze	13.	décimo terceiro
13	treze	14.	décimo quarto
14	catorze	15.	décimo quinto
15	quinze	16.	décimo sexto
16	dezasseis	17.	décimo sétimo
17	dezassete	20.	vigésimo
18	dezoito	21.	vigésimo primeiro
19	dezanove	22.	vigésimo segundo
20	vinte	30.	trigésimo
21	vinte e um	40.	quadragésimo
22	vinte e dois	50.	quinquagésimo
30	trinta	60.	sexagésimo
31	trinta e um	70.	septuagésimo
40	quarenta	80.	octogésimo
50	cinquenta	90.	nonagésimo
60	sessenta	100.	centésimo
70	setenta	101.	centésimo primeiro
80	oitenta	200.	ducentésimo
90	noventa	300.	tricentésimo
100	cem	400.	quadringentésimo
101	cento e um	500.	quingentésimo
200	duzentos	600.	seiscentésimo
300	trezentos	700.	septingentésimo
500	quinhentos	800.	octingentésimo
1.000	mil	900.	nongentésimo
1.107	mil cento e sete	1.000.	milésimo
2.000	dois mil	1.107.	milésimo centésimo sétimo
1.000.000	um milhão	2.000.	dois milésimo

Time

uma hora

uma e cinco

cinco para as duas

uma e dez

dez para as duas

uma e um quarto

um quarto para as duas

uma e vinte

vinte para as duas

uma e vinte e cinco

vinte e cinco para as duas

uma e meia

If you have to indicate that it is a.m. or p.m., add *da manhã, da tarde* or *da noite*.

Thus:

oito da manhã	8 a.m.
duas da tarde	2 p.m.
oito da noite	8 p.m.

Days of the week

domingo	Sunday	*quinta-feira*	Thursday
segunda-feira	Monday	*sexta-feira*	Friday
terça-feira	Tuesday	*sábado*	Saturday
quarta-feira	Wednesday		

Conversion tables /
Tabelas de conversão

C°   F°

100 — 212
40 — 105
36,9 — 98,6
35 —
30 — 90
     — 80
25 —
20 — 70
15 — 60
10 — 50
5 —
     — 40
0 — 32
     — 30
−5 —
     — 20
−10 —
     — 10
−15 —
     — 0
−20 —

Metres and Feet
The figure in the middle stands for both metres and feet, e.g. 1 metre = 3.281 ft. and 1 foot = 0.30 m.

Metros e pés
O algarismo do meio representa, ao mesmo tempo, metros e pés. Por ex.: 1 metro = 3,281 pés e 1 pé = 0,30 m.

Metres/Metros		Feet/Pés
0.30	1	3.281
0.61	2	6.563
0.91	3	9.843
1.22	4	13.124
1.52	5	16.403
1.83	6	19.686
2.13	7	22.967
2.44	8	26.248
2.74	9	29.529
3.05	10	32.810
3.66	12	39.372
4.27	14	45.934
6.10	20	65.620
7.62	25	82.023
15.24	50	164.046
22.86	75	246.069
30.48	100	328.092

Temperature
To convert Centigrade to Fahrenheit, multiply by 1.8 and add 32.
To convert Fahrenheit to Centigrade, subtract 32 from Fahrenheit and divide by 1.8.

Temperatura
Para converter os graus centígrados em graus Fahrenheit, multiplique-os primeiro por 1,8 e adicione 32 ao total.
Para converter graus Fahrenheit em graus centígrados, subtraia 32 e divida o resultado por 1,8.

Some Basic Phrases	Algumas expressões de uso corrente
Please.	Por favor.
Thank you very much.	Muito obrigado.
Don't mention it.	Não tem de quê.
Good morning.	Bom dia.
Good afternoon.	Boa tarde.
Good evening.	Boa noite.
Good night.	Boa noite.
Good-bye.	Adeus.
See you later.	Até logo.
Where is/Where are…?	Onde é/Onde são…?
What do you call this?	Como chama isto?
What does that mean?	O que quer dizer isso?
Do you speak English?	Fala inglês?
Do you speak German?	Fala alemão?
Do you speak French?	Fala francês?
Do you speak Spanish?	Fala espanhol?
Do you speak Italian?	Fala italiano?
Could you speak more slowly, please?	Não se importava de falar mais devagar, por favor?
I don't understand.	Não compreendo.
Can I have…?	Pode dar-me…?
Can you show me…?	Pode indicar-me…?
Can you tell me…?	Pode dizer-me…?
Can you help me, please?	Pode ajudar-me, por favor?
I'd like…	Gostava…
We'd like…	Gostávamos…
Please give me…	Por favor, dê-me…
Please bring me…	Por favor, traga-me…
I'm hungry.	Tenho fome.
I'm thirsty.	Tenho sede.
I'm lost.	Perdi-me.
Hurry up!	Despache-se!

| There is/There are... | Há... |
| There isn't/There aren't... | Não há... |

Arrival

Chegada

Your passport, please.	O seu passaporte, por favor.
Have you anything to declare?	Tem alguma coisa a declarar?
No, nothing at all.	Não, nada.
Can you help me with my luggage, please?	Pode levar-me a bagagem, por favor?
Where's the bus to the centre of town, please?	Onde se apanha o autocarro (ônibus) para o centro da cidade, por favor?
This way, please.	Por aqui, por favor.
Where can I get a taxi?	Onde posso arranjar um táxi?
What's the fare to...?	Qual é o preço do percurso para...?
Take me to this address, please.	Leve-me a esta direcção, por favor.
I'm in a hurry.	Estou com pressa.

Hotel

Hotel

My name is...	Chamo-me...
Have you a reservation?	Reservou?
I'd like a room with a bath.	Queria um quarto com casa de banho (banheiro).
What's the price per night?	Qual é o preço por noite?
May I see the room?	Posso ver o quarto?
What's my room number, please?	Qual é o número do meu quarto, por favor?
There's no hot water.	Não há água quente.
May I see the manager, please?	Posso ver o director, por favor?
Did anyone telephone me?	Não houve nenhum telefonema para mim?
Is there any mail for me?	Há correio para mim?
May I have my bill (check), please?	Pode dar-me a conta, por favor?

Eating out | ## Restaurante

Eating out	Restaurante
Do you have a fixed-price menu?	Tem uma ementa (um cardápio)?
May I see the menu?	Posso ver a lista?
May we have an ashtray, please?	Pode trazer-nos um cinzeiro, por favor?
Where's the toilet, please?	Onde são os lavabos, por favor?
I'd like an hors d'œuvre (starter).	Queria um acepipe.
Have you any soup?	Tem sopa?
I'd like some fish.	Queria peixe.
What kind of fish do you have?	Que peixe tem?
I'd like a steak.	Queria um bife.
What vegetables have you got?	Que legumes tem?
Nothing more, thanks.	Mais nada, obrigado.
What would you like to drink?	Que desejava beber?
I'll have a beer, please.	Queria uma cerveja, por favor.
I'd like a bottle of wine.	Queria uma garrafa de vinho.
May I have the bill (check), please?	Pode trazer-me a conta, por favor?
Is service included?	O serviço está incluído?
Thank you, that was a very good meal.	Obrigado, a comida estava muito boa.

Travelling | ## Excursões

Travelling	Excursões
Where's the railway station, please?	Onde é a estação, por favor?
Where's the ticket office, please?	Onde é a bilheteira (bilheteria), por favor?
I'd like a ticket to…	Queria um bilhete para…
First or second class?	Primeira ou segunda classe?
First class, please.	Primeira classe, por favor.
Single or return (one way or roundtrip)?	Ida ou ida e volta?
Do I have to change trains?	Devo mudar de comboio (trem)?
What platform does the train for… leave from?	De que cais parte o comboio (trem) para…?

Where's the nearest underground (subway) station?	Onde é a estação do metro mais próxima?
Where's the bus station, please?	Onde é a paragem dos autocarros (ônibus), por favor?
When's the first bus to…?	A que horas parte o primeiro autocarro (ônibus) para…?
Please let me off at the next stop.	Por favor, deixe-me na próxima paragem (parada).

Relaxing

Distracções

What's on at the cinema (movies)?	O que vai no cinema?
What time does the film begin?	A que horas começa o filme?
Are there any tickets for tonight?	Ainda há bilhetes para hoje à noite?
Where can we go dancing?	Onde podemos ir dançar?

Meeting people

Encontros

How do you do.	Bom dia.
How are you?	Como está?
Very well, thank you. And you?	Bem, obrigado. E você/a senhora/a menina/o senhor?
May I introduce…?	Posso apresentar-lhe…?
My name is…	Chamo-me…
I'm very pleased to meet you.	Muito prazer em conhecê-lo (la).
How long have you been here?	Há quanto tempo está aqui?
It was nice meeting you.	Tive muito gosto em conhecê-lo (la).
Do you mind if I smoke?	Não se importa que eu fume?
Do you have a light, please?	Tem lume (fogo), por favor?
May I get you a drink?	Posso oferecer-lhe uma bebida?
May I invite you for dinner tonight?	Posso convidá-la para jantar hoje à noite?
Where shall we meet?	Onde nos encontramos?

Shops, stores and services

Where's the nearest bank, please?	Onde é o banco mais próximo, por favor?
Where can I cash some travellers' cheques?	Onde posso trocar cheques de viagem?
Can you give me some small change, please?	Pode-me dar dinheiro trocado, por favor?
Where's the nearest chemist's (pharmacy)?	Onde é a farmácia mais próxima?
How do I get there?	Como posso ir para lá?
Is it within walking distance?	Pode-se ir a pé?
Can you help me, please?	Pode ajudar-me, por favor?
How much is this? And that?	Quanto custa isto? E aquilo?
It's not quite what I want.	Não é bem o que quero.
I like it.	Gosto.
Can you recommend something for sunburn?	Pode aconselhar-me qualquer coisa contra as queimaduras do sol?
I'd like a haircut, please.	Queria cortar o cabelo, por favor.
I'd like a manicure, please.	Queria arranjar as unhas, por favor.

Estabelecimentos

Street directions

Can you show me on the map where I am?	Pode mostrar-me no mapa onde estou?
You are on the wrong road.	Enganou-se na estrada.
Go/Walk straight ahead.	Siga sempre em frente.
It's on the left/on the right.	É à esquerda/à direita.

Direcções

Emergencies

Call a doctor quickly.	Chame depressa um médico.
Call an ambulance.	Chame uma ambulância.
Please call the police.	Chame a polícia, por favor.

Urgências

inglês-português

english-portuguese

Introdução

Este dicionário foi elaborado com um fim prático. A informação linguística é a estritamente necessária. As palavras encontram-se por ordem alfabética, quer sejam simples ou compostas, quer levem ou não traço de união. Única excepção à regra: os verbos reflexos e algumas expressões idiomáticas que foram ordenados em relação ao verbo simples ou à palavra principal.

Quando uma palavra é seguida de expressões correntes ou locuções, estas encontram-se igualmente dispostas por ordem alfabética na rubrica da palavra principal.

Todas as palavras principais trazem a respectiva transcrição fonética e a indicação da classe morfológica (substantivo, verbo, adjectivo, etc.). Quando uma palavra principal pertence a várias classes morfológicas, as respectivas traduções encontram-se a seguir a cada uma delas.

Damos todos os plurais irregulares dos substantivos, assim como certos plurais que possam suscitar dúvidas.

Para evitarmos repetições, usámos um til (~) em lugar da palavra principal.

No plural dos nomes compostos, o travessão (-) substitui o elemento que permanece invariável.

Um asterisco (*) assinala os verbos irregulares. Para mais pormenores, consulte a lista destes verbos.

Este dicionário toma em consideração a ortografia inglesa. As palavras e as definições dos termos tipicamente americanos são indicados como tais (veja a lista das abreviaturas usadas no texto).

Abreviaturas

adj	adjectivo	*n*	nome (substantivo)
adv	advérbio	*nAm*	nome (americano)
Am	americano	*num*	numeral
art	artigo	*p*	imperfeito
Br	brasileiro	*pl*	plural
conj	conjunção	*plAm*	plural (americano)
f	feminino	*pp*	particípio passado
fBr	feminino (brasileiro)	*pr*	presente do indicativo
fpl	feminino plural	*pref*	prefixo
fplBr	feminino plural	*prep*	preposição
	(brasileiro)	*pron*	pronome
m	masculino	*v*	verbo
mBr	masculino (brasileiro)	*vAm*	verbo
mpl	masculino plural		(americano)
mplBr	masculino plural	*vBr*	verbo
	(brasileiro)		(brasileiro)

188

Guia de pronúncia

Cada palavra principal desta parte do dicionário traz uma transcrição
fonética que lhe indica a pronúncia. Deve lê-la como se cada letra
ou grupo de letras tivesse o mesmo valor do que em português. A seguir
figuram unicamente as letras e os símbolos ambíguos ou particularmente difíceis de compreender.

As sílabas estão separadas por traços de união e as tónicas estão
impressas em *itálico*.

É evidente que os sons das duas línguas raras vezes coincidem exactamente, mas, se seguir cuidadosamente as nossas indicações, será capaz
de pronunciar as palavras estrangeiras de maneira a fazer-se entender.
Para facilitar o seu trabalho, as nossas transcrições simplificam, por
vezes, ligeiramente, o sistema fonético da língua, sem deixar, por isso,
de reflectir as diferenças de sons essenciais.

Consoantes

b	sempre como em **b**oca
d	sempre como em **d**ia
ð	parecido com o **d** de na**d**a
gh	como o **g** de **g**ato
h	pronuncia-se expirando rápida e fortemente
k	como o **c** de **c**asa; mas, antes de uma vogal tónica, ouve-se um **h** aspirado depois do **k**
ng	como o **n** de bra**n**co
p	como em **p**orto; mas, antes de uma vogal tónica, ouve-se um **h** aspirado depois do **p**
r	parecido com o **r** de ca**r**a, mas mais fraco
t	como em **t**odo; mas, antes de uma vogal tónica, ouve-se um **h** aspirado depois do **t**
θ	como o **s** de **s**aco, pronunciado com a língua entre os dentes

Vogais e ditongos

a	como em s**a**co
ă	como o **a** de p**o**rta

æ   entre o **a** de saco e o **é** de café

i   parecido com o **i** de fácil

1) As vogais longas estão impressas em duplicado.

2) As letras impressas em caracteres pequenos e elevados (por ex.: **ⁱéç, aiª**) devem pronunciar-se rapidamente e com menos intensidade.

Pronúncia americana

A nossa transcrição corresponde à pronúncia da Grã-Bretanha. Embora existam variações regionais notáveis na língua americana, esta apresenta, em geral, algumas diferenças importantes em relação ao inglês da Grã-Bretanha.

Eis aqui alguns exemplos:

1) O **r**, diante de uma consoante ou no final de uma palavra, pronuncia-se sempre (ao contrário da pronúncia inglesa habitual).

2) Em muitas palavras (por ex.: *ask, castle, laugh,* etc.) o **aa** transforma-se em **ææ**.

3) O som inglês **o** pronuncia-se **a** ou também **óó**.

4) Em palavras como *duty, tune, new,* etc., **uu** transforma-se muitas vezes em **ⁱuu**.

5) Por último, o acento tónico de algumas palavras pode variar consideravelmente.

A

a (ei-ă) *art* (an) um, uma

abbey (æ-bi) *n* abadia *f*

abbreviation (ă-brii-vi-*ei*-chănn) *n* abreviatura *f*

aberration (æ-bă-*rei*-chănn) *n* aberração *f*

ability (ă-*bi*-lă-ti) *n* capacidade *f*; habilidade *f*

able (*ei*-băl) *adj* capaz; *be ~ to *ser capaz de; *poder

abnormal (æb-*nóó*-măl) *adj* anormal

aboard (ă-*bóód*) *adv* a bordo

abolish (ă-*bó*-lich) *v* *abolir

abortion (ă-*bóó*-chănn) *n* aborto *m*

about (ă-*baut*) *prep* acerca de; a respeito de, referente a; em volta de; *adv* cerca de, aproximadamente; à volta, em volta

above (ă-*bav*) *prep* sobre; *adv* em cima

abroad (ă-*bróód*) *adv* no estrangeiro, para o estrangeiro

abscess (æb-*çéç*) *n* abcesso *m*

absence (æb-çănnç) *n* ausência *f*

absent (æb-çănnt) *adj* ausente

absolutely (æb-çă-luut-li) *adv* absolutamente

abstain from (ăb-*çteinn*) *abster-se de

abstract (æb-*çtrækt*) *adj* abstracto

absurd (ăb-*çääd*) *adj* absurdo

abundance (ă-*bann*-dănnç) *n* abundância *f*

abundant (ă-*bann*-dănnt) *adj* abundante

abuse (ă-*b*ⁱ*uuç*) *n* abuso *m*

abyss (ă-*biç*) *n* abismo *m*

academy (ă-*kæ*-dă-mi) *n* academia *f*

accelerate (ăk-*çé*-lă-reit) *v* acelerar

accelerator (ăk-*çé*-lă-rei-tă) *n* acelerador *m*

accent (æk-çănnt) *n* sotaque *m*; acento *m*

accept (ăk-*cépt*) *v* aceitar

access (æk-çéç) *n* acesso *m*

accessary (ăk-*çé*-çă-ri) *n* cúmplice *m*

accessible (ăk-*çé*-çă-băl) *adj* acessível

accessories (ăk-*çé*-çă-riz) *pl* acessórios

accident (æk-çi-dănnt) *n* acidente *m*, desastre *m*

accidental (æk-çi-*dénn*-tăl) *adj* acidental

accommodate (ă-*kó*-mă-deit) *v* acomodar, alojar

accommodation (ă-kó-mă-*dei*-chănn) *n* acomodação *f*, alojamento *m*

accompany (ă-*kamm*-pă-ni) *v* acompanhar

accomplish (ă-*kamm*-plich) *v* terminar; realizar

in accordance with (inn ă-*kóó*-dănnç ᵘiᵈ) conforme

according to (ă-*kóó*-dinng tuu) conforme, segundo

account (ă-*kaunnt*) n conta f; relato m; ~ **for** explicar, justificar; **on** ~ **of** por causa de

accountable (ă-*kaunn*-tă-băl) adj explicável

accurate (æ-kⁱu-rắt) adj exacto

accuse (ă-kⁱ*uuz*) v acusar

accused (ă-kⁱ*uuzd*) n acusado m

accustom (ă-*ka*-çtămm) v acostumar; **accustomed** costumado, habituado

ache (eik) v *doer; n dor f

achieve (ă-*tchiiv*) v alcançar; realizar, *concluir

achievement (ă-*tchiiv*-mănnt) n realização f

acid (æ-çid) n ácido m

acknowledge (ăk-*nó*-lidj) v reconhecer; admitir

acne (æk-ni) n acne f

acorn (*ei*-kóónn) n bolota f

acquaintance (ă-kᵘ*einn*-tănnç) n conhecido m, conhecimento m

acquire (ă-k*uaiᵃ*) v adquirir

acquisition (æ-kᵘi-zi-chănn) n aquisição f

acquittal (ă-kᵘi-tăl) n absolvição f

across (ă-*króç*) prep através; do outro lado de; adv no outro lado

act (ækt) n acto m; número m; v agir; comportar-se; representar

action (æk-chănn) n acção f

active (æk-tiv) adj activo

activity (æk-*ti*-vă-ti) n actividade f

actor (æk-tă) n actor m

actress (æk-triç) n actriz f

actual (æk-tchu-ăl) adj verdadeiro, real, efectivo

actually (æk-tchu-ă-li) adv realmente

acute (ă-kⁱ*uut*) adj agudo

adapt (ă-*dæpt*) v adaptar

add (æd) v adicionar; juntar

adding-machine (æ-dinng-mă-chiinn) n calculador m

addition (ă-*di*-chănn) n adição f

additional (ă-*di*-chă-năl) adj adicional; suplementar; acessório

address (ă-*dréç*) n endereço m; v endereçar; dirigir-se a

addressee (æ-dré-çii) n destinatário m

adequate (æ-di-kᵘăt) adj adequado, apropriado

adjective (æ-djik-tiv) n adjectivo m

adjourn (ă-*djăănn*) v adiar

adjust (ă-*djaçt*) v ajustar

administer (ăd-*mi*-ni-çtă) v administrar

administration (ăd-mi-ni-*çtrei*-chănn) n administração f; gestão f

administrative (ăd-*mi*-ni-çtră-tiv) adj administrativo; ~ **law** direito administrativo

admiral (æd-mă-răl) n almirante m

admiration (æd-mă-*rei*-chănn) n admiração f

admire (ăd-*maiᵃ*) v admirar

admission (ăd-*mi*-chănn) n admissão f

admit (ăd-*mit*) v admitir; reconhecer

admittance (ăd-*mi*-tănnç) n entrada f; **no** ~ entrada proibida

adopt (ă-*dópt*) v adoptar

adorable (ă-*dóó*-ră-băl) adj adorável

adult (æ-dalt) n adulto m; adj adulto

advance (ăd-*vaannç*) n avanço m; adiantamento m; v avançar; adiantar; **in** ~ antecipadamente, adiantadamente

advanced (ăd-*vaannçt*) adj avançado

advantage (ăd-*vaann*-tidj) n vantagem f

advantageous (æd-vănn-*tei*-djăç) adj vantajoso

adventure (ăd-*vénn*-tchă) n aventura f

adverb (*æd*-vääb) *n* advérbio *m*

advertisement (ăd-*vää*-tiç-mănnt) *n* anúncio *m*

advertising (*æd*-vă-tai-zinng) *n* publicidade *f*

advice (ăd-*vaiç*) *n* conselho *m*

advise (ăd-*vaiz*) *v* aconselhar

advocate (*æd*-vă-kăt) *n* advogado *m*, defensor *m*

aerial (*é*ª-ri-ăl) *n* antena *f*

aeroplane (*é*ª-ră-pleinn) *n* avião *m*

affair (ă-*fé*ª) *n* assunto *m*; ligação *f*, aventura *f*

affect (ă-*fékt*) *v* afectar

affected (ă-*fék*-tid) *adj* afectado

affection (ă-*fék*-chănn) *n* afecção *f*; afeição *f*

affectionate (ă-*fék*-chă-nit) *adj* afectuoso

affiliated (ă-*fi*-li-ei-tid) *adj* filiado

affirmative (ă-*fãã*-mă-tiv) *adj* afirmativo

affliction (ă-*flik*-chănn) *n* sofrimento *m*

afford (ă-*fóód*) *v* permitir-se

afraid (ă-*freid*) *adj* assustado, com medo; *be ~ *ter medo

Africa (*æ*-fri-kă) África *f*

African (*æ*-fri-kănn) *adj* africano

after (*aaf*-tă) *prep* depois de; *conj* depois que

afternoon (aaf-tă-*nuunn*) *n* tarde *f*

afterwards (*aaf*-tă-ªădz) *adv* depois; em seguida

again (ă-*ghénn*) *adv* outra vez; de novo; **again and again** repetidamente

against (ă-*ghénnçt*) *prep* contra

age (eidj) *n* idade *f*; **of ~ ** maior; **under ~ ** menor

aged (*ei*-djid) *adj* velho

agency (*ei*-djănn-çi) *n* agência *f*; repartição *f*

agenda (ă-*djénn*-dă) *n* agenda *f*; ordem do dia

agent (*ei*-djănnt) *n* agente *m*, representante *m*

aggressive (ă-*ghré*-çiv) *adj* agressivo

ago (ă-*gho*ᵘ) *adv* há; **long ~ ** há muito tempo

agrarian (ă-*ghré*ª-ri-ănn) *adj* agrário, agrícola

agree (ă-*ghrii*) *v* concordar; *consentir

agreeable (ă-*ghrii*-ă-băl) *adj* agradável

agreement (ă-*ghrii*-mănnt) *n* contrato *m*; acordo *m*

agriculture (*æ*-ghri-kal-tchă) *n* agricultura *f*

ahead (ă-*héd*) *adv* em frente; **~ of** adiante de; **go ~ ** continuar; **straight ~ ** sempre a direito

aid (eid) *n* ajuda *f*; *v* ajudar, auxiliar

ailment (*eil*-mănnt) *n* mal *m*; achaque *m*

aim (eimm) *n* objectivo *m*; **~ at** apontar para, visar; aspirar, aspirar a

air (é*ª*) *n* ar *m*; *v* arejar

air-conditioning (*é*ª-kănn-di-chă-ninng) *n* ar condicionado; **air-conditioned** com ar condicionado

aircraft (*é*ª-kraaft) *n* (pl ~) avião *m*

airfield (*é*ª-fiild) *n* campo de aviação

air-filter (*é*ª-fil-tă) *n* filtro de ar

airline (*é*ª-lainn) *n* companhia de aviação

airmail (*é*ª-meil) *n* correio aéreo

airplane (*é*ª-pleinn) *nAm* avião *m*

airport (*é*ª-póót) *n* aeroporto *m*

air-sickness (*é*ª-çik-năç) *n* enjoo *m*

airtight (*é*ª-tait) *adj* hermético

airy (*é*ª-ri) *adj* arejado

aisle (ail) *n* nave lateral; passagem *f*

alarm (ă-*laamm*) *n* alarme *m*; *v* alarmar

alarm-clock (ă-*laamm*-klók) *n* despertador *m*

album (*æl*-bămm) *n* álbum *m*

alcohol (*æl*-kă-hól) *n* álcool *m*

alcoholic (æl-kă-*hó*-lik) *adj* alcoólico

ale (eil) *n* cerveja *f*

algebra (*æl*-dji-bră) *n* álgebra *f*

Algeria (æl-*dji*ᵃ-ri-ă) Argélia *f*

Algerian (æl-*dji*ᵃ-ri-ănn) *adj* argelino

alien (*ei*-li-ănn) *n* estrangeiro *m*; estranho *m*; *adj* estrangeiro

alike (ă-*laik*) *adj* igual, semelhante; *adv* igualmente

alimony (*æ*-li-mă-ni) *n* pensão alimentícia

alive (ă-*laiv*) *adj* vivo, com vida

all (óól) *adj* todo; tudo; ~ in tudo incluído; ~ right! está bem!; at ~ de todo

allergy (*æ*-lă-dji) *n* alergia *f*

alley (*æ*-li) *n* viela *f*, beco *m*

alliance (ă-*lai*-ănnç) *n* aliança *f*

Allies (*æ*-laiz) *pl* Aliados *mpl*

allot (ă-*lót*) *v* *atribuir

allow (ă-*lau*) *v* permitir, *consentir; ~ to autorizar a; *be allowed *estar autorizado

allowance (ă-*lau*-ănnç) *n* subsídio *m*

all-round (óól-*raunnd*) *adj* polivalente

almanac (óól-mă-næk) *n* almanaque *m*

almond (aa-mănnd) *n* amêndoa *f*

almost (óól-moᵘçt) *adv* quase

alone (ă-*lo*ᵘnn) *adv* só

along (ă-*lónn*) *prep* ao longo de

aloud (ă-*laud*) *adv* em voz alta

alphabet (*æl*-fă-bét) *n* alfabeto *m*

already (óól-*ré*-di) *adv* já

also (óól-çoᵘ) *adv* também, igualmente

altar (óól-tă) *n* altar *m*

alter (óól-tă) *v* alterar

alteration (óól-tă-*rei*-chănn) *n* alteração *f*

alternate (óól-*tă*ă-năt) *adj* alternado

alternative (óól-*tă*ă-nă-tiv) *n* alterna-

tiva *f*

although (óól-*ðo*ᵘ) *conj* embora

altitude (*æl*-ti-tᵘud) *n* altitude *f*

alto (*æl*-toᵘ) *n* (pl ~s) contralto *m*

altogether (óól-tă-*ghé*-ðă) *adv* inteiramente; totalmente; ao todo

always (óól-ᵘeiz) *adv* sempre

am (æmm) *v* (pr be)

amaze (ă-*meiz*) *v* espantar, surpreender

amazement (ă-*meiz*-mănnt) *n* espanto *m*

ambassador (æmm-*bæ*-çă-dă) *n* embaixador *m*

amber (*æmm*-bă) *n* âmbar *m*

ambiguous (æmm-*bi*-gh'u-ăç) *adj* ambíguo; equívoco

ambitious (æmm-*bi*-chăç) *adj* ambicioso

ambulance (*æmm*-b'u-lănnç) *n* ambulância *f*

ambush (*æmm*-buch) *n* emboscada *f*

America (ă-*mé*-ri-kă) América *f*

American (ă-*mé*-ri-kănn) *adj* americano

amethyst (*æ*-mi-θiçt) *n* ametista *f*

amid (ă-*mid*) *prep* entre, no meio de

ammonia (ă-*mo*ᵘ-ni-ă) *n* amoníaco *m*

amnesty (*æmm*-ni-çti) *n* amnistia *f*

among (ă-*mann*g) *prep* entre; ~ other things entre outras coisas

amount (ă-*maunnt*) *n* quantidade *f*; quantia *f*, soma *f*; ~ to importar em; *equivaler a

amuse (ă-*m'uuz*) *v* *divertir

amusement (ă-*m'uuz*-mănnt) *n* divertimento *m*, distracção *m*

amusing (ă-*m'uu*-zinng) *adj* divertido, engraçado

anaemia (ă-*nii*-mi-ă) *n* anemia *f*

anaesthesia (æ-niç-*θii*-zi-ă) *n* anestesia *f*

anaesthetic (æ-niç-*θé*-tik) *n* anestésico *m*

analyse (æ-nǎ-laiz) v analisar

analysis (ǎ-*næ*-lǎ-çiç) n (pl -ses) análise f

analyst (æ-nǎ-liçt) n analista m; psicanalista m

anarchy (æ-nǎ-ki) n anarquia f

anatomy (ǎ-*næ*-tǎ-mi) n anatomia f

ancestor (ænn-çé-çtǎ) n antepassado m

anchor (ænng-kǎ) n âncora f

anchovy (ænn-tchǎ-vi) n anchova f

ancient (einn-chännt) adj antigo, velho; antiquado, envelhecido; velhíssimo

and (ænnd ǎnnd) conj e

angel (einn-djǎl) n anjo m

anger (ænng-ghǎ) n cólera f, ira f; furor m

angle (ænng-ghǎl) v pescar à linha; n ângulo m

angry (ænng-ghri) adj zangado

animal (æ-ni-mǎl) n animal m

ankle (ænng-kǎl) n tornozelo m

annex¹ (æ-nékç) n anexo m

annex² (ǎ-nékç) v anexar

anniversary (æ-ni-vǎǎ-çǎ-ri) n aniversário m

announce (ǎ-*naunnç*) v anunciar

announcement (ǎ-*naunnç*-männt) n anúncio m, participação f

annoy (ǎ-*noi*) v irritar; aborrecer

annoyance (ǎ-*noi*-ǎnnç) n aborrecimento m

annoying (ǎ-*noi*-inng) adj irritante, maçador

annual (æ-n¹u-ǎl) adj anual; n anuário m

per annum (pǎr æ-nǎmm) anualmente

anonymous (ǎ-*nó*-ni-mǎç) adj anónimo

another (ǎ-*na*-ðǎ) adj mais um; um outro

answer (aann-çǎ) v responder a; n resposta f

ant (ænnt) n formiga f

anthology (ænn-*θó*-lǎ-dji) n antologia f

antibiotic (ænn-ti-bai-ó-tik) n antibiótico m

anticipate (ænn-*ti*-çi-peit) v *prever; esperar, *prevenir

antifreeze (ænn-ti-friiz) n anticongelante m

antipathy (ænn-*ti*-pǎ-θi) n antipatia f

antique (ænn-*tiik*) adj antigo; n antiguidade f; ~ **dealer** antiquário m

antiquity (ænn-*ti*-kᵘǎ-ti) n antiguidade f

antiseptic (ænn-ti-*çép*-tik) n antisséptico m

antlers (*ænnt*-lǎz) pl esgalhos mpl

anxiety (ænng-*zai*-ǎ-ti) n ansiedade f

anxious (ænngk-chǎç) adj ansioso; inquieto

any (é-ni) adj qualquer

anybody (é-ni-bó-di) pron qualquer pessoa

anyhow (é-ni-hau) adv de qualquer modo

anyone (é-ni-ᵘann) pron qualquer pessoa

anything (é-ni-θinng) pron qualquer coisa

anyway (é-ni-ᵘei) adv de qualquer maneira

anywhere (é-ni-ᵘéᵃ) adv onde quer que seja; em qualquer lado

apart (ǎ-*paat*) adv à parte, separadamente; ~ **from** fora, à parte

apartment (ǎ-*paat*-männt) nAm apartamento m; andar m; ~ **house** Am prédio de andares; prédio de apartamentos Br

ape (eip) n macaco m

aperitif (ǎ-pé-rǎ-tiv) n aperitivo m

apologize (ǎ-*pó*-lǎ-djaiz) v pedir desculpa, desculpar-se

apology (ǎ-*pó*-lǎ-dji) n desculpa f

apparatus (æ-pă-*rei*-tăç) *n* dispositivo *m*, aparelho *m*

apparent (ă-*pæ*-rănnt) *adj* aparente; óbvio

apparently (ă-*pæ*-rănnt-li) *adv* aparentemente; evidentemente

apparition (æ-pă-*ri*-chănn) *n* aparição *f*

appeal (ă-*piil*) *n* apelo *m*

appear (ă-*pi*ᵃ) *v* parecer; resultar; aparecer; apresentar-se

appearance (ă-*pi*ᵃ-rănnç) *n* aparência *f*; aparecimento *m*

appendicitis (ă-pénn-di-*çai*-tiç) *n* apendicite *f*

appendix (ă-*pénn*-dikç) *n* (pl -dices, -dixes) apêndice *m*

appetite (æ-pă-tait) *n* apetite *m*

appetizer (æ-pă-tai-ză) *n* aperitivos *m*

appetizing (æ-pă-tai-zinng) *adj* apetitoso

applause (ă-*plóóz*) *n* aplausos *mpl*

apple (æ-păl) *n* maçã *f*

appliance (ă-*plai*-ănnç) *n* aparelho *m*

application (æ-pli-*kei*-chănn) *n* aplicação *f*; pedido *m*; candidatura *f*

apply (ă-*plai*) *v* aplicar; solicitar um emprego; aplicar-se a

appoint (ă-*poinnt*) *v* *nomear, designar

appointment (ă-*poinnt*-mănnt) *n* consulta *f*, entrevista *f*; nomeação *f*

appreciate (ă-*prii*-chi-eit) *v* avaliar; apreciar

appreciation (ă-prii-chi-*ei*-chănn) *n* avaliação *f*; apreciação *f*

approach (ă-*prou*tch) *v* aproximar-se; *n* maneira de proceder; acesso *m*

appropriate (ă-*prou*-pri-ăt) *adj* apropriado, justo, adequado

approval (ă-*pruu*-văl) *n* aprovação *f*; on ~ à condição

approve (ă-*pruuv*) *v* aprovar; ~ of concordar com

approximate (ă-*prók*-çi-măt) *adj* aproximado

approximately (ă-*prók*-çi-măt-li) *adv* aproximadamente

apricot (*ei*-pri-kót) *n* alperche *m*

April (*ei*-prăl) Abril

apron (*ei*-prănn) *n* avental *m*

Arab (æ-răb) *adj* árabe

arbitrary (aa-bi-tră-ri) *adj* arbitrário

arcade (aa-*keid*) *n* arcada *f*

arch (aatch) *n* arco *m*; abóbada *f*

archaeologist (aa-ki-ó-lă-djiçt) *n* arqueólogo *m*

archaeology (aa-ki-ó-lă-dji) *n* arqueologia *f*

archbishop (aatch-*bi*-chăp) *n* arcebispo *m*

arched (aatcht) *adj* arqueado

architect (aa-ki-tékt) *n* arquitecto *m*

architecture (aa-ki-ték-tchă) *n* arquitectura *f*

archives (aa-kaivz) *pl* arquivo *m*

are (aa) *v* (pr be)

area (é*ᵃ*-ri-ă) *n* região *f*; zona *f*; área *f*; ~ code indicativo *m*

Argentina (aa-djănn-*tii*-nă) Argentina *f*

Argentinian (aa-djănn-*ti*-ni-ănn) *adj* argentino

argue (aa-ghⁱuu) *v* discutir, argumentar

argument (aa-ghⁱu-mănnt) *n* argumento *m*; discussão *f*; disputa *f*

arid (æ-rid) *adj* árido

*arise (ă-*raiz*) *v* surgir

arithmetic (ă-*riƟ*-mă-tik) *n* aritmética *f*

arm (aamm) *n* braço *m*; arma *f*; *v* armar

armchair (*aamm*-tchéᵃ) *n* cadeira de braços, poltrona *f*

armed (aammd) *adj* armado; ~ forces forças armadas

armour (aa-mă) *n* armadura *f*

army (aa-mi) n exército m

aroma (ă-rou-mă) n aroma m

around (ă-raund) prep em volta de, à volta de; adv à volta de

arrange (ă-reinndj) v ordenar, agrupar, arranjar, organizar

arrangement (ă-reinndj-mănnt) n regulamento m; acordo m

arrest (ă-rést) v prender; n prisão f

arrival (ă-rai-văl) n chegada f

arrive (ă-raiv) v chegar

arrow (æ-rou) n seta f

art (aat) n arte f; habilidade f; ~ **collection** colecção de obras de arte; ~ **exhibition** exposição de arte; ~ **gallery** galeria de arte; ~ **history** história da arte; **arts and crafts** artes e ofícios; ~ **school** academia das belas-artes

artery (aa-tă-ri) n artéria f

artichoke (aa-ti-tchouk) n alcachofra f

article (aa-ti-kăl) n artigo m

artifice (aa-ti-fiç) n artifício m

artificial (aa-ti-fi-chăl) adj artificial

artist (aa-tiçt) n artista m

artistic (aa-ti-çtik) adj artístico

as (æz) conj como; tanto; que; porque, visto que; ~ **from** desde; a partir de; ~ **if** como se

asbestos (æz-bé-çtóç) n amianto m

ascend (ă-cénnd) v ascender; *subir; escalar

ascent (ă-cénnt) n ascensão f; subida f

ascertain (æ-çă-teinn) v constatar; certificar-se de

ash (æch) n cinza f

ashamed (ă-cheimmd) adj envergonhado; *be ~ *ter vergonha

ashore (ă-chóó) adv a terra, em terra

ashtray (æch-trei) n cinzeiro m

Asia (ei-chă) Ásia f

Asian (ei-chănn) adj asiático

aside (ă-çaid) adv de lado; à parte

ask (aaçk) v perguntar; *pedir; convidar

asleep (ă-çliip) adj adormecido

asparagus (ă-çpæ-ră-ghăç) n espargo m

aspect (æ-çpékt) n aspecto m

asphalt (æç-fælt) n asfalto m

aspire (ă-çpaiᵃ) v aspirar

aspirin (æ-çpă-rinn) n aspirina f

ass (æç) n burro m

assassination (ă-çæ-çi-nei-chănn) n assassínio m

assault (ă-çóólt) v atacar; violar

assemble (ă-çémm-băl) v reunir; montar

assembly (ă-çémm-bli) n reunião f, assembleia f

assign to (ă-çainn) *atribuir a

assist (ă-çiçt) v auxiliar, assistir; ~ **at** assistir a

assistance (ă-çi-çtănnç) n ajuda f; assistência f

assistant (ă-çi-çtănnt) n assistente m

associate¹ (ă-çou-chi-ăt) n sócio m, companheiro m; aliado m; membro m

associate² (ă-çou-chi-eit) v associar; ~ **with** andar com, associar-se com

association (ă-çou-çi-ei-chănn) n associação f

assort (ă-çóót) v classificar

assortment (ă-çóót-mănnt) n sortido m, sortimento m

assume (ă-ç'uumm) v *supor

assure (ă-chuᵃ) v assegurar, garantir

asthma (æç-mă) n asma f

astonish (ă-çtó-nich) v espantar

astonishing (ă-çtó-ni-chinng) adj espantoso

astonishment (ă-çtó-nich-mănnt) n espanto m

astronomy (ă-çtró-nă-mi) n astronomia *f*

asylum (ă-*çai*-lămm) *n* asilo *m*

at (æt) *prep* em, a; para

ate (ét) *v* (p eat)

atheist (*ei*-θi-içt) *n* ateu *m*

athlete (æθ-liit) *n* atleta *m*

athletics (æθ-lè-tikç) *pl* atletismo *m*

Atlantic (ăt-*lænn*-tik) Atlântico *m*

atmosphere (æt-măç-fiă) *n* atmosfera *f*; ambiente *m*

atom (æ-tămm) *n* átomo *m*

atomic (ă-tó-mik) *adj* atómico

atomizer (æ-tă-mai-ză) *n* vaporizador *m*; pulverizador *m*

attach (ă-*tætch*) *v* atar, prender; fixar; juntar; **attached to** dedicado a

attack (ă-*tæk*) *v* atacar, *agredir; *n* ataque *m*

attain (ă-*teinn*) *v* atingir

attainable (ă-*tei*-nă-băl) *adj* possível; acessível

attempt (ă-*témmpt*) *v* tentar; *n* tentativa *f*

attend (ă-*ténnd*) *v* assistir a; ~ **on** atender; ~ **to** ocupar-se de, tratar de; prestar atenção a

attendance (ă-*ténn*-dănnç) *n* assistência *f*

attendant (ă-*ténn*-dănnt) *n* guarda *m*

attention (ă-*ténn*-chănn) *n* atenção *f*; *pay ~ prestar atenção

attentive (ă-*ténn*-tiv) *adj* atento

attic (æ-tik) *n* sótão *m*

attitude (æ-ti-t^{i}uud) *n* atitude *f*

attorney (ă-*tăă*-ni) *n* advogado *m*

attract (ă-*trækt*) *v* *atrair

attraction (ă-*træk*-chănn) *n* atracção *f*; atractivo *m*

attractive (ă-*træk*-tiv) *adj* atraente

auburn (óó-*bănn*) *adj* castanho encarnicado

auction (óók-chănn) *n* leilão *m*

audible (óó-di-băl) *adj* audível

audience (óó-di-ănnç) *n* audiência *f*;

auditório *m*

auditor (óó-di-tă) *n* ouvinte *m*

auditorium (óó-di-*tóó*-ri-ămm) *n* auditório *m*

August (óó-*ghăçt*) Agosto

aunt (aannt) *n* tia *f*

Australia (ó-*çtrei*-li-ă) Austrália *f*

Australian (ó-*çtrei*-li-ănn) *adj* australiano

Austria (ó-çtri-ă) Áustria *f*

Austrian (ó-çtri-ănn) *adj* austríaco

authentic (óó-*θénn*-tik) *adj* autêntico

author (óó-θă) *n* autor *m*

authoritarian (óó-θó-ri-té^a-ri-ănn) *adj* autoritário

authority (óó-*θó*-ră-ti) *n* autoridade *f*; poder *m*

authorization (óó-θă-rai-*zei*-chănn) *n* autorização *f*

automatic (óó-tă-*mæ*-tik) *adj* automático

automation (óó-tă-*mei*-chănn) *n* automatização *f*

automobile (óó-tă-mă-biil) *n* automóvel *m*; ~ **club** automóvel clube

autonomous (óó-*tó*-nă-măç) *adj* autónomo

autopsy (óó-tó-pçi) *n* autópsia *f*

autumn (óó-tămm) *n* Outono *m*

available (ă-*vei*-lă-băl) *adj* disponível

avalanche (æ-vă-laannch) *n* avalanche *f*

avaricious (æ-vă-*ri*-chăç) *adj* avarento

avenue (æ-vă-n^{i}uu) *n* avenida *f*

average (æ-vă-ridj) *adj* médio; *n* média *f*; **on the ~** em média

averse (ă-*văăç*) *adj* adverso

aversion (ă-*văă*-chănn) *n* aversão *f*

avert (ă-*văăt*) *v* desviar

avoid (ă-*void*) *v* evitar

await (ă-^{u}eit) *v* esperar

awake (ă-^{u}eik) *adj* acordado

***awake** (ă-^{u}eik) *v* despertar, acordar

award (ă-^{u}óód) *n* prémio *m*; *v* *atribuir

aware (ă-ᵁéª) *adj* ciente

away (ă-ᵁei) *adv* ausente; ***go ~**
*ir-se embora

awful (óó-făl) *adj* terrível, horrível

awkward (óó-kᵁăd) *adj* embaraçoso;
desastrado

awning (óó-ninng) *n* toldo *m*

axe (ækç) *n* machado *m*

axle (æk-çăl) *n* eixo *m*

B

baby (bei-bi) *n* bebé *m*; **~ carriage**
Am carrinho de bebé

babysitter (bei-bi-çi-tă) *n* babysitter
m

bachelor (bæ-tchă-lă) *n* celibatário *m*

back (bæk) *n* costas; *adv* atrás; ***go**
~ regressar

backache (bæ-keik) *n* dores nas costas

backbone (bæk-boᵘnn) *n* espinha dorsal

background (bæk-ghraunnd) *n* fundo
m

backwards (bæk-ᵁădz) *adv* para trás

bacon (bei-kănn) *n* bacon *m*

bacterium (bæk-tii-ri-ămm) *n* (pl -ria)
bactéria *f*

bad (bæd) *adj* mau; grave

bag (bægh) *n* saco *m*; carteira *f*, bolsa *f*; mala *f*

baggage (bæ-ghidj) *n* bagagem *f*;
hand ~ *Am* bagagem de mão

bail (beil) *n* caução *f*

bailiff (bei-lif) *n* oficial de diligências

bait (beit) *n* isca *f*

bake (beik) *v* cozinhar no forno, cozer no forno

baker (bei-kă) *n* padeiro *m*

bakery (bei-kă-ri) *n* padaria *f*

balance (bæ-lănnç) *n* equilíbrio *m*;
balanço *m*; saldo *m*

balcony (bæl-kă-ni) *n* varanda *f*

bald (bóóld) *adj* careca

ball (bóól) *n* bola *f*; baile *m*

ballet (bæ-lei) *n* bailado *m*

balloon (bă-luunn) *n* balão *m*

ballpoint-pen (bóól-poinnt-pénn) *n* caneta esferográfica

ballroom (bóól-ruumm) *n* salão de baile

bamboo (bæmm-buu) *n* (pl ~s) bambu *m*

banana (bă-naa-nă) *n* banana *f*

band (bænnd) *n* banda *f*; ligadura *f*

bandage (bænn-didj) *n* ligadura *f*

bandit (bænn-dit) *n* bandido *m*

bangle (bænng-ghăl) *n* pulseira *f*

banisters (bæ-ni-çtăz) *pl* corrimão *m*

bank (bænngk) *n* beira *f*; banco *m*; *v*
depositar; **~ account** conta bancária

banknote (bænngk-noᵘt) *n* nota de
banco

bank-rate (bænngk-reit) *n* taxa de
desconto

bankrupt (bænngk-rapt) *adj* falido

banner (bæ-nă) *n* estandarte *m*

banquet (bænng-kᵁit) *n* banquete *m*

banqueting-hall (bænng-kᵁi-tinng-
hóól) *n* salão de banquetes

baptism (bæp-ti-zămm) *n* baptismo *m*

baptize (bæp-taiz) *v* baptizar

bar (baa) *n* bar *m*; barra *f*

barber (baa-bă) *n* barbeiro *m*

bare (béª) *adj* nu, despido; descoberto

barely (béª-li) *adv* mal

bargain (baa-ghinn) *n* pechincha *f*; *v*
*regatear

baritone (bæ-ri-toᵘnn) *n* barítono *m*

bark (baak) *n* casca *f*; *v* ladrar

barley (baa-li) *n* cevada *f*

barmaid (baa-meid) *n* empregada de

bar

barman (*baa*-mănn) *n* (pl -men) barman *m*

barn (baann) *n* celeiro *m*

barometer (bă-*ró*-mi-tă) *n* barómetro *m*

baroque (bă-*rók*) *adj* barroco

barracks (*bæ*-răkç) *pl* quartel *m*

barrel (*bæ*-răl) *n* barril *m*, pipa *f*

barrier (*bæ*-ri-ă) *n* barreira *f*; cancela *f*

barrister (*bæ*-ri-çtă) *n* advogado *m*

bartender (*baa*-ténn-dă) *n* empregado de bar

base (beiç) *n* base *f*; alicerce *m*; *v* *basear

baseball (*beiç*-bóól) *n* basebol *m*

basement (*beiç*-mănnt) *n* cave *f*; porão *mBr*

basic (*bei*-çik) *adj* fundamental; básico

basilica (bă-*zi*-li-kă) *n* basílica *f*

basin (*bei*-çănn) *n* bacia *f*, tigela *f*

basis (*bei*-çiç) *n* (pl bases) base *f*, fundamento *m*

basket (*baa*-çkit) *n* cesto *m*

bass[1] (beiç) *n* baixo *m*

bass[2] (bæç) *n* (pl ~) robalo *m*

bastard (*baa*-çtăd) *n* bastardo *m*; patife *m*

batch (bætch) *n* lote *m*

bath (baaθ) *n* banho *m*; ~ **salts** sais de banho; ~ **towel** toalha de banho

bathe (beið) *v* tomar banho, banhar-se

bathing-cap (*bei*-ðinng-kæp) *n* touca de banho

bathing-suit (*bei*-ðinng-çuut) *n* fato de banho; traje de banho *Br*

bathrobe (*baaθ*-roᵘb) *n* roupão de banho

bathroom (*baaθ*-ruumm) *n* quarto de banho; casa de banho; banheiro

mBr

batter (*bæ*-tă) *n* massa *f*

battery (*bæ*-tă-ri) *n* pilha eléctrica; bateria *f*

battle (*bæ*-tăl) *n* batalha *f*; combate *m*, luta *f*; *v* combater

bay (bei) *n* baía *f*; *v* ladrar

*****be** (bii) *v* *ser, *estar

beach (biitch) *n* praia *f*; **nudist** ~ praia para nudistas

bead (biid) *n* conta *f*; **beads** colar *m*; rosário *m*

beak (biik) *n* bico *m*

beam (biimm) *n* raio *m*; viga *f*

bean (biinn) *n* feijão *m*

bear (béᵃ) *n* urso *m*

*****bear** (béᵃ) *v* levar; suportar

beard (biᵃd) *n* barba *f*

bearer (*béᵃ*-ră) *n* portador *m*

beast (biiçt) *n* animal *m*; ~ **of prey** animal de rapina

*****beat** (biit) *v* bater

beautiful (*bⁱuu*-ti-făl) *adj* belo

beauty (*bⁱuu*-ti) *n* beleza *f*; ~ **parlour** instituto de beleza; ~ **salon** salão de beleza; ~ **treatment** tratamento de beleza

beaver (*bii*-vă) *n* castor *m*

because (bi-*kóz*) *conj* porque; já que; ~ **of** por causa de

*****become** (bi-*kamm*) *v* *vir a ser, tornar-se; ficar bem

bed (béd) *n* cama *f*; ~ **and board** pensão completa; ~ **and breakfast** quarto e pequeno almoço

bedding (*bé*-dinng) *n* roupa de cama

bedroom (*béd*-ruumm) *n* quarto de cama

bee (bii) *n* abelha *f*

beech (bii-tch) *n* faia *f*

beef (biif) *n* carne de vaca

beehive (*bii*-haiv) *n* colmeia *f*

been (biinn) *v* (pp be)

beer (biᵃ) *n* cerveja *f*

beet (biit) *n* beterraba *f*

beetle (*bii*-tål) *n* escaravelho *m*

beetroot (*biit*-ruut) *n* beterraba *f*

before (bi-fóó) *prep* antes de; *conj* antes que; *adv* antes; primeiro

beg (bégh) *v* mendigar, *pedir; suplicar

beggar (*bé*-ghå) *n* mendigo *m*

*begin (bi-ghinn) *v* principiar, comecar; iniciar

beginner (bi-*ghi*-nå) *n* principiante *m*

beginning (bi-*ghi*-ninng) *n* princípio *m*; início *m*

on behalf of (ónn bi-*haaf* óv) em nome de; a favor de

behave (bi-heiv) *v* portar-se

behaviour (bi-*hei*-viå) *n* comportamento *m*

behind (bi-hainnd) *prep* atrás de; *adv* atrás

beige (beij) *adj* bege

being (*bii*-inng) *n* ser *m*

Belgian (*bél*-djann) *adj* belga

Belgium (*bél*-djåmm) Bélgica *f*

belief (bi-*liif*) *n* crença *f*

believe (bi-*liiv*) *v* acreditar

bell (bél) *n* sino *m*; campainha *f*

bellboy (*bél*-boi) *n* groom *m*

belly (*bé*-li) *n* ventre *m*

belong (bi-*lónn*) *v* pertencer

belongings (bi-*lónn*-inngz) *pl* bens *mpl*

beloved (bi-*lavd*) *adj* querido

below (bi-*lo*ᵘ) *prep* debaixo de; *adv* em baixo, debaixo

belt (bélt) *n* cinto *m*

bench (bénntch) *n* banco *m*

bend (bénnd) *n* volta *f*, curva *f*; curvatura *f*

*bend (bénnd) *v* dobrar, curvar; ~ down curvar-se

beneath (bi-*niiθ*) *prep* debaixo de; *adv* debaixo

benefit (*bé*-ni-fit) *n* benefício *m*, lucro *m*; vantagem *f*; *v* beneficiar

bent (bénnt) *adj* (pp bend) curvo; curvado; torto

beret (*bé*-rei) *n* boina *f*

berry (*bé*-ri) *n* baga *f*

berth (båản) *n* beliche *m*

beside (bi-*çaid*) *prep* ao lado de

besides (bi-*çaidz*) *adv* além de; além disso; *prep* além de

best (béçt) *adj* o melhor

bet (bét) *n* aposta *f*

*bet (bét) *v* apostar

betray (bi-trei) *v* *trair

better (*bé*-tå) *adj* melhor

between (bi-t*ᵘiinn*) *prep* entre

beverage (*bé*-vå-ridj) *n* bebida *f*

beware (bi-ᵘé*å*) *v* *ter cuidado, *precaver-se

bewitch (bi-ᵘ*itch*) *v* enfeitiçar, encantar

beyond (bi-*ónnd*) *prep* além de; *adv* além

bible (*bai*-bål) *n* bíblia *f*

bicycle (*bai*-çi-kål) *n* bicicleta *f*

big (bigh) *adj* grande; volumoso; importante

bile (bail) *n* bílis *f*

bilingual (bai-*linng*- gh ᵘål) *adj* bilíngue

bill (bil) *n* conta *f*; *v* facturar

billiards (*bil*-iådz) *pl* bilhar *m*

*bind (bainnd) *v* atar, ligar

binding (*bainn*-dinng) *n* encadernação *f*

binoculars (bi-*nó*-kiå-låz) *pl* binóculo *m*

biology (bai-ó-lå-dji) *n* biologia *f*

birch (bååtch) *n* bétula *f*

bird (bååd) *n* ave *f*

birth (bååθ) *n* nascimento *m*

birthday (*bååθ*-dei) *n* dia dos anos

biscuit (*biç*-kit) *n* biscoito *m*

bishop (*bi*-chåp) *n* bispo *m*

bit (bit) *n* pedaço *m*; bocadinho *m*

bitch (bitch) *n* cadela *f*

bite (bait) *n* bocado *m*; mordedura *f*;

picada f
*__bite__ (bait) v morder
__bitter__ (bi-tă) adj amargo
__black__ (blæk) adj preto; ~ __market__ mercado negro
__blackberry__ (blæk-bă-ri) n amora silvestre
__blackbird__ (blæk-bååd) n melro m
__blackboard__ (blæk-bóód) n quadro preto
__black-currant__ (blæk-ka-rănnt) n groselha negra
__blackmail__ (blæk-meil) n chantagem f; v *fazer chantagem
__blacksmith__ (blæk-çmiθ) n ferreiro m
__bladder__ (blæ-dă) n bexiga f
__blade__ (bleid) n lâmina f; ~ __of grass__ folha de erva
__blame__ (bleimm) n culpa f; censura f; v censurar, acusar, culpar
__blank__ (blænngk) adj em branco
__blanket__ (blænng-kit) n cobertor m
__blast__ (blaaçt) n explosão f
__blazer__ (blei-ză) n casaco desportivo
__bleach__ (bliitch) v descolorir
__bleak__ (bliik) adj rigoroso
*__bleed__ (bliid) v sangrar
__bless__ (bléç) v *bendizer, abençoar
__blessing__ (blé-çinng) n benção f
__blind__ (blainnd) n persiana f, estore m; adj cego; v cegar
__blister__ (bli-çtă) n empola f, bolha f
__blizzard__ (bli-zăd) n tempestade de neve
__block__ (blók) v *bloquear, *obstruir; n bloco m; ~ __of flats__ prédio de andares
__blonde__ (blónnd) n loira f
__blood__ (blad) n sangue m; ~ __pressure__ tensão arterial
__blood-poisoning__ (blad-poi-ză-ninng) n septicemia f
__blood-vessel__ (blad-vé-çăl) n vaso sanguíneo

__blot__ (blót) n borrão m; mancha f; __blotting paper__ mata-borrão m
__blouse__ (blauz) n blusa f
__blow__ (blou) n pancada f, golpe m; rajada f
*__blow__ (blou) v assoprar; soprar
__blow-out__ (blou-aut) n furo m
__blue__ (bluu) adj azul; deprimido
__blunt__ (blannt) adj rombo
__blush__ (blach) v corar
__board__ (bóód) n tábua f; quadro m; pensão f; conselho m; ~ __and lodging__ pensão completa
__boarder__ (bóó-dă) n pensionista m
__boarding-house__ (bóó-dinng-hauç) n pensão f
__boarding-school__ (bóó-dinng-çkuul) n colégio interno
__boast__ (bouçt) v gabar-se
__boat__ (bout) n barco m, navio m
__body__ (bó-di) n corpo m
__bodyguard__ (bó-di-ghaad) n guarda-costas m
__body-work__ (bó-di-uăăk) n carroçaria f
__bog__ (bógh) n pântano m
__boil__ (boil) v ferver; n furúnculo m
__bold__ (bould) adj arrojado; atrevido, descarado
__Bolivia__ (bă-li-vi-ă) Bolívia f
__Bolivian__ (bă-li-vi-ănn) adj boliviano
__bolt__ (boult) n ferrolho m; cavilha f
__bomb__ (bómm) n bomba f; v *bombardear
__bond__ (bónnd) n obrigação f
__bone__ (bounn) n osso m; espinha f; v desossar
__bonnet__ (bó-nit) n cobertura do motor
__book__ (buk) n livro m; v reservar; inscrever, registar
__booking__ (bu-kinng) n reserva f
__bookmaker__ (buk-mei-kă) n corretor de apostas
__bookseller__ (buk-çé-lă) n livreiro m
__bookstand__ (buk-çtænnd) n quiosque

de livros

bookstore (*buk*-çtóó) *n* livraria *f*

boot (buut) *n* bota *f*; porta-bagagem *m*

booth (buuð) *n* cabina *f*

border (*bó*-dã) *n* fronteira *f*; borda *f*

bore[1] (bóó) *v* maçar; brocar; *n* maçador *m*

bore[2] (bóó) *v* (p bear)

boring (*bóó*-inng) *adj* maçador, aborrecido

born (bóónn) *adj* nascido

borrow (*bó*-ro^u) *v* *pedir emprestado

bosom (*bu*-zãmm) *n* peito *m*; seio *m*

boss (bóç) *n* patrão *m*, chefe *m*

botany (*bó*-tã-ni) *n* botânica *f*

both (bo^uθ) *adj* ambos; **both ... and** tanto ... como

bother (*bó*-ðã) *v* incomodar, maçar; incomodar-se; *n* incómodo *m*

bottle (*bó*-tãl) *n* garrafa *f*; ~ **opener** abre-garrafas *m*; **hot-water** ~ botija de água quente

bottleneck (*bó*-tãl-nék) *n* passagem estreita

bottom (*bó*-tãmm) *n* fundo *m*; traseiro *m*, rabo *m*; *adj* inferior

bough (bau) *n* ramo *m*

bought (bóót) *v* (p, pp buy)

boulder (*bo^ul*-dã) *n* pedregulho *m*

bound (baunnd) *n* limite *m*; *be ~ to *ter de; ~ **for** a caminho de

boundary (*baunn*-dã-ri) *n* limite *m*; fronteira *f*

bouquet (bu-*kei*) *n* ramo *m*

bourgeois (*bu*-ã-j^uaa) *adj* burguês

boutique (bu-*tiik*) *n* boutique *f*

bow[1] (bau) *v* inclinar

bow[2] (bo^u) *n* arco *m*; ~ **tie** laço *m*

bowels (*bau*^alz) *pl* intestinos *mpl*

bowl (bo^ul) *n* tigela *f*

bowling (*bo^u*-linng) *n* jogo dos paulitos, bowling *m*; ~ **alley** pista de bowling

box[1] (bókç) *v* jogar o boxe; **boxing match** luta de boxe

box[2] (bókç) *n* caixa *f*

box-office (*bókç*-ó-fiç) *n* bilheteira de reservação, bilheteira *f*; bilheteria *fBr*

boy (boi) *n* rapaz *m*; moço *m*, gaiato *m*; criado *m*; ~ **scout** escuteiro *m*

bra (braa) *n* soutien *m*

bracelet (*breiç*-lit) *n* pulseira *f*

braces (*brei*-çiz) *pl* suspensórios *mpl*

brain (breinn) *n* cérebro *m*; inteligência *f*

brain-wave (*breinn*-^ueiv) *n* ideia luminosa

brake (breik) *n* travão *m*; ~ **drum** tambor do travão; ~ **lights** luzes de travão

branch (braanntch) *n* ramo *m*; sucursal *f*

brand (brænnd) *n* marca *f*

brand-new (brænnd-n^i*uu*) *adj* novinho em folha

brass (braaç) *n* latão *m*; ~ **band** fanfarra *f*

brassiere (bræ-zi^ã) *n* soutien *m*

brassware (*braaç*-^ué^ã) *n* utensílios de latão

brave (breiv) *adj* corajoso, valente

Brazil (brã-*zil*) Brasil *m*

Brazilian (brã-*zil*-^iänn) *adj* brasileiro

breach (briitch) *n* brecha *f*; ruptura *f*

bread (bréd) *n* pão *m*; **wholemeal** ~ pão integral

breadth (brédθ) *n* largura *f*

break (breik) *n* fractura *f*; intervalo *m*

*break** (breik) *v* quebrar, partir; ~ **down** avariar-se

breakdown (*breik*-daunn) *n* avaria *f*

breakfast (*brék*-fãçt) *n* pequeno almoço

bream (briimm) *n* (pl ~) pargo *m*

breast (bréçt) *n* peito *m*

breaststroke (bréçt-çtroᵘk) n bruços mpl

breath (bréθ) n respiração f; sopro m

breathe (briið) v respirar

breathing (brii-ðinng) n respiração f

breed (briid) n raça f; espécie f

*breed (briid) v criar

breeze (briiz) n brisa f

brew (bruu) v fabricar cerveja

brewery (bruu-ă-ri) n fábrica de cerveja f

bribe (braib) v subornar

bribery (brai-bă-ri) n suborno m

brick (brik) n tijolo m

bricklayer (brik-leiᵃ) n pedreiro m

bride (braid) n noiva f

bridegroom (braid-ghruumm) n noivo m

bridge (bridj) n ponte f; bridge m

brief (briif) adj breve

briefcase (briif-keiç) n pasta f

briefs (briifç) pl calções mpl, cuecas fpl

bright (brait) adj claro; reluzente; esperto, inteligente

brill (bril) n rodovalho m

brilliant (bril-ⁱănnt) adj brilhante

brim (brimm) n borda f

*bring (brinng) v *trazer; ~ back devolver; ~ up criar, educar; levantar

brisk (briçk) adj vivo

Britain (bri-tănn) Inglaterra f

British (bri-tich) adj britânico

Briton (bri-tănn) n britânico m; inglês m

broad (bróód) adj largo; vasto, amplo; global

broadcast (bróód-kaaçt) n emissão f

*broadcast (bróód-kaaçt) v emitir

brochure (broᵘ-chuᵃ) n brochura f

broke¹ (broᵘk) v (p break)

broke² (broᵘk) adj teso

broken (broᵘ-kănn) adj (pp break)

partido, escangalhado; avariado

broker (broᵘ-kă) n corretor m

bronchitis (brónn-kai-tiç) n bronquite f

bronze (brónnz) n bronze m; adj de bronze

brooch (broᵘtch) n broche m

brook (bruk) n riacho m

broom (bruumm) n vassoura f

brothel (bró-θăl) n bordel m

brother (bra-ðă) n irmão m

brother-in-law (bra-ðă-rinn-lóó) n (pl brothers-) cunhado m

brought (bróót) v (p, pp bring)

brown (braunn) adj castanho

bruise (bruuz) n contusão f, nódoa negra; v magoar

brunette (bruu-nét) n morena f

brush (brach) n escova f; pincel m; v puxar o lustro a, escovar

brutal (bruu-tăl) adj brutal

bubble (ba-băl) n bolha f

bucket (ba-kit) n balde m

buckle (ba-kăl) n fivela f

bud (bad) n botão m

budget (ba-djit) n orçamento m

buffet (bu-fei) n bufete m

bug (bagh) n percevejo m; escaravelho m; nAm insecto m

*build (bild) v *construir

building (bil-dinng) n prédio m

bulb (balb) n bolbo m; cebola f; light ~ lâmpada f

Bulgaria (bal-ghéᵃ-ri-ă) Bulgária f

Bulgarian (bal-ghéᵃ-ri-ănn) adj búlgaro

bulk (balk) n volume m; maior parte f

bulky (bal-ki) adj volumoso

bull (bul) n touro m

bullet (bu-lit) n bala f

bullfight (bul-fait) n tourada f

bullring (bul-rinng) n praça de touros f

bump (bammp) v bater; chocar; n encontrão m, pancada f

bumper (*bamm*-pă) *n* pára-choques *m*

bumpy (*bamm*-pi) *adj* acidentado

bun (bann) *n* brioche *m*

bunch (banntch) *n* ramo *m*; grupo *m*

bundle (*bann*-dăl) *n* molho *m*; *v* atar num molho, atar

bunk (banngk) *n* beliche *m*

buoy (boi) *n* bóia *f*

burden (*băă*-dănn) *n* fardo *m*

bureau (*b¹uᵃ*- roᵘ) *n* (pl ~x, ~s) escrevaninha *f*, secretária *f*; *nAm* cómoda *f*

bureaucracy (*b¹uᵃ*-*ró*-kră-ci) *n* burocracia *f*

burglar (*băă*-ghlă) *n* ladrão *m*

burgle (*băă*-ghăl) *v* assaltar

burial (*bé*-ri-ăl) *n* enterro *m*

burn (băănn) *n* queimadura *f*

*****burn** (băănn) *v* arder; queimar

*****burst** (băăçt) *v* rebentar

bury (*bé*-ri) *v* enterrar

bus (baç) *n* autocarro *m*; ônibus *mBr*

bush (buch) *n* arbusto *m*; mato *m*

business (*biz*-năç) *n* negócios, comércio *m*; negócio *m*, empresa *f*; ocupação *f*; assunto *m*; ~ **hours** horas de serviço, horas de abertura; ~ **trip** viagem de negócios; **on** ~ para negócios

businessman (*biz*-năç-mănn) *n* (pl -men) homem de negócios

bust (baçt) *n* busto *m*

bustle (*ba*-căl) *n* azáfama *f*

busy (*bi*-zi) *adj* ocupado; movimentado, atarefado

but (bat) *conj* mas; todavia; *prep* menos

butcher (*bu*-tchă) *n* talho *m*

butter (*ba*-tă) *n* manteiga *f*

butterfly (*ba*-tă-flai) *n* borboleta *f*; ~ **stroke** mariposa *f*

buttock (*ba*-tăk) *n* nádega *f*

button (*ba*-tănn) *n* botão *m*; *v* abotoar

buttonhole (*ba*-tănn-hoᵘl) *n* casa de botão

*****buy** (bai) *v* comprar; adquirir

buyer (*bai*-ă) *n* comprador *m*

by (bai) *prep* por; com; perto de; por meio de

by-pass (*bai*-paaç) *n* estrada de circunvalação; *v* contornar

C

cab (kæb) *n* táxi *m*

cabaret (*kæ*-bă-rei) *n* cabaré *m*; clube nocturno

cabbage (*kæ*-bidj) *n* couve *f*

cab-driver (*kæb*-drai-vă) *n* motorista de táxi

cabin (*kæ*-binn) *n* cabina *f*; cabana *f*

cabinet (*kæ*-bi-năt) *n* gabinete *m*

cable (*kei*-băl) *n* cabo *m*; telegrama *m*; *v* telegrafar

cadre (*kaa*-dă) *n* quadro *m*

café (*kæ*-fei) *n* café *m*

cafeteria (*kæ*-fă-*ti*ᵃ-ri-ă) *n* cafetaria *f*

caffeine (*kæ*-fiinn) *n* cafeína *f*

cage (keidj) *n* jaula *f*

cake (keik) *n* bolo *m*

calamity (kă-*læ*-mă-ti) *n* catástrofe *f*, calamidade *f*

calcium (*kæl*-çi-ămm) *n* cálcio *m*

calculate (*kæl*-k¹u-leit) *v* calcular

calculation (kæl-k¹u-*lei*-chănn) *n* cálculo *m*

calendar (*kæ*-lănn-dă) *n* calendário *m*

calf (kaaf) *n* (pl calves) vitelo *m*; barriga da perna; ~ **skin** calfe *m*

call (kóól) *v* chamar; telefonar; *n* chamada *f*; visita *f*; *****be called** chamar-se; ~ **names** injuriar; ~ **on** visitar, *****fazer uma visita a; ~ **up** *Am* telefonar

callus (*kæ*-lăç) *n* calo *m*

calm (kaamm) *adj* calmo, tranquilo;
~ **down** acalmar

calorie (*kæ*-lă-ri) *n* caloria *f*

Calvinism (*kæl*-vi-ni-zămm) *n* calvinismo *m*

came (keimm) *v* (p come)

camel (*kæ*-măl) *n* camelo *m*

cameo (*kæ*-mi-o^u) *n* (pl ~s) camafeu *m*

camera (*kæ*-mă-ră) *n* máquina fotográfica; máquina de filmar; ~ **shop** loja de artigos fotográficos

camp (kæmmp) *n* acampamento *m*; *v* acampar

campaign (kæmm-*peinn*) *n* campanha *f*

camp-bed (kæmmp-*béd*) *n* maca *f*, cama de acampamento

camper (*kæmm*-pă) *n* campista *m*

camping (*kæmm*-pinng) *n* campismo *m*; ~ **site** parque de campismo

camshaft (*kæmm*-chaaft) *n* árvore de cames

can (kænn) *n* lata *f*; ~ **opener** abre-latas *m*

***can** (kænn) *v* *poder

Canada (*kæ*-nă-dă) Canadá *m*

Canadian (kă-*nei*-di-ănn) *adj* canadiano

canal (kă-*næl*) *n* canal *m*

canary (kă-*né*^ă-ri) *n* canário *m*

cancel (*kænn*-çăl) *v* anular; cancelar

cancellation (kænn-çă-*lei*-chănn) *n* cancelamento *m*

cancer (*kænn*-çă) *n* cancro *m*

candelabrum (kænn-dă-*laa*-brămm) *n* (pl -bra) candelabro *m*

candidate (*kænn*-di-dăt) *n* candidato *m*

candle (*kænn*-dăl) *n* vela *f*

candy (*kænn*-di) *nAm* rebucado *m*; guloseimas *fpl*

cane (keinn) *n* cana *f*; bengala *f*

canister (*kæ*-ni-çtă) *n* lata *f*

canoe (kă-*nuu*) *n* canoa *f*

canteen (kænn-*tiinn*) *n* cantina *f*

canvas (*kænn*-văc) *n* lona *f*

cap (kæp) *n* boné *m*, barrete *m*

capable (*kei*-pă-băl) *adj* capaz

capacity (kă-*pæ*-çă-ti) *n* capacidade *f*; potência *f*; competência *f*

cape (keip) *n* capa *f*; cabo *m*

capital (*kæ*-pi-tăl) *n* capital *f*; capital *m*; *adj* importante, capital; ~ **letter** maiúscula *f*

capitalism (*kæ*-pi-tă-li-zămm) *n* capitalismo *m*

capitulation (kă-pi-t^i u-*lei*-chănn) *n* capitulação *f*

capsule (*kæp*-çi uul) *n* cápsula *f*

captain (*kæp*-tinn) *n* capitão *m*; comandante *m*

capture (*kæp*-tchă) *v* capturar; *n* captura *f*

car (kaa) *n* carro *m*; ~ **hire** aluguer de carros; ~ **park** parque de estacionamento

carafe (kă-*ræf*) *n* garrafa *f*

caramel (*kæ*-ră-măl) *n* caramelo *m*

carat (*kæ*-răt) *n* quilate *m*

caravan (*kæ*-ră-vænn) *n* caravana *f*; rulote *f*

carburettor (kaa-b^i u-*ré*-tă) *n* carburador *m*

card (kaad) *n* cartão *m*; postal *m*

cardboard (*kaad*-bóód) *n* cartão *m*; papelão *mBr*; *adj* de cartão

cardigan (*kaa*-di-ghănn) *n* casaco de malha

cardinal (*kaa*-di-năl) *n* cardeal *m*; *adj* principal, cardeal

care (ké^ă) *n* cuidado *m*; preocupação *f*; ~ **about** preocupar-se com; ~ **for** gostar de; *take ~ of** tratar de, cuidar de

career (kă-*ri*^ă) *n* carreira *f*

carefree (*ké*^ă-frii) *adj* despreocupado

careful (*ké*^ă-făl) *adj* cuidadoso

careless (ké^ă-lăç) *adj* negligente, descuidado

caretaker (ké^ă-tei-kă) *n* guarda *m*

cargo (kaa-gho^u) *n* (pl ~es) carregamento *m*, carga *f*

carnival (kaa-ni-văl) *n* Carnaval *m*

carp (kaap) *n* (pl ~) carpa *f*

carpenter (kaa-pinn-tă) *n* carpinteiro *m*

carpet (kaa-pit) *n* tapete *m*

carriage (kæ-ridj) *n* carruagem *f*; coche *m*

carriageway (kæ-ridj-^uei) *n* faixa de rodagem

carrot (kæ-răt) *n* cenoura *f*

carry (kæ-ri) *v* transportar; *conduzir; ~ on continuar; *prosseguir; ~ out executar, realizar

carry-cot (kæ-ri-kót) *n* alcofa de bébé

cart (kaat) *n* carroça *f*

cartilage (kaa-ti-lidj) *n* cartilagem *f*

carton (kaa-tănn) *n* caixa de cartão; caixa *m*; caixa de papelão *Br*

cartoon (kaa-tuunn) *n* desenho animado

cartridge (kaa-tridj) *n* cartucho *m*

carve (kaav) *v* trinchar; entalhar

carving (kaa-vinng) *n* obra de talha

case (keiç) *n* caso *m*; causa *f*; mala *f*; estojo *m*; **attaché ~** pasta *f*; **in any ~** seja como for; **in ~** no caso de; **in ~ of** em caso de

cash (kæch) *n* dinheiro *m*; *v* descontar, levantar; ***pay ~** pagar à vista

cashier (kæ-chi^ă) *n* caixa *f*

cashmere (kæch-mi^ă) *n* caxemira *f*

casino (kă-çii-no^u) *n* (pl ~s) casino *m*; cassino *mBr*

cask (kaaçk) *n* barril *m*

cast (kaat) *n* lance *m*

***cast** (kaaçt) *v* lançar, atirar; **cast iron** ferro fundido

castle (kaa-çăl) *n* castelo *m*

casual (kæ-ju-ăl) *adj* à vontade; casual

casualty (kæ-ju-ăl-ti) *n* vítima *f*

cat (kæt) *n* gato *m*

catacomb (kæ-tă-ko^umm) *n* catacumba *f*

catalogue (kæ-tă-lógh) *n* catálogo *m*

catarrh (kă-taa) *n* catarro *m*

catastrophe (kă-tæ-çtră-fi) *n* catástrofe *f*

***catch** (kætch) *v* apanhar; agarrar; surpreender; tomar

category (kæ-ti-ghă-ri) *n* categoria *f*

cathedral (kă-θii-drăl) *n* catedral *f*

catholic (kæ-θă-lik) *adj* católico

cattle (kæ-tăl) *pl* gado *m*

caught (kóót) *v* (p, pp catch)

cauliflower (kó-li-flau^ă) *n* couve-flor *f*

cause (kóóz) *v* causar; provocar; *n* causa *f*; motivo *m*

caution (kóó-chănn) *n* cautela *f*; *v* avisar, *advertir

cautious (kóó-chăç) *adj* prudente

cave (keiv) *n* gruta *f*; caverna *f*

cavern (kæ-vănn) *n* caverna *f*

caviar (kæ-vi-aa) *n* caviar *m*

cavity (kæ-vă-ti) *n* cavidade *f*

cease (çiiç) *v* cessar

ceiling (çii-linng) *n* tecto *m*

celebrate (çé-li-breit) *v* celebrar

celebration (çé-li-brei-chănn) *n* celebração *f*

celebrity (çi-lé-bră-ti) *n* celebridade *f*

celery (çé-lă-ri) *n* aipo *m*

celibacy (çé-li-bă-çi) *n* celibato *m*

cell (çél) *n* célula *f*

cellar (çé-lă) *n* cave *f*; porão *mBr*

cellophane (çé-lă-feinn) *n* celofane *m*

cement (çi-ménnt) *n* cimento *m*

cemetery (çé-mi-tri) *n* cemitério *m*

censorship (çénn-çă-chip) *n* censura *f*

centimetre (çénn-ti-mii-tă) *n* centímetro *m*

central (çénn-trăl) *adj* central; ~ **heating** aquecimento central; ~

station estação central
centralize (çénn-trã-laiz) v centralizar
centre (çénn-tã) n centro m
century (çénn-tchã-ri) n século m
ceramics (çi-ræ-mikç) n cerâmica f
ceremony (çé-rã-mã-ni) n cerimónia f
certain (çãã-tãnn) adj certo
certificate (çã-ti-fi-kãt) n certificado m, atestado m, diploma m, certidão f
chain (tcheinn) n cadeia f
chair (tché⁴) n cadeira f; assento m
chairman (tché⁴-männ) n (pl -men) presidente m
chalet (chæ-lei) n chalé m
chalk (tchóók) n giz m
challenge (tchæ-lãnndj) v desafiar; n desafio m
chamber (tcheimm-bã) n quarto m
chambermaid (tcheimm-bã-meid) n criada de quarto
champagne (chæmm-peinn) n champanhe m
champion (tchæmm-piänn) n campeão m; defensor m
chance (tchaannç) n sorte f; ocasião f, oportunidade f; risco m; azar m; by ~ por acaso
change (tcheinndj) v mudar, modificar; trocar; mudar de roupa; *fazer transbordo; n modificação f, mudança f; troco m
channel (tchæ-nãl) n canal m; **English Channel** Canal da Mancha
chaos (kei-óç) n caos m
chaotic (kei-ó-tik) adj caótico
chap (tchæp) n tipo m
chapel (tchæ-pãl) n capela f
chaplain (tchæ-plinn) n capelão m
character (kæ-rãk-tã) n carácter m
characteristic (kæ-rãk-tã-çtik) adj típico, característico; n característica f; traço caracterial
characterize (kæ-rãk-tã-raiz) v carac-

terizar
charcoal (tchaa-koᵘl) n carvão de lenha
charge (tchaadj) v *pedir; encarregar; acusar; carregar; n preço m; carregamento m, carga f, taxa f; acusação f; ~ **plate** Am cartão de crédito; **free of** ~ gratuito; **in** ~ **of** encarregado de; *take ~ of encarregar-se de
charity (tchæ-rã-ti) n caridade f
charm (tchaamm) n encanto m; amuleto m
charming (tchaa-minng) adj encantador
chart (tchaat) n tabela f; gráfico m; mapa marítimo; **conversion** ~ tabela de conversão
chase (tcheiç) v *perseguir; expulsar, afugentar; n caça f
chasm (kæ-zãmm) n fenda f
chassis (chæ-çi) n (pl ~) chassi m
chaste (tcheiçt) adj casto
chat (tchæt) v conversar, *cavaquear; n conversa f, cavaco m
chatterbox (tchæ-tã-bókç) n tagarela m
chauffeur (choᵘ-fã) n motorista m
cheap (tchiip) adj barato; económico
cheat (tchiit) v enganar; defraudar
check (tchék) v *conferir, verificar; n quadrado m; nAm conta f; cheque m; **check!** xeque!; ~ **in** inscrever-se, registar-se; ~ **out** partir, *sair
check-book (tchék-buk) nAm livro de cheques
checkerboard (tché-kã-bóód) nAm tabuleiro de xadrez
checkroom (tchék-ruumm) nAm vestiário m
check-up (tché-kap) n exame médico
cheek (tchiik) n face f
cheek-bone (tchiik-boᵘnn) n maçã do

rosto

cheer (tchi^ã) v aplaudir, aclamar; ~ **up** animar, alegrar

cheerful (tchi^ã-fål) adj jovial, alegre

cheese (tchiiz) n queijo m

chef (chéf) n cozinheiro-chefe m

chemical (ké-mi-kål) adj químico

chemist (ké-miçt) n farmacêutico m; **chemist's** farmácia f; drogaria f

chemistry (ké-mi-çtri) n química f

cheque (tchék) n cheque m

cheque-book (tchék-buk) n livro de cheques

chequered (tché-kåd) adj em xadrez, quadriculado

cherry (tché-ri) n cereja f

chess (tchéç) n xadrez m

chest (tchéçt) n peito m; arca f; ~ **of drawers** cómoda f

chestnut (tchéç-nat) n castanha f

chew (tchuu) v mastigar

chewing-gum (tchuu-inng-ghamm) n goma de mascar Br, pastilha elástica

chicken (tchi-kinn) n frango m

chickenpox (tchi-kinn-pókç) n varicela f

chief (tchiif) n chefe m; adj principal

chieftain (tchiif-tänn) n chefe m

chilblain (tchil-bleinn) n frieira f

child (tchaild) n (pl children) criança f

childbirth (tchaild-bääθ) n parto m

childhood (tchaild-hud) n infância f

Chile (tchi-li) Chile m

Chilean (tchi-li-änn) adj chileno

chill (tchil) n calafrio m

chilly (tchi-li) adj fresco

chimes (tchaimmz) pl carrilhão m

chimney (tchimm-ni) n chaminé f

chin (tchinn) n queixo m

China (tchai-nä) China f

china (tchai-nä) n porcelana f

Chinese (tchai-niiz) adj chinês

chink (tchinngk) n greta f

chip (tchip) n lasca f; ficha f; v lascar, cortar; **chips** batatas fritas

chiropodist (ki-ró-på-diçt) n calista m

chisel (tchi-zäl) n cinzel m

chives (tchaivz) pl cebolinho m

chlorine (klóó-riinn) n cloro m

chock-full (tchók-ful) adj atestado, repleto

chocolate (tchó-klåt) n chocolate m; bombom m

choice (tchoiç) n escolha f; selecção f

choir (k^uai^ã) n coro m

choke (tcho^uk) v sufocar; estrangular; n choke m; afogador mBr

*choose (tchuuz) v escolher

chop (tchóp) n costeleta f; v picar

Christ (kraiçt) Cristo

christen (kri-çänn) v baptizar

christening (kri-çä-ninng) n baptismo m

Christian (kriç-tchänn) adj cristão; ~ **name** nome próprio; nome de batismo Br

Christmas (kriç-måç) Natal m

chromium (kro^u-mi-ämm) n crómio m

chronic (kró-nik) adj crónico

chronological (kró-nå-ló-dji-kål) adj cronológico

chuckle (tcha-kål) v *rir entre dentes

chunk (tchanngk) n pedaço grosso

church (tchäätch) n igreja f

churchyard (tchäätch-ⁱaad) n cemitério m

cigar (çi-ghaa) n charuto m; ~ **shop** tabacaria f

cigarette (çi-ghå-rét) n cigarro m

cigarette-case (çi-ghå-rét-keiç) n cigarreira f

cigarette-holder (çi-ghå-rét-ho^ul-då) n boquilha f

cigarette-lighter (çi-ghå-rét-lai-tå) n isqueiro m

cinema (çi-nå-mä) n cinema m

cinnamon (*çi*-nă-mănn) *n* canela *f*

circle (*çăă*-kăl) *n* círculo *m*; balcão *m*; *v* circundar, *rodear

circulation (*çăă*-kⁱu-*lei*-chănn) *n* circulação *f*

circumstance (*çăă*-kămm-çtænnç) *n* circunstância *f*

circus (*çăă*-kăç) *n* circo *m*

citizen (*çi*-ti-zănn) *n* cidadão *m*

citizenship (*çi*-ti-zănn-chip) *n* cidadania *f*

city (*çi*-ti) *n* cidade *f*

civic (*çi*-vik) *adj* cívico

civil (*çi*-văl) *adj* civil; educado; ~ **law** direito civil; ~ **servant** funcionário público

civilian (çi-*vil*-ⁱănn) *adj* civil; *n* civil *m*

civilization (çi-vă-lai-*zei*-chănn) *n* civilização *f*

civilized (*çi*-vă-laizd) *adj* civilizado

claim (kleimm) *v* reivindicar; afirmar; *n* pretensão *f*, reivindicação *f*

clamp (klæmmp) *n* grampo *m*

clap (klæp) *v* aplaudir, bater as palmas

clarify (*klæ*-ri-fai) *v* esclarecer, aclarar

class (klaaç) *n* classe *f*

classical (*klæ*-çi-kăl) *adj* clássico

classify (*klæ*-çi-fai) *v* classificar

class-mate (*klaaç*-meit) *n* colega de turma; colega de classe *Br*

classroom (*klaaç*-ruumm) *n* sala de aula

clause (klóóz) *n* cláusula *f*

claw (klóó) *n* garra *f*

clay (klei) *n* argila *f*

clean (kliinn) *adj* puro, limpo; *v* limpar

cleaning (*klii*-ninng) *n* limpeza *f*; ~ **fluid** produto de limpeza

clear (kli^ă) *adj* claro; *v* limpar

clearing (*kli^ă*-rinng) *n* clareira *f*

cleft (kléft) *n* fenda *f*

clergyman (*klăă*-dji-mănn) *n* (pl -men) pastor *m*; clérigo *m*

clerk (klaak) *n* empregado de escritório, funcionário *m*; escrivão *m*; secretário *m*

clever (*klé*-vă) *adj* inteligente; esperto, astuto

client (*klai*-ănnt) *n* cliente *m*

cliff (klif) *n* falésia *f*

climate (*klai*-mit) *n* clima *m*

climb (klaimm) *v* trepar; *n* subida *f*

clinic (*kli*-nik) *n* clínica *f*

cloak (klo^uk) *n* casacão *m*

cloakroom (*klo^uk*-ruumm) *n* guarda-roupa *m*

clock (klók) *n* relógio *m*; **at ... o'clock** às ... horas

cloister (*kloi*-çtă) *n* convento *m*

close[1] (klo^uz) *v* fechar; **closed** fechado, encerrado

close[2] (klo^uç) *adj* próximo

closet (*kló*-zit) *n* armário *m*; *nAm* roupeiro *m*

cloth (klóθ) *n* trapo *m*; pano *m*

clothes (klo^uðz) *pl* vestuário *m*, roupa *f*

clothes-brush (*klo^uðz*-brach) *n* escova de fato

clothing (*klo^u*-ðinng) *n* vestuário *m*

cloud (klaud) *n* nuvem *f*

cloud-burst (*klaud*-băăçt) *n* chuvada *f*

cloudy (*klau*-di) *adj* nublado, encoberto

clover (*klo^u*-vă) *n* trevo *m*

clown (klaunn) *n* palhaço *m*

club (klab) *n* clube *m*; associação *f*, círculo *m*; moca *f*, cacete *m*

clumsy (*klamm*-zi) *adj* desajeitado

clutch (klatch) *n* embraiagem *f*; aperto *m*

coach (ko^utch) *n* autocarro *m*; carruagem *f*; coche *m*; treinador *m*; ônibus *mBr*

coagulate (ko^u-æ-ghⁱu-leit) *v* coagular coal (kou̯l) n carvão m

coarse (kóóç) adj grosseiro

coast (kou̯çt) n costa f

coat (kou̯t) n casacão m, casaco m

coat-hanger (kou̯t-hænng-ă) n cabide m

cobweb (kób-u̯éb) n teia de aranha

cocaine (kou̯-keinn) n cocaína f

cock (kók) n galo m

cocktail (kók-teil) n beberete m; coquetel mBr

coconut (kou̯-kă-nat) n coco m

cod (kód) n (pl ~) bacalhau m

code (kou̯d) n código m

coffee (kó-fi) n café m

cognac (kó-n̆æk) n conhaque m

coherence (kou̯-hi̯ă-rănnç) n coerência f

coin (koinn) n moeda f

coincide (kou̯-inn-çaid) v coincidir

cold (kou̯ld) adj frio; n frio m; constipação f; *catch a ~ constipar-se

collapse (kă-læpç) v sucumbir, desmoronar-se

collar (kó-lă) n coleira f; colarinho m, gola f; ~ stud botão de colarinho

collarbone (kó-lă-bou̯nn) n clavícula f

colleague (kó-liigh) n colega m

collect (kă-lékt) v coleccionar; *ir buscar; *fazer um pedítório

collection (kă-lék-chănn) n colecção f; recolha f

collective (kă-lék-tiv) adj colectivo

collector (kă-lék-tă) n coleccionador m; colector m

college (kó-lidj) n escola universitária; colégio m

collide (kă-laid) v colidir, chocar

collision (kă-li-jänn) n colisão f, choque m; abalroamento m

Colombia (kă-lómm-bi-ă) Colômbia f

Colombian (kă-lómm-bi-ănn) adj colombiano

colonel (kăă-năl) n coronel m

colony (kó-lă-ni) n colónia f

colour (ka-lă) n cor f; v *colorir; ~ film filme a cores

colourant (ka-lă-rănnt) n corante m

colour-blind (ka-lă-blainnd) adj daltónico

coloured (ka-lăd) adj de cor

colourful (ka-lă-făl) adj colorido

column (kó-lămm) n coluna f, pilar m; rubrica f

coma (kou̯-mă) n coma m

comb (kou̯mm) v *pentear; n pente m

combat (kómm-bæt) n combate m, luta f; v combater

combination (kómm-bi-nei-chănn) n combinação f

combine (kămm-bainn) v combinar

*come (kamm) v *vir; ~ across encontrar

comedian (kă-mii-di-ănn) n comediante m; cómico m

comedy (kó-mă-di) n comédia f; musical ~ comédia musical

comfort (kamm-făt) n conforto m, bem-estar m, comodidade f; consolação f; v consolar, confortar

comfortable (kamm-fă-tă-băl) adj confortável

comic (kó-mik) adj cómico

comics (kó-mikç) pl banda desenhada

coming (kă-minng) n chegada f

comma (kó-mă) n vírgula f

command (kă-maannd) v comandar, mandar; n ordem f

commander (kă-maann-dă) n comandante m

commemoration (kă-mé-mă-rei-chănn) n comemoração f

commence (kă-ménnç) v começar, principiar

comment (kó-ménnt) n comentário m; v comentar

commerce (kó-măăç) n comércio m

commercial (kă-măă-chăl) adj comer-

cial; n anúncio m; ~ **law** direito
comercial

commission (kă-*mi*-chănn) n comissão
f

commit (kă-*mit*) v confiar, entregar;
cometer, praticar

committee (kă-*mi*-ti) n comité m, comissão f

common (*kó*-mănn) adj comum; habitual; ordinário

commune (*kó*-mⁱuunn) n comuna f

communicate (kă-*mⁱuu*-ni-keit) v comunicar

communication (kă-mⁱuu-ni-*kei*-chănn)
n comunicação f

communiqué (kă-*mⁱuu*-ni-kei) n comunicado m

communism (*kó*-mⁱu-ni-zămm) n comunismo m

communist (*kó*-mⁱu-niçt) n comunista
m

community (kă-*mⁱuu*-nă-ti) n comunidade f, sociedade f

compact (*kómm*-pækt) adj compacto

companion (kămm-*pæ*-nⁱänn) n companheiro m

company (*kamm*-pă-ni) n companhia
f; firma f, sociedade f

comparative (kămm-*pæ*-ră-tiv) adj relativo; comparativo

compare (kămm-*pé^ă*) v comparar

comparison (kămm-*pæ*-ri-çănn) n
comparação f

compartment (kămm-*paat*-mănnt) n
compartimento m

compass (*kamm*-păç) n bússola f

compel (kămm-*pél*) v obrigar

compensate (*kómm*-pănn-çeit) v compensar

compensation (kómm-pănn-*çei*-chănn)
n compensação f; indemnização f

compete (kămm-*piit*) v *competir

competition (kómm-pă-*ti*-chănn) n
competição f; concorrência f

competitor (kămm-*pé*-ti-tăr) n concorrente m

compile (kămm-*pail*) v compilar

complain (kămm-*pleinn*) v queixar-se

complaint (kămm-*pleinnt*) n queixa f;
complaints book livro de reclamações

complete (kămm-*pliit*) adj completo; v
completar

completely (kămm-*pliit*-li) adv totalmente, completamente, inteira-
mente

complex (*kómm*-plékç) n complexo m;
adj complexo

complexion (kămm-*plék*-chănn) n tez
f; aspecto m

complicated (*kómm*-pli-kei-tid) adj
complicado

compliment (*kómm*-pli-mănnt) n cumprimento m; v felicitar, cumprimentar

compose (kămm-*po^uz*) v *compor

composer (kămm-*po^u*-ză) n compositor m

composition (kómm-pă-*zi*-chănn) n
composição f

comprehensive (kómm-pri-*hénn*-çiv)
adj extensivo

comprise (kămm-*praiz*) v compreender, *conter

compromise (*kómm*-pră-maiz) n compromisso m

compulsory (kămm-*pal*-çă-ri) adj obrigatório

comrade (*kómm*-reid) n camarada m

conceal (kănn-*çiil*) v ocultar, esconder

conceited (kănn-*çii*-tid) adj pretensioso

conceive (kănn-*çiiv*) v compreender,
conceber; imaginar

concentrate (*kónn*-çănn-treit) v concentrar

concentration (kónn-çănn-*trei*-chănn)
n concentração f

conception (kănn-çép-chănn) n concepção f

concern (kănn-çããnn) v *dizer respeito a; n preocupação f; assunto m; empresa f

concerned (kănn-çããnnd) adj preocupado; envolvido

concerning (kănn-çãã-ninng) prep referente a

concert (kónn-căt) n concerto m; ~ hall sala de concertos

concession (kănn-çé-chănn) n concessão f

concierge (kón-çi-éªj) n porteiro m

concise (kănn-çaiç) adj conciso

conclusion (kănng-kluu-jănn) n conclusão f

concrete (kónn-kriit) adj concreto; n betão m; concreto mBr

concurrence (kănng-ka-rănnç) n coincidência f

concussion (kănng-ka-chănn) n comoção cerebral

condition (kănn-di-chănn) n condição f, estado m; circunstância f

conditional (kănn-di-chă-năl) adj condicional

conduct¹ (kónn-dakt) n conduta f

conduct² (kănn-dakt) v *conduzir; acompanhar; dirigir

conductor (kănn-dak-tă) n cobrador m; maestro m

confectioner (kănn-fék-chă-nă) n confeiteiro m

conference (kónn-fă-rănnç) n conferência f

confess (kănn-féç) v reconhecer; confessar-se; professar

confession (kănn-fé-chănn) n confissão f

confidence (kónn-fi-dănnç) n confiança f

confident (kónn-fi-dănnt) adj confiante

confidential (kónn-fi-dénn-chăl) adj confidencial

confirm (kănn-fããmm) v confirmar

confirmation (kónn-fă-mei-chănn) n confirmação f

confiscate (kónn-fi-çkeit) v confiscar

conflict (kónn-flikt) n conflito m

confuse (kănn-fᵘuuz) v confundir; confused confuso

confusion (kănn-fᵘuu-jănn) n confusão f

congratulate (kănng-ghræ-tchu-leit) v felicitar, congratular

congratulation (kănng-ghræ-tchu-lei-chănn) n felicitação f

congregation (kónn-ghri-ghei-chănn) n congregação f, comunidade f, ordem f

congress (kónn-ghréç) n congresso m

connect (kă-nékt) v unir, ligar

connection (kă-nék-chănn) n relação f; ligação f, correspondência f

connoisseur (kó-nă-çãã) n conhecedor m

conquer (kónn-kă) v conquistar; vencer

conqueror (kónn-kă-ră) n conquistador m

conquest (kónn-kᵘéçt) n conquista f

conscience (kónn-chănnç) n consciência f

conscious (kónn-chăç) adj consciente

consciousness (kónn-chăç-năç) n consciência f

conscript (kónn-çkript) n recruta m

consent (kănn-çénnt) v *consentir; aprovar; n consentimento m

consequence (kónn-çi-kᵘănnç) n consequência f

consequently (kónn-çi-kᵘănnt-li) adv consequentemente

conservative (kănn-çãã-vă-tiv) adj conservador

consider (kănn-çi-dă) v considerar;

ponderar; achar

considerable (kănn-çi-dă-ră-băl) *adj* considerável; notável, importante

considerate (kănn-çi-dă-rát) *adj* atencioso

consideration (kănn-çi-dă-rei-chănn) *n* consideracão *f*; atenção *f*

considering (kănn-çi-dă-rinng) *prep* em vista de

consignment (kănn-çainn-mănnt) *n* remessa *f*

consist of (kănn-çiçt) consistir em

conspire (kănn-çpai⁴) *v* conspirar

constant (kónn-çtănnt) *adj* constante

constipated (kónn-çti-pei-tid) *adj* com prisão de ventre

constipation (kónn-çti-pei-chănn) *n* prisão de ventre

constituency (kănn-çti-tchu-ănn-çi) *n* círculo eleitoral

constitution (kónn-çti-t'uu-chănn) *n* constituicão *f*

construct (kănn-çtrakt) *v* *construir; edificar

construction (kănn-çtrak-chănn) *n* construcão *f*, edifício *m*

consul (kónn-çăl) *n* cônsul *m*

consulate (kónn-ç'u-lăt) *n* consulado *m*

consult (kănn-çalt) *v* consultar

consultation (kónn-çăl-tei-chănn) *n* consulta *f*; ~ **hours** horas de consulta

consumer (kănn-ç'uu-mă) *n* consumidor *m*

contact (kónn-tækt) *n* contacto *m*; *v* contactar com; ~ **lenses** lentes de contacto

contagious (kănn-tei-djăç) *adj* contagioso

contain (kănn-teinn) *v* *conter

container (kănn-tei-nă) *n* recipiente *m*

contemporary (kănn-témm-pă-ră-ri) *adj* contemporâneo; de então; *n*

contemporâneo *m*

contempt (kănn-témmpt) *n* desdém *m*, desprezo *m*

content (kănn-ténnt) *adj* satisfeito

contents (kónn-ténntç) *pl* conteúdo *m*

contest (kónn-téçt) *n* luta *f*; concurso *m*

continent (kónn-ti-nănnt) *n* continente *m*

continental (kónn-ti-nénn-tăl) *adj* continental

continual (kănn-ti-n'u-ăl) *adj* contínuo

continue (kănn-ti-n'uu) *v* continuar; durar; *prosseguir

continuous (kănn-ti-n'u-ăç) *adj* contínuo, ininterrupto

contour (kónn-tu⁴) *n* contorno *m*

contraceptive (kónn-tră-çép-tiv) *n* contraceptivo *m*

contract[1] (kónn-trækt) *n* contrato *m*

contract[2] (kănn-trækt) *v* *contrair

contractor (kănn-træk-tă) *n* empreiteiro *m*

contradict (kónn-tră-dikt) *v* *contradizer

contradictory (kónn-tră-dik-tă-ri) *adj* contraditório

contrary (kónn-tră-ri) *n* contrário *m*; *adj* contrário; **on the** ~ pelo contrário

contrast (kónn-traaçt) *n* contraste *m*; diferença *f*

contribution (kónn-tri-b'uu-chănn) *n* contribuicão *f*

control (kănn-tro⁴l) *n* controle *m*; *v* fiscalizar, controlar

controversial (kónn-tră-vără-chăl) *adj* controverso

convenience (kănn-vii-n'ănnç) *n* comodidade *f*

convenient (kănn-vii-n'ănnt) *adj* cómodo; oportuno, apropriado, conveniente

convent (kónn-vănnt) *n* convento *m*

conversation (kónn-vă-_çei_-chănn) *n* conversação *f*, conversa *f*

convert (kănn-_văăt_) *v* converter

convict[1] (kănn-_vikt_) *v* declarar culpado

convict[2] (_kónn_-vikt) *n* condenado *m*

conviction (kănn-_vik_-chănn) *n* convicção *f*; condenação *f*

convince (kănn-_vinnç_) *v* convencer

convulsion (kănn-_val_-chănn) *n* convulsão *f*

cook (kuk) *n* cozinheiro *m*; *v* cozinhar; preparar

cooker (_ku_-kă) *n* fogão *m*; **gas** ~ fogão a gás

cookery-book (_ku_-kă-ri-buk) *n* livro de cozinha

cookie (_ku_-ki) *nAm* biscoito *m*

cool (kuul) *adj* fresco; **cooling system** sistema de arrefecimento

co-operation (ko^u-ó-pă-_rei_-chănn) *n* cooperação *f*

co-operative (ko^u-ó-pă-ră-tiv) *adj* cooperativo; cooperador, colaborador; *n* cooperativa *f*

co-ordinate (ko^u-óó-di-neit) *v* coordenar

co-ordination (ko^u-óó-di-_nei_-chănn) *n* coordenação *f*

copper (_kó_-pă) *n* cobre *m*

copy (_kó_-pi) *n* cópia *f*; exemplar *m*; *v* copiar; imitar; **carbon** ~ cópia *f*

coral (_kó_-răl) *n* coral *m*

cord (kóód) *n* corda *f*; cordão *m*

cordial (_kóó_-di-ăl) *adj* cordial

corduroy (_kóó_-dă-roi) *n* bombazina *f*

core (kóó) *n* núcleo *m*; coração *m*

cork (kóók) *n* rolha *f*

corkscrew (_kóók_-çkruu) *n* saca-rolhas *m*

corn (kóónn) *n* grão *m*; trigo *m*, cereais; calo *m*; ~ **on the cob** macaroca de milho

corner (_kóó_-nă) *n* esquina *f*; canto *m*

cornfield (_kóónn_-fiild) *n* seara *f*

corpse (kóópç) *n* cadáver *m*

corpulent (_kóó_-pⁱu-lănnt) *adj* corpulento; obeso, balofo

correct (kă-_rékt_) *adj* certo, correcto; *v* corrigir

correction (kă-_rék_-chănn) *n* correcção *f*; rectificação *f*

correctness (kă-_rékt_-năç) *n* exactidão *f*

correspond (kó-ri-_çpónnd_) *v* corresponder

correspondence (kó-ri-_çpónn_-dănnç) *n* correspondência *f*

correspondent (kó-ri-_çpónn_-dănnt) *n* correspondente *m*

corridor (_kó_-ri-dóó) *n* corredor *m*

corrupt (kă-_rapt_) *adj* corrupto; *v* corromper

corruption (kă-_rap_-chănn) *n* corrupção *f*

corset (_kóó_-çit) *n* corpete *m*

cosmetics (kóz-_mé_-tikç) *pl* cosméticos *mpl*

cost (kóçt) *n* custo *m*; preço *m*

***cost** (kóçt) *v* custar

cosy (_ko^u_-zi) *adj* íntimo, aconchegado

cot (kót) *nAm* cama de acampamento

cottage (_kó_-tidj) *n* casa de campo

cotton (_kó_-tănn) *n* algodão *m*; de algodão

cotton-wool (_kó_-tănn-^uul) *n* algodão *m*

couch (kautch) *n* divã *m*

cough (kóf) *n* tosse *f*; *v* *tossir

could (kud) *v* (p can)

council (_kaunn_-çăl) *n* conselho *m*

councillor (_kaunn_-çă-lă) *n* conselheiro *m*

counsel (_kaunn_-çăl) *n* conselho *m*

counsellor (_kaunn_-çă-lă) *n* conselheiro *m*

count (kaunnt) v contar; incluir; considerar; n conde m

counter (kaunn-tă) n balcão m

counterfeit (kaunn-tă-fiit) v falsificar

counterfoil (kaunn-tă-foil) n talão m

counterpane (kaunn-tă-peinn) n colcha f

countess (kaunn-tiç) n condessa f

country (kann-tri) n país m; campo m; região f; ~ **house** casa de campo

countryman (kann-tri-mănn) n (pl -men) compatriota m

countryside (kann-tri-çaid) n campo m

county (kaunn-ti) n condado m

couple (ka-păl) n par m; casal m

coupon (kuu-pónn) n cupão m, talão m

courage (ka-ridj) n valentia f, coragem f

courageous (kă-rei-djăç) adj corajoso

course (kóóç) n rota f; prato m; curso m; **intensive** ~ curso intensivo; **of** ~ com certeza, naturalmente

court (kóót) n tribunal m; corte f

courteous (kăă-ti-ăç) adj cortês

cousin (ka-zănn) n prima f, primo m

cover (ka-vă) v *cobrir, tapar; n abrigo m, refúgio m; tampa f; capa f; ~ **charge** preço do talher

cow (kau) n vaca f

coward (kau-ăd) n cobarde m

cowardly (kau-ăd-li) adj cobarde

cow-hide (kau-haid) n pele de vaca

crab (kræb) n caranguejo m

crack (kræk) n estalido m; fenda f; v estalar; rebentar, quebrar, partir

cradle (krei-dăl) n berço m

cramp (kræmmp) n cãibra f

crane (kreinn) n grua f

crankcase (krænngk-keiç) n cárter m

crankshaft (krænngk-chaaft) n cambota f

crash (kræch) n choque m; v colidir; despenhar-se; ~ **barrier** barreira de protecção

crate (kreit) n grade f

crater (krei-tă) n cratera f

crawl (króól) v rastejar

craze (kreiz) n mania f

crazy (krei-zi) adj louco, doido

creak (kriik) v ranger

cream (kriimm) n creme m; nata f; adj creme

creamy (krii-mi) adj cremoso

crease (kriiç) v enrugar, amarrotar; n dobra f; prega f

create (kri-eit) v criar

creature (krii-tchă) n criatura f; ser m

credible (kré-di-băl) adj verosímil

credit (kré-dit) n crédito m; v creditar; ~ **card** cartão de crédito

creditor (kré-di-tă) n credor m

credulous (kré-di'u-lăç) adj crédulo

creek (kriik) n enseada f

***creep** (kriip) v rastejar

creepy (krii-pi) adj horripilante, assustador

cremate (kri-meit) v incinerar

cremation (kri-mei-chănn) n incineração f

crew (kruu) n tripulação f

cricket (kri-kit) n críquete m; grilo m

crime (kraimm) n crime m

criminal (kri-mi-năl) n criminoso m, delinquente m; adj criminal, criminoso; ~ **law** direito penal

criminality (kri-mi-næ-lă-ti) n criminalidade f

crimson (krimm-zănn) adj vermelho

crippled (kri-păld) adj aleijado

crisis (krai-çiç) n (pl crises) crise f

crisp (kriçp) adj quebradiço

critic (kri-tik) n crítico m

critical (kri-ti-kăl) adj crítico; precário

criticism (kri-ti-çi-zămm) n crítica f

criticize (kri-ti-çaiz) v criticar

crochet (kro^u-chei) v *fazer renda
crockery (kró-kă-ri) n faiança f, loiça f
crocodile (kró-kă-dail) n crocodilo m
crooked (kru-kid) adj torto, torcido; desonesto
crop (króp) n colheita f
cross (króç) v atravessar; adj irritado, zangado; n cruz f
cross-eyed (króç-aid) adj estrábico
crossing (kró-çinng) n travessia f; encruzilhada f
crossroads (króç-ro^udz) n cruzamento m
crosswalk (króç-^uóók) nAm passagem de peões; passagem de pedestres Br
crow (kro^u) n gralha f
crowbar (kro^u-baa) n pé-de-cabra m
crowd (kraud) n turba f, multidão f
crowded (krau-did) adj animado; apinhado
crown (kraunn) n coroa f; v coroar
crucifix (kruu-çi-fikç) n crucifixo m
crucifixion (kruu-çi-fik-chänn) n crucificação f
crucify (kruu-çi-fai) v crucificar
cruel (kru^äl) adj cruel
cruise (kruuz) n cruzeiro m
crumb (kramm) n migalha f
crusade (kruu-çeid) n cruzada f
crust (kraçt) n côdea f
crutch (kratch) n muleta f
cry (krai) v chorar; gritar; chamar; n grito m; brado m
crystal (kri-çtăl) n cristal m; adj de cristal
Cuba (kⁱuu-bă) Cuba f
Cuban (kⁱuu-bänn) adj cubano
cube (kⁱuub) n cubo m
cuckoo (ku-kuu) n cuco m
cucumber (kⁱuu-kămm-bă) n pepino m
cuddle (ka-dăl) v acarinhar
cudgel (ka-djăl) n cacete m

cuff (kaf) n punho m
cuff-links (kaf-linngkç) pl botões de punho; abotoaduras fplBr
cul-de-sac (kal-dă-cæk) n beco sem saída
cultivate (kal-ti-veit) v cultivar
culture (kal-tchă) n cultura f
cultured (kal-tchăd) adj culto
cunning (ka-ninng) adj manhoso
cup (kap) n chávena f; taça f; xícara fBr
cupboard (ka-băd) n armário m
curb (kăăb) n beira do passeio; meio-fio mBr; v reprimir, *refrear
cure (kⁱu^ä) v curar; n cura f
curio (kⁱu^ä-ri-o^u) n (pl ~s) curiosidade f
curiosity (kⁱu^ä-ri-ó-çă-ti) n curiosidade f
curious (kⁱu^ä-ri-äç) adj curioso
curl (kăăl) v encaracolar; n caracol m
curler (kăă-lă) n rolo m
curling-tongs (kăă-linng-tónnz) pl ferro de frisar
curly (kăă-li) adj encaracolado
currant (ka-rănnt) n passa de Corinto; groselha f
currency (ka-rănn-çi) n moeda f; foreign ~ moeda estrangeira
current (ka-rănnt) n corrente f; adj corrente; alternating ~ corrente alterna; direct ~ corrente contínua
curry (ka-ri) n caril m
curse (kăăç) v praguejar; amaldiçoar, *maldizer; n praga f
curtain (kăă-tănn) n cortina f; pano m
curve (kăăv) n curva f; volta f
curved (kăăvd) adj curvado, curvo
cushion (ku-chänn) n almofada f
custodian (ka-çto^u-di-änn) n guarda m
custody (ka-çtă-di) n detenção f; custódia f; tutela f

custom (ka-çtămm) n costume m; hábito m

customary (ka-çtă-mă-ri) adj usual, costumado, habitual

customer (ka-çtă-mă) n freguês m; cliente m

Customs (ka-çtămmz) pl alfândega f; ~ **duty** taxa f; ~ **officer** funcionário aduaneiro

cut (kat) n corte m; golpe m

***cut** (kat) v cortar; *reduzir; ~ **off** cortar; interromper

cutlery (kat-lă-ri) n talher m

cutlet (kat-lăt) n costeleta f

cycle (çai-kăl) n velocípede m; bicicleta f; ciclo m

cyclist (çai-klict) n ciclista m

cylinder (çi-linn-dă) n cilindro m; ~ **head** cabeça do motor

cystitis (çi-çtai-tiç) n cistite f

Czech (tchék) adj checo

Czechoslovakia (tché-kă-çlă-vaa-ki-ă) Checoslováquia f

D

dad (dæd) n pai m

daddy (dæ-di) n paizinho m

daffodil (dæ-fă-dil) n junquilho m

daily (dei-li) adj diário; n diário m

dairy (dé-ă-ri) n leitaria f

dam (dæmm) n barragem f; dique m

damage (dæ-midj) n dano m; v danificar

damp (dæmmp) adj húmido; molhado; n humidade f; v humedecer

dance (daannç) v dançar; n dança f

dandelion (dænn-di-lai-ănn) n dente-de-leão m

dandruff (dænn-drăf) n caspa f

Dane (deinn) n dinamarquês m

danger (deinn-djă) n perigo m

dangerous (deinn-djă-răç) adj perigoso

Danish (dei-nich) adj dinamarquês

dare (dé-ă) v ousar; desafiar

daring (dé-ă-rinng) adj temerário

dark (daak) adj escuro; n escuridão f, trevas fpl

darling (daa-linng) n querido m, amor m

darn (daann) v passajar

dash (dæch) v precipitar-se; n traço m

dashboard (dæch-bóód) n painel de instrumentos

data (dei-tă) pl dados mpl

date¹ (deit) n data f; encontro m; v datar; **out of** ~ fora de moda

date² (deit) n tâmara f

daughter (dóó-tă) n filha f

dawn (dóónn) n madrugada f; aurora f

day (dei) n dia m; **by** ~ de dia; ~ **trip** excursão f; **per** ~ por dia; **the** ~ **before yesterday** anteontem

daybreak (dei-breik) n amanhecer m

daylight (dei-lait) n luz do dia

dead (déd) adj morto

deaf (déf) adj surdo

deal (diil) n negócio m

***deal** (diil) v *distribuir; ~ **with** tratar com; *fazer negócios com

dealer (dii-lă) n negociante m

dear (di-ă) adj querido; caro

death (déθ) n morte f; ~ **penalty** pena de morte

debate (di-beit) n debate m

debit (dé-bit) n débito m

debt (dét) n dívida f

decaffeinated (dii-kæ-fi-nei-tid) adj descafeinado

deceit (di-çiit) n engano m

deceive (di-çiiv) v enganar

December (di-çémm-bă) Dezembro

decency (dii-çănn-çi) n decência f

decent (dii-çánnt) *adj* decente

decide (di-çaid) *v* decidir, resolver

decision (di-çi-jánn) *n* decisão *f*

deck (dék) *n* convés *m*; ~ **cabin** camarote de convés; ~ **chair** cadeira de lona

declaration (dé-klã-rei-chánn) *n* declaração *f*

declare (di-kléá) *v* declarar

decoration (dé-kã-rei-chánn) *n* decoração *f*

decrease (dii-kriiç) *v* *diminuir; *n* diminuição *f*

dedicate (dé-di-keit) *v* dedicar

deduce (di-dᵘuuç) *v* *deduzir

deduct (di-dakt) *v* *deduzir, *subtrair

deed (diid) *n* acção *f*

deep (diip) *adj* profundo

deep-freeze (diip-friiz) *n* congelador *m*

deer (diá) *n* (pl ~) veado *m*

defeat (di-fiit) *v* derrotar; *n* derrota *f*

defective (di-fék-tiv) *adj* defeituoso

defence (di-fénnç) *n* defesa *f*

defend (di-fénnd) *v* defender

deficiency (di-fi-chánn-çi) *n* deficiência *f*

deficit (dé-fi-çit) *n* défice *m*

define (di-fainn) *v* definir, determinar

definite (dé-fi-nit) *adj* determinado; definido

definition (dé-fi-ni-chánn) *n* definição *f*

deformed (di-fóómmd) *adj* deformado, disforme

degree (di-ghrii) *n* grau *m*; título *m*

delay (di-lei) *v* atrasar; adiar; *n* atraso *m*, demora *f*; adiamento *m*

delegate (dé-li-ghát) *n* delegado *m*

delegation (dé-li-ghei-chánn) *n* delegação *f*

deliberate¹ (di-li-bã-reit) *v* deliberar, discutir

deliberate² (di-li-bã-rát) *adj* deliberado

deliberation (di-li-bã-rei-chánn) *n* deliberação *f*

delicacy (dé-li-kã-çi) *n* acepipe *m*

delicate (dé-li-kát) *adj* delicado

delicatessen (dé-li-kã-té-çánn) *n* manjar fino; mercearia fina

delicious (di-li-cháç) *adj* delicioso

delight (di-lait) *n* delícia *f*, deleite *m*; *v* deliciar; **delighted** encantado

delightful (di-lait-fál) *adj* encantador, delicioso

deliver (di-li-vã) *v* entregar; livrar

delivery (di-li-vã-ri) *n* entrega *f*; parto *m*; libertação *f*; ~ **van** furgoneta *f*

demand (di-maannd) *v* exigir, *requerer; *n* exigência *f*; procura *f*

democracy (di-mó-krã-çi) *n* democracia *f*

democratic (dé-mã-kræ-tik) *adj* democrático

demolish (di-mó-lich) *v* *demolir

demolition (dé-mã-li-chánn) *n* demolição *f*

demonstrate (dé-mánn-çtreit) *v* demonstrar; manifestar

demonstration (dé-mánn-çtrei-chánn) *n* demonstração *f*; manifestação *f*

den (dénn) *n* toca *f*

Denmark (dénn-maak) Dinamarca *f*

denomination (di-nó-mi-nei-chánn) *n* designação *f*

dense (dénnç) *adj* denso

dent (dénnt) *n* mossa *f*

dentist (dénn-tiçt) *n* dentista *m*

denture (dénn-tchã) *n* dentadura *f*

deny (di-nai) *v* negar, recusar, denegar

deodorant (dii-oᵘ-dã-ránnt) *n* desodorizante *m*; desodorante *mBr*

depart (di-paat) *v* partir, *ir-se; falecer

department (di-paat-mánnt) *n* depar-

tamento *m*; ~ **store** armazém *m*
departure (di-*paa*-tchã) *n* partida *f*,
    despedida *f*
dependant (di-*pénn*-dännt) *adj* depen-
    dente
depend on (di-*pénnd*) depender de
deposit (di-*pó*-zit) *n* depósito *m*; sedi-
    mento *m*; *v* depositar
depository (di-*pó*-zi-tã-ri) *n* armazém
    m
depot (dé-po*ʊ*) *n* armazém *m*; *n*Am
    estação *f*
depress (di-*préç*) *v* deprimir
depression (di-*pré*-chänn) *n* depressão
    f; recessão *f*
deprive of (di-*praiv*) privar de
depth (dépθ) *n* profundidade *f*
deputy (dé-p*i*u-ti) *n* deputado *m*;
    substituto *m*
descend (di-*çénnd*) *v* descer
descendant (di-*çénn*-dännt) *n* descen-
    dente *m*
descent (di-*çénnt*) *n* descida *f*
describe (di-*çkraib*) *v* descrever
description (di-*çkrip*-chänn) *n* descri-
    ção *f*; sinais pessoais
desert[1] (dé-zãt) *n* deserto *m*; *adj* sel-
    vagem, deserto
desert[2] (di-*zäät*) *v* desertar; abando-
    nar
deserve (di-*zããv*) *v* merecer
design (di-*zainn*) *v* desenhar; *n* pro-
    jecto *m*; objectivo *m*
designate (dé-zigh-neit) *v* designar
desirable (di-*zai*ᵃ-rã-bãl) *adj* desejável
desire (di-*zai*ᵃ) *n* desejo *m*; vontade *f*;
    v desejar, cobiçar
desk (déçk) *n* secretária *f*; carteira *f*;
    carteira de escola
despair (di-*çpé*ᵃ) *n* desespero *m*; *v*
    desesperar
despatch (di-*çpätch*) *v* despachar
desperate (dé-çpã-rãt) *adj* desespera-
    do

despise (di-*çpaiz*) *v* desprezar
despite (di-*çpait*) *prep* apesar de
dessert (di-*zäät*) *n* sobremesa *f*
destination (dé-çti-*nei*-chänn) *n* desti-
    no *m*
destine (dé-çtinn) *v* destinar
destiny (dé-çti-ni) *n* sorte *f*, destino *m*
destroy (di-*çtroi*) *v* *destruir
destruction (di-*çtrak*-chänn) *n* destrui-
    ção *f*; ruína *f*
detach (di-*tätch*) *v* separar
detail (dii-teil) *n* particularidade *f*,
    detalhe *m*
detailed (dii-teild) *adj* detalhado
detect (di-*tékt*) *v* *descobrir
detective (di-*ték*-tiv) *n* detective *m*;
    ~ **story** romance policial
detergent (di-*tãã*-djännt) *n* detergente
    m
determine (di-*tãã*-minn) *v* definir, de-
    terminar
determined (di-*tãã*-minnd) *adj* resolu-
    to
detour (dii-tuᵃ) *n* desvio *m*
devaluation (dii-væl-ⁱu-*ei*-chänn) *n* des-
    valorização *f*
devalue (dii-*væl*-ⁱuu) *v* desvalorizar
develop (di-*vé*-lãp) *v* desenvolver; re-
    velar
development (di-*vé*-lãp-männt) *n* de-
    senvolvimento *m*
deviate (dii-vi-eit) *v* desviar-se
devil (dé-vãl) *n* diabo *m*
devise (di-*vaiz*) *v* *planear
devote (di-*voʊt*) *v* dedicar
dew (dⁱuu) *n* orvalho *m*
diabetes (dai-ã-*bii*-tiiz) *n* diabetes *f*
diabetic (dai-ã-*bé*-tik) *n* diabético *m*
diagnose (dai-ãgh-*noʊz*) *v* diagnosti-
    car; constatar
diagnosis (dai-ãgh-*noʊ*-çiç) *n* (pl -ses)
    diagnóstico *m*
diagonal (dai-*æ*-ghã-nãl) *n* diagonal *f*;
    adj diagonal

diagram 221 discard

diagram (*dai*-ă-ghræmm) n diagrama m; gráfico m, esquema m

dialect (*dai*-ă-lékt) n dialecto m

diamond (*dai*-ă-mănnd) n diamante m

diaper (*dai*-ă-pă) nAm fralda f

diaphragm (*dai*-ă-fræmm) n membrana f; diafragma m

diarrhoea (dai-ă-*ri*-ă) n diarreia f

diary (*dai*-ă-ri) n agenda f; diário m

dictaphone (dik-tă-fou nn) n ditafone m

dictate (dik-*teit*) v ditar

dictation (dik-*tei*-chănn) n ditado m

dictator (dik-*tei*-tă) n ditador m

dictionary (*dik*-chă-nă-ri) n dicionário m

did (did) v (p do)

die (dai) v morrer

diet (*dai*-ăt) n dieta f

differ (*di*-fă) v *diferir

difference (*di*-fă-rănnç) n diferença f; distinção f

different (*di*-fă-rănnt) adj diferente; outro

difficult (*di*-fi-kălt) adj difícil

difficulty (*di*-fi-kăl-ti) n dificuldade f; obstáculo m

*dig (digh) v cavar; escavar

digest (di-*djéct*) v *digerir

digestible (di-*djé*-çtă-băl) adj digestivo

digestion (di-*djéc*-tchănn) n digestão f

digit (*di*-djit) n algarismo m

dignified (*digh*-ni-faid) adj distinto

dike (daik) n dique m

dilapidated (di-*læ*-pi-dei-tid) adj delapidado

diligence (*di*-li-djănnç) n aplicação f, zelo m

diligent (*di*-li-djănnt) adj aplicado, zeloso

dilute (dai-*l i uut*) v *diluir

dim (dimm) adj mate, baço; obscuro, vago

dine (dainn) v jantar

dinghy (*dinng*-ghi) n barquinho m

dining-car (*dai*-ninng-kaa) n carruagem-restaurante f

dining-room (*dai*-ninng-ruumm) n sala de jantar

dinner (*di*-nă) n jantar m; almoço m

dinner-jacket (*di*-nă-djæ-kit) n smoking m

dinner-service (*di*-nă-çăă-viç) n serviço de jantar

diphtheria (dif-*θi*ă-ri-ă) n difteria f

diploma (di-*plo*u-mă) n diploma m

diplomat (*di*-plă-mæt) n diplomata m

direct (di-*rékt*) adj directo; v dirigir; encenar

direction (di-*rék*-chănn) n direcção f; instrução f; realização f; administração **directions for use** modo de emprego

directive (di-*rék*-tiv) n directiva f

director (di-*rék*-tă) n director m; encenador m

dirt (dăăt) n sujidade f

dirty (*dăă*-ti) adj porco, sujo

disabled (di-*çei*-băld) adj incapacitado, inválido

disadvantage (di-çăd-*vaann*-tidj) n desvantagem f

disagree (di-çă-*ghrii*) v discordar

disagreeable (di-çă-*ghrii*-ă-băl) adj desagradável

disappear (di-çă-*pi*ă) v desaparecer

disappoint (di-çă-*poinnt*) v desapontar

disappointment (di-çă-*poinnt*-mănnt) n desilusão f

disapprove (di-çă-*pruuv*) v desaprovar

disaster (di-*zaa*-çtă) n desastre m; desgraça f, catástrofe f

disastrous (di-*zaa*-çtrăç) adj desastroso

disc (dićk) n disco m; **slipped** ~ hérnia discal

discard (di-*çkaad*) v *desfazer-se de

discharge (diç-*tchaadj*) v descarregar; ~ **of** dispensar de

discipline (*di*-çi-plinn) n disciplina f

discolour (di-*çka*-lã) v descolorir

disconnect (di-çkã-*nékt*) v desligar

discontented (di-çkänn-*ténn*-tid) adj descontente

discontinue (di-çkänn-*ti*-ni-̌uu) v cessar, suspender

discount (*di*-çkaunnt) n redução f, desconto m

discover (di-*çka*-vã) v *descobrir

discovery (di-*çka*-vã-ri) n descoberta f

discuss (di-*çkaç*) v discutir; debater

discussion (di-*çka*-chänn) n discussão f; conversa f, debate m

disease (di-*ziiz*) n doença f

disembark (di-çimm-*baak*) v desembarcar

disgrace (diç-*ghreiç*) n desonra f; desgraça f

disguise (diç-*ghaiz*) v disfarçar-se; disfarce m

disgusting (diç-*gha*-çtinng) adj repugnante

dish (dich) n prato m, travessa f

dishonest (di-çó-niçt) adj desonesto

disinfect (di-çinn-*fékt*) v desinfectar

disinfectant (di-çinn-*fék*-tännt) n desinfectante m

dislike (di-*çlaik*) v não gostar, detestar; n antipatia f, aversão f, repugnância f

dislocated (*di*-çlã-kei-tid) adj deslocado

dismiss (diç-*miç*) v *despedir

disorder (di-çóó-dã) n desordem f

dispatch (di-*çpætch*) v enviar, *expedir

display (di-*çplei*) v *expor, exibir; mostrar; n exposição f

displease (di-*pliiz*) v desagradar, desgostar

disposable (di-çpo^u-zã-bãl) adj para deitar fora

disposal (di-çpo^u-zãl) n disposição f

dispose of (di-çpo^uz) desembaraçar-se de

dispute (di-çp^iuut) n disputa f; briga f, litígio m; v altercar, contestar

dissatisfied (di-çæ-tiç-faid) adj insatisfeito

dissolve (di-zólv) v *diluir, dissolver

dissuade from (di-ç^ueid) dissuadir

distance (*di*-çtännç) n distância f; ~ **in kilometres** quilometragem m

distant (*di*-çtännt) adj distante

distinct (di-çtinngkt) adj distinto

distinction (di-çtinngk-chänn) n distinção f, diferença f

distinguish (di-çtinng-gh^uich) v distinguir

distinguished (di-çtinng-gh^uicht) adj distinto

distress (di-çtréç) n perigo m; ~ **signal** pedido de socorro

distribute (di-çtri-b^iuut) v *distribuir

distributor (di-çtri-b^iu-tã) n distribuidor m

district (*di*-çtrikt) n distrito m; região f; bairro m

disturb (di-çtãããb) v incomodar

disturbance (di-çtãã-bännç) n perturbação f; distúrbio m

ditch (ditch) n fosso m

dive (daiv) v mergulhar

diversion (dai-vãã-chänn) n desvio m; diversão f

divide (di-vaid) v dividir; repartir; separar

divine (di-vainn) adj divino

division (di-vi-jänn) n divisão f; separação f; secção f

divorce (di-vóóç) n divórcio m; v divorciar-se

dizziness (*di*-zi-näç) n vertigem f

dizzy (*di*-zi) adj atordoado

*do (duu) v *fazer; bastar

dock (dók) n doca f; v entrar em doca

docker (dó-kã) n estivador m

doctor (dók-tã) n médico m; doutor m

document (dó-kʲu-mãnnt) n documento m

dog (dógh) n cão m

dogged (dó-ghid) adj obstinado

doll (dól) n boneca f

dome (doᵘmm) n cúpula f

domestic (dã-mé-çtik) adj doméstico; interno; n empregado doméstico

domicile (dó-mi-çail) n domicílio m

domination (dó-mi-nei-chãnn) n dominação f

dominion (dã-mi-nʲãnn) n domínio m

donate (doᵘ-neit) v *dar

donation (doᵘ-nei-chãnn) n donativo m, doação f

done (dann) v (pp do)

donkey (dónn-ki) n burro m

donor (doᵘ-nã) n doador m

door (dóó) n porta f; **revolving ~** porta giratória; **sliding ~** porta corrediça

doorbell (dóó-bél) n campainha da porta

door-keeper (dóó-kii-pã) n porteiro m

doorman (dóó-mãnn) n (pl -men) porteiro m

dormitory (dóó-mi-tri) n dormitório m

dose (doᵘç) n dose f

dot (dót) n ponto m

double (da-bãl) adj duplo

doubt (daut) v duvidar; n dúvida f; **without ~** sem dúvida

doubtful (daut-fãl) adj duvidoso; incerto

dough (doᵘ) n massa f

down¹ (daunn) adv abaixo, para baixo; adj abatido; prep ao longo de, para baixo; **~ payment** sinal m

down² (daunn) n penugem f

downpour (daunn-póó) n aguaceiro m

downstairs (daunn-çtéᵃz) adv em baixo, para baixo

downstream (daunn-çtriimm) adv rio abaixo

down-to-earth (daunn-tu-ããθ) adj sensato

downwards (daunn-ᵘãdz) adv para baixo

dozen (da-zãnn) n (pl ~, ~s) dúzia f

draft (draaft) n letra f

drag (drægh) v arrastar

dragon (dræ-ghãnn) n dragão m

drain (dreinn) v secar; drenar; n esgoto m

drama (draa-mã) n drama m; tragédia f; teatro m

dramatic (drã-mæ-tik) adj dramático

dramatist (dræ-mã-tiçt) n dramaturgo m

drank (drænngk) v (p drink)

draper (drei-pã) n negociante de tecidos

drapery (drei-pã-ri) n têxteis mpl

draught (draaft) n corrente de ar; **draughts** jogo das damas

draught-board (draaft-bóód) n tabuleiro de damas

draw (dróó) n sorteio m

*draw (dróó) v desenhar; puxar; levantar, sacar; **~ up** redigir

drawbridge (dróó-bridj) n ponte levadiça

drawer (dróó-ã) n gaveta f; **drawers** cuecas fpl

drawing (dróó-inng) n desenho m

drawing-pin (dróó-inng-pinn) n pionés m

drawing-room (dróó-inng-ruumm) n sala f

dread (dréd) v temer; n temor m

dreadful (dréd-fãl) adj espantoso, terrível

dream (driimm) n sonho m

*dream (driimm) v sonhar

dress (dréç) v *vestir; *vestir-se; pensar; n vestido m

dressing-gown (dré-çinng-ghaunn) n roupão m

dressing-room (dré-çinng-ruumm) n quarto de vestir

dressing-table (dré-çinng-tei-băl) n toucador m

dressmaker (dréç-mei-kă) n modista f

drill (dril) v brocar; adestrar; n broca f

drink (drinngk) n bebida f

***drink** (drinngk) v beber

drinking-water (drinng-kinng-ᵁóó-tă) n água potável

drip-dry (drip-drai) adj não passar a ferro

drive (draiv) n estrada f; passeio de carro

***drive** (draiv) v guiar; *conduzir

driver (drai-vă) n condutor m

drizzle (dri-zăl) n chuva miudinha

drop (dróp) v deixar *cair; n gota f

drought (draut) n seca f

drown (draunn) v afogar; *be drowned afogar-se

drug (dragh) n estupefaciente m; medicamento m

drugstore (dragh-çtóó) nAm farmácia f; drogaria f

drunk (dranngk) adj (pp drink) bêbado

dry (drai) adj seco; v secar; enxugar

dry-clean (drai-kliinn) v limpar a seco

dry-cleaner's (drai-klii-năz) n tinturaria f

dryer (drai-ă) n secador m

duchess (da-tchiç) n duquesa f

duck (dak) n pato m

due (dⁱuu) adj esperado; devido; vencido

dues (dⁱuuz) pl direitos mpl

dug (dagh) v (p, pp dig)

duke (dⁱuuk) n duque m

dull (dal) adj enfadonho, insípido; apagado, baço; embotado

dumb (damm) adj mudo; obtuso, estúpido

dune (dⁱuunn) n duna f

dung (danng) n esterco m

dunghill (danng-hil) n estrumeira f

duration (dⁱu-rei-chănn) n duração f

during (dⁱuᵃ-rinng) prep durante

dusk (daçk) n anoitecer m

dust (daçt) n poeira f

dustbin (daçt-binn) n caixote do lixo; lata de lixo Br

dusty (da-çti) adj poeirento

Dutch (datch) adj holandês

Dutchman (datch-mănn) n (pl -men) holandês m

dutiable (dⁱuu-ti-ă-băl) adj sujeito a taxas

duty (dⁱuu-ti) n dever m; tarefa f; direito de importação; **Customs ~** direitos alfandegários

duty-free (dⁱuu-ti-frii) adj isento de direitos

dwarf (dᵁóóf) n anão m

dye (dai) v pintar, tingir; n tinta f

dynamo (dai-nă-moᵁ) n (pl ~s) dínamo m

dysentery (di-çănn-tri) n disenteria f

E

each (iitch) adj cada; ~ other mutuamente

eager (ii-ghă) adj impaciente, desejoso

eagle (ii-ghăl) n águia f

ear (iᵃ) n orelha f

earache (iᵃ-reik) n dor de ouvidos

ear-drum (iᵃ-dramm) n tímpano m

earl (ăăl) n conde m

early (ăă-li) adj cedo

earn (ăănn) v ganhar

earnest (ăă-niçt) n seriedade f

earnings (ăă-ninngz) pl ganhos mpl, rendimentos mpl

earring (iᵃ-rinng) n brinco m

earth (ăăθ) n terra f; solo m

earthenware (ăă-θănn-ᵘéᵃ) n olaria f

earthquake (ăăθ-kᵘeik) n tremor de terra

ease (iiz) n facilidade f, à-vontade m

east (iiçt) n este m

Easter (ii-çtă) Páscoa f

easterly (ii-çtă-li) adj oriental

eastern (ii-çtănn) adj oriental

easy (ii-zi) adj fácil; cómodo; ~ chair poltrona f

easy-going (ii-zi-ghoᵘ-inng) adj descontraído

*eat (iit) v comer

eavesdrop (iivz-dróp) v escutar indiscretamente

ebony (é-bă-ni) n ébano m

eccentric (ik-çénn-trik) adj excêntrico

echo (é-koᵘ) n (pl ~es) eco m

eclipse (i-klipç) n eclipse m

economic (ii-kă-nó-mik) adj económico

economical (ii-kă-nó-mi-kăl) adj económico, poupado

economist (i-kó-nă-miçt) n economista m

economize (i-kó-nă-maiz) v economizar

economy (i-kó-nă-mi) n economia f

ecstasy (ék-çtă-zi) n êxtase m

Ecuador (é-kᵘă-dóó) Equador m

Ecuadorian (é-kᵘă-dóó-ri-ănn) n equatoriano m

eczema (ék-çi-mă) n eczema m

edge (édj) n orla f, borda f

edible (é-di-băl) adj comestível

edition (i-di-chănn) n edição f; morning ~ edição da manhã

editor (é-di-tă) n redactor m

educate (é-dju-keit) v educar, formar

education (é-dju-kei-chănn) n educação f

eel (iil) n enguia f

effect (i-fékt) n efeito m, resultado m; v efectuar; in ~ com efeito

effective (i-fék-tiv) adj eficaz

efficient (i-fi-chănnt) adj eficiente

effort (é-făt) n esforço m

egg (égh) n ovo m

egg-cup (égh-kap) n copinho para os ovos

eggplant (égh-plaannt) n beringela f

egg-yolk (égh-ioᵘk) n gema de ovo

egoistic (é-ghoᵘ-i-çtik) adj egoísta

Egypt (ii-djipt) Egipto m

Egyptian (i-djip-chănn) adj egípcio

eiderdown (ai-dă-daunn) n edredão m

eight (eit) num oito

eighteen (ei-tiinn) num dezoito

eighteenth (ei-tiinnθ) num décimo oitavo

eighth (eitθ) num oitavo

eighty (ei-ti) num oitenta

either (ai-ðă) pron um ou outro; either ... or seja ... seja, ou ... ou

elaborate (i-læ-bă-reit) v elaborar

elastic (i-læ-çtik) adj elástico; flexível; ~ band elástico m

elasticity (é-læ-çti-çă-ti) n elasticidade f

elbow (él-boᵘ) n cotovelo m

elder (él-dă) adj mais velho

elderly (él-dă-li) adj de idade

eldest (él-diçt) adj o mais velho

elect (i-lékt) v escolher, eleger

election (i-lék-chănn) n eleição f

electric (i-lék-trik) adj eléctrico; ~ razor máquina de barbear; barbeador eléctrico Br

electrician (i-lék-tri-chănn) n electricista m

electricity (i-lék-tri-çă-ti) n electricidade f

electronic (i-lék-*tró*-nik) *adj* electrónico

elegance (é-li-ghànnç) *n* elegância *f*

elegant (é-li-ghànnt) *adj* elegante

element (é-li-mànnt) *n* elemento *m*

elephant (é-li-fànnt) *n* elefante *m*

elevator (é-li-vei-tä) *nAm* elevador *m*

eleven (i-*lé*-vänn) *num* onze

eleventh (i-*lé*-vännθ) *num* décimo primeiro

elf (élf) *n* (pl elves) elfo *m*

eliminate (i-*li*-mi-neit) *v* eliminar

elm (élm) *n* ulmeiro *m*

else (élç) *adv* doutro modo

elsewhere (él-ç*uéä*) *adv* noutro lado

elucidate (i-luu-çi-deit) *v* elucidar

emancipate (i-mænn-çi-*pei*-chänn) *n* emancipação *f*

embankment (imm-*bænngk*-männt) *n* paredão *m*

embargo (émm-*baa*-gho*u*) *n* (pl ~es) embargo *m*

embark (imm-*baak*) *v* embarcar

embarkation (émm-baa-*kei*-chänn) *n* embarcação *f*

embarrass (imm-*bæ*-räç) *v* perturbar, embaraçar; estorvar

embassy (émm-bä-çi) *n* embaixada *f*

emblem (émm-blämm) *n* emblema *m*

embrace (imm-*breiç*) *v* abraçar; *n* abraço *m*

embroider (imm-*broi*-dä) *v* bordar

embroidery (imm-*broi*-dä-ri) *n* bordado *m*

emerald (é-mä-räld) *n* esmeralda *f*

emergency (i-*mää*-djänn-çi) *n* emergência *f*; estado de emergência; ~ **exit** saída de emergência

emigrant (é-mi-ghrännt) *n* emigrante *m*

emigrate (é-mi-ghreit) *v* emigrar

emigration (é-mi-*ghrei*-chänn) *n* emigração *f*

emotion (i-*mou*-chänn) *n* emoção *f*

emperor (émm-pä-rä) *n* imperador *m*

emphasize (émm-fä-çaiz) *v* acentuar, frisar

empire (émm-pai*ä*) *n* império *m*

employ (imm-*ploi*) *v* empregar; utilizar, usar

employee (émm-ploi-*ii*) *n* empregado *m*

employer (imm-*ploi*-ä) *n* patrão *m*

employment (imm-*ploi*-männt) *n* emprego *m*; ~ **exchange** agência de colocação

empress (émm-priç) *n* imperatriz *f*

empty (émmp-ti) *adj* vazio; *v* esvaziar

enable (i-*nei*-bäl) *v* possibilitar

enamel (i-*næ*-mäl) *n* esmalte *m*

enamelled (i-*næ*-mäld) *adj* esmaltado

enchanting (inn-*tchaann*-tinng) *adj* encantador, esplêndido

encircle (inn-*çää*-käl) *v* cercar; *rodear

enclose (inng-*klou*z) *v* incluir, juntar

enclosure (inng-*klou*-jä) *n* anexo *m*

encounter (inng-*kaunn*-tä) *v* encontrar; *n* encontro *m*

encourage (inng-*ka*-ridj) *v* encorajar

encyclopaedia (énn-çai-klä-*pii*-di-ä) *n* enciclopédia *f*

end (énnd) *n* extremidade *f*, fim *m*; conclusão *f*; *v* acabar, terminar

ending (énn-dinng) *n* fim *m*

endless (énnd-läç) *adj* infinito

endorse (inn-*dóóç*) *v* endossar

endure (inn-*d*[u]*ä*) *v* suportar

enemy (é-nä-mi) *n* inimigo *m*

energetic (é-nä-*djé*-tik) *adj* enérgico

energy (é-nä-dji) *n* energia *f*; força *f*

engage (inng-*gheidj*) *v* empregar; contratar; comprometer-se; **engaged** noivo; ocupado

engagement (inng-*gheidj*-männt) *n* noivado *m*; compromisso *m*; ~ **ring** anel de noivado

engine (énn-djinn) *n* motor *m*, máquina f; locomotiva f

engineer (énn-dji-*ni*ª) *n* engenheiro *m*

England (*inng*-ghlännd) Inglaterra f

English (*inng*-ghlich) *adj* inglês

Englishman (*inng*-ghlich-männ) *n* (pl -men) inglês *m*

engrave (inng-*ghreiv*) *v* gravar

engraver (inng-*ghrei*-vä) *n* gravador *m*

engraving (inng-*ghrei*-vinng) *n* estampa f; gravação f

enigma (i-*nigh*-mä) *n* enigma *m*

enjoy (inn-*djoi*) *v* desfrutar, gozar

enjoyable (inn-*djoi*-ä-bäl) *adj* agradável

enjoyment (inn-*djoi*-männt) *n* gozo *m*

enlarge (inn-*laadj*) *v* ampliar

enlargement (inn-*laadj*-männt) *n* ampliação f

enormous (i-*nóó*-mäç) *adj* gigantesco, enorme

enough (i-*naf*) *adv* bastante; *adj* suficiente

enquire (inng-k*u*aiª) *v* indagar, perguntar; investigar

enquiry (inng-k*u*aiª-ri) *n* informação f; investigação f; inquérito *m*

enter (*énn*-tä) *v* entrar; inscrever

enterprise (*énn*-tä-praiz) *n* empresa f

entertain (énn-tä-*teinn*) *v* *divertir, *entreter; receber

entertaining (énn-tä-*tei*-ninng) *adj* divertido

entertainment (énn-tä-*teinn*-männt) *n* diversão f, divertimento *m*

enthusiasm (inn-*θ*iuu-zi-æ-zämm) *n* entusiasmo *m*

enthusiastic (inn-θ iuu-zi-æ-çtik) *adj* entusiástico

entire (inn-*tai*ª) *adj* todo, inteiro

entirely (inn-*tai*ª-li) *adv* inteiramente

entrance (*énn*-trännç) *n* entrada f; acesso *m*

entrance-fee (*énn*-trännç-fii) *n* preço de entrada

entry (*énn*-tri) *n* entrada f; lançamento *m*; no ~ proibido entrar

envelope (*énn*-vä-lo*u*p) *n* sobrescrito *m*, envelope *m*

envious (*énn*-vi-äç) *adj* invejoso

environment (inn-*vai*ª-ränn-männt) *n* meio ambiente; arredores *mpl*

envoy (*énn*-voi) *n* emissário *m*

envy (*énn*-vi) *n* inveja f; *v* invejar

epic (*é*-pik) *n* epopeia f; *adj* épico

epidemic (é-pi-*dé*-mik) *n* epidemia f

epilepsy (*é*-pi-lép-çi) *n* epilepsia f

epilogue (*é*-pi-lógh) *n* epílogo *m*

episode (*é*-pi-ço*u*d) *n* episódio *m*

equal (*ii*-k*u*äl) *adj* igual; *v* igualar

equality (i-k*u*ó-lä-ti) *n* igualdade f

equalize (*ii*-k*u*ä-laiz) *v* igualar

equally (*ii*-k*u*ä-li) *adv* igualmente

equator (i-k*u*ei-tä) *n* equador *m*

equip (i-k*u*ip) *v* equipar

equipment (i-k*u*ip-männt) *n* equipamento *m*

equivalent (i-k*u*i-vä-lännt) *adj* equivalente

eraser (i-*rei*-zä) *n* borracha f

erect (i-*rékt*) *v* erigir, edificar; *adj* erecto, em pé

err (ää) *v* errar

errand (*é*-rännd) *n* recado *m*

error (*é*-rä) *n* erro *m*, falta f

escalator (*é*-çkä-lei-tä) *n* escada rolante

escape (i-*çkeip*) *v* escapar; *fugir, evadir; *n* evasão f

escort[1] (*é*-çkóót) *n* escolta f

escort[2] (i-*çkóót*) *v* escoltar

especially (i-*çpé*-chä-li) *adv* principalmente, especialmente

esplanade (é-çplä-*neid*) *n* esplanada f

essay (*é*-çei) *n* ensaio *m*; composição f, tratado *m*

essence (*é*-çännç) *n* essência f; natureza f

essential (i-*çénn*-chäl) *adj* indispensável; essencial

essentially (i-çénn-chă-li) *adv* essencialmente

establish (i-çtǽ-blich) *v* estabelecer

estate (i-çteit) *n* propriedade *f*

esteem (i-çtiimm) *n* estima *f;* *v* estimar

estimate[1] (é-çti-meit) *v* estimar, *fazer a estimativa

estimate[2] (é-çti-măt) *n* estimativa *f*

estuary (éç-tchu-ă-ri) *n* estuário *m*

etching (é-tchinng) *n* água-forte *f*

eternal (i-tăă-năl) *adj* eterno

eternity (i-tăă-nă-ti) *n* eternidade *f*

ether (ii-θă) *n* éter *m*

Ethiopia (i-θi-oᵘ-pi-ă) Etiópia *f*

Ethiopian (i-θi-oᵘ-pi-ănn) *adj* etíope

Europe (ⁱuᵃ-răp) Europa *f*

European (ⁱuᵃ-ră-pii-ănn) *adj* europeu

evacuate (i-vǽ-kⁱu-eit) *v* evacuar

evaluate (i-vǽl-ⁱu-eit) *v* avaliar

evaporate (i-vǽ-pă-reit) *v* evaporar

even (ii-vănn) *adj* liso, igual, plano; constante; par; *adv* mesmo

evening (iiv-ninng) *n* noite *f;* ~ **dress** traje a rigor

event (i-vénnt) *n* acontecimento *m;* caso *m*

eventual (i-vénn-tchu-ăl) *adj* final

ever (é-vă) *adv* jamais; sempre

every (év-ri) *adj* cada

everybody (év-ri-bó-di) *pron* toda a gente; todo o mundo *Br*

everyday (év-ri-dei) *adj* quotidiano

everyone (év-ri-ᵘann) *pron* cada um, toda a gente; todo o mundo *Br*

everything (év-ri-θinng) *pron* tudo

everywhere (év-ri-ᵘéᵃ) *adv* por toda a parte

evidence (é-vi-dănnç) *n* prova *f*

evident (é-vi-dănnt) *adj* evidente

evil (ii-văl) *n* mal *m; adj* mau

evolution (ii-vă-*luu*-chănn) *n* evolução *f*

exact (igh-zǽkt) *adj* exacto

exactly (igh-zǽkt-li) *adv* exactamente

exaggerate (igh-zǽ-djă-reit) *v* exagerar

examination (igh-zæ-mi-*nei*-chănn) *n* exame *m;* interrogatório *m*

examine (igh-zǽ-minn) *v* examinar

example (igh-*zaamm*-păl) *n* exemplo *m;* **for** ~ por exemplo

excavation (ékç-kă-*vei*-chănn) *n* escavação *f*

exceed (ik-*çiid*) *v* exceder; superar

excel (ik-*cél*) *v* *sobressair

excellent (ék-çă-lănnt) *adj* excelente, óptimo

except (ik-*cépt*) *prep* excepto

exception (ik-*cép*-chănn) *n* excepção *f*

exceptional (ik-*cép*-chă-năl) *adj* excepcional, extraordinário

excerpt (ék-çăăpt) *n* trecho *m*

excess (ik-*çéç*) *n* excesso *m*

excessive (ik-*çé*-çiv) *adj* excessivo

exchange (ikç-*tcheinndj*) *v* trocar; troca *f;* bolsa *f;* ~ **office** casa de câmbio; ~ **rate** câmbio *m*

excite (ik-*çait*) *v* excitar

excitement (ik-*çait*-mănnt) *n* excitação *f*

exciting (ik-*çai*-tinng) *adj* emocionante

exclaim (ik-*çkleimm*) *v* exclamar

exclamation (ék-çklă-*mei*-chănn) *n* exclamação *f*

exclude (ik-*çkluud*) *v* *excluir

exclusive (ik-*çkluu*-çiv) *adj* exclusivo

exclusively (ik-*çkluu*-çiv-li) *adv* unicamente, exclusivamente

excursion (ik-*çkăă*-chănn) *n* excursão *f*

excuse[1] (ik-*çkⁱuuç*) *n* desculpa *f*

excuse[2] (ik-*çkⁱuuz*) *v* desculpar

execute (ék-çi-kⁱuut) *v* desempenhar, executar

execution (ék-çi-kⁱuu-chănn) *n* execucão f

executioner (ék-çi-k^{i}uu-chã-nǎ) n carrasco m

executive (igh-zé-k^{i}u-tiv) adj executivo; n poder executivo; director m

exempt (igh-zémmpt) v isentar, dispensar; adj isento

exemption (igh-zémmp-chǎnn) n isenção f

exercise (ék-çǎ-çaiz) n exercício m; v exercitar; exercer

exhale (ékç-heil) v exalar

exhaust (igh-zóóçt) n tubo de escape, escape m; v extenuar; ~ **gases** gases de escape

exhibit (igh-zi-bit) v *expor, exibir

exhibition (ék-çi-bi-chǎnn) n exibição f, exposição f

exile (ék-çail) n exílio m; exilado m

exist (igh-ziçt) v existir

existence (igh-zi-çtǎnnç) n existência f

exit (ék-çit) n saída f

exotic (igh-zó-tik) adj exótico

expand (ik-çpænnd) v expandir; desenvolver

expect (ik-çpékt) v esperar

expectation (ék-çpék-tei-chǎnn) n expectativa f

expedition (ék-çpǎ-di-chǎnn) n expedição f

expel (ik-çpél) v expulsar

expenditure (ik-çpénn-di-tchǎ) n despesa f

expense (ik-çpénnç) n despesa f

expensive (ik-çpénn-çiv) adj caro

experience (ik-çpi^a-ri-ǎnnç) n experiência f; v experimentar, viver; **experienced** experiente

experiment (ik-çpé-ri-mǎnnt) n experiência f, prova f; v experimentar

expert (ék-çpǎǎt) n especialista m, perito m; adj competente

expire (ik-çpai^a) v expirar, terminar;

expired expirado

expiry (ik-çpai^a-ri) n expiração f, vencimento m

explain (ik-çpleinn) v explicar

explanation (ék-çplǎ-nei-chǎnn) n explicação f, esclarecimento m

explicit (ik-çpli-çit) adj explícito, categórico

explode (ik-çplo^{u}d) v *explodir

exploit (ik-çploit) v explorar

explore (ik-çplóó) v explorar

explosion (ik-çplo^u-jǎnn) n explosão f

explosive (ik-çplo^u-çiv) adj explosivo; n explosivo m

export[1] (ik-çpóót) v exportar

export[2] (ék-çpóót) n exportação f

exportation (ék-çpóó-tei-chǎnn) n exportação f

exports (ék-çpóótç) pl exportações fpl

exposition (ék-çpǎ-zi-chǎnn) n exposição f

exposure (ik-çpo^u-jǎ) n exposição f; ~ **meter** fotómetro m

express (ik-çpréç) v expressar, exprimir; manifestar; adj expresso; explícito; ~ **train** comboio rápido

expression (ik-çpré-chǎnn) n expressão f

exquisite (ik-çk^{u}i-zit) adj requintado

extend (ik-çténnd) v prolongar; ampliar; conceder

extension (ik-çténn-chǎnn) n prolongamento m; ampliação f; extensão f; ~ **cord** fio de extensão

extensive (ik-çténn-çiv) adj amplo; extenso, vasto

extent (ik-çténnt) n dimensão f

exterior (ék-çti^a-ri-ǎ) adj exterior; n exterior m

external (ék-çtǎǎ-nǎl) adj exterior

extinguish (ik-çtinng-gh^{u}ich) v apagar, extinguir

extort (ik-çtóót) v *extorquir

extortion (ik-ҫtóó-chănn) *n* extorsão *f*

extra (ék-ҫtră) *adj* suplementar

extract[1] (ik-ҫtrǽkt) *v* *extrair, arrancar

extract[2] (ék-ҫtrǽkt) *n* trecho *m*

extradite (ék-ҫtră-dait) *v* extraditar

extraordinary (ik-ҫtróó-dǎnn-ri) *adj* extraordinário

extravagant (ik-ҫtrǽ-vă-ghǎnnt) *adj* extravagante, exagerado

extreme (ik-ҫtriimm) *adj* extremo; *n* extremo *m*

exuberant (igh-z'uu-bǎ-rǎnnt) *adj* exuberante

eye (ai) *n* olho *m*

eyebrow (ai-brau) *n* sobrancelha *f*

eyelash (ai-lǽch) *n* pestana *f*

eyelid (ai-lid) *n* pálpebra *f*

eye-pencil (ai-pénn-ҫăl) *n* lápis para os olhos

eye-shadow (ai-chǽ-do^u) *n* sombra para os olhos

eye-witness (ai-^uit-năҫ) *n* testemunha ocular

F

fable (fei-băl) *n* fábula *f*

fabric (fǽ-brik) *n* tecido *m*; estrutura *f*

façade (fă-ҫaad) *n* fachada *f*

face (feiҫ) *n* rosto *m*; *v* enfrentar; ~ **massage** massagem facial; **facing** defronte de

face-cream (feiҫ-kriimm) *n* creme de beleza

face-pack (feiҫ-pǽk) *n* máscara facial

face-powder (feiҫ-pau-dǎ) *n* pó-de-arroz *m*

facility (fă-ҫi-lă-ti) *n* facilidade *f*

fact (fǽkt) *n* facto *m*; **in** ~ com efeito

factor (fǽk-tǎ) *n* factor *m*

factory (fǽk-tǎ-ri) *n* fábrica *f*

factual (fǽk-tchu-ăl) *adj* real

faculty (fǽ-kăl-ti) *n* faculdade *f*; aptidão *f*, capacidade *f*

fad (fǽd) *n* capricho *m*

fade (feid) *v* desbotar, desvanecer

faience (fai-ǎҫ) *n* faiança *f*

fail (feil) *v* fracassar; falhar; faltar; omitir; reprovar; **without** ~ sem falta

failure (feil-^iǎ) *n* fracasso *m*; fiasco *m*

faint (feinnt) *v* desmaiar; *adj* vago, desfalecido, fraco

fair (fé^ǎ) *n* feira *f*; *adj* justo; loiro; bonito

fairly (fé^ǎ-li) *adv* bastante, razoavelmente

fairy (fé^ǎ-ri) *n* fada *f*

fairytale (fé^ǎ-ri-teil) *n* história de fadas

faith (feiθ) *n* fé *f*; confiança *f*

faithful (feiθ-ful) *adj* fiel

fake (feik) *n* falsificação *f*

fall (fóól) *n* queda *f*; *nAm* Outono *m* *fall (fóól) *v* *cair

false (fóólҫ) *adj* falso, errado; ~ **teeth** dentadura *f*

falter (fóól-tǎ) *v* vacilar; balbuciar

fame (feimm) *n* fama *f*; reputação *f*

familiar (fă-mil-^iǎ) *adj* familiar

family (fǽ-mǎ-li) *n* família *f*; ~ **name** apelido *m*

famous (fei-mǎҫ) *adj* famoso

fan (fǽnn) *n* ventilador *m*; leque *m*; admirador *m*; fã *mBr*; ~ **belt** correia de ventoinha

fanatical (fă-nǽ-ti-kăl) *adj* fanático

fancy (fǽnn-ҫi) *v* *ter vontade de, gostar de; imaginar; *n* capricho *m*; imaginação *f*

fantastic (fǽnn-tǽ-ҫtik) *adj* fantástico

fantasy (fǽnn-tǎ-zi) *n* fantasia *f*

far (faa) *adj* longe; *adv* muito; **by** ~

de longe; **so ~** até agora
far-away (faa-ră-ᵁei) adj distante
farce (faac) n farsa f
fare (féᵃ) n preco da viagem, preco do bilhete; comida f, alimentação f
farm (faamm) n quinta f; fazenda f
farmer (faa-mă) n lavrador m; **farmer's wife** mulher do lavrador
farmhouse (faamm-hauç) n casal m
far-off (faa-róf) adj longínquo
fascinate (fæ-çi-neit) v fascinar
fascism (fæ-chi-zămm) n fascismo m
fascist (fæ-chiçt) adj fascista
fashion (fæ-chănn) n moda f; maneira f
fashionable (fæ-chă-nă-băl) adj na moda
fast (faaçt) adj rápido; firme
fast-dyed (faaçt-daid) adj de cor fixa, não tinge
fasten (faa-çănn) v prender, atar; fechar
fastener (faa-çă-nă) n fecho m
fat (fæt) adj gordo; n gordura f
fatal (fei-tăl) adj fatal, mortal
fate (feit) n destino m
father (faa-ðă) n pai m; padre m
father-in-law (faa-ðă-rinn-lóó) n (pl fathers-) sogro m
fatherland (faa-ðă-lănnd) n pátria f
fatness (fæt-năç) n obesidade f
fatty (fæ-ti) adj gorduroso
faucet (fóó-çit) nAm torneira f
fault (fóólt) n culpa f; defeito m, imperfeicão f, falha f
faultless (fóólt-lăç) adj impecável; perfeito
faulty (fóól-ti) adj defeituoso, imperfeito
favour (fei-vă) n favor m; v favorecer
favourable (fei-vă-ră-băl) adj favorável
favourite (fei-vă-rit) n favorito m; adj preferido

fawn (fóónn) adj castanho claro; n veadinho m
fear (fiᵃ) n receio m, medo m; v *recear
feasible (fii-ză-băl) adj realizável
feast (fiiçt) n festa f
feat (fiit) n feito m
feather (fé-ðă) n pena f
feature (fii-tchă) n característica f; feição do rosto
February (fé-bru-ă-ri) Fevereiro
federal (fé-dă-răl) adj federal
federation (fé-dă-rei-chănn) n federação f
fee (fii) n honorário m
feeble (fii-băl) adj fraco
***feed** (fiid) v alimentar; **fed up with** farto de
***feel** (fiil) v *sentir; apalpar; **~ like** apetecer
feeling (fii-linng) n sensação f
fell (fél) v (p fall)
fellow (fé-loᵁ) n tipo m
felt¹ (félt) n feltro m
felt² (félt) v (p, pp feel)
female (fii-meil) adj feminino
feminine (fé-mi-ninn) adj feminino
fence (fénnç) n cerca f; v esgrimir
fender (fénn-dă) n pára-choques m
ferment (făă-ménnt) v fermentar
ferry-boat (fé-ri-boᵁt) n ferry-boat m
fertile (făă-tail) adj fértil
festival (fé-çti-văl) n festival m
festive (fé-çtiv) adj festivo
fetch (fétch) v *ir buscar
feudal (fʸuu-dăl) adj feudal
fever (fii-vă) n febre f
feverish (fii-vă-rich) adj febril
few (fʸuu) adj poucos
fiancé (fi-ă-çei) n noivo m
fiancée (fi-ă-çei) n noiva f
fibre (fai-bă) n fibra f
fiction (fik-chănn) n ficção f
field (fiild) n campo m; domínio m; ~

glasses binóculo m

fierce (fiᵃç) adj feroz, violento

fifteen (fif-tiinn) num quinze

fifteenth (fif-tiinnθ) num décimo quinto

fifth (fifθ) num quinto

fifty (fif-ti) num cinquenta

fig (figh) n figo m

fight (fait) n luta f

***fight** (fait) v combater, lutar

figure (fi-ghã) n estatura f, figura f; algarismo m

file (fail) n lima f; arquivo m; fila f

Filipino (fi-li-pii-noᵘ) n filipino m

fill (fil) v encher; ~ **in** preencher; **filling station** estação de serviço; ~ **out** Am encher, preencher; ~ **up** atestar

filling (fi-linng) n obturação f; recheio m

film (film) n filme m; película f; v filmar

filter (fil-tã) n filtro m

filthy (fil-θi) adj imundo

final (fai-nãl) adj final

finance (fai-nænnç) v financiar

finances (fai-nænn-çiz) pl finanças fpl

financial (fai-nænn-chãl) adj financeiro

finch (finntch) n tentilhão m

***find** (fainnd) v achar, encontrar

fine (fainn) n multa f; adj fino; belo; maravilhoso, excelente; ~ **arts** belas-artes fpl

finger (finng-ghã) n dedo m; **little** ~ dedo mínimo

fingerprint (finng-ghã-prinnt) n impressão digital

finish (fi-nich) v terminar, acabar; n fim m; meta f; **finished** acabado

Finland (finn-lãnnd) Finlândia f

Finn (finn) n finlandês m

Finnish (fi-nich) adj finlandês

fire (faiᵃ) n fogo m; incêndio m; v

disparar; *despedir

fire-alarm (faiᵃ-rã-laamm) n alarme de incêndio

fire-brigade (faiᵃ-bri-gheid) n bombeiros mpl

fire-escape (faiᵃ-ri-çkeip) n escada de incêndio

fire-extinguisher (faiᵃ-rik-çtinng-ghᵘi-chã) n extintor m

fireplace (faiᵃ-pleiç) n lareira f

fireproof (faiᵃ-pruuf) adj à prova de fogo; de ir ao forno

firm (fããmm) adj firme; sólido; n firma f

first (fããçt) num primeiro; **at** ~ primeiro; ~ **name** nome próprio; prenome mBr

first-aid (fããçt-eid) n primeiros socorros; ~ **kit** caixa de primeiros socorros; ~ **post** posto de socorros

first-class (fããçt-klaaç) adj de primeira qualidade

first-rate (fããçt-reit) adj excelente, de primeira qualidade

fir-tree (fãã-trii) n pinheiro m, abeto m

fish¹ (fich) n (pl ~, ~es) peixe m; ~ **shop** peixaria f

fish² (fich) v pescar; **fishing gear** equipamento de pesca; **fishing hook** anzol m; **fishing industry** pesca f; **fishing licence** licença de pesca; **fishing line** linha de pesca; **fishing net** rede de pesca; **fishing rod** cana de pesca; **fishing tackle** aparelho de pesca

fishbone (fich-boᵘnn) n espinha de peixe

fisherman (fi-chã-männ) n (pl -men) pescador m

fist (fiçt) n punho m

fit (fit) adj apropriado; n ataque m; v *condizer; **fitting room** gabinete de provas

five (faiv) *num* cinco

fix (fikç) *v* reparar

fixed (fikçt) *adj* fixo

fizz (fiz) *n* efervescência *f*

fjord (fióód) *n* fiorde *m*

flag (flægh) *n* bandeira *f*

flame (fleimm) *n* chama *f*

flamingo (flã-*minng*-gho^u) *n* (pl ~s, ~es) flâmingo *m*

flannel (*flæ*-näl) *n* flanela *f*

flash (flæch) *n* relâmpago *m*

flash-bulb (*flæch*-balb) *n* lâmpada de flash

flash-light (*flæch*-lait) *n* lanterna de mão

flask (flaaçk) *n* frasco *m*; **thermos** ~ termo *m*

flat (flæt) *adj* raso, plano; *n* apartamento *m*; ~ **tyre** pneu furado

flavour (*flei*-vã) *n* sabor *m*; *v* temperar

fleet (fliit) *n* frota *f*

flesh (fléch) *n* carne *f*

flew (fluu) *v* (p fly)

flex (flékç) *n* fio eléctrico

flexible (*flék*-çi-bãl) *adj* flexível; maleável

flight (flait) *n* voo *m*; **charter** ~ voo charter

flint (flinnt) *n* pedra de isqueiro

float (flo^ut) *v* flutuar; *n* flutuador *m*

flock (flók) *n* rebanho *m*

flood (flad) *n* inundação *f*; enchente *f*

floor (flóó) *n* chão *m*; andar *m*, piso *m*; ~ **show** espectáculo de variedades

florist (*fló*-riçt) *n* florista *m*

flour (flau^ã) *n* farinha *f*

flow (flo^u) *v* correr

flower (flau^ã) *n* flor *f*

flowerbed (*flau^ã*-béd) *n* canteiro *m*

flown (flo^unn) *v* (pp fly)

flu (fluu) *n* gripe *f*

fluent (*fluu*-ännt) *adj* fluente

fluid (*fluu*-id) *adj* fluido; *n* líquido *m*

flute (fluut) *n* flauta *f*

fly (flai) *n* mosca *f*; braguilha *f*

***fly** (flai) *v* voar

foam (fo^umm) *n* espuma *f*; *v* espumar

foam-rubber (*fo^umm*-ra-bã) *n* espuma de borracha

focus (*fo^u*-kãç) *n* foco *m*

fog (fógh) *n* nevoeiro *m*

foggy (*fó*-ghi) *adj* enevoado

foglamp (*fógh*-læmmp) *n* farol de nevoeiro

fold (to^uld) *v* dobrar; *n* dobra *f*

folk (fo^uk) *n* povo *m*; ~ **song** canção popular

folk-dance (*fo^uk*-daannç) *n* dança folclórica

folklore (*fo^uk*-lóó) *n* folclore *m*

follow (*fó*-lo^u) *v* *seguir; **following** *adj* seguinte

***be fond of** (bii fónnd óv) gostar de

food (fuud) *n* alimento *m*; comida *f*; ~ **poisoning** intoxicação alimentar

foodstuffs (*fuud*-çtafç) *pl* produtos alimentícios

fool (fuul) *n* idiota *m*, tolo *m*; *v* enganar

foolish (*fuu*-lich) *adj* tolo, maluco; absurdo

foot (fut) *n* (pl feet) pé *m*; ~ **powder** pó para os pés; **on** ~ a pé

football (*fut*-bóól) *n* bola de futebol; ~ **match** jogo de futebol

foot-brake (*fut*-breik) *n* travão de pé

footpath (*fut*-paaθ) *n* passeio *m*; atalho *m*

footwear (*fut*-^ué^ã) *n* calçado *m*

for (fóó) *prep* para; durante; por causa de, por, em consequência de; *conj* porque

***forbid** (fã-*bid*) *v* proibir

force (fóóç) *v* forçar, obrigar; *n* força *f*; **by** ~ forçosamente; **driving** ~

força motriz

ford (fóód) n vau m

forecast (fóó-kaaçt) n previsão f; v
*prever

foreground (fóó-ghraunnd) n primeiro
plano

forehead (fó-réd) n testa f

foreign (fó-rinn) adj estrangeiro; estranho

foreigner (fó-ri-nă) n estrangeiro m;
forasteiro m

foreman (fóó-mănn) n (pl -men) capataz m

foremost (fóó-mouçt) adj primeiro

foresail (fóó-çeil) n traquete m

forest (fó-riçt) n floresta f

forester (fó-ri-çtă) n guarda-florestal
m

forge (fóódj) v falsificar

*forget (fă-ghét) v esquecer

forgetful (fă-ghét-făl) adj esquecido

*forgive (fă-ghiv) v perdoar

fork (fóók) n garfo m; bifurcação f; v
bifurcar

form (fóómm) n forma f; formulário
m; classe f; v formar

formal (fóó-măl) adj formal

formality (fóó-mæ-lă-ti) n formalidade f

former (fóó-mă) adj antigo; antecedente; **formerly** anteriormente, antigamente

formula (fóó-miu-lă) n (pl ~e, ~s)
fórmula f

fort (fóót) n forte m

fortnight (fóót-nait) n quinzena f

fortress (fóó-triç) n fortaleza f

fortunate (fóó-tchă-năt) adj afortunado

fortune (fóó-tchuunn) n fortuna f; sorte f

forty (fóó-ti) num quarenta

forward (fóó-uăd) adv em frente,
avante; v *fazer seguir

foster-parents (fó-çtă-péă-rănntç) pl
pais adoptivos

fought (fóót) v (p, pp fight)

foul (faul) adj porco; infame

found[1] (faunnd) v (p, pp find)

found[2] (faunnd) v fundar, estabelecer, *instituir

foundation (faunn-dei-chănn) n fundação f; ~ **cream** creme de base

fountain (faunn-tinn) n fonte f

fountain-pen (faunn-tinn-pénn) n caneta de tinta permanente

four (fóó) num quatro

fourteen (fóó-tiinn) num catorze

fourteenth (fóó-tiinnθ) num décimo
quarto

fourth (fóóθ) num quarto

fowl (faul) n (pl ~s, ~) aves de criação

fox (fókç) n raposa f

foyer (foi-ei) n entrada f

fraction (fræk-chănn) n fracção f

fracture (fræk-tchă) v quebrar, fracturar; n fractura f

fragile (fræ-djail) adj frágil

fragment (frægh-mănnt) n fragmento
m; bocado m

frame (freimm) n moldura f; armação
f

France (fraannç) França f

franchise (frænn-tchaiz) n direito de
voto

fraternity (fră-tăă-nă-ti) n fraternidade f

fraud (fróód) n fraude f

fray (frei) v desfiar

free (frii) adj livre; ~ **of charge** gratuito; ~ **ticket** bilhete gratuito

freedom (frii-dămm) n liberdade f

*freeze (friiz) v gelar; congelar

freezing (frii-zinng) adj gelado

freezing-point (frii-zinng-poinnt) n
ponto de congelação

freight (freit) n carga f

French (frénntch) *adj* francês
Frenchman (frénntch-mǎnn) *n* (pl -men) francês *m*
frequency (frii-kᵘǎnn-çi) *n* frequência *f*
frequent (frii-kᵘǎnnt) *adj* frequente
fresh (fréch) *adj* fresco; ~ **water** água doce
friction (frik-chǎnn) *n* fricção *f*
Friday (frai-di) sexta-feira *f*
fridge (fridj) *n* frigorífico *m*; geladeira *f Br*
friend (frénnd) *n* amigo *m*; amiga *f*
friendly (frénnd-li) *adj* afável; simpático, amistoso
friendship (frénnd-chip) *n* amizade *f*
fright (frait) *n* susto *m*, medo *m*
frighten (frai-tǎnn) *v* assustar
frightened (frai-tǎnnd) *adj* assustado; *be ~ assustar-se
frightful (frait-fǎl) *adj* terrível, medonho
fringe (frinndj) *n* franja *f*
frock (frók) *n* vestido *m*
frog (frógh) *n* rã *f*
from (frómm) *prep* de; a partir de
front (frannt) *n* frente *f*; in ~ of diante de
frontier (frann-tiǎ) *n* fronteira *f*
frost (fróçt) *n* geada *f*
froth (fróθ) *n* espuma *f*
frozen (froᵘ-zǎnn) *adj* congelado; ~ **food** comida congelada
fruit (fruut) *n* fruta *f*; fruto *m*
fry (frai) *v* fritar
frying-pan (frai-inng-pænn) *n* frigideira *f*
fuel (fⁱuu-ǎl) *n* combustível *m*; ~ **pump** *Am* bomba de gasolina
full (ful) *adj* cheio; ~ **board** pensão completa; ~ **stop** ponto final; ~ **up** repleto
fun (fann) *n* divertimento *m*; prazer *m*

function (fanngk-chǎnn) *n* função *f*
fund (fannd) *n* fundo *m*
fundamental (fann-dǎ-ménn-tǎl) *adj* fundamental
funeral (fⁱuu-nǎ-rǎl) *n* funeral *m*
funnel (fa-nǎl) *n* funil *m*
funny (fa-ni) *adj* engraçado; estranho
fur (fǎǎ) *n* pele *f*; ~ **coat** casaco de peles; **furs** pele *f*
furious (fⁱuǎ-ri-ǎç) *adj* furioso, furibundo
furnace (fǎǎ-niç) *n* forno *m*
furnish (fǎǎ-nich) *v* fornecer, proporcionar; mobilar; ~ **with** *prover de
furniture (fǎǎ-ni-tchǎ) *n* mobília *f*
furrier (fa-ri-ǎ) *n* peleiro *m*
further (fǎǎ-ðǎ) *adj* mais além; ulterior
furthermore (fǎǎ-ðǎ-móó) *adv* além disso
furthest (fǎǎ-ðiçt) *adj* o mais distante
fuse (fⁱuuz) *n* fusível *m*; mecha *f*
fuss (faç) *n* espalhafato *m*
future (fⁱuu-tchǎ) *n* futuro *m*; *adj* futuro

G

gable (ghei-bǎl) *n* empena *f*
gadget (ghæ-djit) *n* engenhoca *f*
gaiety (ghei-ǎ-ti) *n* alegria *f*
gain (gheinn) *v* ganhar; *n* lucro *m*
gait (gheit) *n* passo *m*, andar *m*
gale (gheil) *n* temporal *m*
gall (ghóól) *n* bílis *f*; ~ **bladder** vesícula biliar
gallery (ghæ-lǎ-ri) *n* galeria *f*
gallop (ghæ-lǎp) *n* galope *m*
gallows (ghæ-loᵘz) *pl* forca *f*
gallstone (ghóól-çtoᵘnn) *n* cálculo biliar

game (gheimm) *n* jogo *m;* caça *f;* ~ **reserve** reserva natural
gang (ghænng) *n* quadrilha *f;* turno *m*
gangway (*ghænng*-ᵘei) *n* escada do portaló
gaol (djeil) *n* cadeia *f*
gap (ghæp) *n* brecha *f*
garage (*ghæ*-raaj) *n* garagem *f; v* *pôr na garagem
garbage (*ghaa*-bidj) *n* lixo *m*
garden (*ghaa*-dănn) *n* jardim *m;* **public** ~ jardim público; **zoological gardens** jardim zoológico
gardener (*ghaa*-dă-nă) *n* jardineiro *m*
gargle (*ghaa*-ghăl) *v* gargarejar
garlic (*ghaa*-lik) *n* alho *m*
gas (ghæç) *n* gás *m; nAm* gasolina *f;* ~ **cooker** fogão a gás; ~ **station** *Am* posto de gasolina; ~ **stove** fogão a gás
gasoline (*ghæ*-çă-liinn) *nAm* gasolina *f*
gastric (*ghæ*-çtrik) *adj* gástrico; ~ **ulcer** úlcera gástrica
gasworks (*ghæç*-ᵘăăkç) *n* depósito de gás
gate (gheit) *n* porta *f;* portão *m*
gather (*ghæ*-ðă) *v* coleccionar; reunir; colher
gauge (gheidj) *n* medida *f*
gauze (ghóóz) *n* gaze *f*
gave (gheiv) *v* (p give)
gay (ghei) *adj* alegre; garrido
gaze (gheiz) *v* fitar
gazetteer (ghæ-ză-*tiᵃ*) *n* dicionário geográfico
gear (ghiᵃ) *n* velocidade *f;* equipamento *m;* **change** ~ mudar de velocidade; ~ **lever** alavanca das mudanças
gear-box (*ghiᵃ*-bókç) *n* caixa de velocidades
gem (djémm) *n* jóia *f,* pedra preciosa
gender (*djénn*-dă) *n* género *m*
general (*djé*-nă-răl) *adj* geral; *n* general *m;* ~ **practitioner** médico de clínica geral; **in** ~ em geral
generate (*djé*-nă-reit) *v* *produzir
generation (djé-nă-*rei*-chănn) *n* geração *f*
generator (*djé*-nă-rei-tăr) *n* gerador *m*
generosity (djé-nă-*ró*-çă-ti) *n* generosidade *f*
generous (*djé*-nă-răç) *adj* magnânimo, generoso
genital (*djé*-ni-tăl) *adj* genital
genius (*djii*-ni-ăç) *n* génio *m*
gentle (*djénn*-tăl) *adj* suave; ligeiro, terno; delicado
gentleman (*djénn*-tăl-mănn) *n* (pl -men) cavalheiro *m*
genuine (*djé*-nⁱu-inn) *adj* genuíno
geography (dji-*ó*-ghră-fi) *n* geografia *f*
geology (dji-*ó*-lă-dji) *n* geologia *f*
geometry (dji-*ó*-mă-tri) *n* geometria *f*
germ (djăămm) *n* micróbio *m;* germe *m*
German (*djăă*-mănn) *adj* alemão
Germany (*djăă*-mă-ni) Alemanha *f*
gesticulate (dji-*çti*-kⁱu-leit) *v* gesticular
***get** (ghét) *v* *obter; *ir buscar; *fazer-se, tornar-se; ~ **back** regressar; ~ **off** descer, *apear-se; ~ **on** *subir para; avançar, *progredir; ~ **up** levantar-se, erguer-se
ghost (ghoᵘçt) *n* fantasma *m;* espírito *m*
giant (*djai*-ănnt) *n* gigante *m*
giddiness (*ghi*-di-năç) *n* tontura *f*
giddy (*ghi*-di) *adj* atordoado
gift (ghift) *n* oferta *f,* presente *m;* dom *m*
gifted (*ghif*-tid) *adj* dotado
gigantic (djai-*ghænn*-tik) *adj* gigantesco
giggle (*ghi*-ghăl) *v* *dar risadinhas

gill (ghil) *n* guelra *f*

gilt (ghilt) *adj* dourado

ginger (*djin*-djã) *n* gengibre *m*

gipsy (*djip*-çi) *n* cigano *m*

girdle (ghãã-dãl) *n* cinta *f*

girl (ghããl) *n* rapariga *f*; ~ guide escuteira *f*

*give (ghiv) *v* *dar; entregar; ~ away revelar; ~ in ceder; ~ up desistir, renunciar

glacier (ghlæ-çi-ã) *n* glaciar *m*

glad (ghlæd) *adj* contente; gladly com muito gosto, de boa vontade

gladness (ghlæd-nãç) *n* alegria *f*

glamorous (ghlæ-mã-rãç) *adj* fascinante

glamour (ghlæ-mã) *n* encanto *m*

glance (ghlaannç) *n* relance *m*; *v* *relancear

gland (ghlænnd) *n* glândula *f*

glare (ghlé^ã) *n* brilho *m*; esplendor *m*

glaring (ghlé^ã-rinng) *adj* deslumbrante

glass (ghlaaç) *n* copo *m*; vidro *m*; de vidro; glasses óculos *mpl*; magnifying ~ lupa *f*

glaze (ghleiz) *v* vidrar

glen (ghlénn) *n* ravina *f*

glide (ghlaid) *v* planar; deslizar

glider (ghlai-dã) *n* planador *m*

glimpse (ghlimmpç) *n* vislumbre *m*; *v* vislumbrar

global (ghlou-bãl) *adj* mundial

globe (ghloub) *n* globo *m*

gloom (ghluumm) *n* obscuridade *f*; melancolia *f*

gloomy (ghluu-mi) *adj* sombrio

glorious (ghlóó-ri-ãç) *adj* esplêndido

glory (ghlóó-ri) *n* glória *f*; louvor *m*, honra *f*

gloss (ghlóç) *n* lustro *m*

glossy (ghló-çi) *adj* lustroso

glove (ghlav) *n* luva *f*

glow (ghlou) *v* brilhar; *n* brilho *m*

glue (ghluu) *n* cola *f*

*go (ghou) *v* *ir; andar; *fazer-se; ~ ahead avançar; ~ away *ir-se embora; ~ back regressar; ~ home *ir para casa; ~ in entrar; ~ on continuar, avançar; ~ out *sair; ~ through atravessar, passar por

goal (ghoul) *n* objectivo *m*, baliza *f*; golo *m*

goalkeeper (ghoul-kii-pã) *n* guarda-redes *m*; goleiro *mBr*

goat (ghout) *n* bode *m*, cabra *f*

god (ghód) *n* deus *m*

goddess (ghó-diç) *n* deusa *f*

godfather (ghód-faa-ðã) *n* padrinho *m*

goggles (ghó-ghãlz) *pl* óculos de protecção

gold (ghould) *n* ouro *m*; ~ leaf folha de ouro

golden (ghoul-dãnn) *adj* de ouro

goldmine (ghould-mainn) *n* mina de ouro

goldsmith (ghould-çmiθ) *n* ourives *m*

golf (ghólf) *n* golfe *m*

golf-club (ghólf-klab) *n* clube de golfe

golf-course (ghólf-kóóç) *n* campo de golfe

golf-links (ghólf-linngkç) *n* campo de golfe

gondola (ghónn-dã-lã) *n* gôndola *f*

good (ghud) *adj* bom

good-bye! (ghud-*bai*) adeus!

good-humoured (ghud-h'uu-mãd) *adj* bem humorado

good-looking (ghud-*lu*-kinng) *adj* bonito

good-natured (ghud-*nei*-tchãd) *adj* bondoso

goods (ghudz) *pl* mercadorias *fpl*, bens *mpl*; ~ train comboio de mercadorias

good-tempered (ghud-*témm*-pãd) *adj* bem disposto

goodwill (ghud-*ºil*) *n* boa vontade

goose (ghuuç) *n* (pl geese) ganso *m*

gooseberry (ghuz-bā-ri) *n* groselha verde

goose-flesh (ghuuç-fléch) *n* pele de galinha

gorge (ghóódj) *n* garganta *f*

gorgeous (ghóó-djäç) *adj* magnífico

gospel (ghó-çpäl) *n* evangelho *m*

gossip (ghó-çip) *n* mexerico *m*; *v* mexericar

got (ghót) *v* (p, pp get)

gourmet (ghuª-mei) *n* gastrónomo *m*

gout (ghaut) *n* gota *f*

govern (gha-vänn) *v* governar

governess (gha-vä-niç) *n* governanta *f*

government (gha-vänn-männt) *n* regime *m*, governo *m*

governor (gha-vä-nä) *n* governador *m*

gown (ghaunn) *n* vestido *m*

grace (ghreiç) *n* graça *f*; perdão *m*

graceful (ghreiç-fäl) *adj* gracioso

grade (ghreid) *n* grau *m*; *v* classificar

gradient (ghrei-di-ännt) *n* inclinação *f*

gradual (ghræ-dju-äl) *adj* gradual

graduate (ghræ-dju-eit) *v* diplomar-se

grain (ghreinn) *n* cereal *m*, grão *m*

gram (ghræmm) *n* grama *m*

grammar (ghræ-mä) *n* gramática *f*

grammatical (ghrä-mæ-ti-käl) *adj* gramatical

gramophone (ghræ-mä-foªnn) *n* gramofone *m*

grand (ghrænnd) *adj* grandioso

granddad (ghrænn-dæd) *n* avô *m*

granddaughter (ghrænn-dóó-tä) *n* neta *f*

grandfather (ghrænn-faa-ðä) *n* avô *m*, avozinho

grandmother (ghrænn-ma-ðä) *n* avó *f*, avozinha

grandparents (ghrænn-pé ª-ränntç) *pl* avós *mpl*

grandson (ghrænn-çann) *n* neto *m*

granite (ghræ-nit) *n* granito *m*

grant (ghraannt) *v* conceder, aceder; *n* subsídio *m*, subvenção *f*

grapefruit (ghreip-fruut) *n* toranja *f*

grapes (ghreipç) *pl* uvas *fpl*

graph (ghræf) *n* gráfico *m*

graphic (ghræ-fik) *adj* gráfico

grasp (ghraaçp) *v* agarrar, segurar; *n* aperto *m*

grass (ghraaç) *n* erva *f*

grasshopper (ghraaç-hó-pä) *n* gafanhoto *m*

grate (ghreit) *n* grelha *f*; *v* raspar

grateful (ghreit-fäl) *adj* grato, reconhecido

grater (ghrei-tä) *n* ralador *m*

gratis (ghræ-tiç) *adj* gratuito

gratitude (ghræ-ti-tʲuud) *n* gratidão *f*

gratuity (ghrä-tʲuu-ä-ti) *n* gorjeta *f*

grave (ghreiv) *n* sepultura *f*; *adj* grave

gravel (ghræ-väl) *n* cascalho *m*

gravestone (ghreiv-çtoªnn) *n* lápide *f*

graveyard (ghreiv-ʲaad) *n* cemitério *m*

gravity (ghræ-vä-ti) *n* gravidade *f*; seriedade *f*

gravy (ghrei-vi) *n* molho de carne

graze (ghreiz) *v* pastar; *n* arranhão *m*

grease (ghriiç) *n* gordura *f*; *v* lubrificar

greasy (ghrii-çi) *adj* gordurento, oleoso

great (ghreit) *adj* grande; **Great Britain** Grã-Bretanha *f*

Greece (ghriiç) Grécia *f*

greed (ghriid) *n* cupidez *f*

greedy (ghrii-di) *adj* ganancioso; guloso

Greek (ghriik) *adj* grego

green (ghriinn) *adj* verde; ~ **card** carta verde

greengrocer (ghriinn-ghroª-çä) *n* vendedor de hortaliça

greenhouse (ghriinn-hauç) *n* estufa *f*

greens (ghriinnz) *pl* hortalica *f*
greet (ghriit) *v* cumprimentar
greeting (*ghrii*-tinng) *n* saudação *f*
grey (ghrei) *adj* cinzento
greyhound (*ghrei*-haunnd) *n* galgo *m*
grief (ghriif) *n* desgosto *m*; aflicão *f*, dor *f*
grieve (ghriiv) *v* *ter desgosto; afligir
grill (ghril) *n* grelhador *m*; *v* grelhar
grill-room (*ghril*-ruumm) *n* churrasqueira *f*
grin (ghrinn) *v* *sorrir-se; *n* careta *f*
*grind (ghrainnd) *v* *moer; triturar
grip (ghrip) *v* agarrar; *n* abraço *m*, accão de agarrar; *nAm* saco de mão
grit (ghrit) *n* saibro *m*
groan (ghroᵘnn) *v* gemer
grocer (*ghroᵘ*-çã) *n* merceeiro *m*; grocer's mercearia *f*
groceries (*ghroᵘ*-çã-riz) *pl* artigos de mercearia
groin (ghroinn) *n* virilha *f*
groove (ghruuv) *n* sulco *m*
gross¹ (ghroᵘç) *n* (pl ~) grosa *f*
gross² (ghroᵘç) *adj* grosseiro; bruto
grotto (*ghró*-toᵘ) *n* (pl ~es, ~s) gruta *f*
ground¹ (ghraunnd) *n* solo *m*, fundo *m*; ~ floor rés-do-chão *m*; andar térreo *Br*; grounds terreno *m*
ground² (ghraunnd) *v* (p, pp grind)
group (ghruup) *n* grupo *m*
grove (ghroᵘv) *n* mata *f*
*grow (ghroᵘ) *v* crescer; cultivar; *fazer-se
growl (ghraul) *v* rosnar
grown-up (*ghroᵘnn*-ap) *adj* adulto; *n* adulto *m*
growth (ghroᵘᶿ) *n* crescimento *m*; tumor *m*
grudge (ghradj) *v* invejar
grumble (*ghramm*-bǎl) *v* resmungar
guarantee (ghæ-rǎnn-*tii*) *n* garantia *f*;

caução *f*; *v* garantir
guarantor (ghæ-rǎnn-*tóó*) *n* fiador *m*
guard (ghaad) *n* guarda *m*; *v* guardar
guardian (*ghaa*-di-ǎnn) *n* tutor *m*
guess (ghéç) *v* adivinhar; pensar, *supor; *n* conjectura *f*
guest (ghéçt) *n* hóspede *m*, convidado *m*
guest-house (*ghéçt*-hauç) *n* pensão *f*
guest-room (*ghéçt*-ruumm) *n* quarto de hóspedes
guide (ghaid) *n* guia *m*; *v* guiar
guidebook (*ghaid*-buk) *n* guia *m*
guide-dog (*ghaid*-dógh) *n* cão de cego
guilt (ghilt) *n* culpa *f*
guilty (*ghil*-ti) *adj* culpado
guinea-pig (*ghi*-ni-pigh) *n* porquinho-da-índia *m*
guitar (ghi-*taa*) *n* viola *f*
gulf (ghalf) *n* golfo *m*
gull (ghal) *n* gaivota *f*
gum (ghamm) *n* gengiva *f*; goma *f*; cola *f*
gun (ghann) *n* revólver *m*, espingarda *f*; canhão *m*
gunpowder (*ghann*-pau-dǎ) *n* pólvora *f*
gust (ghaçt) *n* rajada *f*
gusty (*gha*-çti) *adj* ventoso
gut (ghat) *n* intestino *m*; guts coragem *f*
gutter (*gha*-tǎ) *n* valeta *f*
guy (ghai) *n* tipo *m*
gymnasium (djimm-*nei*-zi-ǎmm) *n* (pl ~s, -sia) ginásio *m*
gymnast (*djimm*-næçt) *n* ginasta *m*
gymnastics (djimm-*næ*-çtikç) *pl* ginástica *f*
gynaecologist (ghai-nǎ-*kó*-lǎ-djiçt) *n* ginecologista *m*

H

haberdashery (hæ-bă-dæ-chă-ri) *n* capelista *m*; armarinho *mBr*

habit (hæ-bit) *n* hábito *m*

habitable (hæ-bi-tă-băl) *adj* habitável

habitual (hă-*bi*-tchu-ăl) *adj* habitual

had (hæd) *v* (p, pp have)

haddock (hæ-dăk) *n* (pl ~) arinca *f*

haemorrhage (hé-mă-ridj) *n* hemorragia *f*

haemorrhoids (hé-mă-roidz) *pl* hemorróidas *fpl*

hail (heil) *n* granizo *m*

hair (héªr) *n* cabelo *m*; ~ **cream** creme para o cabelo; ~ **piece** cabelo postico; ~ **rollers** rolos de cabelo; ~ **tonic** tónico capilar

hairbrush (héªr-brach) *n* escova de cabelo

haircut (héªr-kat) *n* corte de cabelo

hair-do (héªr-duu) *n* penteado *m*

hairdresser (héªr-dré-çă) *n* cabeleireiro *m*

hair-dryer (héªr-drai-ă) *n* secador de cabelo

hair-grip (héªr-ghrip) *n* travessão *m*

hair-net (héªr-nét) *n* rede para o cabelo

hair-oil (héªr-roil) *n* óleo capilar

hairpin (héªr-pinn) *n* gancho de cabelo

hair-spray (héªr-çprei) *n* laca para o cabelo

hairy (héªr-ri) *adj* cabeludo

half¹ (haaf) *adj* meio; *adv* meio

half² (haaf) *n* (pl halves) metade *f*

half-time (haaf-*taimm*) *n* intervalo *m*

halfway (haaf-ᵘei) *adv* a meio caminho

halibut (hæ-li-băt) *n* (pl ~) alabote *m*

hall (hóól) *n* vestíbulo *m*; sala *f*

halt (hóólt) *v* parar

halve (haav) *v* dividir ao meio

ham (hæmm) *n* fiambre *m*, presunto *m*

hamlet (hæmm-lăt) *n* aldeola *f*

hammer (hæ-mă) *n* martelo *m*

hammock (hæ-măk) *n* rede *f*

hamper (hæmm-pă) *n* cesta *f*

hand (hænnd) *n* mão *f*; *v* entregar; ~ **cream** creme para as mãos

handbag (hænnd-bægh) *n* mala de mão

handbook (hænnd-buk) *n* manual *m*

hand-brake (hænnd-breik) *n* travão de mão

handcuffs (hænnd-kafç) *pl* algemas *fpl*

handful (hænnd-ful) *n* punhado *m*

handicraft (hænn-di-kraaft) *n* trabalho manual; artesanato *m*

handkerchief (hænng-kă-tchif) *n* lenço de assoar

handle (hænn-dăl) *n* cabo *m*, pega *f*; *v* manejar; tratar

hand-made (hænnd-*meid*) *adj* feito à mão

handshake (hænnd-cheik) *n* aperto de mão

handsome (hænn-çămm) *adj* belo

handwork (hænnd-ᵘăăk) *n* trabalho manual

handwriting (hænnd-rai-tinng) *n* escrita *f*

handy (hænn-di) *adj* jeitoso; à mão, conveniente

***hang** (hænng) *v* pendurar; pender

hanger (hænng-ă) *n* cabide *m*

hangover (hænng-oᵘ-vă) *n* ressaca *mBr*

happen (hæ-pănn) *v* suceder, acontecer

happening (hæ-pă-ninng) *n* acontecimento *m*

happiness (hæ-pi-năç) *n* felicidade *f*

happy (hæ-pi) *adj* contente, feliz

harbour (haa-bă) *n* porto *m*

hard (haad) *adj* duro; difícil; **hardly** mal

hardware (haad-ᵘéª) *n* ferragens *fpl;* ~ **store** loja de ferragens

hare (héª) *n* lebre *f*

harm (haamm) *n* prejuízo *m;* mal *m,* dano *m; v* prejudicar, *fazer mal a

harmful (haamm-fål) *adj* prejudicial, nocivo

harmless (haamm-låç) *adj* inofensivo

harmony (haa-mã-ni) *n* harmonia *f*

harp (haap) *n* harpa *f*

harpsichord (haap-çi-kóód) *n* cravo *m*

harsh (haach) *adj* áspero; severo; cruel

harvest (haa-viçt) *n* colheita *f*

has (hæz) *v* (pr have)

haste (heiçt) *n* rapidez *f,* pressa *f*

hasten (hei-çånn) *v* apressar-se

hasty (hei-çti) *adj* apressado

hat (hæt) *n* chapéu *m;* ~ **rack** bengaleiro *m*

hatch (hætch) *n* alçapão *m*

hate (heit) *v* detestar; *odiar; *n* ódio *m*

hatred (hei-trid) *n* ódio *m*

haughty (hóó-ti) *adj* altivo

haul (hóól) *v* arrastar

***have** (hæv) *v* *ter; mandar; ~ **to** *ter de

hawk (hóók) *n* gavião *m;* falcão *m*

hay (hei) *n* feno *m;* ~ **fever** febre dos fenos

hazard (hæ-zåd) *n* risco *m*

haze (heiz) *n* bruma *f;* névoa *f*

hazelnut (hei-zål-nat) *n* avelã *f*

hazy (hei-zi) *adj* fusco; enevoado

he (hii) *pron* ele

head (héd) *n* cabeça *f; v* dirigir; ~ **of state** chefe de estado; ~ **teacher** director de escola

headache (hé-deik) *n* dor de cabeça

heading (hé-dinng) *n* título *m*

headlamp (héd-læmmp) *n* farol *m*

headland (héd-lånnd) *n* promontório *m*

headlight (héd-lait) *n* farol *m*

headline (héd-lainn) *n* cabeçalho *m*

headmaster (héd-maa-çtå) *n* director de escola; reitor *m*

headquarters (héd-kᵘóó-tåz) *pl* quartel-general *m*

head-strong (héd-çtrónn) *adj* obstinado

head-waiter (héd-ᵘei-tå) *n* chefe de mesa

heal (hiil) *v* sarar, curar

health (hélθ) *n* saúde *f;* ~ **centre** centro de saúde; ~ **certificate** atestado de saúde

healthy (hél-θi) *adj* são

heap (hiip) *n* monte *m,* montão *m*

***hear** (hiª) *v* *ouvir

hearing (hiª-rinng) *n* ouvido *m*

heart (haat) *n* coração *m;* âmago *m;* **by** ~ de cor; ~ **attack** ataque de coração

heartburn (haat-bäänn) *n* azia *f*

hearth (haaθ) *n* lareira *f*

heartless (haat-låç) *adj* insensível

hearty (haa-ti) *adj* efusivo

heat (hiit) *n* calor *m; v* aquecer; **heating pad** almofada eléctrica

heater (hii-tå) *n* aquecedor *m;* **immersion** ~ aquecedor de imersão

heath (hiiθ) *n* charneca *f*

heathen (hii-ðånn) *n* pagão *m*

heather (hé-ðå) *n* urze *f*

heating (hii-tinng) *n* aquecimento *m*

heaven (hé-vånn) *n* céu *m*

heavy (hé-vi) *adj* pesado

Hebrew (hii-bruu) *n* hebreu *m*

hedge (hédj) *n* sebe *f*

hedgehog (hédj-hógh) *n* ouriço *m*

heel (hiil) *n* calcanhar *m;* salto *m*

height (hait) *n* altura *f;* topo *m,* apogeu *m*

hell (hél) *n* inferno *m*

hello! (hé-*lo*ᵘ) olá!; bom dia!

helm (hélm) *n* leme *m*

helmet (hél-mit) *n* capacete *m*

helmsman (hélmz-mănn) *n* timoneiro *m*

help (hélp) *v* ajudar, socorrer; *n* socorro *m*

helper (hél-pă) *n* ajudante *m*

helpful (hélp-făl) *adj* útil

helping (hél-pinng) *n* porção *f*

hem (hémm) *n* bainha *f*

hemp (hémmp) *n* cânhamo *m*

hen (hénn) *n* galinha *f*

henceforth (hénnç-*fóóθ*) *adv* de agora em diante

her (hăă) *pron* lhe, a; *adj* seu

herb (hăăb) *n* erva *f*

herd (hăăd) *n* manada *f*

here (hiă) *adv* aqui; ~ **you are** aqui está

hereditary (hi-ré-di-tă-ri) *adj* hereditário

hernia (hăă-ni-ă) *n* hérnia *f*

hero (hiă-roᵘ) *n* (pl ~es) herói *m*

heron (hé-rănn) *n* garça *f*

herring (hé-rinng) *n* (pl ~, ~s) arenque *m*

herself (hăă-çélf) *pron* se; ela mesma

hesitate (hé-zi-teit) *v* hesitar

heterosexual (hé-tă-ră-çék-chu-ăl) *adj* heterossexual

hiccup (hi-kap) *n* soluço *m*

hide (haid) *n* pele *f*

***hide** (haid) *v* esconder

hideous (hi-di-ăç) *adj* horroroso

hierarchy (haiă-raa-ki) *n* hierarquia *f*

high (hai) *adj* alto

highway (hai-ᵘei) *n* estrada principal; *n Am* auto-estrada *f*

hijack (hai-djæk) *v* *saltear

hijacker (hai-djæ-kă) *n* salteador *m*, raptor *m*

hike (haik) *v* viajar a pé

hill (hil) *n* colina *f*

hillside (hil-çaid) *n* encosta *f*

hilltop (hil-tóp) *n* cume do monte

hilly (hi-li) *adj* acidentado

him (himm) *pron* o, lhe

himself (himm-çélf) *pron* se; ele mesmo

hinder (hinn-dă) *v* estorvar

hinge (hinndj) *n* dobradiça *f*

hip (hip) *n* anca *f*

hire (haiă) *v* alugar; **for** ~ para alugar

hire-purchase (haiă-păă-tchăç) *n* compra a prestações

his (hiz) *adj* seu

historian (hi-çtóó-ri-ănn) *n* historiador *m*

historic (hi-çtó-rik) *adj* histórico

historical (hi-çtó-ri-kăl) *adj* histórico

history (hi-çtă-ri) *n* história *f*

hit (hit) *n* sucesso *m*

***hit** (hit) *v* bater; acertar, atingir

hitchhike (hitch-haik) *v* *pedir boleia; *pedir carona *Br*

hitchhiker (hitch-hai-kă) *n* pessoa que pede boleia

hoarse (hóóç) *adj* rouco

hobby (hó-bi) *n* passatempo *m*

hobby-horse (hó-bi-hóóç) *n* cavalo-de-pau *m*

hockey (hó-ki) *n* hóquei *m*

hoist (hoiçt) *v* içar

hold (hoᵘld) *n* porão *m*

***hold** (hoᵘld) *v* segurar; guardar; ~ **on** agarrar-se; ~ **up** *suster

hold-up (hoᵘl-dap) *n* assalto à mão armada

hole (hoᵘl) *n* buraco *m*

holiday (hó-lă-di) *n* férias *fpl*; feriado *m*; ~ **camp** colónia de férias; ~ **resort** estância de férias; **on** ~ em férias

Holland (hó-lănnd) Holanda *f*

hollow (hó-loᵘ) *adj* oco

holy (hoᵘ-li) *adj* sagrado

homage (hó-midj) n homenagem f

home (hoᵘmm) n lar m; morada f; adv para casa; **at** ~ em casa

home-made (hoᵘmm-meid) adj caseiro

homesickness (hoᵘmm-çik-năç) n nostalgia f

homosexual (hoᵘ-mă-çék-chu-ăl) adj homossexual

honest (ó-niçt) adj honesto; sincero

honesty (ó-ni-çti) n honestidade f

honey (ha-ni) n mel m

honeymoon (ha-ni-muunn) n lua-de-mel f

honour (ó-nă) n honra f; v prestar homenagem, honrar

honourable (ó-nă-ră-băl) adj honroso; honrado

hood (hud) n capuz m; nAm cobertura do motor

hoof (huuf) n casco m

hook (huk) n gancho m

hoot (huut) v buzinar

hooter (huu-tă) n buzina f

hoover (huu-vă) v aspirar

hop¹ (hóp) v saltitar; n pulo m

hop² (hóp) n lúpulo m

hope (hoᵘp) n esperança f; v esperar

hopeful (hoᵘp-făl) adj esperançado

hopeless (hoᵘp-lăç) adj desesperado

horizon (hă-rai-zănn) n horizonte m

horizontal (hó-ri-zónn-tăl) adj horizontal

horn (hóónn) n chifre m; trompa f; buzina f

horrible (hó-ri-băl) adj horrível; atroz, horripilante, horroroso

horror (hó-ră) n horror m, pavor m

hors-d'œuvre (óó-dăăvr) n acepipes mpl

horse (hóóç) n cavalo m

horseman (hóóç-mănn) n (pl -men) cavaleiro m

horsepower (hóóç-pauă) n cavalo-va-

horserace (hóóç-reiç) n corrida de cavalos

horseradish (hóóç-ræ-dich) n rábano silvestre

horseshoe (hóóç-chuu) n ferradura f

horticulture (hóó-ti-kal-tchă) n horticultura f

hosiery (hoᵘ-jă-ri) n malhas

hospitable (hó-çpi-tă-băl) adj hospitaleiro

hospital (hó-çpi-tăl) n hospital m

hospitality (hó-çpi-tæ-lă-ti) n hospitalidade f

host (hoᵘçt) n hospedeiro m

hostage (hó-çtidj) n refém m

hostel (hó-çtăl) n albergue m

hostess (hoᵘ-çtiç) n hospedeira f

hostile (hó-çtail) adj hostil

hot (hót) adj quente

hotel (hoᵘ-tél) n hotel m

hot-tempered (hót-témm-păd) adj irascível

hour (auă) n hora f

hourly (auă-li) adj hora a hora

house (hauç) n casa f; habitação f; prédio m; ~ **agent** agente imobiliário; ~ **block** Am bloco habitacional; **public** ~ bar m

houseboat (hauç-boᵘt) n casa flutuante

household (hauç-hoᵘld) n lar m; família f

housekeeper (hauç-kii-pă) n governanta f

housekeeping (hauç-kii-pinng) n governo de casa, lida da casa

housemaid (hauç-meid) n empregada doméstica

housewife (hauç-ᵘaif) n dona de casa

housework (hauç-ᵘăăk) n lida da casa

how (hau) adv como; que; ~ **many** quantos; ~ **much** quanto

however (hau-é-vă) *conj* todavia, contudo

hug (hagh) *v* abraçar; *n* abraço *m*

huge (h'uudj) *adj* enorme, formidável

hum (hamm) *v* *trautear

human (h'uu-mănn) *adj* humano; ~ **being** ser humano

humanity (h'u-mæ-nă-ti) *n* humanidade *f*

humble (hamm-băl) *adj* humilde

humid (h'uu-mid) *adj* húmido

humidity (h'u-mi-dă-ti) *n* humidade *f*

humorous (h'uu-mă-răç) *adj* espirituoso, engraçado

humour (h'uu-mă) *n* humor *m*

hundred (hann-drăd) *n* cem

Hungarian (hanng-ghéă-ri-ănn) *adj* húngaro

Hungary (hanng-ghă-ri) Hungria *f*

hunger (hanng-ghă) *n* fome *f*

hungry (hanng-ghri) *adj* esfomeado

hunt (hannt) *v* caçar; *n* caça *f*; ~ **for** procurar

hunter (hann-tă) *n* caçador *m*

hurricane (ha-ri-kănn) *n* furacão *m*; ~ **lamp** lâmpada de tempestade

hurry (ha-ri) *v* apressar-se, despachar-se; *n* pressa *f*; **in a** ~ apressadamente

*****hurt** (hăăt) *v* magoar, *ferir; ofender

hurtful (hăăt-făl) *adj* prejudicial

husband (haz-bănnd) *n* marido *m*, esposo *m*

hut (hat) *n* cabana *f*

hydrogen (hai-dră-djănn) *n* hidrogénio *m*

hygiene (hai-djiinn) *n* higiene *f*

hygienic (hai-djii-nik) *adj* higiénico

hymn (himm) *n* hino *m*

hyphen (hai-fănn) *n* hífen *m*

hypocrisy (hi-pó-kră-çi) *n* hipocrisia *f*

hypocrite (hi-pă-krit) *n* hipócrita *m*

hypocritical (hi-pă-kri-ti-kăl) *adj* falso, hipócrita

hysterical (hi-çté-ri-kăl) *adj* histérico

I

I (ai) *pron* eu

ice (aiç) *n* gelo *m*

ice-bag (aiç-bægh) *n* saco de gelo

ice-cream (aiç-kriimm) *n* gelado *m*; sorvete *mBr*

Iceland (aiç-lănnd) Islândia *f*

Icelander (aiç-lănn-dă) *n* islandês *m*

Icelandic (aiç-læn-dik) *adj* islandês

icon (ai-kónn) *n* ícone *m*

idea (ai-diă) *n* ideia *f*; pensamento *m*; noção *f*, conceito *m*

ideal (ai-diăl) *adj* ideal; *n* ideal *m*

identical (ai-dénn-ti-kăl) *adj* idêntico

identification (ai-dénn-ti-fi-kei-chănn) *n* identificação *f*

identify (ai-dénn-ti-fai) *v* identificar

identity (ai-dénn-tă-ti) *n* identidade *f*; ~ **card** bilhete de identidade

idiom (i-di-ămm) *n* expressão idiomática

idiomatic (i-di-ă-mæ-tik) *adj* idiomático

idiot (i-di-ăt) *n* idiota *m*

idiotic (i-di-ó-tik) *adj* idiota

idle (ai-dăl) *adj* ocioso; fútil

idol (ai-dăl) *n* ídolo *m*

if (if) *conj* se

ignition (igh-ni-chănn) *n* ignição *f*; ~ **coil** bobina de ignição

ignorant (igh-nă-rănnt) *adj* ignorante

ignore (igh-nóó) *v* ignorar

ill (il) *adj* doente; mau; maligno

illegal (i-lii-ghăl) *adj* ilegal

illegible (i-lé-djă-băl) *adj* ilegível

illiterate (i-li-tă-răt) *n* analfabeto *m*

illness (il-năç) *n* doença *f*

illuminate (i-luu-mi-neit) *v* iluminar,

alumiar

illumination (i-luu-mi-*nei*-chănn) *n* iluminacão *f*

illusion (i-*luu*-jănn) *n* ilusão *f*

illustrate (*i*-lă-çtreit) *v* ilustrar

illustration (i-lă-*çtrei*-chănn) *n* ilustra-cão *f*

image (*i*-midj) *n* imagem *f*

imaginary (i-*mæ*-dji-nă-ri) *adj* imaginário

imagination (i-mæ-dji-*nei*-chănn) *n* imaginacão *f*

imagine (i-*mæ*-djinn) *v* imaginar

imitate (*i*-mi-teit) *v* imitar

imitation (i-mi-*tei*-chănn) *n* imitacão *f*

immediate (i-*mii*-d¹ăt) *adj* imediato

immediately (i-*mii*-d¹ăt-li) *adv* já, imediatamente

immense (i-*ménnç*) *adj* enorme, imenso

immigrant (*i*-mi-ghrănnt) *n* imigrante *m*

immigrate (*i*-mi-ghreit) *v* imigrar

immigration (i-mi-*ghrei*-chănn) *n* imigracão *f*

immodest (i-*mó*-dịct) *adj* imodesto

immunity (i-m¹*uu*-nă-ti) *n* imunidade *f*

immunize (*i*-m¹u-naiz) *v* imunizar

impartial (imm-*paa*-chăl) *adj* imparcial

impassable (imm-*paa*-çă-băl) *adj* impraticável

impatient (imm-*pei*-chănnt) *adj* impaciente

impede (imm-*piid*) *v* entravar, *impedir

impediment (imm-*pé*-di-mănnt) *n* impedimento *m*

imperfect (imm-*păă*-fikt) *adj* imperfeito

imperial (imm-*pi*ă-ri-ăl) *adj* imperial

impersonal (imm-*păă*-çă-năl) *adj* impessoal

impertinence (imm-*păă*-ti-nănnç) *n*

impertinência *f*

impertinent (imm-*păă*-ti-nănnt) *adj* impertinente, insolente, malcriado

implement¹ (*imm*-pli-mănnt) *n* ferramenta *f*

implement² (*imm*-pli-ménnt) *v* realizar

imply (imm-*plai*) *v* implicar

impolite (imm-pă-*lait*) *adj* grosseiro

import¹ (imm-*póót*) *v* importar

import² (*imm*-póót) *n* importacões *fpl*, importacão *f*; ~ **duty** direitos de importacão

importance (imm-*póó*-tănnç) *n* importância *f*, relevo *m*

important (imm-*póó*-tănnt) *adj* importante, relevante

importer (imm-*póó*-tă) *n* importador *m*

imposing (imm-*po*ᵘ-zinng) *adj* imponente

impossible (imm-*pó*-çă-băl) *adj* impossível

impotence (*imm*-pă-tănnç) *n* impotência *f*

impotent (*imm*-pă-tănnt) *adj* impotente

impound (imm-*paunnd*) *v* apreender

impress (imm-*préç*) *v* impressionar

impression (imm-*pré*-chănn) *n* impressão *f*

impressive (imm-*pré*-çiv) *adj* impressionante

imprison (imm-*pri*-zănn) *v* prender

imprisonment (imm-*pri*-zănn-mănnt) *n* encarceramento *m*

improbable (imm-*pró*-bă-băl) *adj* improvável

improper (imm-*pró*-pă) *adj* impróprio

improve (imm-*pruuv*) *v* melhorar

improvement (imm-*pruuv*-mănnt) *n* melhoramento *m*

improvise (*imm*-pră-vaiz) *v* improvisar

impudent (*imm*-p¹u-dănnt) *adj* desavergonhado

impulse (*imm*-palç) *n* impulso *m*; estímulo *m*

impulsive (imm-*pal*-çiv) *adj* impulsivo

in (inn) *prep* em; dentro de; *adv* dentro

inaccessible (i-næk-*çé*-çã-bãl) *adj* inacessível

inaccurate (i-*næ*-kⁱu-rãt) *adj* incorrecto

inadequate (i-*næ*-di-k^uãt) *adj* inadequado

incapable (inng-*kei*-pã-bãl) *adj* incapaz

incense (*inn*-çénnç) *n* incenso *m*

incident (*inn*-çi-dãnnt) *n* incidente *m*

incidental (inn-çi-*dénn*-tãl) *adj* incidental

incite (inn-*çait*) *v* incitar

inclination (inng-kli-*nei*-chãnn) *n* inclinação *f*

incline (inng-*klainn*) *n* declive *m*

inclined (inng-*klainnd*) *adj* propenso, disposto; *be ~ to* tender

include (inng-*kluud*) *v* incluir

inclusive (inng-*kluu*-çiv) *adj* inclusivo

income (*inng*-kãmm) *n* rendimento *m*

income-tax (*inng*-kãmm-tækç) *n* imposto sobre os rendimentos

incompetent (inng-*kómm*-pã-tãnnt) *adj* incompetente

incomplete (inn-kãmm-*pliit*) *adj* incompleto

inconceivable (inng-kãnn-*çii*-vã-bãl) *adj* inconcebível

inconspicuous (inng-kãnn-*çpi*-kⁱu-ãç) *adj* discreto

inconvenience (inng-kãnn-*vii*-nⁱãnnç) *n* inconveniência *f*, incómodo *m*

inconvenient (inng-kãnn-*vii*-nⁱãnnt) *adj* inconveniente; maçador

incorrect (inng-kã-*rékt*) *adj* inexacto, incorrecto

increase[1] (inng-*kriiç*) *v* aumentar, crescer

increase[2] (*inng*-kriiç) *n* aumento *m*

incredible (inng-*kré*-dã-bãl) *adj* incrível

incurable (inng-*kⁱu^ã*-rã-bãl) *adj* incurável

indecent (inn-*dii*-çãnnt) *adj* indecente

indeed (inn-*diid*) *adv* efectivamente

indefinite (inn-*dé*-fi-nit) *adj* indefinido

indemnity (inn-*démm*-nã-ti) *n* indemnização *f*, compensação *f*

independence (inn-di-*pénn*-dãnnç) *n* independência *f*

independent (inn-di-*pénn*-dãnnt) *adj* independente; autónomo

index (*inn*-dékç) *n* índice *m*; *~ finger* indicador *m*

India (*inn*-di-ã) Índia *f*

Indian (*inn*-di-ãnn) *adj* indiano; índio; *n* indiano *m*; índio *m*

indicate (*inn*-di-keit) *v* indicar, assinalar

indication (inn-di-*kei*-chãnn) *n* indicação *f*, sinal *m*

indicator (*inn*-di-kei-tã) *n* pisca-pisca *m*

indifferent (inn-*di*-fã-rãnnt) *adj* indiferente

indigestion (inn-di-*djéç*-tchãnn) *n* indigestão *f*

indignation (inn-digh-*nei*-chãnn) *n* indignação *f*

indirect (inn-di-*rékt*) *adj* indirecto

individual (inn-di-*vi*-dju-ãl) *adj* particular, individual; *n* indivíduo *m*

Indonesia (inn-dã-*nii*-zi-ã) Indonésia *f*

Indonesian (inn-dã-*nii*-zi-ãnn) *adj* indonésio

indoor (*inn*-dóó) *adj* interno

indoors (inn-*dóóz*) *adv* dentro de casa

indulge (inn-*daldj*) *v* ceder

industrial (inn-*da*-çtri-ãl) *adj* industrial; *~ area* zona industrial

industrious (inn-*da*-çtri-ãç) *adj* traba-

lhador
industry (*inn*-dă-çtri) *n* indústria *f*
inedible (i-*né*-di-băl) *adj* incomestível
inefficient (i-ni-*fi*-chănnt) *adj* ineficiente
inevitable (i-*né*-vi-tă-băl) *adj* inevitável
inexpensive (i-nik-*çpénn*-çiv) *adj* barato
inexperienced (i-nik-*çpi*ă-ri-ănnçt) *adj* inexperiente
infant (*inn*-fănnt) *n* criança de peito
infantry (*inn*-fănn-tri) *n* infantaria *f*
infect (inn-*fékt*) *v* infectar
infection (inn-*fék*-chănn) *n* infecção *f*
infectious (inn-*fék*-chăç) *adj* infeccioso
infer (inn-*făă*) *v* *deduzir
inferior (inn-*fi*ă-ri-ă) *adj* inferior, menor
infinite (*inn*-fi-nătn) *adj* infinito
infinitive (inn-*fi*-ni-tiv) *n* infinitivo *m*
infirmary (inn-*făă*-mă-ri) *n* enfermaria *f*
inflammable (inn-*flæ*-mă-băl) *adj* inflamável
inflammation (inn-flă-*mei*-chănn) *n* inflamacão *f*
inflatable (inn-*flei*-tă-băl) *adj* pneumático
inflate (inn-*fleit*) *v* inchar, encher de ar
inflation (inn-*flei*-chănn) *n* inflação *f*
influence (*inn*-flu-ănnç) *n* influência *f*; *v* influenciar
influential (inn-flu-*énn*-chăl) *adj* influente
influenza (inn-flu-*énn*-ză) *n* gripe *f*
inform (inn-*fóómm*) *v* informar; comunicar, *pôr ao corrente
informal (inn-*fóó*-măl) *adj* sem cerimónia
information (inn-fă-*mei*-chănn) *n* informacão *f*, comunicação *f*; ~

bureau agência de informações
infra-red (inn-fră-*réd*) *adj* infra-vermelho
infrequent (inn-*frii*-kᵁănnt) *adj* raro
ingredient (inng-*ghrii*-di-ănnt) *n* ingrediente *m*
inhabit (inn-*hæ*-bit) *v* habitar
inhabitable (inn-*hæ*-bi-tă-băl) *adj* habitável
inhabitant (inn-*hæ*-bi-tănnt) *n* habitante *m*
inhale (inn-*heil*) *v* inalar
inherit (inn-*hé*-rit) *v* herdar
inheritance (inn-*hé*-ri-tănnç) *n* herança *f*
initial (i-*ni*-chăl) *adj* inicial; *n* inicial *f*; *v* rubricar
initiative (i-*ni*-chă-tiv) *n* iniciativa *f*
inject (inn-*djékt*) *v* injectar
injection (inn-*djék*-chănn) *n* injecção *f*
injure (*inn*-djă) *v* *ferir; ofender
injury (*inn*-djă-ri) *n* ferida *f*, lesão *f*
injustice (inn-*dja*-çtiç) *n* injustica *f*
ink (inngk) *n* tinta *f*
inlet (*inn*-lét) *n* enseada *f*; entrada *f*, passagem *f*
inn (inn) *n* pousada *f*
inner (*i*-nă) *adj* interior; ~ **tube** câmara-de-ar *f*
inn-keeper (*inn*-kii-pă) *n* estalajadeiro *m*
innocence (*i*-nă-çănnç) *n* inocência *f*
innocent (*i*-nă-çănnt) *adj* inocente
inoculate (i-*nó*-kⁱu-leit) *v* inocular
inoculation (i-nó-kⁱu-*lei*-chănn) *n* inoculação *f*
inquire (inng-kᵁ*ai*ă) *v* informar-se, indagar, inquirir
inquiry (inng-kᵁ*ai*ă-ri) *n* pergunta *f*, inquérito *m*; ~ **office** agência de informações
inquisitive (inng-kᵁ*i*-ză-tiv) *adj* curioso
insane (inn-*çeinn*) *adj* louco
inscription (inn-*çkrip*-chănn) *n* inscri

cão f

insect (inn-çékt) *n* insecto *m*

insecticide (inn-çék-ti-çaid) *n* insecticida *m*

insensitive (inn-çénn-çă-tiv) *adj* insensível

insert (inn-çãăt) *v* *inserir

inside (inn-çaid) *n* interior *m*; *adj* interior; *adv* dentro; por dentro; *prep* em, dentro de; ~ **out** do avesso; **insides** entranhas *fpl*

insight (inn-çait) *n* compreensão *f*

insignificant (inn-çigh-ni-fi-kănt) *adj* insignificante; irrelevante; fútil

insist (inn-çiçt) *v* insistir; persistir

insolence (inn-çă-lănnç) *n* insolência *f*

insolent (inn-çă-lănnt) *adj* insolente

insomnia (inn-çómm-ni-ă) *n* insónia *f*

inspect (inn-çpékt) *v* inspeccionar

inspection (inn-çpék-chănn) *n* inspecção *f*

inspector (inn-çpék-tă) *n* inspector *m*

inspire (inn-çpaiă) *v* inspirar

install (inn-çtóól) *v* instalar

installation (inn-çtă-lei-chănn) *n* instalação *f*

instalment (inn-çtóól-mănnt) *n* prestação *f*

instance (inn-çtănnç) *n* exemplo *m*; caso *m*; **for** ~ por exemplo

instant (inn-çtănnt) *n* instante *m*

instantly (inn-çtănnt-li) *adv* instantaneamente, imediatamente

instead of (inn-çtéd óv) em vez de

instinct (inn-çtinngkt) *n* instinto *m*

institute (inn-çti-t^iuut) *n* instituto *m*; instituição *f*; *v* *instituir

institution (inn-çti-t^iuu-chănn) *n* instituição *f*

instruct (inn-çtrakt) *v* *instruir

instruction (inn-çtrak-chănn) *n* instrução *f*

instructive (inn-çtrak-tiv) *adj* instrutivo

instructor (inn-çtrak-tă) *n* instrutor *m*

instrument (inn-çtru-mănnt) *n* instrumento *m*; **musical** ~ instrumento musical

insufficient (inn-çă-fi-chănnt) *adj* insuficiente

insulate (inn-ç^iu-leit) *v* isolar

insulation (inn-ç^iu-lei-chănn) *n* isolamento *m*

insulator (inn-ç^iu-lei-tă) *n* isolador *m*

insult[1] (inn-çalt) *v* insultar

insult[2] (inn-çalt) *n* insulto *m*

insurance (inn-chu^ă-rănnç) *n* seguro *m*; ~ **policy** apólice de seguro

insure (inn-chu^ă) *v* segurar; garantir

intact (inn-tækt) *adj* intacto

intellect (inn-tă-lékt) *n* intelecto *m*

intellectual (inn-tă-lék-tchu-ăl) *adj* intelectual

intelligence (inn-té-li-djănnç) *n* inteligência *f*

intelligent (inn-té-li-djănnt) *adj* inteligente

intend (inn-ténnd) *v* tencionar

intense (inn-ténnç) *adj* intenso

intention (inn-ténn-chănn) *n* intenção *f*

intentional (inn-ténn-chă-năl) *adj* intencional

intercourse (inn-tă-kóóç) *n* relações *fpl*

interest (inn-trăçt) *n* interesse *m*; juro *m*; *v* interessar

interesting (inn-tră-çtinng) *adj* interessante

interfere (inn-tă-fi^ă) *v* *interferir; ~ **with** intrometer-se em

interference (inn-tă-fi^ă-rănnç) *n* interferência *f*

interim (inn-tă-rimm) *n* interim *m*

interior (inn-ti^ă-ri-ă) *n* interior *m*

interlude (inn-tă-luud) *n* interlúdio *m*

intermediary (inn-tă-mii-d^iă-ri) *n* intermediário *m*

intermission (inn-tă-*mi*-chănn) *n* intervalo *m*

internal (inn-tăă-năl) *adj* interno

international (inn-tă-*næ*-chă-năl) *adj* internacional

interpret (inn-*tăă*-prit) *v* interpretar, *traduzir

interpreter (inn-*tăă*-pri-tă) *n* intérprete *m*

interrogate (inn-*té*-ră-gheit) *v* interrogar

interrogation (inn-té-ră-*ghei*-chănn) *n* interrogatório *m*

interrogative (inn-*té*-*ró*-ghă-tiv) *adj* interrogativo

interrupt (inn-tă-*rapt*) *v* interromper

interruption (inn-tă-*rap*-chănn) *n* interrupção *f*

intersection (inn-tă-*çék*-chănn) *n* intersecção *f*

interval (*inn*-tă-văl) *n* intervalo *m*

intervene (inn-tă-*viinn*) *v* *intervir

interview (inn-tă-v'uu) *n* entrevista *f*

intestine (inn-*té*-çtinn) *n* intestino *m*

intimate (*inn*-ti-măt) *adj* íntimo

into (*inn*-tu) *prep* dentro de; para dentro

intolerable (inn-*tó*-lă-ră-băl) *adj* intolerável

intoxicated (inn-*tók*-çi-kei-tid) *adj* embriagado

intrigue (inn-*triigh*) *n* intriga *f*

introduce (inn-tră-d'*uuç*) *v* apresentar; *introduzir

introduction (inn-tră-*dak*-chănn) *n* apresentação *f*; introdução *f*

invade (inn-*veid*) *v* invadir

invalid[1] (*inn*-vă-liid) *n* inválido *m*; *adj* inválido

invalid[2] (inn-*væ*-lid) *adj* sem validade

invasion (inn-*vei*-jănn) *n* invasão *f*

invent (inn-*vénnt*) *v* inventar

invention (inn-*vénn*-chănn) *n* invenção

f

inventive (inn-*vénn*-tiv) *adj* inventivo

inventor (inn-*vénn*-tă) *n* inventor *m*

inventory (*inn*-vănn-tri) *n* inventário *m*

invert (inn-*văăt*) *v* inverter

invest (inn-*véçt*) *v* *investir

investigate (inn-*vé*-çti-gheit) *v* investigar

investigation (inn-vé-çti-*ghei*-chănn) *n* investigação *f*

investment (inn-*véçt*-mănnt) *n* investimento *m*

investor (inn-*vé*-çtă) *n* aquele que faz investimento

invisible (inn-*vi*-ză-băl) *adj* invisível

invitation (inn-vi-*tei*-chănn) *n* convite *m*

invite (inn-*vait*) *v* convidar

invoice (*inn*-voiç) *n* factura *f*

involve (inn-*vólv*) *v* implicar

inwards (*inn*-ᵘădz) *adv* para dentro

iodine (*ai*-ă-diinn) *n* iodo *m*

Iran (i-*raann*) Irão *m*

Iranian (i-*rei*-ni-ănn) *adj* iraniano

Iraq (i-*raak*) Iraque *m*

Iraqi (i-*raa*-ki) *adj* iraquiano

irascible (i-*ræ*-çi-băl) *adj* irascível

Ireland (*ai*ᵃ-lănnd) Irlanda *f*

Irish (*ai*ᵃ-rich) *adj* irlandês

Irishman (*ai*ᵃ-rich-mănn) *n* (pl -men) irlandês *m*

iron (*ai*-ănn) *n* ferro *m*; ferro de engomar; de ferro; *v* passar a ferro

ironical (ai-*ró*-ni-kăl) *adj* irónico

ironworks (*ai*-ănn-ᵘăăkç) *n* fundição *f*

irony (*ai*ᵃ-ră-ni) *n* ironia *f*

irregular (i-*ré*-gh'u-lă) *adj* irregular

irreparable (i-*ré*-pă-ră-băl) *adj* irreparável

irrevocable (i-*ré*-vă-kă-băl) *adj* irrevogável

irritable (*i*-ri-tă-băl) *adj* irritável

irritate (*i*-ri-teit) *v* irritar

is (iz) v (pr be)
island (ai-lånnd) n ilha f
isolate (ai-çă-leit) v isolar
isolation (ai-çă-lei-chänn) n isolamento m
Israel (iz-reil) Israel m
Israeli (iz-rei-li) adj israeliano
issue (i-chuu) v *distribuir; n edição f, emissão f, tiragem f; questão f, ponto m; consequência f, resultado m, fim m, conclusão f; saída f
isthmus (iç-măç) n istmo m
Italian (i-tæl-iänn) adj italiano
italics (i-tæ-likç) pl itálico m
Italy (i-tă-li) Itália f
itch (itch) n comichão f; prurido m; v *ter comichão
item (ai-tämm) n artigo m; ponto m
itinerant (ai-ti-nă-rännt) adj itinerante
itinerary (ai-ti-nă-ră-ri) n itinerário m
ivory (ai-vă-ri) n marfim m
ivy (ai-vi) n hera f

J

jack (djæk) n macaco m
jacket (djæ-kit) n casaco m; paletó mBr; capa f
jade (djeid) n jade m
jail (djeil) n prisão f
jailer (djei-lă) n carcereiro m
jam (djæmm) n doce de fruta; geléia fBr; engarrafamento m
janitor (djæ-ni-tă) n porteiro m
January (djæ-n‘u-ă-ri) Janeiro
Japan (djă-pænn) Japão m
Japanese (djæ-pă-niiz) adj japonês m
jar (djaa) n jarra f
jaundice (djóónn-diç) n icterícia f
jaw (djóó) n maxila f
jealous (djé-lăç) adj ciumento m
jealousy (djé-lă-çi) n ciúme m

jeans (djiinnz) pl calças de ganga
jelly (djé-li) n geleia f
jelly-fish (djé-li-fich) n alforreca f; medusa fBr
jersey (djã-zi) n jersey m; camisola de malha
jet (djét) n jacto m; avião a jacto
jetty (djé-ti) n molhe m
Jew (djuu) n judeu m
jewel (djuu-ăl) n jóia f
jeweller (djuu-ă-lă) n joalheiro m
jewellery (djuu-ăl-ri) n jóias fpl; joalharia f
Jewish (djuu-ich) adj judaico
job (djób) n trabalho m; emprego m
jockey (djó-ki) n jóquei m
join (djoinn) v unir, juntar; associar-se a, *aderir a; reunir
joint (djoinnt) n articulação f; soldadura f; adj unido, conjunto
jointly (djoinnt-li) adv conjuntamente
joke (djoukk) n anedota f, graça f
jolly (djó-li) adj jovial
Jordan (djóó-dänn) Jordânia f
Jordanian (djóó-dei-ni-änn) adj jordaniano
journal (djãă-năl) n jornal m
journalism (djãă-nă-li-zămm) n jornalismo m
journalist (djãă-nă-liçt) n jornalista m
journey (djãă-ni) n viagem f
joy (djoi) n prazer m, alegria f
joyful (djoi-fål) adj contente, alegre
jubilee (djuu-bi-lii) n jubileu m
judge (djadj) n juiz m; v julgar
judgment (djadj-männt) n juízo m; julgamento m
jug (djagh) n jarro m
Jugoslav (‘uu-ghă-çlaav) adj jugoslavo
Jugoslavia (‘uu-ghă-çla-vi-ă) Jugoslávia f
juice (djuuç) n sumo m
juicy (djuu-çi) adj sumarento
July (dju-lai) Julho

jump (djammp) *v* saltar; *n* salto *m*

jumper (*djamm*-pă) *n* camisola *f*

junction (*djanngk*-chănn) *n* cruzamento *m*; junção *f*

June (djuunn) Junho

jungle (*djanng*-ghăl) *n* selva *f*

junior (*djuu*-ni̱ă) *adj* júnior

junk (djanngk) *n* tralha *f*

jury (*dju̱ᵃ*-ri) *n* júri *m*

just (djaçt) *adj* justo; *adv* acabado de; justamente

justice (*dja*-çtiç) *n* direito *m*; justiça *f*

juvenile (*djuu*-vă-nail) *adj* juvenil

K

kangaroo (kænng-ghă-*ruu*) *n* canguru *m*

keel (kiil) *n* quilha *f*

keen (kiinn) *adj* entusiasta; perspicaz

*keep (kiip) *v* *manter; guardar; não cessar de; ~ away from *manter-se à distância; ~ off não tocar; ~ on continuar a, continuar; ~ quiet calar-se; ~ up perseverar; ~ up with não lhe ficar atrás

keg (kégh) *n* barrica *f*

kennel (*ké*-năl) *n* casota do cão; canil *m*

Kenya (*ké*-ni̱ă) Quénia *m*

kerosene (*ké*-ră-çiinn) *n* querosene *m*

kettle (*ké*-tăl) *n* chaleira *f*

key (kii) *n* chave *f*

keyhole (*kii*-ho̱ᵘl) *n* buraco da fechadura *f*

khaki (*kaa*-ki) *n* caqui *m*

kick (kik) *v* *dar um pontapé; *n* pontapé *m*

kick-off (ki-*kóf*) *n* pontapé de saída

kid (kid) *n* criança *f*, garoto *m*; pelica *f*; *v* gozar com

kidney (*kid*-ni) *n* rim *m*

kill (kil) *v* matar

kilogram (*ki*-lă-ghræmm) *n* quilograma *m*

kilometre (*ki*-lă-mii-tă) *n* quilómetro *m*

kind (kainnd) *adj* gentil, bondoso; bom; *n* género *m*

kindergarten (*kinn*-dă-ghaa-tănn) *n* jardim infantil

king (kinng) *n* rei *m*

kingdom (*kinng*-dămm) *n* reino *m*

kiosk (kii-*óçk*) *n* quiosque *m*

kiss (kiç) *n* beijo *m*; *v* beijar

kit (kit) *n* equipamento *m*

kitchen (*ki*-tchinn) *n* cozinha *f*; ~ garden horta *f*

knapsack (*næp*-çæk) *n* mochila *f*

knave (neiv) *n* valete *m*

knee (nii) *n* joelho *m*

kneecap (*nii*-kæp) *n* rótula *f*

*kneel (niil) *v* ajoelhar

knew (ni̱ᵘu) *v* (p know)

knickers (*ni*-kăz) *pl* calcinhas *fpl*

knife (naif) *n* (pl knives) faca *f*

knight (nait) *n* cavaleiro *m*

*knit (nit) *v* tricotar

knob (nób) *n* maçaneta *f*

knock (nók) *v* bater; *n* pancada *f*; ~ against chocar com; ~ down derrubar

knot (nót) *n* nó *m*; *v* *fazer um nó

*know (no̱ᵘ) *v* *saber, conhecer

knowledge (*nó*-lidj) *n* conhecimento *m*

knuckle (*na*-kăl) *n* nó dos dedos; jarrete *m*

L

label (*lei*-băl) *n* etiqueta *f*; *v* etiquetar

laboratory (lă-*bó*-ră-tă-ri) *n* laboratório *m*

labour (*lei*-bă) *n* trabalho *m;* dores; *v* trabalhar arduamente, labutar; **labor permit** *Am* autorização de trabalho

labourer (*lei*-bă-ră) *n* operário *m*

labour-saving (*lei*-bă-çei-vinng) *adj* economisador de trabalho

labyrinth (*læ*-bă-rinnθ) *n* labirinto *m*

lace (leiç) *n* renda *f;* atacador *m*

lack (læk) *n* falta *f,* carência *f; v* carecer de

lacquer (*læ*-kă) *n* verniz *m*

lad (læd) *n* rapaz *m*

ladder (*læ*-dă) *n* escada *f*

lagoon (lă-*ghuunn*) *n* laguna *f*

lake (leik) *n* lago *m*

lamb (læmm) *n* cordeiro *m;* borrego *m*

lame (leimm) *adj* coxo, paralítico

lamentable (*læ*-mănn-tă-băl) *adj* lamentável

lamp (læmmp) *n* candeeiro *m*

lamp-post (*læmmp*-poᵘçt) *n* poste de iluminação

lampshade (*læmmp*-cheid) *n* abajur *m*

land (lænnd) *n* terra *f,* país *m; v* aterrar; desembarcar

landlady (*lænnd*-lei-di) *n* senhoria *f*

landlord (*lænnd*-lóód) *n* senhorio *m,* proprietário *m*

landmark (*lænnd*-maak) *n* ponto de referência; marco *m*

landscape (*lænnd*-çkeip) *n* paisagem *f*

lane (leinn) *n* azinhaga *f,* viela *f;* via *f*

language (*lænng*-ghᵘidj) *n* língua *f;* ~ **laboratory** laboratório de línguas

lantern (*lænn*-tănn) *n* lanterna *f*

lapel (lă-*pél*) *n* lapela *f*

larder (*laa*-dă) *n* despensa *f*

large (laadj) *adj* grande; espaçoso

lark (laak) *n* cotovia *f*

laryngitis (læ-rinn-*djai*-tiç) *n* laringite *f*

last (laaçt) *adj* último; precedente; *v* durar; **at** ~ finalmente

lasting (*laa*-çtinng) *adj* duradouro

latchkey (*lætch*-kii) *n* chave de trinco

late (leit) *adj* tardio; atrasado

lately (*leit*-li) *adv* ultimamente, recentemente

lather (*laa*-ðă) *n* espuma *f*

Latin America (*læ*-tinn ă-*mé*-ri-kă) América Latina

Latin-American (*læ*-tinn-ă-*mé*-ri-kănn) *adj* sul-americano

latitude (*læ*-ti-tⁱuud) *n* grau de latitude

laugh (laaf) *v* *rir; *n* riso *m*

laughter (*laaf*-tă) *n* risada *f*

launch (lóónntch) *v* lançar; *n* barco a motor

launching (*lóónn*-tchinng) *n* lançamento *m*

launderette (*lóónn*-dă-rét) *n* lavandaria automática

laundry (*lóónn*-dri) *n* lavandaria *f;* roupa para lavar

lavatory (*læ*-vă-tă-ri) *n* sanitário *m*

lavish (*læ*-vich) *adj* pródigo

law (lóó) *n* lei *f;* direito *m;* ~ **court** tribunal *m*

lawful (*lóó*-făl) *adj* legal

lawn (lóónn) *n* relvado *m*

lawsuit (*lóó*-çuut) *n* causa judicial, processo *m*

lawyer (*lóó*-ⁱă) *n* advogado *m;* jurista *m*

laxative (*læk*-çă-tiv) *n* laxante *m*

***lay** (lei) *v* pousar, colocar, *pôr; ~ **bricks** *fazer trabalho de pedreiro

layer (*lei*ᵃ) *n* camada *f*

layman (*lei*-mănn) *n* leigo *m*

lazy (*lei*-zi) *adj* preguiçoso

***lead** (liid) *v* dirigir

lead¹ (liid) *n* avanço *m;* direcção *f;* trela *f*

lead² (léd) *n* chumbo *m*

leader (*lii*-dă) *n* chefe *m,* dirigente *m*

leadership (*lii*-dă-chip) *n* direcção *f*

leading (*lii*-dinng) *adj* principal, dominante
leaf (liif) *n* (pl leaves) folha *f*
league (liigh) *n* liga *f*
leak (liik) *v* verter, vazar; *n* fuga *f*
leaky (*lii*-ki) *adj* com fuga
lean (liinn) *adj* magro
***lean** (liinn) *v* apoiar-se
leap (liip) *n* salto *m*
***leap** (liip) *v* saltar
leap-year (*liip*-ⁱiᵃ) *n* ano bissexto
***learn** (lăănn) *v* aprender
learner (*lăă*-nă) *n* principiante *m*
lease (liiç) *n* contrato de arrendamento; arrendamento *m; v* alugar, arrendar
leash (liich) *n* trela *f*
least (liiçt) *adj* mínimo, menos; **at ~** pelo menos
leather (*lé*-ðă) *n* couro *m;* de pele, de cabedal
leave (liiv) *n* licença *f*
***leave** (liiv) *v* deixar, partir, abandonar; **~ out** omitir
Lebanese (lé-bă-*niiz*) *adj* libanês
Lebanon (*lé*-bă-nănn) Líbano *m*
lecture (*lék*-tchă) *n* palestra *f*, conferência *f*
left[1] (léft) *adj* esquerdo
left[2] (léft) *v* (p, pp leave)
left-hand (*léft*-hænnd) *adj* esquerdo
left-handed (léft-*hænn*-did) *adj* canhoto
leg (légh) *n* perna *f*
legacy (*lé*-ghă-çi) *n* legado *m*
legal (*lii*-ghăl) *adj* legal, legítimo; jurídico
legalization (lii-ghă-lai-*zei*-chănn) *n* legalização *f*
legation (li-*ghei*-chănn) *n* legação *f*
legible (*lé*-dji-băl) *adj* legível
legitimate (li-*dji*-ti-măt) *adj* legítimo
leisure (*lé*-jă) *n* vagar *m;* sossego *m*
lemon (*lé*-mănn) *n* limão *m*
lemonade (lé-mă-*neid*) *n* limonada *f*
***lend** (lénnd) *v* emprestar
length (lénngθ) *n* comprimento *m*
lengthen (*lénng*-θănn) *v* alongar
lengthways (*lénngθ*-ᵘeiz) *adv* longitudinalmente
lens (lénnz) *n* lente *f;* **telephoto ~** teleobjectiva *f;* **zoom ~** lente zoom
leprosy (*lé*-pră-çi) *n* lepra *f*
less (léç) *adv* menos
lessen (*lé*-çănn) *v* *diminuir
lesson (*lé*-çănn) *n* lição *f*, aula *f*
***let** (lét) *v* deixar; alugar; **~ down** desiludir
letter (*lé*-tă) *n* carta *f;* letra *f;* **~ of credit** carta de crédito; **~ of recommendation** carta de recomendação
letter-box (*lé*-tă-bókç) *n* caixa do correio
lettuce (*lé*-tiç) *n* alface *f*
level (*lé*-văl) *adj* igual; liso, plano, direito; *n* nível *m; v* aplanar, nivelar; **~ crossing** passagem de nível
lever (*lii*-vă) *n* alavanca *f*
liability (lai-ă-*bi*-lă-ti) *n* responsabilidade *f*
liable (*lai*-ă-băl) *adj* responsável; **~ to** sujeito a
liberal (*li*-bă-răl) *adj* liberal; generoso
liberation (li-bă-*rei*-chănn) *n* libertação *f*
Liberia (lai-*bi*ᵃ-ri-ă) Libéria *f*
Liberian (lai-*bi*ᵃ-ri-ănn) *adj* liberiano
liberty (*li*-bă-ti) *n* liberdade *f*
library (*lai*-bră-ri) *n* biblioteca *f*
licence (*lai*-çănnç) *n* licença *f;* **driving ~** carta de condução; carteira de motorista *Br*
license (*lai*-çănnç) *v* autorizar
lick (lik) *v* lamber
lid (lid) *n* tampa *f*
lie (lai) *v* *mentir; *n* mentira *f*

*lie (lai) v *estar deitado; ~ down deitar-se

life (laif) n (pl lives) vida f; ~ insurance seguro de vida

lifebelt (laif-bélt) n colete salva-vidas

lifetime (laif-taimm) n vida f

lift (lift) v levantar, erguer; n ascensor m; boleia f; carona fBr

light (lait) n luz f; adj leve; claro; ~ bulb lâmpada f

*light (lait) v acender

lighter (lai-tă) n isqueiro m

lighthouse (lait-hauç) n farol m

lighting (lai-tinng) n iluminação f

lightning (lait-ninng) n relâmpago m

like (laik) v gostar de; adj semelhante; conj como

likely (lai-kli) adj provável

like-minded (laik-mainn-did) adj unânime

likewise (laik-ᵘaiz) adv igualmente

lily (li-li) n lírio m

limb (limm) n membro m

lime (laimm) n cal f; tília f; lima f

limetree (laimm-trii) n tília f

limit (li-mit) n limite m; v limitar

limp (limmp) v *coxear; adj frouxo

line (lainn) n linha f; risco m; cordão m; fila f

linen (li-ninn) n linho m; roupa branca

liner (lai-nă) n paquete m

lingerie (lón-jă-rii) n roupa interior

lining (lai-ninng) n forro m

link (linngk) v ligar; n laço m; elo m

lion (lai-ănn) n leão m

lip (lip) n lábio m

lipsalve (lip-çaav) n pomada para os lábios

lipstick (lip-çtik) n baton m

liqueur (li-kᵘă) n licor m

liquid (li-kᵘid) adj líquido; n líquido m

liquor (li-kă) n bebidas alcoólicas

list (liçt) n lista f; v inscrever

listen (li-çănn) v escutar

listener (liç-nă) n ouvinte m

literary (li-tră-ri) adj literário

literature (li-tră-tchă) n literatura f

litre (lii-tă) n litro m

litter (li-tă) n lixo m; ninhada f

little (li-tăl) adj pequeno; pouco

live¹ (liv) v viver; morar

live² (laiv) adj vivo

livelihood (laiv-li-hud) n subsistência f

lively (laiv-li) adj cheio de vida, animado

liver (li-vă) n fígado m

living-room (li-vinng-ruumm) n sala de estar

load (loᵘd) n carregamento m; fardo m; v carregar

loaf (loᵘf) n (pl loaves) pão m

loan (loᵘnn) n empréstimo m

lobby (ló-bi) n átrio m; vestíbulo m

lobster (lób-çtă) n lagosta f

local (loᵘ-kăl) adj local; ~ call chamada local; ~ train comboio suburbano

locality (loᵘ-kæ-lă-ti) n localidade f

locate (loᵘ-keit) v localizar

location (loᵘ-kei-chănn) n localização f

lock (lók) v fechar à chave; n fechadura f; comporta f; ~ up fechar, encerrar

locomotive (loᵘ-kă-moᵘ-tiv) n locomotiva f

lodge (lódj) v hospedar; n pavilhão de caça

lodger (ló-djă) n hóspede m

lodgings (ló-djinngz) pl alojamento m

log (lógh) n toro m

logic (ló-djik) n lógica f

logical (ló-dji-kăl) adj lógico

lonely (loᵘnn-li) adj solitário

long (lónn) adj longo; ~ for desejar; no longer não mais

longing (lónn-inng) n desejo m

longitude (*lónn*-dji-t¹uud) *n* longitude *f*

look (luk) *v* olhar; parecer, *ter ares; *n* olhar *m*, olhadela *f*; aparência *f*, aspecto *m*; ~ **after** ocupar-se de, cuidar de; ~ **at** olhar para; ~ **for** procurar; ~ **out** *ter cuidado, prestar atenção; ~ **up** procurar

looking-glass (*lu*-kinng-ghlaaç) *n* espelho *m*

loop (luup) *n* nó corrediço

loose (luuç) *adj* solto

loosen (*luu*-çănn) *v* desprender, desapertar

lord (lóód) *n* lorde *m*

lorry (*ló*-ri) *n* camião *m*

*lose (luuz) *v* *perder

loss (lóç) *n* perda *f*

lost (lóçt) *adj* perdido; desaparecido; ~ **and found** achados e perdidos; ~ **property office** depósito de objectos perdidos

lot (lót) *n* sorte *f*, destino *m*; quantidade *f*

lotion (*lo*ᵁ-chănn) *n* loção *f*; **after-shave** ~ loção para depois da barba

lottery (*ló*-tă-ri) *n* lotaria *f*

loud (laud) *adj* forte, alto

loud-speaker (laud-çpii-kă) *n* altifalante *m*

lounge (launndj) *n* salão *m*

louse (lauç) *n* (*pl* lice) piolho *m*

love (lav) *v* amar; *n* amor *m*; **in** ~ apaixonado

lovely (*lav*-li) *adj* lindo, encantador, delicioso

lover (*la*-vă) *n* amante *m*

love-story (*lav*-çtóó-ri) *n* história de amor

low (loᵁ) *adj* baixo; deprimido; ~ **tide** baixa-mar *f*

lower (*lo*ᵁ-ă) *v* abaixar; baixar; *adj* inferior

lowlands (*lo*ᵁ-lănndz) *pl* terras baixas

loyal (*loi*-ăl) *adj* leal

lubricate (*luu*-bri-keit) *v* *olear, untar, lubrificar

lubrication (luu-bri-*kei*-chănn) *n* lubrificação *f*; ~ **oil** óleo de lubrificação; ~ **system** sistema de lubrificação

luck (lak) *n* sorte *f*; acaso *m*; **bad** ~ azar *m*

lucky (*la*-ki) *adj* afortunado; ~ **charm** talismã *m*

ludicrous (*luu*-di-krăç) *adj* ridículo, grotesco

luggage (*la*-ghidj) *n* bagagem *f*; **hand** ~ bagagem de mão; **left** ~ **office** depósito de bagagens; ~ **rack** rede da bagagem, bagageira *f*; ~ **van** furgão *m*

lukewarm (*luuk*-ᵁóómm) *adj* morno

lumbago (lamm-*bei*-ghoᵁ) *n* lumbago *m*

luminous (*luu*-mi-năç) *adj* luminoso

lump (lammp) *n* bocado *m*, nó *m*, grumo *m*; alto *m*; ~ **of sugar** torrão de açúcar; ~ **sum** soma global

lumpy (*lamm*-pi) *adj* grumoso

lunacy (*luu*-nă-çi) *n* loucura *f*

lunatic (*luu*-nă-tik) *adj* louco

lunch (lanntch) *n* almoço *m*

luncheon (*lann*-tchănn) *n* almoço *m*

lung (lanng) *n* pulmão *m*

lust (laçt) *n* volúpia *f*

luxurious (lagh-*ju*ᵃ-ri-ăç) *adj* luxuoso

luxury (*lak*-chă-ri) *n* luxo *m*

M

machine (mă-*chiinn*) *n* máquina *f*

machinery (mă-*chii*-nă-ri) *n* maquinaria *f*; mecanismo *m*

mackerel (*mæ*-krăl) *n* (*pl* ~) cavala *f*

mackintosh (*mæ*-kinn-tóch) *n* gabardina f: capa de chuva Br

mad (mæd) adj insensato, maluco, demente; raivoso

madam (mæ-dămm) n senhora f

madness (mæd-năç) n demência f

magazine (mæ-ghă-ziinn) n revista f

magic (mæ-djik) n magia f; adj mágico

magician (mă-dji-chănn) n prestidigitador m

magistrate (mæ-dji-çtreit) n magistrado m

magnetic (mægh-né-tik) adj magnético

magneto (mægh-nii-to^u) n (pl ~s) magneto m

magnificent (mægh-ni-fi-cănnt) adj magnífico; grandioso, esplêndido

magpie (mægh-pai) n pega f

maid (meid) n empregada f

maiden name (mei-dănn neimm) apelido de solteira

mail (meil) n correio m; v *pôr no correio

mailbox (meil-bókç) nAm caixa do correio

main (meinn) adj principal; maior; ~ **deck** convés principal; ~ **line** linha principal; ~ **road** estrada principal; ~ **street** rua principal

mainland (meinn-lănnd) n terra firme

mainly (meinn-li) adv principalmente

mains (meinnz) pl sector principal

maintain (meinn-teinn) v *manter, conservar

maintenance (meinn-tă-nănnç) n manutenção f

maize (meiz) n milho m

major (mei-djă) adj grande; maior; n major m

majority (mă-djó-ră-ti) n maioria f; maioridade f

*make (meik) v *fazer; ganhar; *conseguir; ~ **do with** arranjar-se

com; ~ **good** compensar; ~ **up** *compor

make-up (mei-kap) n maquilhagem f

malaria (mă-lé^a-ri-ă) n malária f

Malay (mă-lei) n malaio m

Malaysia (mă-lei-zi-ă) Malásia f

Malaysian (mă-lei-zi-ănn) adj malaio

male (meil) adj masculino

malicious (mă-li-chăç) adj malicioso

malignant (mă-ligh-nănnt) adj maligno

mallet (mæ-lit) n maço m

malnutrition (mæl-n^{i}u-tri-chănn) n subalimentação f

mammal (mæ-măl) n mamífero m

mammoth (mæ-măθ) n mamute m

man (mænn) n (pl men) homem m; **men's room** lavabos dos homens

manage (mæ-nidj) v administrar; *ter êxito, *conseguir

manageable (mæ-ni-djă-băl) adj manejável

management (mæ-nidj-mănnt) n direcção f; gestão f

manager (mæ-ni-djă) n gerente m, chefe m, director m

mandarin (mænn-dă-rinn) n tangerina f

mandate (mænn-deit) n mandato m

manger (meinn-djă) n manjedoura f

manicure (mæ-ni-k^{i}u^a) n manicura f; v arranjar as unhas

mankind (mænn-kainnd) n humanidade f

mannequin (mæ-nă-kinn) n manequim m

manner (mæ-nă) n maneira f, modo m; **manners** maneiras fpl

man-of-war (mæ-năv-^{u}óó) n navio de guerra

manor-house (mæ-nă-hauç) n solar m

mansion (mænn-chănn) n palacete m

manual (mæ-n^{i}u-ăl) adj manual

manufacture (mæ-n^{i}u-fæk-tchă) v fa-

bricar
manufacturer (mæ-n'u-*fæk*-tchă-ră) *n* fabricante *m*

manure (mă-n'u*ă*) *n* estrume *m*

manuscript (*mæ*-n'u-çkript) *n* manuscrito *m*

many (*mé*-ni) *adj* muitos

map (mæp) *n* mapa *m*; planta *f*

maple (*mei*-păl) *n* ácer *m*

marble (*maa*-băl) *n* mármore *m*; berlinde *m*

March (maatch) Março

march (maatch) *v* marchar; *n* marcha *f*

mare (mé*ă*) *n* égua *f*

margarine (maa-djă-*riinn*) *n* margarina *f*

margin (*maa*-djinn) *n* margem *f*

maritime (*mæ*-ri-taimm) *adj* marítimo

mark (maak) *v* marcar; caracterizar; *n* marca *f*; nota *f*; alvo *m*

market (*maa*-kit) *n* mercado *m*

market-place (*maa*-kit-pleiç) *n* praça do mercado

marmalade (*maa*-mă-leid) *n* doce de laranja

marriage (*mæ*-ridj) *n* casamento *m*

marrow (*mæ*-ro*u*) *n* medula *f*

marry (*mæ*-ri) *v* casar-se, desposar; **married couple** casal *m*

marsh (maach) *n* pântano *m*

marshy (*maa*-chi) *adj* pantanoso

martyr (*maa*-tă) *n* mártir *m*

marvel (*maa*-văl) *n* maravilha *f*; *v* maravilhar-se

marvellous (*maa*-vă-lăç) *adj* maravilhoso

mascara (mæ-*çkaa*-ră) *n* rímel *m*

masculine (*mæ*-çk'u-linn) *adj* masculino

mash (mæch) *v* esmagar

mask (maaçk) *n* máscara *f*

Mass (mæç) *n* missa *f*

mass (mæç) *n* massa *f*; ~ **produc-**

tion produção em série

massage (*mæ*-çaaj) *n* massagem *f*; *v* massajar

masseur (mæ-*çăă*) *n* massagista *m*

massive (*mæ*-çiv) *adj* maciço

mast (maaçt) *n* mastro *m*

master (*maa*-çtă) *n* mestre *m*; patrão *m*; professor *m*; *v* dominar

masterpiece (*maa*-çtă-piiç) *n* obra-prima *f*

mat (mæt) *n* tapete *m*; *adj* baço, mate

match (mætch) *n* fósforo *m*; desafio *m*; *v* *condizer com

match-box (*mætch*-bókç) *n* caixa de fósforos

material (mă-*ti*ă-ri-ăl) *n* material *m*; tecido *m*; *adj* material

mathematical (mæ-θă-*mæ*-ti-kăl) *adj* matemático

mathematics (mæ-θă-*mæ*-tikç) *n* matemática *f*

matrimonial (mæ-tri-*mo*u-ni-ăl) *adj* matrimonial

matrimony (*mæ*-tri-mă-ni) *n* matrimónio *m*

matter (*mæ*-tă) *n* matéria *f*; assunto *m*, questão *f*; *v* *ter importância; **as a ~ of fact** de facto, efectivamente

matter-of-fact (mæ-tă-răv-*fækt*) *adj* realista

mattress (*mæ*-trăç) *n* colchão *m*

mature (mă-*t'u*ă) *adj* maduro

maturity (mă-*t'u*ă-ră-ti) *n* maturidade *f*

mausoleum (móó-çă-*lii*-ămm) *n* mausoléu *m*

mauve (mo*u*v) *adj* lilás

May (mei) Maio

*may (mei) *v* *poder

maybe (*mei*-bii) *adv* talvez

mayor (mé*ă*) *n* presidente da Câmara

maze (meiz) *n* labirinto *m*

me (mii) *pron* me; mim

meadow (mé-do^u) *n* prado *m*

meal (miil) *n* refeição *f*

mean (miinn) *adj* mesquinho; *n* média *f*

*mean (miinn) *v* significar; *querer dizer

meaning (mii-ninng) *n* significado *m*

meaningless (mii-ninng-lặç) *adj* sem sentido

means (miinnz) *n* meio *m*; by no ~ em caso algum, de modo nenhum

in the meantime (inn ða miinn-taimm) entretanto

meanwhile (miinn-^{u}ail) *adv* entretanto

measles (mii-zälz) *n* sarampo *m*

measure (mé-jã) *v* *medir; *n* medida *f*

meat (miit) *n* carne *f*

mechanic (mi-kæ-nik) *n* mecânico *m*

mechanical (mi-kæ-ni-kǎl) *adj* mecânico

mechanism (mé-kǎ-ni-zǎmm) *n* mecanismo *m*

medal (mé-dǎl) *n* medalha *f*

mediaeval (mé-di-ii-vǎl) *adj* medieval

mediate (mii-di-eit) *v* *servir de intermediário

mediator (mii-di-ei-tǎ) *n* intermediário *m*

medical (mé-di-kǎl) *adj* médico

medicine (méd-çinn) *n* medicamento *m*; medicina *f*

meditate (mé-di-teit) *v* meditar

Mediterranean (mé-di-tǎ-rei-ni-ǎnn) Mediterrâneo *m*

medium (mii-di-ǎmm) *adj* médio, mediano

*meet (miit) *v* encontrar

meeting (mii-tinng) *n* reunião *f*, assembleia *f*

meeting-place (mii-tinng-pleiç) *n* ponto de encontro

melancholy (mé-lǎnng-kǎ-li) *n* melancolia *f*

mellow (mé-lo^u) *adj* macio

melodrama (mé-lǎ-draa-mǎ) *n* melodrama *m*

melody (mé-lǎ-di) *n* melodia *f*

melon (mé-lǎnn) *n* melão *m*

melt (mélt) *v* derreter

member (mémm-bǎ) *n* membro *m*; Member of Parliament deputado *m*

membership (mémm-bǎ-chip) *n* filiação *f*

memo (mé-mo^u) *n* (pl ~s) memorando *m*

memorable (mé-mǎ-rǎ-bǎl) *adj* memorável

memorial (mǎ-móó-ri-ǎl) *n* memorial *m*

memorize (mé-mǎ-raiz) *v* decorar

memory (mé-mǎ-ri) *n* memória *f*, recordação *f*

mend (ménnd) *v* remendar, reparar

menstruation (ménn-çtru-ei-chǎnn) *n* menstruação *f*

mental (ménn-tǎl) *adj* mental

mention (ménn-chǎnn) *v* mencionar, *nomear; *n* menção *f*

menu (mé-n^{i}uu) *n* ementa *f*; cardápio *mBr*

merchandise (mǎǎ-tchǎnn-daiz) *n* mercadoria *f*

merchant (mǎǎ-tchǎnnt) *n* comerciante *m*

merciful (mǎǎ-çi-fǎl) *adj* misericordioso

mercury (mǎǎ-k^{i}u-rı) *n* mercúrio *m*

mercy (mǎǎ-çi) *n* clemência *f*, misericórdia *f*

mere (mi^ǎ) *adj* simples

merely (mi^ǎ-li) *adv* somente

merit (mé-rit) *v* merecer; *n* mérito *m*

mermaid (mǎǎ-meid) *n* sereia *f*

merry (*mé*-ri) *adj* alegre

merry-go-round (*mé*-ri-gho^u-raunnd) *n* carrossel *m*

mesh (méch) *n* malha *f*

mess (méç) *n* trapalhada *f*, desordem *f*; ~ **up** estragar

message (*mé*-çidj) *n* mensagem *f*, recado *m*

messenger (*mé*-çinn-djä) *n* mensageiro *m*

metal (*mé*-täl) *n* metal *m*; metálico

meter (*mii*-tä) *n* contador *m*; medidor *mBr*

method (*mé*-θäd) *n* método *m*; ordem *f*

methodical (mä-*θó*-di-käl) *adj* metódico

methylated spirits (*mé*-θä-lei-tid çpi-ritç) álcool desnaturado

metre (*mii*-tä) *n* metro *m*

metric (*mé*-trik) *adj* métrico

Mexican (*mék*-çi-känn) *adj* mexicano

Mexico (*mék*-çi-ko^u) México *m*

mezzanine (*mé*-zä-niinn) *n* sobreloja *f*

microphone (*mai*-krä-fo^unn) *n* microfone *m*

midday (*mid*-dei) *n* meio-dia *m*

middle (*mi*-däl) *n* meio *m*; *adj* médio; **Middle Ages** Idade Média; ~ **class** classe média; **middle-class** *adj* burguês

midnight (*mid*-nait) *n* meia-noite *f*

midst (midçt) *n* meio *m*

midsummer (*mid*-ça-mä) *n* pleno Verão

midwife (*mid*-^uaif) *n* (pl -wives) parteira *f*

might (mait) *n* poder *m*

*might (mait) *v* *poder

mighty (*mai*-ti) *adj* poderoso

migraine (*mi*-ghreinn) *n* enxaqueca *f*

mild (maild) *adj* suave

mildew (*mil*-dⁱu) *n* bolor *m*

mile (mail) *n* milha *f*

milestone (*mail*-çto^unn) *n* marco miliário

milieu (*mii*-lⁱää) *n* meio ambiente

military (*mi*-li-tä-ri) *adj* militar; ~ **force** força armada

milk (milk) *n* leite *m*

milkman (*milk*-männ) *n* (pl -men) leiteiro *m*

milk-shake (*milk*-cheik) *n* batido de leite

milky (*mil*-ki) *adj* leitoso

mill (mil) *n* moinho *m*; fábrica *f*

miller (*mi*-lä) *n* moleiro *m*

milliner (*mi*-li-nä) *n* chapeleira de senhoras

millionaire (mil-ⁱä-*né^ä*) *n* milionário *m*

mince (minnç) *v* picar

mind (mainnd) *n* mente *f*; *v* *fazer objecção a; prestar atenção a, importar-se com, prestar atenção

mine (mainn) *n* mina *f*

miner (*mai*-nä) *n* mineiro *m*

mineral (*mi*-nä-räl) *n* mineral *m*; ~ **water** água mineral

miniature (*minn*-ⁱä-tchä) *n* miniatura *f*

minimum (*mi*-ni-mämm) *n* mínimo *m*

mining (*mai*-ninng) *n* exploração mineira

minister (*mi*-ni-çtä) *n* ministro *m*; pastor *m*; **Prime Minister** primeiro-ministro *m*

ministry (*mi*-ni-çtri) *n* ministério *m*

mink (minngk) *n* vison *m*

minor (*mai*-nä) *adj* menor, pequeno; *n* menor *m*

minority (mai-*nó*-rä-ti) *n* minoria *f*; menoridade *f*

mint (minnt) *n* hortelã *f*

minus (*mai*-näç) *prep* menos

minute¹ (*mi*-nit) *n* minuto *m*; **minutes** acta *f*

minute² (mai-nⁱ*uut*) *adj* minúsculo

miracle (*mi*-ră-kăl) *n* milagre *m*

miraculous (mi-ræ-k[u]-lăç) *adj* milagroso

mirror (*mi*-ră) *n* espelho *m*

misbehave (miç-bi-*heiv*) *v* portar-se mal

miscarriage (miç-kæ-ridj) *n* aborto *m*

miscellaneous (mi-çă-*lei*-ni-ăç) *adj* misturado

mischief (*miç*-tchif) *n* diabrura *f*; maldade *f*, malícia *f*, dano *m*

mischievous (*miç*-tchi-văç) *adj* maroto

miserable (*mi*-ză-ră-băl) *adj* miserável; triste

misery (*mi*-ză-ri) *n* miséria *f*, infelicidade *f*

misfortune (miç-*fóó*-tchénn) *n* infortúnio *m*, infelicidade *f*

*mislay (miç-*lei*) *v* desencaminhar, extraviar

misplaced (miç-*pleict*) *adj* inoportuno; despropositado

mispronounce (miç-pră-*naunnç*) *v* pronunciar mal

miss[1] (miç) *n* menina

miss[2] (miç) *v* *perder

missing (*mi*-çinng) *adj* perdido; ~ person desaparecido *m*

mist (miçt) *n* neblina *f*, nevoeiro *m*

mistake (mi-*çteik*) *n* engano *m*, erro *m*, equívoco *m*

*mistake (mi-*çteik*) *v* confundir

mistaken (mi-*çtei*-kănn) *adj* errado; *be ~ enganar-se

mister (*mi*-çtă) senhor

mistress (*mi*-çtrăç) *n* dona de casa; patroa *f*; amante *f*

mistrust (miç-*traçt*) *v* desconfiar

misty (*mi*-çti) *adj* enevoado

*misunderstand (mi-çann-dă-*çtænnd*) *v* perceber mal, compreender mal

misunderstanding (mi-çann-dă-*çtænn*-dinng) *n* mal-entendido *m*

misuse (miç-[i]*uuç*) *n* abuso *m*

mittens (*mi*-tănnz) *pl* luvas sem dedos

mix (mikç) *v* misturar; ~ with frequentar

mixed (mikçt) *adj* misturado

mixer (*mik*-çă) *n* batedeira *f*

mixture (*mikç*-tchă) *n* mistura *f*

moan (mo[u]nn) *v* gemer; queixar-se

moat (mo[u]t) *n* fosso *m*

mobile (*mo*[u]-bail) *adj* móvel

mock (mók) *v* troçar

mockery (mó-kă-ri) *n* troça *f*

model (mó-dăl) *n* modelo *m*; manequim *m*; *v* modelar, moldar

moderate (mó-dă-răt) *adj* moderado; medíocre

modern (mó-dănn) *adj* moderno

modest (mó-diçt) *adj* modesto

modesty (mó-di-çti) *n* modéstia *f*

modify (mó-di-fai) *v* modificar

mohair (mo[u]-hé[ǎ]) *n* mohair *m*

moist (moiçt) *adj* húmido, molhado

moisten (moi-çănn) *v* humedecer

moisture (moiç-tchă) *n* humidade *f*; moisturizing cream creme hidratante

molar (mo[u]-lă) *n* molar *m*

moment (mo[u]-mănnt) *n* momento *m*, instante *m*

momentary (mo[u]-mănn-tă-ri) *adj* momentâneo

monarch (mó-năk) *n* monarca *m*

monarchy (mó-nă-ki) *n* monarquia *f*

monastery (mó-nă-çtri) *n* mosteiro *m*

Monday (mann-di) segunda-feira *f*

monetary (ma-ni-tă-ri) *adj* monetário; ~ unit unidade monetária

money (ma-ni) *n* dinheiro *m*; ~ exchange casa de câmbio; ~ order ordem postal

monk (manngk) *n* monge *m*

monkey (manng-ki) *n* macaco *m*

monologue (mó-nó-lógh) *n* monólogo *m*

monopoly (mǎ-*nó*-pǎ-li) *n* monopólio *m*

monotonous (mǎ-*nó*-tǎ-nǎç) *adj* monótono

month (mannθ) *n* mês *m*

monthly (*mann*θ-li) *adj* mensal; ~ magazine revista mensal

monument (*mó*-n¹u-mǎnnt) *n* monumento *m*

mood (muud) *n* humor *m*, disposição *f*

moon (muunn) *n* lua *f*

moonlight (*muunn*-lait) *n* luar *m*

moor (muǎ) *n* charneca *f*, urzal *m*

moose (muuç) *n* (pl ~, ~s) alce *m*

moped (*mó*ᵁ-péd) *n* bicicleta a motor

moral (*mó*-rǎl) *n* moral *f*; *adj* moral; morals costumes mpl

morality (mǎ-*ræ*-lǎ-ti) *n* moralidade *f*

more (móó) *adj* mais; once ~ uma vez mais

moreover (móó-*ro*ᵁ-vǎ) *adv* demais a mais, além disso

morning (*móó*-ninng) *n* manhã *f*; ~ paper jornal da manhã

Moroccan (mǎ-*ró*-kǎnn) *adj* marroquino

Morocco (mǎ-*ró*-koᵁ) Marrocos *m*

morphia (*móó*-fi-ǎ) *n* morfina *f*

morphine (*móó*-fiinn) *n* morfina *f*

morsel (*móó*-çǎl) *n* bocado *m*

mortal (*móó*-tǎl) *adj* mortal, fatal

mortgage (*móó*-ghidj) *n* hipoteca *f*

mosaic (mǎ-*zei*-ik) *n* mosaico *m*

mosque (móçk) *n* mesquita *f*

mosquito (mǎ-*çkii*-toᵁ) *n* (pl ~es) mosquito *m*

mosquito-net (mǎ-*çkii*-toᵁ-nét) *n* mosquiteiro *m*

moss (móç) *n* musgo *m*

most (moᵁçt) *adj* mais; at ~ no máximo, quando muito; ~ of all sobretudo

mostly (*mo*ᵁçt-li) *adv* principalmente

motel (moᵁ-*tél*) *n* motel *m*

moth (móθ) *n* traça *f*

mother (*ma*-ðǎ) *n* mãe *f*; ~ tongue língua materna

mother-in-law (*ma*-ðǎ-rinn-lóó) *n* (pl mothers-) sogra *f*

mother-of-pearl (ma-ðǎ-rǎv-*pǎǎl*) *n* madre-pérola *f*

motion (*mo*ᵁ-chǎnn) *n* movimento *m*; moção *f*

motive (*mo*ᵁ-tiv) *n* motivo *m*

motor (*mo*ᵁ-tǎ) *n* motor *m*; *v* viajar de automóvel; starter ~ motor de arranque

motorbike (*mo*ᵁ-tǎ-baik) *n*Am bicicleta a motor

motor-boat (*mo*ᵁ-tǎ-boᵁt) *n* barco a motor

motor-car (*mo*ᵁ-tǎ-kaa) *n* automóvel *m*

motor-cycle (*mo*ᵁ-tǎ-çai-kǎl) *n* motocicleta *f*

motoring (*mo*ᵁ-tǎ-rinng) *n* automobilismo *m*

motorist (*mo*ᵁ-tǎ-riçt) *n* automobilista *m*

motorway (*mo*ᵁ-tǎ-ᵁei) *n* auto-estrada *f*

motto (*mó*-toᵁ) *n* (pl ~es, ~s) divisa *f*

mouldy (*mo*ᵁl-di) *adj* bolorento

mound (maunnd) *n* montículo *m*

mount (maunnt) *v* *subir; *n* monte *m*

mountain (*maunn*-tinn) *n* montanha *f*; ~ pass desfiladeiro *m*; ~ range cordilheira *f*

mountaineering (maunn-ti-*ni*ǎ-rinng) *n* alpinismo *m*

mountainous (*maunn*-ti-nǎç) *adj* montanhoso

mourning (*móó*-ninng) *n* luto *m*

mouse (mauç) *n* (pl mice) rato *m*

moustache (mǎ-*çtaach*) *n* bigode *m*

mouth (mauθ) *n* boca *f*, focinho *m*;

foz f

mouthwash (mau*θ*-ᵘóch) *n* líquido dentífrico

movable (muu-vă-băl) *adj* móvel

move (muuv) *v* mover; deslocar; mexer-se; mudar-se; comover; *n* jogada f, passo m; mudança f

movement (muuv-mănnt) *n* movimento m

movie (muu-vi) *n* filme m

much (match) *adj* muito; **as ~** tanto

muck (mak) *n* porcaria f

mud (mad) *n* lama f

muddle (ma-dăl) *n* confusão f, trapalhada f; *v* *fazer trapalhada

muddy (ma-di) *adj* lamacento

mud-guard (mad-ghaad) *n* guarda-lama m

mug (magh) *n* caneca f

mulberry (mal-bă-ri) *n* amora f

mule (mⁱuul) *n* macho m, mulo m

mullet (ma-lit) *n* tainha f

multiplication (mal-ti-pli-kei-chănn) *n* multiplicação f

multiply (mal-ti-plai) *v* multiplicar

mumps (mammpç) *n* papeira f

municipal (mⁱuu-ni-çi-păl) *adj* municipal

municipality (mⁱuu-ni-çi-pæ-lă-ti) *n* municipalidade f

murder (măă-dă) *n* homicídio m; *v* assassinar

murderer (măă-dă-ră) *n* assassino m

muscle (ma-çăl) *n* músculo m

muscular (ma-çkⁱu-lă) *adj* musculoso

museum (mⁱuu-zii-ămm) *n* museu m

mushroom (mach-ruumm) *n* cogumelo m

music (mⁱuu-zik) *n* música f; **~ academy** conservatório m

musical (mⁱuu-zi-kăl) *adj* musical; *n* comédia musical

music-hall (mⁱuu-zik-hóól) *n* teatro de variedades

musician (mⁱuu-zi-chănn) *n* músico m

muslin (maz-linn) *n* musselina f

mussel (ma-çăl) *n* mexilhão m

***must** (maçt) *v* *ter de, dever

mustard (ma-çtăd) *n* mostarda f

mute (mⁱuut) *adj* mudo

mutiny (mⁱuu-ti-ni) *n* motim m

mutton (ma-tănn) *n* carne de carneiro

mutual (mⁱuu-tchu-ăl) *adj* mútuo, recíproco

my (mai) *adj* meu

myself (mai-çélf) *pron* me; eu mesmo

mysterious (mi-çtiᵃ-ri-ăç) *adj* misterioso

mystery (mi-çtă-ri) *n* mistério m, enigma m

myth (miθ) *n* mito m

N

nail (neil) *n* unha f; prego m

nailbrush (neil-brach) *n* escova de unhas

nail-file (neil-fail) *n* lima de unhas

nail-polish (neil-pó-lich) *n* verniz de unhas

nail-scissors (neil-çi-zăz) *pl* tesoura de unhas

naïve (naa-iiv) *adj* ingénuo

naked (nei-kid) *adj* nu, despido

name (neimm) *n* nome m; *v* chamar, *nomear; **in the ~ of** em nome de

namely (neim-li) *adv* a saber

nap (næp) *n* soneca f

napkin (næp-kinn) *n* guardanapo m

nappy (næ-pi) *n* fralda f

narcosis (naa-koᵘ-çiç) *n* (pl -ses) narcose f

narcotic (naa-kó-tik) *n* narcótico m

narrow (næ-roᵘ) *adj* apertado, estreito

narrow-minded (næ-roᵘ-mainn-did)

adj tacanho

nasty (*naa*-çti) *adj* antipático, desagradável

nation (*nei*-chänn) *n* povo *m*

national (*næ*-chä-näl) *adj* nacional; do
estado; ~ **anthem** hino nacional;
~ **dress** traje nacional; ~ **park**
parque nacional

nationality (næ-chä-*næ*-lä-ti) *n* nacionalidade *f*

nationalize (*næ*-chä-nä-laiz) *v* nacionalizar

native (*nei*-tiv) *n* indígena *m; adj* nativo *m;* ~ **country** pátria *f*, país
natal; ~ **language** língua materna

natural (*næ*-tchä-räl) *adj* natural; nato

naturally (*næ*-tchä-rä-li) *adv* naturalmente, certamente

nature (*nei*-tchä) *n* natureza *f*

naughty (*nóó*-ti) *adj* travesso, maroto

nausea (*nóó*-çi-ä) *n* náusea *f*

naval (*nei*-väl) *adj* naval

navel (*nei*-väl) *n* umbigo *m*

navigable (*næ*-vi-ghä-bäl) *adj* navegável

navigate (*næ*-vi-gheit) *v* navegar

navigation (næ-vi-*ghei*-chänn) *n* navegação *f*

navy (*nei*-vi) *n* marinha *f*

near (ni^{ä}) *prep* perto de; *adj* vizinho,
chegado

nearby (ni^{ä}-bai) *adj* próximo

nearly (*nii^{ä}*-li) *adv* quase

neat (niit) *adj* asseado; puro

necessary (*né*-çä-çä-ri) *adj* necessário

necessity (nä-*cé*-çä-ti) *n* necessidade
f

neck (nék) *n* pescoço *m;* **nape of the**
~ **nuca** *f*

necklace (*nék*-läç) *n* colar *m*

necktie (*nék*-tai) *n* gravata *f*

need (niid) *v* necessitar, precisar; *n*
necessidade *f*, precisão *f;* ~ **to** *ter

de

needle (*nii*-däl) *n* agulha *f*

needlework (*nii*-däl-^{u}ääk) *n* costura *f*

negative (*né*-ghä-tiv) *adj* negativo; *n*
negativo *m*

neglect (ni-*ghlékt*) *v* descuidar; *n* negligência *f*

neglectful (ni-*ghlékt*-fäl) *adj* negligente

negotiate (ni-*ghou*-chi-eit) *v* *negociar

negotiation (ni-gho^u-chi-*ei*-chänn) *n*
negociação *f*

Negro (*nii*-ghro^u) *n* (pl ~es) negro *m*

neighbour (*nei*-bä) *n* vizinho *m*

neighbourhood (*nei*-bä-hud) *n* vizinhança *f*

neighbouring (*nei*-bä-rinng) *adj*
contíguo, vizinho

neither (*nai*-ðä) *pron* nem um nem
outro; **neither ... nor** nem ... nem

neon (*nii*-ónn) *n* néon *m*

nephew (*né*-f^{u}uu) *n* sobrinho *m*

nerve (nääv) *n* nervo *m;* audácia *f*

nervous (*nää*-väç) *adj* nervoso

nest (néçt) *n* ninho *m*

net (nét) *n* rede *f; adj* líquido

the Netherlands (*né*-ðä-länndz) Os
Países Baixos

network (*nét*-^{u}ääk) *n* rede *f*

neuralgia (n^{i}u^ä-*ræl*-djä) *n* nevralgia *f*

neurosis (n^{i}u^ä-*ro^u*-çiç) *n* neurose *f*

neuter (*n^{i}uu*-tä) *adj* neutro

neutral (*n^{i}uu*-träl) *adj* neutral

never (*né*-vä) *adv* nunca

nevertheless (né-vä-ðä-*léç*) *adv* não
obstante

new (n^{i}uu) *adj* novo; **New Year** Ano
Novo

news (n^{i}uuz) *n* notícias, notícia *f;* no-
ticiário *m*

newsagent (*n^{i}uu*-zei-djännt) *n* vendedor de jornais

newspaper (*n^{i}uuz*-pei-pä) *n* jornal *m*

newsstand (*n^{i}uuz*-çtænnd) *n* quiosque

de jornais

New Zealand (n'uu zii-lãnnd) Nova Zelândia

next (nékçt) *adj* próximo, seguinte; ~ to junto a

next-door (nékçt-*dóó*) *adv* ao lado

nice (naiç) *adj* bonito, agradável; bom; simpático

nickel (*ni*-kãl) *n* níquel *m*

nickname (*nik*-neimm) *n* alcunha *f*; apelido *mBr*

nicotine (*ni*-kã-tiinn) *n* nicotina *f*

niece (niiç) *n* sobrinha *f*

Nigeria (nai-*dji^ã*-ri-ã) Nigéria *f*

Nigerian (nai-*dji^ã*-ri-ãnn) *adj* nigeriano

night (nait) *n* noite *f*; by ~ de noite; ~ **flight** voo nocturno; ~ **rate** tarifa nocturna; ~ **train** comboio nocturno

nightclub (*nait*-klab) *n* boate *f*

night-cream (*nait*-kriimm) *n* creme de noite

nightdress (*nait*-dréç) *n* camisa de dormir; camisola *fBr*

nightingale (*nai*-tinng-gheil) *n* rouxinol *m*

nightly (*nait*-li) *adj* nocturno

nil (nil) nada

nine (nainn) *num* nove

nineteen (nainn-*tiinn*) *num* dezanove

nineteenth (nainn-*tiinnθ*) *num* décimo nono

ninety (*nainn*-ti) *num* noventa

ninth (nainnθ) *num* nono

nitrogen (*nai*-trã-djãnn) *n* azoto *m*

no (no^u) não; *adj* nenhum; ~ **one** ninguém

nobility (no^u-*bi*-lã-ti) *n* nobreza *f*

noble (*no^u*-bãl) *adj* nobre

nobody (*no^u*-bó-di) *pron* ninguém

nod (nód) *n* inclinação de cabeça; *v* inclinar a cabeça

noise (noiz) *n* ruído *m*, barulho *m*

noisy (*noi*-zi) *adj* ruidoso

nominal (*nó*-mi-nãl) *adj* nominal

nominate (*nó*-mi-neit) *v* *nomear

nomination (nó-mi-*nei*-chãnn) *n* nomeação *f*

none (nann) *pron* nenhum

nonsense (*nónn*-çãnnç) *n* disparate *m*

noon (nuunn) *n* meio-dia *m*

normal (*nóó*-mãl) *adj* normal

north (nóóθ) *n* norte *m*; *adj* setentrional; **North Pole** pólo norte

north-east (nóóθ-*iiçt*) *n* nordeste *m*

northerly (*nóó*-ðã-li) *adj* do norte

northern (*nóó*-ðãnn) *adj* nórdico

north-west (nóóθ-*u^e*çt) *n* noroeste *m*

Norway (*nóó*-^uei) Noruega *f*

Norwegian (nóó-^u*ii*-djãnn) *adj* norueguês

nose (no^uz) *n* nariz *m*

nosebleed (*no^u*z-bliid) *n* hemorragia nasal

nostril (*nó*-çtril) *n* narina *f*

not (nót) *adv* não

notary (*no^u*-tã-ri) *n* notário *m*

note (no^ut) *n* nota *f*, apontamento *m*; *v* anotar; constatar, observar

notebook (*no^u*t-buk) *n* agenda *f*

noted (*no^u*-tid) *adj* ilustre

notepaper (*no^u*t-pei-pã) *n* papel para escrever, papel de carta

nothing (*na*-θinng) *n* nada *m*

notice (*no^u*-tiç) *v* notar, reparar em; *ver; *n* notícia *f*, aviso *m*; atenção *f*

noticeable (*no^u*-ti-çã-bãl) *adj* perceptível; notável

notify (*no^u*-ti-fai) *v* notificar, participar; avisar

notion (*no^u*-chãnn) *n* noção *f*

notorious (no^u-*tóó*-ri-ãç) *adj* notório

nougat (*nuu*-ghaa) *n* nogado *m*

nought (nóót) *n* zero *m*

noun (naunn) *n* substantivo *m*

nourishing (*na*-ri-chinng) *adj* alimentício

novel (*nó*-vãl) *n* romance *m*

novelist (*nó-vă-lĭçt*) *n* romancista *m*
November (*nou-vémm-bă*) Novembro
now (nau) *adv* agora; actualmente;
~ **and then** de tempos a tempos
nowadays (*nau-ă-deiz*) *adv* hoje em
dia
nowhere (*no^u-^uéa̍*) *adv* em parte alguma
nozzle (*nó-zăl*) *n* bocal *m*
nuance (*n^iuu-ăç*) *n* cambiante *m;*
nuance *f*
nuclear (*n^iuu-kli-ă*) *adj* nuclear; ~
energy energia nuclear
nucleus (*n^iuu-kli-ăç*) *n* núcleo *m*
nude (*n^iuud*) *adj* nu; *n* nu *m*
nuisance (*n^iuu-çănnç*) *n* incómodo *m*
numb (namm) *adj* entorpecido
number (*namm-bă*) *n* número *m*, algarismo *m;* quantidade *f*
numeral (*n^iuu-mă-răl*) *n* numeral *m*
numerous (*n^iuu-mă-răç*) *adj* numeroso
nun (nann) *n* freira *f*
nunnery (*na-nă-ri*) *n* convento *m*
nurse (nää̍ç) *n* enfermeira *f;* ama-seca *f;* v tratar de; amamentar
nursery (*nää̍-çă-ri*) *n* quarto das
crianças; creche *f;* viveiro *m*
nut (nat) *n* noz *f;* porca *f*
nutcrackers (*nat-kræ-kăz*) *pl* quebra-nozes *m*
nutmeg (*nat-mégh*) *n* noz moscada
nutritious (*n^iuu-tri-*chăç) *adj* nutritivo
nutshell (*nat-chél*) *n* casca de noz
nylon (*nai-lónn*) *n* nylon *m*

O

oak (o^uk) *n* carvalho *m*
oar (óó) *n* remo *m*
oasis (*o^u-ei-*çiç) *n* (pl oases) oásis *m*
oath (o^u<) *n* juramento *m*

oats (o^utç) *pl* aveia *f*
obedience (*ă-bii-di-*ănnç) *n* obediência
f
obedient (*ă-bii-*di-ănnt) *adj* obediente
obey (*ă-bei*) *v* obedecer
object[1] (*ób-*djikt) *n* objecto *m*
object[2] (*ăb-*djékt) *v* objectar, *opor;
~ to *opor-se a
objection (*ăb-djék-*chănn) *n* objecção *f*
objective (*ăb-djék-*tiv) *adj* objectivo; *n*
objectivo *m*
obligatory (*ă-bli-ghă-tă-*ri) *adj* obrigatório
oblige (*ă-*blaidj) *v* obrigar; *be obliged to *ser obrigado a; *ter de
obliging (*ă-blai-*djinng) *adj* solícito
oblong (*ób-*lónn) *adj* oblongo; *n* rectângulo *m*
obscene (*ăb-*çiinn) *adj* obsceno
obscure (*ăb-çk^iu^a̍*) *adj* obscuro, confuso, vago, escuro
observation (*ób-ză-vei-*chănn) *n* observação *f*
observatory (*ăb-zăă̍-vă-*tri) *n* observatório *m*
observe (*ăb-zăăv*) *v* observar
obsession (*ăb-çé-*chănn) *n* obsessão *f*
obstacle (*ób-*çtă-kăl) *n* obstáculo *m*
obstinate (*ób-*çti-năt) *adj* obstinado;
teimoso
obtain (*ăb-teinn*) *v* *conseguir, *obter
obvious (*ób-*vi-ăç) *adj* óbvio
occasion (*ă-kei-*jănn) *n* ocasião *f;* motivo *m*
occasionally (*ă-kei-*jă-nă-li) *adv* de vez
em quando, ocasionalmente
occupant (*ó-k^iu-*pănnt) *n* morador *m*
occupation (*ó-k^iu-pei-*chănn) *n* ocupação *f*
occupy (*ó-k^iu-*pai) *v* ocupar
occur (*ă-kăă̍*) *v* suceder, acontecer
occurrence (*ă-ka-*rănnç) *n* ocorrência
f
ocean (*o^u-*chănn) *n* oceano *m*

October (ók-*to*ᵁ-bă) Outubro

octopus (ók-tă-păç) *n* polvo *m*

oculist (ó-kᵁu-liçt) *n* oculista *m*

odd (ód) *adj* invulgar, estranho; ímpar

odour (*o*ᵁ-dă) *n* odor *m*

of (óv ăv) *prep* de

off (óf) *adv* embora; *prep* de

offence (ă-fénnç) *n* falta *f*; ofensa *f*, ultraje *m*

offend (ă-fénnd) *v* ofender; *transgredir

offensive (ă-fénn-çiv) *adj* ofensivo, insultante; *n* ofensiva *f*

offer (ó-fă) *v* oferecer; *n* oferta *f*

office (ó-fiç) *n* escritório *m*; cargo *m*; ~ **hours** horas de serviço

officer (ó-fi-çă) *n* oficial *m*

official (ă-*fi*-chăl) *adj* oficial

off-licence (óf-lai-çănnç) *n* loja de vinhos

often (ó-fănn) *adv* muitas vezes, frequentemente

oil (oil) *n* óleo *m*; petróleo *m*; **fuel** ~ óleo combustível; ~ **filter** filtro de óleo; ~ **pressure** pressão do óleo

oil-painting (oil-*peinn*-tinng) *n* pintura a óleo

oil-refinery (*oil*-ri-fai-nă-ri) *n* refinaria de petróleo

oil-well (*oil*-ᵁél) *n* poço de petróleo

oily (*oi*-li) *adj* oleoso

ointment (*oinnt*-mănnt) *n* unguento *m*

okay! (*o*ᵁ-*kei*) de acordo!

old (*o*ᵁld) *adj* velho; ~ **age** velhice *f*

old-fashioned (*o*ᵁld-*fæ*-chănnd) *adj* antiquado

olive (ó-liv) *n* azeitona *f*; ~ **oil** azeite *m*

omelette (ómm-lăt) *n* omeleta *f*

ominous (ó-mi-năç) *adj* sinistro

omit (ă-*mit*) *v* omitir

omnipotent (ómm-*ni*-pă-tănnt) *adj* omnipotente

on (ónn) *prep* sobre; a

once (ᵁannç) *adv* uma vez; **at** ~ já, imediatamente; ~ **more** uma vez mais

oncoming (ónn-ka-minng) *adj* próximo

one (ᵁann) *num* um; *pron* uma pessoa

oneself (ᵁann-çélf) *pron* si mesmo

onion (a-niᵃănn) *n* cebola *f*

only (*o*ᵁnn-li) *adj* só; *adv* somente, só; *conj* mas

onwards (ónn-ᵁădz) *adv* para a frente

onyx (ó-nikç) *n* ónix *m*

opal (*o*ᵁ-păl) *n* opala *f*

open (*o*ᵁ-pănn) *v* abrir; *adj* aberto; franco

opening (*o*ᵁ-pă-ninng) *n* abertura *f*

opera (ó-pă-ră) *n* ópera *f*

operate (ó-pă-reit) *v* funcionar, actuar; operar

operation (ó-pă-*rei*-chănn) *n* funcionamento *m*; operação *f*

operator (ó-pă-rei-tă) *n* telefonista *f*

operetta (ó-pă-*ré*-tă) *n* opereta *f*

opinion (ă-*pi*-niᵃănn) *n* opinião *f*, parecer *m*

opponent (ă-*po*ᵁ-nănnt) *n* adversário *m*

opportunity (ó-pă-*t'uu*-nă-ti) *n* oportunidade *f*

oppose (ă-*po*ᵁz) *v* *opor-se

opposite (ó-pă-zit) *prep* em frente de; *adj* oposto, contrário

opposition (ó-pă-*zi*-chănn) *n* oposição *f*

oppress (ă-*préç*) *v* oprimir

optician (óp-*ti*-chănn) *n* oculista *m*

optimism (óp-ti-mi-zămm) *n* optimismo *m*

optimist (óp-ti-miçt) *n* optimista *m*

optimistic (óp-ti-*mi*-çtik) *adj* optimista

optional (óp-chă-năl) *adj* facultativo

or (óó) *conj* ou

oral (óó-răl) *adj* oral

orange (ó-rinndj) *n* laranja *f;* *adj* cor-de-laranja

orchard (óó-tchăd) *n* pomar *m*

orchestra (óó-ki-çtră) *n* orquestra *f;* ~ **seat** *Am* plateia *f*

order (óó-dă) *v* mandar, ordenar; encomendar; *n* ordem *f;* comando *m;* encomenda *f;* **in** ~ em ordem; **in** ~ **to** para; **made to** ~ feito por encomenda; **out of** ~ avariado; **postal** ~ vale postal

order-form (óó-dă-fóómm) *n* nota de encomenda

ordinary (óó-dănn-ri) *adj* usual, vulgar

ore (óó) *n* minério *m*

organ (óó-ghănn) *n* orgão *m*

organic (óó-ghæ-nik) *adj* orgânico

organization (óó-ghă-nai-zei-chănn) *n* organização *f*

organize (óó-ghă-naiz) *v* organizar

Orient (óó-ri-ănnt) *n* oriente *m*

oriental (óó-ri-énn-tăl) *adj* oriental

orientate (óó-ri-ănn-teit) *v* orientar-se

origin (ó-ri-djinn) *n* origem *f;* ascendência *f,* proveniência *f*

original (ă-ri-dji-năl) *adj* autêntico, original

originally (ă-ri-dji-nă-li) *adv* originalmente

ornament (óó-nă-mănnt) *n* ornamento *m*

ornamental (óó-nă-ménn-tăl) *adj* ornamental

orphan (óó-fănn) *n* órfão *m*

orthodox (óó-θă-dókç) *adj* ortodoxo

ostrich (ó-çtritch) *n* avestruz *f*

other (a-ðă) *adj* outro

otherwise (a-ðă-ᵘaiz) *conj* senão; *adv* doutro modo

***ought to** (óót) dever

our (auᵃ) *adj* nosso

ourselves (auᵃ-çélvz) *pron* nos; nós próprios

out (aut) *adv* fora; ~ **of** fora de, de

outbreak (aut-breik) *n* explosão *f*

outcome (aut-kamm) *n* resultado *m*

***outdo** (aut-duu) *v* superar

outdoors (aut-dóóz) *adv* ao ar livre

outer (au-tă) *adj* exterior

outfit (aut-fit) *n* equipamento *m*

outline (aut-lainn) *n* contorno *m;* *v* esboçar

outlook (aut-luk) *n* previsão *f;* ponto de vista

output (aut-put) *n* produção *f*

outrage (aut-reidj) *n* ultraje *m*

outside (aut-çaid) *adv* de fora; *prep* fora de; *n* exterior *m*

outsize (aut-çaiz) *n* tamanho extra-grande

outskirts (aut-çkăătç) *pl* arredores *mpl*

outstanding (aut-çtænn-dinng) *adj* eminente

outward (aut-ᵘăd) *adj* externo

outwards (aut-ᵘădz) *adv* para fora

oval (oᵘ-văl) *adj* oval

oven (a-vănn) *n* forno *m*

over (oᵘ-vă) *prep* sobre, por cima de; mais de; *adv* por cima; abaixo; *adj* acabado; ~ **there** ali

overall (oᵘ-vă-róól) *adj* global

overalls (oᵘ-vă-róólz) *pl* fato-macaco *m;* macacão *mBr*

overcast (oᵘ-vă-kaaçt) *adj* nublado

overcoat (oᵘ-vă-koᵘt) *n* sobretudo *m*

***overcome** (oᵘ-vă-kamm) *v* vencer

overdue (oᵘ-vă-dᵘuu) *adj* atrasado

overgrown (oᵘ-vă-ghroᵘnn) *adj* coberto de vegetação

overhaul (oᵘ-vă-hóól) *v* *rever

overhead (oᵘ-vă-héd) *adv* em cima

overlook (oᵘ-vă-luk) *v* deixar passar

overnight (oᵘ-vă-nait) *adv* durante a noite

overseas (oᵘ-vă-çiiz) *adj* ultramarino

oversight (oᵘ-vă-çait) *n* inadvertência *f*

*****oversleep** (oᵘ-vă-çliip) *v* *dormir demais

overstrung (oᵘ-vă-çtranng) *adj* sobre-excitado

*****overtake** (oᵘ-vă-teik) *v* ultrapassar; **no overtaking** ultrapassagem proibida

over-tired (oᵘ-vă-taiᵃd) *adj* exausto

overture (oᵘ-vă-tchă) *n* abertura *f*

overweight (oᵘ-vă-ᵘeit) *n* excesso de peso

overwhelm (oᵘ-vă-ᵘélm) *v* *submergir, desconcertar

overwork (oᵘ-vă-ᵘăăk) *v* trabalhar demais

owe (oᵘ) *v* dever; **owing to** devido a

owl (aul) *n* mocho *m*

own (oᵘnn) *v* *possuir; *adj* próprio

owner (oᵘ-nă) *n* proprietário *m*

ox (ókç) *n* (pl oxen) boi *m*

oxygen (ók-çi-djănn) *n* oxigénio *m*

oyster (oi-çtă) *n* ostra *f*

P

pace (peiç) *n* andar *m*; passo *m*; ritmo *m*

Pacific Ocean (pă-çi-fik oᵘ-chănn) Oceano Pacífico

pacifism (pæ-çi-fi-zămm) *n* pacifismo *m*

pacifist (pæ-çi-fiçt) *n* pacifista *m*

pack (pæk) *v* embalar; ~ **up** embalar

package (pæ-kidj) *n* volume *m*

packet (pæ-kit) *n* pacote *m*

packing (pæ-kinng) *n* embalagem *f*

pad (pæd) *n* almofadinha *f*; bloco de notas

paddle (pæ-dăl) *n* remo *m*

padlock (pæd-lók) *n* cadeado *m*

pagan (pei-ghănn) *adj* pagão; *n* pagão *m*

page (peidj) *n* página *f*

page-boy (peidj-boi) *n* paquete *m*; moço de hotel *Br*

pail (peil) *n* balde *m*

pain (peinn) *n* dor *f*; **pains** dificuldade *f*

painful (peinn-fâl) *adj* doloroso

painless (peinn-lăç) *adj* sem dor

paint (peinnt) *n* tinta *f*; *v* pintar

paint-box (peinnt-bókç) *n* caixa de tintas

paint-brush (peinnt-brach) *n* pincel *m*

painter (peinn-tă) *n* pintor *m*

painting (peinn-tinng) *n* pintura *f*

pair (péᵃ) *n* par *m*

Pakistan (paa-ki-çtaann) Paquistão *m*

Pakistani (paa-ki-çtaa-ni) *adj* paquistanês

palace (pæ-lăç) *n* palácio *m*

pale (peil) *adj* pálido

palm (paamm) *n* palmeira *f*; palma da mão

palpable (pæl-pă-bâl) *adj* palpável

palpitation (pæl-pi-tei-chănn) *n* palpitação *f*

pan (pænn) *n* panela *f*

pane (peinn) *n* vidro *m*

panel (pæ-năl) *n* painel *m*

panelling (pæ-nă-linng) *n* lambril *m*

panic (pæ-nik) *n* pânico *m*

pant (pænnt) *v* arquejar

panties (pænn-tiz) *pl* calcinhas *fpl*

pants (pænntç) *pl* cuecas *fpl*; *plAm* calças *fpl*

pant-suit (pænnt-çuut) *n* fato calça e casaco

panty-hose (pænn-ti-hoᵘz) *n* meia-calça *f*

paper (pei-pă) *n* papel *m*; jornal *m*; de papel; **carbon** ~ papel químico;

papel carbono *Br;* ~ **bag** saco de papel; ~ **napkin** guardanapo de papel; **typing** ~ papel de máquina; **wrapping** ~ papel de embrulho

paperback (*pei*-pă-băk) *n* livro de bolso

paper-knife (*pei*-pă-naif) *n* corta-papel *m*

parade (pă-*reid*) *n* parada *f,* desfile *m*

paraffin (*pæ*-ră-finn) *n* petróleo *m*

paragraph (*pæ*-ră-ghraaf) *n* parágrafo *m,* alínea *f*

parakeet (*pæ*-ră-kiit) *n* periquito *m*

parallel (*pæ*-ră-lél) *adj* paralelo; *n* paralelo *m*

paralyse (*pæ*-ră-laiz) *v* paralisar

parcel (*paa*-căl) *n* embrulho *m,* encomenda *f*

pardon (*paa*-dănn) *n* perdão *m;* indulto *m*

parents (*pé*ᵃ-rănntç) *pl* pais *mpl*

parents-in-law (*pé*ᵃ-rănntç-inn-lóó) *pl* sogros *mpl*

parish (*pæ*-rich) *n* paróquia *f*

park (paak) *n* parque *m; v* estacionar

parking (*paa*-kinng) *n* estacionamento *m;* **no** ~ estacionamento proibido; ~ **fee** tarifa de estacionamento; ~ **light** luz de estacionamento; ~ **lot** *Am* parque de estacionamento; ~ **meter** parcómetro *m;* ~ **zone** zona de estacionamento

parliament (*paa*-lă-mănnt) *n* parlamento *m*

parliamentary (paa-lă-*ménn*-tă-ri) *adj* parlamentar

parrot (*pæ*-răt) *n* papagaio *m*

parsley (*paa*-çli) *n* salsa *f*

parson (*paa*-cănn) *n* vigário *m,* pároco *m*

parsonage (*paa*-că-nidj) *n* presbitério *m*

part (paat) *n* parte *f;* bocado *m; v* separar; **spare** ~ peça sobresselente

partial (*paa*-chăl) *adj* parcial

participant (paa-*ti*-çi-pănnt) *n* participante *m*

participate (paa-*ti*-çi-peit) *v* participar

particular (pă-*ti*-k¹u-lă) *adj* especial; exigente; **in** ~ em particular

parting (*paa*-tinng) *n* despedida *f;* risca *f*

partition (paa-*ti*-chănn) *n* tabique *m*

partly (*paat*-li) *adv* parcialmente, em parte

partner (*paat*-nă) *n* parceiro *m;* sócio *m*

partridge (*paa*-tridj) *n* perdiz *f*

party (*paa*-ti) *n* partido *m;* festa *f;* grupo *m*

pass (paaç) *v* passar, ultrapassar; ~ **by** passar por; ~ **through** atravessar

passage (*pæ*-çidj) *n* passagem *f;* travessia *f;* trecho *m;* viagem *f*

passenger (*pæ*-cănn-djă) *n* passageiro *m;* ~ **train** comboio de passageiros

passer-by (paa-că-*bai*) *n* transeunte *m*

passion (*pæ*-chănn) *n* paixão *f;* fúria *f*

passionate (*pæ*-chă-năt) *adj* apaixonado

passive (*pæ*-çiv) *adj* passivo

passport (*paaç*-póót) *n* passaporte *m;* ~ **control** inspecção de passaportes; ~ **photograph** fotografia de passe

password (*paaç*-ᵘăăd) *n* santo-e-senha *m*

past (paaçt) *n* passado *m; adj* passado; *prep* por, além de

paste (peiçt) *n* pasta *f; v* colar

pastry (*pei*-çtri) *n* pastelaria *f;* ~ **shop** pastelaria *f*

pasture (*paaç*-tchă) *n* pastagem *f*

patch (pætch) *v* remendar; *n* remendo *m*

patent (*pei*-tănnt) *n* patente *f,* alvará

m

path (paaθ) *n* carreiro *m*

patience (*pei*-chännç) *n* paciência *f*

patient (*pei*-chännt) *adj* paciente; *n* doente *m*

patriot (*pei*-tri-ät) *n* patriota *m*

patrol (pä-*tro*ul) *n* patrulha *f*; *v* patrulhar; vigiar

pattern (*pæ*-tänn) *n* desenho *m*, padrão *m*

pause (póóz) *n* intervalo *m*; *v* *fazer uma pausa

pave (peiv) *v* pavimentar

pavement (*peiv*-männt) *n* passeio *m*; pavimento *m*

pavilion (pä-*vil*-iänn) *n* pavilhão *m*

paw (póó) *n* pata *f*

pawn (póónn) *v* empenhar; *n* peão *m*

pawnbroker (*póónn*-brou-kä) *n* penhorista *m*

pay (pei) *n* ordenado *m*, salário *m*

*pay** (pei) *v* pagar; compensar; ~ **attention to** prestar atenção a; **paying** rentável; ~ **off** liquidar; ~ **on account** pagar a prestações

pay-desk (*pei*-déçk) *n* caixa *f*

payee (pei-*ii*) *n* beneficiário *m*

payment (*pei*-männt) *n* pagamento *m*

pea (pii) *n* ervilha *f*

peace (piiç) *n* paz *f*

peaceful (*piiç*-fäl) *adj* tranquilo

peach (piitch) *n* pêssego *m*

peacock (*pii*-kók) *n* pavão *m*

peak (piik) *n* cume *m*; apogeu *m*; ~ **hour** hora de ponta; ~ **season** plena estação

peanut (*pii*-nat) *n* amendoim *m*

pear (péä) *n* pêra *f*

pearl (pääl) *n* pérola *f*

peasant (*pé*-zännt) *n* camponês *m*

pebble (*pé*-bäl) *n* seixo *m*

peculiar (pi-*ki*uul-iä) *adj* estranho; especial, peculiar

peculiarity (pi-kiuu-li-æ-rä-ti) *n* particularidade *f*

pedal (*pé*-däl) *n* pedal *m*

pedestrian (pi-*dé*-çtri-änn) *n* peão *m*; pedestre *mBr*; **no pedestrians** interdito a peões; ~ **crossing** passagem de peões; passagem de pedestres *Br*

pedicure (*pé*-di-kiuä) *n* pedicuro *m*

peel (piil) *v* descascar; *n* casca *f*

peep (piip) *v* espreitar

peg (pégh) *n* gancho *m*

pelican (*pé*-li-känn) *n* pelicano *m*

pelvis (*pél*-viç) *n* pélvis *f*

pen (pénn) *n* caneta *f*

penalty (*pé*-näl-ti) *n* penalidade *f*; castigo *m*; ~ **kick** grande penalidade

pencil (*pénn*-çäl) *n* lápis *m*

pencil-sharpener (*pénn*-çäl-chaap-nä) *n* apara-lápis *m*; apontador *mBr*

pendant (*pénn*-dännt) *n* pingente *m*

penetrate (*pé*-ni-treit) *v* penetrar

penguin (*pénng*-ghuinn) *n* pinguim *m*

penicillin (pé-ni-çi-linn) *n* penicilina *f*

peninsula (pä-*ninn*-çiu-lä) *n* península *f*

penknife (*pénn*-naif) *n* (pl -knives) canivete *m*

pension[1] (pä-çi-ón) *n* pensão *f*

pension[2] (*pénn*-chänn) *n* pensão *f*

people (*pii*-päl) *pl* pessoas, gente *f*; *n* gente *f*, povo *m*

pepper (*pé*-pä) *n* pimenta *f*

peppermint (*pé*-pä-minnt) *n* hortelã-pimenta *f*

perceive (pä-*çiiv*) *v* aperceber

percent (pä-*çénnt*) *n* porcento *m*

percentage (pä-*çénn*-tidj) *n* percentagem *f*

perceptible (pä-*çép*-ti-bäl) *adj* perceptível

perception (pä-*çép*-chänn) *n* percepção *f*

perch (päätch) (pl ~) perca *f*

percolator (păă-kă-lei-tă) *n* cafeteira de filtro

perfect (păă-fikt) *adj* perfeito

perfection (pă-fék-chănn) *n* perfeição *f*

perform (pă-fóómm) *v* desempenhar, executar, cumprir

performance (pă-fóó-mănnç) *n* representação *f*

perfume (păă-fiuumm) *n* perfume *m*

perhaps (pă-hæpç) *adv* talvez; quiçá

peril (pé-ril) *n* perigo *m*

perilous (pé-ri-lăç) *adj* perigoso

period (pi²-ri-ăd) *n* período *m*, época *f*: ponto *m*

periodical (pi²-ri-ó-di-kăl) *n* periódico *m*: *adj* periódico

perish (pé-rich) *v* perecer

perishable (pé-ri-chă-băl) *adj* deteriorável

perjury (păă-djă-ri) *n* perjúrio *m*

permanent (păă-mă-nănnt) *adj* duradouro, permanente; estável, fixo; ~ **press** engomado permanente; ~ **wave** permanente *f*

permission (pă-mi-chănn) *n* autorização *f*; licença *f*

permit[1] (pă-mit) *v* permitir

permit[2] (păă-mit) *n* autorização *f*, licença *f*

peroxide (pă-rók-çaid) *n* água oxigenada

perpendicular (păă-pănn-di-k¹u-lă) *adj* perpendicular

Persia (păă-chă) Pérsia *f*

Persian (păă-chănn) *adj* persa

person (păă-çănn) *n* pessoa *f*; per ~ por pessoa

personal (păă-çă-năl) *adj* pessoal

personality (păă-çă-næ-lă-ti) *n* personalidade *f*

personnel (păă-çă-nél) *n* pessoal *m*

perspective (pă-çpék-tiv) *n* perspectiva *f*

perspiration (păă-çpă-rei-chănn) *n* suor *m*, transpiração *f*, perspiração *f*

perspire (pă-çpai²) *v* transpirar, suar

persuade (pă-ç¹eid) *v* persuadir, convencer

persuasion (pă-ç¹ei-jănn) *n* convicção *f*

pessimism (pé-çi-mi-zămm) *n* pessimismo *m*

pessimist (pé-çi-miçt) *n* pessimista *m*

pessimistic (pé-çi-mi-çtik) *adj* pessimista

pet (pét) *n* animal de estimação; riqueza *f*; favorito

petal (pé-tăl) *n* pétala *f*

petition (pi-ti-chănn) *n* petição *f*

petrol (pé-trăl) *n* gasolina *f*; ~ **pump** bomba de gasolina; ~ **station** posto de gasolina; ~ **tank** depósito da gasolina

petroleum (pi-tro⁰-li-ămm) *n* petróleo *m*

petty (pé-ti) *adj* insignificante, fútil, pequeno; ~ **cash** fundo de maneio

pewit (pii-⁰it) *n* abibe *m*

pewter (p¹uu-tă) *n* peltre *m*

phantom (fænn-tămm) *n* fantasma *m*

pharmacology (faa-mă-kó-lă-dji) *n* farmacologia *f*

pharmacy (faa-mă-çi) *n* farmácia *f*; drogaria *f*

phase (feiz) *n* fase *f*

pheasant (fé-zănnt) *n* faisão *m*

Philippine (fi-li-painn) *adj* filipino

Philippines (fi-li-piinnz) *pl* Filipinas *fpl*

philosopher (fi-ló-çă-fă) *n* filósofo *m*

philosophy (fi-ló-çă-fi) *n* filosofia *f*

phone (fo⁰nn) *n* telefone *m*; *v* telefonar

phonetic (fă-né-tik) *adj* fonético

photo (fo⁰-to⁰) *n* (pl ~s) fotografia *f*

photograph (fo⁰-tă-ghraaf) *n* fotografia f; v fotografar

photographer (fǎ-tó-ghrǎ-fǎ) n fotógrafo m

photography (fǎ-tó-ghrǎ-fi) n fotografia f

photostat (foᵘ-tǎ-çtæt) n fotocópia f

phrase (freiz) n frase f

phrase-book (freiz-buk) n guia linguístico

physical (fi-zi-kǎl) adj físico

physician (fi-zi-chǎnn) n médico m

physicist (fi-zi-çiçt) n físico m

physics (fi-zikç) n ciências naturais, física f

physiology (fi-zi-ó-lǎ-dji) n fisiologia f

pianist (pii-ǎ-niçt) n pianista m

piano (pi-æ-noᵘ) n piano m; **grand ~** piano de cauda

pick (pik) v colher; escolher; n escolha f; **~ up** apanhar; *ir buscar; **pick-up van** furgoneta f

pick-axe (pi-kækç) n picareta f

pickles (pi-kǎlz) pl pickles mpl, conservas em vinagre

picnic (pik-nik) n piquenique m; v piquenicar

picture (pik-tchǎ) n quadro m; gravura f, ilustração f; imagem f; **~ postcard** postal ilustrado; **pictures** cinema m

picturesque (pik-tchǎ-réçk) adj pitoresco

piece (piiç) n fragmento m, peça f

pier (piǎ) n molhe m

pierce (piǎç) v perfurar

pig (pigh) n porco m

pigeon (pi-djǎnn) n pombo m

pig-headed (pigh-hé-did) adj teimoso

piglet (pigh-lǎt) n leitão m

pigskin (pigh-çkinn) n pele de porco

pike (paik) (pl ~) lúcio m

pile (pail) n pilha f; v empilhar, amontoar; **piles** hemorróidas fpl

pilgrim (pil-ghrimm) n peregrino m

pilgrimage (pil-ghri-midj) n peregrinação f

pill (pil) n pílula f

pillar (pi-lǎ) n coluna f, pilar m

pillar-box (pi-lǎ-bókç) n caixa do correio

pillow (pi-loᵘ) n almofada f, almofadão m

pillow-case (pi-loᵘ-keiç) n fronha f

pilot (pai-lǎt) n piloto m

pimple (pimm-pǎl) n borbulha f

pin (pinn) n alfinete m; v prender com alfinetes; **bobby ~** Am gancho de cabelo

pincers (pinn-çǎz) pl tenaz f

pinch (pinntch) v beliscar

pineapple (pai-næ-pǎl) n ananás m; abacaxi mBr

pink (pinngk) adj cor-de-rosa

pioneer (pai-ǎ-niǎ) n pioneiro m

pious (pai-ǎç) adj pio

pip (pip) n caroço m

pipe (paip) n cachimbo m; cano m; **~ cleaner** limpa-cachimbos m; **~ tobacco** tabaco para cachimbo

pirate (paiǎ-rǎt) n pirata m

pistol (pi-çtǎl) n pistola f

piston (pi-çtǎnn) n pistão m; **~ ring** segmento do pistão

piston-rod (pi-çtǎnn-ród) n biela f

pit (pit) n cova f; mina f

pitcher (pi-tchǎ) n bilha f

pity (pi-ti) n piedade f; v *condoer-se de, *ter pena de; **what a pity!** que pena!

placard (plæ-kaad) n cartaz m

place (pleiç) n lugar m; v colocar, pousar; **~ of birth** lugar de nascimento; *take ~ *ter lugar, acontecer

plague (pleigh) n praga f

plaice (pleiç) (pl ~) solha f

plain (pleinn) adj claro; comum, simples; n planície f

plan (plænn) *n* plano *m*; *v* *planear
plane (pleinn) *adj* plano; *n* avião *m*;
~ **crash** desastre de aviação
planet (*plæ*-nit) *n* planeta *m*
planetarium (plæ-ni-*té*^{a}-ri-ămm) *n* planetário *m*
plank (plænngk) *n* prancha *f*
plant (plaannt) *n* planta *f*; fábrica *f*; *v*
plantar
plantation (plænn-*tei*-chănn) *n* plantação *f*
plaster (*plaa*-çtă) *n* estuque *m*, gesso
m; penso rápido; esparadrapo *mBr*
plastic (*plæ*-çtik) *adj* de plástico; *n*
plástico *m*
plate (pleit) *n* prato *m*; chapa *f*
plateau (*plæ*-to^u) *n* (pl ~x, ~s) planalto *m*
platform (*plæt*-fóómm) *n* plataforma
f; ~ **ticket** bilhete de gare
platinum (*plæ*-ti-nămm) *n* platina *f*
play (plei) *v* jogar; tocar; *n* jogo *m*;
peça de teatro; **one-act** ~ peça
num acto; ~ **truant** *fazer gazeta
player (plei^a) *n* jogador *m*
playground (*plei*-ghraunnd) *n* recreio
m
playing-card (*plei*-inng-kaad) *n* carta
de jogar
playwright (*plei*-rait) *n* dramaturgo *m*
plea (plii) *n* defesa *f*
plead (pliid) *v* advogar
pleasant (*plé*-zănnt) *adj* simpático,
agradável
please (pliiz) se faz favor; *v* agradar;
pleased satisfeito; **pleasing** agradável
pleasure (*plé*-jă) *n* prazer *m*, divertimento *m*
plentiful (*plénn*-ti-făl) *adj* abundante
plenty (*plénn*-ti) *n* abundância *f*; fartura *f*
pliers (plai^{a}z) *pl* alicate *m*
plimsolls (*plimm*-çălz) *pl* sapatos de

ginástica
plot (plót) *n* conspiração *f*, conjura *f*;
enredo *m*; parcela *f*
plough (plau) *n* arado *m*; *v* lavrar
plucky (*pla*-ki) *adj* valente
plug (plagh) *n* ficha *f*; ~ **in** ligar
plum (plamm) *n* ameixa *f*
plumber (*pla*-mă) *n* canalizador *m*
plump (plammp) *adj* rolico
plural (*plu*^{a}-răl) *n* plural *m*
plus (plaç) *prep* mais
pneumatic (n^{i}uu-*mæ*-tik) *adj* pneumático
pneumonia (n^{i}uu-*mo*^{u}-ni-ă) *n* pneumonia *f*
poach (po^{u}tch) *v* caçar furtivamente
pocket (*pó*-kit) *n* bolso *m*
pocket-book (*pó*-kit-buk) *n* carteira *f*
pocket-comb (*pó*-kit-ko^{u}mm) *n* pente
de bolso
pocket-knife (*pó*-kit-naif) *n* (pl
-knives) canivete *m*
pocket-watch (*pó*-kit-^{u}ótch) *n* relógio
de bolso
poem (*po*^{u}-imm) *n* poema *m*
poet (*po*^{u}-it) *n* poeta *m*
poetry (*po*^{u}-i-tri) *n* poesia *f*
point (poinnt) *n* ponto *m*; bico *m*; *v*
apontar; ~ **of view** ponto de vista;
~ **out** indicar, apontar
pointed (*poinn*-tid) *adj* pontiagudo
poison (*poi*-zănn) *n* veneno *m*; *v* envenenar
poisonous (*poi*-ză-năç) *adj* venenoso
Poland (*po*^{u}-lănnd) Polónia *f*
Pole (po^{u}l) *n* polaco *m*
pole (po^{u}l) *n* poste *m*
police (pă-*liiç*) *pl* polícia *f*
policeman (pă-*liic*-mănn) *n* (pl -men)
polícia *m*, guarda *m*
police-station (pă-*liiç*-çtei-chănn) *n*
posto da polícia; delegacia de polícia *Br*
policy (*pó*-li-çi) *n* política *f*; apólice *f*

polio (*po*^u-li-o^u) *n* pólio *f*, paralisia infantil

Polish (*po*^u-lich) *adj* polaco

polish (*pó*-lich) *v* *polir

polite (pă-*lait*) *adj* educado

political (pă-*li*-ti-kăl) *adj* político

politician (pó-li-*ti*-chănn) *n* político *m*

politics (*pó*-li-tikç) *n* política *f*

pollution (pă-*luu*-chănn) *n* poluição *f*

pond (pónnd) *n* tanque *m*

pony (*po*^u-ni) *n* pónei *m*

poor (pu^ă) *adj* pobre; fraco

pope (po^up) *n* papa *m*

poplin (*pó*-plinn) *n* popelina *f*

pop music (*póp m*ⁱ*uu*-zik) música pop

poppy (*pó*-pi) *n* papoila *f*; papoula *f*

popular (*pó*-pⁱu-lă) *adj* popular

population (pó-pⁱu-*lei*-chănn) *n* populacão *f*

populous (*pó*-pⁱu-lăç) *adj* populoso

porcelain (*pó*ó-çă-linn) *n* porcelana *f*

porcupine (*pó*ó-kⁱu-painn) *n* porco-espinho *m*

pork (*pó*ók) *n* carne de porco

port (*pó*ót) *n* porto *m*; bombordo *m*

portable (*pó*ó-tă-băl) *adj* portátil

porter (*pó*ó-tă) *n* carregador *m*; porteiro *m*

porthole (*pó*ót-ho^ul) *n* vigia *f*

portion (*pó*ó-chănn) *n* porção *f*

portrait (*pó*ó-trit) *n* retrato *m*

Portugal (*pó*ó-tⁱu-ghăl) Portugal *m*

Portuguese (*pó*ó-tⁱu-*ghiiz*) *adj* português

position (pă-*zi*-chănn) *n* posição *f*; atitude *f*; situação *f*

positive (*pó*-ză-tiv) *adj* positivo; *n* positivo *m*

possess (pă-*zéç*) *v* *possuir; possessed possesso

possession (pă-*zé*-chănn) *n* posse *f*; possessions bens *mpl*

possibility (pó-çă-*bi*-lă-ti) *n* possibilidade *f*

possible (*pó*-çă-băl) *adj* possível; eventual

post (po^uçt) *n* poste *m*; posto *m*; correio *m*; *v* deitar no correio; post-office correios

postage (*po*^u-çtidj) *n* franquia *f*; ~ paid porte pago; ~ stamp selo postal

postcard (*po*^uçt-kaad) *n* bilhete postal; postal ilustrado

poster (*po*^u-çtă) *n* cartaz *m*

poste restante (po^uçt ré-*çtă*t) posta-restante

postman (*po*^uçt-mănn) *n* (pl -men) carteiro *m*

post-paid (po^uçt-*peid*) *adj* porte pago

postpone (pă-*çpo*^unn) *v* adiar, *transferir

pot (pót) *n* vaso *m*

potato (pă-*tei*-to^u) *n* (pl ~es) batata *f*

pottery (*pó*-tă-ri) *n* cerâmica *f*; loiça *f*

pouch (pautch) *n* bolsa *f*

poulterer (*po*^ul-tă-ră) *n* vendedor de aves de criação

poultry (*po*^ul-tri) *n* aves de criação

pound (paunnd) *n* libra *f*

pour (póó) *v* deitar, verter

poverty (*pó*-vă-ti) *n* pobreza *f*

powder (*pau*-dă) *n* pó *m*; ~ compact caixa de pó-de-arroz; talc ~ pó de talco

powder-puff (*pau*-dă-paf) *n* borla de pó-de-arroz

powder-room (*pau*-dă-ruumm) *n* lavabos das senhoras

power (*pau*^ă) *n* energia *f*, potência *f*; poder *m*

powerful (*pau*^ă-făl) *adj* poderoso; forte

powerless (*pau*^ă-lăç) *adj* impotente

power-station (*pau*^ă-çtei-chănn) *n* central eléctrica

practical (*præk*-ti-kăl) *adj* prático

practically (*præk-ti-kli*) *adv* praticamente

practice (*præk-tiç*) *n* prática *f*

practise (*præk-tiç*) *v* praticar; exercitar-se

praise (preiz) *v* louvar; *n* elogio *m*

pram (præmm) *n* carrinho de bebé

prawn (próónn) *n* gamba *f*, camarão grande

pray (prei) *v* rezar

prayer (pré*ª*) *n* oração *f*

preach (priitch) *v* pregar

precarious (pri-ké*ª*-ri-âç) *adj* precário

precaution (pri-kóó-chânn) *n* precaução *f*

precede (pri-çiid) *v* preceder

preceding (pri-çii-dinng) *adj* precedente

precious (pré-châç) *adj* precioso; caro

precipice (pré-çi-piç) *n* precipício *m*

precipitation (pri-çi-pi-tei-chânn) *n* precipitação *f*

precise (pri-çaiç) *adj* exacto, preciso; meticuloso

predecessor (prii-di-çé-çâ) *n* predecessor *m*

predict (pri-dikt) *v* *predizer

prefer (pri-fãã) *v* *preferir, *dar preferência a

preferable (pré-fã-râ-bâl) *adj* preferível

preference (pré-fã-rânnç) *n* preferência *f*

prefix (*prii*-fikç) *n* prefixo *m*

pregnant (prégh-nânnt) *adj* grávida

prejudice (pré-djã-diç) *n* preconceito *m*

preliminary (pri-*li*-mi-nã-ri) *adj* preliminar

premature (pré-mã-tchu*ª*) *adj* prematuro

premier (prémm-i*ª*) *n* primeiro-ministro *m*

premises (pré-mi-çiz) *pl* local *m*

premium (*prii*-mi-âmm) *n* prémio *m*

prepaid (prii-*peid*) *adj* pago adiantado

preparation (pré-pã-rei-chânn) *n* preparação *f*

prepare (pri-pé*ª*) *v* preparar

preposition (pré-pã-zi-chânn) *n* preposição *f*

prescribe (pri-çkraib) *v* prescrever, receitar

prescription (pri-çkrip-chânn) *n* receita *f*

presence (pré-zânnç) *n* presença *f*

present[1] (pré-zânnt) *n* presente *m;* *adj* actual, presente

present[2] (pri-zénnt) *v* apresentar; oferecer

presently (pré-zânnt-li) *adv* a seguir, dentro em pouco

preservation (pré-zã-vei-chânn) *n* conservação *f*

preserve (pri-zããv) *v* conservar; *pôr em conserva

president (pré-zi-dânnt) *n* presidente *m*

press (préç) *n* imprensa *f;* *v* carregar em, carregar, oprimir; passar a ferro; ~ **conference** conferência de imprensa

pressing (pré-çinng) *adj* urgente

pressure (pré-chã) *n* pressão *f;* tensão *f;* **atmospheric** ~ pressão atmosférica

pressure-cooker (pré-chã-ku-kã) *n* panela de pressão

prestige (pré-çtiij) *n* prestígio *m*

presumable (pri-z*ª*uu-mã-bâl) *adj* presumível

presumptuous (pri-zammp-châç) *adj* presunçoso

pretence (pri-ténnç) *n* pretexto *m*

pretend (pri-ténnd) *v* fingir

pretext (*prii*-tâkçt) *n* pretexto *m*

pretty (pri-ti) *adj* bonito; *adv* assaz, bastante, um tanto

prevent (pri-*vénnt*) *v* *impedir; evitar

preventive (pri-*vénn*-tiv) *adj* preventivo

previous (*prii*-vi-ăç) *adj* anterior, precedente, prévio

pre-war (prii-ᵘóó) *adj* do anteguerra

price (praiç) *n* preço *m*; *v* fixar o preço de

priceless (*praiç*-lăç) *adj* inestimável

price-list (*praiç*-liçt) *n* lista de preços

prick (prik) *v* picar

pride (praid) *n* orgulho *m*

priest (priiçt) *n* padre *m*

primary (*prai*-mă-ri) *adj* primário; primeiro, primordial; elementar

prince (prinnç) *n* príncipe *m*

princess (prinn-*çéç*) *n* princesa *f*

principal (*prinn*-çă-păl) *adj* principal; *n* reitor *m*, director *m*

principle (*prinn*-çă-păl) *n* princípio *m*

print (prinnt) *v* imprimir; *n* prova *f*; gravura *f*: **printed matter** impresso *m*

prior (praiᵃ) *adj* anterior

priority (prai-ó-ră-ti) *n* prioridade *f*

prison (*pri*-zănn) *n* prisão *f*

prisoner (*pri*-ză-nă) *n* prisioneiro *m*, detido *m*: ~ **of war** prisioneiro de guerra

privacy (*prai*-vă-çi) *n* intimidade *f*

private (*prai*-vit) *adj* privado, particular; pessoal

privilege (*pri*-vi-lidj) *n* privilégio *m*

prize (praiz) *n* prémio *m*; recompensa *f*

probable (*pró*-bă-băl) *adj* provável

probably (*pró*-bă-bli) *adv* provavelmente

problem (*pró*-blămm) *n* problema *m*

procedure (pră-*çii*-djă) *n* processo *m*

proceed (pră-*çiid*) *v* *prosseguir; proceder

process (*pro*ᵘ-çéç) *n* processo *m*, procedimento *m*

procession (pră-*çé*-chănn) *n* procissão *f*, cortejo *m*

proclaim (pră-*kleimm*) *v* proclamar

produce¹ (pră-*d*ᶦ*uuç*) *v* *produzir

produce² (*pród*-ᶦuuç) *n* produto *m*

producer (pră-*d*ᶦ*uu*-çă) *n* produtor *m*

product (*pró*-dakt) *n* produto *m*

production (pră-*dak*-chănn) *n* produção *f*

profession (pră-*fé*-chănn) *n* profissão *f*

professional (pră-*fé*-chă-năl) *adj* profissional

professor (pră-*fé*-çă) *n* professor *m*

profit (*pró*-fit) *n* benefício *m*, lucro *m*; vantagem *f*; *v* aproveitar-se

profitable (*pró*-fi-tă-băl) *adj* lucrativo

profound (pră-*faunnd*) *adj* profundo

programme (*pro*ᵘ-ghræmm) *n* programa *m*

progress¹ (*pro*ᵘ-ghréç) *n* progresso *m*

progress² (pră-*ghréç*) *v* progredir

progressive (pră-*ghré*-çiv) *adj* progressista; progressivo

prohibit (pră-*hi*-bit) *v* proibir

prohibition (pro*ᵘ*-i-*bi*-chănn) *n* interdição *f*

prohibitive (pră-*hi*-bi-tiv) *adj* proibitivo

project (*pró*-djékt) *n* plano *m*, projecto *m*

promenade (pró-mă-*naad*) *n* passeio *m*

promise (*pró*-miç) *n* promessa *f*; *v* prometer

promote (pră-*mo*ᵘt) *v* promover

promotion (pră-*mo*ᵘ-chănn) *n* promoção *f*

prompt (prómmpt) *adj* imediato, pronto

pronoun (*pro*ᵘ-naunn) *n* pronome *m*

pronounce (pră-*naunnç*) *v* pronunciar

pronunciation (pră-nann-çi-*ei*-chănn) *n* pronúncia *f* proof (pruuf) n prova f

propaganda (pró-pă-*ghænn*-dă) n propaganda f

propel (pră-*pél*) v impulsionar, propulsionar

propeller (pră-*pé*-lă) n hélice f

proper (*pró*-pă) adj justo; apropriado, devido, indicado

property (*pró*-pă-ti) n propriedade f

prophet (*pró*-fit) n profeta m

proportion (pră-*póó*-chănn) n proporção f

proportional (pră-*póó*-chă-năl) adj proporcional

proposal (pră-*po*ᵘ-zăl) n proposta f

propose (pră-*po*ᵘz) v *propor

proposition (pró-pă-zi-chănn) n proposta f

proprietor (pră-*prai*-ă-tă) n proprietário m

prospect (*pró*-çpékt) n perspectiva f

prospectus (pră-*çpék*-tăç) n prospecto m

prosperity (*pró*-çpé-ră-ti) n prosperidade f

prosperous (*pró*-çpă-răç) adj próspero

prostitute (*pró*-çti-t¹uut) n prostituta f

protect (pră-*tékt*) v proteger

protection (pră-*ték*-chănn) n protecção f

protein (*pro*ᵘ-tiinn) n proteína f

protest¹ (*pro*ᵘ-téçt) n protesto m

protest² (pră-*téçt*) v protestar

Protestant (*pró*-ti-çtănnt) adj protestante

proud (praud) adj vaidoso; orgulhoso

prove (pruuv) v provar, demonstrar; revelar-se

proverb (*pró*-văăb) n provérbio m

provide (pră-*vaid*) v fornecer; provided that contanto que

province (*pró*-vinnç) n província f

provincial (pră-*vinn*-chăl) adj provincial

provisional (pră-*vi*-jă-năl) adj provisório

provisions (pră-*vi*-jănnz) pl provisões fpl

prune (pruunn) n ameixa passada

psychiatrist (çai-*kai*-ă-triçt) n psiquiatra m

psychic (çai-kik) adj psíquico

psychoanalyst (çai-ko°-æ-nă-liçt) n psicanalista m

psychological (çai-kó-*ló*-dji-kăl) adj psicológico

psychologist (çai-*kó*-lă-djiçt) n psicólogo m

psychology (çai-*kó*-lă-dji) n psicologia f

pub (pab) n taberna f; cervejaria f

public (*pa*-blik) adj público; geral; n público m; ~ garden jardim público; ~ house bar m

publication (pa-bli-*kei*-chănn) n publicação f

publicity (pa-*bli*-çă-ti) n publicidade f

publish (*pa*-blich) v publicar

publisher (*pa*-bli-chă) n editor m

puddle (*pa*-dăl) n charco m

pull (pul) v puxar; ~ out partir; ~ up parar

pulley (*pu*-li) n (pl ~s) roldana f

Pullman (*pul*-mănn) n carruagem-cama f

pullover (*pu*-lo°-vă) n pulóver m

pulpit (*pul*-pit) n púlpito m, tribuna f

pulse (palç) n pulso m

pump (pammp) n bomba f; v *dar à bomba; *bombear vBr

punch (panntch) v socar; n soco m

punctual (*panngk*-tchu-ăl) adj pontual

puncture (*panngk*-tchă) n furo m

punctured (*panngk*-tchăd) adj furado

punish (*pa*-nich) v castigar

punishment (*pa*-nich-mănnt) n castigo m

pupil (p'uu-păl) n aluno m

puppet-show (pa-pit-cho^u) n teatro de fantoches

purchase (păă-tchăç) v comprar; n compra f; ~ **price** preço de compra; ~ **tax** imposto de consumo

purchaser (păă-tchă-çă) n comprador m

pure (p'u^ă) adj puro

purple (păă-păl) adj purpúreo

purpose (păă-păç) n intento m, intenção f, propósito m; **on** ~ propositado

purse (păăç) n porta-moedas m

pursue (pă-ç'uu) v *prosseguir; pretender

pus (paç) n pus m

push (puch) n empurrão m; v empurrar

push-button (puch-ba-tănn) n botão m

***put** (put) v pousar, colocar, *pôr; meter; formular; ~ **away** guardar; ~ **off** adiar; ~ **on** *vestir; ~ **out** apagar

puzzle (pa-zăl) n puzzle m; enigma m; v embaraçar; **jigsaw** ~ quebra-cabeças m

puzzling (paz-linng) adj incompreensível

pyjamas (pă-djaa-măz) pl pijama m

Q

quack (k^uæk) n curandeiro m, charlatão m

quail (k^ueil) n (pl ~, ~s) codorniz f

quaint (k^ueinnt) adj estranho; antiquado

qualification (k^uó-li-fi-kei-chănn) n habilitação f; restrição f, reserva f

qualified (k^uó-li-faid) adj qualificado; competente

qualify (k^uó-li-fai) v qualificar-se

quality (k^uó-lă-ti) n qualidade f; característica f

quantity (k^uónn-tă-ti) n quantidade f; número m

quarantine (k^uó-rănn-tiinn) n quarentena f

quarrel (k^uó-răl) v disputar, discutir; n briga f, litígio m

quarry (k^uó-ri) n pedreira f

quarter (k^uóó-tă) n quarto m; trimestre m; bairro m; ~ **of an hour** quarto de hora

quarterly (k^uóó-tă-li) adj trimestral

quay (kii) n cais m

queen (k^uiinn) n rainha f

queer (k^ui^ă) adj estranho, esquisito

query (k^ui^ă-ri) n pergunta f; v indagar; *pôr em dúvida

question (k^uéç-tchănn) n pergunta f; questão f, problema m; v interrogar; pôr em dúvida; ~ **mark** ponto de interrogação

queue (k^uuu) n bicha f; v *fazer bicha

quick (k^uik) adj rápido

quick-tempered (k^uik-témm-păd) adj irascível

quiet (k^uai-ăt) adj calmo, tranquilo, sossegado; n silêncio m, tranquilidade f

quilt (k^uilt) n colcha f

quinine (k^ui-niinn) n quinina f

quit (k^uit) v cessar

quite (k^uait) adv completamente; bastante, relativamente; muito

quiz (k^uiz) n (pl ~zes) concurso m

quota (k^uo^u-tă) n quota f

quotation (k^uo^u-tei-chănn) n citação f; ~ **marks** aspas fpl

quote (k^uo^ut) v citar

R

rabbit (ræ-bit) n coelho m

rabies (rei-biz) n raiva f

race (reiç) n corrida f; raça f

race-course (reiç-kóóç) n pista de corridas, hipódromo m

race-horse (reiç-hóóç) n cavalo de corridas

race-track (reiç-træk) n pista de corridas

racial (rei-chăl) adj racial

racket (ræ-kit) n alarido m

racquet (ræ-kit) n raqueta f

radiator (rei-di-ei-tă) n radiador m

radical (ræ-di-kăl) adj radical

radio (rei-di-oᵘ) n rádio m

radish (ræ-dich) n rabanete m

radius (rei-di-ăç) n (pl radii) raio m

raft (raaft) n jangada f

rag (rægh) n trapo m

rage (reidj) n raiva f, furor m; v enfurecer

raid (reid) n incursão f

rail (reil) n barra f, balaustrada f

railing (rei-linng) n gradeamento m

railroad (reil-roᵘd) nAm caminho-de-ferro; via férrea; estrada de ferro Br

railway (reil-ᵘei) n via férrea, caminho-de-ferro; estrada de ferro Br

rain (reinn) n chuva f; v chover

rainbow (reinn-boᵘ) n arco-íris m

raincoat (reinn-koᵘt) n impermeável m; capa de chuva Br

rainproof (reinn-pruuf) adj impermeável

rainy (rei-ni) adj chuvoso

raise (reiz) v levantar; aumentar; criar, educar, cultivar; v tributar; nAm aumento de salário

raisin (rei-zănn) n passa f

rake (reik) n ancinho m

rally (ræ-li) n reunião f

ramp (ræmmp) n rampa f

ramshackle (ræmm-chæ-kăl) adj desmantelado

rancid (rænn-çid) adj rançoso

rang (rænng) v (p ring)

range (reinndj) n alcance m

range-finder (reinndj-fainn-dă) n telémetro m

rank (rænngk) n patente f; fila f

ransom (rænn-çămm) n resgate m

rape (reip) v violar

rapid (ræ-pid) adj rápido, veloz

rapids (ræ-pidz) pl rápidos mpl

rare (réᵃ) adj raro

rarely (réᵃ-li) adv raramente

rascal (raa-çkăl) n patife m, malandro m

rash (ræch) n erupção f; adj irreflectido, precipitado

raspberry (raaz-bă-ri) n framboesa f

rat (ræt) n ratazana f

rate (reit) n preço m, tarifa f; velocidade f; at any ~ de qualquer modo, seja como for; ~ of exchange taxa do câmbio

rather (raa-ðă) adv bastante, um tanto; antes

ration (ræ-chănn) n ração f

rattan (ræ-tænn) n rotim m

raven (rei-vänn) n corvo m

raw (róó) adj cru; ~ material matéria-prima f

ray (rei) n raio m

rayon (rei-ónn) n seda artificial

razor (rei-ză) n aparelho para barbear; navalha f

razor-blade (rei-ză-bleid) n lâmina de barbear

reach (riitch) v alcançar; n alcance m

reaction (ri-æk-chănn) n reacção f

*read (riid) v *ler

reading (rii-dinng) n leitura f

reading-lamp (*rii*-dinng-læmmp) *n* candeeiro de mesa

reading-room (*rii*-dinng-ruumm) *n* sala
de leitura

ready (*ré*-di) *adj* pronto, preparado

ready-made (*ré*-di-*meid*) *adj* de con-
fecção

real (ri³l) *adj* verdadeiro

reality (ri-æ-lã-ti) *n* realidade *f*

realizable (ri³-lai-zã-bãl) *adj* realizável

realize (ri³-laiz) *v* perceber; realizar

really (ri³-li) *adv* verdadeiramente,
realmente; na realidade

rear (ri³) *n* retaguarda *f; v* criar

rear-light (ri³-*lait*) *n* luz da retaguarda

reason (*rii*-zãnn) *n* razão *f,* causa *f;*
senso *m; v* raciocinar

reasonable (*rii*-zã-nã-bãl) *adj* razoável

reassure (rii-ã-*chu³*) *v* tranquilizar

rebate (*rii*-beit) *n* redução *f,* desconto
m

rebellion (ri-*bél*-¹ãnn) *n* revolta *f,* rebelião *f*

recall (ri-*kóól*) *v* recordar-se; chamar;
revogar

receipt (ri-*çiit*) *n* recibo *m;* recepção *f*

receive (ri-*çiiv*) *v* receber

receiver (ri-*çii*-vã) *n* auscultador *m*

recent (*rii*-çãnnt) *adj* recente

recently (*rii*-çãnnt-li) *adv* recentemente, há pouco tempo

reception (ri-*çép*-chãnn) *n* recepção *f;*
acolhimento *m;* ~ **office** recepção
f

receptionist (ri-*çép*-chã-niçt) *n* recepcionista *f*

recession (ri-*çé*-chãnn) *n* recessão *f*

recipe (*ré*-çi-pi) *n* receita *f*

recital (ri-*çai*-tãl) *n* recital *m*

reckon (*ré*-kãnn) *v* calcular; considerar; *crer

recognition (*ré*-kãgh-*ni*-chãnn) *n* reconhecimento *m*

recognize (*ré*-kãgh-naiz) *v* reconhecer

recollect (ré-kã-*lékt*) *v* recordar-se

recommence (rii-kã-*ménnç*) *v* recome-
car

recommend (ré-kã-*ménnd*) *v* recomendar; aconselhar

recommendation (ré-kã-ménn-*dei*-
chãnn) *n* recomendação *f*

reconciliation (ré-kãnn-çi-li-*ei*-chãnn)
n reconciliação *f*

record¹ (*ré*-kóód) *n* disco *m;* recorde
m; registo *m;* **long-playing** ~ disco
de longa duração

record² (ri-*kóód*) *v* registar

recorder (ri-*kóó*-dã) *n* gravador *m*

recording (ri-*kóó*-dinng) *n* gravação *f*

record-player (*ré*-kóód-plei³) *n* gira-discos *m;* toca-discos *mBr*

recover (ri-ka-vã) *v* recuperar; curar-se, restabelecer-se

recovery (ri-ka-vã-ri) *n* cura *f,* restabelecimento *m*

recreation (ré-kri-*ei*-chãnn) *n* recreação *f;* ~ **centre** centro recreativo;
~ **ground** campo de jogos

recruit (ri-*kruut*) *n* recruta *m*

rectangle (*rék*-tænng-ghãl) *n* rectângulo *m*

rectangular (rék-*tænng*- gh¹u-lã) *adj*
rectangular

rector (*rék*-tã) *n* pastor *m,* reitor *m*

rectory (*rék*-tã-ri) *n* reitoria *f*

rectum (*rék*-tãmm) *n* recto *m*

red (réd) *adj* encarnado

redeem (ri-*diimm*) *v* redimir

reduce (ri-d¹uuç) *v* *reduzir, *diminuir

reduction (ri-dak-chãnn) *n* redução *f,*
desconto *m*

redundant (ri-dann-dãnnt) *adj* supérfluo

reed (riid) *n* cana *f*

reef (riif) *n* recife *m*

reference (*réf*-rãnnç) *n* referência *f;*

relação f; with ~ to relativo a

refer to (ri-fáǎ) *referir a

refill (rii-fil) n recarga f

refinery (ri-fai-nǎ-ri) n refinaria f

reflect (ri-flékt) v *reflectir

reflection (ri-flék-chänn) n reflexão f; imagem reflectida

reflector (ri-flék-tǎ) n reflector m

reformation (ré-fǎ-mei-chänn) n Reforma f

refresh (ri-fréch) v refrescar

refreshment (ri-fréch-männt) n refresco m

refrigerator (ri-fri-djä-rei-tǎ) n frigorífico m

refund¹ (ri-fannd) v reembolsar

refund² (rii-fannd) n reembolso m

refusal (ri-fⁱuu-zǎl) n recusa f

refuse¹ (ri-fⁱuuz) v recusar

refuse² (ré-fⁱuuç) n lixo m

regard (ri-ghaad) v considerar; n respeito m; **as regards** quanto a, respeitante a, no que diz respeito a

regarding (ri-ghaa-dinng) prep relativamente a, relativo a; com respeito a

regatta (ri-ghæ-tǎ) n regata f

régime (rei-jiimm) n regime m

region (rii-djänn) n região f

regional (rii-djä-nǎl) adj regional

register (ré-dji-çtǎ) v inscrever-se, registar-se; registar; **registered letter** carta registada

registration (ré-dji-çtrei-chänn) n registo m; ~ **form** formulário de inscrição; ~ **number** número de matrícula; ~ **plate** chapa da matrícula

regret (ri-ghrét) v lamentar; n pena f

regular (ré-ghⁱu-lä) adj regular; normal, corrente

regulate (ré-ghⁱu-leit) v regular

regulation (ré-ghⁱu-lei-chänn) n regulamento m; regulamentação f

rehabilitation (rii-hǎ-bi-li-tei-chänn) n reabilitação f

rehearsal (ri-hǎǎ-çǎl) n ensaio m

rehearse (ri-hǎǎç) v ensaiar

reign (reinn) n reinado m; v reinar

reimburse (rii-imm-bǎǎç) v reembolsar

reindeer (reinn-diǎ) n (pl ~) rena f

reject (ri-djékt) v recusar, rejeitar; reprovar

relate (ri-leit) v contar, relatar

related (ri-lei-tid) adj aparentado

relation (ri-lei-chänn) n relação f; parente m

relative (ré-lä-tiv) n parente m; adj relativo

relax (ri-lækç) v *descontrair-se

relaxation (ri-læk-çei-chänn) n descontracção f

reliable (ri-lai-ǎ-bǎl) adj de confiança

relic (ré-lik) n relíquia f

relief (ri-liif) n alívio m; assistência f; relevo m

relieve (ri-liiv) v aliviar; render

religion (ri-li-djänn) n religião f

religious (ri-li-djäç) adj religioso

rely on (ri-lai) contar com

remain (ri-meinn) v ficar; sobejar

remainder (ri-meinn-dä) n remanescente m, restante m, resto m

remaining (ri-mei-ninng) adj restante

remark (ri-maak) n observação f; v observar

remarkable (ri-maa-kä-bǎl) adj notável

remedy (ré-mä-di) n remédio m

remember (ri-mémm-bǎ) v recordar-se, lembrar-se

remembrance (ri-mémm-bränng) n lembrança f, recordação f

remind (ri-mainnd) v recordar, lembrar

remit (ri-mit) v remeter

remittance (ri-mi-tännç) n remessa f

remnant (*rémm*-nännt) *n* excedente *m*, remanescente *m*

remote (ri-*mo*ᵘt) *adj* distante, remoto

removal (ri-*muu*-väl) *n* remoção *f*

remove (ri-*muuv*) *v* remover

remunerate (ri-*m*ⁱ*uu*-nä-reit) *v* remunerar

remuneration (ri-m*ⁱ*uu-nä-*rei*-chänn) *n* remuneração *f*

renew (ri-*n*ⁱ*uu*) *v* renovar, prolongar

rent (*rénnt*) *v* arrendar, alugar; *n* renda *f*

repair (ri-*pé*ᵃ) *v* reparar; *n* conserto *m*

reparation (ré-pä-*rei*-chänn) *n* reparação *f*

***repay** (ri-*pei*) *v* reembolsar

repayment (ri-*pei*-männt) *n* reembolso *m*

repeat (ri-*piit*) *v* *repetir

repellent (ri-*pé*-lännt) *adj* repugnante, repelente

repentance (ri-*pénn*-tännç) *n* arrependimento *m*

repertory (*ré*-pä-tä-ri) *n* repertório *m*

repetition (ré-pä-*ti*-chänn) *n* repetição *f*

replace (ri-*pleiç*) *v* *substituir

reply (ri-*plai*) *v* responder; *n* resposta *f*; in ~ em resposta

report (ri-*póót*) *v* relatar; participar; apresentar-se; *n* relatório *m*, relação *f*

reporter (ri-*póó*-tä) *n* repórter *m*

represent (ré-pri-*zénnt*) *v* representar

representation (ré-pri-zénn-*tei*-chänn) *n* representação *f*

representative (ré-pri-*zénn*-tä-tiv) *adj* representativo

reprimand (ré-pri-*maannd*) *v* repreender

reproach (ri-*pro*ᵘtch) *n* censura *f*; *v* censurar

reproduce (rii-prä-*d*ⁱ*uuç*) *v* *reprodu-

zir

reproduction (rii-prä-*dak*-chänn) *n* reprodução *f*

reptile (*rép*-tail) *n* réptil *m*

republic (ri-*pa*-blik) *n* república *f*

republican (ri-*pa*-bli-känn) *adj* republicano

repulsive (ri-*pal*-çiv) *adj* repelente

reputation (ré-p*ⁱ*u-*tei*-chänn) *n* reputação *f*; renome *m*

request (ri-*k*ᵘéçt) *n* pedido *m*; *v* *requerer

require (ri-*k*ᵘ*ai*ᵃ) *v* exigir

requirement (ri-k*ᵘai*ᵃ-männt) *n* necessidade *f*

requisite (*ré*-k*ᵘ*i-zit) *adj* necessário

rescue (*ré*-çk*ⁱ*uu) *v* salvar; *n* salvação *f*

research (ri-*çää*tch) *n* investigação *f*

resemblance (ri-*zémm*-blännç) *n* semelhança *f*

resemble (ri-*zémm*-bäl) *v* assemelhar-se

resent (ri-*zénnt*) *v* levar a mal, melindrar-se por

reservation (ré-zä-*vei*-chänn) *n* reserva *f*

reserve (ri-*zääv*) *v* reservar; *n* reserva *f*

reserved (ri-*zääv*d) *adj* reservado

reservoir (*ré*-zä-v*ᵘ*aa) *n* reservatório *m*

reside (ri-*zaid*) *v* residir

residence (*ré*-zi-dännç) *n* residência *f*; ~ **permit** autorização de residência

resident (*ré*-zi-dännt) *n* residente *m*; *adj* residente; interno

resign (ri-*zainn*) *v* demitir-se

resignation (ré-zigh-*nei*-chänn) *n* demissão *f*

resin (*ré*-zinn) *n* resina *f*

resist (ri-*ziçt*) *v* resistir

resistance (ri-zi-*çtä*nnç) *n* resistência

f

resolute (ré-ză-luut) *adj* decidido, resoluto

respect (ri-çpékt) *n* respeito *m*; veneração *f*, estima *f*; *v* respeitar

respectable (ri-çpék-tă-băl) *adj* respeitável

respectful (ri-çpékt-făl) *adj* respeitoso

respective (ri-çpék-tiv) *adj* respectivo

respiration (ré-çpă-rei-chănn) *n* respiração *f*

respite (ré-çpait) *n* protelação *f*

responsibility (ri-çpónn-çă-bi-lă-ti) *n* responsabilidade *f*

responsible (ri-çpónn-çă-băl) *adj* responsável

rest (réçt) *n* descanso *m*; resto *m*; *v* repousar, descansar

restaurant (ré-çtă-rón) *n* restaurante *m*

restful (réçt-făl) *adj* sossegado

rest-home (réçt-ho**u**mm) *n* casa de repouso

restless (réçt-lăç) *adj* inquieto

restrain (ri-çtreinn) *v* *conter, *reter

restriction (ri-çtrik-chănn) *n* restrição *f*

result (ri-zalt) *n* resultado *m*; consequência *f*; *v* resultar

resume (ri-z**i**uumm) *v* recomeçar

résumé (ré-z**i**u-mei) *n* resumo *m*

retail (rii-teil) *v* vender a retalho; ~ **trade** comércio a retalho

retailer (rii-tei-lă) *n* retalhista *m*; revendedor *m*

retina (ré-ti-nă) *n* retina *f*

retired (ri-tai**ă**d) *adj* reformado

return (ri-tăănn) *v* voltar; *n* regresso *m*; ~ **flight** voo de regresso; ~ **journey** viagem de regresso

reunite (rii-**i**uu-nait) *v* reunir

reveal (ri-viil) *v* revelar

revelation (ré-vă-lei-chănn) *n* revelação *f*

revenge (ri-vénndj) *n* vingança *f*

revenue (ré-vă-n**i**uu) *n* receita *f*, rendimento *m*

reverse (ri-văăç) *n* contrário *m*; reverso *m*; marcha atrás; revés *m*, reviravolta *f*; *adj* inverso; *v* *fazer marcha atrás; *fazer marcha à ré Br*

review (ri-v**i**uu) *n* crítica *f*; revista *f*

revise (ri-vaiz) *v* *rever

revolt (ri-vo**u**lt) *v* revoltar-se; *n* rebelião *f*, revolta *f*

revolting (ri-vo**u**l-tinng) *adj* chocante, nojento, revoltante

revolution (ré-vă-luu-chănn) *n* revolução *f*; rotação *f*

revolutionary (ré-vă-luu-chă-nă-ri) *adj* revolucionário

revolver (ri-vól-vă) *n* revólver *m*

revue (ri-v**i**uu) *n* revista *f*

reward (ri-**u**óód) *n* recompensa *f*; *v* recompensar

rheumatism (ruu-mă-ti-zămm) *n* reumatismo *m*

rhinoceros (rai-nó-çă-răç) *n* (pl ~, ~es) rinoceronte *m*

rhubarb (ruu-baab) *n* ruibarbo *m*

rhyme (raimm) *n* rima *f*

rhythm (ri-ðămm) *n* ritmo *m*

rib (rib) *n* costela *f*

ribbon (ri-bănn) *n* fita *f*

rice (raiç) *n* arroz *m*

rich (ritch) *adj* rico

riches (ri-tchiz) *pl* riqueza *f*

riddle (ri-dăl) *n* adivinha *f*

ride (raid) *n* passeio *m*, volta *f*

***ride** (raid) *v* andar de automóvel; montar a cavalo

rider (rai-dă) *n* cavaleiro *m*

ridge (ridj) *n* cumeada *f*

ridicule (ri-di-k**i**uul) *v* troçar, ridicularizar

ridiculous (ri-di-k**i**u-lăç) *adj* ridículo

riding (rai-dinng) *n* equitação *f*

riding-school (*rai*-dinng-çkuul) *n* escola de equitação

rifle (*rai*-fǎl) *v* espingarda *f*

right (rait) *n* direito *m*; *adj* correcto;
recto; direito; equitativo, justo; **all
right!** de acordo!; * **be** ~ *ter razão; ~ **of way** prioridade *f*

righteous (*rai*-tchǎç) *adj* justo

right-hand (*rait*-hænnd) *adj* à direita,
direito

rightly (*rait*-li) *adv* justamente

rim (rimm) *n* jante *f*; borda *f*

ring (rinng) *n* anel *m*; círculo *m*; pista
f

*ring (rinng) *v* tocar; ~ **up** telefonar

rinse (rinnç) *v* enxaguar; *n* enxaguadela *f*

riot (*rai*-ǎt) *n* motim *m*, desordem *f*

rip (rip) *v* rasgar

ripe (raip) *adj* maduro

rise (raiz) *n* aumento *m*; elevação *f*;
subida *f*; origem *f*

*rise (raiz) *v* erguer-se, levantar-se;
*subir

rising (*rai*-zinng) *n* insurreição *f*

risk (riçk) *n* risco *m*; perigo *m*; *v* arriscar

risky (*ri*-çki) *adj* perigoso, arriscado

rival (*rai*-vǎl) *n* rival *m*; *v* rivalizar

rivalry (*rai*-vǎl-ri) *n* rivalidade *f*; concorrência *f*

river (*ri*-vǎ) *n* rio *m*; ~ **bank** margem
f

riverside (*ri*-vǎ-çaid) *n* beira-rio *f*

roach (ro^utch) *n* (pl ~) robalo *m*

road (ro^ud) *n* estrada *f*; ~ **fork** bifurcação *f*; ~ **map** mapa de estra-
das; ~ **system** rede rodoviária; ~
up estrada em obras

roadhouse (*ro^ud*-hauç) *n* estalagem *f*

roadside (*ro^ud*-çaid) *n* berma *f*

roam (ro^umm) *v* *vagabundear

roar (róó) *v* rugir, bramir; *n* rugido
m, rumor *m*

roast (ro^uçt) *v* grelhar, assar

rob (rób) *v* roubar

robber (*ró*-bǎ) *n* ladrão *m*

robbery (*ró*-bǎ-ri) *n* roubo *m*

robe (ro^ub) *n* vestido comprido; veste
f

robin (*ró*-binn) *n* pintarroxo *m*

robust (ro^u-baçt) *adj* robusto

rock (rók) *n* rocha *f*; *v* baloiçar

rocket (*ró*-kit) *n* foguete *m*

rocky (*ró*-ki) *adj* rochoso

rod (ród) *n* vara *f*, varão *m*

roe (ro^u) *n* ova *f*

roll (ro^ul) *v* rolar; *n* rolo *m*; pãozinho
m

roller-skating (*ro^u*-lǎ-çkei-tinng) *n* patinagem *f*

Roman Catholic (*ro^u*-mǎnn *kæ*-θǎ-lik)
católico

romance (rǎ-*mænnç*) *n* romance *m*

romantic (rǎ-*mænn*-tik) *adj* romântico

roof (ruuf) *n* telhado *m*; **thatched** ~
telhado de colmo

room (ruumm) *n* quarto *m*; espaço *m*,
lugar *m*; ~ **and board** cama e mesa; ~ **service** serviço de quarto; ~
temperature temperatura ambiente

roomy (*ruu*-mi) *adj* espaçoso

root (ruut) *n* raiz *f*

rope (ro^up) *n* corda *f*

rosary (*ro^u*-zǎ-ri) *n* rosário *m*

rose (ro^uz) *n* rosa *f*; *adj* rosado

rotten (*ró*-tǎnn) *adj* podre

rouge (ruuj) *n* rouge *m*

rough (raf) *adj* áspero; brusco

roulette (ruu-*lét*) *n* roleta *f*

round (raunnd) *adj* redondo; *prep* em
torno de, à volta; *n* volta *f*; ~ **trip**
Am ida e volta

roundabout (*raunn*-dǎ-baut) *n* rotunda
f

rounded (*raunn*-did) *adj* arredondado

route (ruut) *n* rota *f*

routine (ruu-*tiinn*) *n* rotina *f*

row[1] (ro[u]) *n* fila *f;* *v* remar

row[2] (rau) *n* zaragata *f*

rowdy (*rau*-di) *adj* turbulento

rowing-boat (*ro*[u]-inng-bo[u]t) *n* barco a remos

royal (*roi*-ăl) *adj* real

rub (rab) *v* esfregar

rubber (*ra*-bă) *n* borracha *f;* ~ **band** elástico *m*

rubbish (*ra*-bich) *n* lixo *m;* disparates, asneira *f;* bobagem *fBr;* **talk** ~ *dizer disparates

rubbish-bin (*ra*-bich-binn) *n* caixote do lixo; lata de lixo *Br*

ruby (*ruu*-bi) *n* rubi *m*

rucksack (*rak*-çăk) *n* mochila *f*

rudder (*ra*-dă) *n* leme *m*

rude (ruud) *adj* rude

rug (ragh) *n* tapete *m*

ruin (*ruu*-inn) *v* arruinar; *n* ruína *f*

ruination (ruu-i-*nei*-chănn) *n* ruína *f*

rule (ruul) *n* regra *f;* governo *m,* regime *m,* domínio *m;* *v* governar; **as a** ~ em regra, geralmente

ruler (*ruu*-lă) *n* governante *m,* monarca *m;* régua *f*

Rumania (ruu-*mei*-ni-ă) Roménia *f*

Rumanian (ruu-*mei*-ni-ănn) *adj* romeno

rumour (*ruu*-mă) *n* rumor *m*

*run (rann) *v* correr; ~ **into** deparar com

runaway (*ra*-nă-[u]ei) *n* fugitivo *m*

rung (rann) *v* (pp ring)

runway (*rann*-[u]ei) *n* pista de descolagem

rural (*ru*[ă]-răl) *adj* rural

ruse (ruuz) *n* ardil *m*

rush (rach) *v* apressar-se; *n* junco *m*

rush-hour (*rach*-au[ă]) *n* hora de ponta

Russia (*ra*-chă) Rússia *f*

Russian (*ra*-chănn) *adj* russo

rust (raçt) *n* ferrugem *f*

rustic (*ra*-çtik) *adj* rústico

rusty (*ra*-çti) *adj* ferrugento

S

saccharin (*çæ*-kă-rinn) *n* sacarina *f*

sack (çăk) *n* saca *f*

sacred (*çei*-krid) *adj* sagrado

sacrifice (*çæ*-kri-faiç) *n* sacrifício *m;* *v* sacrificar

sacrilege (*çæ*-kri-lidj) *n* sacrilégio *m*

sad (çăd) *adj* triste; desgostoso, melancólico

saddle (*çæ*-dăl) *n* sela *f*

sadness (*çæd*-năç) *n* tristeza *f*

safe (çeif) *adj* seguro; *n* cofre-forte *m*

safety (*çeif*-ti) *n* segurança *f*

safety-belt (*çeif*-ti-bélt) *n* cinto de segurança

safety-pin (*çeif*-ti-pinn) *n* alfinete de segurança

safety-razor (*çeif*-ti-rei-ză) *n* gilete *f*

sail (çeil) *v* navegar; *n* vela *f*

sailing-boat (*çei*-linng-bo[u]t) *n* barco à vela

sailor (*çei*-lă) *n* marinheiro *m*

saint (çeinnt) *n* santo *m*

salad (*çæ*-lăd) *n* salada *f*

salad-oil (*çæ*-lăd-oil) *n* óleo para salada, azeite *m*

salary (*çæ*-lă-ri) *n* ordenado *m,* salário *m*

sale (çeil) *n* venda *f;* **clearance** ~ liquidação *f;* **for** ~ à venda; **sales** saldos *mpl*

saleable (*çei*-lă-băl) *adj* vendável

salesgirl (*çeilz*-ghăăl) *n* vendedora *f*

salesman (*çeilz*-mănn) *n* (pl -men) vendedor *m*

salon (*çæ*-lón) *n* salão *m*

saloon (çă-*luunn*) *n* bar *m*

salt (çóólt) *n* sal *m*

salt-cellar (*cóólt*-cé-lă) n saleiro m

salty (*cóól*-ti) adj salgado

salute (că-*luut*) v saudar

salve (caav) n unguento m

same (ceimm) adj mesmo

sample (*caamm*-păl) n amostra f

sanatorium (că-nă-*tóó*-ri-ămm) n (pl ~s, -ria) sanatório m

sand (cænnd) n areia f

sandal (*cænn*-dăl) n sandália f

sandpaper (*cænnd*-pei-pă) n lixa f

sandwich (*cænn*-ᵁidj) n sanduíche f

sandy (*cænn*-di) adj arenoso

sanitary (*cæ*-ni-tă-ri) adj sanitário; ~ **towel** penso higiénico

sapphire (*cæ*-faiᵃ) n safira f

sardine (caa-*diinn*) n sardinha f

satchel (*cæ*-tchăl) n pasta da escola

satellite (*cæ*-tă-lait) n satélite m

satin (*cæ*-tinn) n cetim m

satisfaction (*cæ*-tiç-fæk-chănn) n satisfacão f

satisfy (*cæ*-tiç-fai) v *satisfazer

Saturday (*cæ*-tă-di) sábado m

sauce (cóóç) n molho m

saucepan (*cóóç*-pănn) n caçarola f

saucer (*cóó*-çă) n pires m

Saudi Arabia (cau-di-ă-*rei*-bi-ă) Arábia Saudita

Saudi Arabian (cau-di-ă-*rei*-bi-ănn) adj saudita

sauna (*cóó*-nă) n sauna f

sausage (*có*-çidj) n salsicha f

savage (*cæ*-vidj) adj selvagem

save (ceiv) v salvar; poupar

savings (*cei*-vinngz) pl economias fpl; ~ **bank** caixa económica

saviour (*cei*-vᴵă) n salvador m

savoury (*cei*-vă-ri) adj saboroso; picante

saw¹ (cóó) v (p see)

saw² (cóó) n serra f

sawdust (*cóó*-daçt) n serradura f

saw-mill (*cóó*-mil) n serracão f

*say (çei) v *dizer

scaffolding (*çkæ*-făl-dinng) n andaime m

scale (çkeil) n escala f; escama f; **scales** balança f

scandal (*çkænn*-dăl) n escândalo m

Scandinavia (çkænn-di-*nei*-vi-ă) Escandinávia f

Scandinavian (çkænn-di-*nei*-vi-ănn) adj escandinavo

scapegoat (*çkeip*-ghoᵁt) n bode expiatório

scar (çkaa) n cicatriz f

scarce (çkéᵃç) adj escasso

scarcely (*çkéᵃ*-çli) adv raramente

scarcity (*çkéᵃ*-çă-ti) n escassez f

scare (çkéᵃ) v assustar; n susto m

scarf (çkaaf) n (pl ~s, scarves) lenço do pescoço, lenço da cabeça

scarlet (*çkaa*-lăt) adj escarlate

scary (*çkéᵃ*-ri) adj assustador

scatter (*çkæ*-tă) v dispersar

scene (çiinn) n cena f

scenery (*çii*-nă-ri) n paisagem f

scenic (*çii*-nik) adj pitoresco

scent (çénnt) n perfume m

schedule (*ché*-dᵁul) n horário f

scheme (çkiimm) n esquema m; plano m

scholar (*çkó*-lă) n erudito m; aluno m

scholarship (*çkó*-lă-chip) n bolsa de estudos

school (çkuul) n escola f

schoolboy (*çkuul*-boi) n escolar m

schoolgirl (*çkuul*-ghăăl) n escolar f

schoolmaster (*çkuul*-maa-çtă) n professor de escola

schoolteacher (*çkuul*-tii-tchă) n professor de escola

science (*çai*-ănnç) n ciência f

scientific (çai-ănn-*ti*-fik) adj científico

scientist (*çai*-ănn-tiçt) n cientista m

scissors (*çi*-zăz) pl tesoura f

scold (çkoᵁld) v repreender; ralhar

scooter (çkuu-tä) n scooter f; trotineta f

score (çkóó) n resultado m; v marcar

scorn (çkóónn) n escárnio m, desprezo m; v desprezar

Scot (çkót) n escocês m

Scotch (çkótch) adj escocês

Scotland (çkót-lännd) Escócia f

Scottish (çkó-tich) adj escocês

scout (çkaut) n escuteiro m

scrap (çkräp) n pedaço m

scrap-book (çkräp-buk) n álbum de recortes

scrape (çkreip) v raspar

scrap-iron (çkræ-paiänn) n sucata f

scratch (çkrætch) v arranhar, riscar; n risco m, arranhão m

scream (çkriimm) v gritar; n grito m

screen (çkriinn) n biombo m; tela f, écran m

screw (çkruu) n parafuso m; v aparafusar

screw-driver (çkruu-drai-vä) n chave de parafusos

scrub (çkrab) v esfregar; n moita f

sculptor (çkalp-tä) n escultor m

sculpture (çkalp-tchä) n escultura f

sea (çii) n mar m

sea-bird (çii-bääd) n ave marinha

sea-coast (çii-kouçt) n litoral m

seagull (çii-ghal) n gaivota f

seal (çiil) n selo m; foca f

seam (çiimm) n costura f

seaman (çii-männ) n (pl -men) marinheiro m

seamless (çiimm-läç) adj sem costura

seaport (çii-póót) n porto marítimo

search (çäätch) v procurar; revistar, rebuscar, pesquisar; n busca f

searchlight (çäätch-lait) n holofote m

seascape (çii-çkeip) n paisagem marítima

sea-shell (çii-chél) n concha f

seashore (çii-chóó) n beira-mar f

seasick (çii-çik) adj enjoado

seasickness (çii-çik-näç) n enjoo m

seaside resort estação balnear

season (çii-zänn) n estação f; high ~ alta estação; low ~ baixa estação; off ~ fora da época

season-ticket (çii-zänn-ti-kit) n assinatura de temporada

seat (çiit) n assento m; sítio m, lugar m; sede f

seat-belt (çiit-bélt) n cinto de segurança

sea-urchin (çii-ää-tchinn) n ouriço-do-mar m

sea-water (çii-uóó-tä) n água do mar

second (cé-kännd) num segundo; n segundo m; instante m

secondary (cé-känn-dä-ri) adj secundário; ~ school escola secundária

second-hand (cé-kännd-hænnd) adj em segunda mão

secret (çii-krät) n segredo m; adj secreto

secretary (cé-krä-tri) n secretária f; secretário m

section (cé-kännn) n secção f; divisão f

secure (çi-kiuä) adj seguro

security (çi-kiuä-rä-ti) n segurança f; fiança f

sedate (çi-deit) adj calmo

sedative (cé-dä-tiv) n sedativo m

seduce (çi-diuuç) v *seduzir

*see (çii) v *ver; perceber, compreender; ~ to tratar de

seed (çiid) n semente f

*seek (çiik) v procurar

seem (çiimm) v parecer

seen (çiinn) v (pp see)

seesaw (çii-çóó) n balancé m; gangorra f Br

seize (çiiz) v agarrar

seldom (cél-dämm) adv raramente

select (çi-lékt) v escolher, seleccionar; *adj* seleccionado, selecto

selection (çi-*lék*-chănn) *n* selecção *f*, escolha *f*

self-centred (célf-*çénn*-tăd) *adj* egocêntrico

self-employed (cél-fimm-*ploid*) *adj* independente

self-government (célf-*gha*-vă-mănnt) *n* autonomia *f*

selfish (*cél*-fich) *adj* egoísta

selfishness (*cél*-fich-năç) *n* egoísmo *m*

***sell** (cél) *v* vender

semblance (*cémm*-blănnç) *n* aparência *f*

semi- (*cé*-mi) semi-

semicircle (*cé*-mi-çăă-kăl) *n* semi-círculo *m*

semi-colon (*cé*-mi-*ko*ᵘ-lănn) *n* ponto e vírgula

senate (*cé*-năt) *n* senado *m*

senator (*cé*-nă-tă) *n* senador *m*

***send** (cénnd) *v* enviar, mandar; ~ **back** devolver; ~ **for** mandar vir; ~ **off** *expedir

senile (*cii*-nail) *adj* senil

sensation (cénn-*cei*-chănn) *n* sensação *f*

sensational (cénn-*cei*-chă-năl) *adj* sensacional

sense (cénnç) *n* sentido *m*; juízo *m*, razão *f*; *v* perceber, *sentir; ~ **of honour** sentimento de honra

senseless (*cénnç*-lăç) *adj* sem sentido

sensible (*cénn*-çă-băl) *adj* sensato

sensitive (*cénn*-çi-tiv) *adj* sensível

sentence (*cénn*-tănnç) *n* frase *f*; sentença *f*; *v* condenar

sentimental (cénn-ti-*ménn*-tăl) *adj* sentimental

separate¹ (*cé*-pă-reit) *v* separar

separate² (*cé*-pă-răt) *adj* distinto, separado

separately (*cé*-pă-răt-li) *adv* à parte

September (cép-*témm*-bă) Setembro

septic (*cép*-tik) *adj* séptico; ***become** ~ infectar

sequel (*cii*-kᵘăl) *n* continuação *f*

sequence (*cii*-kᵘănnç) *n* sequência *f*; série *f*

serene (că-*riinn*) *adj* sereno

serial (*ci*ᵃ-ri-ăl) *n* folhetim *m*

series (*ci*ᵃ-riiz) *n* (pl ~) série *f*

serious (*ci*ᵃ-ri-ăç) *adj* sério

seriousness (*ci*ᵃ-ri-ăç-năç) *n* seriedade *f*

sermon (*căă*-mănn) *n* sermão *m*

serum (*ci*ᵃ-rămm) *n* soro *m*

servant (*căă*-vănnt) *n* criado *m*

serve (căăv) *v* *servir

service (*căă*-viç) *n* serviço *m*; ~ **charge** taxa de serviço; ~ **station** estação de serviço

serviette (căă-vi-*ét*) *n* guardanapo *m*

session (*cé*-chănn) *n* sessão *f*

set (cét) *n* grupo *m*; jogo *m*

***set** (cét) *v* pousar, *pôr; ~ **menu** ementa fixa; ~ **out** partir

setting (*cé*-tinng) *n* cenário *m*; ~ **lotion** loção fixadora

settle (*cé*-tăl) *v* regularizar, resolver; ~ **down** fixar-se

settlement (*cé*-tăl-mănnt) *n* ajuste *m*, acordo *m*

seven (*cé*-vănn) *num* sete

seventeen (cé-vănn-*tiinn*) *num* dezassete

seventeenth (cé-vănn-*tiinn*θ) *num* décimo sétimo

seventh (*cé*-vănnθ) *num* sétimo

seventy (*cé*-vănn-ti) *num* setenta

several (*cé*-vă-răl) *adj* vários

severe (ci-*vi*ᵃ) *adj* violento, grave, rigoroso

***sew** (çoᵘ) *v* coser; ~ **up** suturar

sewer (*çuu*-ă) *n* esgoto *m*

sewing-machine (*ço*ᵘ-inng-mă-chiinn) *n* máquina de costura

sex (cékç) *n* sexo *m*; sexualidade *f*

sexton (cék-çtänn) n sacristão m

sexual (cék-chu-ãl) adj sexual

sexuality (cék-chu-æ-lã-ti) n sexualidade f

shade (cheid) n sombra f; tom m

shadow (chæ-do^u) n sombra f

shady (chei-di) adj sombrio

****shake** (cheik) v *sacudir, abanar

shaky (chei-ki) adj vacilante

****shall** (chæl) v dever

shallow (chæ-lo^u) adj pouco profundo

shame (cheimm) n vergonha f; desonra f; **shame!** que vergonha!

shampoo (chæmm-puu) n champô m

shamrock (chæmm-rók) n trevo m

shape (cheip) n forma f; v formar

share (ché^ã) v partilhar; n parte f; acção f

shark (chaak) n tubarão m

sharp (chaap) adj afiado

sharpen (chaa-pänn) v afiar

shave (cheiv) v *fazer a barba, *barbear-se

shaver (chei-vä) n máquina de barbear; barbeador eléctrico Br

shaving-brush (chei-vinng-brach) n pincel da barba

shaving-cream (chei-vinng-kriimm) n creme para a barba

shaving-soap (chei-vinng-ço^up) n sabão da barba

shawl (chóól) n xaile m, xale m

she (chii) pron ela

shed (chéd) n arrecadação f

****shed** (chéd) v derramar, vazar; espalhar

sheep (chiip) n (pl ~) ovelha f

sheer (chi^ã) adj puro, absoluto; delicado, translúcido, fino

sheet (chiit) n lençol m; folha f; chapa f

shelf (chélf) n (pl shelves) prateleira f

shell (chél) n concha f; casca f

shellfish (chél-fich) n marisco m

shelter (chél-tä) n refúgio m, abrigo m; v abrigar

shepherd (ché-päd) n pastor m

shift (chift) n turno m

****shine** (chainn) v brilhar; *reluzir

ship (chip) n navio m; v *expedir; **shipping line** companhia de navegação

shipowner (chi-po^u-nä) n armador m

shipyard (chip-¹aad) n estaleiro m

shirt (chäät) n camisa f

shiver (chi-vä) v tremer, tiritar; n arrepio m

shivery (chi-vä-ri) adj trémulo

shock (chók) n choque m; v chocar; ~ **absorber** amortecedor m

shocking (chó-kinng) adj chocante

shoe (chuu) n sapato m; **gym shoes** sapatos de ginástica; ~ **polish** graxa f

shoe-lace (chuu-leiç) n atacador m

shoemaker (chuu-mei-kä) n sapateiro m

shoe-shop (chuu-chóp) n sapataria f

shook (chuk) v (p shake)

****shoot** (chuut) v disparar

shop (chóp) n loja f; v *fazer compras; ~ **assistant** empregado de balcão; **shopping bag** saco das compras; **shopping centre** centro comercial

shopkeeper (chóp-kii-pä) n lojista m

shop-window (chóp-^uinn-do^u) n montra f

shore (chóó) n margem f, beira-mar f

short (chóót) adj curto; baixo; ~ **circuit** curto-circuito m

shortage (chóó-tidj) n escassez f, carência f

shortcoming (chóót-ka-minng) n falha f

shorten (chóó-tắnn) v encurtar

shorthand (chóót-hænnd) n estenografia f

shortly (chóót-li) adv dentro em breve, brevemente, daqui a pouco

shorts (chóótç) pl calções mpl; plAm cuecas fpl

short-sighted (chóót-çai-tid) adj míope m

shot (chót) n tiro m; injecção f

*****should** (chud) v dever

shoulder (chouʰl-dǎ) n ombro m

shout (chaut) v gritar; n grito m

shovel (cha-vǎl) n pá f

show (chouʰ) n representação f, espectáculo m; exposição f

*****show** (chouʰ) v mostrar; exibir, *expor; demonstrar

show-case (chouʰ-keiç) n vitrina f

shower (chauʰᵃ) n duche m; aguaceiro m

showroom (chouʰ-ruumm) n sala de exposições

shriek (chriik) v gritar; n guincho m

shrimp (chrimmp) n camarão m

shrine (chrainn) n santuário m

*****shrink** (chrinngk) v encolher

shrinkproof (chrinngk-pruuf) adj não encolhe

shrub (chrab) n arbusto m

shudder (cha-dǎ) n estremecimento m

shuffle (cha-fǎl) v baralhar

*****shut** (chat) v fechar; **shut** fechado, encerrado; ~ **in** fechar

shutter (cha-tǎ) n janela de madeira, persiana f

shy (chai) adj tímido

shyness (chai-nǎç) n timidez f

Siamese (çai-ǎ-miiz) adj siamês

sick (çik) adj doente; enjoado

sickness (çik-nǎç) n doença f; enjoo m

side (çaid) n lado m; partido m;

one-sided unilateral

sideburns (çaid-bǎǎnnz) pl suíças fpl

sidelight (çaid-lait) n luz lateral

side-street (çaid-çtriit) n transversal f

sidewalk (çaid-ʰóók) nAm passeio m

sideways (çaid-ʰeiz) adv de lado

siege (çiidj) n cerco m

sieve (çiv) n peneira m; v peneirar

sift (çift) v peneirar

sight (çait) n vista f, espectáculo m; ponto de interesse

sign (çainn) n sinal m, marca f, gesto m; v assinar

signal (çigh-nǎl) n sinal m; v *fazer sinais

signature (çigh-nǎ-tchǎ) n assinatura f

significant (çigh-ni-fi-kǎnnt) adj significativo

signpost (çainn-pouʰçt) n poste indicador

silence (çai-lǎnnç) n silêncio m; v calar

silencer (çai-lǎnn-çǎ) n silencioso m

silent (çai-lǎnnt) adj calado, silencioso

silk (çilk) n seda f

silken (çil-kǎnn) adj sedoso

silly (çi-li) adj palerma, disparatado

silver (çil-vǎ) n prata f; de prata

silversmith (çil-vǎ-çmiθ) n ourives m

silverware (çil-vǎ-ʰéᵃ) n pratas fpl

similar (çi-mi-lǎ) adj semelhante, análogo

similarity (çi-mi-læ-rǎ-ti) n semelhança f

simple (çimm-pǎl) adj ingénuo; simples; ordinário

simply (çimm-pli) adv simplesmente

simulate (çi-mʰu-leit) v simular

simultaneous (çi-mǎl-teï-ni-ǎç) adj simultâneo

sin (çinn) n pecado m

since (çinnç) prep desde; adv desde

então; *conj* desde que; visto que

sincere (çinn-çi^ă) *adj* sincero

sinew (çi-nⁱuu) *n* tendão *m*

*sing (çinng) *v* cantar

singer (çinng-ă) *n* cantor *m;* cantora *f*

single (çinng-ghăl) *adj* só; solteiro; ~ room quarto individual

singular (çinng-ghⁱu-lă) *n* singular *m; adj* singular

sinister (çi-ni-çtă) *adj* sinistro

sink (çinngk) *n* lava-louça *m*

*sink (çinngk) *v* afundar-se

sip (çip) *n* sorvo *m*

siphon (çai-fănn) *n* sifão *m*

sir (çăă) senhor

siren (çai^ă-rănn) *n* sirene *f*

sister (çi-çtă) *n* irmã *f*

sister-in-law (çi-çtă-rinn-lóó) *n* (pl sisters-) cunhada *f*

*sit (çit) *v* *estar sentado; ~ down sentar-se

site (çait) *n* sítio *m*

sitting-room (çi-tinng-ruumm) *n* sala de estar

situated (çi-tchu-ei-tid) *adj* situado

situation (çi-tchu-ei-chănn) *n* situação *f*

six (çikç) *num* seis

sixteen (çikç-tiinn) *num* dezasseis

sixteenth (çikç-tiinnθ) *num* décimo sexto

sixth (çikçθ) *num* sexto

sixty (çikç-ti) *num* sessenta

size (çaiz) *n* medida *f,* tamanho *m,* dimensão *f;* formato *m*

skate (çkeit) *v* patinar; *n* patim *m*

skating (çkei-tinng) *n* patinagem *f*

skating-rink (çkei-tinng-rinngk) *n* ringue de patinagem no gelo

skeleton (çké-li-tănn) *n* esqueleto *m*

sketch (çkétch) *n* esboço *m,* desenho *m; v* desenhar, esboçar

sketch-book (çkétch-buk) *n* caderno de desenho

ski¹ (çkii) *v* esquiar

ski² (çkii) *n* (pl ~, ~s) esqui *m; ~ boots* botas de esqui; ~ *pants* calças de esqui; ~ *sticks* varas de esqui

skid (çkid) *v* derrapar

skier (çkii-ă) *n* esquiador *m*

skiing (çkii-inng) *n* esqui *m*

ski-jump (çkii-djammp) *n* salto de esqui

skilful (çkil-făl) *adj* hábil, destro

ski-lift (çkii-lift) *n* telesqui *m*

skill (çkil) *n* perícia *f*

skilled (çkild) *adj* perito, hábil; especializado

skin (çkinn) *n* pele *f;* casca *f;* ~ *cream* creme para a pele

skip (çkip) *v* saltitar; saltar

skirt (çkăăt) *n* saia *f*

skull (çkal) *n* crânio *m*

sky (çkai) *n* céu *m;* ar *m*

skyscraper (çkai-çkrei-pă) *n* arranha-céus *m*

slack (çlæk) *adj* lento

slacks (çlækç) *pl* calças *fpl*

slam (çlæmm) *v* fechar violentamente

slander (çlaann-dă) *n* calúnia *f*

slant (çlaannt) *v* inclinar-se

slanting (çlaann-tinng) *adj* oblíquo, inclinado

slap (çlæp) *v* bater; *n* bofetada *f*

slate (çleit) *n* ardósia *f*

slave (çleiv) *n* escravo *m*

sledge (çlédj) *n* trenó *m*

sleep (çliip) *n* sono *m*

*sleep (çliip) *v* *dormir

sleeping-bag (çlii-pinng-bægh) *n* saco-cama *m*

sleeping-car (çlii-pinng-kaa) *n* carruagem-cama *f*

sleeping-pill (çlii-pinng-pil) *n* comprimido para dormir

sleepless (çliip-lăç) *adj* sem dormir

sleepy (çlii-pi) *adj* sonolento

sleeve (çliiv) *n* manga *f*; capa *f*

sleigh (çlei) *n* trenó *m*

slender (çlénn-dă) *adj* esbelto

slice (çlaiç) *n* fatia *f*

slide (çlaid) *n* deslize *m*; escorrega-douro *m*; slide *m*

*__**slide** (çlaid) *v* deslizar

slight (çlait) *adj* ligeiro

slim (çlimm) *adj* delgado; *v* emagrecer

slip (çlip) *v* escorregar, deslizar; escapar; *n* escorregadela *f*; saia de baixo

slipper (çlí-pă) *n* pantufa *f*

slippery (çlí-pă-ri) *adj* escorregadio

slogan (çlóu-ghănn) *n* slogan *m*, lema *m*

slope (çlóup) *n* vertente *f*; *v* inclinar, *ter declive

sloping (çlóu-pinng) *adj* inclinado

slot (çlót) *n* fenda *f*

slot-machine (çlót-mă-chiinn) *n* slot-machine *f*

slovenly (çlá-vănn-li) *adj* descuidado

slow (çlóu) *adj* lento; ~ **down** abrandar, afrouxar; travar; *frear *vBr*

sluice (çluuç) *n* comporta *f*

slum (çlamm) *n* bairro pobre

slump (çlammp) *n* baixa de preços

slush (çlach) *n* neve meio derretida

sly (çlai) *adj* astuto

smack (çmæk) *v* bater; *n* palmada *f*

small (çmóól) *adj* pequeno

smallpox (çmóól-pókç) *n* varíola *f*

smart (çmaat) *adj* elegante; esperto, inteligente

smell (çmél) *n* cheiro *m*

*__**smell** (çmél) *v* cheirar; cheirar mal

smelly (çmé-li) *adj* mal cheiroso

smile (çmail) *v* *sorrir; *n* sorriso *m*

smith (çmiθ) *n* ferreiro *m*

smoke (çmóuk) *v* fumar; *n* fumo *m*; **no smoking** proibido fumar

smoker (çmóu-kă) *n* fumador *m*; compartimento para fumadores

smoking-compartment (çmóu-kinng-kămm-paat-mănnt) *n* compartimento para fumadores

smoking-room (çmóu-kinng-ruumm) *n* sala de fumo

smooth (çmuuð) *adj* plano, liso; suave

smuggle (çma-ghăl) *v* *contrabandear

snack (çnæk) *n* refeição ligeira

snail (çneil) *n* caracol *m*

snake (çneik) *n* serpente *f*

snapshot (çnæp-chót) *n* instantâneo *m*

sneakers (çnii-kăz) *plAm* sapatos de ginástica

sneeze (çniiz) *v* espirrar

sniper (çnai-pă) *n* franco-atirador *m*

snooty (çnuu-ti) *adj* arrogante

snore (çnóó) *v* ressonar

snorkel (çnóó-kăl) *n* tubo respirador

snout (çnaut) *n* focinho *m*

snow (çnóu) *n* neve *f*; *v* nevar

snowy (çnóu-i) *adj* nevado

so (çóu) *conj* portanto; *adv* assim; tão; **and** ~ **on** assim por diante; ~ **far** até agora; ~ **that** para que, de modo que, a fim de

soak (çóuk) *v* embeber, ensopar, molhar, pôr de molho

soap (çóup) *n* sabão *m*; ~ **powder** sabão em pó

sober (çóu-bă) *adj* sóbrio; ponderado

so-called (çóu-kóóld) *adj* pretenso

soccer (çó-kă) *n* futebol *m*; ~ **team** equipa *f*

social (çóu-chăl) *adj* social

socialism (çóu-chă-li-zămm) *n* socialismo *m*

socialist (çóu-chă-liçt) *adj* socialista; *n* socialista *m*

society (çă-çai-ă-ti) *n* sociedade *f*, associacão *f;* companhia *f*

sock (çók) *n* peúga *f*

socket (çó-kit) *n* casquilho *m*

soda-water (çoᵘ-dã-ᵘóó-tã) *n* soda *f,* água gasificada

sofa (çoᵘ-fã) *n* sofá *m*

soft (çóft) *adj* mole; ~ drink bebida não alcoólica

soften (çó-fãnn) *v* suavizar

soil (çoil) *n* solo *m;* terra *f*

soiled (çoild) *adj* sujo

sold (çoᵘld) *v* (p, pp sell) ; ~ out esgotado

solder (çól-dã) *v* soldar

soldering-iron (çól-dã-rinng-aiãnn) *n* ferro de soldar

soldier (çoᵘl-djã) *n* soldado *m*

sole¹ (çoᵘl) *adj* único

sole² (çoᵘl) *n* sola *f;* linguado *m*

solely (çoᵘl-li) *adv* exclusivamente

solemn (çó-lãmm) *adj* solene

solicitor (çã-*li*-çi-tã) *n* advogado *m*

solid (çó-lid) *adj* robusto, sólido; macico; *n* sólido *m*

soluble (çó-lᵘu-bãl) *adj* solúvel

solution (çã-*luu*-chãnn) *n* solução *f*

solve (çólv) *v* resolver

sombre (çómm-bã) *adj* sombrio

some (çamm) *adj* alguns; *pron* certos, uns; ~ day qualquer dia; ~ more um pouco mais; ~ time alguma vez

somebody (çamm-bã-di) *pron* alguém

somehow (çamm-hau) *adv* duma maneira au doutra

someone (çamm-ᵘann) *pron* alguém

something (çamm-θinng) *pron* alguma coisa

sometimes (çamm-taimmz) *adv* às vezes

somewhat (çamm-ᵘót) *adv* um tanto

somewhere (çamm-ᵘéã) *adv* em qualquer parte

son (çann) *n* filho *m*

song (çónn) *n* canção *f*

son-in-law (ça-ninn-lóó) *n* (pl sons-) genro *m*

soon (çuunn) *adv* brevemente, rapidamente, em breve; as ~ as assim que

sooner (çuu-nã) *adv* antes

sore (çóó) *adj* doloroso; *n* dor *f;* úlcera *f;* ~ throat dor de garganta

sorrow (çó-roᵘ) *n* desgosto *m,* tristeza *f,* dor *f*

sorry (çó-ri) *adj* desolado; sorry! desculpe!, perdão!

sort (çóót) *v* ordenar, classificar; *n* género *m,* categoria *f;* all sorts of toda a espécie de

soul (çoᵘl) *n* alma *f;* espírito *m*

sound (çaunnd) *n* som *m; v* parecer, soar; *adj* seguro

soundproof (çaunnd-pruuf) *adj* à prova de som

soup (çuup) *n* sopa *f*

soup-plate (çuup-pleit) *n* prato de sopa

soup-spoon (çuup-çpuunn) *n* colher de sopa

sour (çauᵃ) *adj* azedo

source (çóóç) *n* fonte *f*

south (çauθ) *n* sul *m;* South Pole pólo sul

South Africa (çauθ æ-fri-kã) África do Sul

south-east (çauθ-iiçt) *n* sueste *m*

southerly (ça-ðã-li) *adj* meridional

southern (ça-ðãnn) *adj* do sul

south-west (çauθ-ᵘéçt) *n* sudoeste *m*

souvenir (çuu-vã-niᵃ) *n* recordação *f*

sovereign (çóv-rinn) *n* soberano *m*

Soviet (çoᵘ-vi-ãt) *adj* soviético; ~ Union União Soviética

*sow (çoᵘ) *v* *semear

spa (çpaa) *n* termas *fpl*

space (çpeiç) *n* espaço *m;* distância *f,* intervalo *m; v* espaçar spacious (*cpei*-chăç) *adj* espaçoso

spade (çpeid) *n* pá *f*

Spain (çpeinn) Espanha *f*

Spaniard (*cpæ*-niăd) *n* espanhol *m*

Spanish (*cpæ*-nich) *adj* espanhol

spanking (*cpæng*-kinng) *n* tareia *f*

spanner (*cpæ*-nă) *n* chave de porcas

spare (çpéᵃ) *adj* de reserva, sobressalente; *v* dispensar; ~ part peça sobressalente; ~ room quarto de hóspedes; ~ time tempo livre; ~ tyre pneu sobresselente; ~ wheel roda sobresselente

spark (çpaak) *n* faísca *f*

sparking-plug (*cpaa*-kinng-plagh) *n* vela de ignição

sparkling (*cpaa*-klinng) *adj* cintilante; espumante

sparrow (*cpæ*-roᵘ) *n* pardal *m*

*speak (çpiik) *v* falar

spear (çpiᵃ) *n* lança *f*

special (*cpé*-chăl) *adj* particular, especial; ~ delivery distribuição expressa

specialist (*cpé*-chă-liçt) *n* especialista *m*

speciality (*cpé*-chi-æ-lă-ti) *n* especialidade *f*

specialize (*cpé*-chă-laiz) *v* especializar-se

specially (*cpé*-chă-li) *adv* particularmente

species (*cpii*-chiiz) *n* (pl ~) espécie *f*

specific (çpă-*çi*-fik) *adj* específico

specimen (*cpé*-çi-männ) *n* amostra *f*, exemplar *m*

speck (çpék) *n* mancha *f*

spectacle (*cpék*-tă-kăl) *n* espectáculo *m*: spectacles óculos *mpl*

spectator (çpék-*tei*-tă) *n* espectador *m*

speculate (*cpé*-kⁱu-leit) *v* especular

speech (çpiitch) *n* fala *f*; discurso *m*, alocução *f*; linguagem *f*

speechless (*cpiitch*-lăç) *adj* mudo

speed (çpiid) *n* velocidade *f*; pressa *f*, rapidez *f*; cruising ~ velocidade de cruzeiro; ~ limit limitação de velocidade, velocidade máxima

*speed (çpiid) *v* guiar com excesso de velocidade

speeding (*cpii*-dinng) *n* excesso de velocidade

speedometer (çpii-*dó*-mi-tă) *n* velocímetro *m*

spell (çpél) *n* encantamento *m*

*spell (çpél) *v* soletrar

spelling (*cpé*-linng) *n* ortografia *f*

*spend (çpénnd) *v* gastar; passar, empregar

sphere (çfiᵃ) *n* esfera *f*

spice (çpaiç) *n* especiaria *f*

spiced (çpaiçt) *adj* condimentado

spicy (*cpai*-çi) *adj* picante

spider (*cpai*-dă) *n* aranha *f*; spider's web teia de aranha

*spill (çpil) *v* entornar

*spin (çpinn) *v* fiar; *fazer girar

spinach (*cpi*-nidj) *n* espinafres *mpl*

spine (çpainn) *n* espinha dorsal

spinster (*cpinn*-çtă) *n* solteirona *f*

spire (çpaiᵃ) *n* agulha *f*

spirit (*cpi*-rit) *n* espírito *m*; humor *m*; spirits bebidas alcoólicas; moral *m*; ~ stove lamparina de álcool

spiritual (çpi-ri-tchu-ăl) *adj* espiritual

spit (çpit) *n* cuspo *m*, saliva *f*; espeto *m*

*spit (çpit) *v* *cuspir

in spite of (inn çpait óv) apesar de

spiteful (*cpait*-făl) *adj* malévolo

splash (çplæch) *v* salpicar

splendid (*cplénn*-did) *adj* esplêndido, magnífico

splendour (*cplénn*-dă) *n* esplendor *m*

splint (çplinnt) *n* tala *f*

splinter (*cplinn*-tă) *n* farpa *f*

*split (çplit) *v* fender

*spoil (çpoil) v estragar; amimar

spoke[1] (çpouk) v (p speak)

spoke[2] (çpouk) n raio m

sponge (çpanndj) n esponja f

spook (çpuuk) n fantasma m

spool (çpuul) n bobina f

spoon (çpuunn) n colher f

spoonful (çpuunn-ful) n colherada f

sport (çpóót) n desporto m; esporte mBr; divertimento m; brincadeira f; v brincar, passar o tempo; adj desportivo

sports-car (çpóótç-kaa) n carro de desporto

sports-jacket (çpóótç-djæ-kit) n casaco desportivo

sportsman (çpóótç-männ) n (pl -men) desportista m

sportswear (çpóótç-ᵘéª) n vestuário de desporto

spot (çpót) n mancha f, nódoa f; local m

spotless (çpót-läç) adj sem mancha; impecável

spotlight (çpót-lait) n projector m

spotted (çpó-tid) adj sarapintado

spout (çpaut) n jorro m

sprain (çpreinn) v torcer, deslocar; n distensão f

*spread (çpréd) v espalhar

spring (çprinng) n Primavera f; mola f; nascente f

springtime (çprinng-taimm) n Primavera f

sprouts (çprautç) pl couve-de-bruxelas

spy (çpai) n espião m

squadron (çkᵘó-dränn) n esquadrilha f

square (çkᵘéª) adj quadrado; n quadrado m; praça f

squash (çkᵘóch) n sumo m

squirrel (çkᵘi-räl) n esquilo m

squirt (çkᵘäät) n esguicho m

stable (çtei-bäl) adj estável; n estábulo m

stack (çtæk) n pilha f

stadium (çtei-di-ämm) n estádio m

staff (çtaaf) n pessoal m

stage (çteidj) n palco m; fase f; etapa f

stain (çteinn) v manchar; n nódoa f, mancha f; **stained glass** vidro colorido; ~ **remover** tira-nódoas m

stainless (çteinn-läç) adj imaculado; ~ **steel** aço inoxidável

staircase (çtéª-keiç) n escada f

stairs (çtéªz) pl escada f

stale (çteil) adj velho, estragado

stall (çtóól) n tenda f; plateia f

stamina (çtæ-mi-nä) n resistência f

stamp (çtæmmp) n selo m; v franquiar; calcar; ~ **machine** distribuidor automático de selos

stand (çtænnd) n stand m; tribuna f

*stand (çtænnd) v *estar de pé

standard (çtænn-däd) n padrão m, norma f; normal; ~ **of living** nível de vida

stanza (çtænn-zä) n estrofe f

staple (çtei-päl) n agrafo m; grampo mBr

star (çtaa) n estrela f

starboard (çtaa-bäd) n estibordo m

starch (çtaatch) n goma f; v engomar

stare (çtéª) v fitar

starling (çtaa-linng) n estorninho m

start (çtaat) v começar; n começo m; **starter motor** motor de arranque

starting-point (çtaa-tinng-poinnt) n ponto de partida

state (çteit) n estado m; v declarar

the States (ðä çteitç) Estados Unidos

statement (çteit-männt) n declaração f

statesman (çteitç-männ) n (pl -men) estadista m

station (çtei-chänn) n estação f; posto

m

stationary (çtei-chă-nă-ri) *adj* estacionário

stationer's (çtei-chă-năz) *n* papelaria *f*

stationery (çtei-chă-nă-ri) *n* artigos de escritório

station-master (çtei-chănn-maa-çtă) *n* chefe de estação

statistics (çtă-*ti*-çtikç) *pl* estatística *f*

statue (çtæ-tchuu) *n* estátua *f*

stay (çtei) *v* ficar; permanecer, hospedar-se; *n* estadia *f*

steadfast (çtéd-faaçt) *adj* constante

steady (çté-di) *adj* firme

steak (çteik) *n* bife *m*

***steal** (çtiil) *v* roubar

steam (çtiimm) *n* vapor *m*

steamer (çtii-mă) *n* barco a vapor

steel (çtiil) *n* aço *m*

steep (çtiip) *adj* íngreme, escarpado

steeple (çtii-păl) *n* campanário *m*

steering-column (çti-ă-rinng-kó-lămm) *n* coluna de direcção

steering-wheel (çti-ă-rinng-ůil) *n* volante *m*

steersman (çti-ă z-mănn) *n* (pl -men) timoneiro *m*

stem (çtémm) *n* haste *f*

stenographer (çté-nó-ghră-fă) *n* estenógrafo *m*

step (çtép) *n* passo *m*; degrau *m*; *v* caminhar, andar

stepchild (çtép-tchaild) *n* (pl -children) enteado *m*; enteada *f*

stepfather (çtép-faa-ðă) *n* padrasto *m*

stepmother (çtép-ma-ðă) *n* madrasta *f*

sterile (çté-rail) *adj* estéril

sterilize (çté-ri-laiz) *v* esterilizar

steward (çt¡uu-ăd) *n* comissário de bordo

stewardess (çt¡uu-ă-déç) *n* hospedeira *f*

stick (çtik) *n* pau *m*

***stick** (çtik) *v* colar, pegar

sticky (çti-ki) *adj* pegajoso

stiff (çtif) *adj* teso

still (çtil) *adv* ainda; todavia; *adj* tranquilo

stillness (çtil-năç) *n* silêncio *m*

stimulant (çti-m¡u-lănnt) *n* estimulante *m*

stimulate (çti-m¡u-leit) *v* estimular

sting (çtinng) *n* picadela *f*, picada *f*

***sting** (çtinng) *v* picar

stingy (çtinn-dji) *adj* mesquinho

***stink** (çtinngk) *v* cheirar mal

stipulate (çti-p¡u-leit) *v* estipular

stipulation (çti-p¡u-*lei*-chănn) *n* estipulação *f*

stir (çtăă) *v* mexer

stirrup (çti-răp) *n* estribo *m*

stitch (çtitch) *n* ponto *m*, pontada *f*; sutura *f*

stock (çtók) *n* stock *m*; *v* *ter em stock; ~ exchange bolsa de valores, bolsa *f*; ~ market bolsa *f*; stocks and shares acções *fpl*

stocking (çtó-kinng) *n* meia *f*

stole[1] (çto ůl) *v* (p steal)

stole[2] (çto ůl) *n* estola *f*

stomach (çta-măk) *n* estômago *m*

stomach-ache (çta-mă-keik) *n* dor de barriga, dor de estômago

stone (çto ůnn) *n* pedra *f*; pedra preciosa; caroço *m*; de pedra; **pumice ~** pedra-pomes *f*

stood (çtud) *v* (p, pp stand)

stop (çtóp) *v* acabar, parar; cessar; *n* paragem *f*; parada *f Br*; stop! alto!

stopper (çtó-pă) *n* rolha *f*

storage (çtóó-ridj) *n* armazenagem *f*

store (çtóó) *n* reserva *f*; loja *f*; *v* armazenar

store-house (çtóó-hauç) *n* armazém *m*

storey (çtóó-ri) *n* andar *m*

stork (çtóók) *n* cegonha *f*

storm (çtóómm) *n* tempestade *f*

stormy (çtóó-mi) *adj* tempestuoso

story (çtóó-ri) *n* história *f*

stout (çtaut) *adj* obeso, corpulento, gordo

stove (çtoᵘv) *n* fogão *m*

straight (çtreit) *adj* direito; recto; *adv* directamente; ~ ahead sempre em frente; ~ away imediatamente, directamente; ~ on sempre em frente

strain (çtreinn) *n* esforço *m*; tensão *f*; *v* forçar; filtrar

strainer (çtrei-nă) *n* coador *m*

strange (çtreinndj) *adj* estranho; insólito

stranger (çtreinn-djă) *n* estrangeiro *m*; forasteiro *m*

strangle (çtrænng-ghăl) *v* estrangular

strap (çtræp) *n* correia *f*

straw (çtróó) *n* palha *f*

strawberry (çtróó-bă-ri) *n* morango *m*

stream (çtriimm) *n* ribeiro *m*; corrente *f*; *v* correr

street (çtriit) *n* rua *f*

streetcar (çtriit-kaa) *n* Am eléctrico *m*; bonde *m* Br

street-organ (çtrii-tóó-ghănn) *n* realejo *m*

strength (çtrénngθ) *n* força *f*, resistência *f*

stress (çtréç) *n* tensão *f*; ênfase *f*; *v* acentuar, sublinhar

stretch (çtrétch) *v* esticar; *n* trecho *m*

strict (çtrikt) *adj* severo; rigoroso

*stride *dar passadas

strife (çtraif) *n* luta *f*

strike (çtraik) *n* greve *f*

*strike (çtraik) *v* bater; atacar; impressionar; *fazer greve

striking (çtrai-kinng) *adj* impressionante, notável

string (çtrinng) *n* cordel *m*; fio *m*,

cordão *m*

strip (çtrip) *n* faixa *f*

stripe (çtraip) *n* risca *f*

striped (çtraipt) *adj* às riscas

stroke (çtroᵘk) *n* ataque *m*

stroll (çtroᵘl) *n* passeio *m*

strong (çtrónn) *adj* forte; possante

stronghold (çtrónn-hoᵘld) *n* praça-forte *f*

structure (çtrak-tchă) *n* estrutura *f*

struggle (çtra-ghăl) *n* combate *m*, luta *f*; *v* lutar

stub (çtab) *n* talão *m*

stubborn (çta-bănn) *adj* teimoso

student (çt'uu-dănnt) *n* estudante *m*; estudante *f*

study (çta-di) *v* estudar; *n* estudo *m*; escritório *m*

stuff (çtaf) *n* substância *f*; coisa *f*

stuffed (çtaft) *adj* recheado

stuffing (çta-finng) *n* recheio *m*

stuffy (çta-fi) *adj* sufocante

stumble (çtamm-băl) *v* tropeçar

stung (çtanng) *v* (p, pp sting)

stupid (çt'uu-pid) *adj* estúpido

style (çtail) *n* estilo *m*

subject¹ (çab-djikt) *n* assunto *m*; súbdito *m*; ~ to sujeito a

subject² (çăb-djékt) *v* submeter

submit (çăb-mit) *v* submeter-se

subordinate (çă-bóó-di-năt) *adj* subordinado; secundário

subscriber (çăb-çkrai-bă) *n* assinante *m*

subscription (çăb-çkrip-chănn) *n* assinatura *f*

subsequent (çab-çi-kᵘănnt) *adj* subsequente

subsidy (çab-çi-di) *n* subsídio *m*

substance (çab-çtănnç) *n* substância *f*

substantial (çăb-çtænn-chăl) *adj* material; real; substancial

substitute (çab-çti-t'uut) *v* *substituir; *n* substituto *m* subtitle (ѕab-tai-tăl) n legenda f

subtle (ҫa-tăl) adj subtil

subtract (ѕăb-trӕkt) v *deduzir, *subtrair

suburb (ҫa-bӑăb) n subúrbio m

suburban (ҫă-bӑă-bănn) adj suburbano

subway (ѕab-ᵘei) n Am metropolitano m

succeed (ҫăk-ҫiid) v *ter êxito; suceder

success (ҫăk-ҫéҫ) n sucesso m

successful (ҫăk-ҫéҫ-făl) adj bem sucedido

succumb (ҫă-kamm) v sucumbir

such (ҫatch) adj tal; adv tão; ~ as tal como

suck (ҫak) v chupar

sudden (ҫa-dänn) adj repentino

suddenly (ҫa-dänn-li) adv repentinamente

suede (ҫᵘeid) n camurça f

suffer (ҫa-fă) v sofrer; suportar

suffering (ҫa-fă-rinng) n sofrimento m

suffice (ҫă-faiҫ) v bastar

sufficient (ҫă-fi-chănnt) adj bastante, suficiente

suffrage (ҫa-fridj) n sufrágio m

sugar (chu-ghă) n açúcar m

suggest (ҫă-djéct) v *sugerir

suggestion (ҫă-djéҫ-tchănn) n sugestão f

suicide (ҫuu-i-ҫaid) n suicídio m

suit (ҫuut) v *convir; adaptar a; ficar bem; n fato m; terno m Br

suitable (ҫuu-tă-băl) adj apropriado

suitcase (ҫuut-keiҫ) n mala f

suite (ҫᵘiit) n apartamento m

sum (ҫamm) n soma f

summary (ҫa-mă-ri) n resumo m

summer (ҫa-mă) n Verão m; ~ time horário de Verão

summit (ҫa-mit) n cima m

summons (ҫa-männz) n (pl ~es) con-

vocação f

sun (ҫann) n sol m

sunbathe (ҫann-beið) v tomar um banho de sol

sunburn (ҫann-bӑănn) n queimadura do sol

Sunday (ҫann-di) domingo m

sun-glasses (ҫann-ghlaa-ҫiz) pl óculos escuros

sunlight (ҫann-lait) n luz do sol

sunny (ҫa-ni) adj soalheiro

sunrise (ҫann-raiz) n nascer do sol

sunset (ҫann-ҫét) n pôr do sol

sunshade (ҫann-cheid) n pára-sol m

sunshine (ҫann-chainn) n sol m

sunstroke (ҫann-ҫtroᵘk) n insolação f

suntan oil (ҫann-tänn-oil) óleo de bronzear

superb (ҫu-pӑăb) adj grandioso, soberbo

superficial (ҫuu-pă-fi-chăl) adj superficial

superfluous (ҫu-pӑă-flu-ăҫ) adj supérfluo

superior (ҫu-piᵃ-ri-ă) adj superior, melhor, maior

superlative (ҫu-pӑă-lă-tiv) adj superlativo; n superlativo m

supermarket (ҫuu-pă-maa-kit) n supermercado m

superstition (ҫuu-pă-ҫti-chănn) n superstição f

supervise (ҫuu-pă-vaiz) v superintender

supervision (ҫuu-pă-vi-jänn) n supervisão f, fiscalização f

supervisor (ҫuu-pă-vai-ză) n superintendente m

supper (ҫa-pă) n ceia f

supple (ҫa-păl) adj flexível, ágil, maleável

supplement (ҫa-pli-männt) n suplemento m

supply (ҫă-plai) n abastecimento m,

fornecimento m; provisão f; oferta f; v fornecer

support (çă-póót) v suportar; n suporte m; ~ hose meias de descanso

supporter (çă-póó-tă) n adepto m; torcedor mBr

suppose (çă-po*u*z) v *supor; supposing that supondo que

suppository (çă-pó-zi-tă-ri) n supositório m

suppress (çă-préç) v reprimir; suprimir

surcharge (çăă-tchaadj) n sobretaxa f

sure (chuă) adj certo

surely (chuă-li) adv certamente

surface (çăă-fiç) n superfície f

surf-board (çăăf-bóód) n prancha de surf

surgeon (çăă-djănn) n cirurgião m; veterinary ~ veterinário m

surgery (çăă-djă-ri) n operação f; consultório m

surname (çăă-neimm) n apelido m; sobrenome m

surplus (çăă-plăç) n excedente m

surprise (çă-praiz) n surpresa f; v surpreender

surrender (çă-rénn-dă) v render-se; n rendição f

surround (çă-raunnd) v cercar, *rodear

surrounding (çă-raunn-dinng) adj em redor

surroundings (çă-raunn-dinngz) pl arredores mpl

survey (çăă-vei) n resumo m

survival (çă-vai-văl) n sobrevivência f

survive (çă-vaiv) v sobreviver

suspect[1] (çă-çpékt) v suspeitar

suspect[2] (çă-çpékt) n suspeito m

suspend (çă-çpénnd) v suspender

suspenders (çă-çpénn-dăz) plAm suspensórios mpl; suspender belt cinto de ligas

suspension (çă-çpénn-chănn) n suspensão f; ~ bridge ponte pênsil

suspicion (çă-çpi-chănn) n suspeita f; desconfiança f

suspicious (çă-çpi-chăç) adj suspeito; desconfiado

sustain (çă-çteinn) v suportar

Swahili (çuă-hii-li) n suaíli m

swallow (çuó-lo*u*) v *engolir; n andorinha f

swam (çu*ă*emm) v (p swim)

swamp (çu*ó*mmp) n pântano m

swan (çu*ó*nn) n cisne m

swap (çu*ó*p) v trocar

*swear (çu*é*ă) v jurar; praguejar

sweat (çu*é*t) n suor m; v suar

sweater (çu*é*-tă) n camisola f; suéter mBr

Swede (çu*u*id) n sueco m

Sweden (çu*u*ii-dănn) Suécia f

Swedish (çu*u*ii-dich) adj sueco

*sweep (çu*u*iip) v varrer

sweet (çu*u*iit) adj doce; encantador; n rebuçado m; doce m; sweets doces mpl, rebuçados mpl; balas fplBr

sweeten (çu*u*ii-tănn) v adoçar

sweetheart (çu*u*iit-haat) n querido m, meu amor

sweetshop (çu*u*iit-chóp) n confeitaria f

swell (çu*é*l) adj formidável

*swell (çu*é*l) v inchar

swelling (çu*é*-linng) n inchaço m

swift (çu*ă*ift) adj rápido

*swim (çu*ă*imm) v nadar

swimmer (çu*ă*i-mă) n nadador m

swimming (çu*ă*i-minng) n natação f; ~ pool piscina f

swimming-trunks (çu*ă*i-minng-tranngkç) pl calções de banho

swim-suit (çu*ă*imm-çuut) n fato de banho

swindle (çu*ă*inn-dăl) v burlar; n burla f

swindler (çu*ă*inn-dlă) n burlão m

swing (çᵘinng) *n* baloiço *m*; balanço *mBr*

*****swing** (çᵘinng) *v* balançar

Swiss (çᵘiç) *adj* suíço

switch (çᵘitch) *n* interruptor *m*; *v* trocar; ~ **off** desligar; ~ **on** ligar

switchboard (çᵘitch-bóód) *n* quadro de distribuição

Switzerland (çᵘit-çă-lănnd) Suíça *f*

sword (çóód) *n* espada *f*

swum (çᵘamm) *v* (pp swim)

syllable (çi-lă-băl) *n* sílaba *f*

symbol (çimm-băl) *n* símbolo *m*

sympathetic (çimm-pă-θé-tik) *adj* cordial, compreensivo

sympathy (çimm-pă-θi) *n* simpatia *f*; compaixão *f*

symphony (çimm-fă-ni) *n* sinfonia *f*

symptom (çimm-tămm) *n* sintoma *m*

synagogue (çi-nă-ghógh) *n* sinagoga *f*

synonym (çi-nă-nimm) *n* sinónimo *m*

synthetic (çinn-θé-tik) *adj* sintético

syphon (çai-fănn) *n* sifão *m*

Syria (çi-ri-ă) Síria *f*

Syrian (çi-ri-ănn) *adj* sírio

syringe (çi-rinndj) *n* seringa *f*

syrup (çi-răp) *n* xarope *m*

system (çi-çtămm) *n* sistema *m*; **decimal** ~ sistema decimal

systematic (çi-çtă-*mæ*-tik) *adj* sistemático

T

table (tei-băl) *n* mesa *f*; tabela *f*; ~ **of contents** índice *m*; ~ **tennis** ténis de mesa

table-cloth (tei-băl-klóθ) *n* toalha de mesa

tablespoon (tei-băl-çpuunn) *n* colher de sopa

tablet (tæ-blit) *n* pastilha *f*

taboo (tă-buu) *n* tabu *m*

tactics (tæk-tikç) *pl* táctica *f*

tag (tægh) *n* etiqueta *f*

tail (teil) *n* cauda *f*

tail-light (teil-lait) *n* farol traseiro

tailor (tei-lă) *n* alfaiate *m*

tailor-made (tei-lă-meid) *adj* feito à medida

*****take** (teik) *v* tomar; agarrar; levar; perceber, entender, compreender; ~ **away** levar, tirar; ~ **off** descolar; ~ **out** tirar; ~ **over** tomar conta de; ~ **place** acontecer

take-off (tei-kóf) *n* descolagem *f*

tale (teil) *n* narrativa *f*, conto *m*

talent (tæ-lănnt) *n* talento *m*

talented (tæ-lănn-tid) *adj* dotado

talk (tóók) *v* falar; *n* conversa *f*

talkative (tóó-kă-tiv) *adj* falador

tall (tóól) *adj* alto

tame (teimm) *adj* domesticado, manso; *v* domesticar

tampon (tæmm-pănn) *n* tampão *m*

tangerine (tænn-djă-riinn) *n* tangerina *f*

tangible (tænn-dji-băl) *adj* tangível

tank (tænngk) *n* tanque *m*

tanker (tænng-kă) *n* navio-cisterna *m*

tanned (tænnd) *adj* bronzeado

tap (tæp) *n* torneira *f*; pancadinha *f*; *v* bater

tape (teip) *n* fita *f*; **adhesive** ~ fita adesiva; adesivo *m*; esparadrapo *mBr*

tape-measure (teip-mé-jă) *n* fita métrica

tape-recorder (teip-ri-kóó-dă) *n* gravador *m*

tapestry (tæ-pi-çtri) *n* tapeçaria *f*

tar (taa) *n* alcatrão *m*

target (taa-ghit) *n* alvo *m*, objectivo *m*

tariff (tæ-rif) *n* tarifa *f*

tarpaulin (taa-póó-linn) *n* toldo impermeável

task (taack) n tarefa f

taste (teiçt) n gosto m, paladar m; v *saber a; provar

tasteless (teiçt-lăç) adj insípido

tasty (tei-çti) adj saboroso

taught (tóót) v (p, pp teach)

tavern (tæ-vänn) n taberna f

tax (tækç) n imposto m; v lançar impostos

taxation (tæk-çei-chănn) n impostos mpl

tax-free (tækç-frii) adj isento de imposto

taxi (tæk-çi) n táxi m; ~ **rank** praça de táxis; ponto de táxis Br; ~ **stand** Am paragem de táxis

taxi-driver (tæk-çi-drai-vă) n motorista de táxi

taxi-meter (tæk-çi-mii-tă) n taxímetro m

taxiplane (tæk-çi-pleinn) n táxi aéreo

tea (tii) n chá m

*teach** (tiitch) v ensinar

teacher (tii-tchă) n professor m; professora f, mestre m

teachings (tii-tchinngz) pl ensinamentos mpl

tea-cloth (tii-klóθ) n pano da loiça

teacup (tii-kap) n chávena de chá

team (tiimm) n equipa f

teapot (tii-pót) n bule m

*tear** (téă) v rasgar

tear¹ (tiă) n lágrima f

tear² (téă) n rasgão m

tear-jerker (tiă-djă-kă) n lamechice f

tease (tiiz) v arreliar

tea-set (tii-çét) n serviço de chá

tea-shop (tii-chóp) n salão de chá

teaspoon (tii-çpuunn) n colher de chá

technical (ték-ni-kăl) adj técnico

technician (ték-ni-chănn) n técnico m

technique (ték-niik) n técnica f

technology (ték-nó-lă-dji) n tecnologia

f

teenager (tii-nei-djă) n adolescente m

teetotaller (tii-to^u-tă-lă) n abstémio m

telegram (té-li-ghræmm) n telegrama m

telegraph (té-li-ghraaf) v telegrafar

telepathy (ti-lé-pă-θi) n telepatia f

telephone (té-li-fo^unn) n telefone m; ~ **book** Am lista telefónica, lista dos telefones; ~ **booth** cabina telefónica; ~ **call** chamada telefónica, telefonema m; ~ **directory** lista telefónica, lista dos telefones; ~ **exchange** central telefónica; ~ **operator** telefonista f

telephonist (ti-lé-fă-niçt) n telefonista f

television (té-li-vi-jănn) n televisão f; ~ **set** aparelho de televisão

*tell** (tél) v *dizer; contar

temper (témm-pă) n mau génio m

temperature (témm-pră-tchă) n temperatura f

tempest (témm-piçt) n tempestade f

temple (témm-păl) n templo m; fonte f

temporary (témm-pă-ră-ri) adj temporário, provisório

tempt (témmpt) v tentar

temptation (témmp-tei-chănn) n tentação f

ten (ténn) num dez

tenant (té-nănnt) n inquilino m

tend (ténnd) v *ter tendência; cuidar; ~ **to** tender para

tendency (ténn-dănn-çi) n tendência f, inclinação f

tender (ténn-dă) adj terno, delicado; tenro

tendon (ténn-dănn) n tendão m

tennis (té-niç) n ténis m; ~ **shoes** sapatos de ténis

tennis-court (té-niç-kóót) n campo de

ténis

tense (ténnç) *adj* tenso

tension (ténn-chänn) *n* tensão *f*

tent (ténnt) *n* tenda *f*

tenth (ténnθ) *num* décimo

tepid (té-pid) *adj* tépido

term (täämm) *n* termo *m*; período *m*; condição *f*

terminal (tää-mi-näl) *n* terminal *m*

terrace (té-räç) *n* terraco *m*

terrain (té-reinn) *n* terreno *m*

terrible (té-ri-bäl) *adj* medonho, terrível, tremendo

terrific (tä-ri-fik) *adj* fantástico

terrify (té-ri-fai) *v* aterrorizar; **terrifying** aterrador

territory (té-ri-tä-ri) *n* território *m*

terror (té-rä) *n* terror *m*

terrorism (té-rä-ri-zämm) *n* terror *m*, terrorismo *m*

terrorist (té-rä-riçt) *n* terrorista *m*

test (téçt) *n* prova *f*, teste *m*; *v* experimentar

testify (té-çti-fai) *v* testemunhar

text (tékçt) *n* texto *m*

textbook (tékç-buk) *n* compêndio *m*

textile (ték-çtail) *n* tecido *m*; *adj* têxtil

texture (tékç-tchä) *n* contextura *f*

Thai (tai) *adj* tailandês

Thailand (tai-lænnd) Tailândia *f*

than (ðænn) *conj* que

thank (θænngk) *v* agradecer; ~ **you** obrigado

thankful (θænngk-fäl) *adj* agradecido

that (ðæt) *adj* esse, aquele; *pron* aquele, isso; que; *conj* que

thaw (θóó) *v* degelar, descongelar; *n* degelo *m*

the (ðä-ði) *art* o *art*; **the ... the** quanto mais ... mais

theatre (θi-ä-tä) *n* teatro *m*

theft (θéft) *n* roubo *m*

their (ðéª) *adj* deles

them (ðémm) *pron* os; lhes

theme (θiimm) *n* tema *m*, assunto *m*

themselves (ðämm-çélvz) *pron* se; eles mesmos

then (ðénn) *adv* então; em seguida, depois

theology (θi-ó-lä-dji) *n* teologia *f*

theoretical (θiª-ré-ti-käl) *adj* teórico

theory (θiª-ri) *n* teoria *f*

therapy (θé-rä-pi) *n* terapia *f*

there (ðéª) *adv* lá; para ali

therefore (ðéª-fóó) *conj* portanto

thermometer (θä-mó-mi-tä) *n* termómetro *m*

thermostat (θää-mä-çtæt) *n* termóstato *m*

these (ðiiz) *adj* estes

thesis (θii-çiç) *n* (pl theses) tese *f*

they (ðei) *pron* eles

thick (θik) *adj* grosso; espesso

thicken (θi-känn) *v* engrossar

thickness (θik-näç) *n* grossura *f*

thief (θiif) *n* (pl thieves) ladrão *m*

thigh (θai) *n* coxa *f*

thimble (θimm-bäl) *n* dedal *m*

thin (θinn) *adj* fino; magro

thing (θinng) *n* coisa *f*

*think (θinngk) *v* pensar; *reflectir; ~ **of** pensar em; ~ **over** ponderar

thinker (θinng-kä) *n* pensador *m*

third (θääd) *num* terceiro

thirst (θääçt) *n* sede *f*

thirsty (θää-çti) *adj* sedento

thirteen (θää-tiinn) *num* treze

thirteenth (θää-tiinnθ) *num* décimo terceiro

thirtieth (θää-ti-äθ) *num* trigésimo

thirty (θää-ti) *num* trinta

this (ðiç) *adj* este; *pron* este

thistle (θi-çäl) *n* cardo *m*

thorn (θóónn) *n* espinho *m*

thorough (θa-rä) *adj* minucioso

thoroughbred (θa-rä-bréd) *adj* puro sangue

thoroughfare (θ*a*-rǎ-fé*ǎ*) n artéria principal, estrada principal

those (ðó*u*z) adj esses; pron aqueles

though (ðó*u*) conj ainda que, se bem que, embora; adv no entanto

thought¹ (θóót) v (p, pp think)

thought² (θóót) n pensamento m

thoughtful (θóót-fǎl) adj pensativo; atencioso

thousand (θ*au*-zǎnnd) num mil

thread (θréd) n fio m; linha f; v enfiar

threadbare (θréd-bé*ǎ*) adj coçado

threat (θrét) n ameaça f

threaten (θré-tǎnn) v ameaçar; **threatening** ameaçador

three (θrii) num três

three-quarter (θrii-k*u*óó-tǎ) adj três quartos

threshold (θré-cho*u*ld) n limiar m

threw (θruu) v (p throw)

thrifty (θrif-ti) adj económico

throat (θro*u*t) n garganta f

throne (θro*u*nn) n trono m

through (θruu) prep através

throughout (θruu-*aut*) adv por toda a parte

throw (θro*u*) n lançamento m

*throw (θro*u*) v atirar, lançar, deitar

thrush (θrach) n tordo m

thumb (θamm) n polegar m

thumbtack (θamm-tæk) nAm pionés m

thump (θammp) v martelar

thunder (θann-dǎ) n trovão m; v troar

thunderstorm (θann-dǎ-çtóómm) n trovoada f

thundery (θann-dǎ-ri) adj tempestuoso

Thursday (θǎǎz-di) quinta-feira f

thus (ðaç) adv assim

thyme (taimm) n tomilho m

tick (tik) n marca f; ~ **off** marcar

ticket (ti-kit) n bilhete m; multa f; ~

collector revisor m; ~ **machine** bilheteira automática

tickle (ti-kǎl) v *fazer cócegas

tide (taid) n maré f; **high** ~ maré cheia; **low** ~ maré baixa

tidings (tai-dinngz) pl notícias fpl

tidy (tai-di) adj asseado; ~ **up** arrumar

tie (tai) v atar, *dar um nó; n gravata f

tiger (tai-ghǎ) n tigre m

tight (tait) adj apertado; estreito; adv fortemente

tighten (tai-tǎnn) v apertar, estreitar; apertar-se

tights (taitç) pl collants mpl

tile (tail) n azulejo m; telha f

till (til) prep até; conj até que

timber (timm-bǎ) n madeira de construção

time (taimm) n tempo m; vez f; **all the** ~ continuamente; **in** ~ a tempo; ~ **of arrival** hora de chegada; ~ **of departure** hora de partida

time-saving (taimm-çei-vinng) adj economizador de tempo

timetable (taimm-tei-bǎl) n horário m

timid (ti-mid) adj tímido

timidity (ti-mi-dǎ-ti) n timidez f

tin (tinn) n estanho m; lata f; **tinned food** conservas fpl

tin-opener (ti-no*u*-pǎ-nǎ) n abre-latas m

tiny (tai-ni) adj minúsculo

tip (tip) n ponta f; gorjeta f

tire¹ (tai*ǎ*) n pneu m

tire² (tai*ǎ*) v cansar

tired (tai*ǎ*d) adj fatigado, cansado; ~ **of** farto de

tiring (tai*ǎ*-rinng) adj fatigante

tissue (ti-chuu) n tecido m; lenço de papel

title (tai-tǎl) n título m

to (tuu) prep até; a, para

toad (to^ud) *n* sapo *m*

toadstool (to^ud-çtuul) *n* cogumelo *m*

toast (to^uçt) *n* torrada *f*; brinde *m*

tobacco (tă-bæ-ko^u) *n* (pl ~s) tabaco *m*; ~ **pouch** bolsa de tabaco

tobacconist (tă-bæ-kă-niçt) *n* tabacaria *f*; **tobacconist's** tabacaria *f*

today (tă-dei) *adv* hoje

toddler (tód-lă) *n* criança pequenina

toe (to^u) *n* dedo do pé

toffee (tó-fi) *n* caramelo *m*

together (tă-ghé-ðă) *adv* juntos

toilet (toi-lăt) *n* retretes *fpl*; ~ **case** estojo de toalete

toilet-paper (toi-lăt-pei-pă) *n* papel higiénico

toiletry (toi-lă-tri) *n* artigos de toalete

token (to^u-kănn) *n* sinal *m*; prova *f*; ficha *f*

told (to^uld) *v* (p, pp tell)

tolerable (tó-lă-ră-băl) *adj* tolerável

toll (to^ul) *n* portagem *f*

tomato (tă-maa-to^u) *n* (pl ~es) tomate *m*

tomb (tuumm) *n* túmulo *m*

tombstone (tuumm-çto^unn) *n* pedra tumular

tomorrow (tă-mó-ro^u) *adv* amanhã

ton (tann) *n* tonelada *f*

tone (to^unn) *n* tom *m*; timbre *m*

tongs (tónnz) *pl* tenaz *f*

tongue (tanng) *n* língua *f*

tonic (tó-nik) *n* tónico *m*

tonight (tă-nait) *adv* esta noite

tonsilitis (tónn-çă-lai-tiç) *n* amigdalite *f*

tonsils (tónn-çălz) *pl* amígdalas *fpl*

too (tuu) *adv* demasiado; também

took (tuk) *v* (p take)

tool (tuul) *n* ferramenta *f*, instrumento *m*; ~ **kit** caixa de ferramenta

tooth (tuuθ) *n* (pl teeth) dente *m*

toothache (tuu-θeik) *n* dor de dentes

toothbrush (tuuθ-brach) *n* escova de dentes

toothpaste (tuuθ-peiçt) *n* pasta de dentes

toothpick (tuuθ-pik) *n* palito *m*

toothpowder (tuuθ-pau-dă) *n* pós dentífricos

top (tóp) *n* cimo *m*; parte de cima; tampa *f*; superior; **on** ~ **of** em cima de; ~ **side** parte superior

topcoat (tóp-ko^ut) *n* sobretudo *m*

topic (tó-pik) *n* tópico *m*

topical (tó-pi-kăl) *adj* actual

torch (tóótch) *n* archote *m*; lanterna de bolso

torment¹ (tóó-ménnt) *v* atormentar

torment² (tóó-ménnt) *n* tormento *m*

torture (tóó-tchă) *n* tortura *f*; *v* torturar

toss (tóç) *v* lançar, arremessar

tot (tót) *n* criança pequena

total (to^u-tăl) *adj* total; completo, absoluto; *n* total *m*

totalitarian (to^u-tæ-li-té^ă-ri-ănn) *adj* totalitário

totalizator (to^u-tă-lai-zei-tă) *n* totalizador *m*

touch (tatch) *v* tocar; *dizer respeito a; *n* contacto *m*, toque *m*; tacto *m*

touching (ta-tchinng) *adj* tocante

tough (taf) *adj* duro

tour (tu^ă) *n* circuito turístico

tourism (tu^ă-ri-zămm) *n* turismo *m*

tourist (tu^ă-riçt) *n* turista *m*; ~ **class** classe turística; ~ **office** agência de turismo

tournament (tu^ă-nă-mănnt) *n* torneio *m*

tow (to^u) *v* rebocar

towards (tă-^uóódz) *prep* em direcção a; para com

towel (tau^ăl) *n* toalha *f*

towelling (tau^ă-linng) *n* pano para toalhas

tower (tau^ă) *n* torre *f*

town (taunn) *n* cidade *f*; ~ **centre** centro da cidade; ~ **hall** câmara municipal

townspeople (*taunnz*-pii-păl) *pl* citadinos *mpl*

toxic (*tók*-çik) *adj* tóxico

toy (toi) *n* brinquedo *m*

toyshop (*toi*-chóp) *n* loja de brinquedos

trace (treiç) *n* rasto *m*; *v* *seguir o rasto de

track (træk) *n* via *f*; pista *f*

tractor (*træk*-tă) *n* tractor *m*

trade (treid) *n* comércio *m*; ofício *m*; *v* comerciar, *negociar

trademark (*treid*-maak) *n* marca de fábrica

trader (*trei*-dă) *n* comerciante *m*

tradesman (*treidz*-männ) *n* (pl -men) comerciante *m*

trade-union (treid-*i*uu-n[i]ănn) *n* sindicato *m*

tradition (tră-*di*-chănn) *n* tradição *f*

traditional (tră-*di*-chă-năl) *adj* tradicional

traffic (*træ*-fik) *n* trânsito *m*; ~ **jam** engarrafamento de trânsito; ~ **light** semáforo *m*

trafficator (*træ*-fi-kei-tă) *n* indicador de direcção

tragedy (*træ*-djă-di) *n* tragédia *f*

tragic (*træ*-djik) *adj* trágico

trail (treil) *n* pista *f*, atalho *m*

trailer (*trei*-lă) *n* reboque *m*; *nAm* caravana *f*

train (treinn) *n* comboio *m*; trem *mBr*; *v* treinar, adestrar; **stopping** ~ comboio correio; **through** ~ comboio directo; ~ **ferry** ferry-boat *m*

training (*trei*-ninng) *n* treino *m*

trait (treit) *n* traço *m*

traitor (*trei*-tă) *n* traidor *m*

tram (trämm) *n* eléctrico *m*; bonde

mBr

tramp (trämmp) *n* vagabundo *m*, vadio *m*; *v* vadiar

tranquil (*trænng*-k[u]il) *adj* tranquilo

tranquillizer (*trænng*-k[u]i-lai-ză) *n* calmante *m*

transaction (trænn-*zæk*-chănn) *n* transacção *f*

transatlantic (trænn-*zăt*-*lænn*-tik) *adj* transatlântico

transfer (trænnç-*făă*) *v* *transferir

transform (trænnç-*fóómm*) *v* transformar, mudar

transformer (trænnç-*fóó*-mă) *n* transformador *m*

transition (trænn-*çi*-chănn) *n* transição *f*

translate (trænnç-*leit*) *v* *traduzir

translation (trænnç-*lei*-chănn) *n* tradução *f*

translator (trænnç-*lei*-tă) *n* tradutor *m*

transmission (trænnz-*mi*-chănn) *n* transmissão *f*

transmit (trænnz-*mit*) *v* transmitir

transmitter (trænnz-*mi*-tă) *n* emissor *m*

transparent (trænn-*çpé*[ă]-rännt) *adj* transparente

transport[1] (*trænn*-çpóót) *n* transporte *m*

transport[2] (trænn-*çpóót*) *v* transportar

transportation (trænn-çpóó-*tei*-chănn) *n* transporte *m*

trap (træp) *n* armadilha *f*

trash (træch) *n* lixo *m*

travel (*træ*-văl) *v* viajar; ~ **agency** agência de viagens; ~ **agent** agente de viagens; ~ **insurance** seguro de viagem; **travelling expenses** despesas de viagem

traveller (*træ*-vă-lă) *n* viajante *m*; **traveller's cheque** cheque de viagem

tray (trei) *n* tabuleiro *m*

treason (*trii*-zǎnn) *n* traição *f*

treasure (tré-jǎ) *n* tesouro *m*

treasurer (tré-jǎ-rǎ) *n* tesoureiro *m*

treasury (tré-jǎ-ri) *n* tesouro público; caixa *f*

treat (triit) *v* tratar

treatment (triit-mǎnnt) *n* tratamento *m*

treaty (*trii*-ti) *n* tratado *m*

tree (trii) *n* árvore *f*

tremble (trémm-bǎl) *v* tremer, tiritar; vibrar

tremendous (tri-ménn-dǎç) *adj* formidável

trespass (tréç-pǎç) *v* infringir

trespasser (tréç-pǎ-çǎ) *n* intruso *m*

trial (trai^ǎl) *n* julgamento *m*; experiência *f*

triangle (trai-ænng-ghǎl) *n* triângulo *m*

triangular (trai-ænng-ghⁱu-lǎ) *adj* triangular

tribe (traib) *n* tribo *f*

tributary (*tri*-bⁱu-tǎ-ri) *n* afluente *m*

tribute (*tri*-bⁱuut) *n* homenagem *f*

trick (trik) *n* manha *f*; truque *m*

trigger (*tri*-ghǎ) *n* gatilho *m*

trim (trimm) *v* aparar

trip (trip) *n* viagem *f*, passeio *m*

triumph (*trai*-ǎmmf) *n* triunfo *m*; *v* triunfar

triumphant (trai-*amm*-fǎnnt) *adj* triunfante

trolley-bus (tró-li-baç) *n* troleicarro *m*

troops (truupç) *pl* tropas *fpl*

tropical (tró-pi-kǎl) *adj* tropical

tropics (*tró*-pikç) *pl* trópicos *mpl*

trouble (tra-bǎl) *n* incómodo *m*, preocupação *f*; *v* incomodar

troublesome (tra-bǎl-çǎmm) *adj* macador

trousers (trau-zǎz) *pl* calças *fpl*

trout (traut) *n* (pl ∼) truta *f*

truck (trak) *nAm* camião *m*

true (truu) *adj* verdadeiro, real; fiel, leal

trumpet (*tramm*-pit) *n* trombeta *f*

trunk (tranngk) *n* baú *m*; tronco *m*; *nAm* mala *f*; **trunks** calções de ginástica

trunk-call (*tranngk*-kóól) *n* chamada interurbana

trust (traçt) *v* confiar em; *n* confiança *f*

trustworthy (traçt-^uǎǎ-ði) *adj* digno de confiança

truth (truuθ) *n* verdade *f*

truthful (*truu*θ-fǎl) *adj* verídico

try (trai) *v* experimentar, tentar, esforçar-se; *n* tentativa *f*; ∼ **on** provar

tube (tⁱuub) *n* cano *m*, tubo *m*

tuberculosis (tⁱuu-bǎǎ-kⁱu-lo^u-çiç) *n* tuberculose *f*

Tuesday (*tⁱuuz*-di) terça-feira *f*

tug (tagh) *v* rebocar; *n* rebocador *m*; estição *m*

tuition (tⁱuu-*i*-chǎnn) *n* instrução *f*

tulip (*tⁱuu*-lip) *n* tulipa *f*

tumbler (*tamm*-blǎ) *n* copo *m*

tumour (*tⁱuu*-mǎ) *n* tumor *m*

tuna (*tⁱuu*-nǎ) *n* (pl ∼, ∼s) atum *m*

tune (tⁱuunn) *n* melodia *f*; ∼ **in** sintonizar

tuneful (*tⁱuunn*-fǎl) *adj* melodioso

tunic (*tⁱuu*-nik) *n* túnica *f*

Tunisia (tⁱuu-*ni*-zi-ǎ) Tunísia *f*

Tunisian (tⁱuu-*ni*-zi-ǎnn) *adj* tunisino

tunnel (ta-nǎl) *n* túnel *m*

turbine (tǎǎ-bainn) *n* turbina *f*

turbojet (tǎǎ-bo^u-djét) *n* motor a jacto-propulsão

Turk (tǎǎk) *n* turco *m*

Turkey (tǎǎ-ki) Turquia *f*

turkey (tǎǎ-ki) *n* peru *m*

Turkish (tǎǎ-kich) *adj* turco; ∼ **bath**

banho turco

turn (tăănn) *v* virar; rodar; *n* viragem *f*, volta *f*; curva *f*; vez *f*; ~ **back** voltar atrás; ~ **down** rejeitar; ~ **into** transformar em; ~ **off** fechar; ~ **on** ligar, acender; abrir; ~ **over** inverter; ~ **round** voltar; virar-se

turning (*tăă*-ninng) *n* curva *f*

turning-point (*tăă*-ninng-poinnt) *n* momento decisivo

turnover (*tăă*-no^{u}-vă) *n* movimento de negócios; ~ **tax** imposto sobre a cifra de negócios

turnpike (*tăănn*-paik) *nAm* estrada com portagem

turpentine (*tăă*-pănn-tainn) *n* terebentina *f*

turtle (*tăă*-tăl) *n* tartaruga *f*

tutor (*t^{i}uu*-tă) *n* preceptor *m*; tutor *m*

tuxedo (tak-*çii*-do^{u}) *nAm* (pl ~s, ~es) smoking *m*

tweed (t^{u}iid) *n* tweed *m*

tweezers (*t^{u}ii*-zăz) *pl* pinça *f*

twelfth (t^{u}élfθ) *num* décimo segundo

twelve (t^{u}élv) *num* doze

twentieth (*t^{u}énn*-ti-ăθ) *num* vigésimo

twenty (*t^{u}énn*-ti) *num* vinte

twice (t^{u}aiç) *adv* duas vezes

twig (t^{u}igh) *n* raminho *m*

twilight (*t^{u}ai*-lait) *n* crepúsculo *m*

twine (t^{u}ainn) *n* guita *f*

twins (t^{u}innz) *pl* gémeos *mpl*; **twin beds** duas camas

twist (t^{u}içt) *v* torcer; *n* torção *f*

two (tuu) *num* dois

two-piece (tuu-*piiç*) *adj* de duas peças

type (taip) *v* escrever à máquina, dactilografar; *n* tipo *m*

typewriter (*taip*-rai-tă) *n* máquina de escrever

typewritten (*taip*-ri-tănn) dactilografado

typhoid (*tai*-foid) *n* tifo *m*

typical (*ti*-pi-kăl) *adj* típico, característico

typist (*tai*-piçt) *n* dactilógrafa *f*

tyrant (*tai^{ă}*-rănnt) *n* tirano *m*

tyre (tai^{ă}) *n* pneu *m*; ~ **pressure** pressão dos pneus

U

ugly (*a*-ghli) *adj* feio

ulcer (*al*-çă) *n* úlcera *f*

ultimate (*al*-ti-măt) *adj* último, final

ultraviolet (al-tră-*vai^{ă}*-lăt) *adj* ultravioleta

umbrella (amm-*bré*-lă) *n* guarda-chuva *m*

umpire (*amm*-pai^{ă}) *n* árbitro *m*

unable (a-*nei*-băl) *adj* incapaz

unacceptable (a-năk-*çép*-tă-băl) *adj* inaceitável

unaccountable (a-nă-*kaunn*-tă-băl) *adj* inexplicável

unaccustomed (a-nă-*ka*-çtămmd) *adj* desacostumado

unanimous (^{i}uu-*næ*-ni-măç) *adj* unânime

unanswered (a-*naann*-çăd) *adj* sem resposta

unauthorized (a-*nóó*-θă-raizd) *adj* ilícito

unavoidable (a-nă-*voi*-dă-băl) *adj* inevitável

unaware (a-nă-*^{u}é^{ă}*) *adj* inconsciente

unbearable (ann-*bé^{ă}*-ră-băl) *adj* insuportável

unbreakable (ann-*brei*-kă-băl) *adj* inquebrável

unbroken (ann-*bro^{u}*-kănn) *adj* inteiro

unbutton (ann-*ba*-tănn) *v* desabotoar

uncertain (ann-*çăă*-tănn) *adj* incerto

uncle (*anng*-kăl) *n* tio *m*

unclean (ann-*kliinn*) *adj* sujo

uncomfortable (ann-*kamm*-fã-tã-bãl) *adj* desconfortável

uncommon (ann-*kó*-mãnn) *adj* insólito, raro

unconditional (ann-kãnn-*di*-chã-nãl) *adj* incondicional

unconscious (ann-*kónn*-chãç) *adj* inconsciente

uncork (ann-*kóók*) *v* desarrolhar

uncover (ann-*ka*-vã) *v* destapar

uncultivated (ann-*kal*-ti-vei-tid) *adj* inculto

under (*ann*-dã) *prep* debaixo de

undercurrent (*ann*-dã-ka-rãnnt) *n* ressaca *f*

underestimate (ann-dã-*ré*-çti-meit) *v* menosprezar

underground (*ann*-dã-ghraunnd) *adj* subterrâneo; *n* metropolitano *m*

underline (ann-dã-*lainn*) *v* sublinhar

underneath (ann-dã-*niiθ*) *adv* debaixo

undershirt (*ann*-dã-chãất) *n* camisola interior; camiseta *fBr*

undersigned (ann-dã-*cainnd*) *n* abaixo-assinado *m*

***understand** (ann-dã-*çtænnd*) *v* compreender, perceber

understanding (ann-dã-*çtænn*-dinng) *n* compreensão *f*

***undertake** (ann-dã-*teik*) *v* empreender

undertaking (ann-dã-*tei*-kinng) *n* empresa *f*

underwater (*ann*-dã-ᵘóó-tã) *adj* submarino

underwear (*ann*-dã-ᵘéᵃ) *n* roupa interior

undesirable (ann-di-*zai*ᵃ-rã-bãl) *adj* indesejável

***undo** (ann-*duu*) *v* *desfazer

undoubtedly (ann-*dau*-tid-li) *adv* sem dúvida

undress (ann-*dréç*) *v* *despir-se

undulating (*ann*-dᵘu-lei-tinng) *adj* ondulante

unearned (a-*nããnd*) *adj* imerecido

uneasy (a-*nii*-zi) *adj* pouco à vontade

uneducated (a-*né*-dᵘu-kei-tid) *adj* inculto

unemployed (a-nimm-*ploid*) *adj* desempregado

unemployment (a-nimm-*ploi*-mãnnt) *n* desemprego *m*

unequal (a-*nii*-kᵘãl) *adj* desigual

uneven (a-*nii*-vãnn) *adj* desigual, rugoso; irregular

unexpected (a-nik-*çpék*-tid) *adj* inesperado, imprevisto

unfair (ann-*féᵃ*) *adj* injusto

unfaithful (ann-*feiθ*-fãl) *adj* infiel

unfamiliar (ann-fã-*mil*-¹ã) *adj* desconhecido

unfasten (ann-*faa*-çãnn) *v* soltar, desprender

unfavourable (ann-*fei*-vã-rã-bãl) *adj* desfavorável

unfit (ann-*fit*) *adj* inadequado

unfold (ann-*fo*ᵘld) *v* desdobrar

unfortunate (ann-*fóó*-tchã-nãt) *adj* desgraçado

unfortunately (ann-*fóó*-tchã-nãt-li) *adv* infelizmente

unfriendly (ann-*frénnd*-li) *adj* antipático

unfurnished (ann-*fãã*-nicht) *adj* desmobilado

ungrateful (ann-*ghreit*-fãl) *adj* ingrato

unhappy (ann-*hæ*-pi) *adj* infeliz

unhealthy (ann-*hél*-θi) *adj* doentio

unhurt (ann-*hãất*) *adj* ileso

uniform (ᶦ*uu*-ni-fóómm) *n* uniforme *m*; *adj* uniforme

unimportant (a-nimm-*póó*-tãnnt) *adj* insignificante

uninhabitable (a-ninn-*hæ*-bi-tã-bãl) *adj* inabitável

uninhabited (a-ninn-*hæ*-bi-tid) *adj* desabitado

unintentional (a-ninn-*ténn*-chă-năl) *adj* involuntário

union (*i*uu-n*i*änn) *n* união *f*; confederação *f*, liga *f*

unique (*i*uu-*niik*) *adj* único

unit (*i*uu-nit) *n* unidade *f*

unite (*i*uu-*nait*) *v* unir, reunir

United States (*i*uu-*nai*-tid çteitç) Estados Unidos

unity (*i*uu-nă-ti) *n* unidade *f*

universal (*i*uu-ni-*vää*-çăl) *adj* geral, universal

universe (*i*uu-ni-vääç) *n* universo *m*

university (*i*uu-ni-*vää*-çă-ti) *n* universidade *f*

unjust (ann-*djaçt*) *adj* injusto

unkind (ann-*kainnd*) *adj* desagradável, pouco amável

unknown (ann-*no*u*nn*) *adj* desconhecido

unlawful (ann-*lóó*-făl) *adj* ilegal

unlearn (ann-*läänn*) *v* desaprender

unless (ănn-*léç*) *conj* a não ser que

unlike (ann-*laik*) *adj* diferente

unlikely (ann-*lai*-kli) *adj* improvável

unlimited (ann-*li*-mi-tid) *adj* ilimitado, sem fim

unload (ann-*lo*u*d*) *v* descarregar

unlock (ann-*lók*) *v* abrir

unlucky (ann-*la*-ki) *adj* infortunado

unnecessary (ann-*né*-çă-çă-ri) *adj* desnecessário

unoccupied (a-*nó*-k*i*u-paid) *adj* desocupado

unofficial (a-nă-*fi*-chăl) *adj* oficioso

unpack (ann-*pæk*) *v* desempacotar

unpleasant (ann-*plé*-zännt) *adj* desagradável; maçador, aborrecido

unpopular (ann-*pó*-p*i*u-lă) *adj* pouco popular, impopular

unprotected (ann-pră-*ték*-tid) *adj* desprotegido

unqualified (ann-k*u*ó-li-faid) *adj* incompetente

unreal (ann-*ri*ă*l*) *adj* irreal

unreasonable (ann-*rii*-ză-nă-băl) *adj* desarrazoado

unreliable (ann-ri-*lai*-ă-băl) *adj* indigno de confiança

unrest (ann-*réçt*) *n* agitação *f*; desassossego *m*

unsafe (ann-*çeif*) *adj* inseguro

unsatisfactory (ann-çæ-tiç-*fæk*-tă-ri) *adj* insatisfatório

unscrew (ann-*çkruu*) *v* desaparafusar

unselfish (ann-*çél*-fich) *adj* desinteressado

unsound (ann-*çaunnd*) *adj* doentio

unstable (ann-*çtei*-băl) *adj* instável

unsteady (ann-*çté*-di) *adj* vacilante, instável

unsuccessful (ann-çăk-*çéç*-făl) *adj* mal sucedido

unsuitable (ann-*çuu*-tă-băl) *adj* inadequado

unsurpassed (ann-çă-*paaçt*) *adj* insuperável

untidy (ann-*tai*-di) *adj* desalinhado; desarrumado

untie (ann-*tai*) *v* desatar

until (ănn-*til*) *prep* até

untrue (ann-*truu*) *adj* falso

untrustworthy (ann-*traçt*-u*ää*-ði) *adj* indigno de confiança

unusual (ann-*i*uu-ju-ăl) *adj* desusado

unwell (ann-u*él*) *adj* indisposto

unwilling (ann-u*i*-linng) *adj* de má vontade

unwise (ann-u*aiz*) *adj* imprudente

unwrap (ann-*ræp*) *v* desembrulhar

up (ap) *adv* em cima, acima, para cima

upholster (ap-*ho*u*l*-çtă) *v* forrar, estofar

upkeep (ap-*kiip*) *n* manutenção *f*

uplands (ap-*länndz*) *pl* terras altas

upon (ă-*pónn*) *prep* sobre

upper (a-pă) *adj* superior

upright (*ap*-rait) *adj* direito; *adv* em pé

*upset (ap-*çét*) *v* transtornar; *adj* transtornado

upside-down (ap-çaid-*daunn*) *adv* de pernas para o ar

upstairs (ap-*çté*ª*z*) *adv* em cima; para cima

upstream (ap-*çtriimm*) *adv* rio acima

upwards (*ap*-ᵘădz) *adv* para cima

urban (*ăă*-bănn) *adj* urbano

urge (ăădj) *v* incitar; *n* impulso *m*

urgency (*ăă*-djănn-çi) *n* urgência *f*

urgent (*ăă*-djănnt) *adj* urgente

urine (*ⁱuª*-rinn) *n* urina *f*

Uruguay (*ⁱuª*-ră-gh ᵘai) Uruguai *m*

Uruguayan (ⁱuª-ră-*gh*ᵘ*ai*-ănn) *adj* uruguaio

us (ac) *pron* nós

usable (*ⁱuu*-ză-băl) *adj* utilizável

usage (*ⁱuu*-zidj) *n* uso *m*

use¹ (ⁱuuz) *v* usar; ***be used to *es**tar habituado a; ~ **up *consumir**

use² (ⁱuuç) *n* uso *m*; utilidade *f*; ***be of** ~ ***servir**

useful (*ⁱuu*ç-făl) *adj* útil

useless (*ⁱuu*ç-lăç) *adj* inútil

user (*ⁱuu*-ză) *n* o que usa, utente *m*

usher (a-chă) *n* arrumador *m*

usherette (a-chă-*rét*) *n* arrumadora *f*

usual (*ⁱuu*-ju-ăl) *adj* usual

usually (*ⁱuu*-ju-ă-li) *adv* habitualmente

utensil (ⁱuu-*ténn*-çăl) *n* utensílio *m*, ferramenta *f*

utility (ⁱuu-*ti*-lă-ti) *n* utilidade *f*

utilize (*ⁱuu*-ti-laiz) *v* utilizar

utmost (*at*-moᵘçt) *adj* máximo

utter (a-tă) *adj* completo, total; *v* emitir

V

vacancy (*vei*-kănn-çi) *n* vaga *f*

vacant (*vei*-kănnt) *adj* vago

vacate (vă-*keit*) *v* vagar

vacation (vă-*kei*-chănn) *n* férias *fpl*

vaccinate (*væk*-çi-neit) *v* vacinar

vaccination (væk-çi-*nei*-chănn) *n* vacinação *f*

vacuum (*væ*-kⁱu-ămm) *n* vácuo *m*; ~ **cleaner** aspirador *m*; ~ **flask** garrafa termos

vagrancy (*vei*-ghrănn-çi) *n* vadiagem *f*

vague (veigh) *adj* vago

vain (veinn) *adj* vaidoso; vão; **in** ~ em vão, inutilmente

valet (*væ*-lit) *n* criado *m*, criado de quarto

valid (*væ*-lid) *adj* válido

valley (*væ*-li) *n* vale *m*

valuable (*væ*-lⁱu-băl) *adj* valioso, de valor; **valuables** valores *mpl*

value (*væ*-lⁱuu) *n* valor *m*; *v* avaliar

valve (vælv) *n* válvula *f*

van (vænn) *n* furgoneta *f*

vanilla (vă-*ni*-lă) *n* baunilha *f*

vanish (*væ*-nich) *v* desaparecer

vapour (*vei*-pă) *n* vapor *m*

variable (*vé*ª-ri-ă-băl) *adj* variável

variation (vé ª-ri-*ei*-chănn) *n* variação *f*; mudança *f*

varied (*vé*ª-rid) *adj* variado

variety (vă-*rai*-ă-ti) *n* variedade *f*; ~ **show** espectáculo de variedades; ~ **theatre** teatro de variedades

various (*vé*ª-ri-ăç) *adj* diversos

varnish (*vaa*-nich) *n* verniz *m*; *v* envernizar

vary (*vé*ª-ri) *v* variar; mudar; ***diferir**

vase (vaaz) *n* vaso *m*

vast (vaaçt) *adj* vasto, imenso

vault (vóólt) *n* abóbada *f*; casa-forte *f*

veal (viil) *n* vitela *f*

vegetable (*vé*-djä-tä-bäl) *n* legume *m*

vegetarian (*vé*-dji-*té*ª-ri-änn) *n* vegetariano *m*

vegetation (*vé*-dji-*tei*-chänn) *n* vegetação *f*

vehicle (*vii*-ä-käl) *n* veículo *m*

veil (veil) *n* véu *m*

vein (veinn) *n* veia *f*; **varicose ~** variz *f*

velvet (*vél*-vit) *n* veludo *m*

velveteen (*vél*-vi-*tiinn*) *n* belbutina *f*

venerable (*vé*-nä-rä-bäl) *adj* venerável

venereal disease (vi-*ni*ª-ri-äl di-*ziiz*) doença venérea

Venezuela (*vé*-ni-z*u*ei-lä) Venezuela *f*

Venezuelan (*vé*-ni-z*u*ei-länn) *adj* venezuelano

ventilate (*vénn*-ti-leit) *v* ventilar, arejar

ventilation (*vénn*-ti-*lei*-chänn) *n* ventilação *f*; arejamento *m*

ventilator (*vénn*-ti-lei-tä) *n* ventilador *m*

venture (*vénn*-tchä) *v* aventurar

veranda (vä-* rænn*-dä) *n* varanda *f*

verb (vääb) *n* verbo *m*

verbal (*vää*-bäl) *adj* verbal

verdict (*vää*-dikt) *n* sentença *f*, veredicto *m*

verge (väädj) *n* borda *f*

verify (*vé*-ri-fai) *v* verificar

verse (vääç) *n* verso *m*

version (*vää*-chänn) *n* versão *f*

versus (*vää*-çäç) *prep* contra

vertical (*vää*-ti-käl) *adj* vertical

vertigo (*vää*-ti-ghoᵘ) *n* vertigem *f*

very (*vé*-ri) *adv* muito; *adj* preciso, verdadeiro; extremo

vessel (*vé*-çäl) *n* embarcação *f*, navio *m*; vasilha *f*

vest (véçt) *n* camisa *f*; *nAm* colete *m*

veterinary surgeon (*vé*-tri-nä-ri *çää*-djänn) veterinário *m*

via (vai*ª*) *prep* via

viaduct (*vai*ª-dakt) *n* viaduto *m*

vibrate (vai-*breit*) *v* vibrar

vibration (vai-*brei*-chänn) *n* vibração *f*

vicar (*vi*-kä) *n* vigário *m*

vicarage (*vi*-kä-ridj) *n* presbitério *m*

vice-president (vaiç-*pré*-zi-dännt) *n* vice-presidente *m*

vicinity (vi-*çi*-nä-ti) *n* vizinhança *f*, proximidades *fpl*

vicious (*vi*-chäç) *adj* vicioso

victim (*vik*-timm) *n* vítima *f*

victory (*vik*-tä-ri) *n* vitória *f*

view (v*i*uu) *n* vista *f*; opinião *f*, parecer *m*; *v* observar

view-finder (*v*iuu-fainn-dä) *n* visor *m*

vigilant (*vi*-dji-länt) *adj* vigilante

villa (*vi*-lä) *n* vivenda *f*; vila *fBr*

village (*vi*-lidj) *n* aldeia *f*

villain (*vi*-länn) *n* patife *m*

vine (vainn) *n* videira *f*

vinegar (*vi*-ni-ghä) *n* vinagre *m*

vineyard (*vinn*-ⁱäd) *n* vinha *f*

vintage (*vinn*-tidj) *n* vindima *f*

violation (vaiª-*lei*-chänn) *n* violação *f*

violence (*vai*ª-lännç) *n* violência *f*

violent (*vai*ª-lännt) *adj* violento; impetuoso

violet (*vai*ª-lät) *n* violeta *f*

violin (vaiª-*linn*) *n* violino *m*

virgin (*vää*-djinn) *n* virgem *f*

virtue (*vää*-tchuu) *n* virtude *f*

visa (*vii*-zä) *n* visto *m*

visibility (vi-zä-*bi*-lä-ti) *n* visibilidade *f*

visible (*vi*-zä-bäl) *adj* visível

vision (*vi*-jänn) *n* visão *f*

visit (*vi*-zit) *v* visitar; *n* visita *f*; **visiting hours** horas de visita

visiting-card (*vi*-zi-tinng-kaad) *n* cartão de visita

visitor (*vi*-zi-tä) *n* visitante *m*

vital (*vai*-täl) *adj* vital

vitamin (*vi*-tä-minn) *n* vitamina *f*

vivid (*vi*-vid) *adj* vivo

vocabulary (vä-*kæ*-bⁱu-lä-ri) *n* vocabu-

lário m
vocal (voᵘ-kăl) adj vocal
vocalist (voᵘ-kă-liçt) n vocalista m
voice (voiç) n voz f
void (void) adj nulo; vazio; n vácuo m
volcano (vól-kei-noᵘ) n (pl ~es, ~s) vulcão m
volt (voᵘlt) n volt m
voltage (voᵘl-tidj) n voltagem f
volume (vó-lᵘumm) n volume m
voluntary (vó-lănn-tă-ri) adj voluntário
volunteer (vó-lănn-tiᵃ) n voluntário m
vomit (vó-mit) v vomitar
vote (voᵘt) v votar; n voto m; votacão f
voucher (vau-tchă) n vale m
vow (vau) n juramento m, voto m; v jurar
vowel (vauᵃl) n vogal f
voyage (voi-idj) n viagem f
vulgar (val-ghă) adj vulgar; popular, ordinário
vulnerable (val-nă-ră-băl) adj vulnerável
vulture (val-tchă) n abutre m

W

wade (ᵘeid) v patinhar
wafer (ᵘei-fă) n bolacha de baunilha
waffle (ᵘó-făl) n bolacha f
wages (ᵘei-djiz) pl salário m
waggon (ᵘæ-ghănn) n vagão m
waist (ᵘeiçt) n cintura f
waistcoat (ᵘeiç-koᵘt) n colete m
wait (ᵘeit) v esperar; ~ on *servir
waiter (ᵘei-tă) n criado m, empregado de mesa; garcom mBr
waiting (ᵘei-tinng) n espera f
waiting-list (ᵘei-tinng-liçt) n lista de espera

waiting-room (ᵘei-tinng-ruumm) n sala de espera
waitress (ᵘei-triç) n empregada de mesa; garconete fBr
*wake (ᵘeik) v acordar; ~ up despertar, acordar
walk (ᵘóók) v andar; *passear; n passeio m; walking a pé
walker (ᵘóó-kă) n passeante m
walking-stick (ᵘóó-kinng-çtik) n bengala f
wall (ᵘóól) n muro m; parede f
wallet (ᵘó-lit) n carteira f
wallpaper (ᵘóól-pei-pă) n papel de parede
walnut (ᵘóól-nat) n noz f
waltz (ᵘóólç) n valsa f
wander (ᵘónn-dă) v *vaguear, errar
want (ᵘónnt) v *querer; desejar; n necessidade f; carência f, falta f
war (ᵘóó) n guerra f
warden (ᵘóó-dănn) n guarda m
wardrobe (ᵘóó-droᵘb) n roupeiro m, guarda-roupa m
warehouse (ᵘéᵃ-hauç) n armazém m
wares (ᵘéᵃz) pl mercadorias fpl
warm (ᵘóómm) adj quente; v aquecer
warmth (ᵘóómmθ) n calor m
warn (ᵘóónn) v *prevenir, avisar
warning (ᵘóó-ninng) n aviso m
wary (ᵘéᵃ-ri) adj prudente
was (ᵘóz) v (p be)
wash (ᵘóch) v lavar; ~ and wear não passar a ferro; ~ up lavar a loica
washable (ᵘó-chă-băl) adj lavável
wash-basin (ᵘóch-bei-çănn) n lavatório m
washing (ᵘó-chinng) n lavagem f; roupa para lavar
washing-machine (ᵘó-chinng-mă-chiinn) n máquina de lavar
washing-powder (ᵘó-chinng-pau-dă) n detergente em pó

washroom (ᵘóch-ruumm) *n Am* lavabos *mpl*

wash-stand (ᵘóch-çtænnd) *n* lavatório *m*

wasp (ᵘóçp) *n* vespa *f*

waste (ᵘeiçt) *v* desperdiçar; *n* desperdício *m*; *adj* inculto

wasteful (ᵘeiçt-fäl) *adj* gastador

wastepaper-basket (ᵘeiçt-*pei*-pä-baaçkit) *n* cesto dos papéis

watch (ᵘótch) *v* observar; vigiar; *n* relógio *m*; ~ **for** espreitar; ~ **out** tomar cuidado

watch-maker (ᵘótch-mei-kä) *n* relojoeiro *m*

watch-strap (ᵘótch-çtræp) *n* correia de relógio

water (ᵘóó-tä) *n* água *f*; **iced** ~ água gelada; **running** ~ água corrente; ~ **pump** bomba de água; ~ **ski** esqui aquático

water-colour (ᵘóó-tä-ka-lä) *n* tinta de água; aguarela *f*

watercress (ᵘóó-tä-kréç) *n* agrião *m*

waterfall (ᵘóó-tä-fóól) *n* queda de água

watermelon (ᵘóó-tä-mé-länn) *n* melancia *f*

waterproof (ᵘóó-tä-pruuf) *adj* impermeável

water-softener (ᵘóó-tä-çóf-nä) *n* produto amaciador da água

waterway (ᵘóó-tä-ᵘei) *n* via navegável

watt (ᵘót) *n* watt *m*

wave (ᵘeiv) *n* onda *f*, ondulação *f*; *v* acenar

wave-length (ᵘeiv-lénngθ) *n* comprimento de onda

wavy (ᵘei-vi) *adj* ondulado

wax (ᵘækç) *n* cera *f*

waxworks (ᵘækç-ᵘääkç) *pl* museu das ceras

way (ᵘei) *n* maneira *f*, modo *m*; caminho *m*; lado *m*, direcção *f*; distância *f*; **any** ~ de qualquer maneira; **by the** ~ a propósito; **one-way traffic** sentido único; **out of the** ~ afastado; **the other** ~ **round** ao contrário; ~ **back** volta *f*; ~ **in** entrada *f*; ~ **out** saída *f*

wayside (ᵘei-çaid) *n* beira do caminho

we (ᵘii) *pron* nós

weak (ᵘiik) *adj* fraco

weakness (ᵘiik-näç) *n* fraqueza *f*

wealth (ᵘélθ) *n* riqueza *f*

wealthy (ᵘél-θi) *adj* rico

weapon (ᵘé-pänn) *n* arma *f*

*wear (ᵘéª) *v* usar, *trazer vestido; ~ **out** gastar

weary (ᵘiª-ri) *adj* cansado

weather (ᵘé-ðä) *n* tempo *m*; ~ **forecast** boletim meteorológico

*weave (ᵘiiv) *v* tecer

weaver (ᵘii-vä) *n* tecelão *m*

wedding (ᵘé-dinng) *n* casamento *m*

wedding-ring (ᵘé-dinng-rinng) *n* aliança *f*

wedge (ᵘédj) *n* cunha *f*

Wednesday (ᵘénnz-di) quarta-feira *f*

weed (ᵘiid) *n* erva daninha

week (ᵘiik) *n* semana *f*

weekday (ᵘiik-dei) *n* dia de semana

weekend (ᵘii-kénnd) *n* fim-de-semana *m*

weekly (ᵘii-kli) *adj* semanal

*weep (ᵘiip) *v* chorar

weigh (ᵘei) *v* pesar

weighing-machine (ᵘei-inng-mächiinn) *n* balança *f*

weight (ᵘeit) *n* peso *m*

welcome (ᵘél-kämm) *adj* benvindo; *n* acolhimento *m*; *v* acolher

weld (ᵘéld) *v* soldar

welfare (ᵘél-féª) *n* bem-estar *m*

well[1] (ᵘél) *adv* bem; *adj* bom; **as** ~ também; **as** ~ **as** assim como;

well! bem!

well² (ᵁél) n poço m

well-founded (ᵁél-*faunn*-did) adj fundamentado

well-known (ᵁél-noᵁnn) adj conhecido

well-to-do (ᵁél-tă-*duu*) adj abastado

went (ᵁénnt) v (p go)

were (ᵁăă) v (p be)

west (ᵁést) n ocidente m, oeste m

westerly (ᵁé-çtă-li) adj ocidental

western (ᵁé-çtănn) adj ocidental

wet (ᵁét) adj molhado; húmido

whale (ᵁeil) n baleia f

wharf (ᵁóóf) n (pl ~s, wharves) cais m

what (ᵁót) pron o quê; o que; ~ **for** para quê

whatever (ᵁó-*té*-vă) pron tudo o que

wheat (ᵁiit) n trigo m

wheel (ᵁiil) n roda f

wheelbarrow (ᵁiil-bæ-roᵁ) n carrinho de mão

wheelchair (ᵁiil-tchéᵃ) n cadeira de rodas

when (ᵁénn) adv quando; conj quando, logo que

whenever (ᵁé-*né*-vă) conj sempre que

where (ᵁéᵃ) adv onde; conj onde

wherever (ᵁéᵃ-*ré*-vă) conj onde quer que

whether (ᵁé-ðǎ) conj se; **whether ... or** quer ... quer

which (ᵁitch) pron qual; que

whichever (ᵁi-*tché*-vă) adj qualquer

while (ᵁail) conj enquanto; n momento m

whilst (ᵁailçt) conj enquanto

whim (ᵁimm) n capricho m, veleidade f

whip (ᵁip) n chicote m; v bater

whiskers (ᵁi-çkăz) pl suíças fpl

whisper (ᵁi-çpă) v murmurar, sussurrar; n sussurro m

whistle (ᵁi-çăl) v assobiar; n apito m

white (ᵁait) adj branco

whitebait (ᵁait-beit) n peixe miúdo

whiting (ᵁai-tinng) n (pl ~) pescada f

Whitsun (ᵁit-çănn) Pentecostes m

who (huu) pron quem; que

whoever (huu-é-vă) pron quem quer que

whole (hoᵁl) adj completo, inteiro; intacto; n todo m

wholesale (hoᵁl-çeil) n venda por grosso; ~ **dealer** armazenista m

wholesome (hoᵁl-cămm) adj saudável

wholly (hoᵁl-li) adv completamente

whom (huumm) pron a quem

whore (hóó) n prostituta f

whose (huuz) pron cujo; de quem

why (ᵁai) adv porquê

wicked (ᵁi-kid) adj mau

wide (ᵁaid) adj vasto, largo

widen (ᵁai-dănn) v alargar

widow (ᵁi-doᵁ) n viúva f

widower (ᵁi-doᵁ-ă) n viúvo m

width (ᵁidθ) n largura f

wife (ᵁaif) n (pl wives) esposa f, mulher f

wig (ᵁigh) n peruca f

wild (ᵁaild) adj selvagem; feroz

will (ᵁil) n vontade f; testamento m

***will** (ᵁil) v *querer

willing (ᵁi-linng) adj disposto

willingly (ᵁi-linng-li) adv de boa vontade

will-power (ᵁil-pauᵃ) n força de vontade

***win** (ᵁinn) v ganhar

wind (ᵁinnd) n vento m

***wind** (ᵁainnd) v serpentear; *dar corda, enrolar

winding (ᵁainn-dinng) adj sinuoso

windmill (ᵁinnd-mil) n moinho de vento

window (ᵁinn-doᵁ) n janela f

window-sill (ᵘinn-doᵘ-çil) *n* peitoril *m*

windscreen (ᵘinnd-çkriinn) *n* pára-brisas *m*; ~ **wiper** limpa pára-brisas

windshield (ᵘinnd-chiild) *nAm* pára-brisas *m*

windy (ᵘinn-di) *adj* ventoso

wine (ᵘainn) *n* vinho *m*

wine-cellar (ᵘainn-cé-lä) *n* adega *f*

wine-list (ᵘainn-liçt) *n* lista dos vinhos

wine-merchant (ᵘainn-mää-tchännt) *n* negociante de vinhos

wine-waiter (ᵘainn-ᵘei-tä) *n* sommelier *m*

wing (ᵘinng) *n* asa *f*

winkle (ᵘinng-käl) *n* búzio *m*

winner (ᵘi-nä) *n* vencedor *m*

winning (ᵘi-ninng) *adj* vencedor; **winnings** lucros

winter (ᵘinn-tä) *n* Inverno *m*; ~ **sports** desportos de inverno

wipe (ᵘaip) *v* limpar

wire (ᵘaiᵃ) *n* fio *m*; arame *m*

wireless (ᵘaiᵃ-läç) *n* rádio *m*

wisdom (ᵘiz-dämm) *n* sabedoria *f*

wise (ᵘaiz) *adj* erudito; sensato

wish (ᵘich) *v* desejar, ambicionar; *n* desejo *m*

witch (ᵘitch) *n* bruxa *f*

with (ᵘið) *prep* com

*****withdraw** (ᵘið-dróó) *v* retirar

within (ᵘi-ðinn) *prep* dentro de; *adv* por dentro

without (ᵘi-ðaut) *prep* sem

witness (ᵘit-näç) *n* testemunha *f*

wits (ᵘitç) *pl* razão *f*

witty (ᵘi-ti) *adj* espirituoso

wolf (ᵘulf) *n* (pl wolves) lobo *m*

woman (ᵘu-männ) *n* (pl women) mulher *f*

womb (ᵘuumm) *n* útero *m*

won (ᵘann) *v* (p, pp win)

wonder (ᵘann-dä) *n* milagre *m*; admiração *f*; *v* perguntar a si próprio

wonderful (ᵘann-dä-fäl) *adj* maravi-

lhoso, estupendo; delicioso

wood (ᵘud) *n* madeira *f*; bosque *m*

wood-carving (ᵘud-kaa-vinng) *n* talha *f*

wooded (ᵘu-did) *adj* arborizado

wooden (ᵘu-dänn) *adj* de madeira; ~ **shoe** tamanco *m*

woodland (ᵘud-lännd) *n* região arborizada

wool (ᵘul) *n* lã *f*; **darning** ~ linha de passajar

woollen (ᵘu-länn) *adj* de lã

word (ᵘääd) *n* palavra *f*

wore (ᵘóó) *v* (p wear)

work (ᵘääk) *n* trabalho *m*; faina *f*; *v* trabalhar; funcionar; **working day** dia útil; ~ **of art** obra de arte; ~ **permit** autorização de trabalho

worker (ᵘää-kä) *n* trabalhador *m*

working (ᵘää-kinng) *n* funcionamento *m*

workman (ᵘääk-männ) *n* (pl -men) operário *m*

works (ᵘääkç) *pl* fábrica *f*

workshop (ᵘääk-chóp) *n* oficina *f*

world (ᵘääld) *n* mundo *m*; ~ **war** guerra mundial

world-famous (ᵘääld-fei-mäç) *adj* mundialmente famoso

world-wide (ᵘääld-ᵘaid) *adj* mundial

worm (ᵘäämm) *n* verme *m*

worn (ᵘóónn) *adj* (pp wear) gasto

worn-out (ᵘóónn-aut) *adj* gasto

worried (ᵘa-rid) *adj* preocupado

worry (ᵘa-ri) *v* afligir-se; *n* preocupação *f*

worse (ᵘääç) *adj* pior; *adv* pior

worship (ᵘää-chip) *v* adorar; *n* culto *m*

worst (ᵘääçt) *adj* o pior; *adv* pior

worsted (ᵘu-çtid) *n* lã cardada

worth (ᵘääθ) *n* valor *m*; *****be** ~ *****valer; *****be worth-while** *****valer a pena

worthless (ᵘääθ-läç) *adj* sem valor

worthy of (ᵘǟ-ð̯i äv) digno de

would (ᵘud) v (p will)

wound¹ (ᵘuunnd) n ferida f; v *ferir, ofender

wound² (ᵘaunnd) v (p, pp wind)

wrap (ræp) v envolver; embrulhar

wreck (rék) n carcaça f; v *destruir

wrench (rénntch) n chave-inglesa f; torcedura f; v torcer

wrinkle (rinng-kǎl) n ruga f

wrist (riçt) n pulso m

wrist-watch (riçt-ᵘótch) n relógio de pulso

*write (rait) v escrever; in writing por escrito; ~ down anotar

writer (rai-tǎ) n escritor m

writing-pad (rai-tinng-pæd) n bloco de notas, bloco de papel

writing-paper (rai-tinng-pei-pǎ) n papel para escrever

written (ri-tänn) adj (pp write) por escrito

wrong (rónn) adj errado, impróprio; n mal m; v lesar; *be ~ *estar errado

wrote (roᵘt) v (p write)

X

Xmas (kriç-mǎç) Natal m

X-ray (ékç-rei) n radiografia f; v radiografar

Y

yacht (ᶦót) n iate m

yacht-club (ᶦót-klab) n clube náutico

yachting (ᶦó-tinng) n vela f

yard (ᶦaad) n pátio m

yarn (ᶦaann) n fio m

yawn (ᶦóónn) v bocejar

year (ᶦiǎ) n ano m

yearly (ᶦiǎ-li) adj anual

yeast (ᶦiiçt) n levedura f

yell (ᶦél) v berrar; n berro m

yellow (ᶦé-loᵘ) adj amarelo

yes (ᶦéç) sim

yesterday (ᶦé-çtǎ-di) adv ontem

yet (ᶦét) adv ainda; conj contudo, mas

yield (ᶦiild) v render; ceder

yoke (ᶦoᵘk) n canga f

yolk (ᶦoᵘk) n gema f

you (ᶦuu) pron tu; te; você; o senhor; ao senhor; vocês; os senhores

young (ᶦanng) adj jovem

your (ᶦóó) adj seu; teu; vosso, teus

yourself (ᶦóó-çélf) pron te; tu mesmo; você mesmo; o senhor mesmo

yourselves (ᶦóó-çélvz) pron se; vocês mesmos; os senhores mesmos

youth (ᶦuuθ) n juventude f; ~ hostel albergue de juventude

Yugoslav (ᶦuu-ghǎ-çlaav) n jugoslavo m

Yugoslavia (ᶦuu-ghǎ-çlaa-vi-ǎ) Jugoslávia f

Z

zeal (ziil) n zelo m

zealous (zé-lǎç) adj zeloso

zebra (zii-brǎ) n zebra f

zenith (zé-niθ) n zénite m; apogeu m

zero (ziǎ-roᵘ) n (pl ~s) zero m

zest (zéçt) n gosto m

zinc (zinngk) n zinco m

zip (zip) n fecho éclair; ~ code Am código postal

zipper (zi-pǎ) n fecho éclair

zodiac (zoᵘ-di-æk) n zodíaco m

zone (zoᵘnn) n zona f; região f

Léxico gastronómico

Comidas

almond amêndoa

anchovy anchova

angel (food) cake bolo fofo à base de claras

angels on horseback ostras envolvidas em bacon, grelhadas e servidas sobre torradas

appetizer aperitivo

apple maçã
~ **dumpling** espécie de pastel recheado de compota de maçã
~ **sauce** molho de maçã

apricot alperce (Bras. damasco)

Arbroath smoky arinca fumado

artichoke alcachofra

asparagus espargo
~ **tip** cabeça de espargo

assorted sortido, variado

aubergine beringela

avocado (pear) abacate

bacon toucinho fumado
~ **and eggs** ovos estrelados com toucinho fumado

bagel rosca

baked cozido no forno
~ **Alaska** sobremesa composta duma camada de bolo fino e outra de gelado (Bras. sorvete), recoberta de claras em castelo e açúcar e levada ao forno rapidamente a alourar
~ **beans** feijão branco guisado com molho de tomate adocicado
~ **potato** batata no forno com pele

Bakewell tart tarte de amêndoa com doce (Bras. geléia) de fruta

baloney espécie de mortadela

banana split banana cortada ao comprido com gelado (Bras. sorvete) e nozes e coberta de calda de fruta ou de chocolate

barbecue 1) carne de vaca picada servida com um molho de tomate picante 2) churrasco ao ar livre
~ **sauce** molho de tomate picante

barbecued grelhado nas brasas

basil manjericão

bass robalo

bean feijão

beef carne de vaca (Bras. boi)
~ **olive** trouxa, rolinho de vaca

beefburger hamburger, sanduíche de bife de vaca picado

beet, beetroot beterraba

bilberry uva-do-monte

bill conta
~ **of fare** lista (Bras. cardápio)

biscuit 1) biscoito, bolacha (GB) 2) pãozinho (EUA)

black pudding chouriço de sangue, morcela

blackberry amora

blackcurrant groselha negra

bloater arenque salgado e fumado

blood sausage chouriço de sangue, morcela

blueberry uva-do-monte (Bras. mirtilo)

boiled cozido

Bologna (sausage) espécie de mortadela

bone osso

boned desossado, sem ossos

Boston baked beans feijão branco guisado com toucinho fumado e melaço

Boston cream pie bolo recheado com chantilly ou creme de pasteleiro e coberto com glace de chocolate

brains miolos

braised estufado, assado

bramble pudding pudim de amoras (geralmente servido com maçãs)

braunschweiger chouriço de fígado

bread pão

breaded panado

breakfast pequeno almoço (Bras. café da manhã)

breast peito (de aves)

brisket peito (de animais)

broad bean fava

broth caldo

brown Betty espécie de pudim de maçã coberto de pão ralado

brunch pequeno almoço (Bras. café da manhã) abundante que substitui o almoço

Brussels sprout couve-de-bruxelas

bubble and squeak batatas e couve fritas como uma omeleta e misturadas, por vezes, com bocados de carne

bun 1) pãozinho de leite com frutas secas (GB) 2) pãozinho redondo (EUA)

butter manteiga

buttered barrado com manteiga

cabbage couve

Caesar salad salada de alface com alho, anchovas, crostões de pão e queijo ralado

cake bolo

cakes bolos, pastéis

calf vitela

Canadian bacon lombo de porco fumado cortado às fatias

cantaloupe variedade de melão

caper alcaparra

capercaillie, capercailzie galo (silvestre)

carp carpa

carrot cenoura

cashew castanha de caju

casserole espécie de guisado

catfish gata (peixe)

catsup ketchup

cauliflower couve-flor

celery aipo

cereal cornflakes

   hot ~ papas de aveia

check conta

Cheddar (cheese) queijo de gosto um pouco ácido, parecido com o queijo da ilha

cheese queijo

   ~ board tabuleiro de queijos variados

   ~ cake tarte de requeijão

cheeseburger sanduíche de bife picado com uma fatia de queijo

chef's salad salada mista de presunto, frango, ovos cozidos, tomates, alface e queijo

cherry cereja

chestnut castanha

chicken frango

chicory 1) endívia (GB) 2) escarola, chicória (EUA)

chili con carne carne de vaca picada com malaguetas e feijão encarnado

chili pepper piripiri, malagueta

chips 1) batatas fritas (GB) 2) batatas chips (EUA)

chitt(er)lings tripas de porco

chive cebolinho

choice 1) escolha 2) primeira qualidade

chop costeleta

~ **suey** prato chinês; tiras muito finas de carne ou de galinha e de legumes variados (feijão, soja, aipo, junça) cortados finos

chopped cortado aos bocados pequenos

chowder sopa creme de marisco

Christmas pudding pudim escuro com frutas cristalizadas e passas, por vezes flamejado com conhaque, e servido com creme de baunilha

chutney condimento indiano agridoce que acompanha os pratos à base de caril

cinnamon canela

clam amêijoa

club sandwich sanduíche americana composta de várias tostas intercaladas de frango, toucinho fumado, alface, tomate e maionese

cobbler espécie de tarte de frutas

cock-a-leekie soup sopa de frango e alho-porro

coconut coco

cod bacalhau fresco

Colchester oyster ostra inglesa muito apreciada

cold cuts/meat prato de carnes frias

coleslaw salada de couve

cooked cozido, cozinhado

cookie bolacha, biscoito

corn 1) trigo (GB) 2) milho (EUA)

~ **on the cob** espiga de milho, maçaroca

corned beef carne enlatada

cornflakes flocos de milho

Cornish pasty pastel recheado com bocados de batata e de carneiro

cottage cheese espécie de requeijão

cottage pie empadão de batata

course prato

cover charge preço do talher

crab caranguejo

cracker bolacha de água e sal

cranberry arando

~ **sauce** molho de arandos

crawfish, crayfish 1) lagostim-do-rio 2) lagostim

cream 1) natas (Bras. creme de leite) 2) sopa creme 3) creme (sobremesa)

~ **cheese** queijo fresco muito cremoso

~ **puff** espécie de farto recheado com chantilly

creamed potatoes batatas cozidas, cortadas aos quadrados e envolvidas em béchamel

creole prato muito condimentado, preparado com tomates, pimentos e cebolas e acompanhado de arroz à crioula

cress agrião

crisps batatas chips

crumpet espécie de pãozinho achatado geralmente torrado

cucumber pepino

Cumberland ham presunto muito apreciado

Cumberland sauce molho agri-doce composto de vinho, sumo de laranja, raspa de limão, condimentos e geleia de groselhas

cupcake queque

cured marinado, salgado e, por vezes, fumado

currant 1) passa de uva (GB) 2) groselha (EUA)

curried com caril

custard creme de baunilha
~ **pie** pastel de nata

cutlet 1) costeleta 2) posta de peixe 3) escalope (EUA)

dab solhão (peixe)

Danish pastry pastel folhado

date tâmara

Derby cheese queijo cremoso e picante de cor amarela pálida

dessert sobremesa

devil(l)ed com molho muito picante

devil's food cake bolo de chocolate

devils on horseback ameixas cozidas em vinho tinto, recheadas de amêndoas e anchovas, envolvidas em toucinho fumado e grelhadas

Devonshire cream natas (Bras. creme de leite) muito espessas

diced cortado aos quadradinhos

diet food comida dietética

dill endro, aneto

dinner jantar

dish prato

donut, doughnut bola de Berlim

double cream natas (Bras. creme de leite) muito espessas

Dover sole linguado de Dôver, muito apreciado

dressing 1) molho para a salada 2) recheio para aves

Dublin Bay prawn camarão grande

duck pato

duckling pato novo

dumpling bolinha de massa, por vezes recheada, cozida em água ou caldo

Dutch apple pie tarte de maçã polvilhada de açúcar mascavado ou coberta de melaço

eel enguia, eiró

egg ovo
boiled ~ semi-cozido (5 min.)
fried ~ estrelado
hard-boiled ~ cozido
poached ~ escalfado (Bras. escaldado)
scrambled ~ mexido
soft-boiled ~ semi-cozido (3 min.) (Bras. ovo quente)

eggplant beringela

endive 1) escarola, chicória (GB) 2) endívia (EUA)

entrée 1) primeiro prato (GB) 2) prato principal (EUA)

fennel funcho

fig figo

fillet lombo de carne ou filete de peixe

finnan haddock arinca, pequeno bacalhau fumado

fish peixe
~ **and chips** filete de peixe com batatas fritas
~ **cake** croquete de peixe panada
~ **finger** palito de peixe panado

flan tarte

flapjack crepe (Bras. panqueca) espesso

flounder patruça

fool mousse de fruta com natas (Bras. creme de leite) batidas

forcemeat recheio, picado

fowl criação

frankfurter salsicha

French bean feijão verde (Bras. vagem)

French bread cacete (pão)

French dressing 1) molho de vinagre para a salada (GB) 2) molho de maionese com ketchup para a salada (EUA)

french fries batatas fritas

French toast rabanada, fatia dourada

fresh fresco

fried frito

fritter frito

frogs' legs pernas de rã

frosting glace, cobertura

fruit fruta

fry fritada

game caça

gammon carne de porco fumada

garfish peixe-agulha

garlic alho

garnish acompanhamento, guarnição

gherkin pickle, pequeno pepino conservado em vinagre

giblets miúdos

ginger gengibre

goose ganso

gooseberry groselha verde

grape uva
~**fruit** toranja

grated ralado

gravy molho de carne

grayling peixe do lago parecido com a truta

green bean feijão verde (Bras. vagem)

green pepper piment(ã)o verde

greens legumes verdes, hortaliça

grilled grelhado

grilse salmão novo

grouse galinha-do-mato

gumbo 1) quiabo, gombo 2) prato crioula à base de quiabo com legumes, carne, peixe ou mariscos

haddock arinca, pequeno bacalhau geralmente salgado e fumado

haggis bucho de carneiro recheado de flocos de aveia

hake pescada

half meio, metade

halibut alabote (peixe)

ham fiambre (Bras. presunto)
~ **and eggs** com ovos estrelados

hare lebre

haricot bean feijão verde (Bras. vagem)

hash restos cortados aos bocadinhos e aquecidos (geralmente carne de vaca e batatas)

hazelnut avelã

heart coração

herbs ervas de cheiros

herring arenque

home-made caseiro

hominy grits milho pilado, cozido em água salgada

honey mel

honeydew melon melão muito doce, cujo interior é amarelo esverdeado

horse-radish rábano silvestre

hot 1) muito quente 2) muito condimentado, apimentado
~ **cross bun** pãozinho de leite com passas
~ **dog** cachorro (Bras. cachorro quente)

huckleberry uva-do-monte (Bras. mirtilo)

hush puppy frito de farinha de milho com cebolas picadas

ice-cream gelado (Bras. sorvete)

iced gelado, muito fresco

icing glace, cobertura

Idaho baked potato batata muito apreciada cozida no forno

Irish stew guisado de carneiro com cebolas e batatas

Italian dressing molho vinagrete com alho para a salada

jam doce (Bras. geléia) de fruta
~ **tart** tartelete de doce de fruta

jellied em gelatina

Jell-O sobremesa de gelatina

jelly geleia de fruta

Jerusalem artichoke tupinambo (Bras. topinamba)

John Dory peixe-galo, São Pedro

jugged hare lebrada

juniper berry baga de zimbro

junket requeijão com açúcar

kale espécie de couve frisada

kedgeree arroz de peixe com ovos cozidos e manteiga

kidney rim

kipper arenque fumado

Lady Curzon soup sopa de tartaruga com natas (Bras. creme de leite) e caril

lamb borrego

Lancashire hot-pot guisado de costeletas, rins de carneiro, batatas e cebolas

laver alga marinha comestível

lean magro, com pouca gordura

leek alho-porro, alho francês

leg perna

lemon limão
~ **sole** azevia, espécie de linguado

lentil lentilha

lettuce alface

lima bean 1) fava (EUA) 2) feijão encarnado (GB)

lime lima, limão verde

liver fígado

lobster lavagante

loin lombo

Long Island duck pato de Long Island, muito apreciado

low-calorie pobre em calorias

lox salmão fumado

lunch almoço

macaroon bolinho de claras, coco ou amêndoas

mackerel sarda

maize milho seco

maple syrup xarope de ácer

marinated marinado

marjoram manjerona

marmalade marmelada de laranjas

marrow 1) tutano 2) variedade de abóbora (GB)
~**bone** osso com tutano

marshmallow rebuçado de malvaísco

marzipan massa de amêndoas, maçapão

mashed potatoes puré de batata

mayonnaise maionese

meal refeição

meat carne
~ **ball** almôndega
~ **loaf** bolo de carne

medium (done) mal passado

melon melão

melted derretido

Melton Mowbray pie empadão de carne

menu lista (Bras. cardápio)

meringue merengue

milk leite

mince picado
~-**pie** empada de frutas cristali-

zadas cortadas aos bocados com passas e condimentos

minced picado

~ **meat** carne picada

mint hortelã

mixed misto, variado

~ **grill** 1) espetada mista (EUA) 2) prato guarnecido geralmente de tomate, cogumelos, ovo estrelado, toucinho fumado e, por vezes, feijão branco e carne grelhada

molasses melaço

morel funcho, cogumelo muito apreciado

mulberry amora

mullet tainha

mulligatawny soup canja de galinha muito condimentada de origem indiana

mushroom cogumelo

muskmelon variedade de melão muito doce

mussel mexilhão

mustard mostarda (geralmente agridoce)

mutton carneiro

noodle nuilha, espécie de massa às tiras

nut noz

oatmeal papas de aveia

oil óleo

okra quiabo (Bras. gombo)

olive azeitona

omelet omelete

onion cebola

orange laranja

ox tongue língua de vaca

oxtail rabo de boi

oyster ostra

pancake crepe (Bras. panqueca)

paprika colorau

parsley salsa

parsnip pastinaga, cenoura

branca

partridge perdiz

pastry 1) massa 2) pastel, bolo

pasty pastel de carne ou de peixe

pâté espécie de pasta de fígado enformada, também feita com carnes diversas

pea ervilha

peach pêssego

peanut amendoim

~ **butter** manteiga de amendoim

pear pêra

pearl barley cevadinha

pepper pimenta

peppermint hortelã-pimenta

perch perca

persimmon dióspiro, caqui

pheasant faisão

pickerel lúcio pequeno

pickled conservado em vinagre, em salmoura

pie empada, empadão recheado de carne, legumes ou frutas

pig porco

pigs' feet/trotters chispe, pé de porco

pigeon pombo

pike lúcio

pineapple ananás (Bras. abacaxi)

plaice solha

plain ao natural, simples

plate prato

plum ameixa

~ **pudding** pudim escuro com frutas cristalizadas e passas, por vezes flamejado com conhaque, e servido com creme de baunilha

poached escalfado, cozido ligeiramente

popcorn pipoca

popover pãozinho de leite

pork porco

porridge papas (Bras. mingau) de aveia

porterhouse steak grande bife de lombo de vaca

potato batata

~ **chips** 1) batatas fritas (GB) 2) batatas chips (EU)

~ **in its jacket** cozida com a pele

potted shrimps camarões conservados em manteiga condimentada e servidos frios

poultry criação

prawn camarão

prune ameixa seca

ptarmigan perdiz da montanha

pudding pudim

pumpernickel pão de centeio integral

pumpkin abóbora

quail codorniz

quince marmelo

rabbit coelho

radish rabanete

rainbow trout truta arco-íris

raisin passa (de uva)

rare muito mal passado

raspberry frambocsa

raw cru

red mullet salmonete

red (sweet) pepper pimentão vermelho

redcurrant groselha

relish pickles

rhubarb ruibarbo

rib (of beef) costeleta (de vaca)

rib-eye steak bife de lombo

rice arroz

river trout truta

roast assado

~ **beef** rosbife

Rock Cornish hen variedade de frango alimentado com grãos

roe ovas

roll pãozinho

rollmop herring filete de arenque marinado em vinho branco e enrolado à volta dum pepino de conserva

round steak bife do alto da perna de vaca

Rubens sandwich fatia de pão de centeio guarnecida com carne de vaca fumada e chucrute, temperada com molho para salada e alourada no forno

rumpsteak bife do alto da perna de vaca

rusk tosta

rye bread pão de centeio

saddle sela, lombo

saffron açafrão

sage salva

salad salada

~ **bar** saladas variadas à descrição

~ **cream** espécie de maionese adocicada

~ **dressing** molho para a salada

salmon salmão

~ **trout** truta-das-fontes

salt sal

salted salgado

sandwich sande (Bras. sanduíche)

sardine sardinha

sauce molho

sauerkraut chucrute, couve picada em salmoura

sausage enchido

sautéed salteado

scallop concha de vieira

scampi rabo de lagostim descascado

scone espécie de pãozinho

Scotch broth sopa de legumes com carne de carneiro ou de vaca

Scotch egg ovo cozido, enrolado em miolo de salsicha e frito

Scotch woodcock torrada com pasta de anchovas e ovos mexidos

sea bass robalo

sea bream goraz (peixe)

sea kale espécie de couve

seafood marisco

(in) season (da) época

seasoning condimento

service charge serviço

service (not) included serviço (não) incluído

set menu ementa fixa (Bras. menu) do dia

shad sável

shallot chalota

shellfish marisco de concha

sherbet sorvete (Bras. sorvete com água)

shortbread biscoito areado

shoulder pá

shredded cortado em tiras finas
~ **wheat** espécie de flocos de trigo

shrimp camarão

silverside (of beef) peça grande de carne de vaca

sirloin steak bife de lombo de vaca

skewer espetada

slice fatia

sliced cortado às fatias

sloppy Joe picado de vaca com um molho de tomate bem condimentado servido dentro dum pãozinho

smelt biqueirão (peixe)

smoked fumado

snack refeição ligeira

sole linguado

soup sopa

sour azedo

soused herring arenque de escabeche

spare rib entrecosto de porco

spice especiaria

spinach espinafre

spiny lobster lagosta

(on a) spit (no) espeto

sponge cake espécie de pão-de-ló

sprat espadilha

squash espécie de abóbora

starter entrada, primeiro prato

steak-and-kidney pie empadão de vaca recheado de carne de vaca e rins

steamed cozido ao vapor

stew guisado

Stilton (cheese) queijo inglês muito apreciado, branco com veios azuis

strawberry morango

string bean feijão verde (Bras. vagem)

stuffed recheado

stuffing recheio

suck(l)ing pig leitão

sugar açúcar

sugarless sem açúcar

sundae taça de gelado (Bras. sorvete) guarnecida

supper ceia

swede rutabaga

sweet 1) doce 2) sobremesa
~-**corn** milho tenro (Bras. milho doce)
~ **potato** batata doce

sweetbread moleja (de vitela ou de borrego)

Swiss cheese queijo adocicado com buracos

Swiss roll torta enrolada

Swiss steak carne de vaca estufada com legumes

T-bone steak grande bife de vaca com um osso ao meio

table d'hôte ementa (Bras. menu) do dia

tangerine tangerina

tarragon estragão

tenderloin lombo

Thousand Island dressing maionese com ketchup, pimentos, azeitonas e ovos cozidos

thyme tomilho

toad-in-the-hole pudim de massa de crepes (Bras. panquecas) com salsichas

toast torrada

toasted torrado

~ **cheese** tosta de queijo

~ **sandwich** tosta mista (Bras. misto quente)

tomato tomate

tongue língua

treacle melaço

trifle bolo de massa lêveda com doce de fruta, amêndoas raladas, demolhado em vinho e servido com chantilly e creme de baunilha

tripe tripas

trout truta

truffle trufa

tuna, tunny atum

turbot pregado

turkey perú

turnip nabo

turnover espécie de pastel de massa tenra geralmente recheado de puré de maçã doce

turtle soup sopa de tartaruga

underdone muito mal passado

vanilla baunilha

veal vitela

~ **bird** trouxa de vitela

~ **cutlet** escalope

vegetable legume

~ **marrow** abobrinha

venison caça

vichyssoise sopa fria de alhos--porros, batatas e natas (Bras. creme de leite)

vinegar vinagre

Virginia baked ham presunto (Bras. pernil) assado no forno com cravinhos, guarnecido de ananás (Bras. abacaxi) e cerejas e regado com o sumo (Bras. suco) das frutas

vol-au-vent vol-au-vent, pequena forma de massa folhada, recheada com um creme de carne, molejas e cogumelos

wafer espécie de bolacha de baunilha

waffle panqueca de máquina

walnut noz

water ice sorvete, gelado feito com água (Bras. sorvete de água)

watercress agrião

watermelon melancia

well-done bem passado

Welsh rabbit/rarebit tosta de queijo

whelk búzio

whipped cream chantilly

whitebait espadilha

Wiener Schnitzel escalope

wine list lista dos vinhos

woodcock galinhola

Worcestershire sauce molho inglês, condimento líquido picante à base de soja, alho e vinagre

yoghurt iogurte

York ham presunto de York

Yorkshire pudding pudim de massa de crepes (Bras. panquecas) cozido no forno sob uma peça de rosbife

zucchini abobrinha

zwieback tosta

ale cerveja levemente adocicada e fermentada a uma elevada temperatura
  bitter ~ cerveja a copo, bastante amarga e pesada
  brown ~ cerveja preta de garrafa, ligeiramente adocicada
  light ~ cerveja branca de garrafa
  mild ~ cerveja preta a copo, de gosto acentuado
  pale ~ cerveja branca de garrafa
angostura amargo de angustura, essência aromática amarga que se adiciona aos cocktails
applejack aguardente de maçã
Athol Brose bebida escocesa composta de whisky, mel, água e, por vezes, flocos de aveia
Bacardi cocktail cocktail à base de rum, gin, xarope de romã e sumo (Bras. suco) de limão verde
barley water refresco aromatizado à base de cevada
barley wine cerveja preta de garrafa, muito alcoólica
beer cerveja
  bottled ~ de garrafa
  draft/draught ~ a copo, imperial
bitters aperitivos e digestivos, feitos à base de raízes, cascas de frutas ou ervas aromáticas
black velvet champanhe misturado com *stout* (bebida que acompanha normalmente as ostras)
bloody Mary vodka com sumo (Bras. suco) de tomate e condimentos
bottle garrafa
bourbon whisky americano à base de milho
brandy 1) nome que designa todas as aguardentes de vinho ou de frutas 2) conhaque
  ~ **Alexander** mistura de conhaque, creme de cacau e natas (Bras. creme de leite)
British wines vinhos «ingleses», feitos de uvas ou de sumo (bras. suco) de uvas importados
champagne champanhe
cherry brandy licor de cereja
cider sidra
claret vinho tinto de Bordéus
cobbler *long drink* à base de sumo (Bras. suco) de frutas misturado com vinho ou licor e servido muito gelado
cocoa cacau
coffee café
  ~ **with cream** com natas magras (Bras. creme de leite)
  black ~ simples
  caffeine-free ~ sem cafeína
  iced ~ café gelado servido em copo, geralmente com chantilly
  white ~ com leite
coke coca-cola
cordial 1) licor 2) espécie de xarope
cream 1) natas (Bras. creme de leite) 2) licor espresso
cup 1) chávena 2) refresco à base de vinho, água gaseificada,

aguardente e frutas variadas servido com uma concha

daiquiri cocktail de rum, sumo (Bras. suco) de lima e de ananás (Bras. abacaxi)

double dose dupla

Drambuie licor de whisky com mel

dry seco
~ **martini** 1) vermute seco (GB) 2) cocktail de gin com vermute seco (EUA)
medium ~ meio-seco

egg flip/nog gemada de bar

fizzy gazeificado

gill medida utilizada para servir as aguardentes (0,142 litro na GB e 0,118 litro nos EUA)

gin and it cocktail de gin

gin-fizz gin com sumo (Bras. suco) de limão, açúcar e soda

ginger beer limonada de gengibre, ligeiramente alcoólica

grasshopper mistura de creme de hortelã-pimenta, de creme de cacau e de natas (Bras. creme de leite)

Guinness (stout) cerveja preta ligeiramente adocicada, de gosto acentuado, contendo grande quantidade de malte e de lúpulo

half pint medida que corresponde aproximadamente a 3 decilitros

highball aguardente ou whisky a que se junta uma boa quantidade de gasosa

iced gelado, muito frio

Irish coffee café com açúcar e whisky irlandês, coberto de chantilly

Irish Mist licor irlandês de whisky com mel

Irish whiskey whisky irlandês feito quase exclusivamente de cevada e menos amargo que o escocês

juice sumo (Bras. suco)

lager cerveja branca e leve, servida muito fresca

lemonade limonada

lime juice amargo de lima (Bras. suco de limão verde)

liqueur licor

liquor bebida espirituosa

long drink aguardente ou whisky a que se junta uma boa quantidade de gasosa

Manhattan cocktail de whisky de milho e vermute com amargo de angustura

mead hidromel

milk leite
~ **shake** batido

mineral water água mineral

mulled wine vinho quente com especiarias

neat puro, simples

old-fashioned cocktail de whisky e marrasquino com cerejas e amargo de angustura

on the rocks com gelo

Ovaltine Ovomaltine

Pimm's cup(s) bebida alcoólica misturada com sumo (Bras. suco) de frutas ou soda
~ **No. 1** à base de gin
~ **No. 2** à base de whisky
~ **No. 3** à base de rum
~ **No. 4** à base de aguardente

pink champagne champanhe rosé

pink lady mistura de claras com aguardente de sidra, sumo (Bras. suco) de limão, xarope de romã e gin

pint medida que corresponde

aproximadamente a 6 deci-
litros

port (wine) vinho do Porto

porter cerveja preta e amarga

quart medida que corresponde a
1,14 litro (EUA 0,95 litro)

red tinto

root beer refresco doce gaseifica-
do, com essências aromáticas

rye (whiskey) whisky de centeio,
mais pesado e mais áspero que
o *bourbon*

screwdriver mistura de vodka e
sumo (Bras. suco) de laranja

shandy *bitter ale* misturada com
limonada ou *ginger beer*

sherry xerez

short drink expressão que designa
uma bebida espirituosa pura

shot dose de licor ou de espirituoso

sloe gin-fizz licor de ameixas sil-
vestres com soda e sumo

(Bras. suco) de limão

soft drink bedina não alcoólica,
refresco

spirits bebidas espirituosas

stinger conhaque com creme de
hortelã

stout cerveja preta, muito alcoólica

straight puro, simples

sweet doce

tea chá

toddy grogue

Tom Collins mistura de gin com
sumo (Bras. suco) de limão,
açúcar e água gaseificada

water água
tonic ~ água tónica

whisky sour whisky com sumo
(Bras. suco) de limão, açúcar e
soda

white branco

wine vinho
sparkling ~ espumante

Verbos irregulares ingleses

Segue-se a lista dos verbos irregulares ingleses. Os verbos compostos ou com prefixo conjugam-se como os verbos principais. Por exemplo: *withdraw* conjuga-se como *draw* e *mistake* como *take*.

Infinitivo	Imperfeito	Particípio passado	
arise	arose	arisen	*surgir*
awake	awoke	awoken/awaked	*despertar*
be	was	been	*ser, estar*
bear	bore	borne	*trazer; suportar*
beat	beat	beaten	*bater*
become	became	become	*tornar-se*
begin	began	begun	*começar*
bend	bent	bent	*curvar*
bet	bet	bet	*apostar*
bid	bade/bid	bidden/bid	*fazer um lanço; ordenar*
bind	bound	bound	*ligar*
bite	bit	bitten	*morder*
bleed	bled	bled	*sangrar*
blow	blew	blown	*soprar*
break	broke	broken	*quebrar*
breed	bred	bred	*criar*
bring	brought	brought	*trazer*
build	built	built	*construir*
burn	burnt/burned	burnt/burned	*queimar*
burst	burst	burst	*rebentar*
buy	bought	bought	*comprar*
can*	could	–	*poder*
cast	cast	cast	*lançar; fundir*
catch	caught	caught	*apanhar*
choose	chose	chosen	*escolher*
cling	clung	clung	*agarrar-se*
clothe	clothed/clad	clothed/clad	*vestir*
come	came	come	*vir*
cost	cost	cost	*custar*
creep	crept	crept	*arrastar-se*
cut	cut	cut	*cortar*
deal	dealt	dealt	*tratar; distribuir*
dig	dug	dug	*cavar*
do (he does*)	did	done	*fazer*
draw	drew	drawn	*puxar; desenhar*
dream	dreamt/dreamed	dreamt/dreamed	*sonhar*
drink	drank	drunk	*beber*
drive	drove	driven	*conduzir*
dwell	dwelt	dwelt	*morar*
eat	ate	eaten	*comer*
fall	fell	fallen	*cair*

* presente do indicativo

feed	fed	fed	*alimentar*
feel	felt	felt	*sentir*
fight	fought	fought	*lutar*
find	found	found	*achar, encontrar*
flee	fled	fled	*fugir*
fling	flung	flung	*arremessar*
fly	flew	flown	*voar*
forsake	forsook	forsaken	*abandonar*
freeze	froze	frozen	*gelar*
get	got	got	*obter*
give	gave	given	*dar*
go (he goes*)	went	gone	*ir*
grind	ground	ground	*moer*
grow	grew	grown	*crescer*
hang	hung	hung	*pendurar*
have (he has*)	had	had	*ter*
hear	heard	heard	*ouvir*
hew	hewed	hewed/hewn	*talhar*
hide	hid	hidden	*esconder*
hit	hit	hit	*dar (uma) pancada*
hold	held	held	*segurar*
hurt	hurt	hurt	*ferir; doer*
keep	kept	kept	*guardar*
kneel	knelt	knelt	*ajoelhar-se*
knit	knitted/knit	knitted/knit	*tricotar*
know	knew	known	*saber, conhecer*
lay	laid	laid	*deitar*
lead	led	led	*dirigir; levar*
lean	leant/leaned	leant/leaned	*apoiar-se*
leap	leapt/leaped	leapt/leaped	*saltar*
learn	learnt/learned	learnt/learned	*aprender*
leave	left	left	*partir; deixar*
lend	lent	lent	*emprestar*
let	let	let	*deixar (licença); alugar*
lie	lay	lain	*estar deitado*
light	lit/lighted	lit/lighted	*acender*
lose	lost	lost	*perder*
make	made	made	*fazer*
may*	might	–	*poder*
mean	meant	meant	*significar*
meet	met	met	*encontrar (pessoas)*
mow	mowed	mowed/mown	*ceifar*
must*	must	–	*ter de*
ought* (to)	ought	–	*dever*
pay	paid	paid	*pagar*
put	put	put	*pôr*
read	read	read	*ler*
rid	rid	rid	*desembaraçar*
ride	rode	ridden	*montar, andar*

---

* presente do indicativo

ring	rang	rung	*tocar (campainha)*
rise	rose	risen	*subir, levantar-se*
run	ran	run	*correr*
saw	sawed	sawn	*serrar*
say	said	said	*dizer*
see	saw	seen	*ver*
seek	sought	sought	*procurar*
sell	sold	sold	*vender*
send	sent	sent	*enviar, mandar*
set	set	set	*pôr; fixar*
sew	sewed	sewed/sewn	*coser*
shake	shook	shaken	*sacudir*
shall*	should	–	*dever*
shed	shed	shed	*despojar-se; derramar*
shine	shone	shone	*brilhar*
shoot	shot	shot	*disparar*
show	showed	shown	*mostrar*
shrink	shrank	shrunk	*encolher*
shut	shut	shut	*fechar*
sing	sang	sung	*cantar*
sink	sank	sunk	*afundar(-se)*
sit	sat	sat	*sentar(-se)*
sleep	slept	slept	*dormir*
slide	slid	slid	*escorregar*
sling	slung	slung	*arrojar*
slink	slunk	slunk	*esquivar-se*
slit	slit	slit	*fender*
smell	smelled/smelt	smelled/smelt	*cheirar*
sow	sowed	sown/sowed	*semear*
speak	spoke	spoken	*falar*
speed	sped/speeded	sped/speeded	*acelerar*
spell	spelt/spelled	spelt/spelled	*soletrar*
spend	spent	spent	*gastar; passar*
spill	spilt/spilled	spilt/spilled	*derramar, entornar*
spin	spun	spun	*fiar; girar*
spit	spat	spat	*cuspir*
split	split	split	*rachar(-se); dividir*
spoil	spoilt/spoiled	spoilt/spoiled	*estragar*
spread	spread	spread	*espalhar*
spring	sprang	sprung	*pular; brotar*
stand	stood	stood	*estar de pé*
steal	stole	stolen	*roubar*
stick	stuck	stuck	*colar*
sting	stung	stung	*picar*
stink	stank/stunk	stunk	*cheirar mal, feder*
strew	strewed	strewed/strewn	*espargir*
stride	strode	stridden	*andar a passos largos*
strike	struck	struck/stricken	*golpear; fazer greve*
string	strung	strung	*esticar cordas*

---

* presente do indicativo

strive	strove	striven	*esforçar-se*
swear	swore	sworn	*jurar*
sweep	swept	swept	*varrer*
swell	swelled	swollen/swelled	*inchar*
swim	swam	swum	*nadar*
swing	swung	swung	*balouçar-se*
take	took	taken	*tomar, pegar*
teach	taught	taught	*ensinar*
tear	tore	torn	*rasgar*
tell	told	told	*contar, dizer*
think	thought	thought	*pensar*
throw	threw	thrown	*atirar*
thrust	thrust	thrust	*empurrar*
tread	trod	trodden	*pisar*
wake	woke/waked	woken/waked	*acordar*
wear	wore	worn	*trazer ou levar (vestido) gastar com o uso*
weave	wove	woven	*tecer*
weep	wept	wept	*chorar*
will *	would	—	*querer*
win	won	won	*ganhar*
wind	wound	wound	*enroscar*
wring	wrung	wrung	*torcer*
write	wrote	written	*escrever*

---

* presente do indicativo

Abreviaturas inglesas

AA	*Automobile Association*	Automóvel Clube da Grã--Bretanha
AAA	*American Automobile Association*	Automóvel Clube dos Estados Unidos
ABC	*American Broadcasting Company*	Companhia particular americana de Rádio e Televisão
A.D.	*anno Domini*	depois de Cristo
Am.	*America; American*	América; americano
a.m.	*ante meridiem (before noon)*	antes do meio-dia (da meia-noite ao meio-dia)
Amtrak	*American railroad corporation*	Companhia particular americana dos Caminhos-de-Ferro
AT & T	*American Telephone and Telegraph Company*	Companhia particular americana de Telefones e Telégrafos
Ave.	*avenue*	avenida
BBC	*British Broadcasting Corporation*	Companhia nacional britânica de Rádio e Televisão
B.C.	*before Christ*	antes de Cristo
bldg.	*building*	prédio, edifício
Blvd.	*boulevard*	alameda
B.R.	*British Rail*	Caminhos-de-Ferro Britânicos
Brit.	*Britain; British*	Grã-Bretanha; britânico
Bros.	*brothers*	irmãos
¢	*cent*	centésima parte do dólar
Can.	*Canada; Canadian*	Canadá; canadiano
CBS	*Columbia Broadcasting System*	Companhia particular americana de Rádio e Televisão
CID	*Criminal Investigation Department*	polícia judiciária britânica
CNR	*Canadian National Railways*	Caminhos-de-Ferro Canadianos
c/o	*(in) care of*	ao cuidado de
Co.	*company*	companhia
Corp.	*corporation*	tipo de sociedade americana
CPR	*Canadian Pacific Railways*	Companhia particular canadiana de Caminhos-de-Ferro
D.C.	*District of Columbia*	Distrito de Colúmbia (Washington, D.C.)
DDS	*Doctor of Dental Science*	dentista
dept.	*department*	repartição; ministério

EEC	*European Economic Community*	CEE (Comunidade Económica Europeia), Mercado Commun
e.g.	*for instance*	por exemplo
Eng.	*England; English*	Inglaterra; inglês
excl.	*excluding; exclusive*	não incluído, exclusive
ft.	*foot/feet*	pé/pés (30,48 cm)
GB	*Great Britain*	Grã-Bretanha
H.E.	*His/Her Excellency; His Eminence*	Sua Excelência; Sua Eminência
H.H.	*His Holiness*	Sua Santidade
H.M.	*His/Her Majesty*	Sua Majestade
H.M.S.	*Her Majesty's ship*	navio da marinha real britânica
hp	*horsepower*	cavalos-vapor
Hwy	*highway*	estrada nacional americana
i.e.	*that is to say*	isto é
in.	*inch*	polegada (2,54 cm)
Inc.	*incorporated*	Sociedade Anónima
incl.	*including, inclusive*	incluído, inclusive
£	*pound sterling*	libra esterlina
L.A.	*Los Angeles*	Los Angeles
Ltd.	*limited*	LDA, (companhia) limitada
M.D.	*Doctor of Medicine*	médico
M.P.	*Member of Parliament*	membro do Parlamento britânico
mph	*miles per hour*	milhas à hora
Mr.	*Mister*	Senhor
Mrs.	*Missis*	Senhora
Ms.	*Missis/Miss*	Senhora/Menina, Senhorita
nat.	*national*	nacional
NBC	*National Broadcasting Company*	companhia particular americana de Rádio e Televisão
No.	*number*	número
N.Y.C.	*New York City*	cidade de Nova Iorque
O.B.E.	*Officer (of the Order) of the British Empire*	Oficial (da Ordem) do Império Britânico
p.	*page; pence*	página; centésima parte da libra esterlina
p.a.	*per annum*	por ano, anual
Ph.D.	*Doctor of Philosophy*	doutorado em filosofia
p.m.	*post meridiem (after noon)*	depois do meio-dia (do meio-dia à meia-noite)
PO	*Post Office*	estação dos correios

POO	*post office order*	vale postal
P.T.O.	*please turn over*	volte, se faz favor
RAC	*Royal Automobile Club*	Automóvel Clube Real da Grã-Bretanha
RCMP	*Royal Canadian Mounted Police*	Polícia Real Montada Canadiana
Rd.	*road*	estrada, rua
ref.	*reference*	veja, confira
Rev.	*reverend*	pastor da Igreja anglicana
RR	*railroad*	caminho-de-ferro
RSVP	*please reply*	responda, se faz favor
$	*dollar*	dólar
Soc.	*society*	sociedade
St.	*saint ; street*	são, santo; rua
STD	*Subscriber Trunk Dialling*	telefone automático
UN	*United Nations*	Nações Unidas
UPS	*United Parcel Service*	Companhia particular de expedição de encomendas (Bras. pacotes)
US	*United States*	Estados Unidos
USS	*United States Ship*	navio da marinha de guerra americana
VAT	*value added tax*	Imposto de Transacção
VIP	*very important person*	personalidade que goza de privilégios particulares
Xmas	*Christmas*	Natal
yd.	*yard*	jarda (91,44 cm)
YMCA	*Young Men's Christian Association*	Associação Cristã de Rapazes
YWCA	*Young Women's Christian Association*	Associação Cristã de Raparigas
ZIP	*Zip code*	código postal

Numerais

Numerais cardinais		Numerais ordinais	
0	zero	1st	first
1	one	2nd	second
2	two	3rd	third
3	three	4th	fourth
4	four	5th	fifth
5	five	6th	sixth
6	six	7th	seventh
7	seven	8th	eighth
8	eight	9th	ninth
9	nine	10th	tenth
10	ten	11th	eleventh
11	eleven	12th	twelfth
12	twelve	13th	thirteenth
13	thirteen	14th	fourteenth
14	fourteen	15th	fifteenth
15	fifteen	16th	sixteenth
16	sixteen	17th	seventeenth
17	seventeen	18th	eighteenth
18	eighteen	19th	nineteenth
19	nineteen	20th	twentieth
20	twenty	21st	twenty-first
21	twenty-one	22nd	twenty-second
22	twenty-two	23rd	twenty-third
23	twenty-three	24th	twenty-fourth
24	twenty-four	25th	twenty-fifth
25	twenty-five	26th	twenty-sixth
30	thirty	27th	twenty-seventh
40	forty	28th	twenty-eighth
50	fifty	29th	twenty-ninth
60	sixty	30th	thirtieth
70	seventy	40th	fortieth
80	eighty	50th	fiftieth
90	ninety	60th	sixtieth
100	a/one hundred	70th	seventieth
230	two hundred and thirty	80th	eightieth
		90th	ninetieth
1,000	a/one thousand	100th	hundredth
10,000	ten thousand	230th	two hundred and thirtieth
100,000	a/one hundred thousand		
1,000,000	a/one million	1,000th	thousandth

As horas

Os Británicos e os Americanos usam o sistema das doze horas. A expressão «a.m.» (ante meridiem) designa as horas que precedem o meio-dia, «p.m.» (post meridiem) as da tarde e da noite (até à meia-noite). Contudo, na Grã-Bretanha, os horários são progressivamente redigidos segundo o modelo continental.

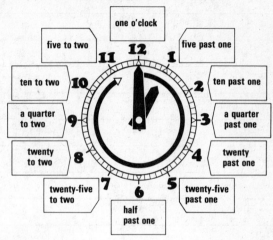

I'll come at seven a.m.   Venho às 7 da manhã.
I'll come at one p.m.   Venho à 1 da tarde.
I'll come at eight p.m.   Venho às 8 da noite.

Os dias da semana

Sunday	domingo	*Thursday*	quinta-feira
Monday	segunda-feira	*Friday*	sexta-feira
Tuesday	terça-feira	*Saturday*	sábado
Wednesday	quarta-feira		

Notes

Notes

Notes _____

Notes

Notes

Notas

Notas

Notas

Notas _____
_____
_____
_____
_____
_____
_____
_____
_____
_____
_____
_____
_____
_____
_____
_____
_____
_____
_____
_____
_____
_____

Notas

DICIONÁRIOS BERLITZ

Bilingues, os dicionários Berlitz contêm 12 500 vocábulos em cada uma das línguas e todas as palavras estrangeiras trazem a respectiva transcrição fonética. Eles incluem também uma lista das abreviaturas correntes e um vasto repertório de termos gastronómicos. Uma ajuda preciosa para todos os que viajam.

Alemão	Inglês
Francês	Sueco
Holandês	

GUIA DE CONVERSAÇÃO BERLITZ

Um guia de conversação de 196 páginas que contém não só as palavras e expressões indispensáveis para se fazer entender nos Estados Unidos, mas também uma transcrição fonética, informações úteis à sua estadia e conselhos práticos a propósito de gorjetas.